Lecture Notes in Computer Science 9974

Commenced Publication in 1973
Founding and Former Series Editors:
Gerhard Goos, Juris Hartmanis, and Jan van Leeuwen

More information about this series at http://www.springer.com/series/7409

Isabelle Comyn-Wattiau · Katsumi Tanaka
Il-Yeol Song · Shuichiro Yamamoto
Motoshi Saeki (Eds.)

Conceptual Modeling

35th International Conference, ER 2016
Gifu, Japan, November 14–17, 2016
Proceedings

 Springer

Editors
Isabelle Comyn-Wattiau
CEDRIC-CNAM and ESSEC Business
  School
Cergy-Pontoise
France

Katsumi Tanaka
Kyoto University
Kyoto
Japan

Il-Yeol Song
Drexel University
Philadelphia, PA
USA

Shuichiro Yamamoto
Nagoya University
Nagoya
Japan

Motoshi Saeki
Tokyo Institute of Technology
Tokyo
Japan

ISSN 0302-9743   ISSN 1611-3349 (electronic)
Lecture Notes in Computer Science
ISBN 978-3-319-46396-4   ISBN 978-3-319-46397-1   (eBook)
DOI 10.1007/978-3-319-46397-1

Library of Congress Control Number: 2015950889

LNCS Sublibrary: SL3 – Information Systems and Applications, incl. Internet/Web, and HCI

Printed on acid-free paper

This Springer imprint is published by Springer Nature
The registered company is Springer International Publishing AG
The registered company address is: Gewerbestrasse 11, 6330 Cham, Switzerland

Preface

This volume contains a collection of research papers that constitute the technical program of the 35th International Conference on Conceptual Modeling (ER 2016), held in Gifu, Japan, during November 14–17, 2016. Chen's seminal work on the entity relationship (ER) model coincided with the emergence of conceptual modeling as a distinct field. One of the unique and valuable dimensions of the ER conference series is the way it brings researchers and practitioners from around the world to discuss ways to raise new challenges in conceptual modeling. Also known as the "Entity Relationship" or "ER" conference, this conference series has been held at an interesting variety of locations, rotating in successive years between Europe, Asia, and the Americas, attracting a diverse international community of scholars. Conceptual modeling is a process aiming at abstracting some aspects of the real world and representing them in the form of a model that can be used for understanding and communication; conceptual models typically are used in the development of computer-based information systems. The technical program for ER 2016 included papers addressing a number of current and emerging topics in conceptual modeling. In response to the call for papers, we received 113 abstracts and 89 full papers. The Program Committee provided at least three reviews for each paper, and on the basis of these reviews we selected 23 full papers (an acceptance rate of 25.84 %) and 18 short papers (a combined acceptance rate of 46.60 %). These papers can be grouped into several topical areas, including modeling and executing business processes, semantic annotations, conceptual modeling guidance, ontologies, business process management and modeling, requirements engineering, goal modeling, schema mapping, and applications of conceptual modeling. We express gratitude to all who helped make ER 2016 a success. It required the significant efforts of many people to make this conference possible. We thank the 93 Program Committee members along with the numerous external reviewers who reviewed and discussed the submitted manuscripts. These reviewers represent 26 different countries, which serves to bring a broad set of perspectives to the research arena. We especially thank the authors who took the time to carefully write up the results of their research and submit papers for consideration. The quality of these papers is a tribute to the authors and also to the reviewers who have guided any necessary improvement. Last but not least, we are greatly indebted to the three keynotes speakers: Prof. Tok Wang Ling of National University of Singapore, Prof. Oscar Pastor of Polytechnic University of Valencia, Spain, and Prof. Hideaki Takeda of National Institute of Informatics, Japan for accepting our invitation to address this conference.

July 2016

Isabelle Comyn-Wattiau
Katsumi Tanaka
Il-Yeol Song
Shuichiro Yamamoto
Motoshi Saeki

Organizing Committee

Honorary Chair

Kiyoshi Agusa — Nanzan University, Japan

Conference Co-chairs

Shuichiro Yamamoto — Nagoya University, Japan
Motoshi Saeki — Tokyo Institute of Technology, Japan

Program Committee Co-chairs

Isabelle Comyn-wattiau — CEDRIC-CNAM and ESSEC Business School, France
Katsumi Tanaka — Kyoto University, Japan
Il-Yeol Song — Drexel University, USA

Workshop Co-chairs

Juan Trujillo — University of Alicante, Spain
Sebastian Link — University of Auckland, New Zealand

Tutorial Co-chairs

Atsushi Ohnishi — Ritsumeikan University, Japan
Panos Vassiliadis — University of Ioannia, Greece

Panel Co-chairs

Sudha Ram — University of Arizona, USA
Esteban Zimányi — Université Libre de Bruxelles, Belgium

Tool Demonstration and Poster Co-chairs

Aditya Ghose — University of Wollongong, Australia
Takashi Kobayashi — Tokyo Institute of Technology, Japan

PhD Symposium Co-chairs

Tsuneo Ajisaka — Wakayama University, Japan
Carson Woo — The University of British Columbia, Canada

Symposium on Conceptual Modeling Education (SCME 2016) Co-chairs

Karen Davis   University of Cincinnatti, USA
Xavier Franch   Universitat Politècnica de Catalunya, Spain

Treasurer

Takako Nakatani   The Open University of Japan, Japan

Local Organizing Co-chairs

Shuji Morisaki   Nagoya University, Japan
Atsushi Yoshida   Nanzan University, Japan

Liasons to IPSJ

Isamu Hasegawa   Square Enix, Japan

Publicity Chair and Web Master

Shinpei Hayashi   Tokyo Institute of Technology, Japan

Student Volunteer Co-chairs

Noritoshi Atsumi   Kyoto University, Japan
Hiroaki Kuwabara   Nanzan University, Japan

Liaison to Steering Committee

Sudha Ram   University of Arizona, USA

Advisor

Mikio Aoyama   Nanzan University, Japan

Program Committee

Jacky Akoka   CNAM and TEM, France
Yuan An   Drexel University, USA
Joao Araujo   Universidade Nova de Lisboa, Portugal
Zhifeng Bao   University of Tasmania, Australia
Ladjel Bellatreche   ENSMA, France
Sandro Bimonte   IRSTEA, France
Mokrane Bouzeghoub   UVSQ/CNRS, France
Shawn Bowers   Gonzaga University, USA

Stephane Bressan	National University of Singapore, Singapore
Stefano Ceri	Politecnico di Milano, Italy
Roger Chiang	AIS, USA
Dickson K.W. Chiu	The University of Hong Kong, SAR China
Byron Choi	Hong Kong Baptist University, SAR China
Alfredo Cuzzocrea	University of Trieste, Italy
Fabiano Dalpiaz	Utrecht University, The Netherlands
Karen Davis	University of Cincinnati, USA
Valeria De Antonellis	University of Brescia, Italy
Sergio De Cesare	Brunel University, UK
José Palazzo M. de Oliveira	Federal University of Rio Grande do Sul, Brazil
Lois Delcambre	Portland State University, USA
Gill Dobbie	University of Auckland, New Zealand
Johann Eder	Alpen Adria Universität Klagenfurt, Austria
Xavier Franch	Universitat Politècnica de Catalunya, Spain
Avigdor Gal	Technion, Israel
Sepideh Ghanavati	Luxembourg Institute of Science and Technology, Luxembourg
Aditya Ghose	University of Wollongong, Australia
Paolo Giorgini	University of Trento, Italy
Georg Grossmann	University of South Australia, Australia
Giancarlo Guizzardi	Federal University of Espirito Santo, Brazil
Renata Guizzardi	Universidade Federal do Espirito Santo, Brazil
Arantza Illarramendi	Basque Country University, Spain
Matthias Jarke	RWTH Aachen University, Germany
Manfred Jeusfeld	University of Skövde, Sweden
Ivan Jureta	University of Namur, Belgium
Dimitris Karagiannis	University of Vienna, Austria
Kamalakar Karlapalem	CDE, IIIT Hyderabad, India
David Kensche	RWTH Aachen University, Germany
Dik Lee	Hong Kong University of Science and Technology, SAR China
Mong Li Lee	National University of Singapore, Singapore
Julio Cesar Leite	PUC-Rio, Brazil
Guoliang Li	Tsinghua University, China
Stephen Liddle	Brigham Young University, USA
Tok Wang Ling	National University of Singapore, Singapore
Sebastian Link	The University of Auckland, New Zealand
Pericles Loucopoulos	The University of Manchester, UK
Hui Ma	Victoria University of Wellington, New Zealand
Wolfgang Maass	Saarland University, Germany
Heinrich C. Mayr	Alpen-Adria-Universität Klagenfurt, Austria
Haralambos Mouratidis	University of Brighton, UK
John Mylopoulos	University of Toronto, Canada
Wilfred Ng	Hong Kong University of Science and Technology, SAR China

Additional Reviewers

Fatma Başak Aydemir	Amador Durán Toro	Diana Marosin
Kamel Barkaoui	Christophe Feltus	Michele Melchiori
Nabila Berkani	Jesús García Galán	Yassine Ouhammou
Vincent Bertram	Mohamad Gharib	Elda Paja
Devis Bianchini	Oliver Kautz	Mattia Salnitri
Dominik Bork	Lu Li	Arik Senderovich
Andrea Burattin	Mingzhao Li	Nikolaos Tantouris
Brice Chardin	Achim Lindt	Marc van Zee
Adela Del Río Ortega	Garm Lucassen	Peng Wang

Organized by

- Special Interest Group on Software Engineering, Information Processing Society of Japan
- The ER Institute (ER Steering Committee)

In Cooperation with

- The Database Society of Japan
- Special Interest Group on Database Systems, Information Processing Society of Japan
- Information and Systems Society and Technical Committee on Data Engineering, The Institute of Electronics, Information and Communication Engineers
- IEEE Computer Society Japan Chapter
- ACM SIGMOD Japan
- Software Engineers Association

Industrial Sponsors

HITACHI
Inspire the Next

株式会社 デンソークリエイト

Abstracts of the Keynotes

Improving the Correctness of Some Database Research Using ORA-Semantics

Tok Wang Ling, Zhong Zeng, Mong Li Lee, and Thuy Ngoc Le

National University of Singapore, Singapore, Singapore
{lingtw,zengzh,leeml,ltngoc}@comp.nus.edu.sg

Abstract. We refer to the concepts of object class, relationship type, and attribute of object class and relationship type in the ER model as ORA-semantics. Common database models such as the relational model and the XML data model do not capture these ORA-semantics which leads to many serious problems in relational and XML database design, data and schema integration, and keyword query processing in these databases. In this paper, we highlight the limitations and problems of current database research in these areas, and discuss how ORA-semantics can be utilized to resolve these problems.

Conceptual Modeling of Life: Beyond the Homo Sapiens

Oscar Pastor

Centro de I+D en Métodos de Producción de Software (PROS),
Universitat Politècnica de València, Camino de Vera s/n, 46022 Valencia, Spain
opastor@dsic.upv.es

Abstract. Our strong capability of conceptualization makes us, human beings, different from any other species in our planet. We, as conceptual modelers, should apply in the right direction such fascinating capability to make it play an essential role in the design of the world to come. What does it mean that "right direction" requires a challenging discussion. Halfway between the need of having a sound philosophical characterization and an effective, practical computer science application, conceptual modeling emerges as the ideal discipline needed for understanding life and improving our life style. This keynote explores this argument by delimiting the notion and scope of conceptual modeling, and by introducing and discussing two possible scenarios of fruitful application. The first one is oriented to better understand why conceptual modeling can help to manage the social challenges of the world of the emerging information era, and how this world that comes could benefit from it. The second one focuses on how understanding the human genome can open new ways to go beyond what we can consider "traditional Homo Sapiens capabilities", with especial implications in the health domain and the new medicine of precision.

Towards Knowledge-Enabled Society

Hideaki Takeda

National Institute of Informatics, 2-1-2, Hitotsubashi, Chiyoda-ku, Tokyo, Japan
takeda@nii.ac.jp

Abstract. Nowadays, most activities in our society is performed with computers or even by computers. It means that we have data about almost all activities in our society. But data for the society as a total is a mess, i.e., scattered and meaningless. Knowledge can help to interpret and organize it. The knowledge engineering research has developed how knowledge is represented and used such as ontology in computer science. Then combining it with Web, Semantic Web is emerged to offer knowledge representation on the Web. Now web is not just for human readable texts but it is used to represent any information from products to sensor data. Linked Data is the direct application of Semantic Web to represent things and knowledge in our society through the Web. So, the knowledge graph, the representation of things and knowledge, is becoming the basis of our society in the digital age.

What is the value of the knowledge graph? All applications and systems in our society will be society-sensitive just like every human activity cannot be performed without relationship with society. The knowledge graph is the interface between such society-sensitive applications and the society.

The status of the knowledge graph is still in the very early stage. DBpedia, Linked Data generated from Wikipedia is the core of the knowledge graph. But it is not enough. In particular, metadata and ontology is not sufficient. Schema.org is the typical activity for it. There are some other similar activities like Japanese IMI Core vocabulary. There need more domain ontologies. Agriculture Activity Ontology is the example how terms can be organized logically to improve interoperability and machine-readability.

Keywords: Semantic web · Linked data · Knowledge graph · Society-sensitive application · DBpedia

Contents

Modeling and Executing Business Processes

Business Process Management and Modeling

Applications and Experiments of Conceptual Modeling

Schema Mapping

Conceptual Modeling Guidance

Goal Modeling

Keynotes

Improving the Correctness of Some Database Research Using ORA-Semantics

Tok Wang Ling[⊠], Zhong Zeng, Mong Li Lee, and Thuy Ngoc Le

National University of Singapore, Singapore, Singapore
{lingtw,zengzh,leeml,ltngoc}@comp.nus.edu.sg

Abstract. We refer to the concepts of object class, relationship type, and attribute of object class and relationship type in the ER model as ORA-semantics. Common database models such as the relational model and the XML data model do not capture these ORA-semantics which leads to many serious problems in relational and XML database design, data and schema integration, and keyword query processing in these databases. In this paper, we highlight the limitations and problems of current database research in these areas, and discuss how ORA-semantics can be utilized to resolve these problems.

1 Introduction

The three basic concepts in the Entity Relationship (ER) Model are the object class, relationship type, and attribute of object class/relationship type [2]. We call these concepts *ORA-semantics*. We observe that the schemas of both the relational and XML data models do not capture the ORA-semantics in the ER model explicitly.

In the relational model [3], functional dependencies (FDs) are integrity constraints, many of which are artificially imposed. Multivalued dependencies (MVDs) are relation-sensitive, that is, the existence of a MVD depends on the relation that contains the attributes of the MVD [14]. A MVD occurs when some independent attributes (of an object class or a relationship type) are wrongly grouped in a relation, and it is difficult to detect MVDs. FDs and MVDs are used to remove redundancy and obtain normal form relations in database schema design. However, there is no concept of ORA-semantics in the relational model. Note that relation names in relational database is not the same as relationship type.

In the XML data model, the DTD/XML Schema can only represent simple constraints in the hierarchical structures and there is no concept of ORA-semantics. The ID in the DTD is not the same as object identifier, and a multivalued attribute of an object class cannot be represented directly as an attribute in DTD/XML Schema. Further, XML cannot distinguish between an attribute of an object class vs an attribute of a relationship type. The parent-child relationship in XML does not indicate any relationship type, in fact, relationship types (especially n-ary) are not explicitly captured in DTD/XML Schema.

© Springer International Publishing AG 2016
I. Comyn-Wattiau et al. (Eds.): ER 2016, LNCS 9974, pp. 3–17, 2016.
DOI: 10.1007/978-3-319-46397-1_1

In this paper, we re-visit the relational and XML data models and discuss the issues that arise due to the inability of these models to capture and represent object classes and relationship types together with their attributes explicitly in their schema languages. We show how ORA-semantics can overcome serious problems in relational and XML database schema design, data and schema integration, and keyword query processing.

2   ER Model and ORA-Semantics

The Entity Relationship (ER) Model [2] describes the data involved in a real-world enterprise in terms of objects and their relationships, and is widely used to develop an initial database design. Figure 1 shows an example ER diagram for a university database. It captures the information of **Student**, **Course**, **Textbook**, **Lecturer** and **Department** objects that interact with each other via **Enrol**, **Use**, **Teach**, **WorkFor** and **Prereq** relationships.

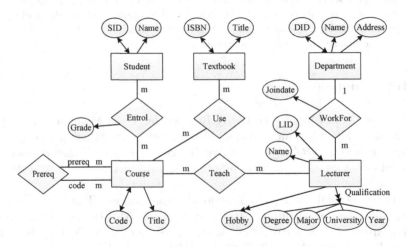

Fig. 1. The ER diagram for a university database

We call the concepts of object class, relationship type, and their attributes in the ER model as Object-Relationship-Attribute (ORA) semantics. We advocate that a database designer must know the ORA-semantics in order to design a good schema for the database. Further, programmers must know the ORA-semantics of the database (or part of the database involved) in order to write their SQL or XQuery programs correctly. Similarly, users also need to know ORA-semantics in order to ask sensible queries to get the information they want.

3   Limitations of Relational Model

In this section, we discuss the limitations of the relational model on capturing ORA-semantics in databases, which leads to problems in database design.

3.1 FDs and MVDs

FDs and MVDs are integrity constraints among attributes in the relational model. Most of FDs are imposed by database designers and/or organizations. On the other hand, the existence of MVDs in relations are mainly because of the following wrong designs:

Case 1. Single valued attributes and multivalued attributes of an object class or a relationship type are put in one relation.

Case 2. Two independent multivalued attributes of an object class or a relationship type are put in one relation.

Case 3. Two independent relationship types are put in one relation.

Example 1. Consider the ER diagram for the university database in Fig. 1. Suppose we capture the lecturer ids, names, and their hobbies in one relation:

```
Lecturer (LID, Name, Hobby)
```

This relation will have an MVD: LID $\twoheadrightarrow$ Hobby because the hobbies of a lecturer only depends on the lecturer identifier LID, and is independent of the lecturer name (Case 1).

On the other hand, suppose we put the hobbies and qualifications of lecturers together in one relation (Case 2):

```
Lecturer_hobby_qual(LID, Hobby, Degree, Major, University,Year)
```

This relation will have two MVDs: LID $\twoheadrightarrow$ Hobby and LID $\twoheadrightarrow$ {Degree, Major, University, Year}, because hobbies and qualifications are two independent multivalued attributes of lecturers.

Finally, suppose we combine the Use and Teach relationships in Fig. 1 into one relation as follows (Case 3):

```
CTL(Code, ISBN, LID)
```

We will have Code $\twoheadrightarrow$ ISBN and Code $\twoheadrightarrow$ LID. This is because the textbooks of a course are independent of the lecturers of the course.   □

MVDs are problematic because they are **relation sensitive** [14]. In Example 1, the relation CTL(Code, ISBN, LID) has two MVDs: Code $\twoheadrightarrow$ ISBN and Code $\twoheadrightarrow$ LID. Suppose we add one more attribute percentage to the relation and obtain CTL'(Code, ISBN, LID, percentage). A tuple (c, i, l, p) in the CTL' relation means lecturer l teaches course c and p percentages of his material is from textbook i. We have the FD: {Code, ISBN, LID} $\rightarrow$ percentage. However, Code $\twoheadrightarrow$ ISBN and Code $\twoheadrightarrow$ LID are no longer hold in CTL'. Note that MVD is different from multivalued attribute and many-to-many relationship, and we cannot determine MVDs until we have the relations.

Further, FDs/MVDs cannot be automatically discovered from database instances. The relation Student (SID, Name) stores the information of students in Fig. 1. Given an instance of this relation, even if the student names are unique, the FD: Name → SID is incorrect in general. This is because the number of students in the current relation instance is limited. In addition, the relation may have frequent updates. We cannot use a static instance of a relation to discover FDs and MVDs. In other words, the discovered FDs and MVDs are just potential FDs and MVDs, and new inserts and/or updates may make these potential FDs and MVDs invalid.

Clearly, FDs/MVDs do not capture ORA-semantics. The ER diagram in Fig. 1 indicates that each lecturer works for only one department. Suppose we store all the information of lecturers and departments in a relation, we will have the FD: LID → Joindate. However, this FD does not indicate if Joindate is an attribute of lecturers or an attribute of relationships between lecturers and departments [12].

3.2   Relational Database Design

The three common methods for relational database schema design are the decomposition method, the synthesis method and the ER approach.

Decomposition Method. This method is based on the Universal Relation Assumption (URA) that a database can be represented by a universal relation containing all the attributes of the database. The universal relation is then decomposed into smaller relations to remove redundant data using the given FDs and MVDs. However, since MVDs are relation sensitive [14], it is almost impossible to obtain MVDs before the decomposition process because MVDs may change when relations are decomposed. The process is non-deterministic, depending on the order of FDs and MVDs that are used for decompositions. Different orders may lead to different sets of relations. In addition, this method cannot handle recursive relationship (e.g., manager of employee), ISA relationship (e.g., a manager is also an employee), and more than one relationship type among object classes in the ER model naturally and directly.

Synthesis Method [1]. This method is also based on URA and assumes that a database can be represented by a set of attributes together with a set of FDs. It then synthesizes a set of 3NF relations. Each step of the method makes sure the closure of the set of FDs remains unchanged, and does not consider MVDs. Similar to the decomposition method, the synthesis depends on the non-redundant covering of FDs to generate 3NF relations. Recursive relationship, ISA relationship, more than one relationship type among object classes, multivalued attribute of object classes and relationship types, and many-to-many relationship type without attribute cannot be handled naturally. Finally, the synthesis method does not guarantee the re-constructibility and the resulting relations may contain global redundant attributes [16].

The ER Approach. This approach first constructs an ER diagram (ERD) based on the database specifications and requirements, including recursive relationship, isa relationship, more than one relationship type defined among object classes, etc. Then it normalizes the ERD to a normal form ERD [15]. Finally it translates the normal form ERD to a set of normal form relations together with a set of constraints (e.g., role name, inclusion dependency, etc.) which cannot be represented in the relational schema. The ER approach is based on the relaxed URA, that is, only object identifier names have to be unique. Users do not need to consider MVDs which are relation sensitive. Further, it captures ORA-semantics and thus can avoid the problems of the decomposition method and synthesis method.

Summary. The relational model only considers integrity constraints and does not capture the important ORA-semantics which exists in the ER model. The decomposition method and the synthesis method use FDs and MVDs to generate relational database schema. However, they are non-deterministic, sensitive to the changes of FDs and MVDs, and cannot handle recursive relationship, ISA relationship, and more than one relationship type defined among object classes, etc. naturally. These problems can be solved by the ER approach, which translates a normal form ERD to a set of normal form relations [15].

4   Limitations of XML Data Model

XML (eXtensible Markup Language) has become a de facto standard of information representation and exchange over the Internet. Compared to HTML, XML does not have predefined elements and attributes, and provides a flexible way for users to define their own elements, attributes and the structure of the data.

4.1   XML DTD and XML Schema

An XML document is organized in a hierarchical structure, where the data is bounded in a pair of starting and ending tags. The constraints on the structure and content of the document can be described by DTD or XML Schema.

Figure 2 shows an example DTD for the database in Fig. 1. It indicates that the XML document starts with a **db** element, and **db** contains 0 or more occurrences of **Lecturer** and **Course** elements. A **Lecturer** element has attributes **LID**, **Name** and **Course**. Further, **LID** is the unique identifier of lecturer elements.

We see that DTD/XML Schema only specifies the structural representation of XML documents with simple constraints, and has no concept of ORA-semantics. This is reflected in the following aspects:

ID in DTD Is Not the Same as Object Identifier. Although ID defines unique values for an attribute, an object class cannot have the ID attribute if it has a m:m or 1:m relationship with its higher level object class. For instance,

```
<IDOCTYPE universitydb [
        <IELEMET db (Lecturer*, Course*)>
        <IELEMET Lecturer (Hobby*, Qualification*, Department)>
        <IATTLIST Lecturer LID  ID  #REQUIRED
                    Name  cdata
                    Course  IDREFS  #IMPLIED>
        ....
        <IELEMET Course (Textbook*, Student*)>
        <IATTLIST Course Code  ID  #REQUIRED
                    Title  cdata
                    Prereq  IDREFS  #IMPLIED>
        <IELEMET Student (Name, Grade)>
        <IATTLIST Student SID  cdata  #REQUIRED>
        ....
    ]>
```

Fig. 2. An XML DTD for the university database in Fig. 1

we cannot define SID as the unique ID identifier of Student elements in Fig. 2. This is because the same Student element may occur multiple times in the XML as the student may enrol in more than one course.

Multivalued Attribute Cannot Be Defined as an Attribute. In Fig. 2, the hobbies and qualifications of lecturers are given by the elements Hobby and Qualification under the Lecturer elements. They cannot be defined as attributes of Lecturer elements.

Relationship Type Is Implicit via Parent-Child Relationship. This leads to the problems of capturing the type of relationships and distinguishing between object attribute vs relationship attribute. For example, both Name and Grade are elements of Student in Fig. 2. However, from ORA-semantics in the ER diagram in Fig. 1, we know that name is a property of students while grade is an attribute of enrol relationships between students and courses. Further, DTD cannot distinguish 2 binary relationships vs one binary relationship together with a ternary relationship in a hierarchical path that involve 3 object classes.

4.2   ORA-SS Data Model

In contrast to the DTD/XML Schema, the ORA-SS data model [4] is designed to capture the ORA-semantics in XML data. This model distinguishes between objects, relationships and their attributes. The identifier of an object class is highlighted, while the other attributes are associated with cardinalities to indicate whether they are single valued or multivalued attributes. The relationship type is explicitly expressed with its name, degree and the cardinality of participating object classes. The attributes of a relationship type are labeled by the relationship name in order to distinguish from attributes of an object class.

Figure 3 shows an ORA-SS schema diagram for the XML document based on the ER diagram of the university database in Fig. 1. We see that this diagram

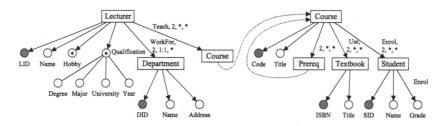

Fig. 3. An ORA-SS schema diagram for the university database in Fig. 1

fully captures the information of **Student**, **Course**, **Textbook**, **Lecturer** and **Department** objects, as well as the information of their relationships. In fact, an ORA-SS schema diagram is an ER diagram augmented with hierarchical structure. It solves the problems of DTD/XML Schema, and can be used to detect redundancy in XML data and define normal form for XML schema.

5   ORA-Semantics in Data and Schema Integration

Data and schema integration has been widely studied. However, the importance of ORA-semantics in data/schema integration is largely ignored. We list the problems in data and schema integration, and show that how ORA-semantics can solve these problems and improve the correctness of the integration.

Different Data Models. Databases may have different data models such as RDB, XML, NoSQL, etc. This requires us to transform the schemas of different data models into an ER schema diagram, and then integrate the data based on the integrated ERD. The transformation can only be done semi-automatically with ORA-semantics enrichment manually. This ER approach can improve the correctness of the integrated database/schema because ERDs capture ORA-semantics in databases.

Different Relationship Types. Entity resolution (i.e., object identification and record linking) is used to identify if two records refer to the same object across different data sources. However, this is not enough for data/schema integration, as we need to consider the relationship types as well.

Example 2. Consider two databases about person and house:

> DB1: **PersonHouse(SSN, Address)**
> DB2: **PersonHouse(SSN, Address)**

Assuming both **SSN** and **Address** uniquely identify a person and a house respectively, we cannot simply integrate the two databases together although they have the same schema. This is because the two relationship types between persons and houses may be different, e.g., DB1 may capture the relationship type **Own** (person owns house), while DB2 captures the relationship type Live (person lives in house). This indicates that we need the proper identification of both objects and relationships in order to integrate database or schema correctly. □

Local/Global Object Identifier. We need to consider local object identifier vs global object identifier during integration, otherwise, we may obtain incorrect integrated database/schema.

Suppose we have two databases with the same schema Enrol(SID, Code, Grade) that store the information of student enrolment. We cannot directly integrate them into one relation because the databases may come from two universities, and the same SID and Code may refer to different students and courses. In other words, SID and Code are local identifiers.

Local/Global FD. Similarly, we need to consider whether an FD is local or global during integration.

Example 3. Consider two bookstore databases:

    DB1: Book(ISBN, Title, First_author, Price)
    DB2: Book(ISBN, Title, First_author, Price)

We cannot integrate them into one relation because the same book may have different prices in different stores. Theoretically, we have the global FD: ISBN → {Title, First_author}, and the local FD: ISBN → Price. The global FD for price is {ISBN, Store} → Price. The integrated schema of these two databases should consists of 2 relations: Book_info(ISBN, Title, First_author) and Book_price(ISBN, Store, Price).   □

Semantic Dependency. The work in [12] introduces the notion of semantic dependency to capture the semantic relationship between two sets of attributes.

Example 4. Consider the following relations that store the information of employees and departments:

    R1: Emp(EID, Ename, Jointdate, DID)
    R2: Dept(DID, Dname)

The FDs that hold on these relations are: EID → {Ename, Joindate, DID} and DID → Dname. Based on the FDs, it is unclear whether Joindate is an attribute of employees (i.e., the date when an employee joined the company) or an attribute of the relationship between employees and departments (i.e., the date when an employee started working for a department). However, if we have the semantic dependency {EID, DID} $\xrightarrow{Sem}$ Joindate, then we know that Joindate indicates the date when an employee started working for a department. In order to discover semantic dependencies in a database, we need ORA-semantics.   □

Schematic Discrepancy. This occurs when the name of an attribute or a relation in one database corresponds to attribute values in the other databases [5].

Example 5. Suppose we want to store the quantities of parts supplied by suppliers in each month of the year. Depending on whether the values of months are stored as attribute values or names of attributes or names of relations, we can have 3 equivalent designs of the database as follows:

```
DB1: Supply(SID, PID, Month, Quantity)
DB2: Supply(SID, PID, Jan, Feb, ..., Dec)
DB3: Jan_Supply(SID, PID, Quantity),
     Feb_Supply(SID, PID, Quantity),
     ...
     Dec_Supply(SID, PID, Quantity)
```

The value of attribute Month in DB1 corresponds to an attribute name in DB2, and a relation name in DB3. When we integrate these 3 databases, we need to resolve schematic discrepancy using ORA-semantics. In particular, we remove the context of schema constructs by transforming attributes that cause schematic discrepancy into object classes, relationship types and their attributes.   □

In summary, we see that many issues must be considered during data/schema integration: different data models, different relationship types, local/global object identifier, local/global FD, semantic dependency, schematic discrepancy. All these require ORA-semantics if we want to achieve a good quality integration.

6   ORA-Semantics in Relational Keyword Search

The success of web search has made keyword search a major form of retrieval method. Given the rapid growth of relational data, the ability to support keyword search in relational database has gained traction. Existing works in relational keyword search can be classified into data graph approach [7] and schema graph approach [6]. In data graph approach, an RDB is represented as a graph where each node represents a tuple and each edge represents a foreign key-key reference. An answer to a keyword query is typically defined as a minimal connected subgraph (Steiner tree) which contains all the keywords. On the other hand, schema graph approach considers an RDB as a schema graph where each node represents a relation and each edge represents a foreign key-key constraint. Based on the schema graph, it translates a keyword query into a set of SQL statements, and leverages on RDBMSs to evaluate the SQL statements and retrieve answers.

We choose data graph approach as a representative and use the database in Fig. 4 to illustrate the serious problems of current relational keyword search approaches. The data graph of the database is shown in Fig. 5. Schema graph approach suffers from the similar problems. More details can be found in [19].

Student

SID	Name
S1	Bill
S2	John
S3	Mary

Course

Code	Title	LID
CS301	IR	L2
CS521	DB	L1
CS203	Java	L1

Department

DID	Name	Address
D1	Computing	Smith Street
D2	Business	Queen Street

Enroll

	SID	Code	Grade
E1	S1	CS521	A
E2	S2	CS203	B
E3	S2	CS521	A
E4	S3	CS203	A
E5	S3	CS301	B

Lecturer

LID	Name	DID
L1	Smith	D1
L2	Smith	D2
L3	Steven	D1

Qualification

	DID	Degree	Major	University	Year
Q1	L1	PhD	CS	NUS	2016
Q2	L3	PhD	CS	SMU	2015
Q3	L3	Master	EE	NTU	2013

Fig. 4. University database

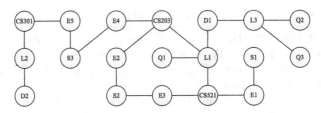

Fig. 5. The data graph for the RDB in Fig. 4

Incomplete Object Answer. Suppose a user issues the keyword query Q1 = {Steven} to retrieve all the information about him. Existing works only return his id and name, i.e., the tuple $L3$ in the Lecturer relation. However, information of his multivalued attributes such as degrees, majors, universities and years of Steven, which are stored in the Qualification relation, are not retrieved.

Incomplete Relationship Answer. Suppose a user wants to know the information of the course where a student Bill obtains grade A, and issues the keyword query Q2 = {Bill A}. Existing works retrieve a Steiner tree which contains the tuples $S1$ and $E1$, as the two query keywords occur in these tuples respectively and there exists a foreign key reference between them. This answer is not informative as the course title is not retrieved.

Meaningless Answer. Suppose a user issues the keyword query Q3 = {S1 S3}. Existing works returns two answers: (a) $S1 - E1 - CS521 - L1 - CS203 - E4 - S3$ and (b) $S1 - E1 - CS521 - E3 - S2 - E2 - CS203 - E4 - S3$. The first answer indicates that student S1 is enrolled in the course CS521 and student S3 is enrolled in the course CS203. Both the courses are taught by the same lecturer L1. In other words, L1 is the common lecturer of S1 and S3. The second answer means that some other student S2 is enrolled in the same course CS521 as S1; S2 is also enrolled in the same course CS203 as S3. We observe that the second answer is most likely meaningless to the user.

Complex Answers. Given a query answer which is a Steiner tree, e.g., $S1 - E1 - CS521 - L1 - CS203 - E4 - S3$ for query Q3, the user may feel difficult to understand. This is because the answer may consists of many nodes that are connected in a complex structure.

Inconsistent Types of Answers. Consider queries Q3 and Q4 = {S1 S2}. Both the queries comprise of two student ids. However, existing works retrieve answer $S1 - E1 - CS521 - L1 - CS203 - E4 - S3$ for query Q3 and answer $S1 - E1 - CS521 - E3 - S2$ for query Q4. The former indicates the common lecturer while the latter indicates the common course of these two students. This can be confusing as two similar queries have inconsistent answers. The reason is that existing keyword search methods do not interpret the user's search intention and blindly return Steiner trees of keyword match nodes.

Schema Dependence. Given the same data source, the relations in RDB are often denormalized to improve runtime performance. This denormalization leads to data duplication and affects the database schema. Existing works do not consider unnormalized relations in RDB, and thus may suffer from the problems of duplicated answers and missing answers. For example, suppose we join the Student, Enrol and Course relations in Fig. 4 and obtain an unnormalized relation Enrolment(SID, Name, Code, Title, LID, Grade) to store information of students, courses and the many-to-many relationships between students and courses. Given the query {Bill}, existing works will retrieve duplicated answers as information of student Bill are duplicated in the Enrolment relation. On the other hand, the data graph of this relation has no edges because of no foreign key references. Then existing works will not retrieve any answers for query Q3.

From the above problems, we see that existing works on relational keyword search are highly dependent on foreign key-key references and return Steiner trees as query answers. These answers are difficult to understand and often fail to satisfy users' search intention. This is because existing methods do not consider ORA-semantics and thus cannot interpret keyword queries.

In contrast, we exploit ORA-semantics and utilize them to solve these problems. We classify relations in RDB into object relations, relationship relations, mixed relations and component relations [19]. An object (relationship resp.) relation captures the information of objects (relationships resp.). The multivalued attributes of an object class (relationship type) are captured in component relations. A mixed relation contains information of both objects and relationships, which occurs when we have a many-to-one relationship.

Based on the different types of relations, we build an ORM data graph that consists of object, relationship and mixed nodes. Each node includes some tuple in the corresponding relation. Tuples in component relations are attached to their corresponding object/relationship/mixed nodes. Two nodes are connected via an edge if there is a foreign key-key reference between tuples in the nodes.

We search over the ORM data graph and process queries based on the types of keyword match nodes. The information of objects and relationships in the

ORM data graph enable us to retrieve more complete and informative answers. We further extend keyword queries to include metadata keywords and aggregate functions to enhance the expressive power and evaluation of keyword queries. More details are described in [18, 20].

7   ORA-Semantics in XML Keyword Search

Similar to relational keyword search, XML keyword search has also been widely studied [17, 21]. Existing works in XML keyword search typically consider an XML document without ID references and model it as a tree. An answer to a keyword query is defined as an LCA (Least Common Ancestor) of keyword match nodes, or its variants such as SLCA [17] and ELCA [21].

We choose the LCA-based approach as a representative and use Fig. 6 to illustrate the problems of current XML keyword search. More details are in [11].

Meaningless Answer. Consider query Q5 = {Bill}. The LCA-based approach returns node Bill_(21). However, this is not useful since it does not provide any relevant information about Bill. This happens when a returned node is a non-object node, e.g., an attribute or a value. The reason is that the LCA-based approach cannot differentiate object and non-object nodes. Returning object node is meaningful while returning non-object node is not. The expected answer should be the object node Student_(17), which includes the id and name of Bill and excludes his grade as grade is a relationship attribute.

Missing Answer. Consider query Q6 = {DB Java}. The LCA-based approach only returns Lecturer_(7). However, it can never recognize that Student_(24) and Student_(36) refer to the same object Student S2. This is the common student taking the DB and Java courses. The LCA-based approach should also return the common student taking these two courses, namely, Student S2 appearing as Student_(24) or Student_(36) as an answer.

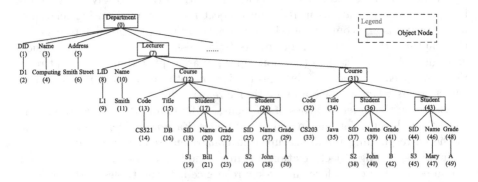

Fig. 6. University.xml

Duplicated Answer. Consider query Q7 = {S2 John}. The LCA-based approach returns two answers Student_(24) and Student_(36). These two answers are duplicated as they actually refer to the same object Student S2. This problem is caused by the duplications of student objects as DTD/XML Schema cannot declare SID as the ID of students, and the LCA-based approach are unaware of these duplications. Users expect that either Student_(24) or Student_(36) is returned, but not both.

Problems Related to Relationships. Consider query Q8 = {Bill A}. The LCA-based approach returns node Student_(17). This answer is incomplete because A grade is not an attribute of a student, but the grade of a student taking a course instead. In other words, grade is an attribute of relationships between students and courses. The LCA-based approach cannot distinguish between an object attribute and a relationship attribute under an object node, as DTD cannot express this semantics. The answer should be moved up to contain other objects (i.e., Course_(12)) participating in the relationship that A grade belongs to. It means that the student Bill takes the Course_(12) and obtains an A grade.

Inconsistent Types of Answers. Similar to RDB keyword search, the LCA-based approach returns inconsistent types of answers for similar queries. For example, the LCA-based approach returns answer {Course_(12)} for query {S1 S2} and answer {Lecturer_(7)} for query {S1 S3}. These two answers refer to objects of different classes and users may get confused as the queries are similar.

Schema Dependence. There may be several designs for the same data source. The XML data in Fig. 6 can be represented by another design where Student objects become the parents of Course objects. Since the LCA-based approach replies on the hierarchical structure of the XML data, it may return different answers for different designs even though these designs refer to exactly the same information and we are dealing with the same query.

From the above, we see that existing LCA-based approach only depends on the hierarchical structure of XML and is unaware of ORA-semantics in the data. This approach suffers from serious problems as it cannot distinguish between objects, relationships and their attributes, and it cannot detect duplications of objects/relationships.

We have designed an approach to discover ORA-semantics in XML [13]. Based on the ORA-semantics, we construct an Object tree for the XML data by keeping only object nodes and associating all non-object nodes to the corresponding object nodes. The Object tree contains a much smaller number of nodes than the original XML and every node represents an object.

Given a keyword query, we search for lowest common object ancestors (LCOAs) over the Object tree. Since each LCOA contains all the information of an object, we can avoid returning meaningless answers and duplicated answers. We also search for highest common object descendants (HCODs) to find answers that are missed by LCOAs. Finally, we introduc common relatives (CRs) to perform a schema independent keyword search. More details are given in [8,10].

We also support queries involving aggregates and GROUPBY in XML keyword search [9]. We show that ORA-semantics is sufficient and necessary to compute aggregate functions correctly. Without ORA-semantics, we may answer aggregate queries incorrectly.

8   Conclusion

In this paper, we identify the expressive limitations of common database models such as the relational model and the XML data model due to the lack of ORA-semantics. First of all, both FDs/MVDs in the relational model and DTD/XML Schema in the XML data model do not have concepts of ORA-semantics. They are just integrity constraints and many are imposed artificially by database designers/organizations. This may lead to problematic database schemas in relational/XML database design. Next, without ORA-semantics, data and schema integration suffers from many problems such as different data models, different relationship types, local/global object identifier, local/global FD, semantic dependency, and schematic discrepancy. Finally, existing works on RDB/XML keyword search do not consider ORA-semantics and thus return incomplete answers, duplicated answers, meaningless answers, inconsistent types of answers and schema dependent answers. We point out the reasons of these serious problems and show how ORA-semantics can improve the correctness of database research in these areas. In future, we plan to study ORA-semantics on NoSQL databases, and keyword search on multiple databases that are represented by various data models including RDB, XML and NoSQL.

References

1. Bernstein, P.A.: Synthesizing third normal form relations from functional dependencies. ACM Trans. Database Syst. **1**, 277–298 (1976)
2. Chen, P.P.: The entity-relationship model: toward a unified view of data. ACM Trans. Database Syst. **1**, 9–36 (1976)
3. Codd, E.F.: A relational model of data for large shared data banks. ACM Commun. **13**, 377–387 (1970)
4. Dobbie, G., Wu, X., Ling, T.W., Lee, M.L.: ORA-SS: an object-relationship-attribute model for semistructured data. Technical report, National University of Singapore (2000)
5. He, Q., Ling, T. W.: Extending and inferring functional dependencies in schema transformation. In: CIKM (2004)
6. Hristidis, V., Papakonstantinou, Y., Discover: keyword search in relational databases. In: VLDB (2002)
7. Hulgeri, A., Nakhe, C.: Keyword searching and browsing in databases using BANKS. In: ICDE (2002)
8. Le, T.N., Bao, Z., Ling, T.W.: Schema-independence in XML keyword search. In: Yu, E., Dobbie, G., Jarke, M., Purao, S. (eds.) ER 2014. LNCS, vol. 8824, pp. 71–85. Springer, Heidelberg (2014). doi:10.1007/978-3-319-12206-9_6

9. Le, T.N., Bao, Z., Ling, T.W., Dobbie, G.: Group-by and aggregate functions in XML keyword search. In: Decker, H., Lhotská, L., Link, S., Spies, M., Wagner, R.R. (eds.) DEXA 2014. LNCS, vol. 8644, pp. 105–121. Springer, Heidelberg (2014). doi:10.1007/978-3-319-10073-9_10

10. Le, T.N., Ling, T.W., Jagadish, H.V., Lu, J.: Object semantics for XML keyword search. In: Bhowmick, S.S., Dyreson, C.E., Jensen, C.S., Lee, M.L., Muliantara, A., Thalheim, B. (eds.) DASFAA 2014. LNCS, vol. 8422, pp. 311–327. Springer, Heidelberg (2014). doi:10.1007/978-3-319-05813-9_21

11. Le, T.N., Wu, H., Ling, T.W., Li, L., Lu, J.: From structure-based to semantics-based: towards effective XML keyword search. In: Ng, W., Storey, V.C., Trujillo, J.C. (eds.) ER 2013. LNCS, vol. 8217, pp. 356–371. Springer, Heidelberg (2013). doi:10.1007/978-3-642-41924-9_29

12. Lee, M., Ling, T.W.: Resolving structural conflicts in the integration of entity-relationship schemas. In: Papazoglou, M.P. (ed.) OOER 1995. LNCS, vol. 1021, pp. 424–433. Springer, Heidelberg (1995). doi:10.1007/BFb0020552

13. Li, L., Le, T.N., Wu, H., Ling, T.W., Bressan, S.: Discovering semantics from data-centric XML. In: Decker, H., Lhotská, L., Link, S., Basl, J., Tjoa, A.M. (eds.) DEXA 2013. LNCS, vol. 8055, pp. 88–102. Springer, Heidelberg (2013). doi:10.1007/978-3-642-40285-2_10

14. Ling, T.W.: An analysis of multivalued and join dependencies based on the entity-relationship approach. Data Knowl. Eng. 1, 253–271 (1985)

15. Ling, T.W., Teo, P.K.: A normal form object-oriented entity relationship diagram. In: Loucopoulos, P. (ed.) ER 1994. LNCS, vol. 881, pp. 241–258. Springer, Heidelberg (1994). doi:10.1007/3-540-58786-1_83

16. Ling, T.W., Tompa, F.W., Kameda, T.: An improved third normal form for relational databases. ACM Trans. Database Syst. 6, 329–346 (1981)

17. Xu, Y., Papakonstantinou, Y.: Efficient keyword search for smallest LCAs in XML databases. In: SIGMOD (2005)

18. Zeng, Z., Bao, Z., Le, T.N., Lee, M.L., Ling, W.T.: ExpressQ: identifying keyword context and search target in relational keyword queries. In: CIKM (2014)

19. Zeng, Z., Bao, Z., Lee, M.L., Ling, T.W.: A semantic approach to keyword search over relational databases. In: Ng, W., Storey, V.C., Trujillo, J.C. (eds.) ER 2013. LNCS, vol. 8217, pp. 241–254. Springer, Heidelberg (2013). doi:10.1007/978-3-642-41924-9_21

20. Zeng, Z., Lee, M.L., Ling, W.T.: Answering keyword queries involving aggregates and groupby on relational databases. In: EDBT (2016)

21. Zhou, R., Liu, C., Li, J.: Fast ELCA computation for keyword queries on XML data. In: EDBT (2010)

Conceptual Modeling of Life: Beyond the Homo Sapiens

Oscar Pastor[✉]

Centro de I+D en Métodos de Producción de Software (PROS),
Universitat Politècnica de València, Camino de Vera s/n, 46022 Valencia, Spain
opastor@dsic.upv.es

Abstract. Our strong capability of conceptualization makes us, human beings, different from any other species in our planet. We, as conceptual modelers, should apply in the right direction such fascinating capability to make it play an essential role in the design of the world to come. What does it mean that "right direction" requiresa challenging discussion. Halfway between the need of having a sound philosophical characterization and an effective, practical computer science application, conceptual modeling emerges as the ideal discipline needed for understanding life and improving our life style. This keynote explores this argument by delimiting the notion and scope of conceptual modeling, and by introducing and discussing two possible scenarios of fruitful application. The first one is oriented to better understand why conceptual modeling can help to manage the social challenges of the world of the emerging information era, and how this world that comes could benefit from it. The second one focuses on how understanding the human genome can open new ways to go beyond what we can consider "traditional Homo Sapiens capabilities", with especial implications in the health domain and the new medicine of precision.

Keywords: Conceptual modeling · Conceptual models · Applications of conceptual modeling

1 Introduction

I live Conceptual Modeling (CM) with passion. For a person with this working passion, conceptualizing—as the basic process of CM—is present in almost every aspect of life. How to use it successfully becomes a challenge whose analysis is the objective of this keynote paper. The selected title is the first consequence of the faced topic. Conceptual modeling of life because behind any section of the paper there is always a concrete goal: to analyze how CM could be seen as a scientific approach to understand and improve life.

This covers a too open spectrum, and as time and space are limited, two main perspectives are going to be explored. The first one (Sect. 3) is a so-called "social perspective", intended to discuss how CM could help to better design the world to come, the world that in the information and hyperconnectivity era is already approaching. The second one (Sect. 4) is a so-called "biological perspective", which is closer to the scientific meaning of life, focused on arguing on how CM could help to understand

© Springer International Publishing AG 2016
I. Comyn-Wattiau et al. (Eds.): ER 2016, LNCS 9974, pp. 18–31, 2016.
DOI: 10.1007/978-3-319-46397-1_2

the human genome transforming us, the current Homo Sapiens "version", into an evolved species able tomanage and transform life in our planet.

To make this discussion meaningful, the first aspect to be studied is necessarily to determine as much precisely as possible the scope and the definition of CM. It is a concept largely discussed but without a universally accepted definition, and the second section will be dedicated to this problem. Based on this positioning, the two previous perspectives will be then analyzed. Conclusions and references will close as usual the work. The idea of this paper is to introduce the guidelines of the keynote, in which more concrete details and examples will be given.

2 Conceptual Modeling Fundamentals: What Are We Talking About

The capability of conceptualizing is essential for human beings as it makes us different for any other species in our planet. It should then be massively accepted as an essential tool in the scope of software engineering (SE) and information systems (IS) engineering. This is not the case, and programming (as the act) and programmers (as the actors) are frequently socially recognized as their main roles. Conceptual models should be the key artefacts to make true that "the model is the code" instead "the code is the model". Unfortunately, this does not appear to be the case... yet! In current practice, software production methods are mainly code-centric, and it is the latter statement the one still guiding traditionally a software production process.

In a world heavily influenced by "doers", just doing something without understanding with a sound conceptual basis why to do it and how to do it better, appears to be too often the selected approach. Working as a Conceptual Modeler, or being nowadays a participant in a Conceptual Modeling conference, could be seen in some way close to the famous call for participation done by Shackleton, British explorer and adventurer, when looking for candidates for his expedition to cross the Antarctic (see Fig. 1).

Fig. 1. Conceptual modelers wanted to face the challenges of the world to come: an analogy with the famous Shackleton call to cross the Antarctic.

In practical terms, conceptual modeling-based software production tools should be widely used and conceptual programmers should be the basic actors of any sound, well-defined software production process. As said before, even if a significant set of concrete proposals already exist (i.e. the conceptual programming manifesto presented in [1], the fundamentals of a conceptual model compiler introduced in [2]), this does not appear to be the case. Any discussion around this fact should start clarifying the definition and the scope of CM to try to envision scenarios of fruitful use. In this context, this keynote has three main goals:

- to discuss the notion and the scope of Conceptual Modeling,
- to analyze how conceptual modeling can help us to understand the world that comes (within what we could call a "social perspective"), and
- to analyze how conceptual modeling can open promising and challenging scenarios in the domain of the genome understanding.

2.1   Definitions for Conceptual Modeling/Conceptual Model

Teaching conceptual modeling since the early nineties, I have faced many times the very simple question of "what is conceptual modeling" and "what is a conceptual model". While some common, basic understanding could be said to be shared by many conceptual modelers, it is amazing to realize that so many years after the introduction by Chen of the seminal ER model [3] as a widely recognized conceptual model, the discussion for providing a universal, widely-accepted simple definition is still an open problem. Let me analyze some basic definitions to understand how CM is perceived commonly, and to explore the commented, shared understanding of the two notions.

Starting from a so elementary source as Wikipedia, we can find this first definition: "a conceptual model is a model made of the composition of concepts, which are used to help people know, understand, or simulate a subject the model represents". If a conceptual model is a model, the problem is transferred to the definition of "model". If we want to find what is a "model", what we have is that a model may refer to a conceptual model, a physical model, a scale model or a scientific model. Loop and back to the beginning…

Probably, Wikipedia is not the best option from a formal point of view. But if we look at some of the most well-known definition of "model" [4], we find that a model is defined as a simplification of a system built with an intended goal in mind [5], as an abstraction of a system to reason about it (either a physical system [6] or a real or language-based system [7]), as a description of specification of a system and its environment for some certain purpose [8], … One main conclusion that we can reach is that the distinction between "model" and "conceptual model" is not always as precise at it should be. As stated in [4], "while much has already been written on this topic, there is however neither precise description about we do when we model, nor rigorous description about of the relations among modeling artifacts". Looking for a kind of universal definition, it appears to be true what JochenLudewig states in [9]: "nobody can just define what a model is, and expect that other people will accept this definition: endless discussions have proven that there is no consistent problem understanding of models".

I would not agree with such a statement as a major conclusion. As said before, conceptualizing provides the key notion to characterize a modeling process. As a "conceptual" process, it is difficult to imagine a "model" that has not behind its essence a process of conceptualizing. This is why in this keynote we will explore the use of the "conceptual model" term assuming that a conceptual model is a model where the main components are concepts resulting from a process of conceptualizing a part of reality.

Back to Wikipedia to understand how CM is defined in non-formal contexts, more complexity arises. Exploring the definition it can be immediately discovered that there is another different proposed definition for conceptual model in the context of computer science: "A Conceptual model in the field of computer science is also known as a domain model. Conceptual modeling should not be confused with other modeling disciplines such as data modelling, logical modelling and physical modelling. The conceptual model is explicitly chosen to be independent of design or implementation concerns...". We see that the distinction between modeling and conceptual modeling is again unclear. What it is interesting is how an ontological perspective is introduced: "the aim of a conceptual model is to express the meaning of terms and concepts used by domain experts to discuss the problem, and to find the correct relationships between different concepts. The conceptual model attempts to clarify the meaning of various, usually ambiguous terms, and ensure that problems with different interpretations of the terms and concepts cannot occur. Such differing interpretations could easily cause confusion amongst stakeholders, especially those responsible for designing and implementing a solution, where the conceptual model provides a key artifact of business understanding and clarity". This ontological perspective will be explored in more detail later.

Another important aspect in this context is the connection between the conceptual model and the corresponding software product that materializes it. Once concepts of the domain have been modeled, the model becomes a stable basis for subsequent development of applications in the domain. The concepts of the conceptual model can be mapped into physical design or implementation constructs using either manual or automated code generation approaches. This is the basis of any model-driven development approach.

At least, this "computer science" perspective of CM—that I will prefer to refer to as SE/IS perspective—opens a more precise way to define CM, where we can find a significant agreement. Let me first refer to the John Mylopoulos's seminal paper [10] that defines the discipline of conceptual modeling as "the activity of formally describing some aspects of the physical and social world around us for purposes of understanding and communication. Conceptual modelling supports structuring and inferential facilities that are psychologically grounded. After all, the descriptions that arise from conceptual modelling activities are intended to be used by humans, not machines... The adequacy of a conceptual modelling notation rests on its contribution to the construction of models of reality that promote a common understanding of that reality among their human users..."

Back to the conceptualization human capability, we can conclude that a conceptual model is then the result of making explicit a conceptualization process applied to a part of the world considered relevant for the conceptual modeler purpose. This idea is clearly developed by Olivé in [11]: "In the information systems field, we use the name conceptual modeling for the activity that elicits and describes the general knowledge a particular information system needs to know. The main objective of conceptual modeling is to obtain that description, which is called a conceptual schema. Conceptual schemas are written in languages called conceptual modeling languages. Conceptual modeling is an important part of requirements engineering, the first and most important phase in the development of an information system".

This statement raises an interesting concern: how the terms "conceptual model" and "conceptual schema" are traditionally mixed up probably incorrectly. As an example taken from the database field, this mistake does not appear when we distinguish between "relational model" and "relational schema". Even it is frequent to see that these terms are used in a undistinguishable way, we have to be at least aware that what it is frequently referred to as a "conceptual model", it is really representing a particular "conceptual schema".

In the considered SE/IS context, we can then conclude that conceptual modeling is about describing the semantics of software applications at a high level of abstraction. Specifically, conceptual modelers have to (1) describe structure models in terms of entities, relationships, and constraints; (2) describe behavior or functional models in terms of states, transitions among states, and actions performed in states and transition; and (3) describe interactions and user interfaces in terms of messages sent and received, information exchanged, and look-and-feel navigation and appearance. Conceptual model diagrams are high-level abstractions that enable clients and analysts to understand one another and enable analysts to communicate successfully with application programmers. An immediate challenge is to facilitate the long-time dream of being able to develop information systems strictly by conceptual modeling, to be able to say that conceptual modeling is programming.

If behind a conceptual model there is a conceptualization process, the ontological perspective of conceptual modeling becomes a first-order issue to understand what CM is. Let's develop this aspect in the next section.

2.2   Foundational Ontological Background

Recovering Olive's ideas [11], in the field of information systems we make the fundamental assumption that a domain consists of a number of objects and the relationships between them, which are classified into concepts. The set of concepts used in a particular domain constitutes a conceptualization of that domain. The specification of this conceptualization is what conforms a particular conceptual model of the domain (sometimes called an ontology of the domain, although to see the conceptual schema as anontology-based representation of a domain provides a more precise picture). Note that in this context, the term ontology is used—in computer science terms—as a specification of the basic conceptual primitives used in the process of conceptualization. There may be several conceptualizations of the same domain and thus several possible conceptual schemas, all of them based on the same ontological primitives. Additionally, an ontology provides a concrete view of a particular domain. Therefore, it is also an ontological commitment for the people who observe and act on this domain.

In the field of information systems, ontologies are the basis for creating conceptual schemas, and the languages in which they are written are called conceptual modeling languages.

This perspective provides a solid basis to link ontologies and CM, through the use of a foundational ontology. Conceptual models provide a precise definition of structural knowledge in a specific field that can be instantiated across different application domains in the corresponding field. Such a conceptual model should always be built based on a foundational ontology that must determine the basic conceptual building units to be used to specify any concrete application domain.

The notion of foundational ontology is essential. A foundational ontology can be defined as an ontology that "defines a range of top-level domain-independent onto-logical categories, which form a general foundation for more elaborated domain-specific ontologies" [12, 13]. Rephrasing Guizzardi in [14], on the basis of a foundational ontology "a domain ontology is constructed with the goal of making the best possible description of the domain in reality". It can be represented as a conceptual model, as an engineering artifact with the additional requirement of representing a model of consensus within a community. Once users have already agreed on a common conceptualization, operational versions of the reference (foundational) ontology can be created. Selecting a foundational ontology determines the kind of conceptualization that must be performed.

Contrary to foundational ontologies, operational ontologies are designed with the focus on guaranteeing desirable computational properties. This makes a clear distinction between the foundational ontological perspective of conceptual modeling, and the operational perspective of ontologies represented by OWL, that it is not then a good choice for representing "foundational" ontologies. As a representation of a foundational ontology, a particular OWL ontology could consequently be seen as a conceptual model for the considered application domain.

In this context of ontology-driven conceptual modeling it is very important to characterize the different sets of meta-ontological choices that can produce different types of conceptual models. As analyzed in the OntoCom workshop series [15], "the effects of these differences resonate further into the overall information systems (IS) development lifecycle, with potentially significant economic impact on the evolution and integration of information systems. This especially affects the intended quality of the conceptual models that are generated to represent a given domain". It is important to know and to understand what methaphysical choices are taken when a given foundational ontology is proposed, because these choices characterizes the type of conceptual models that can be generated. In some sense, these metaphysical options determine what kind of conceptualization is applied to elaborate a specific conceptual model and not another one. As it is stated in [15], "sound knowledge of a foundational ontology's metaphysical choices better enables the IS modeler and practitioner to assess the consequences of selecting one foundational ontology over another, including the effects on the quality of the conceptual models underpinning the requirements and design of information systems".

Examples of meta-ontological choices were discussed in [15] and include [16–18]:

- Realism vs. idealism: there exists an objective reality (realism) or reality is individually constructed by one's own concepts (or ideas) resulting from one's subjective interpretation (idealism).
- Endurantism vs. perdurantism: individual objects are fully present at any given time and do not extend temporally (endurantism) or individual objects extend spatially and temporally, therefore, an individual is never wholly present at a specific instant in time (perdurantism).
- Physical vs. abstract objects: all individual objects are physical and no abstract objects exist (physical objects) or not all objects are physical therefore some objects are abstract (abstract objects).
- Higher order types: types can instantiate other types.
- Possible worlds: Our actual world is one of many possible worlds.

These different dimensions can help to classify different types of conceptualization supported by different proposals of foundational ontologies. Since the application of meta-ontology to conceptual modeling and IS development is still relatively underexplored and with a scarce literature, this perspective can really help to conduct comparative analyses of two or more foundational ontologies (and their subsequent conceptual modeling languages). This would allow to, for example, make explicit their theoretical differences, understand the different expressiveness of the resultant conceptual and investigating the implications of such differences on conceptual modelling within information systems development.

3 Conceptual Modeling and Life: A Social View and a Biological View

After emphasizing the link between conceptualizing and conceptual modeling, and the subsequent importance of conceptual modeling for human beings, let's explore in this section how we could benefit from recognizing and improving our CM capabilities. Understanding how our process of conceptualizing works in order to better understand our world and how to adapt it to our purposes, would allow us to go beyond the current, conventional "Homo Sapiens" rational capabilities. CM should be the basic tool of a future, evolved human being, able to use a level of knowledge never reached before, based on the rational use of universal information and advanced technologies. We are going to develop these ideas from two points of view:

- a social one, intended to analyze how CM can help us to look at the world to come as a better world, and
- a biological one, oriented to discover the secrets of life in our planet through the detailed understanding of the genome language, in order to profit this knowledge in the right direction.

3.1 The Social Perspective: Conceptual Modeling for Understanding the World That Is Coming

Understanding the world to come can be seen as a challenge whose solution should be CM-based. The sequence of social and technological advances that we are witnessing in the last decades is the source of a new era for the humanity. A CM-based exercise is required to understand those big changes and their immediate consequences. Once more, conceptualization is the key activity to guide adequately this new world that comes. This conceptualization process should be oriented to identify the basic issues that lead the change, to understand how they affect the current social context and to develop strategies to implement an accurate transformation.

Many works study this attractive social perspective. For instance, in [19], the basic issues whose continuous development is creating the context for the new world to come includes:

1. Hyperconnectity: the global net platform that has been created gives a big power to individuals and it allows the whole world to be more and more connected, having immediate access at any information and knowledge in the planet. This also blurs geographical barriers and it creates world of total, open competition.
2. Technological acceleration: the technological improvement is following an exponential growth. This technological explosion opens the way for a technological revolution whose intensity and social implications have never seen before.
3. Raising of world-wide emerging citizens, coming potentially from any country of the world and ready to consume and compete. The emergence of this new actor will impact economics and politics.

What role can CM play in this context? The combination of these three issues requires to perform an intense CM exercise to understand how they interact among them and to analyze the possible scenarios that could be generated as a result of these interactions. "Just doing it" does not appear to be an adequate approach.

A precise understanding of the concepts that participate in those potential scenarios is strongly required. Beyond its conventional use in the design and development of IS, conceptual modeling should provide a solid basis to discuss and materialize the opportunities demanded by this new world that is coming. The IS that must support this human evolution should be conceptually well-founded, and concepts as relevant as context, adaptability, decision, luck, user experience, satisfaction, sustainability… should have a strong conceptual support to represent them appropriately in those ISs.

Educating conceptual modeling skills will be the essential challenge to form citizens whose capabilities are expected to go beyond the Homo Sapiens traditional behavior. To do it, the role of a conceptual modeler is to understand the mental models used to abstract and represent the concepts that are relevant for a given domain. Identifying concepts and their relationships should guide the conceptual discussion intended to elaborate the most adequate solution.

An interesting conceptual starting point to characterize the types of knowledge that must be considered are proposed by Gervasi et al. [20] and explored in by Sutcliffe et al. [21] from a RE perspective. A Tacit Knowledge Framework is introduced, using the properties of expressible, i.e. known knowledge; articulated, as documented known knowledge; accessible, which is known but not in the foreground of the stakeholder's mind and therefore a memory recall problem; and relevant to the project and domain. As a result this work defines:

- Known knowns: expressible, articulated, and relevant.
- Known unknowns: not expressible or articulated, but accessible and potentially relevant.
- Unknown knowns: potentially accessible but not articulated.
- Unknown unknowns: not expressible, articulated or accessible but still potentially relevant.

While conventional CM focus on identifying "known knowns", these definitions provides an attractive taxonomy to be used in the conception process of a conceptual model. Conceptual modelers should act as the knowledge architects of those relevant data and the information generated by this hyperconnected world, composed by last-generation technologies in continuous evolution and reached by virtually all the human population.

One of the most appealing and challenging applications of this advanced technologies are those that focus on understanding the Human Genome. In the next subsection we are going to discuss another perspective of conceptual modeling of life: a biological one centered around facing the problem of how conceptual modeling can be applied to the never-answered question of understanding why we are as we are, and how the challenge of managing life could be faced.

3.2 The Biological Perspective: Conceptual Modeling for Understanding the Human Genome

Philosophers are for centuries trying to answer the question of why we—human beings —are as we are. Why do we behave as we behave? What is our origin and our destiny? Understanding and manipulating life has historically being out of our scope, and considered closer to religion than to pure science.

But again a new world is coming where CM can play an essential role. From a SE/IS perspective software products can be generated from a conceptual schema following a binary, silicon-based execution model based on 0s and 1s. Using an analogy, from a biological point of view we have the programs—any living being—executing an execution model that is carbon-based and instead uses four letters (A, C, G, T, the four nucleotides that conforms the basic elements of a DNA sequence). In this case we have the program instances, but we don't have the models. Analyzing this as a reverse engineering model-driven problem, we have the program and but don't know—yet!— the conceptual schema that a given program represent. This analogy is represented in Fig. 2.

A huge amount of data is generated continuously in the genome domain. While the sequencing technologies are making more feasible and accessible to obtain our genome sequenced, what do we do with a data file that contains approximately 3,200,000,000 nucleotides of DNA whose meaning is mainly unknown for us? We could go further in our analogy with conventional code, wondering what we would do with a huge

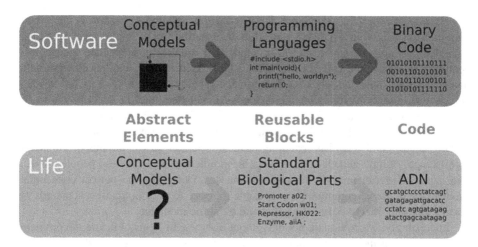

Fig. 2. Conceptual models for software versus conceptual models for life

sequence of 0–1s of an executable program if this sequence of millions of 0–1s were our only documentation of the program.

The technologies that are sequencing DNA improve at an impressive speed, Converting the initial sample of blood or saliva in a final sequence requests a sophisticated process where again the data perspective is essential. The so-called bioinformatics pipeline (see Fig. 3) follows a precise process where firstly, after a raw data capturing step the initial physical sample is converted into a given file visualization format (usually technology dependent). Secondly a sequence estimation process and an alignment to a reference sequence process generate a set of files with a de-facto, widely accepted data file formats (FAST, FASTQ, SAM, BAM). Finally, a comparative report with the relevant genome variants is generated using another text file format especially created for the case (VCF).

Fig. 3. The bioinformatics pipeline: sequence of actions, each one generating a type of file with a particular data format.

The problem is that this is just one concern of the problem. Beyond this technological perspective, once we have for instance the VCF file with the reported variants, the other concern of the problem is how to interpret the semantics of these variants in terms of what phenotype implications they may have. In clinical terms, we want to know what variations are related to what diseases. Considering the big number of diseases and the short amount of knowledge that we currently have, it is easy to conclude how much work is still to be done in the next decades.

To improve our knowledge of DNA variation and the consistency in variant classification will require a massive effort in data sharing. As we will discuss next, this data sharing implies a CM exercise to identify the relevant concepts and their corresponding relationships. Only having such a CM-based background, an efficient data analysis can be done and assessed. For instance, a recent analysis of the ClinVar data source on variant interpretation comparisons concluded that 11 % (12,895 up to 118,169) of variants had two or more submitters, and 17 % (2229 up to 12,895) were interpreted differently [22, 23]. Increasingly, genetic tests provide ambiguous results, leaving doctors and scientists searching to make sense of these "variants of unknown significance". Clinic genetics may have a big problem that is affecting people's lives. One again, CM can provide the required answer. Designing the correct conceptual models, the genomic community could come together to develop its own standards to ensure safe and effective use of genetic and genomic medicine.

Interestingly, we could talk not only about diseases. In terms of facing the problem of understanding the human genome, the final challenge is to understand any characteristic related with our way of living: physiognomy, personality features... The capability of being able to know and manipulate this type of properties opens scientific and ethical challenges that we have never faced in our history. Never in the past the Homo Sapiens has been able to understand how life works in order to manage this knowledge to transform life according to his interests. This is a strong, cultural revolution, that justifies why in the title of this keynote the term "beyond the Homo Sapiens" has been introduced. A Homo Sapiens with the capability of transforming herself appears to conform an evolved Homo Sapiens. Without any doubt, an interesting topic for a rich, long discussion!

Bioinformatics and CM. If we wonder what it is the role of CM in this context, the answer is immediate. More and more data are generated every day. Just for the human case, the size of a complete genome for an individual person is approximately 2.5–3 GB, but the data involved in the process is ten times bigger. We can imagine the Big Data problem related to the setup and maintenance of a sort of Genome database where we could for instance store the genomes of all the humanity. The most similar experience, the 1000 Genomes database, stores several TB of data. Still worse, it is not just a problem of data loading, it is a problem of data management. We should be able to "read" any particular genome, to compare different genomes, to edit a genome as we do with a conventional program... Genome editing technologies start to be a reality and the practical implications of all these facts are anticipating a revolution in our human concept of medicine, leading to the medicine of precision, a personalized medicine where any treatment will be dependent on the personal "genomic" code of the patient.

Additionally, we do not should forget that life in our planet is not only limited to humans! Any life as we understand it on the Earth is genome-based. This means that whatever we are saying for the human genome could be generalized and could be applied to any genome of any kind of species. Giving a unifying data treatment to the problem of representing life as a whole is a problem whose dimension is even hard to delimit.

This context provides a challenging working environment for the CM community. It is surprising to realize that in such a complex context, where data management and data understanding is a first-order problem, CM practice is ignored too frequently. To make things worse, current data are spread over a very diverse set of heterogeneous data sources, where data consistency is not warranted and data integration is tremendously complex - when just not possible.

The only feasible strategy to provide a sustainable solution should be centered around the use of the well-known IS principles, using CM techniques and proposing a kind of Genome IS approach based on a precise conceptual schema of the human genome (CSGH). While steps in this direction are already under development [24], much more work is to be done to assess that a sound conceptual background is provided to make possible an effective and efficient genome data management policy. This CSHG will act as conceptual repository designed to include all the knowledge accumulated around the human genome, and unifying the management of that heterogeneous set of data sources from a holistic perspective. Only with such an "oracle" of valid, well-designed data, a sustainable progress can be performed, based on storing and managing more and more right ("curated") data to be obtained as research in the domain progresses and to be provided to the community in the form of accurate results.

The steps towards a successful and reliable universal medicine of precision are fully dependent on the success of this IS and CM perspective, and this is probably the most promising scenario for CM practices in the next future.

4 Conclusions

This keynote emphasizes the intended importance of conceptualizing from two perspectives: from an Information Systems/Software Engineering perspective on the one side, and from a social, human being-oriented perspective on the other side. The world to come is plenty of social and technological challenges, and the discussed approach is that its fruitful development should be CM-based.

Assuming that CM is the essential discipline to develop such an evolved, better world where technology and information were properly used, conceptual modelers should play a central role. To understand this role, what CM is and what its scope is has been analyzed, focusing on the ontological background that such a sound definition requires.

An initial analysis of practical implications is discussed, If we want to build a better world, we must know what we are trying to build. The hardest part for most designers of complex systems is not knowing how to design such a complex system, but what it is what they are trying to design. This is where CM can provide the needed answers and tools. Using CM to understand and manage life—from both those social and biological points of view—will help us to use adequately our rational power of conceptualization, going beyond the capabilities traditionally attached to human beings and opening the door to an improved version of our species: beyond the Homo Sapiens, for developing a challenging, improved world that is already coming, with a sound CM background as the essential strategy to make it viable and real.

References

1. Embley, D.W., Liddle, S.W., Pastor, O.: Conceptual-model programming: a manifesto. In: Embley, D.W., Thalheim, B. (eds.) Handbook of Conceptual Modeling, pp. 3–16. Springer, Heidelberg (2011)
2. Pastor, O., Molina, J.C.: Model-Driven Architecture in Practice: A Software Production Environment Based on Conceptual Modeling. Springer, Heidelberg (2007). pp. I–XVI, 1–302. ISBN 978-3-540-71867-3
3. Chen, P.P.: The entity-relationship model - toward a unified view of data. ACM Trans. Database Syst. 1(1), 9–36 (1976)
4. Muller, P.-A., Fondement, F., Baudry, B.: Modeling modeling. In: Schürr, A., Selic, B. (eds.) MODELS 2009. LNCS, vol. 5795, pp. 2–16. Springer, Heidelberg (2009)
5. Bézivin, J., Gerbé, O.: Towards a precise definition of the OMG/MDA framework. Presented at ASE, Automated Software Engineering, November 2001
6. Brown, A.W.: Model driven architecture: principles and practice. SoSyM 3(3), 314–327 (2004)
7. Kuehne, T.: Matters of (meta-) modeling. SoSyM 5(4), 369–385 (2006)
8. OMG, Model Driven Architecture, Electronic Source: Object Management Group. http://www.omg.org/mda/
9. Ludewig, J.: Models in software engineering - an introduction. SoSyM 2(3), 5–14 (2003)
10. Mylopoulos, J.: Conceptual modeling and telos. In: Loucopoulos, P., Zicari, R. (eds.) Conceptual Modeling, Databases, and CASE: an Integrated View of Information Systems Development, pp. 49–68. Wiley, New York (1992)
11. Olivé, A.: Conceptual Modeling of Information Systems. Springer, Heidelberg (2007). pp. I–XXV, 1–455
12. Guizzardi, G., Wagner, G.: A unified foundational ontology and some applications of it in business modeling. In: CAiSE Workshops, vol. 3, pp. 129–143 (2004)
13. Guizzardi, G.: Towards ontological foundations for conceptual modeling: the unified foundational ontology (UFO) story. Appl. Ontol. 10, 259–271 (2015)
14. Guizzardi, G.: On ontology, ontologies, conceptualizations, modeling languages and (meta)models. In: Vasilecas, O., Edler, J., Caplinskas, A. (eds.) Databases and Information Systems IV, pp. 18–39. IOS Press, Amsterdam (2007)
15. de Cesare, S., Gailly, F., Guizzardi, G., Lycett, M., Partridge, C., Pastor, O.: 4th International Workshop on Ontologies and Conceptual Modeling, Onto.Com 2016 (together with FOIS 2016). http://www.mis.ugent.be/ontocom2016/workshop-program-presentations/
16. Masolo, C., Borgo, S., Gangemi, A., Guarino, N., Oltramari, A.: WonderWeb Deliverable D18: Ontology Library. Ontology Infrastructure for the Semantic Web. Laboratory For Applied Ontology - ISTC-CNR, Trento (2003)
17. Partridge, C.: Note: A Couple of Meta-Ontological Choices for Ontological Architectures. LADSEB CNR, Padova (2002)
18. Sem, S.K., Pulvermacher, M.K., Obrst, L.J.: Toward the Use of an Upper Ontology for U.S. Government and U.S. Military Domains: An Evaluation. The MITRE Corporation, Bedford (2004)
19. Martinez-Barea, J.: The world to come, Ed. Gestión 200, 144 pages. ISBN: 978-84-9875-374-5
20. Gervasi, V., Gacitua, R., Rouncefield, M., Sawyer, P., Kof, L., Ma, L., Nuseibeh, B., Piwek, P., de Roeck, A., Willis, A., Yang, H.: Unpacking tacit knowledge for requirements engineering. In: Maalej, W., Thurimella, A.K. (eds.) Managing Requirements Knowledge. Springer, Heidelberg (2013)

21. Sutcliffe, A., Sawyer, P.: Requirements elicitation: towards the unknown unknowns. In 21st IEEE International Requirements Engineering Conference, RE 2013, pp. 92–104. IEEE (2013). ISBN 978-1-4673-5765-4/13

22. Rehm, H.L:. Deciphering the genome: community driven approaches. In: BioIT World, Boston, MA (2016). http://www.bio-itworldexpo.com/

23. Rehm, H.L., et al.: ClinGen: the clinical genome resource. New Engl. J. Med. Spec. Rep. NEJM **372**, 2235–2242 (2015)

24. Pastor, O., Casamayor, J.C., Celma, M., Mota, L., Pastor, M., Levin, A.M.: Conceptual modeling of human genome: integration challenges. In: Düsterhöft, A., Klettke, M., Schewe, K.-D. (eds.) Conceptual Modelling and Its Theoretical Foundations. LNCS, vol. 7260, pp. 231–250. Springer, Heidelberg (2012)

Analytics and Conceptual Modeling

A Conceptual Modeling Framework for Business Analytics

Soroosh Nalchigar[1(✉)], Eric Yu[1], and Rajgopal Ramani[2]

[1] Department of Computer Science, University of Toronto, Toronto, Canada
{soroosh,eric}@cs.toronto.edu
[2] Deloitte, Global Technology Services, Toronto, Canada
rramani@deloitte.ca

Abstract. Data analytics is an essential element for success in modern enterprises. Nonetheless, to effectively design and implement analytics systems is a non-trivial task. This paper proposes a modeling framework (a set of metamodels and a set of design catalogues) for requirements analysis of data analytics systems. It consists of three complementary modeling views: business view, analytics design view, and data preparation view. These views are linked together and act as a bridge between enterprise strategies, analytics algorithms, and data preparation activities. The framework comes with a set of catalogues that codify and represent an organized body of business analytics design knowledge. The framework has been applied to three real-world case studies and findings are discussed.

Keywords: Conceptual modeling · Data analytics · Machine learning · Goal-oriented requirements engineering · Business analytics

1 Introduction

The effective design and implementation of data analytics solutions has proven to be difficult. This difficulty is, in part, due to challenges such as determining the right analytics needs, utilizing the right analytics algorithms, as well as connecting them with high-level business objectives and strategies.

Requirements elicitation for data analytics systems is a complex task [12,27]. Analytics requirements are often unclear and incomplete at the early phases of projects. While business users often have a clear understanding of their strategic goals (e.g., improve marketing campaigns, reduce inventory levels), they are not clear on how analytics can help them achieve those goals. This is, to a great extent, due to a huge conceptual distance between business strategies, decision processes and organizational performance on one hand, and the implementation of analytics systems in terms of databases, preprocessing activities, and machine learning algorithms on the other hand. Previous researches report that the leading barrier to using analytics techniques is lack of understanding of how to use analytics and unlock its value to improve the business [17,19].

© Springer International Publishing AG 2016
I. Comyn-Wattiau et al. (Eds.): ER 2016, LNCS 9974, pp. 35–49, 2016.
DOI: 10.1007/978-3-319-46397-1_3

Moreover, *designing analytics solutions* includes making critical design decisions while taking into account softgoals and tradeoffs [18]. A large number of machine learning and data mining algorithms exists and new ones are being developed continuously. During analytics projects, one needs to make design choices such as what are potential algorithms that can address the problem at hand? What criteria should be considered to evaluate those algorithms? What/how data should be prepared to be used by algorithms? These decisions have important implications in several aspects of the eventual analytics solution, such as scalability, understandability, tolerance to noisy data and missing values.

On the other hand, *aligning analytics with business strategies* is critical for achieving value through analytics [14,17]. Lack of this alignment can result in unclear expectations of how analytics contribute to business strategies, lack of executive sponsorship, and analytics project failures. It is important for organizations to discover, justify, and establish why there is a need for the organization to allocate resources to analytics initiatives. Towards this end, discovering the business goals and translating them into analytics goals is a critical step [4,15].

This paper presents a modeling framework (i.e., a set of metamodels and a set of design catalogues) for overcoming these challenges. The framework includes three complementary modeling views: (i) The *Business View* represents an enterprise in terms of strategies, decisions, analytics questions, and required insights. This view is used to systematically elicit analytics requirements and to inform the types of analytics that the user needs. (ii) The *Analytics Design View* represents the core design of an analytics system in terms of analytical goals, (machine learning) algorithms, softgoals, and metrics. This view identifies design tradeoffs, captures the experiments (to be) performed with a range of algorithms, and supports algorithm selection. (iii) The *Data Preparation View* represents data preparation processes in terms of mechanisms, algorithms and preparation tasks. This view expresses the structure and content of data sources and the design of data preparation tasks. The three views are used together to link enterprise strategies to analytics algorithms and data preparation activities. The framework comes with three catalogues, each corresponding to a modeling view. Catalogues codify and represent reusable analytics knowledge for users.

Organization. Section 2 presents an illustration of the proposed framework in a real analytics project. Section 3 introduces primitive concepts and presents metamodels. Section 4 offers three analytics design catalogues. Section 5 discusses findings from applying the framework in three analytics projects. Section 6 reviews related work and Sect. 7 concludes the paper.

2   An Illustration

We illustrate the framework using a project aimed at developing an analytics system to predict upcoming software system outages. The company has around 300 globally accessible software applications hosted in its data centers across the world. Software system outages are costly and predicting them can enable preventive maintenance activities.

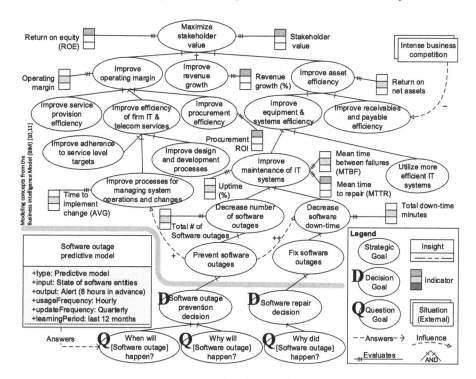

Fig. 1. Business View for the software outage prediction project (partial). This model is constructed based on interviews with domain experts, review of reporting dashboards and metrics in place, supplemented with some assumptions.

Figure 1 illustrates the *Business View* for the software outage prediction project. The purpose of this view is to represent the analytics needs of an organization and to ensure that those needs are driven by organizational decisions and strategies. This view models the business motivation for the analytics project in terms of its *strategic goals, indicators, decision goals, question goals,* and *insights.*

The model in Fig. 1 shows that Improve maintenance of IT systems is a strategic goal of the company. It also shows that Mean time between failures and Uptime (%) are among the indicators that the company uses to evaluate the goal. Strategic goals are decomposed into lower level strategic goals and eventually into decision goals. Software outage prevention decision is an example of a decision goal. The model indicates that in order to Prevent software outages, the corresponding actor[1] needs to decide on how to prevent a software from failing. Decision goals are further decomposed into question goals. When will [Software outage] happen? is an example of a question goal. The model depicts that for making Software outage prevention decision, the corresponding actor needs to know if a software outage will happen in the near future. Question goals are answered by insights. Software outage predictive model is an example of an insight to be generated by

---

[1] Actors are not shown here due to space limitations.

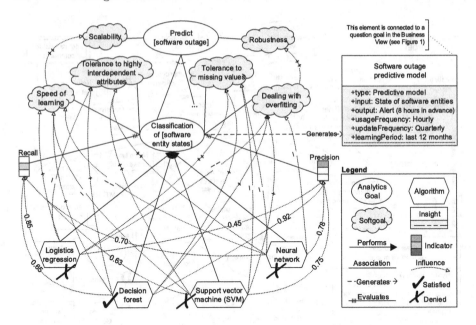

Fig. 2. Analytics Design View for software outage prediction project (partial).

the intended analytics system. It is a Predictive model that, in runtime, will be used Hourly to generate Alerts before an upcoming outage.

By modeling *decision goals*, this view represents the areas that need support from analytics insights. It ensures the connection between analytics, organizational decision processes, and strategic goals. This concept also facilitates linking and turning analytics-driven insights into actions, because the actions are indeed the decision outcomes. Through the *question goals*, the framework captures the business needs that the analytics work is intended to address. The catalogue of question goals (introduced in Sect. 4) can be used while performing modeling activities in this view. Eliciting the questions at the early phases of analytics will help perform the right analysis for the right user. Later in the analytics process and once the findings are generated, the questions can also facilitate the process of interpreting and framing the findings. By modeling *insights*, this view represents the knowledge that is extracted from data for answering the questions. The insight elements connect business view to analytics design view.

Figure 2 illustrates the *Analytics Design View* for the software outage prediction project. The purpose of this view is to represent the design of the analytics system, including algorithm selection. This view models an analytics system in terms of *analytics goals*, *(machine learning) algorithms*, *softgoals*, and *indicators*.

In Fig. 2, Predict software outage is an example of an analytics goal. To achieve this goal, the system needs to achieve the Classification of software entity states goal[2]. The model shows that Neural networks and Decision forest are alternative algorithms that perform classification. Moreover, the model represents the contributions from algorithms towards indicators and softgoals. For example, the link from Decision Forest algorithm towards Precision means that during experiments, the algorithm resulted in the value of 0.92 for Precision. Also, this algorithm has a positive contribution towards the Speed of learning. By capturing these, the view supports algorithm selection while designing the analytics systems[3]. The algorithms catalogue (introduced in Sect. 4) assists users in this modeling view and supports designing analytics systems. The analytics goals connect this view to the data preparation view.

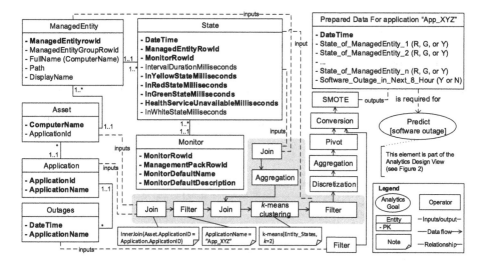

Fig. 3. Data Preparation View for software failure prediction project (partial).

Figure 3 illustrates the *Data Preparation View* for the software outage prediction project. The purpose of this view is to support the design and documentation of data preparations workflows. This view models data preparation processes in terms of *entities, attributes, mechanisms, algorithms,* and *preparation tasks.*

The model in Fig. 3 shows the content and structure of data sources[4]. It shows that an Application is related to many Assets and each asset in turn can have many ManagedEntities. The State data captures the status of the software

---

2 There were several instances of classification goal that each addressed a specific prediction period, such as 8, 16, 24 h. Each of the goals is connected to a different instance of the insight element. Due to space limitations, only one pair of analytics goal and insight is illustrated here.

3 In the first case study, the indicator Precision had highest priority which justified the choice of Decision Forest for the corresponding classification goal.

4 The company has a cross-platform data center management system that logs computer systems operations.

entities over time. The model shows the sequence of data preparation mechanism and algorithms. Join and Filter are examples of mechanism. SMOTE is an example of an algorithm for data preparation. A set of mechanisms and algorithms together form a data preparation task. In Fig. 3 the gray shaded area shows a Data numerosity reduction task. This task is responsible for removing managed entities whose State data is not showing any meaningful relationship with software outage. The k-means clustering is an example of an algorithm which, in this case, performs the main part of the data reduction task. The main outcome of the workflows is the prepared dataset that is required for the analytics goal To predict [software outage]. The data preparation catalogue (see Sect. 4) assists users in this modeling view and supports designing data preparation workflows.

3   Metamodels

3.1   Business View

Figure 4 shows metamodel of the Business View in terms of a UML class diagram. Concepts in the gray shaded area are adopted from the Business Intelligence Model (BIM) [10,11]. Here we explain concepts that are added to extend BIM.

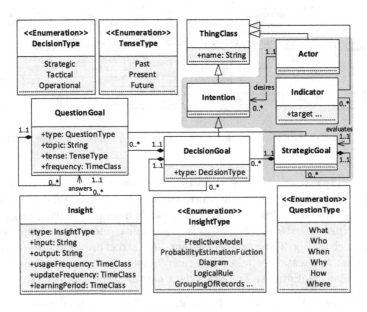

Fig. 4. Part of metamodel for the Business View.

Decision Goals. This concept represents intention of an actor for taking actions towards achieving strategic goals. Strategic goals can be decomposed into one or more decision goals.

Question Goals. This concept represents the desire of an actor for understanding or knowing something that is required for making decisions (i.e., achieving decisions goals). It captures "needs to know" of an actor. Decision goals are decomposed into one or more questions. Questions can be refined into one or more questions.

Question goals are analyzed into a *type* and *topic* as in NFR framework [5], and also *tense* (see the metamodel in Fig. 4). The question type denotes the question phrase (e.g., When in Fig. 1), while the question topic denotes the subject and focus of the (intended) analysis (e.g. [Software outage] in Fig. 1). The question tense captures the time horizon that a question goal addresses. Elicitation of question type and tense together allows specifying what kinds of analytics and machine learning algorithms are required as part of the intended system. Moreover, identification of topic allows specifying what kind of data (or what parts of database) will the intended analytics system use for mining. In addition, as shown in Fig. 4, question goals are specified in terms of their *frequency*. This attribute captures time scales and frequencies that the corresponding question is being raised. High frequency analytics question have more potential to be embedded into automated analytics systems and tools [21].

Insights. This concept represents a structured, (machine) understandable pattern (i.e., relationship among data) that is extracted from data by applying analytics algorithms. It represents a piece of information/knowledge that (partially) answers a question goal, and thereafter facilitates decision making and contributes to strategic goals. This concept has the following subtypes: *Predictive model*, *Probability Estimation Function*, *Diagrams* (e.g., trees, graphs), *Logical Rule* (e.g., association rules) and *Groupings of Records* (e.g., clusters). This concept connects to the question goals through the *answers* link. It represents the immediate output of the data analytics activities.

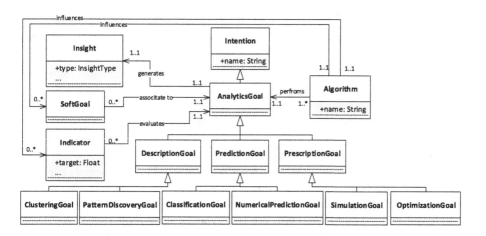

Fig. 5. Part of metamodel for the Analytics Design View.

3.2 Analytics Design View

Analytics Goals. This concept (see the metamodel in Fig. 5) represents the top-goal of the data analytics system, i.e., to extract insight from data. Analytics goals connect to insights via the link *generates*. There are three types of analytics goals. *Prediction Goal* represents an intention to predict value of a target data attribute (i.e., label attribute) by using other existing attributes in the dataset. It shows the desire to find the relationship between the target feature and other existing features in the dataset. Two subtypes of this concept are *Classification* (predicts categorical values) and *Numeric Prediction*. *Description Goal* represents an intention to summarize and describe the dataset and includes two subtypes: *Clustering* and *Pattern Discovery*. *Prescription Goal* represents an intention to find the optimal alternative among a set of potential alternatives. *Optimization* and *Simulation* are subtypes of prescription goals.

Algorithms. This concept represents a procedure that addresses an analytics goal. An algorithm is a set of steps that are necessary for an analytics goal to be achieved. It is a way through which insight is extracted from data in order to satisfy an analytics goal. This concept is connected to analytics goal through the *performs* links, representing a means-end relationship.

Indicators and Softgoals. Indicators [10] are numeric metrics that measure performance with regard to some goal (analytics goal in this modeling view). Softgoals [28] capture qualities that should sufficiently hold when performing analytics. Algorithms connect to indicators and softgoals through the *influence* links. Influence links that are directed towards an indicator, can be labeled with the corresponding numeric value.Contributions that are directed towards qualities can range from positive to negative, following *i** guidelines [28].

Analytics projects involve experimenting with different algorithms. During design time, indicators and softgoals represent criteria to be considered for evaluation/comparison of alternative algorithms that perform the analytics task at hand. They can be used to reduce the domain of experiments. During runtime they can be used for monitoring the performance of the running analytics system.

3.3 Data Preparation View

Data Preparation Tasks. This concept (see the metamodel in Fig. 6) represents the general task of preparing the data that is required for achieving some analytics goal. A data preparation task consists of one or more *Operator(s)*. It has four subtypes [9]: *Data reduction* generates a data set that is smaller in size than the input data set and yet produces the same analytical results (i.e., serves the same analytical goals). *Data numerosity reduction* (see an example in Fig. 3) and *Data dimensionality reduction* are two types of data reduction tasks. *Data cleaning* represents the tasks that remove errors from the input dataset and also treat missing values in it. *Clean missing value* and *Clean noisy attribute* are subtypes of this concept. *Data transformation* transforms the shape of data in a

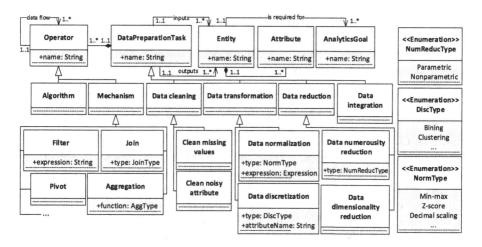

Fig. 6. Part of metamodel for the Data Preparation View.

way that is more appropriate for analytics algorithms to mine and find patterns. *Data normalization* and *Data discretization* are subtypes of this concept. *Data integration* merges data from different data sources.

Operator. It represents an atomic activity that performs (part of) a data preparation task. Operators are linked by *data flows* to represent the sequence. There are two types of operators. *Mechanism* represents fundamental data preparation operations such as *Join* and *Filter* [6,24]. *Algorithm* is identical with algorithm in the previous view. In the data preparation view, this concept captures situations where machine learning algorithms are used for preparing data, and not for performing the actual analytics task (see examples in Fig. 3).

Table 1. High-level structure of question goals catalogue. Due to space limitations, instances of each category of question goals are not provided here.

Type	Tense		
	Past	*Present*	*Future*
What	What happened?✍	What is happening?✍➻	What will happen?✶➻
Who	Who was involved in it?✍	Who is involved in it?✍	Who will be involved?✶
When	When did it happened?✍	Is it happening now?✍✶	When will it happen?✶
Where	Where did it happen?✍	Where is it happening?✍	Where will it happen?✶
Why	Why did it happen?✍	Why is it happening?✍	Why will it happen?✶➻
How	How did it happen?✍	How is it happening?✍	How will it happen?✶➻

Symbols ✍,✶, ➻ refer to analytics goal of description, prediction, and prescription respectively.

4   Cataloguing Analytics Design Knowledge

The proposed framework comes with three kinds of design catalogues. These catalogues bring relevant analytics knowledge to the attention of the project team for use and re-use during the design and development processes. They provide an organized body of analytics knowledge, accumulated from surveys (e.g., [16]), textbooks (e.g., [9]), formal ontologies (e.g., [25]), and previous experiences.

Business Questions Catalogue. This catalogue represents knowledge about the types of question goals, and their associated analytics types. It categorizes question goals based on their *type* and *tense* (see Sect. 3.1) and associates each category with relevant analytics goal(s). Table 1 presents the high level schema of the catalogue. This catalogue is populated with a wide collection of instances for each category of questions goals. For example, the question goal of Who will be [leaving the firm]? belongs to the Who will be involved in it? category in Table 1, and can be addressed by Prediction type of analytics. As another example, the question goal of When will [Software outage] happen? from Fig. 1, belongs to the When will it happen? category in Table 1. This catalogue can be used by analytcis team and stakeholders during the modeling activities of business view. It can facilitate the elicitation of analytics requirements (i.e., needs to know) by suggesting and refining question goals. It also guides users to the kinds of analytics solutions that can address their needs.

Algorithms Catalogue. This catalogue systematically organizes machine learning algorithms that are available for addressing different types of analytics goals. The catalogue provides existing metrics to be taken into account while comparing/evaluating performances of different algorithms. It also presents critical softgoals that need to be taken into account while developing analytics solutions. In addition, it encodes the knowledge on how each algorithm perform with regard to different softgoals (influence links). A portion of this catalogue is illustrated in Fig. 7. As an example, it shows that Support Vector Machine (SVM) is an algorithm that performs Numeric prediction and its performance can be evaluated using the Mean Absolute Error (MAE) metric.

The *context* semantics from [1] are used to associate context with machine learning algorithms. In this way, the catalogue represents when certain machine learning algorithms are shown to perform well based on a collection of previous evidences and experiments in the literature or relevant sources. This can guide the decision on which algorithms are more appropriate for the analytics goal and shorten the experimentation phase of the projects. In Fig. 7, context C1 shows that the Classification goal is activated when Target attribute type (the value to be predicted) is categorical. On the other hand, C2 shows that Neural network can be used for Numeric prediction, when Input dataset is scaled to a narrow range around zero. Due to space limitations, not all the contexts are given in Fig. 7.

Data Preparation Techniques Catalogue. This catalogue captures knowledge on available methods for different types of data preparation tasks. It makes use of the same modeling elements as in the algorithm catalogue. As shown in

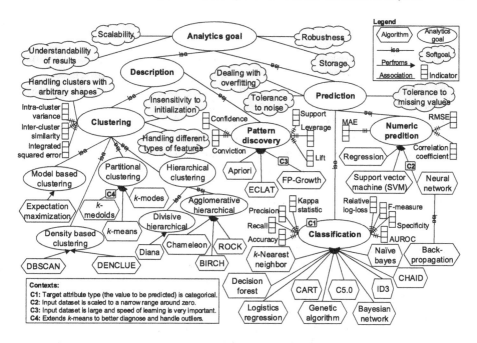

Fig. 7. A portion of algorithm catalogue. Influence links from algorithms towards softgoals are not shown here to keep the model readable.

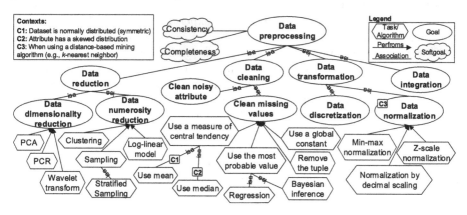

Fig. 8. A portion of data preparation catalogue. Not all the contexts are shown.

Fig. 8, Using median is a method for Cleaning missing values when the corresponding Attribute has a skewed distribution. Analytics development team can browse through this catalogue and design data preparation workflows.

5   Case Studies

The proposed framework has been applied to three analytics projects. The first two case studies were reconstructions of completed projects. The third case study was an application of the framework to an on-going analytics project. These cases together serve as an initial validation of the framework. In Sect. 2, we used the first case study for illustrating the modeling views. The *second project* focused on finance analytics. The purpose of this project was to predict an upcoming event regarding financial metrics in company's network. The *third project* focuses on search engine analytics. The purpose of this project is to use analytics to provide query suggestions to online users.

Our main observation from the first and second cases is that the modeling views together provide an adequate set of concepts for connecting strategic goals to analytics algorithms and data preparation activities. The three modeling views were instantiated for these case studies, presented to and understood by stakeholders. We observed that the framework can be used for representing analytics requirements, can show design tradeoffs and support algorithm selection, can capture data preparation activities, and can represent the alignment between analytics systems and business strategies.

Our main observation from the third case is that the framework can be useful in guiding analytics projects. A model from business view was constructed, in collaboration with stakeholders, at the requirements elicitation phase of the project. While at the beginning the focus of the project was broad and imprecise (to use analytics for improving users' search experience), the models effectively helped the team to narrow down the scope and reach an agreement about the "to-be" analytics system (to use analytics to provide query suggestions). We observed that users are able to understand the content of the model and can work with analytics team to construct and elaborate on the models. The models raised effective discussions during meetings and resulted in removing some and adding new question goals. These suggest that the framework can enhance the communication between domain experts and data scientists (who develop analytics systems). Models from data analytics design view were constructed and updated during the project, mostly by the project manager and data scientists. The softgoals (most importantly Scalability) were used for making design decisions.

6   Related Work

Conceptual Modeling for Data Warehouses. These works propose conceptual modeling approaches for requirements engineering of data warehouses. For example, the work in [20] proposes a goal-oriented, model-driven approach for development of data warehouses. Authors in [23] propose goal-decision-information model for analyzing data warehouse requirements. Reference [8] proposes a Tropos-based methodology for requirements analysis in data warehouses. While we adopt some of concepts from these works (e.g., decision goals in [20,23]), the proposed framework supports requirements engineering for predictive and prescriptive types of analytics systems, in addition to descriptive ones.

Conceptual Modeling for ETL Processes. These works propose conceptual modelings for ETL (Extraction-Transformation-Loading) processes. The work in [26] presents a metamodel and notation for modeling ETL processes in the early stages of data warehouse projects. In [24] authors define a set of common ETL activities in terms of stereotyped classes and use UML dependencies to link them together. Reference [22] defines a model–driven architecture approach to transform ETL conceptual models to code. In [6], a BPMN-based modeling approach for ETL processes is presented. While the proposed framework reuses modeling constructs from these works (e.g., mechanism from [24]), it captures machine learning and organizational aspects of analytics solutions.

Modeling for BI. The Business Intelligence Model (BIM) [11] represents a business in terms of strategic goals, processes, performance indicators, influences, and situations. BIM supports a wide range of automated reasoning and business analyses techniques [2,10]. It is shown that the language can facilitate design and development of BI solutions [3]. BIM lacks primitive concepts for supporting design of advanced analytics solutions. This work uses and extends the modeling constructs to capture analytics work from data preparation tasks to algorithms, and thereafter to insights and question goals.

Data Mining Process Models. These models describe the sequence of tasks that should be done in order to carry out data mining projects. The work by Fayyad et al. [7] is often considered as the first reported data mining process model. The CRISP-DM model [4] is often mentioned as the most used and the *de facto* standard process model. These works do not offer a modeling language.

Data Mining Ontologies. Several efforts have been made to establish formal ontologies for supporting users during data mining processes. For example, references [13] propose ontologies for facilitating algorithm selection and designing the data mining workflows. The ontology in [25] formally represents data mining experiments to enable meta-learning. Concepts that express business and requirements aspect of analytics solutions are not included in these works.

7   Conclusion

This paper presented initial research results towards a conceptual modeling framework for business analytics. The framework has been tested in three case studies. The case studies suggest that the proposed framework can support the design and implementation of analytics solutions. It is notable that all these case studies belong to a single domain and company. In future we plan to extend the framework and evaluate it in different domains, completing other pieces of the design science research approach. We plan to conduct empirical studies with users who are not the researchers. Usage, comprehensibility and learning curve of the modeling views can be examined for different types of roles (from business decision makers to data scientists) that are typically involved in analytics projects. These studies can lead to definition of a model-based methodology, as part of the framework, for developing analytics systems. The content of analytics catalogues can be extended, validated, and their usage can be examined in real cases. We also plan to develop tools that support the framework.

References

1. Ali, R., Dalpiaz, F., Giorgini, P.: A goal-based framework for contextual requirements modeling and analysis. Requirements Eng. **15**(4), 439–458 (2010)
2. Barone, D., Jiang, L., Amyot, D., Mylopoulos, J.: Composite indicators for business intelligence. In: Jeusfeld, M., Delcambre, L., Ling, T.-W. (eds.) ER 2011. LNCS, vol. 6998, pp. 448–458. Springer, Heidelberg (2011). doi:10.1007/978-3-642-24606-7_35
3. Barone, D., Topaloglou, T., Mylopoulos, J.: Business intelligence modeling in action: a hospital case study. In: Ralyté, J., Franch, X., Brinkkemper, S., Wrycza, S. (eds.) CAiSE 2012. LNCS, vol. 7328, pp. 502–517. Springer, Heidelberg (2012). doi:10.1007/978-3-642-31095-9_33
4. Chapman, P., Clinton, J., Kerber, R., Khabaza, T., Reinartz, T., Shearer, C., Wirth, R.: CRISP-DM 1.0 Step-by-Step Data Mining Guide. SPSS Inc. (2000)
5. Chung, L., Nixon, B.A., Yu, E., Mylopoulos, J.: Non-functional Requirements in Software Engineering. Springer Science & Business Media, New York (2012)
6. Akkaoui, Z., Mazón, J.-N., Vaisman, A., Zimányi, E.: BPMN-based conceptual modeling of ETL processes. In: Cuzzocrea, A., Dayal, U. (eds.) DaWaK 2012. LNCS, vol. 7448, pp. 1–14. Springer, Heidelberg (2012). doi:10.1007/978-3-642-32584-7_1
7. Fayyad, U., Piatetsky-Shapiro, G., Smyth, P.: From data mining to knowledge discovery in databases. AI Mag. **17**(3), 37–54 (1996)
8. Giorgini, P., Rizzi, S., Garzetti, M.: GRAnD: a goal-oriented approach to requirement analysis in data warehouses. Decis. Support Syst. **45**(1), 4–21 (2008)
9. Han, J., Kamber, M., Pei, J.: Data Mining: Concepts and Techniques. Elsevier, Waltham (2012)
10. Horkoff, J., Barone, D., Jiang, L., Eric, Y., Amyot, D., Borgida, A., Mylopoulos, J.: Strategic business modeling: representation and reasoning. Softw. Syst. Model. **13**(3), 1015–1041 (2014)
11. Jiang, L., Barone, D., Amyot, D., Mylopoulos, J.: Strategic models for business intelligence. In: Jeusfeld, M., Delcambre, L., Ling, T.-W. (eds.) ER 2011. LNCS, vol. 6998, pp. 429–439. Springer, Heidelberg (2011). doi:10.1007/978-3-642-24606-7_33
12. Kandogan, E., Balakrishnan, A., Haber, E.M., Pierce, J.S.: From data to insight: work practices of analysts in the enterprise. IEEE Comput. Graphics Appl. **34**(5), 42–50 (2014)
13. Keet, C.M., Lawrynowicz, A., dAmato, C., Hilario, M.: Modeling issues and choices in the Data Mining OPtimization Ontology. In: OWLED 2013, Montpellier, France, May 2013
14. Kohavi, R., Mason, L., Parekh, R., Zheng, Z.: Lessons and challenges from mining retail e-Commerce data. Mach. Learn. **57**, 83–113 (2004)

15. Kohavi, R., Rothleder, N.J., Simoudis, E.: Emerging trends in business analytics. Commun. ACM **45**(8), 45–48 (2002)
16. Kotsiantis, S.B.: Supervised machine learning: a review of classification techniques. Informatica **31**(3) (2007)
17. LaValle, S., Hopkins, M.S., Lesser, E., Shockley, R., Kruschwitz, N.: Analytics: the new path to value. MIT Sloan Manag. Rev. (2010)
18. Luca, M., Kleinberg, J., Mullainathan, S.: Algorithms need managers, too. Harvard Bus. Rev. **94**, 96–101 (2016)
19. Manyika, J., Chui, M., Brown, B., Bughin, J., Dobbs, R., Roxburgh, C., Byers, A.H.: Big data: the next frontier for innovation, competition, and productivity. Technical report, McKinsey Global Institute (2011)
20. Mazón, J.-N., Pardillo, J., Trujillo, J.: A model-driven goal-oriented requirement engineering approach for data warehouses. In: Hainaut, J.-L., et al. (eds.) ER 2007. LNCS, vol. 4802, pp. 255–264. Springer, Heidelberg (2007). doi:10.1007/978-3-540-76292-8_31
21. Menzies, T., Zimmermann, T.: Software analytics: so what? IEEE Softw. **30**(4), 31–37 (2013)
22. Muñoz, L., Mazón, J.-N., Trujillo, J.: Automatic generation of ETL processes from conceptual models. In: DOLAP 2009, pp. 33–40 (2009)
23. Prakash, N., Gosain, A.: An approach to engineering the requirements of data warehouses. Requirements Eng. **13**(1), 49–72 (2008)
24. Trujillo, J., Luján-Mora, S.: A UML based approach for modeling ETL processes in data warehouses. In: Song, I.-Y., Liddle, S.W., Ling, T.-W., Scheuermann, P. (eds.) ER 2003. LNCS, vol. 2813, pp. 307–320. Springer, Heidelberg (2003). doi:10.1007/978-3-540-39648-2_25
25. Vanschoren, J., Blockeel, H., Pfahringer, B., Holmes, G.: Experiment databases - a new way to share, organize and learn from experiments. Mach. Learn. **87**(2), 127–158 (2012)
26. Vassiliadis, P., Simitsis, A., Skiadopoulos, S.: Conceptual modeling for ETL processes. In: DOLAP 2002, pp. 14–21 (2002)
27. Viaene, S., Van den Bunder, A.: The secrets to managing business analytics projects. MIT Sloan Manag. Rev. **53**(1), 65–69 (2011)
28. Yu, E.: Modelling strategic relationships for process reengineering. Ph.D. thesis, University of Toronto, Canada (1995)

NOSQL Design for Analytical Workloads: Variability Matters

Victor Herrero$^{(\boxtimes)}$, Alberto Abelló, and Oscar Romero

Universitat Politècnica de Catalunya - BarcelonaTech, Barcelona, Spain
{vherrero,aabello,oromero}@essi.upc.edu

Abstract. Big Data has recently gained popularity and has strongly questioned relational databases as universal storage systems, especially in the presence of analytical workloads. As result, co-relational alternatives, commonly known as NOSQL (Not Only SQL) databases, are extensively used for Big Data. As the primary focus of NOSQL is on performance, NOSQL databases are directly designed at the physical level, and consequently the resulting schema is tailored to the dataset and access patterns of the problem in hand. However, we believe that NOSQL design can also benefit from traditional design approaches. In this paper we present a method to design databases for analytical workloads. Starting from the conceptual model and adopting the classical 3-phase design used for relational databases, we propose a novel design method considering the new features brought by NOSQL and encompassing relational and co-relational design altogether.

Keywords: NOSQL · DW · Big data · Relational · Co-relational · Database design

1 Introduction

Deriving valuable information from raw data is nowadays a priority for most companies [21], which see in today's business the need to effectively monitor and analyse own and external data to predict future trends and make informed decisions. The success of Business Intelligence (BI) and the data-driven society paradigm [15] gave rise to data-oriented companies and the consequent data deluge, which requires non-traditional sources (e.g., logs, sensors, free-text data, images, etc.) to be included in current analytical processes. Such paradigm shift is known as Big Data (BD), a wide concept commonly defined by the so-called 3 V's [11], which enable data analysis in the presence of very large volumes (Volume) of heterogeneous (Variety) data in near real time environments (Velocity).

The data warehouse (DW) is the current de-facto implementation standard in BI, where data is multidimensionally modeled (with a star-join schema), stored in Relational Database Management System (RDBMS), and exploited by two means [10]: OLAP and Data Mining/Machine Learning (DM/ML). Thus, the DW is actually modeled according to OLAP needs, while for DM/ML

I. Comyn-Wattiau et al. (Eds.): ER 2016, LNCS 9974, pp. 50–64, 2016.
DOI: 10.1007/978-3-319-46397-1_4

database dumps are generated from the DW and loaded into specialised tools (e.g., SAS or R). The two exploitation means are still present in BD as Small (OLAP) and Big (DM/ML) Analytics [19]. However, Small and Big Analytics require a specific management when combined with any of the aforementioned 3 V's. As result, Not Only SQL (NOSQL) databases [22] raised as an alternative.

NOSQL systems focus almost exclusively on performance and are based on distributed database principles, also using flexible data models to reduce the impedance mismatch [2]. Aiming at exploiting the data locality principle [16], they discourage dumping data to a file for DM/ML. Consequently, the data scientist role emerged: a data analyst with strong Computer Science skills able to access NOSQL systems and perform advanced analysis inside them. In parallel, several BD tools were developed for them to conduct both Small (e.g., Hive[1]) and Big Analytics (e.g., SparkR[2]) in BD ecosystems. As result, NOSQL systems must **consider** the access patterns of DM/ML to better design the database. However, there are no systematic design methods for them, and traditional ones cannot be reused as-they-are since they do not consider Big Analytics.

In this paper, we present a novel database design method to support analytical workloads (i.e., Small **and** Big Analytics). Currently, some approaches have discussed how to model OLAP in BD (e.g., [17]) but, to our knowledge, there is no systematic unified modeling strategy also considering DM/ML. To accommodate NOSQL novel features, we build on the ideas in [14], where the relationship between relational and NOSQL databases is shown to actually be different faces of the same coin. They claim for the co-existence of the relational (whose core data structure is the relation) and the co-relational (whose core is a finer-grained structure; such as the key-value) data models. In our approach, we benefit from the well-researched relational design techniques and extend them for the co-relational model, and from DW concepts that also apply in BD.

Currently, NOSQL design is, at best, performed at the logical level, in a performance-wise manner and not following the classical ANSI/SPARC architecture. However, this results to be problematic as BD requirements are more dynamic than in DW. Data scientists frequently ask for new attributes, entities or relationships that were not considered in their statistical models before. Thus, since the schema will change and we cannot assume a complete view of the user needs will be available at design time, we need to accommodate *variability* [9] during the design phase (not only that coming from schema evolution, but also caused by heterogeneity of data). For this reason, we claim for starting the design at the conceptual level and for identifying relevant *subject* areas of analysis [10]. Oppositely, purely performance-oriented solutions work at the attribute level and denormalise relational tables (to avoid joins) and cluster attributes according to their *affinity* [16] (i.e., how often they are queried together). However, such solutions do not accommodate evolution as entity correspondences are not preserved. Therefore, we advocate for a high level subject-oriented (i.e., coarser) design preserving the main focus of analysis, which is further refined

---

[1] https://hive.apache.org.
[2] https://spark.apache.org.

according to the characteristics of each subject identified (to accommodate variability inside). Such refinement includes the decision per subject of using either the relational or co-relational data model (i.e., the degree of denormalisation). Finally, performance is considered at the physical level and, according to the expected workload, each subject is vertically fragmented to improve the effective read ratio [16]. We apply our method to an anonimised real-world BD case study and discuss the pros and cons compared to a purely performance-oriented solution.

Contributions. In particular, our main contributions are as follows:

– We follow the traditional 3-phase design: conceptual, logical and physical.
– Integrate both relational and co-relational design into a single quantitative method, also considering classical DW subject orientation.
– We showcase the use of our method in a real use case.

Outline. Section 2 briefly introduces co-relational data models considered. Section 3 introduces the use case. Section 4 details the proposed method. Sections 5 the impact of our method and Sect. 6 the related work. Finally, Sect. 7 concludes the paper.

2   Co-relational Models

The three co-relational models considered in this paper are *key-value*, *document* and *column-family*. Figure 1 classifies their underlying structures with respect to the schema nature. Schemas are explicit if they are declared, which allows the database to automatically parse the instance data. Explicit schemas can in turn be either fix or variable. In the former, all instances' data follow the same schema, which is globally declared once, while in the latter, instance data is individually embedded with its schema. A DBMS with implicit schema does not manage any information about the instance structure, which is a black-box for the system, and data must be parsed at the application level.

To exemplify those three models, we will use a toy example. Let us suppose the following information: "the city of Barcelona (BCN) has a population of 2,000,000 inhabitants and it is located in Catalonia (CAT)". This could be captured in a single relation (*city*), with three attributes: *name*, *population* and *region*. Using SQL notation, it would look like: `city(name, population, region) VALUES ('BCN', '2,000,000', 'CAT')`.

Key-value stores have the simplest layout. Instance data is stored in tables and represented with a key (i.e., identifier), and a value (i.e., associated data). Neither the key nor the value are tied to a specific format. The former is typically a string and the value a binary object. Thus, no declarative query language and optimizer can be provided to accesss the data, and only simple actions (such as get and put by key) are provided via low-level APIs. Consequently, the application layer is responsible for interpreting each instance, and we consider the schema to be implicit. Our example could be represented as: `['BCN', '2,000,000;CAT']`.

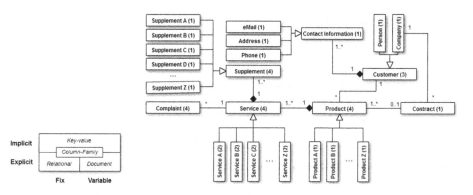

Fig. 1. DBMS based on their schema properties

Fig. 2. Use case conceptual schema

Document stores keep documents within collections (i.e., namespace). A document is a key-value structure where the value is a semi-structured document (typically JSON or XML), that can be seen as a set of entries in the form of (potentially nested) key-value pairs. Thus, the schema is explicit but variable, since the XML or JSON structure is stored with the instance. In our example, the corresponding document would be [id:'BCN', population:'2,000,000', region:'CAT']. So structuring the value opens the door for higher-level query languages and optimization. Typically, document stores use a *query-by-example* approach. Given a pattern document (e.g., *name = 'BCN' or salary > 5000*), all documents fulfilling such pattern are retrieved.

Column-family stores are key-value stores that further structure the value into families, which contain groups of attributes (aka columns). Similar to documents, we could query and retrieve the whole instance, a family, or a specific attribute within a family. Families actually denote vertical fragments, and each is physically stored in a different disk file. From the schema point of view, families are static and defined at table creation time, whereas attributes can be dynamically specified at data insertion time (i.e., the attribute name is stored together with the instance data). Thus, the table schema (i.e., the families) is (i) explicitly declared, static, and shared by all instances, but also (ii) explicit and variable within families, since attributes may vary among instances, and finally (iii) data types are implicit since the attribute value is stored in the form of key-values. Our example could result in a table with two families, namely *population* and *region*, and a constant attribute in each of them, named *value*, to store each attribute: ['BCN', population:{value:'2,000,000'}, region:{value:'CAT'}].
Alternatively, we could use a family *all* containing both attributes: ['BCN', all:{population:'2,000,000',region:'CAT'}]. Similar to key-value stores, we may use a single column inside the family: ['BCN', all:{value:'2,000,000;CAT'}].

3   Motivating Use Case

This section presents a BD real-world use case where our method was applied to create a decisional NOSQL repository as a complement to the existing relational DW. We choose this use case for being representative of all the problems typically due to variability in BD projects. We outline the limitations of traditional approaches, and define the objectives to be tackled by a design method.

Figure 2 shows the conceptual schema of the use case domain (due to a disclosure agreement, class names have been altered but relationships between them remain the same). Customers (either individual Persons or Companies) buy Products that are composed of Services which, in turn, are complemented by different Supplements. Complaints can be filed if services do not fulfill the customer expectations. To contact customers, their Contact Information is registered in the form of eMails, Addresses or Phone numbers. Finally, companies can agree on Contracts that comprise several products. Our company needed to **predict** actions from customers regarding products.

The *large heterogeinity* involving some entities becomes the first limitation (e.g., dozens of products, several hundreds of services and some thousands of supplements). Relational tables provide a homogeneous representation of entities and we would need to either create a table for each possible *specialised* entity or a single *general* table containing the union of all attributes. This would poorly perform since deploying thousands of tables, that would be joined to produce the general entity, or creating a table with thousands of attributes (Supplement alone has almost one hundred) results unpractical and generates expensive queries [22]. Furthermore, new products are constantly developed and released. In the OLTP system, this was solved by implementing specialisations with ad-hoc tables containing generic columns storing different attributes depending on the specialised entity. For example, the product table contained hundreds of columns of type varchar(50). A row representing productA stores in column C the product model, while those of type productB use C to store location). A dictionary at the application level keeps track of the mapping of each product column (e.g., C) to its real meaning (e.g., productA → model).

Schema evolution becomes extremely important in the context of Big Analytics as analysts constantly look for new patterns and therefore ask for new data to be included in the decisional datasets. Reflecting such changes in the relational model is possible, but turns out to be costly as it either requires to alter the current table (massively updating the new columns for existing instances) or create a sibling one (same key) for the new attributes (this was the approach followed in the data sources of our company). Thus, in our use case, changes affecting the DW were simply ignored, resulting in data scientists spending most of their time collecting data from different sources, and cleaning and merging them by themselves prior to conduct the analysis.

Data matrices are the query output for Big Analytics. Traditional DW relies on star-join schemas [12] and data is organised in factual and dimensional tables, which represent subjects of analysis (e.g., `Sales`) and analysis facets (e.g., `Store`, `Time`), respectively. Dimensional data contains hierarchies representing the different levels to which aggregate factual data for each facet. This, e.g., allows aggregating to count `sales` per `store` and `year`, and later easily disaggregate them per `day`. However, star-join schemas cannot be easily used to produce data matrices, because joins between different cuboids are necessary. Consider `Product` to be the subject and `Customer` one of its facets, and we want to produce a flatten data matrix where each row represents a product bought by a customer. The matrix columns hold any type of information regarding such event, and limitations arise when they must contain data at coarser levels, like `totalAmountBought` (i.e., the total amount bought by the customer of the product in a given matrix row). Since this is not an atomic value, but an aggregated one through the `Product-Customer` relationship, a parallel aggregation on `Product` per `Customer` must be computed and subsequently joined so that all products from the same customer show the same value. Such requirement is usual in DM/ML, but goes against the star-join query pattern [12]. In BI, this issue is tackled once data is loaded in specialised software (such as R) and never considered when designing the database.

Design Objectives: Given those limitations, we present the list of objectives to be overcome by considering co-relational data models.

(a) Simplify the representation of large specialisations so that queries on such entities are kept simple.
(b) Consider schema evolution at design time and acknowledge the possibility of adding new features or values later.
(c) Generate flatten data matrices (i.e., without nested structures).
(d) Performance must be considered first-class citizen.

Note that (a) and (b) correspond to dealing with variability.

4   Design Method for Relational and Co-relational

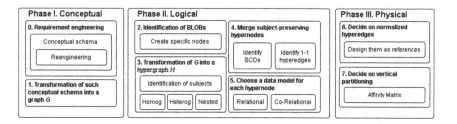

Fig. 3. Summary of steps composing the design method

In current BD settings, the lack of know-how to address database design results in most solutions being designed only considering performance. Oppositely, our

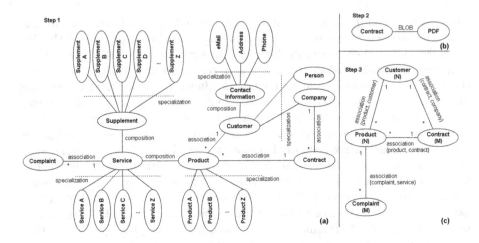

Fig. 4. Graph representation after the first three steps

method advocates for a top-down approach: we drive the design from the conceptual schema and find a physical design resilient to variability while performance penalisation is minimised. Spanning the 3-phases shown in Fig. 3, in the first phase we assume that a requirement engineering (RE) process, tailored for analysis-oriented systems [7], has been conducted. During RE the conceptual schema must be produced (in BI/BD settings typically by using reengineering techniques [3]) and entity evolution likelihood quantified. Such *quantification* is typical of DW, where it is used to identify Slowly Changing Dimensions (SCD) [12]. Note we assume a correct RE process was conducted and thus, although the conceptual schema may evolve, **the current knowledge is correct**. Starting from the conceptual schema, the second phase decides the degree of normalization after identifying subjects of analysis and, accordingly, proposes a relational or co-relational data model. The last phase accommodates performance issues and, according to the currently known workload, vertically fragments the identified subjects to improve the effective read ratio [16].

4.1   Phase I: Conceptual Schema

Step 1. Firstly, we transform the conceptual schema (assumed to have been reified) into an undirected graph $G = (V, E)$ where nodes V denote entities, and edges E denote relationships between them (tagged with the relationship **type** and its **multiplicity**). We consider three relationship types (i.e., "*specialisation*", "*composition*", or "*association*"). Aggregations, unlike compositions, cannot guarantee membership between entities and for our goal they are treated as "associations". Finally, multiplicities are also kept in G.

Use case. We produced the conceptual schema by reverse engineering from the available data sources. The result is depicted in Fig. 2 (numbers by the entities denote their evolving likelihood, being 4 the highest probability), and its transformation into G is shown in Fig. 4(a).

4.2   Phase II: Logical Schema

Step 2. Binary large objects (BLOBs), such as images, videos or other non-detachable objects, cannot be decomposed in smaller subcomponents and are directly understood by the application (i.e., its schema is implicit). Thus, key-value stores rise as a natural option to store them. Any entity containing a BLOB entails the creation of a new node v_{BLOB} in G. This is linked to the entity node v by means of a edge of type "*BLOB*". Although this is a physical decision, since BLOBs are separated because of performance reasons (i.e., unknown format, large size, and rarely retrieved together with other attributes), doing it earlier does not affect the result and simplifies the process.

Use case. BLOBs could be found in `Contract`, where PDF documents were stored. Figure 4(b) shows how the `Contract` vertex is updated accordingly.

Step 3. We then explore the conceptual schema to identify two different types of entity sets: first, sets of *nested entities* and, second, sets of *heterogeneous* entities. Nested entities essentially refer to compositions where the content can only exist within the container's scope (compositions). Heterogeneous entities are those where the schema may vary among instances (specialisations). Thus, **general entities** (e.g., `Contact Information`) are narrowed in other **specialised entities** (e.g., `Address`, `Phone`, etc.). Entities not involved in any specialisation are considered homogeneous as their schema is fix. Thus, the goal of this step is to group entities regarding the aforementioned types and synthesise G in groups of independent domain concepts (i.e., subjects). This process accordingly results in a hypergraph $H = (X, E')$ where a hypernode $x \in X$ maps to a subgraph of G representing each group entity and E' represents the set of hyperedges. Note an entity can be part of several heterogeneous hypernodes if involved in specialisations belonging to different groups. In these cases, such entity must be replicated in each hypernode. Hypernodes are adorned with its type: Nested, heTerogeneous or hoMogeneous. Also, they take the name of their *main* entity; either the *container* entity from compositions or the most *general* entity from specialisations. Note a hypernode might be adorned with more than one type. We define a dominant function $\gg$ among the tags as follows: $(N) \gg (T) \gg (M)$ so that only one tag prevails over others. Hyperedges E' are created from "associations" in G, from where they inherit their multiplicity.

Use case. Figure 4(c) shows H. The hypernodes in H (named after the main hypernode entity) contain the following entities:

$X_{customer} = \{$`Customer, Person, Company, Contact Inf, eMail, Address, Phone`$\}$
$X_{product} = \{$`Product, Service, Supplement, (plus all their subclasses)`$\}$
$X_{contract} = \{$`Contract`$\}$
$X_{complaint} = \{$`Complaint`$\}$.

Step 4. We now identify hypernodes to be potentially merged in order to improve performance. Note, however, this compromises the variability resilience as modifications in a graph node will impact on the hypernodes it has been placed in. To prevent this, we only merge hypernodes detected as part of the same **subject**. Following well-known DW principles [12], only hypernodes connected by hyperedges with *1-1* and *1-** multiplicities are considered. Merging hypernodes related by *1-1* hyperedges clearly preserves the subject, and the main entity in this case corresponds to the hypernode with higher likelihood to evolve (as it facilitates further changes in the merged hypernode schema). Similarly, hypernodes related by a *1-** hyperedge can only be merged if the to-one end of the hyperedge represents an SCD. Since the SCD evolution likelihood is very low, the main entity of the merged hypernode is its counterpart hypernode in the hyperedge. Replication of an SCD in different merged hypernodes can occur if such SCD is connected to several hypernodes. Finally, the created hypernode acquires the most dominant adornment of the merged ones.

Use case. In the use case, no *1-1* hyperedge exists. `Contract`, however, was identified as an SCD. We thus merged $X_{product}$ and $X_{contract}$ and created $X_{product\_contract}$. The merged hypernode is adorned as (N) and `Product` is accordingly identified as main entity. Incident hyperedges on the merged hypernodes are now related to $X_{product\_contract}$.

Step 5. For each hypernode, we decide whether it should be designed following the relational or co-relational model depending on the adornments defined. We use the evolution likelihood threshold t_e as indicator to resolve situations where more than one solution is possible.

1. Hypernodes adorned with (M) should be designed by means of relational structures unless they are expected to evolve, as their fix schema can be separately declared and shared by all instances. Oppositely, if their evolution likelihood is above t_e, then they should be designed with co-relational structures to facilitate the accommodation of schema changes.
2. Hypernodes adorned with (T) can be either represented by relational or co-relational structures. Several alternatives exist in case of the former [4], while the most natural way to model heterogeneous entities in case of the latter is with explicit but variable schemas. Deciding between the two data models depends on the degree of heterogeneity. Co-relational should be chosen when the number of heterogeneous entities involved is large (e.g., `Product`). Alternatively, we can consider relational if only few specialised entities exist (e.g., `Contact Information`). In the latter case, two types of schema evolution must be considered: (i) if only new attributes can be added to existing entities, an analogous rationale to M holds, (ii) if new specialisations are regularly created (e.g., new types of `Supplement`), then a co-relational model is a better option. Note that the expertise of the database designer is key to decide, given the RE process artefacts, in which case each hypernode falls.
3. Finally, hypernodes adorned with (N) must be stored in co-relational structures by means of nested lists, which allow recursively storing lists of lists.

This way, the container holds its components. In case (N) hypernodes contain entities with fix schema, these are stored in co-relational structures by embedding their schema into the instance. Note that relational structures may also be used, but each of the entities must then be mapped to a relational table and their relationships represented with foreign keys (heavily penalizing performance). Schema evolution in (N) hypernodes is smoothly absorbed by the co-relational model.

Use case. The data model chosen for the hypernodes are the following:

Co-relational for $X_{customer}$ and $X_{product\_contract}$ (adorned both with (N))
Relational for $X_{complaint}$ (adorned with (M)).

4.3 Phase III: Physical Schema

Step 6. We now focus on the remaining hyperedges (i.e., "associations"). Since two data models are being considered, these hyperedges might be relating two hypernodes to be modeled with different data models. Design rules are introduced in Table 1, where all situations are shown. Rows denote what reference direction is possible given the case in the columns, where R is used to refer to a relational hypernode, and Co to a co-relational hypernode. The feasibility of a certain reference is given by considering whether the source hypernode accepts mono-valued or multi-valued attributes, or both. The relational model can only take mono-valued attributes and designing R-R hyperedges can be devised in a traditional manner [4], although *-* can also be designed by transforming one end into Co. Co-Co hyperedges can be indifferently designed, as multi-valued attributes are natively supported. Similarly, for R-Co hyperedges, references from the R-end are only possible when the Co-end has a to-one multiplicity, whereas references from the Co-end are always possible.

Table 1. Feasible reference directions for hyperedges

	R-R				Co-Co				R-Co			
Reference	1-1	1-*	*-1	*-*	1-1	1-*	*-1	*-*	1-1	1-*	*-1	*-*
"->"	✓	✗	✓	✗	✓	✓	✓	✓	✓	✗	✓	✗
"<-"	✓	✓	✗	✗	✓	✓	✓	✓	✓	✓	✓	✓

Use case. (i) The hyperedge relating $X_{complaint}$ and $X_{product\_contract}$ has a *-1 multiplicity relating a relational to a co-relational hypernode. Consequently, this hyperedge is designed through a reference from $X_{complaint}$ to $X_{product\_contract}$. (ii) Two hyperedges relate $X_{product\_contract}$ and $X_{customer}$: one originally relating **Product** and **Customer**, and the other **Contract** and **Company**. Both hyperedges connect two co-relational hypernodes and have a *-1 multiplicity. Thus, they are implemented as two references from $X_{product\_contract}$ to $X_{customer}$ (each reference corresponds to a hyperedge).

Step 7. We aim to improve performance by maximizing the effective read ratio by grouping/splitting entities according to the known workload. Unlike other approaches, we fragment honouring the subjects identified, which cannot be split. Importantly, fragmentation is implemented in most RDBMS and given by all column-family stores. For each hypernode, we identify the vertical fragments checking how often two attributes are queried together. To compute such *affinity*, we can use well-known techniques such as the *affinity matrix* (AM) [16]. Columns and rows in AM represent attributes and a cell describes the frequency these two attributes are queried together. Given a certain threshold t_a, fragments are identified. AM assumes the query workload is given, but this might not be true (e.g., a situation where the solution is built from scratch and there is no past experience on how the database is queried). In such cases, the expected workload is identified during RE. Such process requires the participation of data analysts and techniques such as observation [7].

Use case. For each hypernode, an AM must be created. Figure 5 illustrates the resulting AM for hypernode $X_{product\_contract}$. Attributes from the use case entities have been renamed to numbered table prefixes in order to honour the disclosure agreement, and cells are percentages. At the bottom of the figure, we sketch a simplified version of the query workload corresponding to four parametrised batch processes creating different matrices. Frequencies represent how many times queries were run per month and we transform them into percentages. $Q1$, $Q3$ and $Q4$ were executed 20 times/month and $Q2$ 15 times/month. In our use case, t_a was set to 73.4 % and led to two fragments: one containing $\{pr1, pr2, pr3, pr5, su1, su2\}$ and another with the rest of attributes.

	pr1	pr2	pr3	pr4	pr5	pr6	pr7	se1	se2	se3	se4	su1	su2
pr1	—	73.4	73.4	100	46.7	46.7	46.7	46.7	46.7	46.7	46.7	73.4	73.4
pr2		—	73.4	46.7	73.4	46.7	46.7	46.7	46.7	46.7	46.7	73.4	73.4
pr3			—	46.7	73.4	46.7	46.7	46.7	46.7	46.7	46.7	73.4	73.4
pr4				—	46.7	46.7	46.7	46.7	46.7	46.7	46.7	46.7	46.7
pr5					—	46.7	46.7	46.7	46.7	46.7	46.7	73.4	73.4
pr6						—	46.7	46.7	46.7	46.7	46.7	46.7	46.7
pr7							—	46.7	46.7	46.7	46.7	46.7	46.7
se1								—	46.7	46.7	46.7	46.7	46.7
se2									—	46.7	46.7	46.7	46.7
se3										—	46.7	46.7	46.7
se4											—	46.7	46.7
su1												—	73.4
su2													—

Attributes

Customer(cus1,cus2,cus3,cus4)
Address(ad1,ad2)
Contract(con1,con2)
Product(pr1,pr2,pr3,pr4,pr5,pr6,pr7)
Service(se1,se2,se3,se4)
Supplement(su1,su2)
Complaint(com1,com2,com3,com4)

Query workload

$Q1(pr1,pr2,pr3,pr4,pr5,pr6,pr7,se1,se2,se3,se4,su1,su2)$
$Q2(cus1,cus2,cus3,cus4,ad1,ad2,con1,con2,pr1,pr2,pr3,pr4,pr5,pr6,pr7,se1,se2,se3,se4,su1,su2,com1,com2,com3,com4)$
$Q3(pr1,pr2,pr3,pr5,su1,su2,com4)$
$Q4(pr1,pr5,com2,com1,com4)$

Fig. 5. Affinity matrix for hypernode $X_{product\_contract}$

Deployment. Importantly, note that deciding relational or co-relational to design a hypernode is not bind to the choice of a specific kind of DBMS, but to unveil its **nature**. Although our method remains agnostic of the chosen product, we finish our case study showing how to deploy the hypergraph in a commercial relational DBMS (i.e., Oracle) and in an open source co-relational store (i.e., HBase plus Hive). The output of our method then hints the best storage model, but the subsequent technological instantiation and the corresponding product-oriented tuning fall out of the scope of this paper.

Despite having a relational architecture underneath, Oracle[3] supports data structures traditionally not considered relational-like. Of special relevance for this paper are the data types *XMLType* and *NESTED TABLE*. The former corresponds to XML data and the latter to tables embedded in other table columns. These data structures map to co-relational structures introduced in Sect. 2. Documents in Oracle can therefore be stored through the data type *XMLType*, and vertical fragments be implemented with *NESTED TABLE*. Thus, relational hypernodes would be designed as regular relational tables whereas co-relational hypernodes can be designed through *XMLType* structures (if no vertical fragmentation is applied), and *NESTED TABLES* for hypernodes vertically fragmented.

Another example coming from the open-source world is HBase[4] plus Hive (see Footnote 1). HBase is a column-family system. Consequently, vertically fragmented hypernodes can be naturally stored, regardless being relational or co-relational. Similarly, both relational and co-relational hypernodes where vertical fragmentation did not apply can still be designed as single-family HBase tables. Nevertheless, benefits from using relational structures (HBase has no global schemas and therefore embeds the schema into each instance) and document stores (column values are stored as string and parsing relies on the application level) are then lost in HBase. This cannot be solved from the point of view of the storage, but Hive can be added on top to provide a relational view so that queries can be run as if the underlying storage was relational.

5   Scrutinizing Our Method

This section discusses how our method meets design objectives in Sect. 3.

Objective (a): Our method properly deals with large specialisations by means of Steps 3 and 5. In Step 3, entities related by specialisations are grouped as part of the same subject. In Step 5, subjects are evaluated to decide the data model to design them. If classified as too heterogeneous, then the co-relational model is chosen. In the use case, for **Product**, **Service** and **Supplement** the number of potential tables was reduced from dozens, hundreds or thousands, respectively, to one entity with explicit and variable schema.

Objective (b): Two key characteristics of our method facilitate schema evolution. Firstly, the main entities from the conceptual model are identified as centroids of a clustered subject-oriented design. Secondly, schema evolution likelihood, quantified per entity in Step 1, is used in Step 5 to decide the data model

---

[3] https://www.oracle.com/database.
[4] https://hbase.apache.org.

of each subject. In our use case, we easily added new attributes to entities as well as specialisation and composition relationships. During the project we added 205 new attributes/relationships and none required to reconsider the current design.

Objective (c): Conceptually, the multidimensional model is a good starting point for creating matrices. However, the star-join schema statically binds the subjects of analysis with dimensions at design time. To accommodate variability our method identifies subjects (Steps 3 and 5) reflecting them in the database schema. However, unlike a star-join schema, we do not identify dimensions at design time but at query time, depending on analysts concrete needs. Thus, we deploy a *dimensionless* decisional schema, relieving dimensional data of meeting well-formedness OLAP characteristics (e.g., multidimensional normal forms [13]). Decoupling both concepts in the schema provides us with the needed flexibility to tackle unforeseen dimensional concepts. For example, in our use case, several new features were required by data scientists throughout the project. Many times, such features were computed by aggregating data in an already identified dimension but at a coarser granularity, which would have raised the problems discussed in Sect. 3.

Objective (d): To evaluate performance, we compare the subject-oriented result obtained for our case study (S) against a performance-oriented (P) design for the same workload, built by computing the AM at the attribute level over the universal relation [16]. Considering the same t_a we chose (i.e., 73.4 %), we obtain one fragment per entity Customer, Address, Contract and Service; plus two more fragments $P_1 : \{pr1, pr5, com4\}$, and $P_2 : \{pr2, pr3, su1, su2\}$, corresponding to a vertical fragmentation of Product⋈Supplement⋈Complaint. Despite S only proposed three hypernodes, the number of joins needed is larger than in P, since attribute grouping in P is perfectly tailored to the queries in the current workload (Table 2 reports on the number of joins). Thus, average number of joins of S turns to be 6.3 % worse than that of P, a reasonable price for the gain obtained. Note, furthermore, that the effective read ratio of S matches that of P since we apply vertical fragmentation per hypernode (see Step 7).

Table 2. Join operations in the subject- (S) and performance-oriented (P) designs

Query	Frequency	Joins (S)	Joins (P)
Q1	26.7 %	0	1
Q2	20.0 %	3	4
Q3	26.7 %	1	0
Q4	26.7 %	1	0
Average:		1.134	1.063

6   Related Work

Operational (write-intensive) RDBMS use normalization to avoid redundancy and therefore insert, update and delete anomalies [8]. Oppositely, decision support (read-intensive) systems use denormalisation in order to avoid joins and improve performance. Multidimensional modeling [12], the de-facto standard for DW, is a simple yet powerful metaphor that focuses on subjects of analysis and their facets, which is implemented with a star-join relational schema. However, the star-join schema is not appropriate for flexible BD settings since not only the subject, but also the potential dimensions of analysis are fixed at design time. Furthermore, adding new dimensional or factual data is a costly operation in the DW, since it is typically implemented with relational technology.

Column-oriented engines take vertical fragmentation to the extreme, and redesign the DBMS architecture enabling the combination of light-weight encoding and vector processing [16]. Such engines have shown excellent performance for read-intensive workloads [20] and adaptive systems dynamically exploit vertical or horizontal layouts depending on the workload [1]. However, current techniques for fragmenting a database vertically, such as attribute clustering or AM [16], do not consider evolution and assume static workloads. Also, vertical fragmentation is not always the best modeling choice [1]. Finally, several guidelines specific for NOSQL design are nowadays available [6,18,22] presenting high-level guidelines that map either to phase two or three of our method. Other approaches bet for the integration of heterogeneous data by means of functional SQL-like languages [5] and, thus, integration occurs at query time rather than at design time. To our knowledge, this is the first holistic approach encompassing the relational and co-relational design altogether.

7   Conclusions

We have presented a novel method to holistically address the design of relational and co-relational databases in the presence of analytical workloads. Unlike most spread habits among BD practitioners, we underline the importance of the conceptual schema and propose a method resembling traditional database design following the classical 3-phase design: conceptual, logical and physical. However, we do not diminish the importance of performance in BD, but rather balance it with other equally important aspects such as data structural variability, which we have shown that can be managed by subject-oriented design (a well-known DW concept). We have exemplified our method with a real case study paradigmatic of the typical modeling complexities found in BD projects, and shown the benefits of our design approach.

Acknowledgments. We would like to thank Antoni Olivé for revising the paper.

References

1. Alagiannis, I., et al.: H2O: a hands-free adaptive store. In: SIGMOD (2014)
2. Ambler, S.: Agile Database Techniques: Effective Strategies for the Agile Software Developer. Wiley, New York (2003)
3. Blaha, M.: On reverse engineering of vendor databases. In: WCRE (1998)
4. Blaha, M.: Patterns of Data Modeling. CRC Press, Inc., Boca Raton (2010)
5. Bondiombouy, C., Kolev, B., Levchenko, O., Valduriez, P.: Integrating big data and relational data with a functional SQL-like query language. In: Databaseand Expert Systems Applications - 26th International Conference, DEXA 2015, Valencia, Spain, 1–4 September 2015, Proceedings, Part I, pp. 170–185 (2015). http://dx.doi.org/10.1007/978-3-319-22849-5_13
6. Bugiotti, F., Cabibbo, L., Atzeni, P., Torlone, R.: Database design for NoSQL systems. In: Yu, E., Dobbie, G., Jarke, M., Purao, S. (eds.) ER 2014. LNCS, vol. 8824, pp. 223–231. Springer, Heidelberg (2014). doi:10.1007/978-3-319-12206-9_18
7. Garcia, S., et al.: DSS from an RE perspective: a systematic mapping. J. Syst. Softw. **117**, 488–507 (2016)
8. Garcia-Molina, H., et al.: Database Systems - The Complete Book. Pearson Education, Harlow (2009)
9. Gartner: Focus on the 'Three Vs' of Big Data Analytics: Variability, Veracity and Value. https://www.gartner.com/doc/2921417/focus-vs-big-data-analytics
10. Inmon, W.H., et al.: Corporate Information Factory. Wiley, New York (2001)
11. Jagadish, H.V., et al.: Big data and its technical challenges. Commun. ACM **57**(7), 86–94 (2014)
12. Kimball, R.: The Data Warehouse Toolkit: Practical Techniques for Building Dimensional Data Warehouses. Wiley, New York (1996)
13. Mazón, J.-N., Trujillo, J., Lechtenbörger, J.: A set of QVT relations to assure the correctness of data warehouses by using multidimensional normal forms. In: Embley, D.W., Olivé, A., Ram, S. (eds.) ER 2006. LNCS, vol. 4215, pp. 385–398. Springer, Heidelberg (2006). doi:10.1007/11901181_29
14. Meijer, E., Bierman, G.M.: A co-relational model of data for large shared data banks. Commun. ACM **54**(4), 49–58 (2011)
15. OCDE: Data-driven Innovation for Growth and Well-being. http://www.oecd.org/sti/inno/data-driven-innovation-interim-synthesis.pdf
16. Özsu, M.T., Valduriez, P.: Principles of Distributed DB Systems. Springer, New York (2011)
17. Romero, O., et al.: Tuning small analytics on big data: data partitioning and secondary indexes in the Hadoop ecosystem. Inf. Syst. **54**, 336–356 (2015)
18. Sadalage, P., Fowler, M.: NoSQL Distilled: A Brief Guide to the Emerging World of Polyglot Persistence. Addison-Wesley Professional, Upper Saddle River (2012)
19. Stonebraker, M.: What Does 'Big Data' Mean? http://cacm.acm.org/blogs/blog-cacm/155468-what-does-big-data-mean/fulltext
20. Stonebraker, M., et al.: C-store: a column-oriented DBMS. In: VLDB (2005)
21. TDWI: TDWI Best Practices Report, Achieving Greater Agility with Business Intelligence. https://tdwi.org/research/2013/01/tdwi-best-practices-report-achieving-greater-agility-with-business-intelligence.aspx
22. Wiese, L.: Advanced Data Management for SQL, NoSQL, Cloud and Distributed Databases. DeGruyter, Boston (2015)

Translating Bayesian Networks into Entity Relationship Models

Frank Rosner[1]([envelope]) and Alexander Hinneburg[2]([envelope])

[1] Global Data and Analytics, Allianz SE, Munich, Germany
frank.rosner@allianz.com
[2] Computer Science, Martin-Luther-University Halle-Wittenberg, Halle, Germany
hinneburg@informatik.uni-halle.de

Abstract. Big data analytics applications drive the convergence of data management and machine learning. But there is no conceptual language available that is spoken in both worlds. The main contribution of the paper is a method to translate Bayesian networks, a main conceptual language for probabilistic graphical models, into usable entity relationship models. The transformed representation of a Bayesian network leaves out mathematical details about probabilistic relationships but unfolds all information relevant for data management tasks.

1 Introduction

The implementation of a big data analytics application requires to join data management software with machine learning tools. However, the fields of data management and machine learning developed quite different models and notations. The former frequently uses entity-relationship models (ERM) while the latter uses probabilistic graphical models to communicate key concepts. In this paper, we pick Bayesian networks (BN) as a widely used graphical notation for machine learning models. Note that the presented ideas can be transferred to other common graphical notions like undirected Markov models or factor graphs as well.

The notations of ERMs and BNs are designed to serve the needs of the respective fields. They are stressing information relevant in the particular domain while visually suppressing less important details. E.g. an ERM highlights the existence and cardinalities of relationships between distinguishable entities. On the other hand, a BN represents a joint probability distribution as a factorization of several hierarchically linked conditional probabilities. Even while both kinds of graphical notations show many details of the data, information explicit on one side remains implicit on the other one and vice versa—there is no natural understanding of the two worlds. However, a common conceptual description of the contribution from both worlds is crucial for the successes of big data analytics projects.

The data management part of a big data analytics project typically represents more details of the data than the machine learning part. Therefore, it is

© Springer International Publishing AG 2016
I. Comyn-Wattiau et al. (Eds.): ER 2016, LNCS 9974, pp. 65–72, 2016.
DOI: 10.1007/978-3-319-46397-1_5

reasonable to translate the machine learning part to the conceptual language of data management. Attempts into this direction include machine learning libraries with APIs in one or multiple programming languages [8,13,14], and new declarative languages or extension of existings ones [1,2,6,10,11]. However, none of these approaches solves the problem of integrating the information about machine learning that is relevant for data management into the conceptual view of this side. The advantages of a formal conceptual view of machine learning models integrated into the conceptual view of the data management side would be (i) no black box behind an abstract API in the data management model and (ii) developers from the data management side understand the basic in- and outputs of the machine learning part.

We propose a rule-based method to translate a graphical BN model in plate notation into an ERM. Such ERM can be easily integrated into the overall ERM of the whole application. As an example, we look at topic modeling of documents [3]. Latent Dirichlet allocation (LDA) [4] – shown in Fig. 3a – is one of the most popular topic models. Although not limited to this application, it is often used to find a hidden structure in text documents, called *topics*. Topics are modeled as probability distributions over a vocabulary. They are often presented as word lists each ordered by descending probabilities.

The given data in this example include documents consisting of word tokens. Each token corresponds to a particular occurrence of a word from the vocabulary. Documents, tokens and words have additional information attached like title, publication date or part-of-speech (POS) tags. The entities and relationships about the given data are shown in Fig. 1 (left). The BN describing the LDA topic model shown in Fig. 3a represents the given word tokens d_{nm} as shaded circles, which indicates random variables with given values. The hidden random variables represented by empty circles are the token-topic assignments z_{nm}, document specific topic proportions θ_n and topic-vocabulary distributions μ_k. For those variables, either expectations or probable value assignments are computed during machine learning inference. The black dots represent fixed hyper-parameters that determine the prior distributions for the hidden variables. The descriptions of the boxes (plates) correspond to the entities **Document** and **Token**. However, some entities like **Word** do not appear in the BN as they are implicit in the definition of vectors. Further, the plate named **Topics** introduces a new entity.

The result of the whole translation is shown in Fig. 1 (right). The ERM of the BN represents all relevant entities with respective primary keys. Further, the relationships between topics on one side and documents, tokens and vocabulary words on the other side are shown with their respective cardinalities. The ERMs about the given data and the translated one from BN can be combined into a single one by merging the matching entities. We believe that such an overall ERM helps to improve the efficiency of the development process as now the developers on the data management side can see what data is needed and contributed from the machine learning part with respect to relational aspects.

Our main contribution is a rule-based translation from BN in plate notation to ERMs, described in Sect. 2. This method provides semantic guidelines for

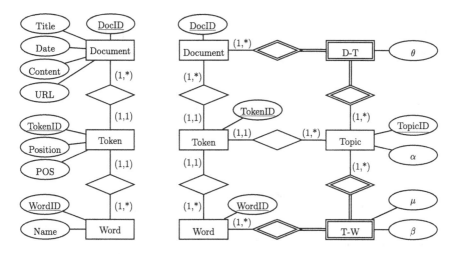

Fig. 1. ERM of given Data (left) and translated ERM for LDA (right).

building a conceptual representation of a BN that addresses the needs of the data management side of a big data analytics project. However, a BN is not a unique way to describe a probabilistic model, i.e. the same probabilistic model can be described by multiple BNs that differ in complexity. Therefore, our proposed translation constructs an intermediate atomic plate model (APM) in several steps (Sect. 2.1). It gradually uncovers implicit information not represented in the original BN. Further, the subsequent translation from an APM to an ERM (Sect. 2.2) can include different probabilistic relationships between the generated entities. Finally, a reduction step is applied to eliminate possible translation artifacts (Sect. 2.3). Last, we discuss related work in Sect. 3 and conclude the paper in Sect. 4.

2 Translation of Bayesian Networks in Plate Notation

BNs mainly describe data with random variables at the level of data items, e.g. word tokens. The BN for LDA in Fig. 3a has an observed random variable d_{nm} for each of the M_n tokens of the nth document. As plotting all data items one by one is not possible, the visual notation of plates is used. A plate groups a set of random variables sharing an index set. Due to this, plates convey information about entities and relationships. However, some random variables are implicitly denoted in BNs: (i) multidimensional vector notation of random variables and (ii) functions that implicitly describe data transformations coupled with joins. Therefore, we propose a stepwise approach to transform a given BN in plate notation into a well-formed ERM. This is done in three steps:

1. Make implicit relational information explicit: The resulting model is called an atomic plate model (APM).

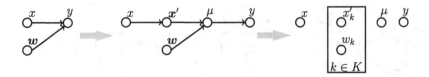

Fig. 2. Conversion of data transformation in BNs to atomic plate models

2. Convert the APM into an ERM based on graphical rules.
3. Reduce the ERM to avoid translation artifacts.

We use the standard ERM notation [5] with min-max cardinalities [7, p. 82]. We call an ERM *well-formed* iff it (1) is syntactically correct, (2) is explicit and (3) does not have redundant constructs. Explicitness means that all real world constructs which have a corresponding construct in the ERM notation are modeled using those. Thus, a well-formed ERM does not contain explicit foreign key attributes but uses relationships instead. Having no redundant constructs means that no entity or relationship is duplicate, i.e. semantically expressing the same thing. However, those duplicates may appear as intermediate results of the translation procedure. The following subsections offer detailed explanations of all steps to translate a BN to an ERM.

2.1 Construction of Atomic Plate Models

Plate models (BN in plate notation) may contain multidimensional random variables (e.g. vectors or matrices), hidden deterministic data transformations, and relationships. A plate model is converted to an APM by explicitly including those hidden transformations and relationships and any variables associated with it, as well as splitting multidimensional variables into their components.

For example, a word token is coded as a bit vector $\boldsymbol{d}_{nm} \in \{0,1\}^{|V|}$ that has exactly a single 1 at the index associated with the respective word $v \in V$. Thus, the respective APM for LDA (Fig. 3b) includes a word plate for the dimensions this vector and the vector variable is split into the respective components d_{nmv}. In this translation, edges are discarded. If they would be preserved, they conveyed wrong semantics about the conditional probabilities of the BN after the decomposition.

Detecting the deterministic relationships and data transformations hidden in BNs is a bit more subtle. Figure 2 illustrates this on the example of polynomial regression. The one-dimensional input x is transformed into a vector $\boldsymbol{x}'$ of several inputs $x'_k = x^k$ by taking different powers $k \in K \subset \mathbb{N}$. All powers are multiplied with weights that are components of the vector $\boldsymbol{w} \in \mathbb{R}^{|K|}$. Finally, the weighted powers are summed up and this sum is used as the mean μ of a normal distribution that governs a univariate random variable y. As we introduced another multidimensional variable $\boldsymbol{x}' \in \mathbb{R}^{|K|}$, splitting all multidimensional variables yields a common plate with index set K including all x'_k and w_k.

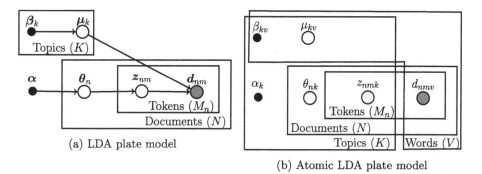

(a) LDA plate model

(b) Atomic LDA plate model

Fig. 3. Transformation of the LDA plate model to an APM.

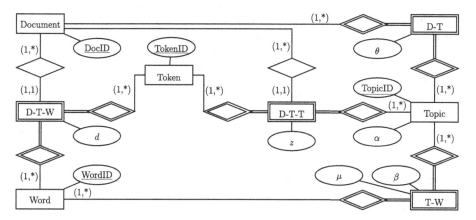

Fig. 4. Intermediate ERM for LDA, translated from an APM.

2.2   Translation of APM to ERM

After converting a plate model to an APM, it is translated to an ERM. For this step, we extend the mapping from plate models to DAPER models [9]. We defer the discussion of the differences between our mapping and DAPER models to the related work section. We briefly state the translation rules. Due to space restrictions, we refer to [12] for extended graphical explanations. Further, we explain the handling of special model constraints. The rules are illustrated by examples included in the translation of the APM (Fig. 3b) of LDA to an intermediate verbose ERM (Fig. 4) and then to the final ERM (Fig. 1 right).

Translate plates to entity types. Each plate of an APM is represented as an entity type. Usually there is an index set associated with each plate. Each entity type gets an artificial key (ID) that enumerates the index set. Thus, the plates word, document, token and topic become entities in Fig. 4.

Translate plate intersections to relationships. Plate intersections represent many-to-many relationships between the corresponding entity types. In contrast to [9], we express all relationships as association entity types [7, pp. 86–88]. This allows a generic translation procedure that can easily be used for n-ary relationships. E.g. the intersection between the plates for topics and words is translated as the association entity T-W in Fig. 4.

Translate variables to attributes. The translation of attributes depends on the number of plates surrounding them. If a variable is surrounded by exactly one plate, the entity type of that plate gets an additional attribute representing this variable. If a variable resides inside multiple plates, it becomes an attribute of the corresponding association entity. Variables that are associated with no plate are assigned to an artificial entity type called Global. There exists only one entity of type Global.

Translate nested plates to one-to-many relationships. If a plate is nested in another plate, the resulting relationship has one-to-many cardinality instead of many-to-many. This works well in the simple case of a binary relation, but falls short when one or both plates are additionally intersected or nested with further plates. Therefore, nested plates are translated using an additional weak entity, the parent of which is the entity of the inside plate. For example, the token plate, which is nested inside the document plate (Fig. 3b), is translated to a one-to-many relationship between the token and document entity via the association entity D-T-W in Fig. 4. This case shows the benefit of our approach as the word entity also becomes a parent of D-T-W due to the intersections of the word, document and token plates. In case of only binary relationships, the weak entity is not necessary. Such cases will be fixed in the reduction step that follows the translation to ERM.

In addition to these basic rules, we propose two additional transformation rules that consider the effects of constraints for random variables on the resulting ERM and cope with self relationships as a result of matrix or tensor variable translations.

Adjust cardinalities depending on variable constraints. In some applications there are variables that solely express associations between objects. In the LDA example, a token m inside a document n is assigned to a topic k through $z_{nm} \in \{0,1\}^K$ with $\sum_{k=1}^{K} z_{nmk} = 1$. In this case the plate intersection of the topic plate should not be translated as a many-to-many relationship but as one-to-many relationship. The one-to-many relationship is expressed by an additional weak entity with only a single parent as in the previous rule to allow the translation to continue with further plate intersections covering z_k. The entity index set of which is summed over, becomes not a parent of the weak entity. Finally, the constrained attribute z_k of the association entity is removed since now the association information is expressed by the relationships. In case of only two overlapping plates, the more complex expression of the one-to-many relationship is simplified in the final reduction step. The intermediate ERM in Fig. 4 shows the situation between the token and the topic entity before applying this rule, Fig. 1 shows the final result after the reduction. A more detailed example is found in [12].

Translate overlapping plates with same index set to self relationships.
When converting plate models with matrix or tensor variables to APMs, the
translation procedure will produce overlapping plates. Given a matrix with equal
dimensions $N = M$, this will result in two overlapping plates of the same index
set. These are simply translated as a many-to-many self relationship. The matrix
components are then represented as an attribute of the resulting association
entity.

With this set of rules it is possible to translate any given plate model into an
ERM. However, in some cases the resulting model might not be well-formed. It
might express simple one-to-many relationships in a complicated way. Therefore,
a reduction step is performed as described in the next section.

2.3   Reduction of Translated Entity-Relationship Models

In order to produce well-formed ERMs from plate models, it is necessary to
apply a reduction step after the conversion from APM to ERM. This reduction
will make sure that all translation artifacts are eliminated that are caused by
straight application of the translation rules. Those artifacts are weak entities
without primary key extension and duplicate relationships.

Plate intersections are translated to association entities having a weak relationship to all entities that form the intersection. However, 1-of-K coded variables and nested plates turn weak entity relationships into normal ones. In case
only one weak relationship is left after the completed translation, the construct
is not well-formed when it does not extend the primary key. The weak entity
relationship is then a degenerated one-to-one relationship and the weak entity is
merged with parent entity. After removing the degenerated weak relationships
as described above there may be duplicate relationships left. The translating
person can decide to merge these relationships if they are expressing the same
fact [12]. The right part of Fig. 1 shows the result of applying the reduction steps
to the intermediate ERM from Fig. 4.

3   Related Work

Directed acyclic probabilistic entity-relationship (DAPER) models [9] are closely
related to our work. However, they are designed to unify probabilistic relational
models and plate models. While we discard all facts about probabilistic relationships in our translation, DAPER models can still be used to express such
relationships. As a consequence, vector variables and other implicit information
are not resolved in DAPER models like in the proposed translation to APMs.
Thus, DAPER models are not used and also not intended to work as ERMs for
conceptional design of data management.

Our work is closely related in spirit to a recently proposed conceptual modeling framework work for network analytics [15]. In contrast, we target BNs, but
we believe that our proposed translation method is a core building block for a
conceptual framework for probabilistic models that can yield similar benefits.

4 Conclusion

Our proposed translation shows that modeling an ERM for a given BN is a non-trival task. Knowledge of the translation procedure helps data architects to pose the right questions for machine learning experts to uncover implicit information in a BN. Future work includes building a library of ERMs for widely used BNs. Based on such library, we want to work out a framework that gives guidelines how to effectively build an integrated conceptual model that includes details about domain specific aspects as well as the machine learning side of a big data analytics application. Within such framework, efficiency optimizations can be embedded when translating an integrated conceptual model to a particular implementation.

References

1. Akdere, M., Cetintemel, U., Riondato, M., et al.: The case for predictive database systems: opportunities and challenges. In: CIDR, pp. 167–174 (2011)
2. Armbrust, M., Xin, R.S., Lian, C., et al.: Spark SQL: relational data processing in spark. In: SIGMOD, pp. 1383–1394 (2015)
3. Blei, D.M.: Probabilistic topic models. Commun. ACM **55**(4), 77–84 (2012)
4. Blei, D.M., Ng, A.Y., Jordan, M.I.: Latent Dirichlet allocation. J. Mach. Learn. Res. **3**, 993–1022 (2003)
5. Chen, P.P.-S.: The entity-relationship model–toward a unified view of data. ACM Trans. Database Syst. (TODS) **1**(1), 9–36 (1976)
6. Domingos, P., Richardson, M.: Markov logic: a unifying framework for statistical relational learning. In: Introduction to Statistical Relational Learning, pp. 339–371 (2007)
7. Elmasri, R., Navathe, S.B.: Fundamentals of Database Systems. Pearson, Boston (2007)
8. Hall, M., Frank, E., Holmes, G., et al.: The WEKA data mining software: an update. ACM SIGKDD Explor. Newsl. **11**(1), 10–18 (2009)
9. Heckerman, D., Meek, C., Koller, D.: Probabilistic entity-relationship models, PRMs, and plate models. In: Introduction to statistical relational learning, pp. 201–238 (2007)
10. Hellerstein, J.M., Ré, C., Schoppmann, F., et al.: The MADlib analytics library: or MAD skills, the SQL. J. VLDB **5**(12), 1700–1711 (2012)
11. Kumar, A., Niu, F., Ré, C.: Hazy: making it easier to build and maintain big-data analytics. Commun. ACM **56**(3), 40–49 (2013)
12. Rosner, F., Hinneburg, A.: Translating Bayesian networks into entity relationship models (Extended Version). arXiv e-prints, 1607.02399 (2016)
13. Scikit: scikit-learn. Machine Learning in Python (2014)
14. Sparks, E.R., Smith, V., et al.: MLI: an API for distributed machine learning. In: ICDM, pp. 1187–1192 (2013)
15. Wang, Q.: A conceptual modeling framework for network analytics. Data Knowl. Eng. **99**, 59–71 (2015)

Key Performance Indicator Elicitation and Selection Through Conceptual Modelling

Alejandro Maté[1]([✉]), Juan Trujillo[1], and John Mylopoulos[2]

[1] Lucentia Research Group, Department of Software and Computing Systems,
University of Alicante, Alicante, Spain
{amate,jtrujillo}@dlsi.ua.es
[2] Department of Computer Science, University of Trento, Trento, Italy
jm@cs.toronto.edu

Abstract. Key Performance Indicators (KPIs) operationalize ambiguous enterprise goals into quantified variables with clear thresholds. Their usefulness has been established in multiple domains yet it remains a difficult and error-prone task to find suitable KPIs for a given strategic goal. A careful analysis of the literature on both strategic modeling, planning and management reveals that this difficulty is due to a number of factors. Firstly, there is a general lack of adequate conceptualizations that capture the subtle yet important differences between performance and result indicators. Secondly, there is a lack of integration between modelling and data analysis techniques that interleaves analysis with the modeling process. In order to tackle these deficiencies, we propose an approach for selecting explicitly KPIs and Key Result Indicators (KRIs). Our approach is comprised of (i) a novel modeling language that exploits the essential elements of indicators, covering KPIs, KRIs and measures, (ii) a data mining-based analysis technique for providing data-driven information about the elements in the model, thereby enabling domain experts to validate the KPIs selected, and (iii) an iterative process that guides the discovery and definition of indicators. In order to validate our approach, we apply our proposal to a real case study on water management.

Keywords: Business intelligence · KPIs · KRIs · Conceptual modeling

1 Introduction

Key Performance Indicators (KPIs) constitute a popular tool for monitoring the performance of an enterprise [11]. KPIs translate ambiguous enterprise goals, such as "Increase revenue", into measurable ones with concrete thresholds, such as "Revenue increased by 5 %", which can be objectively assessed in order to obtain a clear picture of the current status of an enterprise. However, whenever KPIs are defined to monitor strategic goals in any area the same question arises "is this an adequate KPI?" Answering this question is far from trivial.

First, the selection of a wrong KPI can have a severely detrimental effect for an organization. A wrong KPI wastes resources in the wrong place and those

© Springer International Publishing AG 2016
I. Comyn-Wattiau et al. (Eds.): ER 2016, LNCS 9974, pp. 73–80, 2016.
DOI: 10.1007/978-3-319-46397-1_6

responsible for its improvement develop a resilience over time to change the KPI they are focusing on [14]. Second, even though domain experts do know their business, once we start moving from measures related to results (e.g. number of products sold) to measures related to actual performance it is no longer clear which are the KPIs that the enterprise should focus on, their priorities and even more, their interrelationships and influences [2]. This is aggravated by the fact that value thresholds that should be established for each KPI are also unknown. Third, although organizations within the same industry sector typically share a common set of candidate KPIs [5], each of them actually operates in a slightly different fashion and different priorities, leading to subtle yet significant differences in the KPIs they use.

In order to tackle this problem, in this paper we present an approach for eliciting, assessing, and selecting KPIs and KRIs (Key Result Indicators). The main objective of our proposal, is to establish a baseline for improving indicator elicitation and selection, and it is comprised of the following contributions:

1. A modeling language that extends the expressivity of traditional models by including KPIs, KRIs, and measures as first class citizens.
2. A data mining approach to analyze the relationship between indicators by exploiting the conceptual model created by the domain experts.
3. A three step iterative process that covers the definition of the indicator map, as well as its refinement and assessment through data analysis, thereby connecting objectives to data through data mining.

The rest of the paper is structured as follows. Section 2 describes related work. Section 3 presents the proposed approach. Section 4 describes a case study based on water management for the validation of the proposal. Finally, Sect. 5 presents the conclusions and directions for future works.

2   Related Work

There is a broad literature on performance indicators due to their attractiveness as a monitoring tool. Strategic modeling works [6,8,10,13] treat KPIs are as a quantification, with no distinction between performance and result indicators. This is because strategic modeling provides the tools for representing indicators, but their selection is responsibility of the domain expert and the business strategy modeler. Management literature [4,7,11] aims to improve business management by providing tools to identify problems within organizations. It includes numerous research works on the use of predefined set of indicators and their effectiveness [1,4], as well as on the differentiation between *lag* (provides information when the target has been met) versus *lead* (provides information ahead of time, inaccurate) indicators [7]. The main drawback is that this knowledge has not been mapped into formal models which can be used for analysis.

Aside from these disciplines it is worth mentioning data analysis approaches [9,12]. These approaches are strongly data driven, with clear inputs and outputs to a process where domain experts have limited interaction. They are effective but not flexible, which limits their application when there are additional factors (e.g. recession) with no associated no data available.

As we can see, there has been a lot of interest on the topic of performance indicators. However, the lack of adequate tools has maintained indicator selection as one of the key problems in strategic management.

3 Eliciting and Selecting Business Indicators

Selecting adequate indicators for business objectives requires exploring the business strategy together with domain experts, while providing data-driven insights whenever confirmation or additional information is required. Therefore, the ideal solution is an iterative approach that alternates conceptual modeling with data analysis for enriching the strategic model obtained. Our proposal is a 3-step iterative process, based on strategic modeling, data analysis, and model update. In the following, we describe the main components involved in our process: the modeling language and the analysis process.

3.1 Business Modeling and Indicator Metamodel

Business strategy modeling can be a very complex task. Existing modeling languages [6,10,13] include a large set of concepts that are required for analyzing different aspects of the business strategy, such as dependencies across organizations, or the business mission and vision. However, these are unnecessary for the task at hand and, additionally, do not provide the expressiveness required for the indicator analysis. In order to keep the analysis simple, we propose a reduced metamodel that can be integrated as an extension for any of the existing modeling languages. Our metamodel is shown in Fig. 1. In this Figure we can see the following concepts included in the modeling language:

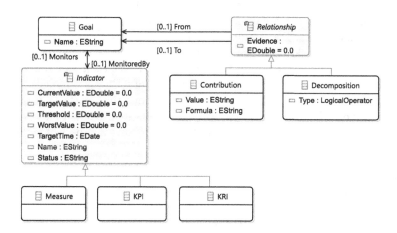

Fig. 1. Metamodel with the concepts and relationships for our modeling language

1. **Goals** are desired state of affairs. They are included in pretty much every strategic modeling language [6,10,13].
2. **Relationships** allow domain experts and analysts to express the expected relationships between goals and, therefore, between their associated indicators. They can be either contributions (with positive or negative effect) or decomposition. In our language, relationships have the evidence property, which captures the results from the analysis step showing whether the relationship is supported by the data or not.
3. **Indicators** measure the satisfaction of goals. In order to make indicators from our model compatible with existing proposals [6,13] all indicators can have a formula, current value, target value, threshold, worst value, and target time. Furthermore they have a status, which provides information on the status of the indicator with respect to the data. They are further specialized into three types, not found in current modeling languages:
   (a) **Measures** are the simplest form of indicators. They represent known formulas for measuring business activities with no known targets or thresholds. Their are potential as KPI and KRI candidates.
   (b) **Key Result Indicators** are indicators which directly correlate with the satisfaction of a goal. For example, "Increment in sales by 5 %" is a KRI, since it provides information about the results of the business objective "Increase sales". Every KRI must have clear defined thresholds and values, and its usefulness comes from the capability to determine the exact status of the associated business objective. However, compared to KPIs, (i) KRIs always provide information at the same point in time when the associated objective should be fulfilled and (ii) organizations cannot effect KRIs directly. Following our examples, we cannot increase sales directly, we have to effect them through promotions.
   (c) **Key Performance Indicators** are indicators that measure the performance of key activities related to KRIs. As KRIs, KPIs have clear defined thresholds, but they may not have a target time since they can monitor continuous tasks. For example, "Average response time under 3 days" is a continuous task. KPIs are important for the company due to the ability to effect them directly and, thus, indirectly effect their associated KRIs. Therefore, if KRIs change, it is likely the set of KPIs also changes. Finally, KPIs provide information ahead of time about the satisfaction of KRIs. Intuitively, if we perform well, we will obtain good results. However, this information is not accurate, as KPIs only measure a subset of the factors influencing a KRI.

With this metamodel, we can construct strategic models focused on indicators in collaboration with domain experts. The process for building the initial strategic model is approached in a top-bottom fashion as follows. First, the main objectives pursued by the organization are listed as top level goals. For each of these top level goals assign a candidate KRI (if known) or a measure that quantifies it. Next, using the information provided by the main objectives established and the KRIs and measures, we start refining the goals. Goals that are coarse grained can be decomposed into simpler goals. Once we have simpler goals, we can ask how/what are we doing (or plan to do) in order to achieve them, and what effect these actions have any of the current goals in our strategic model. The lower level goals obtained will be candidates to be monitored through KPIs. Finally, any candidate KRI, KPI, or measure not related to any goal is listed and included into the model with no relationship to the rest of elements.

3.2 Analysis

Indicators included in the strategic model represent specific formulas that allow us to evaluate their behavior over time. However, quality data is often scarce, and can be present in different formats. Therefore, we have defined a multi-step analysis process that accounts for several challenges that can be found during data analysis. Due to space constrains we mention only the key aspects.

If we have enough time data, then we start our time series by analyzing the correlation between indicators, in order to obtain candidate relationships within the data. These relationships are further analyzed though cross-correlation to estimate the time difference between the behavior of one variable and its effect on the other. Finally, we fit an ARIMA [3] to estimate the confidence and direction of the relationship identified.

If there is not enough time data and instead we rely on large number of instances with few time points, then we require simpler models. As previously, we start by analyzing the correlation between indicators. Then, we generate multiple linear regressions (one per region) in order to compare the behavior of indicators across regions and confirm the existence and direction of the relationship. Finally, we estimate the confidence of the relationship using simple sentinel-like rules [9]. These rules are calculated by using the difference in values across time for each indicator and comparing if a positive (negative) value for the predicting indicator results in a positive (negative) value for the affected indicator. Occurrences of the same type (direct/inverse relationship) are added, while occurrences of the opposite type subtract from each other.

The information obtained during the analysis is used to update the model in order to feed the next iteration of the process. New contribution relationships are added between goals whose indicator have a correlation with a confidence rate higher than the threshold defined during model update. If there is no associated goal, then a new goal is created with? As its description. The rest of the modifications are omitted due to paper constraints. With the newly added information, domain experts and analysts can begin the next iteration of the process, by defining composite measures and re-designing the strategic model using the newly obtained insights.

4   Case Study: Performance Indicators for Water Supply Management

Water supply management companies focus on ensuring water supply to multiple zones. It is a complex activity that involves multiple elements and processes.

The water supply network incurs into loses, and must be renovated once critical points are reached. However, finding the specific parts of the network that require renovation is a challenging task, and thus entire blocks of the network have to be renovated, which is costly. Therefore, in the following we apply our approach in order to help the company explore their objectives and metrics and improve both their performance monitoring as well as decision making.

We start with a simple indicator model depicting the high level goals pursued and including the whole list of measures (cropped due to space constraints, and mostly anonymized due to privacy reasons). The highest level goal is to provide an efficient water supply, which does not have any known measure associated. In order to track this high level objective, it is further decomposed into minimizing water lost and improve network efficiency. In order to minimize water lost, intuitively the company wishes to minimize breakdowns and leaks, which are avoided by maintaining the supply network and renovating it when needed. However, renovating the supply network involves a costly process, and thus harms the reduction of maintenance costs. With regards to improving network efficiency, Measure 9 is proposed, which is related to the population density and cannot be directly effected by the company. Therefore, no further goals are related to this objective, which acts merely as a monitoring tool (Fig. 2).

Due to space constraints, we can only provide a summary of the data analysis performed. For the first iteration of the analysis we start with 21 measures, which contain yearly readings for the period of 2008 to 2014 (6 data points) for 574 instances of the data. We start the preprocessing by extending the set of measures, calculating water lost (not directly available), from water supplied and water registered. Furthermore, due to the presence of missing values across different measures, we remove Measure 15, which presents largest number of missing values (382) and limits the application of statistical methods.

After performing the analysis, we identify a number of potential relationships (see Fig. 3) between result indicators, generating new potential goals that may be hidden and require exploration. Conversely, an initially expected relationship between Measure 14 and water lost is not supported by the data. This indicates that we need to review either the way we are monitoring our goal. i.e.

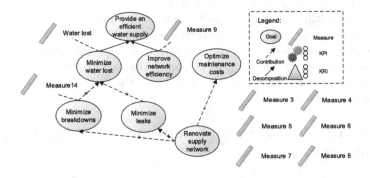

Fig. 2. Subset of the initial model for our case study

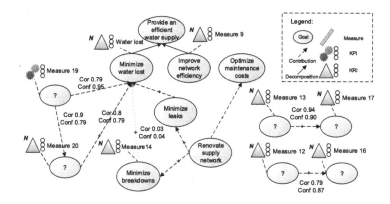

Fig. 3. Subset of the indicator model updated with data analysis results

how are we measuring breakdowns, or review the suitability of the relationship, i.e. breakdowns not cause severe water loses? During the first step of the next iteration we identified three relationships (Measures 12–16, 13–17, 20-water lost) as not interesting, since the measures involved calculated in a similar fashion, while another three relationships (4–5, 7–11, 19–20) were marked as of special interest.

At the moment we gathering additional data that leads us to more insights, but our approach has already successfully helped us to both simplify the initial indicator list as well as enrich the strategic model.

5   Conclusions and Future Work

We have presented an iterative approach for the elicitation, assessment and selection of KPIs and KRIs. To the best of our knowledge, it is the first proposal that explicitly includes the distinction between KPIs, KRIs, and measures within its modeling language and exploits this information in order to drive the analysis. Thanks to this information, our proposal enables domain experts to explore their candidate indicators, helping them to iteratively build an indicator map that reflects their priorities and is aligned with the results pursued. Furthermore, we have applied our approach to a real case study based on the water management sector, where we needed to elicit and select indicators for improving water efficiency. As shown in the case study, the combination of strategic models together with data analysis contributes greatly to progress in this search.

In the short term, we plan to focus on defining a methodology to cover the whole process and improving the data analysis to detect more complex relationships between indicators. This will likely contribute to create more detailed models and possibly extend the modeling language, where these complex relationships provide additional insights and ideas for domain experts.

Acknowledgments. This work has been partially supported by the European Research Council (ERC) through advanced grant 267856, titled "Lucretius: Foundations for Software Evolution" (04/2011/2016) http://www.lucretius.eu. Alejandro Maté is funded by the Generalitat Valenciana (APOSTD/2014/064). This work has been partially funded by the Spanish Ministry of Economy and Competitiveness (MINECO/FEDER) under the Granted Project SEQUOIA-UA (Management requirements and methodology for Big Data analytics) (TIN2015-63502-C3-3-R).

References

1. American productivity and quality center. https://www.apqc.org/
2. Angoss: Key Performance Indicators, Six Sigma and Data Mining. White Paper (2011). http://www.angoss.com/white-papers/key-performance-indicators-six-sigma-data-mining/
3. Box, G.E., Jenkins, G.M., Reinsel, G.C., Ljung, G.M.: Time Series Analysis: Forecasting and Control. Wiley, New York (2015)
4. Chae, B.: Developing key performance indicators for supply chain: an industry perspective. Supply Chain Manag. Int. J. **14**(6), 422–428 (2009)
5. Chan, A.P., Chan, A.P.: Key performance indicators for measuring construction success. Benchmarking Int. J. **11**(2), 203–221 (2004)
6. Horkoff, J., Barone, D., Jiang, L., Yu, E., Amyot, D., Borgida, A., Mylopoulos, J.: Strategic business modeling: representation and reasoning. Softw. Syst. Model. **13**(3), 1015–1041 (2014)
7. Laursen, G., Thorlund, J.: Business Analytics for Managers: Taking Business Intelligence Beyond Reporting. Wiley, New York (2010)
8. Maté, A., Trujillo, J., Mylopoulos, J.: Conceptualizing and specifying key performance indicators in business strategy models. In: Atzeni, P., Cheung, D., Ram, S. (eds.) ER 2012. LNCS, vol. 7532, pp. 282–291. Springer, Heidelberg (2012). doi:10.1007/978-3-642-34002-4_22
9. Middelfart, M., Pedersen, T.B.: Implementing sentinels in the TARGIT BI suite. In: 2011 IEEE 27th International Conference on Data Engineering (ICDE), pp. 1187–1198. IEEE (2011)
10. Object Management Group: Business Motivation Model (BMM) 1.3. (2014). http://www.omg.org/spec/BMM/1.3
11. Parmenter, D.: Key Performance Indicators: Developing, Implementing, and Using Winning KPIs. Wiley, New York (2015)
12. Rodriguez, R.R., Saiz, J.J.A., Bas, A.O.: Quantitative relationships between key performance indicators for supporting decision-making processes. Comput. Ind. **60**(2), 104–113 (2009)
13. Silva Souza, V.E., Mazón, J.N., Garrigós, I., Trujillo, J., Mylopoulos, J.: Monitoring strategic goals in data warehouses with awareness requirements. In: Proceedings of the 27th Annual ACM Symposium on Applied Computing, pp. 1075–1082. ACM (2012)
14. Van Thiel, S., Leeuw, F.L.: The performance paradox in the public sector. Public Perform. Manag. Rev. **25**(3), 267–281 (2002)

Conceptual Modeling and Ontologies

Insights on the Use and Application of Ontology and Conceptual Modeling Languages in Ontology-Driven Conceptual Modeling

Michael Verdonck$^{(\boxtimes)}$ and Frederik Gailly

Faculty of Economics and Business Administration, Ghent University,
Ghent, Belgium
{michael.verdonck,frederik.gailly}@UGent.be

Abstract. In this paper, we critically survey the existing literature in ontology-driven conceptual modeling in order to identify the kind of research that has been performed over the years and establish its current state of the art by describing the use and the application of ontologies in mapping phenomena to models. We are interested if there exist any connections between representing kinds of phenomena with certain ontologies and conceptual modeling languages. To understand and identify any gaps and research opportunities, our literature study is conducted in the form of a systematic mapping review, which aims at structuring and classifying the area that is being investigated. Our results indicate that there are several research gaps that should be addressed, which we translated into several future research opportunities.

1 Introduction

Modeling, in all its various forms, plays an important role in representing and supporting complex human design activities. Especially in the development, the analysis, as well as in the re-engineering of information systems, modeling has proved to be an essential element in achieving high performing information systems [1]. More specifically, conceptual models are descriptions of the organizational context for which a particular system is developed [2]. According to Stachowiak [3], a model possesses three features. The *mapping feature*, of a model can be seen as a representation of the 'original' system and is expressed through a modeling language. Second, the *reduction feature* characterizes the model as only a subset of the original system. Finally, every model is created with an intended purpose or objective, i.e. the *pragmatic feature*. Due to many project failures that were the consequence of faulty requirement analysis in the 1960s, the importance of conceptual modeling grew substantially as a means to enable early detection and correction of errors. As a consequence, a wide range of conceptual modeling-based approaches and techniques were introduced. Criticism however arose, stating that most of these modeling-based approaches and techniques were based on common sense and the intuition of their developers, therefore lacking sound theoretical foundations [4, 5]. This led to the introduction of ontologies, which provide a foundation for conceptual modeling by means of a formal specification of the semantics

© Springer International Publishing AG 2016
I. Comyn-Wattiau et al. (Eds.): ER 2016, LNCS 9974, pp. 83–97, 2016.
DOI: 10.1007/978-3-319-46397-1_7

of models and describe precisely which modeling constructs represent which phenomena [6]. Although ontologies were originally used in the domain of conceptual modeling to analyze the constructs used in the models and evaluate conceptual grammars for their ontological expressiveness, the role of ontological theories evolved towards improving and extending conceptual modeling languages (CML). From now on, we refer to all of these techniques as *ontology-driven conceptual modeling* (ODCM) approaches. We define ODCM as the utilization of ontological theories, coming from areas such as formal ontology, cognitive science and philosophical logics, to develop engineering artifacts (e.g. modeling languages, methodologies, design patterns and simulators) for improving the theory and practice of conceptual modeling [7]. In this paper, we intend to examine the mapping feature of conceptual models more closely in the context of ODCM. We aim to describe the use and the application of ontologies in mapping phenomena to models and are interested if there exist any connections between representing kinds of phenomena with certain ontologies and modeling languages. As such, we will survey the existing literature and determine which phenomena, ontologies and CMLs occur the most in the area of ODCM. Our survey of the literature will be conducted in the form of a systematic mapping review (SMR). The purpose of a SMR is to summarize prior research and to describe and classify what has been produced by the literature. Therefore, this paper aims to make the following contributions: (1) provide a classification founded on previously developed research that will categorize the different kinds of phenomena; (2) present two frequency tables that describe the types of ontologies and CMLs that occur the most; and (3) discuss the current and past use and application of ontologies and CMLs in representing phenomena.

2 Research Methodology

In order to achieve a rigorous mapping study, we based our method on the systematic literature study methods described in [8–10]. A mapping study aims to outline the structure of the investigated research area. In this paper, we thus perform a SMR on the use and application of ontologies and CMLs in the domain of ODCM. To conduct our SMR, we rely on the guidelines defined by [8]: (1) definition of the research questions; (2) formulation of a search strategy and the paper selection criteria; (3) construction of the classification and frequency table; (4) extraction of data and (5) synthesis of the results. In this section, we will describe guidelines (1) through (4). The synthesis of the results will be discussed in Sect. 3. We would like to note that this SMR is being performed by building further upon the literature set that was collected in [11]. In this paper, a literature study was conducted on the existing literature of ODCM in order to assess the kind of research that has been performed over the years. While this literature study focused more on the general research trends that occurred in ODCM, our paper intends to be more specific. Our objective is to focus on the type of ontologies and the kind of CMLs that have been applied in ODCM to represent different phenomena. As such, both the literature study as the SMR of this paper target the same research domain, i.e. ODCM, but perform their study on a different level of depth and focus. Therefore, for a full explanation of the formulation of the search strategy and paper selection criteria, we refer to [11].

The **research questions**, as defined below, act as the foundation for all further steps of the literature study. The research questions should be formulated in such a way that they represent the objectives of this literature study. Our questions serve multiple purposes: RQ1 aims at gaining more insight into the kind of phenomena the modeling languages represent. The purpose of this question is to reveal which type of phenomena research in ODCM has been focusing upon, and to discover which phenomena have been disregarded. We define phenomena as: elements or concepts that embody real-world occurrences and can be represented by a conceptual modeling grammar which provides a set of rules and constructs that show how to model and represent these real-world domains and phenomena [12]. RQ2 aims to discover which type of ontology and which type of CML has been used in a specific article. This question will allow us to determine the ontologies and CMLs that have been applied the most in previous research efforts. Finally, RQ3 intends to deliver more insights on the relationship between phenomena, ontologies and CMLs. As such, we compare the results of RQ1 and RQ2, and aim to reveal if there exists any influence between the kind of phenomena that are being represented by a conceptual model and the kind of ontology and CML that is being used to construct this conceptual model.

- *RQ1*: Which kinds of phenomena are considered the most in ODCM?
- *RQ2*: Which type of ontologies and CMLs are being used in ODCM?
- *RQ3:* How are ontologies and CMLs applied to represent phenomena?

Our **classification and frequency tables** are based upon these first two research questions. To answer RQ1, we construct a classification that will allow us to categorize between different kinds of phenomena. We base our classification on the structuring principles defined by [12, 13]. In this paper, various perspectives or structuring principles are being distinguished, based upon previous research performed in classifying phenomena. A structuring principle or perspective is defined as a rule or assumption indicating how phenomena should be structured. We therefore construct our classification scheme and assign phenomena into different categories based upon these perspectives. Each of these categories is discussed in more detail below:

- *Static perspective*: Phenomena that are characterized within the static perspective tend to describe the structure of a system. These kinds of phenomena are often represented with constructs named as entity, thing or object. These entities are being distinguished with a unique principle of identity and often hold a number of attributes, which represent specific values of the entity. Generally, these entities are also connected through a variety of relationships.
- *Dynamic perspective*: The dynamic structure collects phenomena that represent change and time. These phenomena are generally translated in constructs that describe events and processes. The happening of an operation or activity that has

been triggered by an external factor is called an event. A process is the trace of the events during the existence of an entity.

- *Behavioral & Functional (B&F) perspective*: The main phenomena that belong to the B&F perspective are social phenomena and states and their transitions or transformations. Social phenomena relate to entities such as actors and the roles they assume and actions they perform. Also rules and goals can be categorized as social phenomena since they influence the behavior of an actor. A transformation of a state can be defined as an activity, based on a set of phenomena that transforms them to another set of phenomena. Other terms used are function or task.

For example, if a paper introduces a new method to model and describes data structures used for representing and exchanging database information, we would add a reference from this paper to the static perspective. Similarly, if a paper focuses on the semantic incompleteness of models in the area of business process modeling, a reference is added to the dynamic perspective. Finally, a paper that aims to represent role-related and goal-related concepts in agent-oriented modeling will be classified as a reference to the B&F perspective.

In order to answer RQ2, we will construct a frequency table that lists all CMLs, and another frequency table that lists all ontologies that are being used in the papers of our literature set. We thus start of with an 'empty' frequency table, and populate this table during the analysis and the reading of the articles. Whenever we encounter a yet undefined CML or ontology, we insert this as a new category of our frequency table. It is important for the reader to realize that one paper can address multiple CMLs, ontologies or perspectives of phenomena. For example, if a paper performs an onto-logical analysis with the Bunge Wand Weber (BWW) ontology [14] on both the languages UML and EER, then this paper has one reference to the BWW ontology, and one reference each to respectively UML and EER. Similarly, if a paper introduces an ontological framework based upon Unified Foundational Ontology (UFO) [15] and explains how this framework can be adopted without specifically demonstrating this framework to a CML, this paper will only be assigned a reference to UFO.

After we collected our research articles, we applied our classification and started to perform our **data extraction**. In total, the literature set represents 200 articles that are related to research in ODCM, and that were published from 1993 to 2015. All articles, classifications and other data of the SMR can be found at http://www.mis.ugent.be/ER2016/. To extract the data, we first gathered all the collected literature from our search strategy into the reference manager Mendeley[1], to organize the general demographic information such as title, author, publication year etc. Next, the extraction was performed through the qualitative analysis tool Nvivo[2] to analyze and structure our data. Both the data from Mendeley and Nvivo were then merged in the statistical software tool SPSS[3] to conduct some additional qualitative analyses. The results of this analysis can be found in the section below.

---

[1] https://www.mendeley.com/.

[2] http://www.qsrinternational.com/products_nvivo.aspx.

[3] http://www-01.ibm.com/software/be/analytics/spss/.

3   Systematic Mapping Study Results

3.1   RQ1: Which Kinds of Phenomena Are Considered the Most in ODCM?

In order to answer RQ1, we classified the articles according to our classification scheme. In total, 104 articles belonged to the Static Perspective (45,8 %), 74 articles (32,6 %) to the B&F perspective and 49 articles (21,6 %) could be classified to the dynamical perspective. These findings are in line with the results of Fettke [16] and Davies et al. [17]. In their research, they investigated how practitioners applied conceptual modeling and which tools and techniques where the most popular. When asking the practitioners for the purpose of conceptual modeling use, the highest ranked application areas were: database design & management and software development. These domains mostly require rather static phenomena to be modeled. Other main application areas were improvement of internal business processes and workflow management. These domains encompass more phenomena of the B&F perspective and the dynamic perspective. It seems logical that academic research would also focuses on the same kind of areas and types of phenomena that are deemed important to practitioners and enterprises. To gain more insight at the evolution of which kind of phenomena have been the topic of interest in the field of ODCM, we display in Fig. 1 the number of references per type of perspective over the period 1993–2015. As the figure

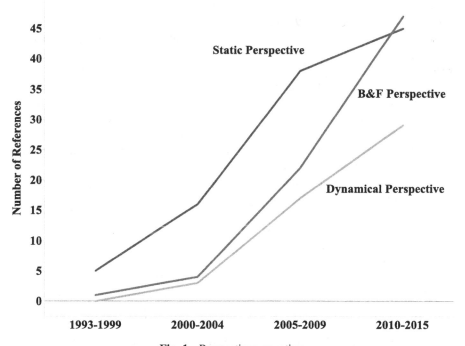

Fig. 1. Perspectives over time

demonstrates, phenomena of the static perspective have been dominating ODCM for almost its entire life span.

Only in the last five years has the B&F perspective overruled the interest in the static perspective. Starting from 2005, both the phenomena of the dynamic and B&F perspectives have increased in interest. A possible explanation to this trend is that ontologies were first applied to analyze constructs that represented static phenomena, while after several years of successfully applying these practices, the research community shifted the application of ontologies to constructs belonging to the dynamic and B&F perspective. Moreover our observation is in line with Recker and Rosemann [18], where they state that an increasing demand for a more disciplined approach towards process modeling and business process management (BPM) triggered related academic and commercial work aiming towards advanced process and business modeling solutions. Since these areas require concepts and elements that represent phenomena from both the dynamical and B&F perspective, it is likely that the increased demand in process modeling and BPM solutions caused the ODCM community to focus more on this domain.

3.2   RQ2: Which Type of Ontologies and CMLs Are Being Used in ODCM?

To answer our second research question, we display the frequency tables in Tables 1 and 2, which represent respectively all the ontologies that have been applied and all of the modeling languages that have been used in the field of ODCM. As we can see from our first frequency table, the BWW ontology (68) is by far the most occurring ontology. The second most occurring ontology is UFO (24). Both ontologies are by no coincidence foundational ontologies. Foundational ontologies are suitable for many different target domains since they provide a broad view of the world [19]. Therefore, they are a popular means to employ for different kind of phenomena and modeling languages. This assumption is again confirmed when regarding the many domain ontologies in the table and their frequency. Many of these ontologies have been referenced only once in a paper. Evidently, since a domain ontology is often developed for a specific purpose and targets a certain domain, its number of references is significantly lower compared to the domain-independent foundational ontologies. In our frequency table, we have made a distinction between foundational ontologies and domain ontologies, where we further categorized every domain ontology according to their application domain. Most of the domain ontologies in ODCM seem to apply to the business and enterprise domain, followed by domain ontologies in software systems development & architecture and the semantic web. The most frequently referenced domain ontology was the Resource-Event-Agent (REA) ontology.

To get a closer look at the kinds of modeling languages that have been used by ODCM researchers, we summarize our results in frequency Table 2. As with ontologies, we can see that several CMLs dominate the field of ODCM. The most popular modeling language is by far the Unified Modeling Language (UML) with 68 references. EER holds second place, with a total number of 25 references. Again, these

Table 1. Frequency table - type of ontology

Type of Ontology	Frequency	Type of Ontology	Frequency
Foundational Ontology		*Semantic Web*	
BWW	68	Web Service Modeling Ontology (WSMO)	3
UFO	24	DAML ontology	1
General Formal Ontology (GFO)	4	FOAF ontology	1
Discrete Event Simulation Ontology (DESO)	3	Geographic Ontology	1
DOLCE	3	MUSIC Ontology	1
Chisholm Ontology	2	RICO Ontology	1
SUMO	2	USMO ontology	1
BORO	1	*Software Systems Development & Architecture*	
Basic Formal Ontology (BFO)	1	Architectural Style Ontology	2
Searle's Ontology	1	FRISCO	1
Business/Enterprise		GUIMeta Ontology	1
REA	5	IT Service Configuration Management Ontology	1
UEML Ontology	2	ONTOMADEM	1
CM Task Ontology (CMTO)	1	Software Measurement Ontology	2
Construction Core Ontology (CCO)	1	Technology Risk Ontology	1
Domain Ontology for Resource (DORe)	1	Vulnerability-Centric Ontology	2
EAF Ontology	1	**Medicine & Healthcare**	
e-Business Model Ontology (e-BMO)	1	HOTMES Ontology	2
Project-Collaboration Ontology (PCO)	1	ECG Ontology	1
PRONTO	1	Neuroweb Reference Ontology	1
e3 Service Ontology	3	Public Health Informatics (PHI) Ontology	1
SOA Ontology	1	*Conceptual Design Knowledge*	
Database Design & Architecture		Activity-Space Ontology	1
AERDIA ontology	1	CAM ontology	1
Context Ontology	1	Port Ontology	1
ITSM Knowledge Ontology	1	Scale-extended Geo-Ontology	1
Transportation		Tactile information ontology	1
Public Transportation Ontology	1		

observations are similar to those of Fettke [16] and Davies et al. [17]. Their findings identified that the modeling languages UML and EER are two of the most frequently used modeling techniques of practitioners.

It is again no coincidence that the modeling languages UML and EER are most frequently applied to model static phenomena in areas such as database design and software development. Many modeling languages have been developed for specific purposes. For example, the EER modeling language was specifically developed for the purpose of describing the data and information aspects of databases while the Business Process Modeling Notation (BPMN) is more focused on specifying business processes. Other modeling languages that were frequently identified are the Web Ontology Language (OWL) and OntoUML. While most of the identified modeling languages are used to represent concepts and elements of a domain, the OWL language is often used to represent the structure of the ontology. One of the main advantages of using OWL is that it provides a machine-readable ontology, which can then be processed by applications. The language OntoUML is an example of a CML whose metamodel has been designed to comply with the ontological distinctions and axiomatic theories put forth by a foundational ontology, in this case UFO. When a model is built in OntoUML, the language induces the user to construct the resulting models via the combination of existing ontologically motivated design patterns. It is an interesting development to observe this kind of ontologically supported modeling language ranking fifth in the frequency table.

Table 2. Frequency table - type of CML (CML)

Type of CML	Frequency	Type of CML	Frequency
UML	68	Multiagent-based Integrative Business Modeling Language	2
ER & EER	25	ADONIS	1
OWL	24	AIML	1
BPMN	16	Information flow diagram (IFD)	1
OntoUML	9	LItER	1
Petri Nets	5	Misuse case maps (MUCM)	1
ArchiMate	4	OPEN Modeling Language (OML)	1
ARIS	4	ORM	1
Event-driven Process Chain (EPC)	3	REA	1
Unified Enterprise Modelling Language (UEML)	3	Reference Model of Open Distributed Processing (RM-ODP) language	1
e3 Value	2	Value Delivery Modeling Language (VDML)	1
iStar	2		

3.3   RQ3: How Are Ontologies and CMLs Applied to Represent Phenomena?

To gain a better understanding of the two most applied ontologies in ODCM, we have mapped their frequency of references over time. As we can see from Fig. 2, the BWW ontology has been especially popular in the years 2005-2009. However, since UFO's introduction in 2005, researchers performing ODCM have keenly adopted the ontology. It is clear that many users of BWW have switched to UFO in the years 2010–2015.

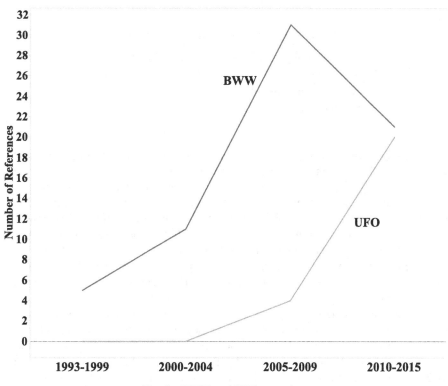

Fig. 2. BWW and UFO over time

To better explain this shift in ontologies, we take a closer look at which phenomena the ontologies have been applied for in ODCM. As displayed in Table 3, more than half of all the phenomena that are related to the BWW ontology are categorized into the static perspective. Both the dynamic and B&F perspective each represent around 25 % of the phenomena that correspond with the BWW ontology. Contrary to the UFO ontology, more than half of the phenomena belong to the B&F perspective. These results imply that the BWW and UFO ontologies are being applied for specific kind of phenomena. Our results would suggest that the BWW ontology is more convenient to apply to static phenomena while the UFO ontology is more suited to deal with B&F

phenomena. A similar, theoretical observation has also been made by [20], where they contribute a lack of social or behavioral aspects in the BWW ontology that are necessary to model a social environment. Our assumption is further supported when observing the structure of UFO. The UFO ontology is divided into three incrementally layered compliance sets: (1) UFO-A, which defines the core of UFO, describing Endurants, i.e. entities that persist through time; (2) UFO-B defining terms related to Perdurants, entities that do not persist through time such as events, and finally (3) UFO-C which describes social entities (both Endurants and Perdurants) and their behavior, or more specifically the social aspects of actors, roles and goals. UFO thus has a layer that specifically targets behavioral phenomena.

Table 3. BWW and UFO per type of perspective

Type of phenomena	BWW	Percentage	UFO	Percentage
Static Perspective	40	52,0 %	8	27,6 %
Dynamical Perspective	19	24,7 %	5	17,2 %
B&F Perspective	18	23,3 %	16	55,2 %

Our results suggest that certain ontologies are more preferred depending on the kind of phenomena the modeler is dealing with. An interesting research opportunity would therefore be to investigate if certain ontologies are in fact more advantageous to apply depending on the kind of phenomena. Further, as described in Fig. 1, since the year 2005, the B&F perspective has gained much attention in the field of ODCM. Similarly in Fig. 2, we also notice an increase starting from 2005 in the utilization of the UFO ontology. When linking both trends, the shift from BWW to UFO could therefore be explained that the increased interest in modeling phenomena from the B&F perspective has persuaded more researchers into applying UFO instead of BWW, because of UFO's beneficial ability to deal with this kind of phenomena.

To gain a better understanding in how CMLs are applied in ODCM, we map the ten most frequently used CMLs to the phenomena they should represent accordingly. The results are displayed in Fig. 3. For the static perspective, UML (39) is by far the most occurring modeling language, followed by the EER language (19) and OWL (16). Concerning the dynamic perspective, these phenomena seem to be represented the most through the UML language (12) and BPMN (11). Also languages such as EPC and Petri-nets are the most used for this perspective. Finally, when looking at modeling languages in the B&F perspective, we see that UML (27) is the most dominating modeling language. It seems that there does not really exist a second 'competing' or preferred modeling language in this perspective. We can see that modeling languages such as BPMN, ArchiMate and UEML are also applied to represent B&F phenomena, although they clearly are still far behind of UML. Despite UML offering many types of diagrams (class, activity, interaction, statechart etc.) to model a wide variety of phenomena, it is curious that one modeling language dominates all three perspectives. As mentioned above, many CMLs have been developed to represent and be applied in certain kind of application areas. Even though UML is a standard modeling language for a wide spectrum of application domains, it still has it deficiencies in representing certain kind of phenomena. Research by [21] for example, expressed the deficiencies of UML diagrams to model business organizations and the inadequate use of UML for abstracting high-level business-specific concepts. We should therefore carefully consider during the modeling process which kind of CML we will apply in order to represent certain kind of phenomena.

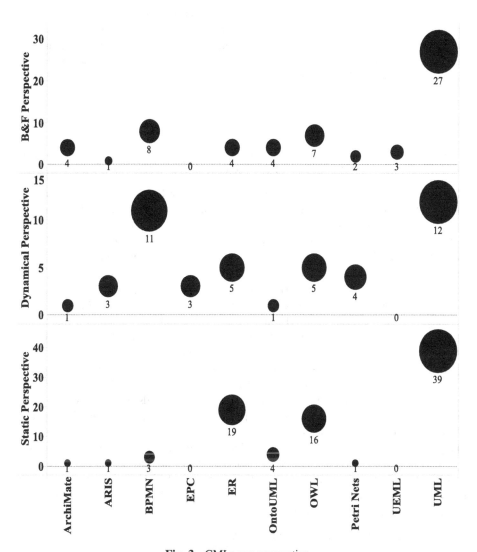

Fig. 3. CMLs per perspective

3.4   Additional Results

Beyond the investigation into the state of the research in ODCM, we describe here additional results that can be of interest for producers and consumers of research in ODCM. We have identified the top five journal and conference papers that were the most occurring publication forums in our literature set. These forums allow us to identify the main targets for ODCM research and to determine were previous research efforts can be found. The top five journals, with the respective number of papers are: Information Systems Journal (14), Data and Knowledge Engineering (9), Scandinavian Journal of Information Systems (7), Decision Support Systems (6) and Journal of Database Management (5). The top five conferences are the International Conference on Conceptual Modelling (8), Americas Conference on Information Systems (7), European Conference on Information Systems (7), International Conference on Information Systems (7) and Enterprise Distributed Object Computing Conference (6).

4   Discussion

In order to contribute to the field of ODCM, we discuss certain shortcomings and possible research opportunities that have been identified within this literature study.

Research Opportunity 1. As observed in Sect. 3.1, the field of ODCM has focused mostly on phenomena of the static perspective. Only in the last decade did we observe an increased interest in the dynamic and especially the B&F perspective. Similarly, the BWW ontology was by far the most applied in ODCM. We did recognize a growing interest in the UFO ontology, which is likely related to the growing interest in the B&F perspective. Furthermore, our results indicated that UML is the principal modeling language in ODCM. Moreover, UML was the most applied CML in every perspective. Although we do not doubt that both the BWW ontology and the UML modeling language are very adequate in performing ODCM, we can ask ourselves if this rather unilateral approach is much desired. As mentioned by Guizzardi [7], research in ODCM aims to develop engineering artifacts for improving the theory and practice of conceptual modeling. This research process is essential, not only to support acceptance among IS professionals, but also to establish the credibility of ODCM research among the larger body of researchers in the various engineering fields. If the field of ODCM produces artifacts that are mostly based upon the same and existing knowledge base, we tend to transform this research process into routine design [22]. As such, we believe many opportunities in ODCM still lie in addressing *important and unsolved problems with new ontologies and different conceptual modeling languages.* This diversification will lead to unique and innovative ways into solving these problems. A good example of such an innovative solution is the pattern language OntoUML, which was referenced by several papers in our literature set.

Research Opportunity 2. Our results would suggest that certain ontologies are more advantageous to apply, depending on which kind of phenomena the modeler is dealing with. However, as observed in [11], many researchers remain vague in defining the specific application of the ontology and in motivating their choice of ontological theories for the intended purpose. As displayed in Table 3, we observed that more than half of all the phenomena that were applied together with the BWW ontology where phenomena from the static perspective, while more than half of the phenomena that were used with the UFO ontology belong to the B&F perspective. These results would suggest that the BWW ontology is more convenient to apply to static phenomena while the UFO ontology is more suited to deal with B&F phenomena. These implications could serve as a testing hypothesis for future research to investigate these topics more thoroughly. This opportunity can also be approached from a different perspective, by relating the choice of an ontology (and the choice of a CML) to the pragmatic feature of a model [3]. Since every model is created with an intended purpose (its pragmatics), the ontology should correspond to this purpose. In other words, we believe that an opportunity lies in properly investigating *which ontology can be applied according to the pragmatics of the model.*

Research Opportunity 3. Ontologies are increasingly seen as key to successfully achieve semantic interoperability between models and languages. As identified in frequency Table 1, many different types of ontologies are being applied. Consequently, the field of ODCM has a wide variety of ontological analyses, ontology-based models and numerous methods in how to create or perform such analyses and models. However, this has re-introduced the interoperability problem, as also mentioned by Khan and Keet [23]. Especially on the long term, this raises the ambiguity between different ontology-founded models and increases the terminological confusion, which as a result leads to more complexity for both modelers and practitioners of ODCM. By *increasing the interoperability between ontologies*, we could facilitate their ease of use. By creating a mapping of elements between different ontological concepts and structures, this would reduce the workload for new research efforts since they could be based upon already earlier performed research. Efforts to increase interoperability can occur in many different forms. For example, as a way to increase the interoperability between ontologies, Khan and Keet [23] have created an online library of foundational ontologies called ROMULUS (Repository of Ontologies for MULtiple USes). ROMULUS maintains a catalogue of mappable and non-mappable elements among several foundational ontologies, and the pairwise machine-processable mapped ontologies.

5   Conclusion

This paper conducted a systematic mapping review in the field of ODCM. In total, our mapping study investigated 200 articles that originated from six digital libraries. We have provided a classification founded on previously developed research and two frequency tables, in order to clearly and thoroughly categorize papers dealing with ODCM. The classification scheme was used to identify which types of phenomena occurred the most, while the frequency tables aimed to discover the most frequently applied ontologies and CMLs. The results of the classification scheme indicate that phenomena of the static perspective have been considered the most in ODCM. However, during the last decade, we noticed an increased interest in phenomena of the dynamic and the B&F perspective. Our frequency tables determined that the BWW ontology and the UML modeling language have been applied most often. Originating from these results, we formulated several research opportunities: (1) we emphasized the importance of applying new kind of ontologies and types of modeling languages; (2) we suggest that the kind of ontology which is used to produce ODCM is of importance, and should be justified as a design choice in the modeling process; and (3) by increasing the interoperability between ontologies, we can link many of their analyses, models and frameworks and facilitate the overall ease of use in ODCM.

References

1. Karimi, J.: Strategic planning for information systems: requirements and information engineering methods. J. Manag. Inf. Syst. **4**, 5–24 (1988)
2. Evermann, J., Wand, Y.: Ontology based object-oriented domain modelling: fundamental concepts. Requir. Eng. **10**, 146–160 (2005)
3. Stachowiak, H.: Allgemeine Modelltheorie. Springer-Verlag, Wien (1973)
4. Siau, K., Rossi, M.: Evaluation techniques for systems analysis and design modelling methods - a review and comparative analysis. Inf. Syst. J. **21**, 249–268 (2007)
5. Batra, D., Marakas, G.M.: Conceptual data modelling in theory and practice. Eur. J. Inf. Syst. **4**, 185–193 (1995)
6. Opdahl, A.L., Berio, G., Harzallah, M., Matulevičius, R.: An ontology for enterprise and information systems modelling. Appl. Ontol. **7**, 49–92 (2012)
7. Guizzardi, G.: Ontological foundations for conceptual modeling with applications. In: Ralyté, J., Franch, X., Brinkkemper, S., Wrycza, S. (eds.) CAiSE 2012. LNCS, vol. 7328, pp. 695–696. Springer, Heidelberg (2012). doi:10.1007/978-3-642-31095-9_45
8. Kitchenham, B., Charters, S.: Guidelines for performing systematic literature reviews in software engineering (2007)
9. Dybå, T., Dingsøyr, T., Hanssen, G.K.: Applying systematic reviews to diverse study types: an experience report. In: Proceedings of 1st International Symposium Empirical Software Engineering and Measurement, 2007, pp. 225–234 (2007)
10. Petersen, K.: Measuring and predicting software productivity: a systematic map and review. Inf. Softw. Technol. **53**, 317–343 (2011)
11. Verdonck, M., Gailly, F., de Cesare, S., Poels, G.: Ontology-driven conceptual modeling: a systematic literature mapping and review. Appl. Ontol. **10**, 197–227 (2015)
12. Wand, W.: Research commentary: information systems and conceptual modeling— a research agenda. Inf. Syst. Res. **13**, 363–376 (2002)
13. Krogstie, J.: Perspectives to process modeling. In: Glykas, M. (ed.) Business Process Management. SCI, vol. 444, pp. 1–40. Springer, Heidelberg (2013)
14. Wand, W.R.: On the ontological expressiveness of information systems analysis and design grammars. Inf. Syst. J. **3**, 217–237 (1993)
15. Guizzardi, G.: Ontological Foundations for Structural Conceptual Models. CTIT, Centre for Telematics and Information Technology (2005)
16. Fettke, P.: How conceptual modeling is used. Commun. Assoc. Inf. **25**, 43 (2009)
17. Davies, I., Green, P., Rosemann, M., Indulska, M., Gallo, S.: How do practitioners use conceptual modeling in practice? Data Knowl. Eng. **58**, 358–380 (2006)
18. Recker, J., Rosemann, M.: Integration of models for understanding continuance of process modeling techniques. In: Proceedings of the 13th Americas Conference on Information Systems 2007, pp. 1–12 (2007)

19. Guarino, N., Oberle, D., Staab, S.: What is an ontology? In: Handbook on Ontologies, pp. 1–17 (2009)
20. Johnston, R.B., Milton, S.K.: The foundational role for theories of agency in understanding of information systems design. Australas. J. Inf. Syst. **10**, 40–49 (2002)
21. De Cesare, S. De Lycett, M.: Business modelling with UML: distilling directions for future research. In: International Conference on Enterprise Information Systems, pp. 570–579 (2002)
22. Hevner, A.R., March, S.T., Park, J., Ram, S.: Design science in information systems research. MIS Q. **28**, 75–105 (2004)
23. Khan, Z.C., Keet, C.: The foundational ontology library ROMULUS. In: Cuzzocrea, A., Maabout, S. (eds.) MEDI 2013. LNCS, vol. 8216, pp. 200–211. Springer, Heidelberg (2013). doi:10.1007/978-3-642-41366-7_17

An Ontological Approach for Identifying Software Variants: Specialization and Template Instantiation

Iris Reinhartz-Berger[1(✉)], Anna Zamansky[1], and Yair Wand[2]

[1] Department of Information Systems, University of Haifa, 31905 Haifa, Israel
{iris,annazam}@is.haifa.ac.il
[2] Sauder School of Business, University of British Columbia,
Vancouver, Canada
yair.wand@ubc.ca

Abstract. Software is a crucial component of many products and often is a product in itself. Software artifacts are typically developed for particular needs. Often, identifying software variants is important for increasing reuse, reducing time and costs of development and maintenance, increasing quality and reliability, and improving productivity. We propose a method for utilizing variability mechanisms of Software Product Line Engineering (SPLE) to allow identification of variants of software artifacts. The method is based on an ontological framework for representing variability of behaviors. We demonstrate the feasibility of the method on two common variability mechanisms – specialization and template instantiation. The method has been implemented using reverse engineered code. This provides a proof-of-concept of its feasibility.

Keywords: Variability · Reuse · Software Product Line Engineering

1 Introduction

Development has become increasingly complex while reducing time-to-market remains a critical issue. Therefore, identifying variants of software artifacts, such as requirements, design models, and code, plays a central role in software engineering. Variability is specifically researched and studied in the field of Software Product Line Engineering (SPLE) [7, 20], which aims at providing techniques, methods, and tools for effectively and efficiently developing and maintaining similar software products. This is done by promoting systematic reuse through what is commonly called variability mechanisms (namely, reuse or variation mechanisms). These are techniques applied to adapt generic (reusable) artifacts to the context of particular products. Different variability mechanisms have been suggested for different development stages, e.g., implementation [1], architecture design [3], and reference models [5]. Specialization (a.k.a. inheritance) and template instantiation are two examples of such mechanisms relevant throughout the whole development lifecycle. *Specialization* deals with refining behaviors (commonly by introducing new attributes or restricting the ranges of existing attributes) or adding behaviors. Unlike code inheritance, which

© Springer International Publishing AG 2016
I. Comyn-Wattiau et al. (Eds.): ER 2016, LNCS 9974, pp. 98–112, 2016.
DOI: 10.1007/978-3-319-46397-1_8

sometimes "just" promotes software reuse or behavior substitution (through operation overriding), in specialization, the specialized element is expected not to "violate" the laws (i.e., the intended behavior) of the generalized element, but to refine it. *Template instantiation* enables adapting types or filling product-specific parts in a generic behavior. In Java and C#, for example, it is achieved using the concept of generics.

Despite the benefits of reuse in general and SPLE in particular, in practice artifacts are often not developed for reuse. Cloning, for instant, involves copying artifacts and adapting them to the particular needs and related requirements. It provides a common, available, and simple practice [13] whose consequences are identified in adaptation, bug fixing, and maintenance.

When dealing with software product lines, a recent industrial survey [4] reveals that SPLE is commonly adopted extractively (i.e., existing product artifacts are re-engineered into a software product line) or reactively (i.e., one or several products are built before the product line artifacts are developed). In those scenarios identification of variants is required to support adaptation and improve maintenance or bug fixing.

To this end, we propose a method for identifying variants of software artifacts and associating them with variability mechanisms to help increase their reuse and improve their future development and maintenance. A formal framework for representing properties of variability has already been presented in [22] and used to define different variability mechanisms. In that framework, software products and software product lines are defined as things exhibiting behavior. The framework identifies relationships among software product lines and software products and enables mathematical definition of well-known variability mechanisms.

In this paper we suggest using the above framework to identify variants and recommend which variability mechanisms may potentially be applied in those cases. The method is composed of three stages, as depicted in Fig. 1. In the first stage the information regarding the software products (P_1, …, P_n) is extracted from their artifacts and represented in a repository. Next, the commonality and variability are analyzed utilizing properties of different variability mechanisms, such as specialization and template instantiation. Finally, the analysis results are presented in variability models, expressed in languages such as feature diagrams [12] or Orthogonal Variability Models (OVM) [20]. The actual application of the mechanisms is currently left to software designers and implementers.

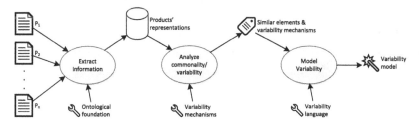

Fig. 1. A high level description of the suggested approach

Below, Sect. 2 reviews the relevant literature. Section 3 briefly presents the onto-logical foundations. Section 4 introduces the formal basis for the suggested method, while Sect. 5 presents its realization and refers to preliminary results. Finally, Sect. 6 concludes and sets the ground for future research.

2 Related Work

Identifying variants of software artifacts has been studied for several purposes. First, techniques have been suggested to detect code clones and manage them through refactoring or tracking [18, 23]. Roy and Cordy [23] refer to four categories of clone detection approaches: textual, lexical, syntactic, and semantic. After being detected, the clones can be divided to those that should be refactored (i.e., merged into a single fragment) and those that should be tracked in order to improve management (e.g., to support consistent update of all clones). In the context of SPLE, Faust et al. [9] propose a method for migrating multiple instances of code units of a "successful" single information system to a software product line. The method is based on a two phase model: (1) grow, in which the code is copied and modified to implement additional similar functionality, and (2) prune, in which the different variants are merged to support easy percolation of changes. Mende et al. [16] further suggest a tool to support the maintenance of code developed following the grow-and-prune model. In order to identify similar functions that may be merged, token-based clone detection is used to detect pairs of functions sharing code. Then, textual similarity measures are utilized to lift sufficiently similar functions to the architectural level.

Detection of variants is also studied for analyzing variability. Ryssel et al. [25], for example, propose how to automatically identify variation points, namely, places where variability occurs, in function-block-based models. These are models that decompose the functionality of systems into components (function blocks). Yoshimura et al. [28] describe an approach to detect variability in a software product line from the change history of the software. Several studies offer methods for generating variability models from existing artifacts, e.g., [8, 11, 19, 27]. Overall, these studies concentrate on identification of particular types of artifacts (most notably, code or requirements) and create feature diagrams or OVM models for representing variability. Moreover, many approaches for managing cloned variants make assumptions on the project context or the application domain [24].

In this paper we suggest identifying variants utilizing properties of commonly used variability mechanisms, such as specialization and template instantiation. The study in [2] has already referred to variability mechanisms as techniques to guide customization or modification of existing components. Our approach formalizes such guidance for the general case and demonstrates it on two variability mechanisms and object-oriented design and code artifacts.

3 The Ontological Foundations

Our approach is based on the ontological model of Bunge [6]. We chose this general purpose ontology because it has been widely used in conceptual modeling of information systems analysis and design [26]. It can be therefore considered a natural candidate for defining software artifacts and providing the semantics of variability mechanisms. Although other, more expressive ontological models could be used, we show next how Bunge's concepts can be used for defining variability mechanisms and analyzing the differences between them. Elaboration on Bunge's ontological model in the context of software variability analysis can be found at [22].

3.1 Things, States, and Behaviors

The elementary unit in Bunge's ontology is a *thing*, which possesses properties (intrinsic and mutual) and manifests behaviors. Properties are known to humans via attributes. A chosen set of attributes forms the *state variables* by which we model things. The values of state variables change in time, due to the occurrence of an *event* which triggers changes of state. Events can be *external* – caused by changes in other things, or *internal* – caused by the thing itself. From an external view, the *behavior* of things can be modeled by the initial state of the thing before the behavior occurs (S_1), the sequence of external events triggering the behavior ($<e>$), and the final state of the thing after the behavior occurs ($S*$) [21]. Table 1 summarizes these concepts and exemplifies them using library management systems. *Book Copy* is a thing, characterized by status (available or unavailable) and an indicator whether it can be borrowed or not (due to library's policies).

Table 1. The relevant concepts based on Bunge's ontological model

Concept	Definition	Example
State variable	An expression of the form x_i, which has an associated set Range(x_i) of values that can be assigned to it	Range (status) = {available, unavailable}; Range (borrowable?) = {yes, no}
State (of the thing)	A (potentially partial) assignment of values (from the associated ranges) at a given time to the state variables of the thing	$s' = $ (available, yes); $s'' = $ (unavailable, yes)
External event	A (trigger that causes) change in the state of a thing as a result of an action of another thing	User borrows User returns
Behavior	A triple b = (S_1, $<e>$, $S*$). S_1 and $S*$ are the initial and final states. $<e>$ is a sequence of external events	Borrowing: (s', $<$user borrows$>$, s''); Returning: (s'', $<$user returns$>$, s')
Thing	Described by T = (SV, E, B): SV is the state variables of interest E is a set of external events of interest B is a set of allowed behaviors	Book copy = ({status, borrowable?}, {user borrows, user returns}, {borrowing, returning})

3.2   The Formal Framework for Representing Variability Mechanisms

Using Bunge's ontology, software product lines and software products are represented by things exhibiting behaviors. *Product artifacts* are descriptions of software products and *core assets* are descriptions of software product lines which determine (part of) the behavior of software products. Product artifacts are obtained by introducing modifications to core assets.

Modifications can be classified along two dimensions: product and element. In the *product dimension* we examine the relationship between the whole set of behaviors B_P of a product (as specified in the relevant product artifact) and the whole set of the software product line behaviors B_{SPL} (as specified in the relevant core asset). Along this dimension, we can find for example configuration – choosing alternative functions and implementations [10]. However, in this paper we focus on the *element dimension* which deals with the relationship between a single behavior of a software product, b_P, and the corresponding (single) behavior of the software product line - b_{SPL}. The premise is that b_P "concretizes" b_{SPL}. Concretization allows for changes in the use of state variables (from the core asset) and in their allowed values. This is described by a *state mapping* from the set of states for the software product line to the set of states for a software product. The state mapping is induced by the relevant state variable mapping and the value mapping (see [22] for the full definitions of these mappings).

Concretization of a behavior $b_{SPL} = (S_1, <e>, S^*)$ can be achieved in different ways, two of which are specialized and template-instantiated behaviors (see Table 2). We refer to events as the triggers of transformations. Thus, we currently do not involve them in the definitions of specialized and template-instantiated behaviors, concentrating on the essence of the transformation depicted by the initial and final states.

Table 2. Properties and examples of specialized and template-instantiated behaviors

Variability of behaviors	Effect	Example
Specialized behavior ($S'_1 \subseteq S_1$ and $S'^* \subseteq S^*$)	Addition of state variables which are used in existing behaviors (to refine them)	b_{SPL}: *Book Copy is available* $\xrightarrow{user\ borrows}$ *Book Copy is unavailable* (status: {available, unavailable})
		b_P: *Book Copy is available and borrowable* $\xrightarrow{user\ borrows}$ *Book Copy is unavailable and borrowable* (status: {available, unavailable}; borrowable?:{yes, no})
Template-instantiated behavior ($S_1 \twoheadrightarrow S'_1$ and $S^* \twoheadrightarrow S'$)	Different state variables and their values which change similarly	b_{SPL}: *Item is available* $\xrightarrow{user\ borrows}$ *Item is unavailable* (ItemStatus: {available, unavailable})
		b_P: *Disk is on shelf* $\xrightarrow{user\ borrows}$ *Disk is off shelf* (DiskLocation: {on shelf, off shelf})

A *specialized behavior* $b_P = (S'_1, <e'>, S'^*)$ refines the initial state and/or the final state of the original behavior (b_{SPL}) by considering additional state variables or more detailed values. This means that the set S_1' is a refinement (specialization) of the set S_1 and similarly for S'^* and S^*. We denote these relations by $S'_1 \subseteq S_1$ and $S'^* \subseteq S^*$.

A *template-instantiated behavior* $b_P = (S'_1, <e'>, S'^*)$ applies to different state variables than the original behavior (b_{SPL}), but its effect in terms of transformation is similar. Formally, there are two bijections $m_1:S_1 \rightarrow S'_1$, $m^*: S^* \rightarrow S'^*$ (i.e., m_1 and m^* are total, onto, and 1-to-1). We denote these bijections by $S_1 \rightarrowtail S'_1$ and $S^* \rightarrowtail S'$.

4 Identifying Variants Through Variability Mechanisms

The above framework describes the relations between core assets and product artifacts in the element dimension, in terms of state variables and values. Due to the great popularity of object-orientation in the software engineering community, we adapt the general framework described in Sect. 3 to object-oriented artifacts (design & code). The mapping between the object-oriented terminology and the ontological concepts is straightforward: (objects of) classes can be mapped to things, attributes – to state variables, types – to (potential) values, and operations (methods) – to behaviors.

Below we adapt the notions of specialized and template-instantiated behaviors to object-oriented concepts in order to identify places where specialization and/or template instantiation can be applied. A method to use these adapted notions in practice and preliminary results are described in Sect. 5.

4.1 Basic Definitions and Notations

We consider a set of classes, along with their attributes and operations.

As a simple example, consider a class *BookCopy* whose attributes are:

- BorrowingPeriod (specifying for how many days the book copy can be borrowed);
- AvailabilityStatus (specifying whether the book is available or not, i.e., borrowed);
- ReturnDate (specifying the date in which the book copy is expected to be returned, if it is borrowed).

The operations of the class (besides the constructor) include:

- A borrow operation (changing the AvailabilityStatus from true to false and the ReturnDate to the current date plus BorrowingPeriod);
- A return operation (changing the AvailabilityStatus from false to true and resetting the ReturnDate).

We use the following representations of attributes and operations.

Definition 1. An *attribute* att is represented by a pair (name, vals), where *name* is the attribute name and *vals* is its type, representing the values it can assume.

We denote by att.name and att.vals the first and second constituents of att, respectively. The three attributes of the BookCopy class are depicted in Table 3.

Table 3. Attributes of the book copy class

	a_1	a_2	a_3
Name	BorrowingPeriod	AvailabilityStatus	ReturnDate
Vals	{i | i is of type int}	{true, false}	{d | d is of type Date}

An operation o is represented by two descriptors. One, named *shallow* (external), is equivalent to the operation signature (interface) and includes what other classes or operations "know" regarding the behavior. The second, named *deep*, reflects the (internal) impact of the operation on attributes. In other words, it specifies the transformation performed by the operation and its impact on the attributes. As shown later, the shallow and deep behavior descriptors enable specifying the behavior captured by the operation in terms of initial state (S_1), external events ($<e>$), and final state (S^*).

Definition 2. The ***shallow behavior descriptor*** of an operation o is denoted by $b_{shallow}(o) = $ (op_name, params, ret_type) where op-name is the operation name, params is a set of pairs (name, vals) denoting the operation's parameters and types, and ret_type is the returned type (all types have the form of sets of possible values).

We denote by $b_{shallow}(o).$op-name, $b_{shallow}(o).$params, and $b_{shallow}(o).$ret-type the three constituents of $b_{shallow}(o)$, respectively. The shallow behavior descriptors of the two operations of class BookCopy are depicted in Table 4.

Table 4. Operations of the book copy class

		o_1	o_2
Shallow	Op-name	Borrow	Return
	Params	$\varnothing$	$\varnothing$
	Ret-type	$\varnothing$	$\varnothing$
Deep	Att-used	(AvailabilityStatus, {true})	(AvailabilityStatus, {false})
	Att-modified	(AvailabilityStatus, {false}) (ReturnDate, {now() +BorrowingPeriod})	(AvailabilityStatus, {true}) (ReturnDate, {null})

Definition 3. The ***deep behavior descriptor*** of an operation o has the form $b_{deep}(o) = $ (att_used, att_modified): att_used is the set of attributes involved in the operation having the form (name, type) where name is the name of an attribute a, and type is a subset of values of the type of a; att_modified is the set of the attributes being modified by the operation which have the same form.

We denote by $b_{deep}(o).$att_used and $b_{deep}(o).$att_modified the two constituents of $b_{deep}(o)$, respectively. The deep behavior descriptors of the BookCopy class are depicted in Table 4. Note that since we are interested in an external view of a behavior, as reflected in the triplet (S_1, $<e>$, S^*), we currently ignore the impact of the behavior on the local variables of the operation.

Attributes and operations are used to represent the *ontological* counterparts, which are state variables and behaviors of things. State variables have names and a range of possible values, as reflected by the name and range of values (type) of attributes.

Ontological behaviors have the form $b = (S_1, <e>, S^*)$, reflected by S_1 = att_used $\cup$ params (namely, all attributes and parameters being used by the operation before being modified by it) and S^* = att_modified $\cup$ ret_type (i.e., all attributes modified by the operation and the returned parameter). $<e>$ is derived from the semantics of op_name.

4.2   Similarity-Based Relations

In order to identify whether operations, and consequently classes, can be considered variants of each other or variants of core asset classes, we use the notion of similarity. Similarity between classes is based on the similarity of their attributes and operations. Similarity of attributes is calculated with their names and possible values. Similarity of operations is calculated with respect to shallow and deep behavior descriptors. We therefore assume the existence of a similarity measure of the following form:

Definition 4. Let C be a set of classes $\{C_1, ..., C_n\}$. A *similarity measure* for C is a function from pairs of class constituents (attributes, shallow behavior descriptors, or deep behavior descriptors) to a Boolean value[1] indicating whether the pair of constituents is similar or not. Formally expressed:

sim: $Atts(C) x Atts(C) \cup B_{shallow}(C) x B_{shallow}(C) \cup B_{deep}(C) x B_{deep}(C) \rightarrow \{0,1\}$, where:

$Atts(C) = \{(a.att\_name, a.vals) \mid a$ is an attribute of $C_i \in C\}$
$B_{shallow}(C) = \{b_{shallow}(o) \mid o$ is an operation of $C_i \in C\}$
$B_{deep}(C) = \{b_{deep}(o) \mid$ is an operation of $C_i \in C\}$

Using the example of class BookCopy, assume another class MediaItem with an attribute *Location* of type enumeration and possible values: on-the-shelf and off-the-shelf (meaning borrowed). The operations of this class are similar to those of BookCopy, *borrow* and *return*, where *borrow* changes the *Location* from on-the-shelf to off-the-shelf, and *return* changes this attribute in the opposite direction. We can argue that the similarity of the attributes Location and AvailabilityStatus is 1 due to their isomorphic types and the similar roles they play in borrow and return. The similarity of the operations, in terms of both shallow and deep, is also 1.

Based on the similarity measure above, we define two relations between behaviors: inclusion similarity ($\subseteq_{sim}$) and replacement similarity ($\rightarrowtail_{sim}$). Using these relations we can adapt the notions of specialized and template-instantiated behaviors to object-oriented design and programming.

---

[1] Note that for simplicity, we assume that the similarity measure returns a Boolean value, 0 (different) or 1 (similar), rather than a range of values indicating the degree of similarity. In the method implementation, we realized the similarity measure by ranges and thresholds.

Definition 5 (inclusion similar). Operation o_i of class C_i is *inclusion similar* to operation o_j of class C_j if the components of $b_{shallow}(o_i)$, (op-name, params, ret-type), are included in the components of $b_{shallow}(o_j)$ and the components of $b_{deep}(o_i)$, (att-used and att-modified), are included in the components of $b_{deep}(o_j)$, up to the similarity measure for $\{C_i, C_j\}^2$. We denote this by $o_i \subseteq {}_{sim} o_j$.

Definition 6 (replacement similar). Operation o_i of class C_i is *replacement similar* to operation o_j of class C_j if there is a bijection b, which maps each component c of $b_{shallow}(o_i)$ and $b_{deep}(o_i)$, (namely, op-name, params, ret-type, att-used and att-modified) to a corresponding component b(c) of $b_{shallow}(o_j)$ and $b_{deep}(o_j)$, respectively, such that sim(c, b(c)) = 1. We denote this by $o_i \twoheadrightarrow {}_{sim} o_j$.

Using the examples of classes BookCopy and MediaItem, assume an extra Boolean attribute of MediaItem, borrowable?, indicating whether the media item is borrowable or not. The operation *borrow* changes the media item's *location* from "on-the-shelf" to "off-the-shelf" if borrowable is true. It is easy to check that BookCopy.borrow $\subseteq_{sim}$ MediaItem.borrow, as op-name, params, ret-type, att-used and att-modified of Book-Copy.borrow are similar (as explained above) to the corresponding components of MediaItem.borrow. The latter also has an additional attribute (borrowable?) which does not match any attributes of BookCopy.borrow, but influences the behavior of the operation 'borrow'. Thus, actually, BookCopy.borrow $\subset_{sim}$ MediaItem.borrow.

Now consider two classes: CatalogOfBooks and CatalogOfItems. Both have similar operations, such as addToCatalog and Browse. However, they work on different objects: CatalogOfBooks works on objects of the class BookCopy, while Cata-logOfItems works on items (such as BookCopy and MediaItem). Defining a bijection mapping between Item and BookCopy, it can be shown that:

CatalogOfItems.addToCatalog $\twoheadrightarrow_{sim}$ CatalogOfBooks.addToCatalog;
CatalogOfItems.browse $\twoheadrightarrow_{sim}$ CatalogOfBooks.browse.

4.3   Identifying Specialization and Template Instantiation

So far we have discussed specialization and template instantiation on the behavior (or operation) level. However, these concepts are usually used on the class-level.

Specialization deals with refinement of behavior by addition of state variables (attributes) or by restricting values of existing state variables. We concentrate here on cases where specialized classes do not violate the intended behaviors of the generalized classes (as may occur in code inheritance, e.g., through overriding). Since our approach is behavioral, we refer to attributes implicitly, through the changes they undergo (described in att-used and att-modified of the deep behavior descriptor). We next define specialization in terms of behaviors and inclusion similarity.

---

[2] By 'up to the similarity measure' we mean that for each pair of components of either shallow or deep behavior descriptors, A and B, B includes A means that for each element $a \in A$ there is an element $b \in B$, such that sim(a, b) = 1.

Definition 7. Let C_1, C_2 be classes. C_1 is a *specialization of* C_2 if for each operation o_2 of C_2 there is an operation o_1 of C_1 such that o_2 is inclusion similar to o_1 ($o_2 \subseteq_{sim} o_1$).

Note that the behavior of C_2 can be extended in C_1, namely, C_1 has operations with no counterparts in C_2, and operations from C_2 can be used as they are (without specialization) in C_1. As an example consider a variation of the class BookCopy, named BookCopy1, with an additional attribute – last? – which indicates whether the book copy is considered the last to be borrowed. Borrowing the last book copy requires special handling, e.g., notifying the librarian. According to the definition above, BookCopy1 is a specialization of BookCopy.

As noted, template instantiation deals with type adaptation and generic behaviors and can be characterized using replacement similarity as follows:

Definition 8. Let C_1, C_2 be classes. C_1 is template instantiation of C_2 if:

- For each operation o_2 of C_2 there is an operation o_1 of C_1 such that o_2 is replacement similar to o_1 ($o_2 \rightarrowtail_{sim} o_1$).
- For each operation o_1 of C_1 there is an operation o_2 of C_2 such that o_1 is replacement similar to o_2 ($o_1 \rightarrowtail_{sim} o_2$).

The class CatalogOfBooks demonstrated above is a template instantiation of the class CatalogOfItems.

5 Implementation and Preliminary Results

To evaluate our approach, we developed and implemented a proof-of-concept, following the stages in Fig. 1. The inputs are object-oriented code artifacts belonging to different products (P_1, …, P_n). The outputs are variability models specifying similar classes and the variability mechanisms associated with them. Note that we do not assume the existence of core assets. Instead we use our formal foundations in order to set the ground for the definition of core assets. We next elaborate on each stage of the implemented method and on some preliminary results.

Extract Information The input software artifacts (object-oriented code) are transformed (reverse engineered) into: (i) class diagrams from which the attributes and shallow behavior descriptors can be extracted and (ii) Program Dependence Graphs (PDG)[3] [15] from which the deep behavior descriptors are extracted. These particular models have the ability to represent structure and behavior (rather than specific scenarios). Moreover, they are common and mature as can be reflected by the availability of a variety of tools to reverse engineer object-oriented code. Finally, these models enabled ignoring low level details, such as comments and syntactic differences.

While the attributes and the shallow behavior descriptors are directly and simply derived from the class diagrams, the extraction of deep behavior descriptors deserves special attention. We utilize only the vertices getField and putField from the PDGs. These vertices get or set a value of static/object field. The use and modification of

---

[3] PDG explicitly represents the data and control dependencies of a program.

attributes may be done directly in the operation or through other operations invoked by the operation at hand. Hence, we consider a third type of vertices – CallSite. Through these vertices our method can recursively check getField and putField vertices in the invoked operations. Listing 1 describes how the initial state of a (behavior induced by a) given operation o is derived. The final state is similarly computed on put field vertices.

OperationInitialState(operation o, Set s1): Set

    Set combinedS1=s1∪retrieveGetField(o)

    Set invoked=retrieveCallSite()

    For each op in invoked

        combinedS1=OperationInitialState(op, combinedS1)

    return combinedS1

Listing 1. Deriving the initial state of a given operation

Analyze Commonality/Variability Similarity plays an important role in analyzing variability. We decided to measure the similarity of names (attributes, operations, and parameters) by using semantic metrics [17]. It provides for not considering the exact same written names, but commonly utilizes semantic nets or statistical techniques to measure the distances among words and terms[4]. As for similarity of types, for the sake of simplicity, we used equality, namely, two types are similar if and only if they are the same. This metric can be replaced in the future by more sophisticated measures, such as a metric that measures whether two types are isomorphic or not.

Shallow similarity was computed as the weighted average of the similarities of their operation names, parameters, and returned types. Parameters similarity was computed as the weighted average of name and type similarities. The weights can be manually tuned by software designers to reflect the specific characteristics of the given products.

Finally, deep similarity was calculated based on the symmetric difference (for multisets) of the attributes used and attributes modified. Formally expressed, let AU_o and AM_o be the attributes_used and attributes_modified of operation o, respectively, and $AU_{o'}$, $AM_{o'}$ – the attributes_used and attributes_modified of operation o', respectively. The deep similarity of o and o' is defined as:

$$1 - \frac{|\Delta(AU_o, AU_{o'})| + |\Delta(AM_o, AM_{o'})|}{|AU_o| + |AU_{o'}| + |AM_o| + |AM_{o'}|}$$

where $\Delta(A, B)$ is the symmetric difference operator for multisets, calculated as $(A - B) \cup (B - A)$ and $|A|$ is the number of elements in A.

For grouping similar shallow behavior descriptors and deep behavior descriptors, we used a hierarchical agglomerative clustering algorithm [14]. This algorithm starts by putting each element in a separate cluster and merges in each iteration the closest

---

[4] We assume that in order to make the code comprehensible attributes and operations have meaningful names (potentially including several words separated by underscores or capital letters).

clusters, namely, clusters whose average similarity is the highest. Those clusters are used for examining inclusion similarity and replacement similarity. Note that the method associates a variability mechanism (specialization or template instantiation) if potentially the classes satisfy the mechanism relation (inclusion or replacement similarity, respectively).

Model Variability To visualize the analysis results, we use Orthogonal Variability Modeling (OVM) [20]. OVM represents variability through the concepts of variation point and variant. A *variation point*, denoted by triangles, represents a variable item or a property of an item. A *variant*, denoted by a rectangle, defines a possibility to realize the variable item or property. OVM further supports relating variability information to software artifacts (such as requirements, design, and code) that are affected by the variability. For each cluster of similar classes, our method defines a variation point and associates with it the variability mechanisms utilized to identify the variants. The method further defines variants – one for each class in the cluster – and associates them with the variation point via an OR relation (see Fig. 2 for an example). Currently, we do not handle dependencies between variation points and variants.

Preliminary Evaluation We explored the code of two open-source versions of a SuperSnake game[5]: Supersnake 1.0 (released in 2008, containing 8 classes) and Supersnake 2.0 (released in 2010, containing 14 classes, some of which are exact copies or adaptations of classes from version 1.0). Running the method on the representations reversed engineered from this code resulted in 20 cases of specialization and 18 cases of template instantiation[6]. While 7 of the specialization and 5 of the template instantiation cases were trivial (i.e., included exact classes from the previous version), the rest of the cases were found relevant based on manual examination. Particularly, these cases pointed on high degrees of similarity between classes, in terms of their exhibited behaviors. We further observed some limitations which we plan to address in future research. First, the use of a general purpose vocabulary for measuring the semantic similarities led to irrelevant cases, such as menu (in the context of GUI) and food. These can be easily eliminated by using programming-related or domain-specific vocabularies. Second, the implemented method tries to locate for each element in one class similar elements in the other class without controlling multiplicities, thus leading to over generalization (e.g., classes with similar GUI controls). Finally, the presence of numerous getter and setter operations led to identification of template instantiation, regardless of the semantics of the corresponding transformations. This can be addressed in the future by a more in-depth analysis of code representations and refinement of the similarity measure for deep behaviors.

---

[5] The two versions were taken from http://sourceforge.net/.

[6] See details in http://mis.hevra.haifa.ac.il/ ~ iris/research/VarMech/InhTmpAnalysis.xlsx.

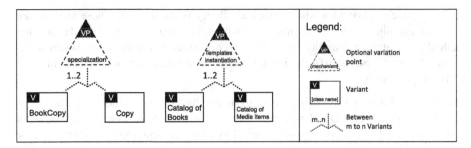

Fig. 2. Examples of the method outputs

6 Conclusions and Future Directions

Identification of variants of software artifacts is important for improving software development and maintenance. While current approaches mainly aim to avoid variants (through refactoring) or track them, we propose a method for utilizing variability mechanisms, and specifically specialization and template instantiation, to analyze and represent variability. The method is based on ontological foundations, which allow focusing on behaviors rather than on implementation. The method can be used to identify situations and places in software artifacts where different variability mechanisms may need to be applied in order to increase and systematize reuse. A proof-of-concept implementation of the method was applied to open-source code.

Immediate directions for future research are evaluating the method with software designers and developers and extending it to other well-known variability mechanisms, such as parameterization, configuration, and analogy. Another direction is refining the analysis of similarity of attributes and operations, e.g., by considering isomorphic types and semantics of deep descriptors. Furthermore, employing other representations in addition to class diagrams and PDGs may lead to a more wide-spread analysis. These directions will facilitate the development of a tool for an automatic construction of core assets for the analyzed software artifacts, based on the relations at the basis of different variability mechanisms.

References

1. Anastasopoulos, M., Gracek, C.: Implementing product line variabilities. ACM SIGSOFT Softw. Eng. Notes **26**(3), 109–117 (2001)
2. Anguswamy, R., Frakes, W.B.: Reuse design principles. In: International Workshop on Designing Reusable Components and Measuring Reusability (DReMeR 2013) (2013)
3. Bass, L., Clements, P., Kazman, R.: Software Architecture in Practice. SEI Series in Software Engineering, 3rd edn. Addison Wesley, Boston (2012)
4. Berger, T., Rublack, R., Nair, D., Atlee, J.M., Becker, M., Czarnecki, K., Wasowski, A.: A survey of variability modeling in industrial practice. In: Proceedings of the 7th International Workshop on Variability Modelling of Software-Intensive Systems (VaMoS 2013), pp. 7:1–7:8 (2013)

5. Brocke, J.: Design principles for reference modelling - reusing information models by means of aggregation, specialisation, instantiation, and analogy. In: Fettke, P., Loos, P. (eds.) Reference Modeling for Business Systems Analysis, pp. 47–75. Idea Group, Hershey (2007)

6. Bunge, M.: Treatise on Basic Philosophy. Ontology I: The Furniture of the World, vol. 3. Reidel, Boston, Massachusetts (1977)

7. Clements, P., Northrop, L.: Software Product Lines: Practices and Patterns. Addison-Wesley, Reading (2001)

8. Chen, K., Zhang, W., Zhao, H., Mei, H.: An approach to constructing feature models based on requirements clustering. In: 13th IEEE International Conference on Requirements Engineering, pp. 31–40 (2005)

9. Faust, D., Verhoef, C.: Software product line migration and deployment. J. Softw. Pract. Exp. **30**(10), 933–955 (2003)

10. Jacobson, I., Griss, M., Jonsson, P.: Software Reuse: Architecture. Process and Organization for Business Success. ACM/Addison-Wesley, New York (1997)

11. Itzik, N., Reinhartz-Berger, I., Wand, Y.: Variability analysis of requirements: considering behavioral differences and reflecting stakeholders perspectives. IEEE Trans. Softw. Eng. **42**, 7687–7706 (2016)

12. Kang, K.C., Cohen, S.G., Hess, J.A., Novak, W.E., Peterson, A.S.: Feature-oriented domain analysis (FODA) feasibility study. Technical report, SEI (1990)

13. Kapser, C.J., Godfrey, M.W.: "Cloning Considered Harmful" considered harmful: patterns of cloning in software. Empir. Softw. Eng. **13**, 645–692 (2008)

14. Kurita, T.: An efficient agglomerative clustering algorithm using a heap. Pattern Recogn. **24**(3), 205–209 (1991)

15. Krinke, J.: Identifying similar code with program dependence graphs. In: 8th Working Conference on Reverse Engineering, pp. 301–309 (2001)

16. Mende, T., Koschke, R., Beckwermert, F.: An evaluation of code similarity identification for the grow-and-prune model. J. Softw. Maint. Evol. Res. Pract. **21**(2), 143–169 (2009)

17. Mihalcea, R., Corley, C., Strapparava, C.: Corpus-based and knowledge-based measures of text semantic similarity. In: American Association for Artificial Intelligence (AAAI 2006), pp. 775–780 (2006)

18. Mondal, M., Roy, C.K., Schneider, K.A.: Automatic identification of important clones for refactoring and tracking. In: 14th IEEE International Working Conference on Source Code Analysis and Manipulation (SCAM 2014), pp. 11–20 (2014)

19. Niu, N., Easterbrook, S.: Extracting and modeling product line functional requirements. In: International Conference on Requirements Engineering (RE 2008), pp. 155–164 (2008)

20. Pohl, K., Böckle, G., van der Linden, F.: Software Product-Line Engineering: Foundations, Principles, and Techniques. Springer, Heidelberg (2005)

21. Reinhartz-Berger, I., Sturm, A., Wand, Y.: External variability of software: classification and ontological foundations. In: Jeusfeld, M., Delcambre, L., Ling, T.-W. (eds.) ER 2011. LNCS, vol. 6998, pp. 275–289. Springer, Heidelberg (2011)

22. Reinhartz-Berger, I., Zamansky, A., Wand, Y.: Taming software variability: ontological foundations of variability mechanisms. In: Johannesson, P., et al. (eds.) ER 2015. LNCS, vol. 9381, pp. 399–406. Springer, Heidelberg (2015). doi:10.1007/978-3-319-25264-3_29

23. Roy, C.K., Cordy, J.R.: Scenario-based comparison of clone detection techniques. In: The 16th IEEE International Conference on Program Comprehension (ICPC 2008), pp. 153–162 (2008)

24. Rubin, J., Czarnecki, K., Chechik, M.: Managing cloned variants: a framework and experience. In: 17th ACM International Software Product Line Conference, pp. 101–110 (2013)

25. Ryssel, U., Ploennigs, J., Kabitzsch, K.: Automatic variation-point identification in function-block-based models. In: 9th International Conference on Generative Programming and Component Engineering (GPCE 2010), pp. 23–32 (2010)
26. Wand, Y., Weber, R.: An ontological model of an information system. IEEE Trans. Softw. Eng. **16**, 1282–1292 (1990)
27. Weston, N., Chitchyan, R., Rashid, A.: A framework for constructing semantically composable feature models from natural language requirements. In: 13th International Software Product Line Conference, pp. 211–220 (2009)
28. Yoshimura, K., Narisawa, F., Hashimoto, K., Kikuno, T.: Factor analysis based approach for detecting product line variability from change history. In: 5th Working Conference on Mining Software Repositories, pp. 11–18 (2008)

The Role of Ontology Design Patterns in Linked Data Projects

Valentina Presutti[1]([envelope]), Giorgia Lodi[1]([envelope]), Andrea Nuzzolese[1],
Aldo Gangemi[1,3], Silvio Peroni[2], and Luigi Asprino[1,2]([envelope])

[1] Institute of Cognitive Sciences and Technologies,
National Research Council of Italy, Rome, Italy
{valentina.presutti,giorgia.lodi,andrea.nuzzolese,aldo.gangemi,
luigi.asprino}@istc.cnr.it
[2] DISI, University of Bologna, Bologna, Italy
{silvio.peroni,luigi.asprino}@unibo.it
[3] LIPN, Université Paris 13 Sorbonne Cité, CNRS, Paris, France

Abstract. The contribution of this paper is twofold: (i) a UML stereotype for component diagrams that allows for representing ontologies as a set of interconnected Ontology Design Patterns, aimed at supporting the communication between domain experts and ontology engineers; (ii) an analysis of possible approaches to ontology reuse and the definition of four methods according to their impact on the sustainability and stability of the resulting ontologies and knowledge bases. To conceptually prove the effectiveness of our proposals, we present two real LOD projects.

Keywords: Ontology · Ontology design patterns · Linked data · Ontology reuse · eXtreme Design

1 Introduction

Linked Data (LD) is rapidly increasing, especially in the public sector where opening data is becoming a consolidated institutional activity. However, the importance of providing LD with a high quality ontology modelling is still far from being fully perceived. The result is that LD are mostly modelled by direct reuse of individual classes and properties defined in external ontologies, overlooking the possible risks caused by such a practice. We claim that this practice may compromise the level of semantic interoperability that can be achieved. Therefore, the need of clear practices for motivated guidelines for ontology reuse arise. Ontology Design Patterns (ODPs) proved to be an effective means for improving the quality of ontologies. Another neglected aspect in ontology projects is the need of proper tools for sharing ontology details with domain experts, without requiring training sessions in knowledge representation.

Starting from the eXtreme Design (XD) methodology, the contribution of this paper is twofold. Firstly, we introduce a new task in XD concerning the

© Springer International Publishing AG 2016
I. Comyn-Wattiau et al. (Eds.): ER 2016, LNCS 9974, pp. 113–121, 2016.
DOI: 10.1007/978-3-319-46397-1_9

communication with domain experts. We define a UML stereotype that allows representing ontologies as a web of ODPs modelled as UML components. This notation hides the complexity of OWL representations while still conveying the main semantics to domain experts. Secondly, we provide motivated guidelines for reusing external ontologies and ODPs in ontology design projects. To prove the effectiveness of our contributions we discuss two real examples of LOD projects.

Background. Originally ontologies were seen mainly as *portable* components [6], while nowadays one of the most challenging areas of ontology design is *reusability* [5]. Although ontology reuse is a recommended practice in most ontology design methodologies [11], a standardisation of ontology reuse practices is still missing. Most literature on ontology reuse is focused on the challenging issue of ontology selection, while our perspective is on how to implement reuse once the selection finalised. We contribute to this issue with an analysis of possible reuse approaches, emphasising the role of Ontology Design Patterns (ODPs) [1,4] in this process. Design patterns and ontology reuse have been investigated in ontology engineering since early stages and they became hot topics in the context of the Semantic Web. ODPs enabled *pattern-based methodologies* in ontology engineering. These methodologies formalise approaches and provide facilities for re-using ODPs, however they do not provide motivated alternative guidelines on how to implement such a task.

The eXtreme Design (XD) [2,9] is an agile design methodology providing guidelines for performing ontology design through an incremental and iterative process based on the reuse of ontology design patterns (ODP) [8]. It is inspired by the eXtreme Programming (XP) and it recommends pair and test driven development, refactoring, and a divide-and-conquer approach to problem-solving [10].

Paper structure. Section 2 introduces the main contributions; namely, the new UML stereotype for ontology and ODPs representation and different approaches to ontology reuse while Sect. 3 provides real examples where the main contribution of the paper are applied. Section 4 concludes the paper.

2 Extending eXtreme Design

Figure 1 shows the *eXtreme Design* (XD) methodology highlighting in grey the contributions of this paper. The first contribution (involving tasks 7 and 8) regards the need of a *model that describes possible approaches to ODP reuse*, allowing ontology engineers to choose the most appropriate model for their project according to its specific characteristics. The second contribution (task 13 in Fig. 1) regards the need of describing ontologies to domain experts. It is important to provide them with enough insights about the ontology structure, its main concepts and usage, without exposing them to the burden of learning logics and knowledge representation languages.

2.1 Approaches to Semantic Web Ontology Reuse

Ontology reuse models can be classified based on (i) the type of reused ontology (e.g. foundational, top-level, ontology design patterns, domain ontologies),

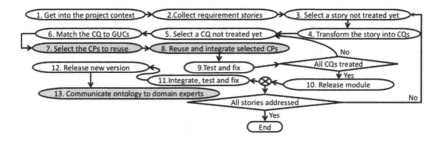

Fig. 1. Extended XD workflow

(ii) the type of reused ontology fragment (e.g. individual entities, modules, ontology design patterns, arbitrary fragments), (iii) the amount of reused axioms (e.g. import of all axioms, of only axioms in a given neighbourhood of an entity, of no axioms), (iv) and the alignment policy (e.g. direct reuse of entities, reuse via equivalent relations such as `rdfs:subClassOf` and `owl:equivalentClass`). The only characteristic that all these models share is to reuse entities with the same logical type as they were defined (e.g. an entity defined as `owl:Class` in an ontology is commonly reused as such).

A certain choice of reuse practice impacts significantly on the semantics of an ontology, its sustainability, and its interoperability.

2.2   Guidelines for Ontology Reuse

In this paper we provide guidelines for ontology reuse in the context of ontology projects that exhibit these characteristics: (i) there is no ontology that addresses all or most of the requirements of the local ontology project; (ii) the ontology under development is meant to be used as a reference ontology for a certain domain, and (iii) there is the willingness to comply with existing standards. We identify the following possible approaches to ontology reuse.

Direct reuse of individual entities. This approach consists on directly introducing individual entities of external ontologies in local axioms. This practice is very common in the LD community, however it is a routine, not a good practice, at all. It is essentially driven by the intuition of the semantics of concepts based on their names, instead of their axioms. In this case, the risk that the formal semantics of the reused entities is incompatible with the intended semantics to be represented is rather high. Moreover, with this practice a strong dependency of the local ontology with all the reused ontologies is created. This dependency may put at risk the sustainability and stability of the local ontology and its associated knowledge bases: if a change in the external ontology introduces incoherences in the local one, they must be dealt with a redesign process and consequential change in the ontology signature.

Indirect reuse of ontology modules and alignments. With this approach, the modelling of some concepts and relations, which are relevant for the domain but applicable to more general scopes, is delegated to external ontologies by means of ontology module reuse. An ontology module is a fragment that may be identified as providing a solution to one or more specific requirements of the local ontology. For example, let us consider an external ontology modelling the participation of an individual (e.g. through a property `ex:isInvolvedIn`) to an event (e.g. a class `ex:Event`). If the local ontology needs to specify a particular involvement in an event (e.g. `lo:hosted`) it should specialize (it indirectly reuses) the relation of the external one (i.e. `ex:isInvolvedIn`). The fragment of the external ontology identified as relevant for the local ontology may be communicated in some usage documentation provided with the ontology. Nevertheless, it is difficult to provide third parties with a formal indication of the fragment that was meant to be relevant. This may lead to high heterogeneity in the usage of external fragments in data modelled through the local ontology. As for ontology sustainability, when a change in the external ontology provokes possible incoherences, the redesign process would be easier dealt with as compared to the previous approach.

Direct reuse of ontology design patterns and alignments. If the fragment is clearly and formally identified, since it is embedded in a dedicated ontology, some of the previous remarked issues can be mitigated. Let us consider that the earlier example class `ex:Event` is defined in an external ontology that implements a specific ODP. In this case, a scenario in which a redesign process must be undertaken may be less frequent. In fact, ODPs are developed for reuse purposes and thus they are unlikely to change. In the light of these observations, it is recommended to reuse ODPs in contrast to individual entities.

Indirect reuse of ontology design patterns and alignments. ODPs are used as templates. This approach is an extension of the previous one. At the same time, the ontology guarantees interoperability by keeping the appropriate alignments with the external ODPs, and provides extensions that satisfy more specific requirements. The alignment axioms may be published separately from the core of the ontology. With this type of reuse, the potential impact of possible changes in the external ODP is minimised. In fact, should incoherences show after a change in the external ODP (which is rather unlikely to happen) the redesign process would be very simple. The ontology signature and axioms would remain unchanged, as incoherences would be resolved by simply removing or revising the alignment axioms.

Table 1 summarises the advantages and disadvantages of the discussed four approaches. In general, among all of them, the recommended one is the fourth approach: in the situation of incoherence raised by a change in an external reused ontology, it guarantees the easiest maintenance.

2.3   UML Profile for Representing ODP-Based Ontologies

Ontology development processes are all supported by languages, notations and tools for producing inputs and outputs of the various phases. XD provides detailed guidelines on how to perform some of its process tasks. For example, user

Table 1. Pros and cons of different approaches to ontology reuse.

Reuse method	Fragment	Pros	Cons
Direct reuse	Individual entity	Linked data practise	Semantic ambiguity, difficulty in verifying the consistency among the diverse reused concepts, dependency on external ontologies, instability and unsustainability
Direct reuse	Ontology module	Stability and sustainability of domain relations and concepts, modularity, interoperability	Possible heterogeneity in module usage, dependency on external modules, instability and unsustainability limited to external modules
Direct reuse	ODP	Stability and sustainability of domain relations and concepts, modularity, interoperability, easier redesign in case of external changes	Dependency on external modules, mitigated risk of instability and unsustainability limited to external ODPs
Indirect reuse	ODP	Stability and sustainability of domain relations and concepts, modularity, interoperability, dependency on external modules limited to alignment axioms	Slightly increased design effort for moulding ODPs

stories are collected by means of *story cards* with a template, OWL is used as ontology modelling language and its related UML profile defined in the Ontology Definition Metamodel (ODM) [7] is used as a graphical notation for representing the ontology in its documentation. ODM provides stereotypes for both class diagrams and packages. The package profile is the only one addressing the representation of whole ontologies or ontology modules and their inter-relations. The relation between packages (i.e., among ontology modules) can only be an *import* relation referring to `owl:import` for its semantics.

This package- and OWL-based notation may be inadequate in some context, in particular when the target user is a domain expert without an expertise in knowledge representation. Our proposal extends the ODM OWL profile by introducing a stereotype for component diagrams that enables the representation of ODPs as components that implement and/or reuse certain interfaces.

The concept of ontology interface has been investigated in the literature related to ontology modularisation and knowledge encapsulation [3]. An ontology module defines its content (e.g. classes and relations) by means of *interfaces* that constitute the access point to its model.

Our main focus is to provide a notation that can be used for sketching the design of an ODP-based ontology and for communicating (sharing) the ontology model and discussing it with domain experts by hiding implementation details. The proposed ODM profile extension is depicted in Fig. 2. We define two stereotypes that can be used with UML components diagrams: *Ontology Module* (OM) and *Ontology Design Pattern* (ODP). The latter inherits from the former and

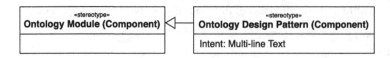

Fig. 2. Ontology module and ODP stereotypes for UML component diagrams

has a tagged value *intent*, i.e., a multi-line text that describes the modelling problem addressed by the ODP.

Each component defines two types of interfaces (compliant with standard UML notation): (i) the interfaces that the ODP *implements* (i.e., realises) denoted by *lollipops*; (ii) the interfaces that a ODP *uses* denoted by *sockets*. An ontology engineer may exploit this profile to sketch an abstract view of the adopted design choices when she has not decided yet what specific implementation of an ODP will be reused. The abstract view can be shared with domain experts in a phase between the collection of requirements (i.e., user stories) and the implementation, in order to share design choices and tune them before the actual reuse happens, if needed. Referring to Fig. 1, this would be between Task 7 and Task 8.

3 Applying the XD Extensions in Linked Data Projects

We applied the described contributions in two real Linked Open Data projects of the e-government sector. The first project was developed in the context of cultural heritage, in collaboration with the Italian Ministry of Cultural Heritage and Activities and Tourism; the second was carried out within the agriculture domain, in collaboration with the Italian Ministry of Agriculture.

3.1 Cultural-ON: Cultural ONtologies

Cultural-ON[1] is a suite of ontology modules for modelling knowledge in the cultural heritage domain. In Cultural-ON we applied the pattern-based ontology engineering approach, extensively reusing ODPs. The class *Cultural Institute or Site* (shortly, *CIS*) is used to model the different types of cultural heritage institutes or sites (e.g., museums, libraries, monumental areas). A number of organizations or juridicial entities (i.e., agents), playing specific roles on CISs, are represented in the ontology by `cis:Agent`. *CISs* are located in specific physical places that are precisely identified by geographical coordinates and/or addresses. CISs host collections (`cis:Collection` using the ODP *Collection*) and/or cultural heritage objects (`cis:CulturalHeritageObject`). Finally, cultural events (i.e., the class `cis:Event` that reuses the ODP *TimeIndexedSituation*) can be hosted in a *CIS*.

ODPs for domain experts communication. In the project we wanted domain experts to be focussed on the requirements. However, it was important

---

[1] http://stlab.istc.cnr.it/documents/mibact/cultural-ON_xml.owl.

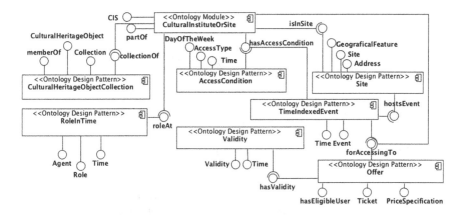

Fig. 3. Cultural-ON: UML component diagram for ODPs representation

to let them understand the main concepts of the ontology in order to facilitate reuse, and favour technological transfer to them who are ultimately responsible for ontology maintenance. In doing so, we faced the same issues as those earlier discussed: several times we were more focussed on explaining details of logics and ontology design best practices, and on convincing them not to concentrate on mere terms, as ontologys classes and properties were mostly seen. In the light of this, we elaborated the UML notation of Sect. 2.3.

Figure 3 illustrates the UML component diagram that describes Cultural-ON as a set of interconnected ODPs. For example, the component CulturalInstitute-OrSite depicts the class CIS and some of its main characterisations such as the composition (i.e., the partOf relation). The component RoleInTime, an application of the TimeIndexed ODP, exposes three main concepts; namely, Role, Time and Agent. It is then linked to a CIS by means of the concept roleAt. Note that this notation allows us to hide the OWL-specific modelling of an n-ary relation, requiring reification, while still conveying its semantics to domain experts.

External ontologies reuse. We adopted the earlier fourth model and we identified most relevant ODPs of external ontologies that were selected during an alignment process. We reproduced those ODPs in Cultural-ON so that to use ODPs as templates.

3.2 FOOD: FOod in Linked Open Data

FOOD[2] aims at publishing LOD data of EU quality schemes, known as PDO and PGI. Each PDO and PGI agriculture product is described, in its characteristics, by a policy document.

The data contained in these documents were modelled as OWL ontologies, reusing ODPs. Specifically, we produced an upper ontology that represents general elements that contribute to form the content of the documents. The upper

---

[2] http://w3id.org/food/.

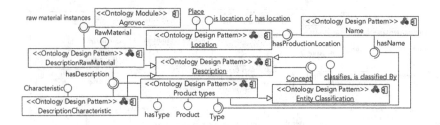

Fig. 4. FOOD: UML component diagram for the upper ontology

ontology represents the product name to be protected, its different types, the geographical area where it is produced and its characteristics[3] (including raw materials, and principal physical, chemical, microbiological or organoleptic characteristics). Specific ontologies per single product category were also produced in order to specialize the elements modelled in the upper ontology.

ODPs reuse in domain experts communication. Figure 4 shows the resulting UML component diagram of the upper ontology. Underlined components represent more general ODPs. The Description ODP applied to raw materials of a product, the component DescriptionRawMaterial exposes the concept RawMaterial and is connected through hasDescription with the component Product Type hiding the OWL representation details.

External ontologies reuse. In FOOD we applied both indirect and direct reuse (Agrovoc has been directly reused for representing raw materials). The direct use of domain dependent controlled vocabularies (coverage-oriented ontologies) such as Agrovoc can be recommended in order to maintain the produced ontologies fully aligned with possible evolutions of those vocabularies, which can be viewed as domain reference standards usually developed by reference bodies in stable processes.

4　Conclusions

In this paper we discussed the role of ODPs in the design of ontologies within Linked Data projects. In particular, we extended the eXtreme Design methodology in order to address two issues we faced in practice: communication with domain experts and approaches to ontology reuse. Two real e-government Linked Data projects are described in order to prove the applicability of the introduced XD extensions. Future works focus on performing user-based surveys for a larger scale evaluation of our proposals by both ontology and domain experts.

---

[3] Reusing http://ontologydesignpatterns.org/wiki/Submissions:Description.

References

1. Blomqvist, E., Sandkuhl, K.: Patterns in ontology engineering: classification of ontology patterns. In: Proceedings of ICEIS, Miami, Florida, USA, pp. 413–416. CEUR-WS (2005)
2. Blomqvist, E., Presutti, V., Daga, E., Gangemi, A.: Experimenting with eXtreme Design. In: Cimiano, P., Pinto, H.S. (eds.) EKAW 2010. LNCS (LNAI), vol. 6317, pp. 120–134. Springer, Heidelberg (2010). doi:10.1007/978-3-642-16438-5_9
3. Ensan, F., Du, W.: A knowledge encapsulation approach to ontology modularization. Knowl. Inf. Syst. **26**(2), 249–283 (2010)
4. Gangemi, A.: Ontology design patterns for semantic web content. In: Gil, Y., Motta, E., Benjamins, V.R., Musen, M.A. (eds.) ISWC 2005. LNCS, vol. 3729, pp. 262–276. Springer, Heidelberg (2005). doi:10.1007/11574620_21
5. Gangemi, A., Presutti, V.: Ontology Design Patterns. In: Staab, S., Studer, R. (eds.) Handbook on Ontologies, 2nd edn, pp. 221–243. Springer, Heidelberg (2009)
6. Gruber, T.R.: A translation approach to portable ontology specifications. Knowl. Acquis. **5**(2), 199–220 (1993)
7. ODM: Version 1.1. OMG, September 2014
8. Presutti, V., Gangemi, A.: Content ontology design patterns as practical building blocks for web ontologies. In: Li, Q., Spaccapietra, S., Yu, E., Olivé, A. (eds.) ER 2008. LNCS, vol. 5231, pp. 128–141. Springer, Heidelberg (2008). doi:10.1007/978-3-540-87877-3_11
9. Presutti, V., et al.: eXtreme Design with content ontology design patterns. In: Proceedings of WOP, Washington, DC USA. CEUR-WS.org (2009)
10. Presutti, V., Blomqvist, E., Daga, E., Gangemi, A.: Pattern-based ontology design. In: Suárez-Figueroa, M.C., Gómez-Pérez, A., Motta, E., Gangemi, A. (eds.) Ontology Engineering in a Networked World, pp. 35–64. Springer, Heidelberg (2012)
11. Simperl, E.P.B., Mochol, M., Bürger, T.: Achieving maturity: the state of practice in ontology engineering in 2009. IJCSA **7**(1), 45–65 (2010)

Bridging the IT and OT Worlds Using an Extensible Modeling Language

Paola Lara[(⊠)], Mario Sánchez, and Jorge Villalobos

Systems and Computing Engineering, Universidad de Los Andes,
Bogotá, Colombia
{p.lara1081,mar-san1,jvillalo}@uniandes.edu.co

Abstract. Enterprise Modeling is used to analyze and improve IT, as well as to make IT more suitable to the needs of the business. However, asset intensive organizations have an ample set of operational technologies (OT) that Enterprise Modeling does not account for. When trying to model such enterprises, there is no accurate form of showing components that belong to the world of OT nor is there a way to bridge the division between OT and IT. Existing languages fall short due to their limited focus that does not consider modeling operational technologies and even less relating them to the IT and Business dimensions. To address these issues, in this paper we present a new modeling language which extends ArchiMate. This language proposes a set of core elements for modeling OT components, based on existing OT standards and ontologies, and makes it possible to associate these components to business and IT elements. Introducing this language makes it possible to apply existing modeling and analysis techniques from Enterprise Modeling in settings that cover Business, OT and IT.

Keywords: Operational Technology · Modeling language · Archimate

1 Introduction

According to IEEE, "Architecture is the fundamental organization of a system embodied in its components, their relationships to each other, and to the environment, and the principle guiding its design and evolution" [4]. Similarly, Enterprise Architecture (EA) is "a coherent whole of principles, methods, and models that are used in the design and realization of an enterprise's organizational structure, business processes, information systems, and infrastructure. Enterprise architecture captures the essentials of the business, IT and its evolution." [5]. Enterprise Modeling (EM), which can be seen as an integral part of building an EA, is the process of creating an integrated enterprise model, which represents certain aspects of the enterprise, in their current or future state, and materializes the knowledge of stakeholders involved in the modeling process [7].

A central element to EM is using a modeling language, which may be standardized and open, or may be proprietary and embedded in modeling tools. Recently, ArchiMate [9] has become a de facto standard, both for its relative simplicity and for its closeness to the Architecture Content Framework from TOGAF [10]. The problem with this is that these tools have a narrow focus limited to the business and IT dimensions: most

© Springer International Publishing AG 2016
I. Comyn-Wattiau et al. (Eds.): ER 2016, LNCS 9974, pp. 122–129, 2016.
DOI: 10.1007/978-3-319-46397-1_10

organizations are interested in modeling a much larger scope than just this. For example, in asset-intensive organizations it is extremely important to monitor other kinds of elements that are central to the business and its success such as drills in the oil and gas industry.

Gartner defines operational technologies (OT) as the "hardware and software that detects or causes a change through the direct monitoring and/or control of physical devices, processes and events in the enterprise" [3]. However, OT encompasses a number of elements that are not typically classified as hardware or software, but are still technological elements fundamental to the success of the business. On top of that, with the advent of advances in technology OT elements are becoming capable of generating lots of information thus closing the gap with IT components. The structure that standards and reference models provide is not very strong for the OT domain. An even more specific problem is that there are no languages to model OT in a way that relates them to the IT and Business dimensions. Considering the current widespread concern about IT and OT convergence [2], it is clear that novel mechanisms are required in order to bridge these two worlds. In this paper we present a language extension to ArchiMate 2.1 that we built to target the OT world. The contribution of our work is thus the structure for the base elements in the OT dimension, as well as establishing their relationships with IT.

The rest of the paper is structured as follows. Section 2 presents an overview of EM and Sect. 3 discusses the operational technologies world. Then Sect. 4 presents the core of our proposal: the OT extension for ArchiMate. Finally, Sect. 5 concludes the paper.

2 Enterprise Modeling and IT

EA is used to align business and IT elements according to the enterprise strategy and stated organizational goals. An architecture landscape comprises three core dimensions (business, software, and hardware) and is analyzed with respect to concerns such as business improvement, information, technology, security, and governance [6]. EM focuses on the integration of different elements and components of an organization to display an abstract representation and its inter-dependencies. This practice enables a view on the current situation of an enterprise which may be utilized for different aspects such as process optimization, business and IT strategic development, and security and issue detection among others. To allow organizations to create accurate models many tools, modeling practices and languages such as UML, BPMN and ArchiMate, have been developed tailored to different needs of the enterprise [7].

It is noticeable that both EA and EM concentrate on the dimensions of IT (hardware and software) and business. The blueprint created through EA enables a clear view of key resources in the organization and how these intertwine to close the gap between business, systems and technology architectures. Such focus allows organizations to vastly cover their needs for analyzing, designing, planning, and modeling their business and its IT support. The caveat is that this is typically valuable only to information intensive organization.

The de facto standard language used nowadays for EA and EM is ArchiMate. Governed by The Open Group it has been described as an enterprise architecture modeling language which provides a "structuring mechanism for architecture domains, layers, and aspects" [9]. As such, it provides a graphical language for representing enterprises that is aligned with TOGAF's Architecture Content Framework which covers business, information systems, and technology elements. Moreover, ArchiMate 2.1 makes it possible to specify inter-related architectures, which span several of those dimensions, and also offers a set of commonly used viewpoints Moreover, what sets ArchiMate apart from other modeling languages such as BPMN and UML is its wide scope, the tradeoff behind this is the lack of detail that ArchiMate 2.1 supports in any of the layers and which have to be covered by other languages.

3   Operational Technologies - OT

In asset intensive industries, such as energy, mining, oil and gas, utilities, and manufacturing, the OT world encompasses the truly critical factors to execute daily tasks and operations. With EA and EM, the world of IT has developed numerous mechanisms for modeling and understanding the technology and business dimensions. However, these tools fall short for asset intensive organizations, where the scope of modeling and analysis is vaster. In fact, there is a lack of alternatives to model both IT and OT architectures for understanding the relationships between these two worlds.

T build a sound conceptual model of the OT domain, the structure of said reality must be understood. It comprises technologies to control and monitor equipment (devices, actuators, sensors and software) in industrial processes and activities executed by personnel. These elements collaborate and interact to achieve industrial objectives aligned with the organization plans and are therefore critical for the company to achieve its planned business goals.

Currently, a few standards propose terminology and industry specific models and topologies for OT. The international standard ANSI/ISA 95 Enterprise – Control System Integration [1], contains terminology and object models developed to be used in all industries for production process. Similarly, there are standards and guides that define industry or equipment specific topology and models. For example, the NSIT Guide to Industrial Control Systems (ICS) Security contains aspects specific to types of technology, operation models, layout and topology models [8].

The goal behind the idea of modeling OT is understanding how these elements support the business and its goals and to design improvements to effectively integrate IT and OT. However, differences between these domains creates gaps that must be understood to bridge this division accurately. For example, elements in OT have longer life cycles compared to those in IT and with the increase of OT elements connected over networks there is a greater exposure and risk of attacks [11]. Likewise, OT and IT are organizational silos as there is a clear difference in ownership and governance [2]. Because of these differences, in many organizations OT elements exist in the world of IT only as mere inventory in ERP systems; also, a great deal of information that these OT elements generate is ignored when analyzing business components because they are only used during operation flows.

While it is not a complete solution for the presented problem, a first step in this direction could be to create mechanisms to enable a better understanding of OT architectures, and their relationships with IT architectures. For this reason, we have created a modeling language based on ArchiMate to enable the modeling of OT architectures and their relationship with IT.

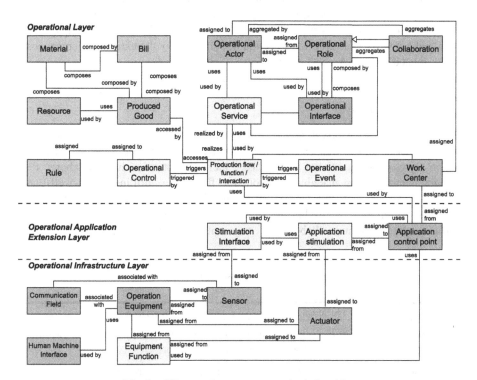

Fig. 1. OT extension concepts and relationships

4   An ArchiMate Extension for OT

This section describes our ArchiMate Extension for modeling Operational Technologies. This extension is intended to be used in three ways. Firstly, it can be used to model OT architectures by using core OT elements. Secondly, it can be used to relate the OT architecture to IT and Business architectures modeled using ArchiMate's core elements. Finally, it can be used as a base for creating industry-specific OT extensions, i.e., OT modeling languages customized to the needs of particular industries.

To design the OT extension, we mimicked the structure of ArchiMate's core: it is organized in three layers that separate elements by the concern they address (business, application, and technology) and three types of elements (active structure elements, behavior elements, and passive structure elements). The OT extension identifies three layers: the operational layer, the operational application layer extension, and the infrastructure layer. In addition to this, it also categorizes elements according to the role they play in the architecture as active structure elements, behavior elements, and passive structure elements. The elements found in each area of the grid are described further along in this section, as well as their graphical notations.

The construction of the OT extension started with the observation of standards and ontologies in the OT world (see Sect. 3): common concepts were identified to form a core set with applicability in a large number of organizations. Each concept was then assigned to a layer and relationships between them were identified. Figure 1 presents the resulting meta-model for the extension: this figure only shows relationships within layers and between adjacent layers. Section 4.4 shows how the extended elements can also be related to core ArchiMate elements.

4.1 Operational Layer

Elements in the *Operational Layer* (Tables 1, 2 and 3) serve to model services, functions, and products that are considered part of the operative areas such as production flows and operational actors. This includes actors such as a laborer that manages manufacturing machinery, production flows (e.g., drilling an oil well), and operational passive elements needed to perform behavioral concepts. Following the principles established by ArchiMate, the operational layer uses concepts such as interface, interaction, and collaboration congruent to the operative context.

Table 1. Active structure concepts in the Operational Layer

Concept	Notation	Description
Operational Actor		An operative entity that is capable of performing (operational) behavior.
Operational Role		A responsibility for performing some behavior, to which an operational actor can be assigned.
Operational Collaboration		Aggregate of two or more operational roles that work together to perform collective behavior.
Operational Interface		A point of access where an operational service is made available to the environment.
Work Center		A subtype of Location under which equipment performs production and storage of material.

4.2 Operational Application Extension Layer

The *Operational Application Layer* (Table 4) extends ArchiMate's Application Layer to support the needs of the Operational Layer. Since it is an extension, it does not add many additional elements. Instead, it builds on top of the existing elements (e.g. Application Component, Application Function, Data Object, etc.).

Table 2. Behavior structure concepts in the Operational Layer

Concept	Notation	Description
Production Flow		It groups behavior based on operational activities to produce products or operational services.
Operational Function		An element that groups behavior based on chosen criteria (resources, materials, competences).
Operational Interaction		A behavior element that describes the behavior of an operational collaboration.
Operational Event		Something that happens internally and influences an operational behavior.
Operational Service		A service that fulfills an operational need for internal use in the organization.
Operational Control		The ability to perform actions or behavioral elements using the available resources.

Table 3. Passive structure concepts in the Operational Layer

Concept	Notation	Description
Resource		An asset that provides capabilities required by the execution of operation activities and/or business process.
Material		A subassembly, part, and/or items used in production of a finished good.
Rule		A norm that directs an operational control.
Produced good		A partial or finished product which has endured processing and production.
Bill		A representation of the needed bills for production such as bill of lading, bill of materials, and bill of resources.

Table 4. Operational Application Extension Layer

Concept	Notation	Description
Application Control Point		An active structure that exercises direction over an application or software system.
Application Stimulation		An application stimulation triggers an occurrence in the operational infrastructure layer.
Stimulation Interface		The stimulation interface the intermediate between the operational data and the application control point that uses the data to take decisions.

4.3   Operational Infrastructure Layer

The *Operational Infrastructure Layer* (Table 5) includes elements to execute, monitor and control the operational context. These include equipment, assets, and functions that support the productivity of the organization. Additionally, this encompasses elements that enable control (e.g., actuators and sensors), assets that may be controlled (e.g., equipment, HMI), and their respective functions.

Table 5. Operational Infrastructure Layer

Concept	Notation	Description
Actuator		An active component responsible for controlling other mechanisms, systems or equipment.
Sensor		An active structure that detects changes in operational equipment.
Operational Equipment		An active structure used in the production of a good through a specific function.
Communication Field		An active structure through which operational equipment interacts with a sensor or an actuator.
Human Machine Interface		A control panel through which an operational actor may interact with operational equipment.
Equipment Function		A behavior element that groups behavior based on an operational equipment role in production.

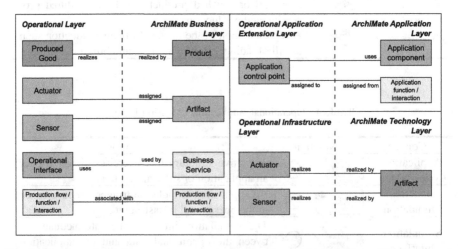

Fig. 2. (a) Operational layer concepts and relationships with ArchiMate (b) Operational application extension layer concepts and relationships with ArchiMate (c) Operational infrastructure layer concepts and relationships with ArchiMate

4.4   Relations with the IT and Business Dimensions

The elements for modeling the OT dimension are also intended to be related to the rest of the organization, and specifically to the business and IT dimensions. To support this, the extension specifies allowed relationships between some of the newly proposed elements and core ArchiMate elements (see Fig. 2). It should be noted that all of these are established between layers in the same "level" (e.g., there are no relationships between the operational and the application layer).

5   Conclusion

This paper presented an extension to ArchiMate for the Operational Technology domain. It expands the scope of ArchiMate beyond business and IT, and makes it possible to model operational elements which are typically studied independently. This extension can be used for three purposes: to model OT architectures using general OT concepts; to model OT architectures and their relationships to Business and IT elements; and to model OT architectures in specific industries, using industry-specific OT concepts. For this last objective, it is necessary to extend even more the proposed OT extension and derive industry specific concepts.

Ultimately, the goal of enterprise modeling languages is to make it possible to apply techniques for the improvement of enterprises, based on the analysis of enterprise models. With the proposed language extension, we expect to bring this possibility to elements that so far have been neglected even though they are of the maximum importance in many organizations and industries.

References

1. ANSI/ISA-95, Enterprise-Control System Integration
2. Atos Scientific Community IT/OT Convergence Track Team: The Convergence of IT and Operational Technology. Atos Scientific Community (2012)
3. Operational Technology (OT): Gartner IT Glossary (2016)
4. IEEE: Recommended practice for architectural description of software intensive systems. Technical report IEEE P1471:2000, ISO/IEC 42010:2007 (2000)
5. Lankhorst, M., et al.: Enterprise Architecture at Work: Modelling Communication and Analysis. Springer, Heidelberg (2009)
6. Land, M., Proper, E., Wage, M., Cloo, J., Steghuis, C.: Enterprise Architecture. Springer, Heidelberg (2009)
7. Sandkuhl, K., Stirna, J., Persson, A., Wißotzki, M.: Enterprise Modeling: Tackling Business Challenges with the 4EM Method. Springer, Heidelberg (2014)
8. Stouffer, K., Falco, J., Scarfone, K.: Guide to Industrial Control Systems (ICS) Security. U.S. Department of Commerce (2011)
9. The Open Group: ArchiMate 2.1 Specification. Van Haren Publishing (2012)
10. The Open Group: TOGAF Version 9.1. Van Haren Publishing (2011)
11. Harp, D., Gregory-Brown, B.: IT/OT Convergence - Bridging the Divide. NEX DEFENSE (2014)

Requirements Engineering

Possibilistic Cardinality Constraints and Functional Dependencies

Tania K. Roblot and Sebastian Link[✉]

Department of Computer Science, University of Auckland,
Auckland, New Zealand
{t.roblot,s.link}@auckland.ac.nz

Abstract. Cardinality constraints and functional dependencies together can express many semantic properties for applications in which data is certain. However, modern applications need to process large volumes of uncertain data. So far, cardinality constraints and functional dependencies have only been studied in isolation over uncertain data. We investigate the more challenging real-world case in which both types of constraints co-occur. While more expressive constraints could easily be defined, they would not enjoy the computational properties we show to hold for our combined class. Indeed, we characterize the associated implication problem axiomatically and algorithmically in linear input time. We also show how to summarize any given set of our constraints as an Armstrong instance. These instances help data analysts consolidate meaningful degrees of certainty by which our constraints hold in the underlying application domain.

Keywords: Data semantics · Integrity constraints · Possibility theory · Requirements engineering · Uncertain data

1 Introduction

Background. Cardinality constraints (CCs) and functional dependencies (FDs) are fundamental for understanding the structure and semantics of data, and have a long and fruitful history in conceptual modeling, database theory and practice. CCs were introduced in the seminal paper by Chen [5], while FDs were introduced in the seminal paper by Codd [6]. We focus on cardinality constraints that define an upper bound on the number of objects that have matching values on a given set of attributes. For example, any project manager should not be looking after more than three projects at any period of time. An FD expresses that the values on some attributes uniquely determine the values on some other attributes. For example, every project has at most one manager. Due to their ability to express desirable properties of many application domains, CCs and FDs have been used successfully for core data management tasks, including database cleaning, design, integration, modeling, querying, and updating.

Motivation. Relational databases were developed for applications with certain data, including accounting, inventory and payroll. Modern applications, such

© Springer International Publishing AG 2016
I. Comyn-Wattiau et al. (Eds.): ER 2016, LNCS 9974, pp. 133–148, 2016.
DOI: 10.1007/978-3-319-46397-1_11

Emp	Dep	Mgr	Degree of possibility	Scope of constraints
Nishikori	Tennis	Federer	α_1 *(fully)*	
Date	Tennis	Federer	α_1 *(fully)*	
Sakita	Physics	Gauss	α_1 *(fully)*	
Sato	Maths	Gauss	α_1 *(fully)*	
Nara	Tennis	Federer	α_2 *(somewhat)*	
Musashimaru	Sumo	Hakuho	α_2 *(somewhat)*	
Musashimaru	Sumo	Taiho	α_2 *(somewhat)*	

β_2 *(somewhat certain)* $\qquad$ β_1 *(fully certain)*

Fig. 1. A possibilistic instance and the scope by which constraints apply to its objects

as information extraction, sensors, and data integration produce large volumes of uncertain data. While different approaches to uncertainty in data exist, our running example considers a simple scenario in which a qualitative approach is applied to the integration of two data sources. The scenario maintains the levels of confidence associated with objects. Indeed, objects that occur in both sources are labeled 'fully possible', while objects that occur in only one source are labeled 'somewhat possible'. The information about the confidence of objects is clearly useful, but probability distributions are unavailable. Instead, a qualitative approach as founded in possibility theory is appropriate [9,10,35]. Figure 1 shows a possibilistic instance (p-instance) where each object is associated with a possibility degree (p-degree) from a finite scale: $\alpha_1 > \ldots > \alpha_{k+1}$. The top degree α_1 is reserved for objects that are 'fully possible', the bottom degree α_{k+1} for objects that are 'impossible' to occur. Intermediate degrees and their linguistic interpretations are used as preferred, such as 'somewhat possible' (α_2).

Interestingly, p-degrees enable us to express CCs and FDs with different degrees of certainty. For example, to express that it is 'impossible' that the same department and manager are associated with more than three employees we declare the CC $card(Dep, Mgr) \leq 3$ to be 'fully certain' by using the label β_1, stipulating that no combination of department and manager can feature in more than three objects that are at least 'somewhat possible'. Similarly, to say it is only 'somewhat possible' that departments with different managers exist we declare the FD $Dep \to Mgr$ as 'somewhat certain' by using the label β_2, stipulating that no department has more than one manager in 'fully possible' objects. We will investigate the combined class of CCs and FDs in this possibilistic data model.

Contributions and impact. Our contributions are as follows. (1) We show that the combination of CCs and FDs in a possibilistic data model constitutes a 'sweet spot' in terms of expressivity and computational behavior. In particular, we unify previous work under a more expressive framework that retains efficient computational properties. Slightly more expressive approaches result in non-axiomatizability, intractability, or even undecidability. (2) We establish a finite axiomatization and a linear-time decision algorithm for the associated implication problem. We illustrate applications from constraint maintenance, query optimization, and pivoting to eliminate data redundancy. (3) We establish an effective construction of Armstrong representations for any given set of our constraints. Here, we overcome the practical challenge that finite Armstrong instances do not frequently exist. We thus provide automated support for the acquisition of the constraints that are meaningful in a given application domain.

Organization. Section 2 discusses related work. Our data model is defined in Sect. 3. In Sect. 4 we characterize the implication problem axiomatically and algorithmically. Applications are highlighted in Sect. 5. Section 6 describes how to compute Armstrong representations. In Sect. 7 we conclude and discuss future work. Proofs are available in [39].

2 Related Work

FDs are probably the most studied class of constraints, due to their expressivity, computational behavior, and impact on practice. FDs were introduced in Codd's seminal paper [6], and are intrinsically linked to conceptual, logical, and physical database design [27,44]. Applications on the conceptual level include graphical reasoning [8] and pivoting [3,17]. CCs are an influential contribution of conceptual modeling to database constraints. They featured in Chen's seminal paper [5]. Cardinality constraints subsume the class of keys as a special case where the upper bound on the cardinality is fixed to 1. Keys are fundamental to most data models [4,11,16,21,22,26,29,30,42,46]. Most languages for conceptual design (description logics, ER, UML, ORM) come with means for specifying CCs. CCs have been studied extensively in database design [7,18,25,31,32,38,43].

Probability theory offers a popular quantitative approach to uncertain data [41]. Research about constraints on probabilistic data is in its infancy [4,40]. Probabilistic FDs, which specify a lower bound on the marginal probability that FDs exhibit on probabilistic databases, are not finitely axiomatizable.

The results of our article unify various previous works under one, more expressive, framework. In fact, our framework subsumes (1) the sole class of possibilistic CCs [15,28], (2) the sole class of possibilistic FDs [35], and (3) the combined class of CCs and FDs over relational data (the special case of possibilistic data with only one degree of confidence, i.e. where $k = 1$) [18]. While our framework is strictly more expressive, it retains the good computational properties of previous work, making it special. Indeed, making our framework more expressive is likely to result in the loss of good computational behavior. For example, using numerical dependencies instead of FDs leaves the implication problem not finitely axiomatizable [14], using multivalued dependencies requires more elaborate possibilistic data models and the interaction with CCs is not well-understood [19,20,23,24,33,34,45], using conditional FDs leaves the implication problem coNP-complete [13], adding inclusion dependencies makes the implication problem undecidable [37], and adding lower bounds to the upper bounds of our CCs' results requires us to solve unsolved problems from combinatorial design theory, even in the special case where $k = 1$ [18]. Further restrictions on what we additionally include are always possible, but our focus here is the natural class of cardinality constraints with upper bounds and functional dependencies.

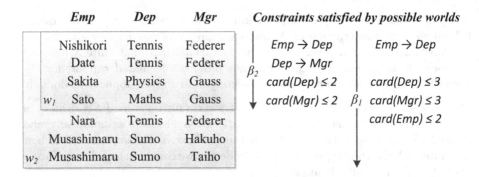

Fig. 2. Nested worlds of the p-instance from Fig. 1 and possibilistic constraints

3 Cardinality Constraints and Functional Dependencies

We extend object types that model certain objects in traditional conceptual modeling to model uncertain objects qualitatively. This allows us to extend CCs and FDs from their use on certain object types to uncertain object types.

An object type, denoted by O, is a finite non-empty set of *attributes*. Each attribute $A \in O$ has a *domain* $dom(A)$ of values. An *object* o over O is an element of the Cartesian product $\prod_{A \in O} dom(A)$. For $X \subseteq O$ we denote by $o(X)$ the *projection* of o on X. An *instance* over O is a set ι of objects over O. For example we use the object type WORK with attributes *Emp*, *Dep*, and *Mgr*. Objects either belong or do not belong to an instance. For example, we cannot express that we have less confidence for Employee **Nara** to work in the department **Tennis** under Manager **Federer** than for the Employee **Nishikori**.

We model uncertain instances by assigning to each object some degree of possibility with which the object occurs in an instance. Formally, we have a *possibility scale*, or p-scale, that is, a strict linear order $\mathcal{S} = (S, <)$ with $k + 1$ elements. We write $\mathcal{S} = \{\alpha_1, \ldots, \alpha_{k+1}\}$ to declare that $\alpha_1 > \cdots > \alpha_k > \alpha_{k+1}$. The elements $\alpha_i \in S$ are called *possibility degrees*, or p-degrees. Here, α_1 is reserved for objects that are 'fully possible' while α_{k+1} is reserved for objects that are 'impossible' to occur in an instance. Humans like to use simple scales in everyday life to communicate, compare, or rank. Here, the word "simple" means that items are classified qualitatively rather than quantitatively by putting precise values on them. Classical instances use two p-degrees, i.e. $k = 1$.

A *possibilistic object type* $(O, \mathcal{S})$, or p-object type, consists of an object type O and a p-scale $\mathcal{S}$. A *possibilistic instance*, or p-instance, over $(O, \mathcal{S})$ consists of an instance ι over O, and a function $Poss$ that assigns to each object $o \in \iota$ a p-degree $Poss(o) \in \mathcal{S} - \{\alpha_{k+1}\}$. We sometimes omit $Poss$ when denoting a p-instance. Figure 1 shows a p-instance over $(\text{WORK}, \mathcal{S} = \{\alpha_1, \alpha_2, \alpha_3\})$.

P-instances enjoy a possible world semantics. For $i = 1, \ldots, k$ let w_i consist of all objects in ι that have p-degree at least α_i, that is, $w_i = \{o \in \iota \mid Poss(o) \geq \alpha_i\}$. Indeed, we have $w_1 \subseteq w_2 \subseteq \cdots \subseteq w_k$. If $o \notin w_k$, then $Poss(o) = \alpha_{k+1}$. Every object that is 'fully possible' occurs in every possible world, and is therefore also 'fully certain'. Hence, instances are a special case of uncertain instances. Figure 2 shows the possible worlds $w_1 \subsetneq w_2$ of the p-instance of Fig. 1.

As CCs and FDs are fundamental to applications with certain data, their possibilistic variants serve similar roles for applications with uncertain data. A *cardinality constraint* over object type O is an expression $card(X) \leq b$ where $X \subseteq O$, and b is a positive integer. The CC $card(X) \leq b$ over O is satisfied by an instance w over O, denoted by $\models_w card(X) \leq b$, if there are no $b+1$ distinct objects $o_1, \ldots, o_{b+1} \in w$ with matching values on all the attributes in X. For example, Fig. 2 shows that $card(Dep, Mgr) \leq 1$ is not satisfied by any instance w_1 or w_2, and $card(Dep, Mgr) \leq 2$ is satisfied by w_1, but not by w_2. A *functional dependency* over object type O is an expression $X \to Y$ where $X, Y \subseteq O$. The FD $X \to Y$ over O is satisfied by an instance w over O, denoted by $\models_w X \to Y$, if for any two objects $o_1, o_2 \in w$ the following holds: if $o_1(X) = o_2(X)$, then $o_1(Y) = o_2(Y)$. For example, Fig. 2 shows that $Dep \to Mgr$ is satisfied by w_1, but not by w_2, and $Emp \to Dep$ is satisfied by w_1 and w_2.

The p-degrees of objects result in degrees of certainty by which constraints hold. Since $Emp \to Dep$ holds in every possible world, it is fully certain to hold on ι. As $Dep \to Mgr$ and $card(Dep, Mgr) \leq 2$ are only violated in a somewhat possible world w_2, they are somewhat certain to hold on ι. Since $card(Dep, Mgr) \leq 1$ is violated in the fully possible world w_1, it is not certain to hold on ι.

Similar to the scale $\mathcal{S}$ of p-degrees α_i for objects, we use a scale $\mathcal{S}^T$ of certainty degrees, or c-degrees, β_j for CCs and FDs. Formally, the correspondence between p-degrees in $\mathcal{S}$ and the c-degrees in $\mathcal{S}^T$ is defined by the mapping $\alpha_i \mapsto \beta_{k+2-i}$ for $i = 1, \ldots, k+1$. Hence, the certainty $C_\iota(\sigma)$ by which the CC $\sigma = card(X) \leq b$ or FD $\sigma = X \to Y$ holds on the uncertain instance ι is either the top degree β_1 if σ is satisfied by w_k, or the minimum amongst the c-degrees β_{k+2-i} that correspond to possible worlds w_i in which σ is violated, that is,

$$C_\iota(\sigma) = \begin{cases} \beta_1 & , \text{ if } \models_{w_k} \sigma \\ \min\{\beta_{k+2-i} \mid \not\models_{w_i} \sigma\} & , \text{ otherwise} \end{cases}.$$

We can now define the semantics of possibilistic CCs and FDs. Let $(O, \mathcal{S})$ denote a p-object type. A possibilistic CC (p-CC) over $(O, \mathcal{S})$ is an expression $(card(X) \leq b, \beta)$ where $card(X) \leq b$ denotes a CC over O and $\beta \in \mathcal{S}^T$. A p-instance $(\iota, Poss)$ over $(O, \mathcal{S})$ satisfies the p-CC $(card(X) \leq b, \beta)$ if and only if $C_\iota(card(X) \leq b) \geq \beta$. A possibilistic FD (p-FD) over $(O, \mathcal{S})$ is an expression $(X \to Y, \beta)$ where $X \to Y$ denotes an FD over O and $\beta \in \mathcal{S}^T$. A p-instance $(\iota, Poss)$ over $(O, \mathcal{S})$ satisfies the p-FD $(X \to Y, \beta)$ if and only if $C_\iota(X \to Y) \geq \beta$.

For example, Fig. 2 shows some of the p-CCs and p-FDs that the p-instance ι from Fig. 1 satisfies. The next example introduces the set Σ of p-CCs and p-FDs we will use as an example constraint set in the remainder of the article.

Example 1. Let Σ denote the set with the following p-CCs and p-FDs over p-object type $(\text{WORK}, \mathcal{S} = \{\alpha_1, \alpha_2, \alpha_3\})$: $(Emp \to Dep, \beta_1)$, $(card(Dep, Mgr) \leq 3, \beta_1)$, $(Dep \to Mgr, \beta_2)$, and $(card(Mgr) \leq 2, \beta_2)$. $\qquad\square$

4   Computational Problems and Their Solutions

We establish fundamental tools to reason about p-CCs and p-FDs. Their applicability will be illustrated in Sect. 5. First, we define the implication problem and then address its solution in terms of inference rules and algorithms.

Let $\Sigma \cup \{\varphi\}$ denote a set of p-CCs and p-FDs over $(O, \mathcal{S})$. We say Σ *implies* φ, denoted by $\Sigma \models \varphi$, if every p-instance $(\iota, Poss)$ over $(O, \mathcal{S})$ that satisfies every element of Σ also satisfies φ. We use $\Sigma^* = \{\varphi \mid \Sigma \models \varphi\}$ to denote the *semantic closure* of Σ. The *implication problem for p-CCs and p-FDs* is to decide, given any p-object type, and any set $\Sigma \cup \{\varphi\}$ of p-CCs and p-FDs over the p-object type, whether $\Sigma \models \varphi$ holds.

Example 2. Let Σ be as in Example 1. Further, let σ denote the CC $card(Dep) \leq 2$. Then the highest c-degree β such that (σ, β) is implied by Σ is β_2. Indeed, Σ does not imply $\varphi = (\sigma, \beta_1)$. We can create a p-instance that has 3 different objects, all of which have matching values for department and manager, but pairwise different employees, and 2 of those objects have p-degree α_1 while the remaining object has p-degree α_2. Then the c-degree of $card(Dep) \leq 2$ in ι is β_2, which means that $(card(Dep) \leq 2, \beta_1)$ is violated. Since the c-degrees of $Emp \rightarrow Dep$, $Dep \rightarrow Mgr$, and $card(Dep,Mgr) \leq 3$ in ι are β_1, and the c-degree of $card(Mgr) \leq 2$ in ι is β_2, ι satisfies Σ, but violates φ.   □

4.1   Using β-Cuts

Our overarching goal is to extend the combined use of CCs and FDs from certain to uncertain data, while maintaining their good computational properties. The core notion for achieving this goal is that of a β-cut for a given set Σ of p-CCs and p-FDs and c-degree $\beta > \beta_{k+1}$. Informally, the β-cut Σ_β of Σ contains all CCs and FDs σ such that there is some p-CCs or p-FD (σ, β') in Σ where β' is at least β. That is, $\Sigma_\beta = \{\sigma \mid (\sigma, \beta') \in \Sigma \text{ and } \beta' \geq \beta\}$ is the β-*cut* of Σ. The following theorem shows how the β-cut can be used to reduce the implication problem for p-CCs and p-FDs to the implication problem of traditional CCs and FDs. The theorem does not hold for CCs with lower bounds or multivalued dependencies.

Theorem 1. *Let $\Sigma \cup \{(\sigma, \beta)\}$ be a set of p-CCs and p-FDs over $(O, \mathcal{S})$ where $\beta > \beta_{k+1}$. Then $\Sigma \models (\sigma, \beta)$ if and only if $\Sigma_\beta \models \sigma$.*

Theorem 1 allows us to apply achievements from CCs and FDs for certain data to p-CCs and p-FDs. It is a major tool to establish our results.

Example 3. Let Σ be as in Example 1. Then Σ_{β_1} consists of $card(Dep,Mgr) \leq 3$ and $Emp \rightarrow Dep$, while Σ_{β_2} contains Σ_{β_1} and includes $card(Mgr) \leq 2$ and $Dep \rightarrow Mgr$. Using knowledge about the interaction of CCs and FDs from relational data [18], we conclude that Σ_{β_1} does not imply $card(Dep) \leq 2$, but Σ_{β_2} does imply $card(Dep) \leq 2$. Theorem 1 shows then that Σ does not imply $(card(Dep) \leq 2, \beta_1)$, but Σ does imply $(card(Dep) \leq 2, \beta_2)$. In fact, the possible world w_1 of the p-instance ι from Example 2 satisfies Σ_{β_1}, and violates $card(Dep) \leq 2$.   □

Table 1. Finite axiomatization of p-CCs and p-FDs

	$\dfrac{(X \rightarrow Y, \beta)}{(X \rightarrow XY, \beta)}$	$\dfrac{(X \rightarrow Y, \beta) \quad (Y \rightarrow Z, \beta)}{(X \rightarrow Z, \beta)}$
$\dfrac{}{(XY \rightarrow X, \beta_1)}$ (reflexivity)	(extension)	(transitivity)
$\dfrac{}{(\mathit{card}(O) \leq 1, \beta_1)}$ (top)	$\dfrac{(\mathit{card}(X) \leq b, \beta)}{(\mathit{card}(X) \leq b+1, \beta)}$ (relax)	$\dfrac{(X \rightarrow Y, \beta) \quad (\mathit{card}(Y) \leq b, \beta)}{(\mathit{card}(X) \leq b, \beta)}$ (pullback)
$\dfrac{(\mathit{card}(X) \leq 1, \beta)}{(X \rightarrow Y, \beta)}$ (key)	$\dfrac{}{(\sigma, \beta_{k+1})}$ (bottom)	$\dfrac{(\sigma, \beta)}{(\sigma, \beta')} \; \beta' \leq \beta$ (weakening)

4.2 Axiomatic Characterization

A finite axiomatization allows us to effectively enumerate all implied p-CCs and p-FDs, that is, to determine the semantic closure $\Sigma^* = \{\sigma \mid \Sigma \models \sigma\}$ of Σ. A finite axiomatization facilitates human understanding of the interaction of the given constraints, and ensures all opportunities for the use of these constraints in applications can be exploited (Sect. 5). We determine the semantic closure by applying *inference rules* of the form $\dfrac{\text{premise}}{\text{conclusion}}$. For a set $\mathfrak{R}$ of inference rules let $\Sigma \vdash_{\mathfrak{R}} \varphi$ denote the *inference* of φ from Σ by $\mathfrak{R}$. That is, there is some sequence $\sigma_1, \ldots, \sigma_n$ such that $\sigma_n = \varphi$ and every σ_i is an element of Σ or is the conclusion that results from an application of an inference rule in $\mathfrak{R}$ to some premises in $\{\sigma_1, \ldots, \sigma_{i-1}\}$. Let $\Sigma_{\mathfrak{R}}^+ = \{\varphi \mid \Sigma \vdash_{\mathfrak{R}} \varphi\}$ be the *syntactic closure* of Σ under inferences by $\mathfrak{R}$. $\mathfrak{R}$ is *sound* (*complete*) if for every set Σ over every $(O, \mathcal{S})$ we have $\Sigma_{\mathfrak{R}}^+ \subseteq \Sigma^*$ ($\Sigma^* \subseteq \Sigma_{\mathfrak{R}}^+$). The (finite) set $\mathfrak{R}$ is a (finite) *axiomatization* if $\mathfrak{R}$ is both sound and complete. Table 1 shows an axiomatization $\mathfrak{C}$ for p-CCs and p-FDs. Here, $(O, \mathcal{S})$ is an arbitrarily given p-object type, $X, Y \subseteq O$, b is a positive integer, $\beta, \beta' \in \mathcal{S}^T$ are c-degrees, and σ uniformly denotes either some CC or FD. In particular, β_{k+1} denotes the bottom c-degree in $\mathcal{S}^T$.

Theorem 2. *The set $\mathfrak{C}$ forms a finite axiomatization for the implication of possibilistic cardinality constraints and functional dependencies.*   □

The application of inference rules in $\mathfrak{C}$ from Table 1 is illustrated next.

Example 4. Consider Σ from Example 1. Applying pullback to $(Dep \rightarrow Mgr, \beta_2)$ and $(\mathit{card}(Mgr) \leq 2, \beta_2)$ results in $(\mathit{card}(Dep) \leq 2, \beta_2) \in \Sigma_{\mathfrak{C}}^+$. For an inference of $(\mathit{card}(Emp, Mgr) \leq 1, \beta_1)$ consider the following steps. Applying reflexivity infers $(Emp, Mgr \rightarrow Emp, \beta_1)$. Then we apply transitivity to $(Emp, Mgr \rightarrow Emp, \beta_1)$ and $(Emp \rightarrow Dep, \beta_1)$ to infer $(Emp, Mgr \rightarrow Dep, \beta_1)$. Next we apply extension to $(Emp, Mgr \rightarrow Dep, \beta_1)$ to infer $(Emp, Mgr \rightarrow Emp, Dep, Mgr, \beta_1)$. The top rule infers $(card(Emp,Dep,Mgr) \leq 1, \beta_1)$. Finally, we apply pullback to $(Emp,Mgr \rightarrow Emp,Dep,Mgr, \beta_1)$ and $(card(Emp,Dep,Mgr) \leq 1, \beta_1)$ to infer $(card(Emp,Mgr) \leq 1, \beta_1) \in \Sigma_{\mathfrak{C}}^+$.   □

4.3 Algorithmic Characterization

While $\mathfrak{C}$ enables us to enumerate all p-CCs and p-FDs that are implied by a set Σ of p-CCs and p-FDs, in practice it often suffices to decide whether a given p-CC or p-FD φ is implied by Σ. Enumerating all implied constraints and checking whether φ is among them is neither efficient nor makes good use of φ. However, our axiomatization $\mathfrak{C}$ provides us with the insight to develop efficient algorithms for deciding the associated implication problem.

First, Theorem 1 tells us that the implication of some p-CC or p-FD (σ, β) by Σ can be decided by considering the β-cut Σ_β. If σ denotes an FD $X \rightarrow Y$, then our axiomatization $\mathfrak{C}$ tells us that the decision only depends on the FDs in Σ_β and the cardinality constraints $card(X) \leq 1 \in \Sigma_\beta$, as the latter implies the FD $X \rightarrow O \in \Sigma_\beta^*$. For a given set Σ of cardinality constraints and functional dependencies, let $\Sigma[\mathrm{FD}]$ denote the set of FDs in Σ together with the FDs $X \rightarrow O$ for every $card(X) \leq 1 \in \Sigma$. The p-FD $(X \rightarrow Y, \beta)$ is therefore implied by Σ if and only if the FD $X \rightarrow Y$ is implied by $\Sigma_\beta[\mathrm{FD}]$. The latter condition is equivalent to Y being a subset of the attribute set closure $X_{\Sigma_\beta[\mathrm{FD}]}^+ = \{A \in X \mid \Sigma_\beta[\mathrm{FD}] \models X \rightarrow A\}$, which can be computed in linear time in the input set $\Sigma_\beta[\mathrm{FD}]$ [1]. This shows condition (i) in Theorem 3 below. If σ denotes a cardinality constraint $card(X) \leq b$, then our axiomatization $\mathfrak{C}$ tells us that the decision only depends on the existence of some cardinality constraint $card(Y) \leq b' \in \Sigma_\beta$ such that $Y \subseteq X_{\Sigma_\beta[\mathrm{FD}]}^+$ and $b' \leq b$. The clause that $b' \leq b$ follows from the relax rule, and the clause that $Y \subseteq X_{\Sigma_\beta[\mathrm{FD}]}^+$ follows from the pullback rule and the fact that $X_{\Sigma_\beta[\mathrm{FD}]}^+$ is the maximal subset of O that is functionally determined by X given $\Sigma_\beta[\mathrm{FD}]$. This shows condition (ii) in Theorem 3 below.

Theorem 3. *Let Σ denote a set of p-CCs and p-FDs over $(O, \mathcal{S})$ with $|\mathcal{S}| = k + 1$. Then (i) Σ implies $(X \rightarrow Y, \beta)$ if and only if $Y \subseteq X_{\Sigma_\beta[FD]}^+$, and (ii) Σ implies $(card(X) \leq b, \beta)$ if and only if $X_{\Sigma_\beta[FD]}^+ = O$, or there is some $card(Y) \leq b' \in \Sigma_\beta$ such that $Y \subseteq X_{\Sigma_\beta[FD]}^+$ and $b' \leq b$.*

The worst-case complexity bound in the following result follows from the well-known fact that the computation of $X_{\Sigma[FD]}^+$ is linear in the total number of attribute occurrences in $\Sigma[FD]$ [1], and this size of $\Sigma[FD]$ is bounded by $|O| \times |\Sigma|$ where $|\mathcal{S}|$ denotes the number of elements in $\mathcal{S}$.

Corollary 1. *An instance $\Sigma \models \varphi$ of the implication problem for p-CCs and p-FDs can be decided in time $\mathcal{O}(|O| \times |\Sigma \cup \{\varphi\}|)$.*   □

We illustrate the use of Theorem 3 on our running example.

Example 5. Let Σ be as in Example 1. Then we can use Theorem 3 to decide whether the p-CC $(card(Dep) \leq 2, \beta_2)$ is implied by Σ. Indeed, $Dep^*_{\Sigma_{\beta_2}[FD]} = \{Dep, Mgr\}$ and $card(Mgr) \leq 2 \in \Sigma_{\beta_2}$. Similarly, Σ implies $(card(Emp, Mgr) \leq 1, \beta_1)$ since $\{Emp, Mgr\}^+_{\Sigma_{\beta_1}[FD]} = O$. $\qquad\square$

5   Applications

We give a series of examples that illustrate core data processing areas on which our solutions have an impact. These include more efficient update and query operations, as well as schema decompositions to avoid data redundancy.

Non-redundant Constraint Maintenance. Constraints ensure data integrity. Whenever database instances are updated, it must be validated that the updated instance satisfies all the given constraints. Data integrity therefore comes at the cost of enforcing it. However, it is redundant to validate any implied constraints, because every instance that satisfies the remaining constraints already satisfies the implied constraints. Unnecessary costs for implied constraints are removed by computing a non-redundant cover of the given constraint set. This is done by successively removing any constraint $\sigma \in \Sigma$ from Σ whenever $\Sigma - \{\sigma\}$ implies σ. Having an efficient algorithm to decide implication means that we also have an efficient algorithm to compute a non-redundant set of constraints. Note that the time complexity refers to the schema size, which is negligible in comparison to the size of the instance. Furthermore, the larger database instances are the more time we save by validating non-redundant sets of constraints. We will now illustrate these ideas on our running example from the introduction. Some of the p-CCs and p-FDs satisfied by the p-instance in Fig. 1 include: $(Emp \rightarrow Dep, \beta_1)$, $(card(Dep) \leq 3, \beta_1)$, $(card(Mgr) \leq 3, \beta_1)$, $(card(Emp) \leq 2, \beta_1)$, $(card(Emp, Dep) \leq 2, \beta_1)$, $(Emp \rightarrow Dep, \beta_2)$, $(Dep \rightarrow Mgr, \beta_2)$, $(Emp \rightarrow Mgr, \beta_2)$, $(card(Dep) \leq 2, \beta_2)$, $(card(Mgr) \leq 2, \beta_2)$, $(card(Dep, Mgr) \leq 2, \beta_2)$, and $(card(Emp, Mgr) \leq 3, \beta_2)$. This set is redundant, and a non-redundant subset that implies all constraints of the given set is shown in Fig. 2.

Query Optimization. Knowing which constraints hold on a given instance also assists us with making the evaluation of queries more efficient. Take, for example, the query

SELECT DISTINCT *Emp* FROM WORK WHERE *p-degree*=α_1;

and assume it is evaluated on the p-instance from Fig. 1. Since the p-instance satisfies the p-CCs and p-FDs in Fig. 2, and these constraints imply the p-CC $card(Emp \leq 1, \beta_2)$, a query optimizer that can reason about our constraints is able to conclude that the DISTINCT clause in the query above is superfluous. The elimination of this clause can save considerable evaluation time because the ordering of tuples and removing of duplicates is an expensive operation. For another query evaluated on the same p-instance consider

SELECT *Dep*, COUNT(*Emp*) FROM WORK WHERE *p-degree*=α_1
GROUP BY *Dep* HAVING Count(*Emp*)$\leq$ 3;

which lists the departments together with the number of their 'certain' employees, if that number does not exceed 3. A query optimizer able to determine that the p-CC (*card*(*Dep*) $\leq$ 3, β_2) is implied by the satisfied set of p-CCs and p-FDs, can remove the HAVING clause from the query without affecting the result.

Removing Data Redundancy by Pivoting. The goal of pivoting is to decompose object schemata at design time in an effort to reduce data redundancy and optimize constraint validation time during the lifetime of the target database. We briefly use our running example to illustrate the impact of possibilistic constraints on pivoting. For this purpose, consider again the (possible worlds of the) p-instance in Fig. 2.

Each occurrence of the *Mgr*-value Federer in world w_1 is redundant in the sense that any update of this occurrence to a different value would result in a violation of the p-FD (*Dep* $\to$ *Mgr*, β_2). In contrast, the occurrence of Federer in w_2 is not redundant, because the p-FD (*Dep* $\to$ *Mgr*, β_2) only applies to objects with p-degree α_1. In other words, we could decompose the schema WORK into the two schemata {*Dep,Mgr,ID*1} and {*Emp,ID*1} for objects with p-degree α_1. For objects with p-degree α_2 we could decompose WORK into the two schemata {*Emp,Dep,ID*2} and {*Mgr,ID*2}, based on the p-FD (*Emp* $\to$ *Dep*, β_1). That is, our framework enables us to first apply a horizontal decomposition of the given database instance into w_1 and $w_2 - w_1$, and then apply traditional pivoting to decompose the schema with respect to the β-cuts Σ_{β_2} and Σ_{β_1}, respectively. The resulting decomposition of the p-instance from Fig. 1 would look like:

Dep	*Mgr*	*ID*1
Tennis	Federer	1
Physics	Gauss	2
Maths	Gauss	3

Emp	*ID*1
Nishikori	1
Date	1
Sakita	2
Sato	3

Emp	*Dep*	*ID*2
Nara	Tennis	1
Musashimaru	Sumo	2

Mgr	*ID*2
Federer	1
Hakuho	2
Taiho	2

in which all redundant data value occurrences have been removed. In addition, the original cardinality constraint (*card*(*Dep,Mgr*) $\leq$ 2, β_2) now becomes a cardinality constraint stipulating that each *ID*1 value in the {*Dep, Mgr, ID*1} instance should occur in at least 1 and at most 2 objects of the {*Emp, ID*1} instance.

6   Armstrong Instances and Representations

We establish computational support for the acquisition of p-CCs and p-FDs that are meaningful in a given application domain. A major inhibitor to the acquisition is the mismatch in expertise between business analysts and domain experts.

The former know database concepts but not the domain, while the latter know the domain but not database concepts. To facilitate effective communication between them, Armstrong instances serve as data samples that perfectly represent the current set of constraint sets. We will sketch how to compute Armstrong instances for any given set of p-CCs and p-FDs, which analysts and experts can jointly inspect to consolidate the set of meaningful constraints.

We first restate the original definition of an Armstrong database [12] in our context. A p-instance ι is said to be *Armstrong* for a given set Σ of p-CCs and p-FDs on a given p-object type $(O, \mathcal{S})$ if and only if for all p-CCs and p-FDs φ over $(O, \mathcal{S})$ it is true that ι satisfies φ if and only if Σ implies φ. As such, Armstrong p-instances exhibit for each cardinality constraint and functional dependency the largest c-degree for which it is implied by the given set Σ.

Example 6. The p-instance from Fig. 1 is Armstrong for the set of p-CCs and p-FDs from Fig. 2. □

We will now explain how to compute an Armstrong p-instance ι for an arbitrarily given set Σ of p-CCs and p-FDs.

For every attribute subset X and every c-degree β_i, we compute the smallest $b_{X,i}$ such that $(card(X) \leq b_{X,i}, \beta_i)$ is implied by Σ. We start with $b_{X,i} = \infty$, and set $b_{X,i} = 1$, if $X^+_{\Sigma_{\beta_i}[\text{FD}]} = O$ holds. Otherwise, we set $b_{X,i}$ to b whenever there is some $card(Y) \leq b \in \Sigma_{\beta_i}$ such that $Y \subseteq X^+_{\Sigma_{\beta_i}[\text{FD}]}$ and $b < b_{X,i}$, see Theorem 3 (ii). Now it suffices to introduce $b_{X,i}$ objects into ι with p-degree α_{k+1-i} and matching values $c_{A,i}$ on all $A \in X$ and unique values on all $A \notin X$. This ensures that all p-CCs implied by Σ are satisfied in ι and all p-CCs not implied by Σ are violated. Several optimizations reduce the number of objects in an Armstrong p-instance: If $b_{X,i} = 1$, no objects need to be introduced in ι. If $Y \subset X$ and $b_{Y,i} = b_{X,i}$, then it suffices to introduce $b_{X,i}$ objects, because they also violate $(card(Y) \leq b_{Y,i}, \beta_i)$. For $j > i$ and $b_{X,j} \leq b_{X,i}$ for which $b_{X,j}$ objects with (at most) p-degree α_{k+1-j} have already been introduced, it suffices to introduce further $b_{X,i} - b_{X,j}$ objects of p-degree α_{k+1-i}, again with matching values $c_{X,j}$ on all $A \in X$ and unique values on all $A \notin X$.

As an illustration, Fig. 3 shows for all attribute subsets X and c-degrees β_1 and β_2 the associated cardinalities $b_{X,i}$ for our running example from Example 1. The bold attribute sets are those that require the insertion of objects into an Armstrong p-instance for the given Σ.

In general, we still need to ensure that all p-FDs not implied by Σ are violated. For all $A \in X$ and every c-degree β_i, we compute all maximal attribute subsets X such that $A \notin X^+_{\Sigma_{\beta_i}[\text{FD}]}$, i.e., for all $B \notin (XA)$ we have $A \in (XB)^+_{\Sigma_{\beta_i}[\text{FD}]}$. These sets are known as the *maximal sets* for $\Sigma_{\beta_i}[\text{FD}]$ and can be computed by an algorithm given in [36]. For each set X that is maximal with respect to $\Sigma_{\beta_i}[\text{FD}]$, we introduce two objects with p-degree α_{k+1-i} and matching values $c_{A,i}$ on all $A \in X$ and unique values on all $A \notin X$. Again, some optimizations reduce the number of objects in the final Armstrong p-instance: If X is maximal with respect to $\Sigma_{\beta_i}[\text{FD}]$ and $\Sigma_{\beta_j}[\text{FD}]$ and $i < j$, then it suffices to introduce the two objects with p-degree α_{k+1-j}. Finally, we do not need

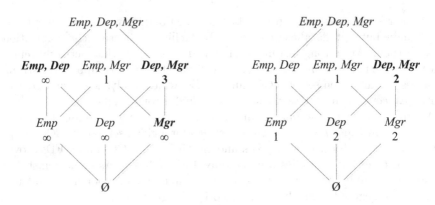

Fig. 3. Attribute sets X with cardinalities $b_{X,i}$ for $i = 1, 2$ from left to right

to introduce the two objects for the maximal set X, if $b_{Y,j}$ objects have previously been introduced for some $j \geq i$ where $X \subseteq Y$ and X is only maximal for attributes $A \notin Y - X$ with respect to $\Sigma_{\beta_i}[\mathrm{FD}]$.

Continuing with the construction of an Armstrong p-instance for the given set Σ from Example 1, the following table lists the attribute subsets (only one maximal set in each case here) that are maximal for the given attributes and $\Sigma_{\beta_i}[\mathrm{FD}]$.

	Emp	Dep	Mgr
Σ_{β_1}	$\{Dep,Mgr\}$	$\{Mgr\}$	$\{Emp,Dep\}$
Σ_{β_2}	$\{Dep,Mgr\}$	$\{Mgr\}$	$\emptyset$

Indeed, only the set $\{Mgr\}$ that is maximal for $\Sigma_{\beta_2}[\mathrm{FD}]$ requires us to insert two objects. In particular, the maximal set $X = \{Dep,Mgr\}$ for $\Sigma_{\beta_2}[\mathrm{FD}]$ is already covered by the $b_{X,2} = 2$ objects introduced previously, see Fig. 3, and the maximal set $\emptyset$ is covered because the p-FD $(\emptyset \to Mgr, \beta_2)$ is already violated after two objects with different Mgr values have been introduced. Similarly, all the maximal sets for $\Sigma_{\beta_1}[\mathrm{FD}]$ have already been covered.

The outlined algorithm ensures that Armstrong p-instances exist for every given set Σ of p-CCs and p-FDs, and that they are computed in time exponential in input. Since there are cases where the minimum number of required objects is exponential in the given input, which is known for traditional FDs [2], no polynomial-time algorithm can exist. However, as our running example illustrates we still need to deal with the following occurring case, which occurs frequently in practice. There are attribute subsets X and c-degrees β_i such that $b_{X,i} = \infty$, that is, there is no finite upper bound b such that $(card(X) \leq b, \beta_i)$ is implied by the input Σ. It follows that every Armstrong p-instance is necessarily infinite, which seems to make our acquisition strategy unfit for its intended purpose. However, we apply the following representation trick that overcomes this challenge. Instead of introducing $b_{X,i}$ different objects with matching values $c_{A,i}$

on all $A \in X$ and unique values on all $A \notin X$, we introduce one single object with $c_{A,i}$ on all $A \in X$ and $*$ on all $A \notin X$, plus its cardinality $b_{X,i}$ in a new column **card**. This single object represents the $b_{X,i}$ different objects, in particular, $*$ for unique values in all columns outside of X. If the objects result from a maximal set, then the cardinality is simply 2. Representations resulting from this transformation of (finite or infinite) Armstrong p-instances are called *Armstrong p-representations* for Σ. We can show that the optimizations applied in our computation result in representations that are bounded by the size of minimum-sized Armstrong p-representations (those Armstrong p-representations with the least number of objects) and the number of given constraints.

Theorem 4. *Given an arbitrary set Σ of poss-CCs and poss-FDs over some given p-object type, the outlined algorithm computes an Armstrong p-representation ζ for Σ whose size is bounded by that of a minimum-sized Armstrong p-representation ζ^{min} for Σ and the number of elements in Σ as follows: $|\zeta| \leq |\zeta^{min}| \times (|\Sigma| + |\zeta^{min}|)$.* □

This construction yields the following Armstrong p-instance for the given set Σ of p-CCs and p-FDs from Example 1.

Emp	Dep	Mgr	p-degree	card
$*$	Tennis	Federer	α_1	2
$*$	$*$	Gauss	α_1	2
$*$	Tennis	Federer	α_2	1
Musashimaru	Sumo	$*$	α_2	∞
$*$	$*$	Taiho	α_2	∞

We list some of the observations we can make by inspecting this Armstrong p-instance. First of all, the given constraint set Σ has not captured any 'fully certain' finite bounds on the cardinalities by which (Emp,Dep)-objects or (Mgr)-objects occur. Indeed, the combination (Musashimaru, Sumo) can occur infinitely many times when 'somewhat possible' objects are involved, and the same applies to (Taiho). In contrast, Σ does guarantee the uniqueness of any (Emp)-objects that are 'fully possible', and a maximum cardinality of two on any (Dep,Mgr)-objects that are 'fully possible'. Similarly, any nontrivial FD $Mgr \to A$ is not even 'somewhat certain'. The FD $Dep \to Mgr$ is 'somewhat certain', because there are two 'somewhat possible' occurrences of the (Sumo) department, but in combination with different managers. While the FD $Emp \to Dep$ is 'fully certain', the FD $Emp \to Mgr$ is only 'somewhat certain', because there are two 'somewhat possible' occurrences of the employee (Musashimaru), but each occurrence is in combination with different managers.

7   Conclusion and Future Work

Cardinality constraints and functional dependencies naturally co-occur in most aspects of life. Consequently, they have received invested interest from the conceptual modeling community over the last three decades. In contrast to various previous works, we have studied cardinality constraints and functional dependencies over uncertain data. Uncertainty has been modeled qualitatively by applying the framework of possibility theory. Our results show that cardinality constraints and functional dependencies form a 'sweet spot' in terms of both expressivity and good computational behavior, as more expressive classes of constraints behave poorly. In particular, we have established a finite axiomatization and a linear time algorithm to decide the implication problem associated with our class, and illustrated their applicability to conceptual design, update and query efficiency. We have also established an algorithm that computes for every given set of our constraints an Armstrong representation. These representations embody the exact certainty with which any constraint in our class is currently perceived to hold by data analysts. The analysts can show our Armstrong representations to domain experts in order to jointly consolidate the actual certainty with which cardinality constraints and functional dependencies shall hold in a given application domain.

Our framework opens up several questions for future investigation, including a detailed study and performance tests for our applications, the interaction with yet other constraint classes despite the limits outlined, and empirical evaluations for the usefulness of Armstrong representations. It is further interesting to investigate possibilistic approaches to more expressive data models, such as SQL with partial and duplicate information, XML, RDF, or graph databases.

Acknowledgement. This research is supported by the Marsden fund council from Government funding, administered by the Royal Society of New Zealand.

References

1. Beeri, C., Bernstein, P.: Computational problems related to the design of normal form relational schemas. ACM Trans. Database Syst. **4**(1), 30–59 (1979)
2. Beeri, C., Dowd, M., Fagin, R., Statman, R.: On the structure of Armstrong relations for functional dependencies. J. ACM **31**(1), 30–46 (1984)
3. Biskup, J., Menzel, R., Polle, T., Sagiv, Y.: Decomposition of relationships through pivoting. In: Thalheim, B. (ed.) ER 1996. LNCS, vol. 1157, pp. 28–41. Springer, Heidelberg (1996). doi:10.1007/BFb0019913
4. Brown, P., Link, S.: Probabilistic keys for data quality management. In: Zdravkovic, J., Kirikova, M., Johannesson, P. (eds.) CAiSE 2015. LNCS, vol. 9097, pp. 118–132. Springer, Heidelberg (2015). doi:10.1007/978-3-319-19069-3_8
5. Chen, P.P.: The Entity-Relationship model - toward a unified view of data. ACM Trans. Database Syst. **1**(1), 9–36 (1976)
6. Codd, E.F.: A relational model of data for large shared data banks. Commun. ACM **13**(6), 377–387 (1970)

7. Currim, F., Neidig, N., Kampoowale, A., Mhatre, G.: The CARD system. In: Parsons, J., Saeki, M., Shoval, P., Woo, C., Wand, Y. (eds.) ER 2010. LNCS, vol. 6412, pp. 433–437. Springer, Heidelberg (2010). doi:10.1007/978-3-642-16373-9_31

8. Demetrovics, J., Molnár, A., Thalheim, B.: Graphical reasoning for sets of functional dependencies. In: Atzeni, P., Chu, W., Lu, H., Zhou, S., Ling, T.-W. (eds.) ER 2004. LNCS, vol. 3288, pp. 166–179. Springer, Heidelberg (2004). doi:10.1007/978-3-540-30464-7_14

9. Dubois, D., Prade, H.: Possibility theory and its applications: Where do we stand? In: Kacprzyk, J., Pedrycz, W. (eds.) Springer Handbook of Computational Intelligence, pp. 31–60. Springer, Heidelberg (2015)

10. Dubois, D., Prade, H.: Practical methods for constructing possibility distributions. Int. J. Intell. Syst. **31**(3), 215–239 (2016)

11. Fagin, R.: A normal form for relational databases that is based on domains and keys. ACM Trans. Database Syst. **6**(3), 387–415 (1981)

12. Fagin, R.: Horn clauses and database dependencies. J. ACM **29**(4), 952–985 (1982)

13. Fan, W., Geerts, F., Jia, X., Kementsietsidis, A.: Conditional functional dependencies for capturing data inconsistencies. ACM Trans. Database Syst. **33**(2), 94–115 (2008)

14. Grant, J., Minker, J.: Inferences for numerical dependencies. Theor. Comput. Sci. **41**, 271–287 (1985)

15. Hall, N., Köhler, H., Link, S., Prade, H., Zhou, X.: Cardinality constraints on qualitatively uncertain data. Data Knowl. Eng. **99**, 126–150 (2015)

16. Hannula, M., Kontinen, J., Link, S.: On the finite and general implication problems of independence atoms and keys. J. Comput. Syst. Sci. **82**(5), 856–877 (2016)

17. Hartmann, S.: Decomposing relationship types by pivoting and schema equivalence. Data Knowl. Eng. **39**(1), 75–99 (2001)

18. Hartmann, S.: On the implication problem for cardinality constraints and functional dependencies. Ann. Math. Artif. Intell. **33**(2–4), 253–307 (2001)

19. Hartmann, S., Link, S.: Multi-valued dependencies in the presence of lists. In: Beeri, C., Deutsch, A. (eds.) Proceedings of the Twenty-Third ACM SIGACT-SIGMOD-SIGART Symposium on Principles of Database Systems, 14–16 June 2004, Paris, France, pp. 330–341. ACM (2004)

20. Hartmann, S., Link, S.: On a problem of Fagin concerning multivalued dependencies in relational databases. Theor. Comput. Sci. **353**(1–3), 53–62 (2006)

21. Hartmann, S., Link, S.: Efficient reasoning about a robust XML key fragment. ACM Trans. Database Syst. **34**(2) (2009)

22. Hartmann, S., Link, S.: Expressive, yet tractable XML keys. In: Kersten, M.L., Novikov, B., Teubner, J., Polutin, V., Manegold, S. (eds.) EDBT 2009, 12th International Conference on Extending Database Technology, Saint Petersburg, Russia, 24–26 March, 2009, Proceedings. ACM International Conference Proceeding Series, vol. 360, pp. 357–367. ACM (2009)

23. Hartmann, S., Link, S., Schewe, K.-D.: Reasoning about functional and multi-valued dependencies in the presence of lists. In: Seipel, D., Turull-Torres, J.M. (eds.) FoIKS 2004. LNCS, vol. 2942, pp. 134–154. Springer, Heidelberg (2004). doi:10.1007/978-3-540-24627-5_10

24. Hartmann, S., Link, S., Schewe, K.: Functional and multivalued dependencies in nested databases generated by record and list constructor. Ann. Math. Artif. Intell. **46**(1–2), 114–164 (2006)

25. Jones, T.H., Song, I.Y.: Analysis of binary/ternary cardinality combinations in entity-relationship modeling. Data Knowl. Eng. **19**(1), 39–64 (1996)

26. Köhler, H., Leck, U., Link, S., Zhou, X.: Possible and certain keys for SQL. VLDB J. **25**(4), 571–596 (2016)
27. Köhler, H., Link, S.: SQL schema design: Foundations, normal forms, and normalization. In: Özcan, F., Koutrika, G., Madden, S. (eds.) Proceedings of the 2016 International Conference on Management of Data, SIGMOD Conference 2016, San Francisco, CA, USA, 26 June–01 July 2016, pp. 267–279. ACM (2016)
28. Koehler, H., Link, S., Prade, H., Zhou, X.: Cardinality constraints for uncertain data. In: Yu, E., Dobbie, G., Jarke, M., Purao, S. (eds.) ER 2014. LNCS, vol. 8824, pp. 108–121. Springer, Heidelberg (2014). doi:10.1007/978-3-319-12206-9_9
29. Köhler, H., Link, S., Zhou, X.: Possible and certain SQL keys. PVLDB **8**(11), 1118–1129 (2015)
30. Köhler, H., Link, S., Zhou, X.: Discovering meaningful certain keys from incomplete and inconsistent relations. IEEE Data Eng. Bull. **39**(2), 21–37 (2016)
31. Lenzerini, M., Nobili, P.: On the satisfiability of dependency constraints in entity-relationship schemata. Inf. Syst. **15**(4), 453–461 (1990)
32. Liddle, S.W., Embley, D.W., Woodfield, S.N.: Cardinality constraints in semantic data models. Data Knowl. Eng. **11**(3), 235–270 (1993)
33. Link, S.: Charting the completeness frontier of inference systems for multivalued dependencies. Acta Inf. **45**(7–8), 565–591 (2008)
34. Link, S.: Characterisations of multivalued dependency implication over undetermined universes. J. Comput. Syst. Sci. **78**(4), 1026–1044 (2012)
35. Link, S., Prade, H.: Possibilistic functional dependencies and their relationship to possibility theory. IEEE Trans. Fuzzy Syst. **24**(3), 757–763 (2016)
36. Mannila, H., Räihä, K.J.: Design by example: an application of Armstrong relations. J. Comput. Syst. Sci. **33**(2), 126–141 (1986)
37. Mitchell, J.C.: The implication problem for functional and inclusion dependencies. Inf. Control **56**(3), 154–173 (1983)
38. Queralt, A., Artale, A., Calvanese, D., Teniente, E.: OCL-lite: finite reasoning on UML/OCL conceptual schemas. Data Knowl. Eng. **73**, 1–22 (2012)
39. Roblot, T.: Cardinality constraints for probabilistic and possibilistic databases. Ph.D. thesis, Department of Computer Science, The University of Auckland, New Zealand (2016)
40. Roblot, T., Link, S.: Probabilistic cardinality constraints. In: Johannesson, P., Lee, M.L., Liddle, S.W., Opdahl, A.L., López, Ó.P. (eds.) ER 2015. LNCS, vol. 9381, pp. 214–228. Springer, Heidelberg (2015). doi:10.1007/978-3-319-25264-3_16
41. Suciu, D., Olteanu, D., Ré, C., Koch, C.: Probabilistic Databases. Synthesis Lectures on Data Management. Morgan & Claypool Publishers, Boston (2011)
42. Thalheim, B.: On semantic issues connected with keys in relational databases permitting null values. Elektronische Informationsverarbeitung und Kybernetik **25**(1/2), 11–20 (1989)
43. Thalheim, B.: Fundamentals of cardinality constraints. In: Pernul, G., Tjoa, A.M. (eds.) ER 1992. LNCS, vol. 645, pp. 7–23. Springer, Heidelberg (1992). doi:10.1007/3-540-56023-8_3
44. Thalheim, B.: Entity-relationship modeling - foundations of database technology. Springer, Heidelberg (2000)
45. Thalheim, B.: Conceptual treatment of multivalued dependencies. In: Song, I.-Y., Liddle, S.W., Ling, T.-W., Scheuermann, P. (eds.) ER 2003. LNCS, vol. 2813, pp. 363–375. Springer, Heidelberg (2003). doi:10.1007/978-3-540-39648-2_29
46. Toman, D., Weddell, G.E.: On keys and functional dependencies as first-class citizens in description logics. J. Autom. Reasoning **40**(2–3), 117–132 (2008)

Exploring Views for Goal-Oriented Requirements Comprehension

Lyrene Silva[1]([✉]), Ana Moreira[2], João Araújo[2], Catarina Gralha[2],
Miguel Goulão[2], and Vasco Amaral[2]

[1] Dimap/IMD, Federal University of Rio Grande do Norte, Natal, Brazil
lyrene@dimap.ufrn.br
[2] NOVA LINCS, DI, FCT, Universidade NOVA de Lisboa, Lisbon, Portugal
{amm,joao.araujo,mgoul,vma}@fct.unl.pt, acg.almeida@campus.fct.unl.pt

Abstract. Requirements documents and models need to be used by many stakeholders with different technological proficiency during software development. Each stakeholder may need to understand the entire (or simply part of the) requirements artifacts. To empower these stakeholders, views of the requirements should be configurable to their particular needs. This paper uses information visualization techniques to help in this process. It proposes different views aiming at highlighting information that is relevant for a particular stakeholder, helping him to query requirements artifacts. We offer three kinds of visualizations capturing language and domain elements, while providing a gradual model overview: the big picture view, the syntax-based view, and the concern-based view. We instantiate these views with i^* models and introduce an implementation prototype in the iStarLab tool.

Keywords: Requirements exploration · Visualization · Comprehension · Views

1   Introduction

Information exploration tasks, such as zooming, obtaining details-on-demand, filtering, extracting, relating, and overviewing [1] are basic tasks for information analysis. They have been used in several areas, including software engineering. For code exploration, for example, these tasks may help the maintenance software engineer to comprehend the structure and behavior of a program through the generation of multiple views [2]. Multiple views are also broadly employed in requirements modeling for very specific purposes. Usually, these views do not offer interactive features to allow stakeholders browsing the information according to their needs [3–6].

Requirements artifacts are usually described textually or graphically (e.g., with use case scenarios, or NFR graphs). These artifacts are often too large or too complex to be quickly understood or easily queried for information of interest by different stakeholders, including clients, domain experts, and software engineers. Therefore, how to navigate through requirements artifacts to

© Springer International Publishing AG 2016
I. Comyn-Wattiau et al. (Eds.): ER 2016, LNCS 9974, pp. 149–163, 2016.
DOI: 10.1007/978-3-319-46397-1_12

get the relevant information? In other words, how can we explore (i.e., examine or study) requirements that have been elicited and documented (often by other people and/or not recently) to accomplish some activity of the software development process? This need for exploration shares some similarities with needs from other domains, such as map exploration, where the information is hierarchically organized, so that zoom and filter mechanisms may be used for seamless navigation through several information abstraction levels.

We aim at providing interactive mechanisms to allow users looking for information pieces they intend to analyze. To achieve this goal, we propose three views focusing on exploratory tasks: *big picture*, *syntax-based view* and *concern-based view*. These views are conceptually abstract, and so can be used with various types of models. Here, we chose i^*, a social goal modeling requirements language [7], to illustrate them. As we will see later, i^* models get complex very quickly. So, it is a good target to illustrate the value of our proposal.

This paper is structured as follows. Section 2 presents an overview of software exploration and i^*. Section 3 defines the three views, illustrates them with i^*, and shows an implementation of the concern-based view. It then discusses how to apply the views to other languages and indicates some challenges on using multiple views for requirements exploration. Section 4 discusses related work and Sect. 5 summarizes our conclusions and discusses ideas for further research.

2   Background

Requirements exploration is a process to navigate through requirements artifacts, aiming at comprehending their structure and content. Each stakeholder engaged in requirements exploration has particular skills and goals, and aims to quickly find specific information to confirm or refute his understanding of the requirements. These skills, goals and understanding can evolve over time. In fact, the faster stakeholders understand artifacts, the faster they may adjust their exploration goals [8]. Similarly to program exploration [9], there are three major reasons to provide mechanisms for requirements exploration:

- Requirements artifacts are often used by people that have not created them. Consequently, these artifacts have unknown structure and content to them.
- Stakeholders need to search information on these artifacts, aiming at completing a software development task or at understanding a domain. Therefore questions may vary from simple (*"Who are the stakeholders?"*) to complex (*"How to modularize the system?"*).
- Requirements are potentially huge, typically written in natural language in several abstraction levels, and scattered among different artifacts which may be specified in distinct languages. Exploration mechanisms can help navigating through the entire documentation to find the elements associated with a specific point of interest.

To illustrate our need for exploration mechanisms, we use the i^* framework. i^* is a goal-oriented requirements framework, whose objective is to analyze and represent how actors collaborate to achieve system goals [7]. $i*$ offers two models: the Strategic Dependency model (SD), focused on the collaboration among actors, and the Strategic Rationale model (SR), focused on identifying how these goals are achieved by detailing them into tasks.

Usually, modeling starts by building the SD model, showing actors, their main goals and dependencies. After that, in the SR model, each actor is detailed to operationalize the defined goals. Therefore, we may understand the SR model as an expansion of the information offered by the SD model—$i*$ defines the *boundary* element to group all the elements relevant to an actor. Despite these two levels of abstraction, $i*$ models may still be considered complex, since its meta-model defines many kinds of elements and relationships. Even using only a subset of these kinds of elements, the model can easily become too large and complex.

Some works have investigated ways to make the $i*$ notation simpler, for example by increasing its semantic transparency [10]. Instead, we aim at providing visualization mechanisms that essentially use the standard notation, enriched with information hiding mechanisms, so that a particular view supports an easier way to focus on the relevant parts of the model, for a particular stakeholder.

Figure 1 presents an SR model for the Health Care System (HCS), modeled with the iStarLab tool [11]. HCS provides costs management of a medical service, considering the trade-offs between Patients, Insurance Companies and Physicians [7]. This model consists of 13 actors, 13 goals, 41 tasks, 26 softgoals, and 165 relationships. If a stakeholder needs to analyze just one of the actors and its internal activity, the boundary element provides this information, and we could cut out all the other external dependencies. However, if we do that, we lose the context of those elements. On the other hand, if we do not cut them out, we need to manage a larger than actually needed model, and struggle to follow the intricate links. This example shows how the size and complexity of $i*$ models can be significant, and consequently decrease our ability to analyze them.

3   Views for Requirements Exploration

Creating multiple views is a strategy for requirements exploration. These exploration views must include interaction. *Zoom, filter, extract, details on demand, history, relate,* and *overview* are examples of exploration tasks supporting interaction with the information [1]. This paper defines three views focusing on filtering and zooming of requirements models. We have taken the classical Visual Information Seeking Mantra, *"Overview first, zoom and filter, then details-on-demand"* [1], into consideration. Thus, the focus is on our need for: top-down and bottom-up navigation; selecting the parts to be detailed; and selecting information types offered for the models, as well as information related to the domain vocabulary.

Our views offer an information subset (raw or pre-processed) of a model taken as source, and represent it by using the same (or similar) notation of the

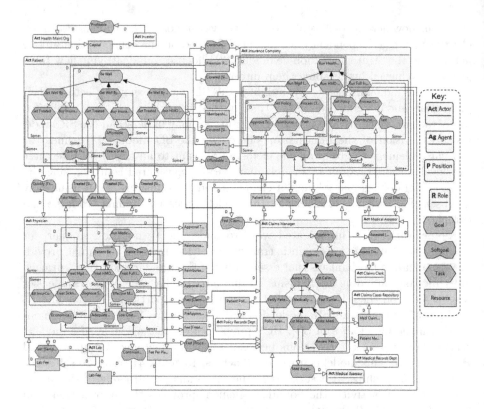

Fig. 1. The HCS strategy dependency model, taken from [11]

source model. Using the representation of the original model may decrease the cognitive effort required from stakeholders. However, this representation should depend on the task that stakeholders are performing and thus other notations may be more appropriated in some situations.

The three views defined in this paper are: the *big picture view*, the *syntax-based view*, and the *concern-based view*. The big picture generates an overview [12] for a source model (or artifact), offering the ability to expand and reduce the details on demand; it organizes the model information on levels of importance or by aggregation. The syntax-oriented view filters the types of language elements that will be visualized. Finally, the concern-oriented view filters concerns, through meta-data, system lexicon (key words) or semantic similarity.

While the big picture generalizes the need of top-down and bottom-up navigation through the information aggregation/disaggregation, the concern and syntax-based views generalize the search for information according to its abstraction level, from instance level to meta-model level, respectively. These views aim to reduce the scope by hiding model elements that are not of interest in a given moment. Next we present a conceptual model of our views.

3.1 Conceptual Model

Figure 2 presents a conceptual model relating our views, the exploration task types and the kind of data that we have taken into consideration. The *visualization* entity consists of *views* and *interaction techniques*. *Views* are projections of a *model* taken as source. A *model* consists of *elements* (*components* and *relationships*), which are characterized by *attributes*. This *model* entity generalizes model approaches (e.g. *i**, use cases, and KAOS). For example, for *i** the set of components includes nodes such as actors, boundaries, goals, softgoals, tasks, and beliefs, while the set of relationships includes dependencies, decomposition, associations, and means-end links.

The *interaction techniques* that we have focused on this paper are *zoom* and *filter*. *Zoom* realizes the *big picture* while *filter* realizes the *syntax* and *concern-based views*. We define the *big picture view* to offer an overview that aggregates *elements* of a model, while the *concern* and *syntax-based views* filter, respectively, data into *attributes* and from the model *elements*.

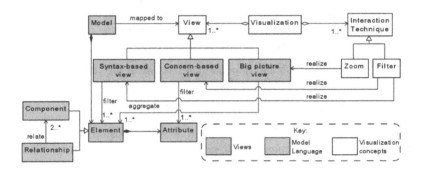

Fig. 2. Conceptual model for exploration views

Although we have classified our views as a kind of zoom and filter, they also include characteristics of the following types of interaction:

- *extract*, because they are slices of an original model, hence representing an information subset of the original model and obeying its syntactic and semantic rules;
- *overview*, because the aggregation proposed in the big picture may generate a collapsed representation at a higher abstraction level;
- *details on demand*, because the aggregations may be gradually expanded according to the user needs.

These views should be used in an interactive and integrative way. This means that it is necessary to provide tools to make the views interactive so that the stakeholder can directly manipulate, as well as combine, them in a non predefined order.

3.2   Exploring i^*

To instantiate our views for i^*, we analyze i^* elements, hierarchy, composition and decomposition characteristics, and intrinsic goal. We model its components and identify which one of them could be filtered and aggregated.

The Big Picture View. We can perceive the SD model as an abstract view of a system, showing its context. The SD model is later refined into SR models, each specifying an actor in the SD model. Here, the SD model can be seen as a Big Picture for the SR models.

SD models usually show more than one dependency between any two actors. The larger the number of links (*i.e.*, the actor's fan-in and fan-out), the more unreadable the model becomes. Hence, an SD overview, or simpler view, may be useful, allowing us to gradually expand and reduce it according to our needs. It is worth mentioning that we want to create ways to aggregate (and disaggregate) information into models, rather than creating new notations to represent them. So, if the source model language does not provide aggregation elements, we must create visual mechanisms to help the user see the collapsed points of information.

The intrinsic characteristics of SD and SR models led to us to identify four ways to reduce their quantity of elements:

- Hiding dependencies: multiple dependencies between any two actors are collapsed into one single relationship. This relationship will be annotated in both directions, defining the quantity of dependencies collapsed into it.
- Hiding actors: *actors* (as well as *roles*, *positions* and *agents*) associated to others by *isa*, *is-part-of*, *plays*, *occupies* or *ins* relationships may be omitted since they do not have dependencies with other actors. For example, if actor1 *isa* actor2, then actor1 may be collapsed.
- Hiding the internal elements of an actor: the boundary element may be used to reduce the size of the model by hiding its internal elements. This is an i^* resource that tools have already explored.
- Hiding relationships among tasks, goals, softgoals and beliefs: any two elements only linked by decomposition relationships are collapsed into the most general element. Note that means-ends and contributions are not hidden, as they are not hierarchical relationships.

Figure 3 depicts the visual mechanisms our approach adds to i^* models, so that the stakeholders are made aware of available model exploration alternatives at a given moment. The plus sign in an actor denotes the possibility of expanding the information on that actor, while the minus sign provides the alternative for collapsing (*i.e.*) that information. Finally, a simple line aggregates several dependencies that can, if necessary, be expanded.

Figure 4 illustrates our big picture view for Fig. 1. It is a simplification of the original model, since it hides several visual elements. This reduction still shows the actors and dependencies among them. Note that dependencies are represented by an annotated relationship, whose ends indicate how many dependencies exist on each direction, if any. Although it uses a different notation for

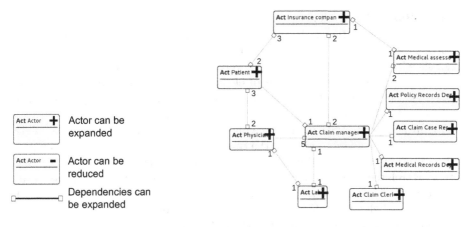

Fig. 3. Visual clues for simplifying *i** models visualization

Fig. 4. The Big Picture with both actors and dependencies collpased

dependencies and actors, there are no new elements involved, hence still representing a subset of an SD model. The number of dependencies collapsed in each relation may be used to identify, for example, actors that accumulate too many responsibilities, or those that have too few (their fan-in and fan-out).

Stakeholders may explore (collapse and expand) actors and relationships (their elements of interest), by directly selecting them or by using other interaction elements such as menus and check boxes. For example, Fig. 5 illustrates the expansion of *Patient* actor and dependencies between *Physician* and *Insurance Company* actors, which were collapsed in Fig. 4.

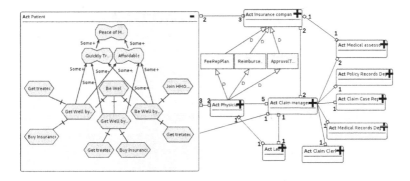

Fig. 5. The Big Picture with an expanded link and actor

Syntax-Based View. This view provides the possibility of choosing the syntactic elements of interest. It is worth noting that hiding some combinations of elements (subsets of the language) may generate semantically invalid models (e.g., showing the boundary but not its related actor). Therefore, it is necessary to define the possible combinations of elements through rules to generate well-formed views. Another alternative is to use visual clues to contrast *focused* with *non-focused* elements.

Figure 6 depicts a SD model showing only the resource dependencies. This view helps stakeholders to identify the resources flow among actors, for example, *Lab* can receive a *Lab fee* from *Claim manager* and *Physician*. Other important filters are related to each dependum, node or relationship kinds. For instance, generating a view that shows only the goals (softgoals, tasks or beliefs) related to each actor helps to understand why those actors depend on each other, or if their goals are not directly related to their dependencies.

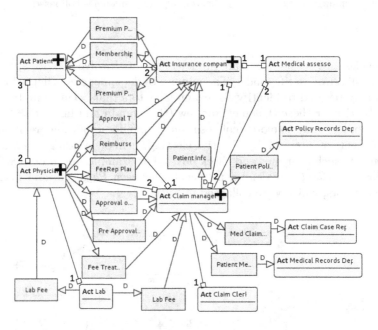

Fig. 6. Syntax-based view: filtering resource dependums

Concern-Based View. This view allows the abstraction of the model by filtering model elements. The focus is not on a type of element of the language, but, instead, on values for these types. For instance, if stakeholders only need to explore one specific actor through its SR model or identify which aspects concerning response time have been addressed, the actor's name and keywords about response time, respectively, may be used as criteria for generating these views. Additionally, we can use the syntax-based view in conjunction with the concern-based view to make the filter more precise. For example, if the name of that actor is being used for naming another kind of element, we could narrow the search by only considering the actor element type.

This kind of visualization also represents a set of views that could be defined by the stakeholders. Basically, they can specify values for particular types of language elements (in this case the syntax and concern based views are used in conjunction), or, more freely, search for a concern on any type of element. It is also necessary to consider that the result of these searches has to include the context (the model elements) related to the concern searched, as this is usually relevant for the analysis. For instance, when stakeholders search for the actor named *Patient*, they probably want actor *Patient* with all its internal elements (those within its boundary), and the actors with dependencies to *Patient*.

In this case, there is a clear need to consider the distance to the elements to be captured by this view. For example, a distance of zero only captures the elements directly searched, a distance of one considers the elements directly searched and those elements linked to them, a distance of two searches all elements in distance of one and those elements linked to them, and so on and so forth. Moreover, some kind of query language could be needed.

Figure 7 illustrates the result for a free search, requiring the elements that match the value *Cost*, with a distance of one. The result is all elements with the string *Cost* and the actors, tasks, goals and softgoals directly linked to them.

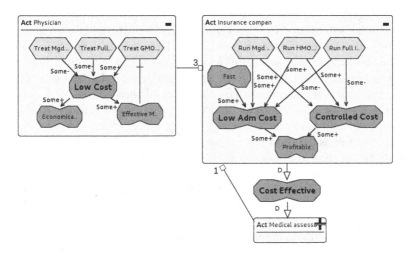

Fig. 7. Concern-based view (considering a distance of one): filtering the string *Cost*

3.3   Implementation

The *i** models presented in this paper were created with our iStarLab tool, an Eclipse-based *i** editor that allows stakeholders to generate *concern-based views* by selecting one or more concerns. After the selection, the tool presents a view that shows which elements of the model are involved or contribute to achieve that concern or set of concerns. The prototype tool was implemented using Domain Specific Language (DSL) construction mechanisms.

The tool can be used to create i^* models as well as to analyze them in terms of concerns. In this context, a concern can be viewed, for example, as a non-functional requirement (NFR) or a symbol of the system lexicon. Each one of the model elements should have one or more concerns associated with it, through tags. The stakeholder can assign one or more concerns to the elements at any time. During or after the modeling process, s/he can choose a set of those concerns, from a list, for further scrutiny. With this analysis, stakeholders can, for example, perceive if there are elements that should have associated a specific concern, which are the most used concerns, and which resources are involved or are needed to achieve a desired concern.

In this implementation of the concern-based view, there are two types of visualizations available: *(i)* highlight model elements with a specific set of concerns, without losing the model context; and *(ii)* view only model elements with a specific set of concerns, i.e., the others should be hidden in the model. After analyzing a given concern, the stakeholder can view the model in its original state, i.e., the model without highlighted elements or deleted ones.

3.4 Discussion and Challenges

Big picture, syntax and concern-base views were defined in an abstract manner. So, they can be instantiated to other types of requirements models. To instantiate these views, it is necessary to analyze the model principles and their syntactic and semantic elements and structure. Also, it is necessary to analyze if the model has aggregation elements that may be used, similarly to the *boundary* element in i^*. To validate this claim about the generality of these views, we successfully applied them to use case diagrams and their scenario descriptions (the results cannot be presented here, due to lack of space).

Taking into consideration the performed literature review and our experience with the i^* and use case models, we enumerate some of the challenges on generating or using multiple views for requirements exploration: *(i)* in the requirements engineering process, many different models are generated; so, it is necessary to provide exploration mechanisms to navigate through them, instead of only navigating an isolated model; *(ii)* the proposed views complement each other, so it is necessary to define, for each model, how they may be composed; *(iii)* the tools implementing these views should provide mechanisms to allow users to interact directly with the visual elements; *(iv)* this interaction includes generating other views from the resulting views, and so, care must be taken to avoid confusion between the source model and its views; *(v)* since users may interact with the source model as well as with the views, it is also necessary to generate a view about the path followed to the achieved result; *(vi)* interaction mechanisms include aspects from human-computer interaction have not been taken into consideration yet.

4   Related Work

For software comprehension, it is necessary to enhance bottom-up and top-down comprehension approaches, facilitate the navigation, provide orientation clues, and reduce disorientation [9]. Tools that support program comprehension should provide requirements such as browse, search and filter mechanisms, as well as abstractions, history and multiples views [13,14]. Actually, software exploration requires flexible and interactive views, i.e., visualization techniques rather than static and isolated views, in order to enable the user navigating through artifacts [14–18].

Visualization includes data types and interaction techniques [1,8,19]. In this paper, we have considered that our data types are basically software, graphs and text, while the task types are filter and zoom. Therefore, there is a wide set of other alternatives that may also be used for requirements comprehension.

Views generated for software comprehension serve firstly to reveal and understand software structures and behavior. Consistency is secondary, as these views are generated when needed and may be discarded soon after, to be regenerated when necessary. This idea comes from the information visualization field, where visualization is an activity rather than an artifact [17]. There is a high potential for this type of visualization in requirements engineering, due to the emphasis on information seeking and creation, with multiple parties and activities involved [16,17].

In this context, we may separate the related works into two categories: those that propose views generated from data sets (that describe requirements and their attributes), and those that propose views generated from constructs (or properties) of a meta-model. In the first category, filters and attributes of requirements are used to generate graphical views, usually graphs or charts [4,6,16,20]. Although they have inspired our work, they are distinct because neither do they deal with the properties of a modeling language nor with the generation of visual clues in the source model (or source model subset).

In the second category (see Table 1) we list approaches that generate views from models like i^* [5,21], theme/doc [22], use cases [23] and NFR graphs [24]. This category is highly related to our work. In general, these views are distinct from the views defined in our research, because: *(i)* they deal with a specific kind of input, while ours are abstract enough to be applied to many kinds of models; *(ii)* they generate static views by using a very specific criterion, while ours use criteria defined by users, so that many views can be generated; or *(iii)* they support only one way of interacting, while in our approach, views abstract three ways to interact with requirements models.

Horkoff and Yu [5] present two views (or filters): one to highlight the starting points for analysis (the leaves of model), and another to indicate the elements involved in a conflict. These views focus on seeking for elements of the meta-meta model that match with pre-defined properties, while our views are generic to accommodate user-defined properties.

Ernst, Yu and Mylopoulos [21] propose a visualization scheme where quality attributes are added to elements of i^* models to enable the projection of views

Table 1. Requirements aggregation and filtering mechanisms

Ref.	Source	Target	Static/Interactive	Pre-defined criteria
[21]	i^*, meta-data	i^*	Interactive	Concern-based
[5]	i^*	i^*	Static	Syntax-based: leaves and elements in conflict
[22]	ThemeDoc	ThemeDoc	Interactive	Aggregation
[23,25]	Use cases	Use cases, UML	Static	Aggregation and concern-oriented
[24]	NFR framework	NFR framework	Static	Syntax-based: objective, problem, alternative and selection patterns
Our views	i^*, use cases, others	i^*, use cases, others	Interactive	Aggregation, concern and syntax-based

based on these attributes. In their work, the quality attributes of efficiency, trustability, certainty and feasibility are defined and showed on the goal model by using visual clues. The difference between this work and ours is that it does not provide other filters types, neither overview.

Baniassad and Clarke [22] define a summarized view of Theme/Doc to deal with the lack of scalability of this kind of model. This view is similar to our Big Picture, and it was idealized to have the same kind of interaction we claim it is needed. However, their view has not been designed to be generalized nor to support filters.

Jacobson and Ng [25] define an approach where use case slices are elaborated, including pieces of the use case model and other UML models that deal with a specific concern. We can understand this use case slice as a static concern-oriented overview of the UML models, but it is not automatically (or semi-automatically) generated. Furthermore, Jacobson, Spence and Bittner [23] reinforce the importance of a Big Picture, but in this case, it is the use case diagram (unchanged). In opposition to that, our approach considers that an integrated model exists and from it a tool should be able to generate the slices, and these slices are user-defined, by considering three abstract criteria.

Supakkul and Chung [24] present a framework for visualization of patterns (objective, problem, alternatives and selection patterns) in NFRs graphs. Therefore, the criterion for visualization is specific for these patterns, so that users cannot make free searches.

5   Conclusions and Future Work

This work presents three views for models exploration: *big picture view*, *syntax-based view* and *concern-based view*. These views are based on the interaction tasks zoom and filter. Therefore, they capture three manners of abstracting a model, by decreasing its amount of elements, making it possible for stakeholders to search and focus on information of interest. Although only an instantiation of these views were shown for *i** models, they are abstract enough to be applied to other kinds of models and we have done so already for use case models.

The related works diverge from our abstract views because they are well tailored to specific languages or concerns. Instead, our views are to be adapted to different languages, and capture many kinds of concerns. Therefore, our proposal provides a strategy to effectively deal with the complexity of requirements models, where our views offer more flexible mechanisms for exploring and understanding such models. Without these kinds of mechanisms, more stakeholders' effort is demanded to find and analyze relevant information in the system model.

For the near future, we are interested in investigating how tools can be prepared for supporting our views. We are already exploring the use of DSLs to query requirements models, and meta-data to provide richer insights. Also, we will focus on other interaction tasks and define the variabilities that are intrinsic to requirements exploration, visualization and comprehension, as well as to define a process to instantiate our views to other requirement models. We plan to conduct experimental evaluations of the impact of introducing the proposed mechanisms in requirements tools and on the efficiency and effectiveness of different stakeholders while performing requirements exploration. Approaches to manage consistency among models such as in [26] will be also considered.

Acknowledgments. This work was funded by UFRN and NOVA LINCS research laboratory (Ref. UID/CEC/04516/2013), CNPq-PDE grant 201848/2014-7, and FCT-MCTES research grant SFRH/BD/108492/2015.

References

1. Shneiderman, B.: The eyes have it: a task by data type taxonomy for information visualizations. In: Symposium on Visual Languages, pp. 336–343. IEEE (1996)
2. Diehl, S.: Software Visualization: Visualizing the Structure, Behaviour, and Evolution of Software. Springer Science & Business Media, New York (2007)
3. Cooper Jr., J.R., Lee, S.W., Gandhi, R., Gotel, O.: Requirements engineering visualization: a survey on the state-of-the-art. In: 4th International Workshop on Requirements Engineering Visualization (REV 2009), pp. 46–55. IEEE (2009)
4. Donzelli, P., Hirschbach, D., Basili, V.: Using visualization to understand dependability: a tool support for requirements analysis. In: 29th Annual IEEE/NASA Software Engineering Workshop, pp. 315–324. IEEE (2005)
5. Horkoff, J., Yu, E.: Visualizations to support interactive goal model analysis. In: 5th International Workshop on Requirements Engineering Visualization (REV 2010), pp. 1–10. IEEE (2010)

6. Reddivari, S., Rad, S., Bhowmik, T., Cain, N., Niu, N.: Visual requirements analytics: a framework and case study. Requirements Eng. **19**(3), 257–279 (2014)
7. Yu, E.: Modelling strategic relationships for process reengineering. Ph.D. thesis, University of Toronto, Canada (1996)
8. Keim, D.: Information visualization and visual data mining. IEEE Trans. Visual Comput. Graphics **8**(1), 1–8 (2002)
9. Storey, M.A.D., Fracchia, F.D., Müller, H.A.: Cognitive design elements to support the construction of a mental model during software exploration. J. Syst. Softw. **44**(3), 171–185 (1999)
10. Moody, D., Heymans, P., Matulevičius, R.: Visual syntax does matter: improving the cognitive effectiveness of the i* visual notation. Requirements Eng. **15**(2), 141–175 (2010)
11. Gralha, C., Goulão, M., Araújo, J.: Identifying modularity improvement opportunities in goal-oriented requirements models. In: Jarke, M., Mylopoulos, J., Quix, C., Rolland, C., Manolopoulos, Y., Mouratidis, H., Horkoff, J. (eds.) CAiSE 2014. LNCS, vol. 8484, pp. 91–104. Springer, Heidelberg (2014). doi:10.1007/978-3-319-07881-6_7
12. Hornbæk, K., Hertzum, M.: The notion of overview in information visualization. Int. J. Hum. Comput. Stud. **69**(7), 509–525 (2011)
13. Kienle, H.M., Müller, H., et al.: Requirements of software visualization tools: a literature survey. In: 4th IEEE International Workshop on Visualizing Software for Understanding and Analysis, (VISSOFT 2007), pp. 2–9. IEEE (2007)
14. Storey, M.A.D.: Theories, methods and tools in program comprehension: past, present and future. In: 13th International Workshop on Program Comprehension (IWPC 2005), pp. 181–191. IEEE (2005)
15. Favre, J.M.: A new approach to software exploration: back-packing with GSEE. In: 6th European Conference on Software Maintenance and Reengineering, pp. 251–262. IEEE (2002)
16. Gotel, O., Marchese, F.T., Morris, S.J.: On requirements visualization. In: 2nd International Workshop on Requirements Engineering Visualization (REV 2007). IEEE (2007)
17. Gotel, O., Marchese, F.T., Morris, S.J.: The potential for synergy between information visualization and software engineering visualization. In: 12th International Conference on Information Visualisation, (IV 2008), pp. 547–552. IEEE (2008)
18. Niu, N., Mahmoud, A., Yang, X.: Faceted navigation for software exploration. In: IEEE International Conference on Program Comprehension, pp. 193–196 (2011)
19. Keller, P.R., Keller, M.M.: Visual Cues: Practical Data Visualization. IEEE Computer Society Press, Los Alamitos (1994)
20. Heim, P., Lohmann, S., Lauenroth, K., Ziegler, J.: Graph-based visualization of requirements relationships. In: 3rd International Workshop on Requirements Engineering Visualization, (REV 2008), pp. 51–55. IEEE (2008)
21. Ernst, N., Yu, Y., Mylopoulos, J.: Visualizing non-functional requirements. In: 1st International Workshop on Requirements Engineering Visualization (REV 2006). IEEE (2006)
22. Baniassad, E., Clarke, S.: Investigating the use of clues for scaling document-level concern graphs. In: Workshop on Early Aspects (held with ECOOP 2004), Vancouver, Canada, pp. 1–7 (2004)
23. Jacobson, I., Spence, I., Bittner, K.: Use Case 2.0: the guide to succeeding with use cases. In: Ivar Jacobson International, pp. 1–55 (2011)

24. Supakkul, S., Chung, L.: Visualizing non-functional requirements patterns. In: 5th International Workshop on Requirements Engineering Visualization (REV 2010), pp. 25–34. IEEE (2010)

25. Jacobson, I., Ng, P.W.: Aspect-Oriented Software Development with Use Cases. Addison-Wesley Object Technology Series. Addison-Wesley Professional, Reading (2004)

26. Bork, D., Buchmann, R., Karagiannis, D.: Preserving multi-view consistency in diagrammatic knowledge representation. In: Zhang, S., Wirsing, M., Zhang, Z. (eds.) KSEM 2015. LNCS, vol. 9403, pp. 177–182. Springer, Heidelberg (2015). doi:10.1007/978-3-319-25159-2_16

Keys with Probabilistic Intervals

Pieta Brown[1], Jeeva Ganesan[1], Henning Köhler[2], and Sebastian Link[1(✉)]

[1] Department of Computer Science, University of Auckland, Auckland, New Zealand
{pieta.brown,j.ganesan,s.link}@auckland.ac.nz
[2] School of Engineering and Advanced Technology, Massey University,
Palmerston North, New Zealand
h.koehler@massey.ac.nz

Abstract. Probabilistic databases accommodate well the requirements of modern applications that produce large volumes of uncertain data from a variety of sources. We propose an expressive class of probabilistic keys which empowers users to specify lower and upper bounds on the marginal probabilities by which keys should hold in a data set of acceptable quality. Indeed, the bounds help organizations balance the consistency and completeness targets for their data quality. For this purpose, algorithms are established for an agile schema- and data-driven acquisition of the right lower and upper bounds in a given application domain, and for reasoning about these keys. The efficiency of our acquisition framework is demonstrated theoretically and experimentally.

Keywords: Data mining · Data semantics · Integrity constraint · Probabilistic data · Requirements acquisition

1 Introduction

Background. Keys allow us to understand the structure and semantics of data. In relational databases, a key is a set of attributes that holds on a relation if no two different tuples in the relation have matching values on all the attributes of the key. The ability of keys to uniquely identify entities makes them invaluable in data processing and applications.

Motivation. Relational databases target applications with certain data, such as accounting and payroll. Modern applications, such as data integration and financial risk assessment produce large volumes of uncertain data from a variety of sources. For instance, RFID (radio frequency identification) can track movements of endangered species of animals, such as the Japanese Serow in central Honshu. Here it is sensible to apply probabilistic databases. Table 1 shows two probabilistic relations (p-relation), which are probability distributions over a finite set of possible worlds, each being a relation.

In requirements acquisition the goal is to specify all keys that apply to the application domain, and those keys only. This goal addresses the consistency and completeness dimensions of data quality. Here, consistency means to specify all

© Springer International Publishing AG 2016
I. Comyn-Wattiau et al. (Eds.): ER 2016, LNCS 9974, pp. 164–179, 2016.
DOI: 10.1007/978-3-319-46397-1_13

Table 1. Probabilistic relations r_1 and r_2

r_1:

W_1 ($p_1 = 0.35$)			W_2 ($p_2 = 0.3$)			W_3 ($p_3 = 0.1$)			W_4 ($p_4 = 0.25$)		
rfid	*time*	*zone*	*rfid*	*time*	*zone*	*rfid*	*time*	*zone*	*rfid*	*time*	*zone*
j1	2pm	z1	j1	2pm	z1	j1	2pm	z1	j1	2pm	z1
j1	3pm	z2	j3	2pm	z3	j1	5pm	z1	j1	5pm	z1
j2	4pm	z1	j1	5pm	z1	j4	2pm	z1	j4	2pm	z1
j3	2pm	z3							j1	2pm	z4

r_2:

W_1 ($p_1 = 0.2$)			W_2 ($p_2 = 0.3$)			W_3 ($p_3 = 0.25$)			W_4 ($p_4 = 0.25$)		
rfid	*time*	*zone*	*rfid*	*time*	*zone*	*rfid*	*time*	*zone*	*rfid*	*time*	*zone*
j1	2pm	z1	j1	2pm	z1	j1	2pm	z1	j1	2pm	z1
j2	3pm	z1	j2	3pm	z1	j3	2pm	z3	j1	5pm	z1
			j1	4pm	z2	j1	5pm	z1	j1	2pm	z4
			j3	2pm	z3				j4	2pm	z1

meaningful keys in order to prevent the occurrence of inconsistent data, while completeness means not to specify any meaningless keys in order to capture any potential meaningful database instance. This situation is exemplified in Fig. 1.

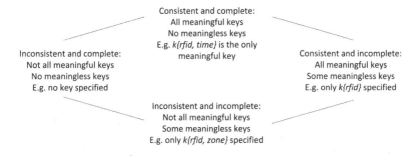

Fig. 1. Consistency and completeness dimensions as controlled by keys

In probabilistic databases, one may speak of a key when it holds in all possible worlds. That is to say that a key holds with marginal probability one, which means that the probabilities of the worlds in which the key holds add up to one. Due to the veracity of probabilistic data and the variety of sources the data originate from, one must not expect to satisfy the completeness criteria with this definition. Neither does such definition make sensible use of probabilities, as one would expect for probabilistic data. In our example, neither r_1 nor r_2 satisfy any non-trivial key with marginal probability one: The key $k\{$ *rfid, time* $\}$ has marginal probability 0.75 in both r_1 and r_2, while $k\{$ *time, zone* $\}$ has marginal probability 0.65 in r_1 and marginal probability 0.75 in r_2.

We propose *keys with probabilistic intervals*, or p-keys for short, which stipulate lower and upper bounds on the marginal probability by which a traditional key holds on probabilistic data. For example, we may specify the p-keys

$k\{rfid, time\} \in (0.75, 1)$ and $k\{time, zone\} \in (0.65, 0.75)$. In particular, the ability to stipulate lower and upper bounds on the marginal probability of keys is useful for probabilistic data. The p-key $k\{time, zone\} \in (0.65, 0.75)$ reflects our observations that different serows may occur at the same time in the same zone at least with probability 0.25 and at most with probability 0.35. Our main motivation for p-keys is their ability to balance the consistency and completeness targets for the quality of probabilistic data. Consistency means that for each key the specified lower (upper) bound on its marginal probability is not too high (low), and completeness means that for each key the specified lower (upper) bound is not too low (high). Once the bounds have been consolidated, p-keys can be utilized to control these data quality dimensions during updates. When new data arrives, p-keys can help detect anomalous patterns of data in the form of p-key violations. That is, automated warnings can be issued whenever data would not meet a desired lower or upper bound of some p-key. In a different showcase, p-keys can be used to infer probabilities that query answers are (non-)unique. In our example, we may wonder about the chance that different serows are in the same zone at the same time, indicating potential mating behavior. We may ask

SELECT DISTINCT $rfid$ FROM TRACKING WHERE $zone$='z2' AND $time$='2pm'.

P-keys enable us to derive a minimum (maximum) probability of 0.65 (0.75) that a unique answer is returned, because different serows are in zone z2 at 2pm at least with probability 0.25 and at most with probability 0.35. These bounds can be inferred without accessing any data at all, only requiring that $k\{time, zone\}$ has a marginal probability between 0.65 and 0.75 on the given data.

Contributions. Our contributions can be summarized as follows. **Modeling:** We propose p-keys $kX \in (p, q)$ as a natural class of integrity constraints over uncertain data. Their main use is to help organizations balance consistency and completeness targets for the quality of their data, and to quantify bounds on the probability for (non-)unique query answers. **Reasoning:** While sets of p-keys can be unsatisfiable, we establish an efficient algorithm to decide satisfiability. The implication problem is to decide for a given set $\Sigma \cup \{\varphi\}$ of p-keys, whether

Table 2. Two PC-tables that form an Armstrong PC-base for the p-keys of Fig. 2

CD table				P table			CD table				P table	
rfid	time	zone	W	W	$\mathcal{P}$		rfid	time	zone	W	W	$\mathcal{P}$
j1	2pm	z1	1, 2, 3, 4	1	.35		j1	2pm	z1	1, 2, 3, 4	1	.2
j1	3pm	z2	1	2	.3		j2	3pm	z1	1, 2	2	.3
j2	4pm	z1	1	3	.1		j1	4pm	z2	2	3	.25
j3	2pm	z3	1, 2	4	.25		j3	2pm	z3	2, 3	4	.25
j1	5pm	z1	2, 3, 4				j1	5pm	z1	3, 4		
j4	2pm	z1	3, 4				j1	2pm	z4	4		
j1	2pm	z4	4				j4	2pm	z1	4		

every p-relation that satisfies all elements of Σ also satisfies φ. We characterize the implication problem of satisfiable sets of p-keys by a finite set of Horn rules, and a linear time decision algorithm. This enables organizations to reduce the overhead of managing p-keys to a minimal level necessary. **Summarization:** For the schema-driven acquisition of the right probabilistic intervals, we show how to perfectly summarize any given satisfiable set of p-keys as an Armstrong PC-base. An Armstrong PC-base consists of two PC-tables: One that satisfies every key with the exact marginal probability that is the perceived best lower bound for the domain, and one that is the perceived best upper bound. Any flaws with these perceptions are explicitly pointed out: Either as unreasonably high lower bounds, or unreasonably low upper bounds. For example, Table 2 shows an Armstrong PC-base for the p-keys shown in Fig. 2. In the CD table, the W column of a tuple shows the identifiers of possible worlds to which the tuple belongs. The P-table shows the probability distribution on the possible worlds. The first PC-table represents the p-relation r_1 and the second PC-table represents the p-relation r_2 from Table 1. While all p-keys that are implied by this p-key set are satisfied by both PC-tables, every non-implied p-key is violated by at least one PC-table. For example, the implied p-key $k\{time,zone\} \in (0.6, 0.8)$ is satisfied by the p-relations the tables represent, while the non-implied p-key $k\{time,zone\} \in (0.7, 0.75)$ is violated by r_1.

Discovery: For the data-driven acquisition of p-keys we compute the probabilistic interval of any key as the smallest and largest marginal probabilities across all given PC-tables. For example, given the two PC-tables in Table 2, our algorithm would discover the profile of p-keys in Fig. 2. **Experiments:** Experiments show that our algorithms are efficient and scale linearly *in our acquisition framework.*

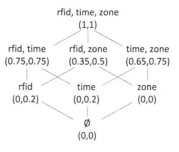

Fig. 2. P-key profile of Table 2

Organization. We discuss related work in Sect. 2. P-keys are introduced in Sect. 3. Computational problems are characterized in Sect. 4. The schema- and data-driven acquisition of p-keys is developed in Sect. 5. Experiment results are presented in Sect. 6. We conclude in Sect. 7.

2   Related Work

Poor data quality inhibits the transformation of data into value [23]. P-keys provide a well-founded, yet simple approach to balance the consistency and completeness targets for the quality of data. Keys are fundamental to most data models [3,6,9,12,15,25,26]. P-keys subsume keys from traditional relations [1,2], covered by the special case where p-relations consist of one possible world only. There is substantial work on the discovery of "approximate" constraints, see [4,16,20] for recent surveys. Approximate means that not all tuples satisfy the given constraint, but exceptions are tolerable. P-keys are not approximate since they are either satisfied or violated by the given p-relation. Future work will investigate approximate p-keys. Possibilistic keys [11] are attributed some degree of certainty saying to which tuples they apply. Possibility theory is a qualitative approach, while probability theory is a quantitative approach to uncertainty. P-keys complements the qualitative approach to possibilistic keys from [11]. Keys with probabilistic intervals extend our own work on keys with lower bounds only [3]. The extension causes significant differences. Keys with intervals are more expressive as upper bounds smaller than 1 can be specified, addressing better any consistency and completeness targets. Sets of keys with intervals may not be satisfiable by any p-relation, while every set of keys with only lower bounds is satisfiable. While implication and inference problems become more complex for intervals, we succeed in establishing linear time algorithms. While keys with only lower bounds enjoy representations by a single Armstrong PC-table, keys with intervals require generally two PC-tables. This is an interesting novelty for Armstrong databases for which more than one database instance have not been considered in previous research. We also generalize the discovery problem for keys with intervals to a collection of input instances, while only single input instances were considered in [3] for keys with lower bounds.

3   Keys with Probabilistic Intervals

We introduce our notion of keys with probabilistic intervals after some preliminaries on probabilistic databases.

A *relation schema* is a finite set R of attributes A. Each attribute A is associated with a domain $dom(A)$ of values. A tuple t over R is a function that assigns to each attribute A of R an element $t(A)$ from the domain $dom(A)$. A *relation* over R is a finite set of tuples over R. Relations over R are also called *possible worlds* of R here. An expression kX over R with $X \subseteq R$ is called a *key*. A key kX is said to hold in a possible world W of R, denoted by $W \models kX$, if and only if there no two tuples $t_1, t_2 \in W$ such that $t_1 \neq t_2$ and $t_1(X) = t_2(X)$. A *probabilistic relation* (p-relation) over R is a pair $r = (\mathcal{W}, P)$ of a finite non-empty set $\mathcal{W}$ of possible worlds over R and a probability distribution $P : \mathcal{W} \rightarrow (0, 1]$ such that $\sum_{W \in \mathcal{W}} P(W) = 1$ holds. Table 1 shows two p-relations over relation schema $\text{TRACKING} = \{rfid, time, zone\}$. World W_2 of r_1, for example, satisfies the keys $k\{rfid, time\}$ and $k\{zone, time\}$, but violates the key $k\{rfid, zone\}$. The *marginal probability* $m_{X,r}$ of a key kX in the p-relation r is the sum of the probabilities of those possible worlds in r which satisfy kX. We will now introduce the central notion of a key with probabilistic intervals.

Definition 1. *A* key with probabilistic intervals, *or* p-key *for short, over relation schema R is an expression $kX \in (l, u)$ where $X \subseteq R$, $l, u \in [0, 1]$, and $l \leq u$. The p-key $kX \in (l, u)$ over R is* satisfied by, *or said to* hold in, *the p-relation r over R if and only if the marginal probability $m_{X,r}$ of kX in r falls into the interval (l, u), that is, $l \leq m_{X,r} \leq u$.*

In our running example over relation schema TRACKING, the p-relation r_2 from Table 1 satisfies the p-keys $k\{rfid, time\} \in (0.7, 0.75)$ and $k\{time, zone\} \in (0.3, 0.8)$, but violates the p-keys $k\{rfid, time\} \in (0.7, 0.7)$ and $k\{time, zone\} \in (0.3, 0.65)$. The reasons are that $m_{\{rfid,time\},r_2} = m_{\{time,zone\},r_2} = 0.75$.

It is useful to separate a p-key into one key that stipulates the lower bound and one key that stipulates the upper bound. This allows users to focus on one bound at a time, but also allows us to gain a better understanding of their interaction. A key with lower bound, or *l-key*, is of the form $kX \in (l, 1)$, and we write $kX_{\geq l}$. A key with upper bound, or *u-key*, is of the form $kX \in (0, u)$, and written as $kX_{\leq u}$. For example, the p-key $k\{time, zone\} \in (0.65, 0.75)$ can be rewritten as the l-key $k\{time, zone\}_{\geq 0.65}$ and the u-key $k\{time, zone\}_{\leq 0.75}$. It follows directly that a p-relation satisfies a p-key iff it satisfies the corresponding l-key and u-key. L-keys were studied in [3]. First, we will study u-keys, and then combine them with l-keys.

4   Reasoning Tools

When using sets of p-keys to enforce the consistency and completeness targets on the quality of data, their overhead must be reduced to a minimal level necessary. In practice, this requires us to reason about p-keys efficiently. We will now establish tools to reason about the interaction of p-keys. This will help us identify efficiently (i) if a given set of p-keys is consistent, and (ii) the most concise interval by which a given key is implied from a given set of p-keys. This helps optimize query and update efficiency, but is also essential for developing our acquisition framework later.

4.1   Computational Problems

Let $\Sigma \cup \{\varphi\}$ denote a set of constraints over relation schema R. We say that Σ is *satisfiable*, if there is some p-relation over R that satisfies all elements of Σ; and say that Σ is *unsatisfiable* otherwise. We say that Σ *implies* φ, denoted by $\Sigma \models \varphi$, if every p-relation r over R that satisfies Σ, also satisfies φ. We use $\Sigma^* = \{\varphi : \Sigma \models \varphi\}$ to denote the *semantic closure* of Σ. Let $\mathcal{C}$ denote a class of constraints. The $\mathcal{C}$-*satisfiability problem* is to decide for a given relation schema R and a given set Σ of constraints in $\mathcal{C}$ over R, whether Σ is satisfiable. The $\mathcal{C}$-*implication problem* is to decide for a given relation schema R and a given satisfiable set $\Sigma \cup \{\varphi\}$ of constraints in $\mathcal{C}$ over R, whether Σ implies φ. If $\mathcal{C}$ denotes the class of p-keys, then the $\mathcal{C}$-*inference problem* is to compute for a given relation schema R, a given satisfiable set Σ of p-keys, and a given key kX over R the largest probability l and the smallest probability u such that Σ implies $kX \in (l, u)$. We will characterize the computational problems for u-keys first. Subsequently, we then show how to combine these results with our previous findings on l-keys to characterize the computational problems for p-keys.

Table 3. Axiomatization $\mathfrak{U} = \{\mathcal{R}, \mathcal{F}, \mathcal{W}\}$

$\dfrac{}{kR_{\leq 1}}$ (Maximum, $\mathcal{M}$)	$\dfrac{kXY_{\leq p}}{kX_{\leq p}}$ (Fragment, $\mathcal{F}$)	$\dfrac{kX_{\leq p}}{kX_{\leq p+q}}$ (Relax, $\mathcal{R}$)

4.2 Keys with Upper Bounds

Satisfiability. Unsatisfiability is strong evidence that a set of keys has been over-specified. While every set of l-keys is satisfiable, this is not the case for every set of u-keys. However, satisfiable sets are easy to characterize for u-keys: Unsatisfiability can only originate from stipulating an upper bound smaller than one for the trivial key kR.

Proposition 1. *A set Σ of u-keys over relation schema R is satisfiable if and only if Σ does not contain a u-key of the form $kR_{\leq u}$ where $u < 1$. The satisfiability problem for u-keys can thus be decided with one scan over the input.* $\square$

Axioms. We determine the semantic closure by applying *inference rules* of the form $\dfrac{\text{premise}}{\text{conclusion}}$. For a set $\mathfrak{R}$ of inference rules let $\Sigma \vdash_{\mathfrak{R}} \varphi$ denote the *inference* of φ from Σ by $\mathfrak{R}$. That is, there is some sequence $\sigma_1, \ldots, \sigma_n$ such that $\sigma_n = \varphi$ and every σ_i is an element of Σ or is the conclusion that results from an application of an inference rule in $\mathfrak{R}$ to some premises in $\{\sigma_1, \ldots, \sigma_{i-1}\}$. Let $\Sigma_{\mathfrak{R}}^+ = \{\varphi : \Sigma \vdash_{\mathfrak{R}} \varphi\}$ be the *syntactic closure* of Σ under inferences by $\mathfrak{R}$. $\mathfrak{R}$ is *sound* (*complete*) if for every satisfiable set Σ over every R we have $\Sigma_{\mathfrak{R}}^+ \subseteq \Sigma^*$ ($\Sigma^* \subseteq \Sigma_{\mathfrak{R}}^+$). The (finite) set $\mathfrak{R}$ is a (finite) *axiomatization* if $\mathfrak{R}$ is both sound and complete. The set $\mathfrak{U}$ of inference rules from Table 3 forms a finite axiomatization for the implication of u-keys. Here, R denotes the underlying relation schema, X and Y form attribute subsets of R, and p, q as well as $p + q$ are probabilities.

Theorem 1. $\mathfrak{U}$ *forms a finite axiomatization for u-keys.* $\square$

It is worth pointing out the soundness of the rules. The maximum rule $\mathcal{M}$ holds trivially, because every marginal probability can at most be one. For the fragment rule $\mathcal{F}$ assume that the marginal probability of kX exceeds p. Since every world that satisfies kX must also satisfy kXY, the marginal probability of kXY exceeds p, too. Finally, for the relax rule $\mathcal{R}$ assume that the marginal probability of kX exceeds $p + q$. Then the marginal probability of kX exceeds p, for sure. Some examples illustrate the use of the inference rule for reasoning about u-keys.

For example, $\Sigma = \{k\{\mathit{rfid}, \mathit{time}\}_{\leq 0.75}\}$ implies $\varphi = k\{\mathit{time}\}_{\leq 0.8}$, but not $\varphi' = k\{\mathit{time}\}_{\leq 0.2}$. Indeed, φ can be inferred from Σ by applying $\mathcal{F}$ to $k\{\mathit{rfid}, \mathit{time}\}_{\leq 0.75}$ to infer $k\{\mathit{time}\}_{\leq 0.75}$, and applying $\mathcal{R}$ to $k\{\mathit{time}\}_{\geq 0.75}$ to infer φ.

Algorithm 1. Inference

Require: R, Σ, kX with satisfiable set Σ of u-keys
Ensure: $\min\{u : \Sigma \models kX_{\leq u}\}$
1: $p \leftarrow 1$;
2: **for all** $kZ_{\leq q} \in \Sigma$ **do**
3:     **if** $X \subseteq Z$ and $q < u$ **then**
4:         $u \leftarrow q$;
5: **return** u;

If a p-relation satisfies a set Σ of p-keys, then it also satisfies every p-key φ implied by Σ. Consequently, it is redundant to verify that a given p-relation satisfies an implied p-key. In particular, the larger the given p-relation, the more time we save by avoiding such redundant validation checks.

Algorithms. In practice, the semantic closure Σ^* of a finite set Σ is infinite and even though it can be represented finitely, it is often unnecessary to determine all implied constraints. In fact, the implication problem has input $\Sigma \cup \{\varphi\}$ and the question is if Σ implies φ. Computing Σ^* and checking if $\varphi \in \Sigma^*$ is not feasible. We will now establish a linear-time algorithm for computing the smallest probability u, such that $kX_{\leq u}$ is implied by Σ. The following theorem allows us to reduce the implication problem for u-keys to a single scan of the input.

Theorem 2. *Let $\Sigma \cup \{kX_{\leq u}\}$ denote a satisfiable set of u-keys over relation schema R. Then Σ implies $kX_{\leq u}$ if and only if (i) $u = 1$ or (ii) there is some $kZ_{\leq q} \in \Sigma$ such that $X \subseteq Z$ and $q \leq u$.* □

Based on Theorem 2, Algorithm 1 returns for a given satisfiable set Σ of u-keys and a given key kX over R, the smallest probability u such that $kX_{\leq u}$ is implied by Σ. Starting with $u = 1$, the algorithm scans all input keys $kZ_{\leq q}$ and sets u to q whenever q is smaller than the current u and X is contained in Z. We use $|S|$ to denote the total number of attributes that occur in set S.

Corollary 1. *On input (R, Σ, kX), Algorithm 1 returns in $\mathcal{O}(|\Sigma| + |R|)$ time the minimum probability u with which $kX_{\leq u}$ is implied by Σ.* □

Given $R, \Sigma, kX_{\leq p}$ as an input to the implication problem for u-keys, Algorithm 1 computes $u := \min\{q : \Sigma \models kX_{\leq q}\}$ and we return an affirmative answer iff $u \leq p$. Hence, the implication problem is linear time decidable in the input.

Corollary 2. *The implication problem of u-keys is decidable in linear time.* □

Given $\Sigma = \{k\{rfid, time\}_{\leq 0.75}\}$ and $k\{time\}$, Algorithm 1 returns $u = 0.75$. For $\varphi' = k\{time\}_{\leq 0.2}$, we conclude that Σ does not imply φ' as $u > 0.2$.

4.3 Keys with Probabilistic Intervals

We will now study p-keys as the combination of l-keys and u-keys. That is, we think of every set Σ of p-keys as the union of the set $\Sigma_l := \{kX_{\leq p} \mid kX \in (p, q) \in \Sigma\}$ of l-keys and the set $\Sigma_u := \{kX_{\geq q} \mid kX \in (p, q) \in \Sigma\}$ of u-keys.

Satisfiability. While satisfiability for l-keys can be decided in constant time [3], and satisfiability for u-keys requires one scan over the input, the satisfiability problem for p-keys requires two scans over the input.

Proposition 2. *A set Σ of p-keys over relation schema R is satisfiable if and only if $\Sigma_l \cup \Sigma_u \cup \{kR_{\geq 1}\}$ does not contain $kX_{\geq p}$, $kXY_{\leq q}$ such that $p > q$. The satisfiability problem for p-keys is decidable with two scans over the input.* □

The set $\Sigma = \{k\{rfid\} \in (0.75, 0.75), k\{rfid, time\} \in (0.6, 0.7)\}$ is unsatisfiable.

No interaction. We reduce the remaining computational problems for p-keys to those of u-keys and l-keys. This is possible since we can show that every satisfiable set of p-keys does not exhibit any interaction between its l-keys and u-keys. Formally, u-keys and l-keys *do not interact* if and only if for every relation schema R, every satisfiable set Σ of p-keys, every l-key $kX_{\geq p}$ and every u-key $kY_{\geq u}$ over R, the following two conditions hold:

- $\Sigma_u \cup \Sigma_l \models kX_{\geq p}$ if and only if $\Sigma_l \models kX_{\geq p}$,
- $\Sigma_u \cup \Sigma_l \models kY_{\leq q}$ if and only if $\Sigma_u \models kY_{\leq q}$.

In other words, the non-interaction between u-keys and l-keys enables us to reduce the implication problem for p-keys to the implication problems for u-keys and l-keys. That is, a p-key $kX \in (p, q)$ is implied by a satisfiable set Σ of p-keys if and only if i) $kX_{\geq p}$ is implied by Σ_l, and ii) $kX_{\leq q}$ is implied by Σ_u.

Theorem 3. *U-keys and l-keys do not interact.*

Proof (Sketch). The non-trivial direction is to show the following: if $\Sigma_l \not\models kX_{\geq p}$, then $\Sigma_u \cup \Sigma_l \not\models kX_{\geq p}$. If $\Sigma_l \not\models kX_{\geq p}$, then any Armstrong p-relation for Σ_l satisfies Σ_l and violates $kX_{\geq p}$. Since $\Sigma_u \cup \Sigma_l$ is satisfiable, it follows that the Armstrong p-relation for Σ_l also satisfies Σ_u. Consequently, $\Sigma_u \cup \Sigma_l \not\models kX_{\geq p}$. The arguments works similarly when we know that $\Sigma_u \not\models kY_{\leq q}$. We can create an Armstrong p-relation for Σ_u, which must also satisfy Σ_l because $\Sigma_u \cup \Sigma_l$ is satisfiable. □

Theorem 3 allows us to reduce the implication and inference problems for p-keys to the implication and inference problems for l-keys and u-keys. As a first consequence, combining our axiomatizations for u-keys and l-keys yields an axiomatization for p-keys.

Corollary 3. *Axiomatization $\mathfrak{U}$ for u-keys from Theorem 1 together with axiomatization $\mathfrak{P}$ for l-keys from [3] form a finite axiomatization for p-keys.* □

As a second consequence, we can also combine our inference algorithms for u-keys and l-keys to obtain an efficient inference algorithm for p-keys.

Corollary 4. *Given relation schema R, a satisfiable set Σ of p-keys, and a key kX over R, we can return in $\mathcal{O}(|\Sigma| + |R|)$ time the maximum probability l and the minimum probability u such that $kX \in (l, u)$ is implied by Σ.* □

Thirdly, the implication problem of p-keys can be decided efficiently.

Corollary 5. *The implication problem of p-keys is decidable in linear time.* □

To decide if $k\{time,zone\} \in (0.6, 0.7)$ is implied by the set Σ of p-keys from Fig. 2, we check if $k\{time,zone\}_{\geq 0.6}$ is implied by Σ_l and if $k\{time,zone\}_{\leq 0.7}$ is implied by Σ_u. As the second condition fails, the p-key is not implied by Σ.

Our results show that it takes quadratic time in the input to keep the enforcement of p-key sets to a minimal level necessary: For a given p-key set, we can remove successively all p-keys from the set that are implied by the remaining set. More validation time is saved the bigger the underlying p-relations grow.

5   Tools for Acquiring Probabilistic Key Intervals

The main inhibitor to the uptake of p-keys is the difficulty to determine the right interval for the marginal probabilities by which keys hold in the underlying application domain. For that purpose, analysts should communicate with domain experts. We establish two major computational tools that help analysts communicate effectively with domain experts. We follow the framework in Fig. 3. Here, analysts use our algorithm to summarize abstract sets Σ of p-keys in the form of some Armstrong PC-base, which is then inspected jointly with domain experts. In particular, the two PC-tables that form together the PC-base represent simultaneously for every key kX their lowest and highest marginal probabilities that quality data sets in the target domain should exhibit.

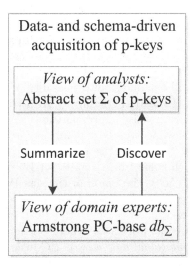

Fig. 3. Acquisition framework

Domain experts may change the PC-tables or supply new PC-tables to the analysts. For that case we establish an algorithm that discovers p-keys from sets of PC-tables. That is, the algorithm computes the lowest and highest marginal probabilities of each key across all the given PC-tables. Such profiles are also useful for query optimization, for example.

5.1   Summarizing Abstract Sets of P-Keys as Armstrong PC-bases

Our results will show that every satisfiable set Σ of p-keys can be summarized in the form of two PC-tables such that all given p-keys are satisfied by the two p-relations the PC-tables represent, and all those p-keys not implied by Σ are violated by at least one of the p-relations. This notion generalizes the concept of an *Armstrong database*, which is a *single* database instance that satisfies a constraint if and only if it is implied by the given constraint set [5]. The reason why p-keys require two database instances is simple: Each instance can only represent one marginal probability, but p-keys generally require a lower and an upper bound on the marginal probability. So, unless every given key has the same lower and upper bounds, we require two database instances. The formal definition is therefore as follows.

Definition 2. *Let Σ be a satisfiable set of p-keys over a given relation schema R. A pair of p-relation r_1, r_2 over R is Armstrong for Σ if and only if for all p-keys φ over R it holds that r_1 and r_2 satisfy φ if and only if Σ implies φ.*

For example, the p-relations r_1, r_2 from Table 1 are Armstrong for the set Σ of p-keys in Fig. 2. It is worth emphasizing the effectiveness of the definition: Knowing that r_1, r_2 are Armstrong for a given Σ enables us to reduce *every* instance $\Sigma \cup \{\varphi\}$ of the implication problem to simply checking if both r_1 and r_2 satisfy φ. Knowing that u-keys and l-keys do not interact, we can compute r_1, r_2 such that *every* instance $\Sigma \cup \{kX\}$ of the inference problem is reduced to simply computing the lower (upper) bound l (u) in $kX \in (l, u)$ as the marginal probability m_{X,r_1} (m_{X,r_2}) of kX in r_1 (r_2). For example, the $k\{time,zone\} \in (0.6, 0.7)$ is not implied by Σ from Fig. 2 as the given upper bound 0.7 is smaller than the marginal probability 0.75 of $k\{time,zone\}$ in r_2.

Instead of computing Armstrong p-relations we compute PC-tables that are more concise representations. We call these *Armstrong* PC-bases. Recall the following standard definition from probabilistic databases [24]. A *conditional table* or *c-table*, is a tuple $CD = \langle r, W \rangle$, where r is a relation, and W assigns to each tuple t in r a finite set W_t of positive integers. The set of *world identifiers* of CD is the union of the sets W_t for all tuples t of r. Given a world identifier i of CD, the possible world associated with i is $W_i = \{t | t \in r$ and $i \in W_t\}$. The semantics of a c-table $CD = \langle r, W \rangle$, called *representation*, is the set $\mathcal{W}$ of possible worlds W_i where i denotes some world identifier of CD. A *probabilistic conditional database* or *PC-table*, is a pair $\langle CD, P \rangle$ where CD is a c-table, and P is a probability distribution over the set of world identifiers of CD. The set of possible worlds of a PC-table $\langle CD, P \rangle$ is the representation of CD, and the probability of each possible world W_i is defined as the probability of its world identifier. For example, the PC-tables from Table 2 form an Armstrong PC-base for the set Σ of p-keys from Fig. 2.

Algorithm 2 in [3] computes a single Armstrong PC-table for every given set Σ of l-keys. In the construction, the number of possible worlds is given by the number of distinct lower bounds that occur in Σ. Indeed, for every given set Σ of l-keys over R and every $p \in (0, 1]$, $\Sigma_p = \{kX : \exists kX_{\geq q} \in \Sigma \wedge q \geq p\}$ denotes the *p-cut* of Σ. If Σ does not contain a p-key $kX_{\geq p}$ where $p = 1$, an Armstrong PC-table for Σ is computed that contains one more possible world than the number of distinct lower bounds in Σ. Processing the bounds in Σ from smallest p_1 to largest p_n, the algorithm computes as possible world with probability $p_i - p_{i-1}$ a traditional Armstrong relation for the p_i-cut Σ_{p_i}. For this purpose, the anti-keys are computed for each p_i-cut, and the set W of those worlds i is recorded for which X is an anti-key with respect to Σ_{p_i}. The CD-table contains one tuple t_0

which occurs in all worlds, and for each anti-key X another tuple t_j that occurs in all worlds for which X is an anti-key and that has matching values with t_0 in exactly the columns of X.

For example, applying this construction to the lower bounds of p-keys in Fig. 2 produces the PC-table on the left of Table 2. Indeed, let Σ consist of $k\{rfid, time\}_{\geq.75}$, $k\{rfid, zone\}_{\geq.35}$, and $k\{time, zone\}_{\geq.65}$. Then $\Sigma_{.35}$ consists of $k\{rfid, time\}$, $k\{rfid, zone\}$, and $k\{time, zone\}$; $\Sigma_{.65}$ consists of $k\{rfid, time\}$, and $k\{time, zone\}$; $\Sigma_{.75}$ consists of $k\{rfid, time\}$; and Σ_1 is empty. The world W_1 has thus probability $p_1 = 0.35$, and is an Armstrong relation for $\Sigma_{0.35}$. Here, we have the three singleton anti-keys $\{rfid\}$, $\{time\}$, and $\{zone\}$. W_1 has four tuples, the first and second tuple have matching values on $\{rfid\}$, the first and third tuple have matching values on $\{zone\}$, and the first and fourth tuple have matching values on $\{time\}$. This gives us the Armstrong relation W_1 of r_1 shown in Table 1. The world W_2 has probability $p_2 = 0.3$, and is an Armstrong relation for $\Sigma_{0.65}$. Here, we have the two anti-keys $\{time\}$ and $\{rfid, zone\}$. The world W_3 has probability $p_3 = 0.1$, and is an Armstrong relation for $\Sigma_{0.75}$. Here, we have the two anti-keys $\{rfid, zone\}$ and $\{time, zone\}$. Finally, W_4 has probability $p_4 = 0.25$, and is an Armstrong relation for Σ_1. Here, we have the three anti-keys $\{rfid, zone\}$, $\{time, zone\}$, and $\{rfid, time\}$. Similar to W_1 it is easy to see how W_2, W_3, and W_4 of r_1 in Table 1 constitute the corresponding Armstrong relations. Finally, we simply record the identifiers of those worlds in which a tuple appears to obtain the CD-table. This results in the CD-table shown in Table 2.

The outlined algorithm can also compute an Armstrong PC-table for every satisfiable set Σ of u-keys. The reason is that the algorithm is independent of whether we view the given probabilities as lower or upper bounds. The only necessary change concerns the definition of Σ_p which becomes $\Sigma_p = \{kX : \exists kX_{\leq q} \in \Sigma \wedge q \geq p\}$ in this case. For example, applying this construction to the upper bounds of p-keys in Fig. 2 results in the PC-table on the right of Table 2.

The use of this algorithm can be taken further when we consider Theorem 3, which states that u-keys and l-keys do not interact in satisfiable sets. This means, given a satisfiable set Σ of p-keys, we can compute an Armstrong PC-base for Σ by applying Algorithm 2 of [3] to compute an Armstrong PC-table for the set Σ_l, and by applying Algorithm 2 of [3] to compute an Armstrong PC-table for the set Σ_u. Indeed, we obtain an Armstrong PC-base for Σ by simply pairing the outputs of both applications together.

Theorem 4. *For every satisfiable set Σ of p-keys over relation schema R, applications of Algorithm 2 in [3] to Σ_l and Σ_u, respectively, result in an Armstrong PC-base for Σ in which the total number of possible worlds coincides with the sum of the distinct non-zero lower bounds in Σ'_l and the distinct non-zero upper bounds in Σ'_u. Here, Σ'_l (Σ'_u) denotes Σ_l (Σ_u) if there is some $X \subseteq R$ such that $kX_{\geq 1} \in \Sigma_l$ ($kX_{\leq 1} \in \Sigma_u$), and $\Sigma_l \cup \{kR_{\geq 1}\}$ ($\Sigma_u \cup \{kR_{\leq 1}\}$) otherwise.* □

The PC-tables of Table 2 form an Armstrong PC-base for the set Σ of p-keys in Fig. 2. Indeed, the number of possible worlds in both PC-tables is 4, which

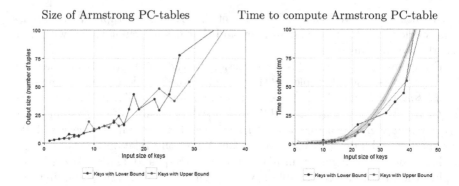

Fig. 4. Results of experiments with visualization

is the number of distinct non-zero lower bounds in Σ and also the number of distinct non-zero upper bounds in Σ. Finally, we derive some bounds on the time complexity of finding Armstrong PC-tables. Additional insight is given by our experiments in Sect. 6.

Theorem 5. *The time complexity to find an Armstrong PC-base for a given set* Σ *of p-keys over relation schema R is precisely exponential in* $|\Sigma|$.

Here, precisely exponential means that there is an algorithm which requires exponential time and that there are cases in which the number of tuples in the output is exponential in the input size. Nevertheless, there are also cases where the number of tuples in some Armstrong PC-base for Σ over R is logarithmic in $|\Sigma|$. Such a case is given by $R_n = \{A_1, \ldots, A_{2n}\}$ and $\Sigma_n = \{k(X_1 \cdots X_n) \in (1,1) : X_i \in \{A_{2i-1}, A_{2i}\}$ for $i = 1, \ldots, n\}$ with $|\Sigma_n| = n \cdot 2^n$.

5.2 Discovery of P-Keys from Collections of PC-tables

The discovery problem of p-keys from a collection of PC-tables over a relation schema R is to determine for all $X \subset R$, the smallest marginal probability $l_{X,r}$ and the largest marginal probability $u_{X,r}$ of kX across all given p-relations $r = (\mathcal{W}, P)$ represented by some given PC-table. The problem of computing the marginal probability $m_{X,r}$ can be solved as follows: For each $X \subset R$, initialize $m_{X,r} \leftarrow 0$ and for all worlds $W \in \mathcal{W}$, add the probability p_W of W to $m_{X,r}$, if X contains some minimal key of W. The set of minimal keys of a world W is given by the set of minimal transversals over the disagree sets of W (the complements of agree sets) [21]. For example, applying this algorithm to the PC-tables from Table 2 returns the p-keys shown in Fig. 2.

6   Experiments

In this section we report on some experiments regarding the computational complexity of our algorithms for the summarization and discovery of p-keys.

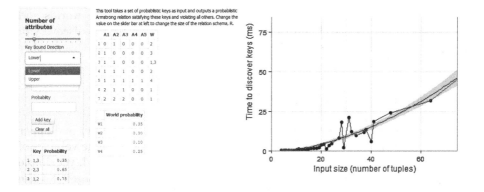

Fig. 5. GUI for summarization and times for discovering p-keys

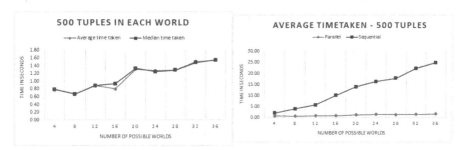

Fig. 6. Results on "Car" data set for MapReduce implementation

Summarization. While the worst-case time complexity of generating Armstrong PC-tables is exponential, these cases occur rarely in practice and at random. In our experiment we simulated average case behavior by generating sets of keys with upper/lower bounds. For each key, the set of attributes, the associated probability, and the type (either upper or lower) were randomly selected. First, we checked whether the created set of p-keys was satisfiable. If it was, one Armstrong PC-table was computed for the set of keys with upper bounds and one for the set of keys with lower bounds. Overall, 24 % of the p-key sets created were unsatisfiable. The average sizes and times to create the Armstrong PC-tables are shown in Fig. 4. The results demonstrate that Armstrong PC-bases exhibit small sizes on average, which makes them a practical tool to acquire keys with meaningful probabilistic intervals in a joint effort with domain experts. A screenshot of our graphical user interface is shown on the left of Fig. 5.

Discovery. The right of Fig. 5 shows the discovery times of p-keys from two given PC-tables. The input size is the total number of tuples in the input. We also applied a MapReduce implementation on a single node machine with 40 processors to the "Car" data set[1] of the UCI Machine Learning Repository. We

---

[1] http://archive.ics.uci.edu/ml/datasets/Car+Evaluation.

converted "Car" into a p-relation with rising numbers of possible worlds and 500 tuples in each world. Figure 6 shows that our algorithm for the discovery of p-keys scales linearly in the number of possible worlds, considering this number is relatively low in our acquisition framework.

7   Conclusion and Future Work

We introduced keys with probabilistic intervals, which stipulate lower and upper bounds on the marginal probability by which keys shall hold on large volumes of uncertain data. Keys with probabilistic intervals provide a principled, yet simple enough mechanism to control the consistency and completeness targets for the quality of an organization's uncertain data. Similar to how lower bounds say that a key is satisfied with some minimum probability, upper bounds provide us with means to say that a key is violated with a minimum probability. Our axiomatic and algorithmic reasoning tools minimize the overhead in using the keys for data quality management and query processing. Our findings for the visualization and discovery of these keys provide effective support for the efficient acquisition of the right probabilistic intervals that apply in a given application domain.

In future research we will apply our algorithms to investigate empirically the usefulness of our framework for acquiring the right probabilistic intervals of keys in a given application domain. This will require us to extend empirical measures from certain [17] to probabilistic data. Particularly intriguing is the question whether PC-bases or their p-relations are more useful. It is also interesting to investigate probabilistic variants of other useful constraint sets, such as functional, multivalued, and inclusion dependencies [7,8,10,13,14,18,19]. However, we have shown that such variants are not finitely axiomatizable. In this sense, our results for p-keys are rather special. An extension that seems feasible is to add lower bounds to the probabilistic cardinality constraints from [22].

References

1. Abedjan, Z., Golab, L., Naumann, F.: Profiling relational data: a survey. VLDB J. **24**(4), 557–581 (2015)
2. Beeri, C., Dowd, M., Fagin, R., Statman, R.: On the structure of Armstrong relations for functional dependencies. J. ACM **31**(1), 30–46 (1984)
3. Brown, P., Link, S.: Probabilistic keys for data quality management. In: Zdravkovic, J., Kirikova, M., Johannesson, P. (eds.) CAiSE 2015. LNCS, vol. 9097, pp. 118–132. Springer, Heidelberg (2015). doi:10.1007/978-3-319-19069-3_8
4. Caruccio, L., Deufemia, V., Polese, G.: Relaxed functional dependencies - a survey of approaches. IEEE Trans. Knowl. Data Eng. **28**(1), 147–165 (2016)
5. Fagin, R.: Horn clauses and database dependencies. J. ACM **29**(4), 952–985 (1982)
6. Hannula, M., Kontinen, J., Link, S.: On the finite and general implication problems of independence atoms and keys. J. Comput. Syst. Sci. **82**(5), 856–877 (2016)
7. Hartmann, S., Link, S.: Multi-valued dependencies in the presence of lists. In: Beeri, C., Deutsch, A. (eds.) Proceedings of the Twenty-third ACM SIGACT-SIGMOD-SIGART Symposium on Principles of Database Systems, Paris, France, 14–16 June 2004, pp. 330–341. ACM (2004)

8. Hartmann, S., Link, S.: On a problem of Fagin concerning multivalued dependencies in relational databases. Theor. Comput. Sci. **353**(1–3), 53–62 (2006)

9. Hartmann, S., Link, S.: Efficient reasoning about a robust XML key fragment. ACM Trans. Database Syst. **34**(2) (2009). Article No.10

10. Hartmann, S., Link, S., Schewe, K.: Functional and multivalued dependencies in nested databases generated by record and list constructor. Ann. Math. Artif. Intell. **46**(1–2), 114–164 (2006)

11. Koehler, H., Leck, U., Link, S., Prade, H.: Logical foundations of possibilistic keys. In: Fermé, E., Leite, J. (eds.) JELIA 2014. LNCS, vol. 8761, pp. 181–195. Springer, Heidelberg (2014). doi:10.1007/978-3-319-11558-0_13

12. Köhler, H., Leck, U., Link, S., Zhou, X.: Possible and certain keys for SQL. VLDB J. **25**(4), 571–596 (2016)

13. Köhler, H., Link, S.: Inclusion dependencies reloaded. In: Bailey, J., Moffat, A., Aggarwal, C.C., de Rijke, M., Kumar, R., Murdock, V., Sellis, T.K., Yu, J.X. (eds.) Proceedings of the 24th ACM International on Conference on Information and Knowledge Management, CIKM 2015, Melbourne, VIC, Australia, 19–23 October 2015, pp. 1361–1370. ACM (2015)

14. Köhler, H., Link, S.: SQL schema design: foundations, normal forms, and normalization. In: Özcan, F., Koutrika, G., Madden, S. (eds.) Proceedings of the 2016 International Conference on Management of Data, SIGMOD Conference 2016, San Francisco, CA, USA, 26 June–01 July 2016, pp. 267–279. ACM (2016)

15. Köhler, H., Link, S., Zhou, X.: Possible and certain SQL keys. PVLDB **8**(11), 1118–1129 (2015)

16. Köhler, H., Link, S., Zhou, X.: Discovering meaningful certain keys from incomplete and inconsistent relations. IEEE Data Eng. Bull. **39**(2), 21–37 (2016)

17. Langeveldt, W., Link, S.: Empirical evidence for the usefulness of Armstrong relations in the acquisition of meaningful functional dependencies. Inf. Syst. **35**(3), 352–374 (2010)

18. Link, S.: Charting the completeness frontier of inference systems for multivalued dependencies. Acta Inf. **45**(7–8), 565–591 (2008)

19. Link, S.: Characterisations of multivalued dependency implication over undetermined universes. J. Comput. Syst. Sci. **78**(4), 1026–1044 (2012)

20. Liu, J., Li, J., Liu, C., Chen, Y.: Discover dependencies from data - a review. IEEE Trans. Knowl. Data Eng. **24**(2), 251–264 (2012)

21. Mannila, H., Räihä, K.J.: Algorithms for inferring functional dependencies from relations. Data Knowl. Eng. **12**(1), 83–99 (1994)

22. Roblot, T., Link, S.: Probabilistic cardinality constraints. In: Johannesson, P., Lee, M.L., Liddle, S.W., Opdahl, A.L., López, Ó.P. (eds.) ER 2015. LNCS, vol. 9381, pp. 214–228. Springer, Heidelberg (2015). doi:10.1007/978-3-319-25264-3_16

23. Sadiq, S. (ed.): Handbook of Data Quality. Springer, Heidelberg (2013)

24. Suciu, D., Olteanu, D., Ré, C., Koch, C.: Probabilistic Databases. Synthesis Lectures on Data Management. Morgan & Claypool Publishers, San Rafael (2011)

25. Thalheim, B.: On semantic issues connected with keys in relational databases permitting null values. Elektronische Informationsverarbeitung und Kybernetik **25**(1/2), 11–20 (1989)

26. Toman, D., Weddell, G.E.: On keys and functional dependencies as first-class citizens in description logics. J. Autom. Reasoning **40**(2–3), 117–132 (2008)

Advanced Conceptual Modeling

On Referring Expressions in Information Systems Derived from Conceptual Modelling

Alexander Borgida[1], David Toman[2(✉)], and Grant Weddell[2]

[1] Department of Computer Science, Rutgers University, New Brunswick, USA
borgida@cs.rutgers.edu
[2] Cheriton School of Computer Science, University of Waterloo, Waterloo, Canada
{david,gweddell}@uwaterloo.ca

Abstract. We apply recent work on referring expression types to the issue of identification in Conceptual Modelling. In particular, we consider how such types yield a separation of concerns in a setting where an Information System based on a conceptual schema is to be mapped to a relational schema plus SQL queries. We start from a simple object-centered representation (as in semantic data models), where naming is not an issue because everything is self-identified (possibly using surrogates). We then allow the analyst to attach to every class a preferred "referring expression type", and to specify uniqueness constraints in the form of generalized functional dependencies. We show (1) how a number of well-formedness conditions concerning an assignment of referring expressions can be efficiently diagnosed, and (2) how the above types attached to classes allow a concrete relational schema and SQL queries over it to be derived from a combination of the conceptual schema and queries over it.

1 Introduction

The Entity Relationship notation, and its many extensions, were designed with the explicit purpose of helping to derive relational database schemata from the conceptual model. One feature of the relational model, namely that attribute fillers are values such as strings and integers, means that relationships between entities need to be represented as relationships between their "names" (primary keys), and therefore all entities need to have primary keys. This resulted in (E)ER modelers having to *pay premature attention to naming issues*. For example:

(a) One cannot create tables representing relationships before one has decided on how entities are going to be externally named.
(b) One needs to distinguish right from the beginning "weak entity sets", like ROOM, with attributes room-num and capacity, which are insufficient to act as an external key, from regular entity sets like BUILDING, with attribute address that can identify it. This is necessary even though no deep ontological factors distinguish ROOM and BUILDING.
(c) If entity set PERSON is identified by ssn, and it has subclass FAMOUS-PERSON, then the latter must inherit its identifier from the superclass. This, despite

© Springer International Publishing AG 2016
I. Comyn-Wattiau et al. (Eds.): ER 2016, LNCS 9974, pp. 183–197, 2016.
DOI: 10.1007/978-3-319-46397-1_14

the fact that we might prefer as identifier the attribute `name` for `FAMOUS-PERSON`; or maybe even add `star-name`, which is only applicable to `FAMOUS-PERSON`.

(d) Certain entity sets are introduced by *generalization* as the union of heterogeneous sub-classes; for example, `LEGAL-ENTITY` is the generalization of `PERSON` and `COMPANY`, for the purpose of acting as participant in relationships such as `owns`. In such cases, one is forced to create an artificial attribute, (e.g., `legal-entity-number`), which replaces the natural keys of `PERSON` (e.g., `ssn`) and `COMPANY` (e.g., `corp-name` and `city`). Since `legal-entity-number` is meaningless to end users, programmers must always remember to perform joins so as to include the usual keys of the subclasses, depending on the individuals returned.

We thank a reviewer for pointing out that Halpin [4] has been investigating, independently, the modeling of reference schemes in languages such as ORM, UML, Barker ER, and OWL, using a plethora of examples. The problems he considers, including so-called compound, disjunctive and context-dependent reference schemes, overlap considerably with the above list. In Sect. 5, we point out which examples our proposed solutions cannot handle.

Returning to issues (a) and (b), note that they do not arise when using an object-centered modelling notation supporting object identity, such as most semantic data models since Taxis [6], because relationships are stated between objects themselves. Our essential starting point is that one can therefore postpone the naming issue to a separate pass. Unfortunately, problems (c) and (d) persist, and naming of weak entities must eventually be handled. We propose a multi-part approach to address these. The following outlines the remainder of the paper and how our results provide a basis for this approach:[1]

(1) After this enumeration, we introduce by example a simple conceptual model, $\mathcal{C}$, that has the common features of so-called "attribute-based" semantic models, such as those surveyed in Table 12 of [5]. The model is based on the familiar object-centered view of the world consisting of individual objects, with attributes that can have as values either other objects or atomic values, such as SQL datatypes. The objects are grouped into classes, satisfying a variety of constraints, such as subclass hierarchies, disjointness, coverage, and a general form of functional dependency. As we hope to illustrate below, $\mathcal{C}$ can serve as a lingua franca for standard conceptual models such as EER, UML class diagrams, DL-Lite ontologies, and so on. The important point is that $\mathcal{C}$ does this without the need to decide external referring expressions for objects. In Sect. 2, we provide a slight syntactic variant, $\mathcal{C}_{AR}$, of $\mathcal{C}$, which gives it more of a relational flavor by making internal object identifiers visible as "abstract" attribute values.

---

[1] The outline is followed by a sequence of examples that illustrate intuitively the entire process. The remainder of the paper is a somewhat more formal development of the ideas.

(2) As with all object-centered conceptual models, one can describe data access using arbitrary SQL-like queries over $\mathcal{C}$, and especially $\mathcal{C}_{AR}$ schemas, using variables that range over extents of classes. In Sect. 2, we also introduce SQL^{path}, a core of SQL in which it is also possible to employ "dotted path notation" (e.g., x.manager.salary) to avoid explicit foreign key joins, and hence make queries shorter[2].

(3) In a separate, orthogonal pass, modellers specify (*i*) functional dependency-like constraints that include keys, and (*ii*) a preferred naming scheme for each class by associating with it a *referring expression type* specified in a language introduced in Sect. 3. The notation makes it possible to address situations like (b), (c) and (d) above.

(4) Given a $\mathcal{C}_{AR}$ schema, a referring expresion type assignment, and a set of SQL^{path} queries, algorithms can be given to perform several key tasks:

   – In Sect. 3, we show how to verify that the referring expression naming schemes in (3) above do indeed uniquely identify objects in tables and queries.
   – In Sect. 4, we how show how the referring expresion types in (3) guide the replacement of abstract attributes in a $\mathcal{C}$ schema with sequences of concrete attributes, thus obtaining a concrete relational schema.
   – In Sect. 4, we also show how to translate any SQL^{path} query into *a provably equivalent* regular SQL query over the concrete relational schema, thereby eliminating all path expressions as well as non-printable object ids that might have been returned by the query.

Let us illustrate the above using a situation where legal entities, which are either persons or companies, can own vehicles (one owner per vehicle), while persons can drive vehicles. A conceptual schema expressed in $\mathcal{C}$ might be given as follows:[3]

```
class PERSON (ssn: INT, name: STRING, isa LEGAL-ENTITY,
    disjoint with VEHICLE)
class COMPANY (corp-name: STRING, city: STRING, isa LEGAL-ENTITY)
class LEGAL-ENTITY (covered by PERSON, COMPANY)
class VEHICLE (vin: INT, make: STRING, owned-by: LEGAL-ENTITY)
class CAN-DRIVE (driver: PERSON, driven: VEHICLE)
```

Given this schema, a modeller will then be able to express the following queries in SQL^{path}:

– *The name of anyone who can drive a vehicle made by Ford*:

```
select d.driver.name from CAN-DRIVE d
where d.driven.make ='Ford'
```

– *The owners of GM vehicles*:

```
select v.owned-by from VEHICLE where v.make ='GM'
```

---

[2] This and other features of $\mathcal{C}$ were already available in Taxis [6] and GEM [9].

[3] We explain the correspondence to a $\mathcal{C}_{AR}$ schema in the next section.

Note that as it stands, the second query does not specify how the (hetero-geneous) owners, which share no common concrete attributes that can identify them, will be described in the final answer.

Concurrently with writing queries, modellers can address external naming preferences. Note that this might require adding (or discovering) functional dependencies from which one can derive key/uniqueness information. The nam-ing process might start by stating that ssn is a key for PERSON, and that the combination of attributes (corp-name,city) is a key for COMPANY; and then asso-ciating referring expresion types "ssn=?" to class PERSON, and "(corp-name=?, city=?)" to class COMPANY, making these key values the references. (Note that PERSON might have had other keys.) A referring expresion type for LEGAL-ENTITY objects might be given as follows:

$$\text{PERSON} \rightarrow \text{ssn=?; COMPANY} \rightarrow \text{(corp-name=?, city=?)}$$

Were it possible for an object to be both a person and a company, the use of ";" expresses a *preference* for using ssn attribute values for identifying the object.

Once it has been verified that this assignment of referring expresion types is *well-formed* in the sense that it resolves all identification issues (see Sect. 3), it then becomes possible to automatically map the schema originally given by mod-ellers to a concrete relational schema with additional primary key attributes and with "object pointer" attributes replaced by (sequences of) concrete attributes. In turn, SQL^{path} queries are similarly translated to executable SQL queries over this schema (see Sect. 4). To illustrate, the following are (parts of) the concrete tables that would be produced for PERSON, LEGAL-ENTITY and VEHICLE:

```
table PERSON (ssn INT, name STRING, primary key (ssn),...)
table LEGAL-ENTITY (disc enum{'PERSON','COMPANY'}, ssn INT,
    corp-name STRING, city STRING, primary key (disc,ssn,corp-name,city))
table VEHICLE (vin, make, owner-disc,owner-ssn,owner-co-name,owner-city,
    foreign key (owner-disc, owner-ssn, owner-corp-name, owner-city)
    references LEGAL-ENTITY (disc, ssn, corp-name, city) )
```

Note how identification for LEGAL-ENTITY objects is ultimately resolved: four attributes are added, with attribute disc acting as a discriminant in variant records. (We assume inapplicable attributes are always initialized with default non-null values.) To illustrate how SQL^{path} queries are mapped, consider the second example query above; it maps to the following executable query:

```
select v.disc, v.ssn, v.corp-name, v.city from VEHICLE v
where v.make ='GM'.
```

2   Abstract Relational Databases

We now introduce $\mathcal{C}_{AR}$, a minor variant of the modeling language used in Sect. 1 examples. Essentially, it makes object identifiers *user visible*, in order to bring data declaration and manipulation syntax closer to SQL, which is more familiar to application programmers.

Definition 1 ($\mathcal{C}_{AR}$: A more relational but still abstract view of $\mathcal{C}$).
Let TAB, AT, and CD be sets of table names, attribute names, and *concrete domains* (data types), respectively, and let OID be an *abstract domain* of *identifiers/surrogates*, disjoint from all concrete domains. A $\mathcal{C}_{AR}$ schema Σ is a set of *abstract table declarations* of the form

$$\text{table } T \text{ (self OID, } A_1\ D_1,\ \ldots,\ A_k\ D_k,\ \varphi_1, \ldots, \varphi_\ell)$$

where $T \in$ TAB, self $\in$ AT is the *primary key* of T (self is a *distinguished attribute* identifying the aggregation $(A_1, \ldots, A_k \in$ AT$))$; $D_i \in$ CD $\cup \{$OID$\}$, and φ_j are *constraints* attached to the abstract table T (see below). $\qquad\square$

To illustrate, we begin translating class PERSON into $\mathcal{C}_{AR}$ as follows:

$$\text{table PERSON(self OID, ssn INT, name STRING, } \ldots$$

Note the occurrence of attribute self — the user visible object identifier. There are five kinds of constraints relevant to identification issues, and which we use in our examples:[4]

1. *(foreign keys)* foreign key A references T
2. *(specialization)* isa T
3. *(cover constraints)* covered by $\{T_1, \ldots, T_m\}$
4. *(disjointness constraints)* disjoint with T
5. *(path functional dependencies)* pathfd $\mathsf{Pf}_1, \ldots, \mathsf{Pf}_n \to \mathsf{Pf}$

Continuing with the translation of class PERSON to $\mathcal{C}_{AR}$, we add three constraints:

$$\ldots \text{isa LEGAL-ENTITY, disjoint with COMPANY, pathfd ssn} \to \text{self)}.$$

The first two constraints assert that self values of PERSON tuples are a subset of self values of LEGAL-ENTITY tuples, and are disjoint from self values of COMPANY tuples; the third asserts that any pair of PERSON tuples agreeing on ssn also agree on self (i.e., ssn is a key for PERSON). In fact, pathfds are more general and powerful: one can declare

```
table OFFICE( self OID, office-num INT, located-in OID,
    foreign key (located-in) references BUILDING,
    pathfd office-numb, located-in.address → self )
```

once one specifies that buildings have addresses. This says that (i) each value of located-in must appear as the self value of a BUILDING tuple, and (ii) the office number and the address of the office's building form a key for offices. The latter addresses the issue (b) of weak entity identification, using the power of *attribute paths*, located-in.address in this case. (For a formal definition of paths, please see [2].)

---

[4] To adhere to SQL'99 syntax, a formulation using a general assertion would be needed in most cases. For formal definitions of constraints, please see [2].

We call attributes ranging over $D_i \in$ CD *concrete*, since their values are atomic, such as the INTegers, and the remaining attributes *abstract*. Also, without loss of generality, we assume that every attribute A_i, other than self, is included in the declaration of at most one abstract table, and write Home(A_i) to refer to this table. If A_i is abstract, we assume there is a "first" foreign key constraint for A_i to some abstract table, referred to as Dom(A_i). Thus, Home(ssn) = PERSON and Dom(located-in) = BUILDING in the above.

For a table T in schema Σ, we write $\Sigma \models (\varphi \in T)$ to denote the fact that a particular constraint φ for T (possibly not explicitly stated) *logically follows* from the constraints in schema Σ. For example, the above declaration of PERSON logically entails that "(pathfd ssn, name → self)" also holds for PERSON. And if $\{T_1, T_2\}$ cover T, then so does $\{T_1, T_2, S\}$ for any S.

The problem of deciding when $\Sigma \models (\varphi \in T)$ holds can be reduced to reasoning about logical consequence in the *description logic* $\mathcal{DLFD}$ [7], which is decidable. If no cover constraints occur in Σ, it also becomes possible to reduce such questions to reasoning about logical consequence in the description logic $\mathcal{CFDI}_{nc}^{\forall-}$ [8], which is decidable in PTIME. (Details are beyond the scope of this paper.)

We introduce next a core relational algebra fragment of SQL that incorporates attribute paths:

Definition 2 (SQL^{path}). The following grammar gives the syntax for (an idealized) SQL-like query language over instances of $\mathcal{C}$ schema:

$$
\begin{aligned}
Q ::=\ & T\ x & & \textit{(table reference)} \\
 |\ & \texttt{select } x_1.\mathsf{Pf}_1, \ldots, x_k.\mathsf{Pf}_k\ Q & & \textit{(projection)} \\
 |\ & \texttt{from } Q, Q & & \textit{(product)} \\
 |\ & Q \texttt{ where } x.\mathsf{Pf}_1 = y.\mathsf{Pf}_2 & & \textit{(selection)} \\
 |\ & Q \texttt{ union } Q & & \textit{(union)} \\
 |\ & Q \texttt{ minus } Q & & \textit{(set difference)}
\end{aligned}
$$

As in SQL, we require that all variables are appropriately *bound* with a "$T\ x$" clause, and denote T by Bound(x); that Pf is well defined for Bound(x) for any term "$x.\mathsf{Pf}$"; that variables in subqueries of the from clause are disjoint; and that the subqueries in the union and minus operations are *union compatible*. We also assume the standard SQL-like interpretation of the above syntax.   □

In summary, SQL^{path} deviates from standard SQL in three ways:

1. In addition to *standard atomic datatypes*, we have introduced an abstract domain OID (which then allows abstract attributes, and the ability to refer directly to abstract identifiers with expressions of the form "$x.A$").
2. We allow the use of attribute paths in place of single attributes in where conditions.
3. We allow "$T\ x$" as a query (where SQL would require "select * from $T\ x$").

We also allow obvious syntactic sugar to make examples more readable, such as using conjunction in the where clauses, and multi-arity from clauses instead of the nested use of from.

Less obviously, terms of the form "$x_1.\mathsf{Pf}.A$" occurring in `select` and `where` clauses can ultimately be replaced by terms of the form "$x_2.A$" by repeatedly applying straightforward rewritings. (More details are given in [2].) For example, applying such rewritings to our introductory query

```
select d.driver.name from CAN-DRIVE d
where d.driven.make ='Ford'
```

would ultimately produce the query

$$\begin{array}{l}\texttt{select p.name from CAN-DRIVE d, PERSON p, VEHICLE v}\\ \texttt{where v.make ='Ford' and d.driven = v.self and d.driver = p.self.}\end{array} \quad (1)$$

Note that this requires confirming, among others, that

$$\Sigma \models ((\texttt{foreign key (driven) references VEHICLE}) \in \texttt{CAN-DRIVE})$$

and that `make` is an attribute of `VEHICLE`.

3 Managing Identity

By introducing the purely abstract domain `OID`, $\mathcal{C}_{\mathrm{AR}}$ frees the user from any need to address identification issues when formulating queries. This enables our main contribution: a separation of concerns in which identification issues can be addressed concurrently with the formulation of data access requirements. But unlike various *object models*, the values of attributes over this domain are *purely abstract* and *are not storable* in concrete table instances.

We now show how these issues can be resolved by using the *referring expression type language* proposed in [1]. Intuitively, a type in this language defines a space of first-order formulas free in one variable, x. The objective is for each formula to be true for *exactly one* object in `OID` in every abstract schema instance that satisfies all schema constraints. The language is given in the following:

Definition 3 (Referring Expressions, Types, and Assignments). Let Σ be a $\mathcal{C}_{\mathrm{AR}}$ schema. A *referring expression type Rt relative to* Σ is an instance of a recursive *pattern* language given by the grammar:

$$Rt \quad ::= \quad \mathsf{Pf} = ? \quad | \quad Rt, Rt \quad | \quad G \to Rt \quad | \quad Rt; Rt$$

where Pf is an attribute path ending in a concrete attribute, and where $G = \{T_1, \ldots, T_\ell\}$ is a set of table names from Tables(Σ), called a *guard*. We write $\mathrm{RE}(Rt)$ to refer to a set of *referring expressions* ϕ_i induced by a given referring expression type Rt relative to Σ as follows:

$$\begin{array}{l}\mathrm{RE}(\mathsf{Pf} = ?) = \{x.\mathsf{Pf} = a \mid a \text{ a constant}\}\\ \mathrm{RE}(Rt_1, Rt_2) = \{\phi_1 \wedge \phi_2 \mid \phi_i \in \mathrm{RE}(Rt_i)\}\\ \mathrm{RE}(\{T_1, \ldots, T_k\} \to Rt) = \{\bigwedge_{i=1}^{k}(\exists y_1, \ldots, y_l.T_i(x, y_1, \ldots, y_l)) \wedge \phi \mid \phi \in \mathrm{RE}(Rt)\}\\ \mathrm{RE}(Rt_1; Rt_2) = \mathrm{RE}(Rt_1) \cup \{\phi \in \mathrm{RE}(Rt_2) \mid \neg\exists\psi \in \mathrm{RE}(Rt_1).(\phi \equiv \psi)\}\end{array}$$

Given $T \in \mathsf{Tables}(\Sigma)$, we say that Rt is *strongly identifying* for T if, for all instances I of Σ,

$$I \models \forall x_1, x_2.(\exists y_1, \ldots, y_l.T(x_1, y_1, \ldots, y_l) \wedge \phi(x/x_1)) \wedge$$
$$(\exists y_1, \ldots, y_l.T(x_2, y_1, \ldots, y_l) \wedge \phi(x/x_2)) \rightarrow x_1 = x_2,$$

holds for all $\phi \in \mathrm{RE}(Rt)$, and

$$I \models \neg\exists x.(\phi_1 \wedge \phi_2)$$

holds for all syntactically distinct $\phi_1, \phi_2 \in \mathrm{RE}(Rt)$. A *referring type assignment* for Σ is a mapping RTA from $\mathsf{Tables}(\Sigma)$ to referring expresion types relative to Σ.   □

For example, RTA might assign either "`ssn=?`" or "`name=?`" as the referring expresion type for `PERSON`. Intuitively, the former would qualify as strongly identifying, but the latter would not, since two people can have the same name.

In [1], it is also shown that any Rt can be converted to a normal form with the following structure:

$$G_1 \rightarrow (\mathsf{Pf}_{1,1} = ?, \ldots, \mathsf{Pf}_{1,k_1} = ?); \ldots; G_k \rightarrow (\mathsf{Pf}_{k,1} = ?, \ldots, \mathsf{Pf}_{k,k_k} = ?).$$

We call each subexpression separated by ";" a *component* of Rt. For the remainder of the paper, we assume $\mathsf{RTA}(T)$ is already in this form, and, that each guard G_i contains at most one table name.[5] To improve readability, we omit mention of empty guards, and write T as shorthand for guard $\{T\}$. Finally, we write $\mathsf{Fix}(Rt, T)$ to denote a normal form Rt with T added to any empty guard. Thus, $\mathsf{Fix}(Rt, T)$ will have the form

$$T_1 \rightarrow (\mathsf{Pf}_{1,1} = ?, \ldots, \mathsf{Pf}_{1,k_1} = ?); \ldots; T_k \rightarrow (\mathsf{Pf}_{k,1} = ?, \ldots, \mathsf{Pf}_{k,k_k} = ?). \quad (2)$$

The next definition deals with situations illustrated by the case when $\mathsf{RTA}(\texttt{PERSON})$ is "`PERSON` → `ssn=?; name=?`". Here, "`name=?`" will be ignored since the guard of the first component has precedence, and will "catch" any `PERSON`.

Definition 4 (Non-redundant Referring Types). Let Σ be a $\mathcal{C}_{\mathrm{AR}}$ schema, RTA a referring type assignment, $T \in \mathsf{Tables}(\Sigma)$, and assume $\mathsf{Fix}(\mathsf{RTA}(T), T)$ has the form (2). We say that the jth component "$T_j \rightarrow (\mathsf{Pf}_{j,1} = ?, \ldots, \mathsf{Pf}_{j,k_j} = ?)$" is *redundant with respect to* T if it satisfies any of the following conditions:

$$(a) \ \Sigma \models ((\texttt{covered by } \{T_1, \ldots, T_{j-1}\}) \in T_j),$$
$$(b) \ \Sigma \models ((\texttt{covered by } \{T_1, \ldots, T_{j-1}\}) \in T), \text{ or}$$
$$(c) \ \Sigma \models ((\texttt{disjoint with } T_j) \in T).$$

Given an arbitrary Rt in normal form, we write $\mathsf{Prune}(Rt, T)$ to denote the referring expression $\mathsf{Fix}(Rt, T)$ from which all components redundant with respect to T have been removed.   □

---

[5] Allowing guards to have more than one table name is a straightforward extension.

The following example illustrates another potential problem with a given RTA: that not all possible referring type assignments can support synthesizing arbitrary concrete SQL queries:

Example 5. Consider the SQL^{path} query

$$\texttt{select } x.\texttt{self from } T_1 \; x, T_2 \; y \texttt{ where } x.\texttt{self} = y.\texttt{self} \qquad (3)$$

over a $\mathcal{C}_{\mathrm{AR}}$ schema Σ in which T_i is declared as follows:

$$\texttt{create } T_i \; (\texttt{self OID}, A_i \texttt{ STRING, pathfd } A_i \rightarrow \texttt{self}). \qquad (4)$$

When $\mathrm{RTA}(T_i)$ is given by "$A_i = ?$", the ability to compare the OID values is lost since the referring expressions associated with T_1 and T_2 do not provide a way to determine if the same object belongs to both tables. The problem is solved, e.g., by instead defining $\mathrm{RTA}(T_2)$ as "$T_1 \rightarrow A_1 = ?; A_2 = ?$" since T_2 objects are then *identified* by A_1 values when also in T_1. $\qquad \Box$

All such mapping issues are avoided when a referring expression type assignment is *identity resolving*, which can be defined as follows:

Definition 6 (Identity Resolving Type Assignments). Let Σ be a $\mathcal{C}_{\mathrm{AR}}$ schema and RTA a referring type assignment for Σ. Given a linear order $\mathcal{O} = (T_{i_1}, \ldots, T_{i_k})$ on the set $\mathsf{Tables}(\Sigma)$, define $\mathcal{O}(\mathsf{RTA})$ as the following referring expression type:

$$\mathsf{Fix}(\mathsf{RTA}(T_{i_1}), T_{i_1}); \ldots; \mathsf{Fix}(\mathsf{RTA}(T_{i_k}), T_{i_k}).$$

We say that RTA is *identity resolving* if there is some linear order $\mathcal{O}$ such that the following conditions hold for each $T \in \mathsf{Tables}(\Sigma)$:

1. $\mathsf{Fix}(\mathsf{RTA}(T), T) = \mathsf{Prune}(\mathcal{O}(\mathsf{RTA}), T)$,
2. $\Sigma \models ((\texttt{covered by } \{T_1, \ldots, T_n\}) \in T)$, where $\{T_1, \ldots, T_n\}$ are all tables occurring in the guards in $\mathsf{Fix}(\mathsf{RTA}(T), T)$, and
3. for each component $T_j \rightarrow (\mathsf{Pf}_{j,1} = ?, \ldots, \mathsf{Pf}_{j,k_j} = ?)$ of $\mathsf{Fix}(\mathsf{RTA}(T), T)$, the following also holds: (i) $\mathsf{Pf}_{j,i}$ is well defined for T_j, for $1 \leq i \leq k_j$, and (ensuring *strong identification*) (ii) $\Sigma \models ((\texttt{pathfd } \mathsf{Pf}_{j,1}, \ldots, \mathsf{Pf}_{j,k_j} \rightarrow \texttt{self}) \in T_j)$.

We write $\mathsf{Order}(\mathsf{RTA})$ for a fixed choice for such an order when one exists. $\qquad \Box$

Given an RTA, the existence of $\mathcal{O}$ can be tested by checking for cycles in a graph with nodes labeled by table names and directed edges connecting tables that appear in consecutive guards of a referring type assigned by RTA. The linear order is then any topological sort of the (acyclic) graph. The remaining conditions can also be checked by appeal to the description logics $\mathcal{DLFD}$ [7], and $\mathcal{CFDI}_{nc}^{\forall -}$ [8] (see previous section).

Example 7. Consider the SQL^{path} query and $\mathcal{C}_{\mathrm{AR}}$ schema Σ given by (3) and (4) in Example 5 above, and also assume $\mathrm{RTA}(T_1)$ and $\mathrm{RTA}(T_2)$ are given respectively by "$A_1 = ?$" and "$T_1 \rightarrow A_1 = ?; A_2 = ?$". Then $\mathrm{RTA}(T_2)$ implies that T_1

must precede T_2 in Order(RTA). Indeed, the linear order $\mathcal{O} = (T_1, T_2)$ satisfies all conditions required for RTA to be identity resolving. In contrast, if RTA(T_1) is instead given by "$T_2 \to A_2 = ?; A_1 = ?$", then no such linear order $\mathcal{O}$ exists and RTA is not identity resolving. This can be blamed on an inherent ambiguity on how objects belonging to both tables should be referenced.

More generally, entity sets/classes are often assumed to be disjoint, unless they participate in an isa hierarchy. In such cases, one should be free to chose the identifying Rt independently. For example, consider where RTA(T_i) is given by "$A_i = ?$", and where the constraint "disjoint with T_2" is added to T_1. RTA is now identity resolving in this case since all conditions hold for $\mathcal{O} = (T_1, T_2)$ (or for $\mathcal{O} = (T_2, T_1)$). □

An identity resolving referring type assignment yields a natural way to *coerce* referring expression types to more general types. This is based on the observation that, for a linear order $(T_{i_1}, \ldots, T_{i_k})$, all referring expression types that are formed as sub-sequences of components of RTA can be simply extended with additional components as long as the result is still a sub-sequence of Rt.

Definition 8 (Coercion). Let Σ be a $\mathcal{C}_{AR}$ schema, RTA an identity resolving referring type assignment for Σ, and Rt_1 and Rt_2 two referring expressions with component orders conforming to Order(RTA). We say that Rt_1 is a *referring supertype of* Rt_2 if all components of Rt_2 are also components of Rt_1, and write $Rt_1 \triangledown Rt_2$ to denote the *least common referring supertype* of both Rt_1 and Rt_2, that is, a referring expression type with components given by the union of the components of Rt_1 and Rt_2 and that are ordered by Order(RTA). □

Example 9. Consider the SQL^{path} query

$$\text{(select } x.\text{self } T_1 \ x\text{) union (select } x.\text{self } T_2 \ x\text{)} \tag{5}$$

over schema (4) in Example 5 above, and also assume RTA(T_1) and RTA(T_2) are given respectively by "$A_1 = ?$" and "$T_1 \to A_1 = ?; A_2 = ?$". As Example 7 shows, RTA is an identity resolving type assignment. However, the union operation requires a coercion to a common referring expression type for T_1 and T_2. In particular, since Order(RTA) $= (T_1, T_2)$, RTA(T_1)$\triangledown$RTA(T_2) defines this as "$T_1 \to A_1 = ?; A_2 = ?$" (matching RTA(T_2)). Thus, an *encoding* of referring expressions given by "$A_1 = ?$" in a *concrete* version of T_1 must be extended to an encoding of "$T_1 \to A_1 = ?; A_2 = ?$" before computing the union operation. In the next section, we present a simple encoding that enables such coercion. □

4   Concrete Relational Databases and SQL^{path}

For a given $\mathcal{C}_{AR}$ schema Σ, an identity resolving referring type assignment can serve as a basis to encoding elements of OID with *sequences of values* for concrete attributes that can serve as surrogate keys for the values. We now present such an encoding, Rep, and show how it leads, in turn, to a concrete relational database for Σ, and finally to SQL queries over this schema that implement SQL^{path} queries. This "closes the loop" on our overall objective for a separation of concerns.

On the Concrete Representation of Referring Expressions

Definition 10 (Rep). Let T and Rt be an abstract table and referring expression type, where $\mathsf{Fix}(Rt, T)$ is given by

$$T_1 \to (\mathsf{Pf}_{1,1} = ?, \ldots, \mathsf{Pf}_{1,k_1} = ?); \ldots; T_k \to (\mathsf{Pf}_{k,1} = ?, \ldots, \mathsf{Pf}_{k,k_k} = ?),$$

and let $D_{i,j}$ be the underlying concrete domain for the final attribute in each $\mathsf{Pf}_{i,j}$. Also let $\mathsf{Nm}(\mathsf{Pf})$, where $\mathsf{Pf} = A_1.\cdots.A_\ell$, denote a new attribute name "$A_1\text{-}\ldots\text{-}A_\ell$". We write $\mathsf{Rep}(Rt, T)$ to denote the sequence of concrete attributes

$$(\texttt{disc enum}\{`T_1\text{'}, \ldots, `T_k\text{'}\}, \mathsf{Nm}(\mathsf{Pf}_{1,1})\ D_{1,1}, \ldots, \mathsf{Nm}(\mathsf{Pf}_{k,k_k})\ D_{k,k_k}).$$

If Rt consists of a single component, then attribute $\texttt{disc}$ is excluded.   □

Note that Rep uses an auxiliary Nm function to invent new attributes names simply by replacing "dots" by "dashes".[6] The following example now illustrates how Rep can be used to encode abstract values occurring in abstract tables:

Example 11. Consider the SQL^{path} query (5) over schema (4) above (see Examples 9 and 5), and assume $\mathsf{RTA}(T_1)$ and $\mathsf{RTA}(T_2)$ are given respectively by "$A_1 = ?$" and by "$T_1 \to A_1 = ?; A_2 = ?$". Then $\mathsf{Rep}(\mathsf{RTA}(T_1))$ and $\mathsf{Rep}(\mathsf{RTA}(T_2))$ are given respectively by "$(A_1\ \texttt{STRING})$" and by

$$\texttt{"(disc enum}\{`T_1\text{'}, `T_2\text{'}\}, A_1\ \texttt{STRING}, A_2\ \texttt{STRING)"}.$$

Now consider where: T_1 has object e_1 with $A_1 = `\texttt{abc'}$, $T_2$ has object $e_2$ with $A_2 = `\texttt{bcd'}$, and both T_1 and T_2 have object e_3 with $A_1 = `\texttt{cde'}$ and $A_2 = `\texttt{def'}$. Referring expressions for each e_i would then be encoded as follows:[7]

$$e_1 : (`\texttt{abc'}),$$
$$e_2 : (`T_2\text{'}, \langle defaultSTRINGvalue\rangle, `\texttt{bcd'})\ \text{and}$$
$$e_3 : (`T_1\text{'}, `\texttt{cde'}, `\texttt{def'}).$$

To compute the union operator, coercion for concrete representations of referring expressions is necessary. In this case, value sequences encoding references to e_i will need to be augmented with additional values to conform to $\mathsf{Rep}(\mathsf{RTA}(T_1) \triangledown \mathsf{RTA}(T_2))$, which matches $\mathsf{Rep}(\mathsf{RTA}(T_2))$ (see Example 9). Thus, the encoding of the referring expression for e_1 is extended to

$$(`T_1\text{'}, `\texttt{abc'}, \langle defaultSTRINGvalue\rangle)$$

prior to evaluating $\texttt{union}$.   □

As the example illustrates, extending our coercion operator for referring expression types to their concrete representations is straightforward. In particular, to

---

[6] Other options for both Nm and Rep are clearly possible, e.g., based on introducing *variant* record types.

[7] We assume a non-null default value exists for each concrete domain.

coerce a $\mathsf{Rep}(Rt_1, T_1)$ tuple to a $\mathsf{Rep}(Rt_2, T_2)$ tuple, where Rt_2 is a *referring supertype* of Rt_1, it suffices to create the $\mathsf{Rep}(Rt_2, T_2)$ tuple by using the values from the $\mathsf{Rep}(Rt_1, T_1)$ tuple for the concrete attributes corresponding to common components, and to assign default values to the remaining columns. We denote this function by $\mathsf{Coerce}_{(Rt_1, T_1)}^{(Rt_2, T_2)}$. To convert a $\mathsf{Rep}(Rt_2, T_2)$ tuple back to a $\mathsf{Rep}(Rt_1, T_1)$ tuple, we first check if the value of the `disc` attribute corresponds to a guard for some component of Rt_1 and, if so, we project the former to attributes in $\mathsf{Rep}(Rt_1, T_1)$; the conversion is undefined otherwise. We denote this function by $\mathsf{Restrict}_{(Rt_2, T_2)}^{(Rt_1, T_1)}$. Note that both functions can be expressed using SQL query constructs, e.g., by using constant expressions in a `select` clause in the case of the Coerce function.

To simplify notation, we extend the Coerce and $\mathsf{Restrict}$ functions to tuples by applying the functions component-wise (assuming values of concrete attributes map to themselves), and omit mention of T_i to improve readability.

The main consequence of a referring expression type assignment RTA that is identity resolving and of Rep, our suggestion for a concrete encoding of referring expressions, is that we now have a way to compare possibly different representations of an OID value:

Lemma 12. Let RTA be an identity resolving type assignment for Σ and $\mathcal{R}$ a set of referring expression types such that $\{\mathsf{RTA}(T) \mid T \in \mathsf{Tables}(\Sigma)\} \subseteq \mathcal{R}$ and such that $\mathcal{R}$ is closed under $\triangledown$. Then, for every $e_1, e_2 \in \mathsf{OID}$, if $\mathsf{Rep}(Rt_1, T_1)$ tuple t_1 and $\mathsf{Rep}(Rt_2, T_2)$ tuple t_2 are concrete representations of referring expressions to e_1 and e_2 induced by types occurring in $\mathcal{R}$, respectively, then $e_1 = e_2$ if and only if

$$\mathsf{Coerce}_{Rt_1}^{Rt_1 \; \triangledown \; Rt_2}(t_1) = \mathsf{Coerce}_{Rt_2}^{Rt_1 \; \triangledown \; Rt_2}(t_2).$$

$\square$

The Coerce and $\mathsf{Restrict}$ functions are naturally extended to *abstract attributes* to produce a list of column names of the representation, to *abstract tuples* that may contain several abstract identifiers (we assume that concrete attributes are *represented* by themselves), and, in turn, to abstract database instances and query answers.

On Concrete Relational Schemata. With Rep, it is straightforward to define a *concrete relational schema* corresponding to a given $\mathcal{C}_{\mathrm{AR}}$ schema (such as "`table PERSON` $(\cdots)$" given in our introduction):

Definition 13 (Mapping Abstract $\mathcal{C}_{\mathrm{AR}}$ Tables to Concrete Relations). Let $T \in \Sigma$ be an abstract table and RTA an identity resolving referring type assignment for Σ. The *concrete relational table schema* $\mathsf{Tab}(T)$ for T is obtained by appending attributes and constraints to an initially empty sequence s, in "`table` T (s)", in the order they occur in T according to the following:

1. For attribute "`self OID`", append columns $\mathsf{Rep}(\mathsf{RTA}(T), T)$ together with a primary key constraint consisting of these columns.

2. For a concrete attribute "A D", append same if not already included.
3. For an abstract attribute "A OID", append columns $\mathsf{Rep}(\mathsf{RTA}(\mathsf{Dom}(A), T))$ after renaming each column by prefixing with "A-". Also add a foreign key constraint from these columns to $\mathsf{Tab}((\mathsf{Dom}(A)))$.
4. For a constraint φ, add a general assertion constraint if φ is not the first occurrence of a foreign key constraint defining $\mathsf{Dom}(A)$ for some attribute A.

□

Observe that assertion constraints are generated for all but the "first" foreign key constraints defined on a given abstract attribute. Such are needed to verify the presence of appropriate values in referenced tables that might differ in their assigned referring expression types. Alternatively, one may add additional columns (using Rep repeatedly) and then enforce integrity locally.

Along similar lines, Rep can also be extended, with respect to a referring type assignment RTA, to *instances* of abstract tables and to bindings of abstract values to variables in queries. We write $\mathsf{Rep}_{\mathsf{RTA}}$ to denote this extension.

Query Translation. To summarize, relational operations on the concrete representation of referring expressions, in particular equality comparisons, requires that *compatibility* issues between referring expression types that can potentially refer to the same value in OID must be addressed. In our setting, Lemma 12 ensures this for Rep in the case of an identity resolving type assignment. Hence, to translate a $\mathsf{SQL}^{path} Q$ to concrete SQL, we can apply rewritings to Q to ensure all terms have the form "$x.A$", for some abstract or concrete attribute A (see Sect. 2 and [2] for more details), and then apply Map, a recursive procedure:

Definition 14 (Query Compilation). Let Q be a SQL^{path} query over the abstract schema Σ, and RTA an identity resolving type assignment for Σ. We define Map, a function that maps Q to concrete SQL by induction on the structure of Q, as follows:

$$\mathsf{Map}(T\ x) \mapsto \mathsf{Tab}(T)\ x$$
$$\mathsf{Map}(\texttt{select}\ x_1.A_1, \ldots, x_k.A_k\ Q) \mapsto \texttt{select}\ \mathsf{Rep}_{\mathsf{RTA}}(x_1.A_1), \ldots, \mathsf{Rep}_{\mathsf{RTA}}(x_k.A_k)\ \mathsf{Map}(Q)$$
$$\mathsf{Map}(\texttt{from}\ Q_1, Q_2) \mapsto \texttt{from}\ \mathsf{Map}(Q_1), \mathsf{Map}(Q_2)$$
$$\mathsf{Map}(Q\texttt{where}\ x_1.A_1 = x_2.A_2) \mapsto Q\texttt{where}$$
$$\mathsf{Coerce}_{Rt(x_1.A_1)}^{Rt(x_1.A_1)\triangledown Rt(x_2.A_2)}(\mathsf{Rep}_{\mathsf{RTA}}(x_1.A_1)) = \mathsf{Coerce}_{Rt(x_1.A_1)}^{Rt(x_1.A_1)\triangledown Rt(x_2.A_2)}(\mathsf{Rep}_{\mathsf{RTA}}(x_2.A_2))$$
$$\mathsf{Map}(Q_1\ \texttt{union}\ Q_2) \mapsto \mathsf{Coerce}_{Rt(Q_1)}^{Rt(Q_1\triangledown Q_2)}(\mathsf{Map}(Q_1))$$
$$\texttt{union}\ \mathsf{Coerce}_{Rt(Q_2)}^{Rt(Q_1\triangledown Q_2)}(\mathsf{Map}(Q_2))$$
$$\mathsf{Map}(Q_1\ \texttt{minus}\ Q_2) \mapsto \mathsf{Restrict}_{Rt(Q_1\triangledown Q_2)}^{Rt(Q_1)}(\mathsf{Coerce}_{Rt(Q_1)}^{Rt(Q_1\triangledown Q_2)}(\mathsf{Map}(Q_1))$$
$$\texttt{minus}\ \mathsf{Coerce}_{Rt(Q_2)}^{Rt(Q_1\triangledown Q_2)}(\mathsf{Map}(Q_2)))$$

Note that $Rt(\cdot)$ denotes the referring types assigned to variables in answer tuples (or, by mild abuse of notation, to all components of a tuple), and also that *equality comparisons* on $\mathsf{Rep}(\cdot)$ are performed component-wise when needed. (The type assignments originate from RTA and "T x" operators, and are preserved through the query save for **union** operators that convert variables to least common referring supertypes with respect to the corresponding referring types in Q_1 and Q_2.) $\square$

Observe that the definition of Map is purely syntactic and produces a concrete SQL query for which the following, our main result, applies:

Theorem 15. *Let Σ be a $\mathcal{C}_{AR}$ schema and let* RTA *an identity resolving type assignment for Σ. For any SQL^{path} query Q over Σ and every database instance I of Σ we have* $\mathsf{Rep}_{RTA}(Q(I)) = (\mathsf{Map}(Q))(\mathsf{Rep}_{RTA}(I))$. $\square$

Example 16. Applying Map to the SQL^{path} query (1) from Sect. 2 then yields the following in SQL when RTA(PERSON) and RTA(VEHICLE) are respectively given by "ssn=?" and "vin=?":

```
select p.name from CAN-DRIVE d, PERSON p, VEHICLE v
where v.make = 'Ford' and d.driven-vin = v.vin and d.driver-ssn = p.ssn.
```

5   Summary and Future Work

This paper was motivated by two problems that seem to inhere in relational DBMS: (i) the need to prematurely commit to an "external key" (printable values) in designing relational schemas; and (ii) the need to choose a *single and simple way* to refer to all entities/tuples in a class/table rather than allow for variations.

To help with this, we started with a simple semantic data model $\mathcal{C}$, where naming is not an issue because objects have identity, together with a simple extension of SQL, SQL^{path}, allowing implicit foreign key joins in the form of "path expressions"[8] In the hope of making SQL programmers more comfortable, we turned $\mathcal{C}$ into $\mathcal{C}_{AR}$, a more relational-like version, where surrogates are visible as columns in tables.

Orthogonally to schema and query specification, analysts can specify uniqueness constraints in the form of path functional dependencies, and, most inovatively, assign complex *preferred naming schemes* for each class/table in the abstract schema. The language for preferred naming schemes allows us to solve the problems raised in the beginning, such as having different naming schemes for subclasses than for superclasses, and not having to invent new names for generalizations. The examples of Halpin [4] can also be handled, especially if one creates special subclasses to guard preferences, as in OWL. The one situation he considers which we cannot accommodate is non-deterministic choice of references. This would immediately cause problems with equality checking.

We emphasize that we view the separation of concerns between naming and schema/query body specification to be a central contribution of this work.

To support this, we provided ways to verify that the naming schemes are indeed unique, based on the dependencies specified, and algorithms for converting the abstract schema and queries into ordinary SQL table declarations and queries, where object (identifiers) are no longer visible.

---

[8] We emphasize that such ideas have been present in database semantic models since Taxis [6] and GEM [9].

There are a number of interesting problems that remain to be investigated. One issue is how to help relieve analysts from the burden of having to write complex referring expressions for *every* class in the schema. One could start with default rules: a single key k for class C results in type expression k=?, which is inherited to all subclasses of C that do not specify keys. This could then be augmented with some form of "default inheritance" that allows subclasses to over-ride superclass reference types. Other directions for work include a richer language for referring expression types, alternatives to the concrete representation, (including support for alternative mappings of class hierarchies to relational tables, which are mentioned in many textbooks).

A different research direction, also suggested by the referee, is to investigate extensively the connection between the rather pragmatic notion of naming considered here and the deep ontological analysis of *principles of individuation* and *identity* considered in [3], among others.

References

1. Borgida, A., Toman, D., Weddell, G.: On referring expressions in query answering over first order knowledge bases. In: International Conference on Principles of Knowledge Representation and Reasoning, pp. 319–328 (2016)
2. Borgida, A., Toman, D., Weddell, G.: On Referring Expressions in Information Systems derived from Conceptual Modelling. Technical report CS-2016-03, Cheriton School of Computer Science, University of Waterloo (2016)
3. Guizzardi, G., Wagner, G., Guarino, N., van Sinderen, M.: An ontologically well-founded profile for UML conceptual models. Adv. Inf. Syst. Eng. CAiSE **2004**, 112–126 (2004)
4. Halpin, T.A.: Modeling of linguistic reference schemes. Int. J. Inf. Syst. Model. Design **6**(4), 1–23 (2015)
5. Hull, R., King, R.: Semantic database modeling: survey, applications, and research issues. ACM Comput. Surv. **19**(3), 201–260 (1987)
6. Mylopoulos, J., Bernstein, P.A., Wong, H.K.T.: A language facility for designing database-intensive applications. ACM Trans. Database Syst. **5**(2), 185–207 (1980)
7. Toman, D., Weddell, G.: On Attributes, roles, and dependencies in description logics and the Ackermann case of the decision problem. In: Description Logics 2001, CEUR-WS, vol. 49, pp. 76–85 (2001)
8. Toman, D., Weddell, G.E.: On adding inverse features to the description logic $\mathcal{CFD}_{nc}^{\forall}$. In: Pacific Rim International Conference on Artificial Intelligence, PRICAI 2014, pp. 587–599 (2014)
9. Zaniolo, C.: The database language GEM. In: ACM SIGMOD International Conference on Management of Data, pp. 207–218 (1983)

DeepTelos: Multi-level Modeling
with Most General Instances

Manfred A. Jeusfeld[1(✉)] and Bernd Neumayr[2]

[1] University of Skövde, Skövde, Sweden
manfred.jeusfeld@his.se
[2] Johannes Kepler University Linz, Linz, Austria
bernd.neumayr@jku.at

Abstract. Multi-level modeling aims to reduce redundancy in data models by defining properties at the right abstraction level and inheriting them to more specific levels. We revisit one of the earliest such approaches, Telos, and investigate what needs to be added to its axioms to get a true multi-level modeling language. Unlike previous approaches, we define levels not with numeric potencies but with hierarchies of so-called most general instances.

Keywords: Multi-level modeling · Telos · Meta modeling

1 Introduction

Multi-level modeling [1,13] (or Deep Modeling) aims at reducing accidental complexity [2] in software, data, and domain models by utilizing abstraction levels to express model statements only once rather than repeating them multiple times, e.g., defining a property `listPrice` for product models or a property `owner` for individual products. Early approaches were materialization [19] and power types [18]. Many current approaches [6,12,16,20] to multi-level modeling assign potencies to relationships, attributes, and classes. Potencies constrain how many times the respective concept can be instantiated until it can no further be instantiated.

Telos [14] is a metamodeling language based on the single concept of *proposition* to represent any model elements, regardless of its abstraction level. ConceptBase [8] is an implementation of the O-Telos [9] variant of Telos that maps all language axioms to Datalog. It shares the simplicity of Telos by solely using a single data structure of propositions to represent objects, classes, attributes, relationships, instantiations, and specializations. The 30+ axioms are forming the rules for propositions, in particular how instantiation, specialization and attribution/relationship interplay.

Telos pioneered core ideas of multi-level modeling. First, Telos models come with an *unrestricted number of meta-levels*. Second, there is no separation between classes and objects: a model element (later referred to as *clabject*) may act both as object and as class, and possibly also as metaclass, and so forth.

© Springer International Publishing AG 2016
I. Comyn-Wattiau et al. (Eds.): ER 2016, LNCS 9974, pp. 198–211, 2016.
DOI: 10.1007/978-3-319-46397-1_15

Third, the reliance on a single language construct, proposition, which is instantiated by model elements at all modeling levels, pioneered what was later referred to as *orthogonal classification architecture*.

Telos, however, lacks a crucial feature of multi-level modeling, namely full support for *deep characterization*. That is, in Telos, there is no easy way to specify with a metaclass a property that is instantiated by the instances of the instances of the metaclass. For example, there is no obvious way to specify that all instances of all instances of `ProductCategory` have a property `listPrice` and their instances in turn have a property `owner`.

The contribution of this paper is to extend Telos with *most general instances* (MGI), a language construct for deep characterization. The result is DeepTelos, a language and system for *Deep Metamodeling* (combining metamodeling and multi-level modeling), akin to MetaDepth [12]. What sets DeepTelos apart are the strengths inherited from Telos and ConceptBase:

- simplicity and conceptual clarity
- formal semantics expressed and implemented in Datalog
- rich query and query optimization facilities

In the remainder of the paper we introduce, in Sect. 2, the relevant O-Telos axioms. The analysis of the axioms reveals that O-Telos as such is unable to support deep characterization by its existing axioms. In Sect. 3 we propose the simple yet powerful construct of *most generic instances* (MGI) to support deep characterization within the axiomatic boundaries of Telos. Telos extended with MGIs allows to combine "linguistic" metamodeling, e.g. modeling the entity-relationship model, and "ontological" multi-level modeling, e.g., specifying product hierarchies with multiple levels. In Sect. 4 we present details about the implementation of the approach and the implementation of the running example. In Sect. 4 we discuss the approach and related work.

1.1 Running Example

The running example is derived from the example discussed in [15]: There are product categories such as car models and phone models, also called product models. Product models subsume products, which themselves subsume individual products. Product categories have persons as category managers. Car models have attributes like the number of doors. Product models have a list price. Finally, products have a person as owner.

The example highlights that some concepts have both the nature of a class (defining attribute and relation types for their instances) and of an object (instantiating attribute and relation types). Such concepts are commonly referred to as *clabject* [1, 7]. In classical two-level models, one would have to separate the class and object flavors into different objects, e.g. using the powertype pattern [4]. Multi-level modeling aims at avoiding this separation by regarding each class also as an object that can have its own properties.

2 Telos

Telos was originally developed for requirements modeling [5] but later mostly applied for the design of interrelated modeling languages [10,17], i.e. for the linguistic flavor of metamodeling. Its O-Telos axioms [9] are defining the interplay between instantiation, specialization, and properties (subsuming attributes and relationships). A proposition in Telos is a quadruple $P(o, x, n, y)$ where o is its identifier, x its source, n its label, and y its target. The components x and y are identifiers of either the same proposition (then it has the form $P(o, o, n, o)$ and is displayed as a node) or of some other propositions (then it is a link between the other propositions). If the label is 'in', then it is an explicit instantiation. If the label is 'isa', then it is an explicit specialization, otherwise it is a relation between two proposition. Telos does not distinguish objects and values. Hence attributes are just relations between propositions, the one being interpreted as an object, the other being interpreted as a value. Propositions are then used to derive the predicates In and Isa:

$$\forall o, x, c \ P(o, x, in, c) \Rightarrow In(x, c) \tag{1}$$

$$\forall o, c, d \ P(o, c, isa, d) \Rightarrow Isa(c, d) \tag{2}$$

Instantiation and specialization interplay via a number of axioms. The first one is about inheritance of class membership, see also left half of Fig. 1:

$$\forall x, c, d \ In(x, c) \land Isa(c, d) \Rightarrow In(x, d) \tag{3}$$

Instantiations are displayed as broken directed links and specializations as directed links with white arrows heads. The instantiation of relations such as the relation labelled m between c and d in the right half of Fig. 1 requires that both the sources and targets of the instance with label n are synchronously instantiated:

$$\forall o, x, n, y, p \ P(o, x, n, y) \land In(o, p) \Rightarrow \exists \ c, m, d \ P(p, c, m, d) \land In(x, c) \land In(y, d) \tag{4}$$

The upper half of Fig. 1 refers to an analogous constraint on the specialization of relations. This synchronous semantics of instantiation and specialization made Telos appear unsuitable for true multi-level modeling, at least on first sight. To show this consider a Telos metaclass **Product** that has an attribute

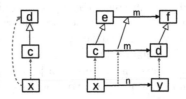

Fig. 1. Instantiation and specialization in Telos

serialnumber whose value is an integer number. An instance of the attribute serialnumber has to instantiate the source of the attribute to an instance of Product, i.e., a simple class, and the destination to an instance of integer. The latter one cannot be further instantiated, the former one is a class. Hence, we cannot define serial numbers of actual products in this manner.

On the other hand, Telos does not distinguish classes from objects. Instead it links them via the instantiation predicate $In(x, c)$. Telos is also agnostic of any pre-defined abstraction levels. Abstractions levels rather follow from chains of instantiation facts such as

$$\ldots, In(x, c), In(c, mc), In(mc, mmc), \ldots$$

Such chains are un-restricted on both sides, i.e. the object x could also have instances, and the object mmc could have classes.

3   Most General Instances

Our running example mentions the concepts product categories, product models, and products. Each of them has describing properties such as the ownership of a product, or the number of doors of a car model. Intuitively, products, product models, and product categories are at different abstraction levels, but how can this be expressed in Telos that has no builtin abstraction levels? We propose the construct of *most general instances* to formalize the relationship between the concepts. The most general instance of a class c is a class m that has all instances of c as subclasses:

$$\boxed{\forall\, x, c, m\ In(x, c) \wedge IN(m, c) \Rightarrow Isa(x, m)} \qquad (5)$$

Figure 2 visualizes the construct. The class c has the (regular) instance x and the most general instance m. The axiom (5) then demands that x is a subclass of m. The axiom is similar to axiom (3). The difference is that it does not derive instantiations but specializations. The predicate $IN(m, c)$ defines m to be the most general instance of c. This should not be confused with the instantiation predicate $In(x, c)$. The most general instance of a class is usually not an instance of the class itself. It rather is a *proxy* of the class at the abstraction level below

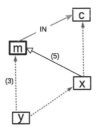

Fig. 2. Most general instance

the class. It has all instances of all instances of class c as its instances. This is defined via the class membership inheritance axiom (3). In Fig. 2 the instantiation $In(y, m)$ is derived via axiom (3).

A most general instance is placed on the top of generalization hierarchies. One may argue that such a class must be abstract, i.e. that it should not have any instance that does not occur in one of its proper subclasses. We leave this open in order to minimize the set of additional axioms. The original axiom set [9] plus the axiom (5) is referred to as *DeepTelos*, since it allows to use multi-level modeling with Telos as discussed subsequently.

3.1 Linguistic Use of Most General Instances

Since Telos was originally developed for linguistic metamodeling, we apply the new construct first to the entity-relationship diagramming language (ERD). It features as constructs entity types, relationship types, role links between relationship types and entity types, domains, and attributes. Further, it defines multiplicity constraints, specialization between entity types, and key attributes. There are several approaches to provide meta models for ERD but to our knowledge none defines the meaning of an entity in contrast to an entity type.

Entity in Fig. 3 is defined as most general instance of EntityType. As a consequence, the two entity types Project and Employee become subclasses of Entity, hence the instances p346 and mary are both instances of Entity. This makes Entity a normal class that can be queried. In a symmetric way, Value is declared as most general instance of Domain. All values of the database can then be queried via the class Value. Even more, one can include a constraint that the two classes Entity and Value are disjoint. This is an implicit assumption in data modeling, which now becomes explicit.

The example can be pushed further in Fig. 4 by applying it to links, such as the the attribution property of EntityType. Links are first class objects in Telos and can also be subjected to the new construct for most general instances.

The link value of Entity is the most general instance of the link property of EntityType. The latter defines that entity types can have describing properties, such as the budget of projects. The most general instance value subsumes all

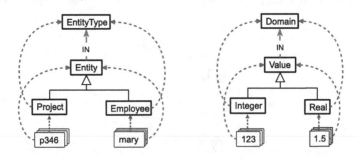

Fig. 3. Defining Entity and Value as most general instances

data level links such as the `pbudget` link. We can thus use the `value` link to query all entities that have a certain property, regardless of the entity type! This allows for schema-less querying.

3.2 Ontological Use of Most General Instances

We now turn to the running example to discuss the ontological use of most general instances for multi-level modeling. The essential idea of multi-level modeling is to define properties of objects and classes (clabjects) at the right level of abstraction in order to avoid redundancy and accidental complexity [2]. Existing approaches rely on potencies on links of clabjects, which are natural numbers specifying how many times the clabject has to be instantiated to reach the most specific incarnation of the clabject or link. For example, the link `property` in Fig. 4 would have the potency 2 since we reach after two instantiations to a link like `pbudget`, which me may classify as a fact that can not be instantiated further.

DeepTelos has no potencies at all and thus we need to show that it can be used for multi-level modeling. The replacement of potencies are hierarchies of most general instances. In the running example, the central hierarchy is formed by `ProductCategory`, `ProductModel`, and `Product`. In OMG terms, `ProductCategory` would be a M3-level class (meta-metaclass), `ProductModel` would be a M2 class (metaclass), and `Product` be an M1 class (simple class).

Figure 5 shows the main chain of most general instances in the running example. The specializations to the MGI `ProductModel` are derived by axiom (5) from the instantiation facts

```
In(CarModel,ProductCategory)
In(PhoneModel,ProductCategory)
```

By declaring `Porsche911` as instance of `CarModel` it also becomes an instance of the MGI `ProductModel` via axiom (3). This again matches axiom (5) and makes `Porsche911` a specialization of the MGI `Product`. Finally, `maryscar` is an instance of `Porsche911` and via axiom (3) an instance of `Product`. The right-hand side on phones works analogously. The MGI chain triggers the two axioms

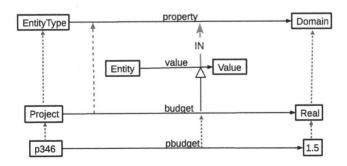

Fig. 4. Entity properties as most general instances

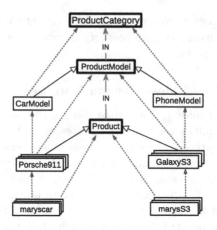

Fig. 5. The product hierarchy as chain of most general instances

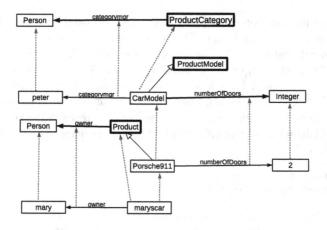

Fig. 6. Multi-level attributes for the product hierarchy

(3) and (5) and results in a set of derived instantiations to the MGI clabjects. These instantiations now allow to define the clabject properties of the running example in a way that does not violate the existing axioms of Telos, in particular the synchronous instantiation of the source and target of a proposition, axiom (4).

Figure 6 shows the use of the product hierarchy to model the properties of the running example. Product categories can have category managers. So, here peter is assigned as category manager of CarModel. Car models have a number of doors, here Porsche911 has 2 doors. And finally, products have owners, e.g. mary owns maryscar. The product hierarchy chain of Fig. 5 replaces the potencies at the expense of having multiple proxies of the 'product' concept, i.e. ProductCategory for potency 3, ProductModel for potency 2, and Product for potency 1. The benefit of the proxies is that we now have meaningful names

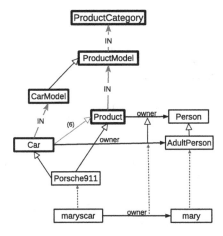

Fig. 7. Multiple MGI hierarchies

for the abstraction levels. Like with Telos instantiation, there is no limit on the number of abstraction levels and they can also be extended at any time.

Several MGI hierarchies can co-exist and interact as shown in Fig. 7. Cars are defined as most general instances of `CarModel`. The 'owner' relation of `Product` is refined by `Car`, demanding that only adult persons may own a car (compare right side of Fig. 1). This case requires however that `Car` is a specialization of `Product`. We can ensure this by a second axiom for most general instances:

$$\forall\, c, d, m, n\ IN(m, c) \wedge IN(n, d) \wedge Isa(c, d) \Rightarrow Isa(m, n) \tag{6}$$

4 Implementation

The described approach is implemented and tested with several examples by extending ConceptBase with the required axioms. ConceptBase has Datalog as underlying computational engine. All user-defined formulas are compiled into an efficient Datalog program. For technical reasons, the Isa predicate is barred from occurring as conclusion of deductive rules. For this reason, the implementation defines a predicate `ISA` which behaves like the Isa predicate with respect to the inheritance of class membership, axiom (3). The code for the implementation uses a textual frame syntax. The new `IN` and `ISA` predicates are declared as attributes of `Proposition`:

```
Proposition with
  attribute
    ISA: Proposition; IN: Proposition
end
```

Subsequently, the new axioms are declared. Rule `mrule2` is equivalent to axiom (3) but now formulated for the user-defined `ISA` attribute of `Proposition`. Rules `mrule1` and `mrule3` are equivalent to axioms (5) and (6), respectively.

```
DeepTelosRules in Class with
  rule
    mrule1: $ forall m,x,c/Proposition
                 (x in c) and (m IN c) ==> (x ISA m) $;
    mrule2: $ forall x,c,d/Proposition
                 (c ISA d) and (x in c) ==> (x in d) $;
    mrule3: $ forall c,d,m,n/Proposition
                 (m IN c) and (n IN d) and (c ISA d) ==> (m ISA n) $
end
```

The product hierarchy is subsequently defined using the new IN relation. Note that the Telos *In* predicate is spelled 'in' in the frame syntax. The source code includes in comments the potencies of clabject, attributes and relations. These comments serve for comparing DeepTelos with dual deep instantiation (DDI) [15,16], see discussion in Sect. 5.

```
ProductCategory with                       {* 3 *}
  attribute
    categoryMgr: Person                    {* 1-1 *}
end
ProductModel  with
  IN c: ProductCategory
  attribute listPrice: Integer             {* 2-1 *}
end
Product  with
  IN c: ProductModel
  attribute owner: Person                  {* 3-1 *}
end
CarModel in ProductCategory with           {* 2 *}
  categoryMgr c: peter                     {* 0-0 *}
  attribute numberOfDoors: Integer         {* 1-1 *}
end
Car with
  IN c: CarModel
  attribute mileage: Integer               {* 2-1 *}
end
Porsche911 in CarModel with                {* 1 *}
  numberOfDoors d: 2                       {* 0-0 *}
  listPrice p: 120000                      {* 0-0 *}
end
marysCar in Porsche911 with                {* 0 *}
  mileage m: 27000                         {* 0-0 *}
  owner o: mary                            {* 0-0 *}
end
Person end                                 {* 1 *}
peter in Person end                        {* 0 *}
mary in Person end                         {* 0 *}
```

Figure 8 shows a ConceptBase screendump of the running example. Not all attributes, instantiations, and specializations are shown in the screendump for

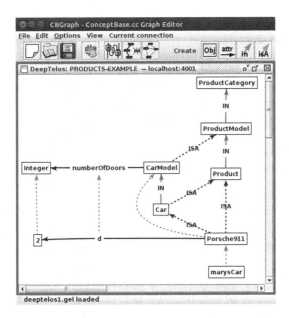

Fig. 8. ConceptBase screendump of the running example

sake of readability. ConceptBase uses a partial evaluation technique for formulas that contain predicates matching $In(x, c)$ with a variable c. Since the new axioms contain such predicates, the formula compiler produces efficient Datalog code for them. The implementation and examples can be downloaded under an open license from http://conceptbase.cc/deeptelos.

5   Discussion and Related Work

MGIs can be regarded as the inverse of Odell's *power types* [18]. Adding to a metaclass c an MGI m results in a base class m with a power type c. The contribution of DeepTelos is to fully integrate this construct in a metamodeling language and system which already comes with support for unbounded deep characterization via 'mediated' [20] properties and full support for metaclasses. This also sets DeepTelos apart from work on the powertype pattern [4] where the powertype role is played by a 'normal' class. For an insightful analysis of power types and their role in multi-level modeling see [3]. We take a perspective that is inverse to power types, because our starting point are metaclasses in Telos. With MGIs we add full support for deep characterization to Telos, making it possible that the metaclass introduces (via its MGI) a property that is directly instantiated by the individual (its instance-instance, i.e., potency 2) without an intermediate instantiation step at the class – this is similar to what Rossini [20] refers to as 'semantics of single-potency'.

DeepTelos is related to the metamodeling system VODAK [11], where a metaclass c comes with own-type, instance-type, and instance-instance-type, which are all specified together with the metaclass. In that way, VODAK supported deep characterization, but limited to two instantiation levels. The added value of DeepTelos is to have unbounded meta-levels. For example, ProductCategory (specifying own-values and instance-type) would typically be created together with its MGI ProductModel (specifying the instance-instance-type of ProductCategory) and its MGI's MGI Product (specifying the instance-instance-instance-type of ProductCategory). While DeepTelos is not restricted to a particular modeling methodology, this example gives a hint of how MGIs are applied by metamodelers.

DeepTelos is also related to our work on Dual Deep Instantiation [15,16]. In DDI, a class together with its MGI chain would be represented by a single clabject where each property has source and target potency. For example (see comments in the example in Sect. 4), ProductCategory, ProductModel, and Product would be represented together by a single clabject with potency 3, with property listPrice having source potency 2 and target potency 1.

Linguistic vs. Ontological Instantiation: In multi-level modeling one often distinguishes two types of classification (or instantiation), namely linguistic classification and ontological classification [6]. It is often argued that these two kinds of instantiation are orthogonal to each other. In a first approach [15] to use O-Telos for multi-level modeling, we specified and implemented dual deep instantiation in ConceptBase. We followed the idea of separating linguistic instantiation (defined by the O-Telos axioms) from DDI's constructs for ontological instantiation (defined by roughly another 30 new axioms). The result was consistent and the axioms were free of redundancy, but it showed that this separation hinders the modeler from making use of Telos' metamodeling features together with DDI's multi-level modeling features, further, the combined set of axioms was relatively large and their execution in ConceptBase rather slow.

The DeepTelos approach, in contrast, preserves all the strengths of Telos and ConceptBase by not distinguishing linguistic and ontological instantiation. Interestingly, there seem to be different kinds or levels of linguistic instantiation: first, all model elements in a DeepTelos model are linguistic instances of Proposition, second, when modeling a modeling language like ERD (see Sect. 3.1) with linguistic classes Entity and EntityType, then some model elements, like mary, which is a linguistic instance of Proposition is also a linguistic instance of Entity. It seems that the former is a linguistic instantiation in DeepTelos and the second is a linguistic instantiation in ERD, which is in turn modeled in DeepTelos. The two scenarios about the linguistic use (see Sect. 3.1) and ontological use (see Sect. 3.2) of MGIs can be combined and create no inconsistency because the two hierarchies are separate. The combination allows to query for products that are also entities, or for the identifier (key attribute) of a given product.

One may ask whether MGI hierarchies are model-specific or universal. This cannot be answered from the axiomatic standpoint used in this paper. The 'ontological' MGI hierarchy for products has more of a model-specific flavor, since there are these 3 levels for product categories, product models, and actual products. This is a deliberate choice of the modeler. The 'linguistic' example for entity types and entities has a more universal nature because of the set-theoretic semantics of entity types as defined by the creator of the entity relationship model. A closer investigation of this question is subject to future research.

Formalization of DeepTelos: The DeepTelos axiomatization requires virtually only a single additional axiom (5) for Telos to realize an environment for multi-level modeling. The main axiom (5) is surprisingly simple and similar to the class membership axiom (3) of Telos. Both axioms closely interact with each other: the specializations derived by axiom (5) feed into the condition of axiom (3) to derive new instantiations. These instantiations then feed again into the condition of axiom (5). A second axiom (6) was added to ensure consistency of hierarchies where subtypes have MGIs. For example, in Fig. 7, CarModel with MGI Car is a specialization of ProductModel with MGI Product; axiom (6) then derives that Car is a specialization of Product.

As an alternative to MGIs, we also investigated extending Telos with singleton hierarchies (which we referred to internally as *most specific classes*). This construct did work for part of the example but finally clashed with a naming axiom in Telos that forbids that objects have multiple attributes/relations with the same label. The singleton approach apparently was also heavier in terms of required additional axioms, so we abandoned it. Both approaches share the idea to have proxy objects at the required level to replace the usual potencies of multi-level modeling approaches.

More Complex MGI Networks: We provided only examples of MGI chains, where a class has at most one MGI and an object is MGI of at most one class. This is the typical case, but it is worth discussing how more complicated MGI networks operate. First, consider the case that a class c has two MGIs m_1 and m_2. Axiom (5) will then derive the same subclasses for both m_1 and m_2. If the two MGIs are abstract classes, then they shall always have the same set of instances. One may then argue that they are redundant and multiple MGIs of the same class should be excluded. Even if the two MGIs had different attributes, then every instance of the first MGI would also be an instance of the other one. Hence, they always can use all attributes. As a consequence, we may want to forbid multiple MGIs of the same class c.

A second case is that an object m is the most general instance of two different classes c_1 and c_2. In this case, it shall have the instances of c_1 and the instances of c_2 as subclasses. This is useful when having different classifications for the same kind of objects. In our running example instead of a single ProductCategory class there may be multiple categorizations of product models, e.g., SalesProductCategory and LogisticsProductCategory which have different instances, e.g., LuxuryCar and GoodsForResale, respectively, but ProductModel as most general instance.

A network of MGI relations could be cyclic, e.g. $IN(m_1, m_2), IN(m_2, m_1)$. The instances of the one would then be subclasses of the other. We see no real-world application of such a pattern but did not forbid it in the axioms. We rather followed a minimalistic approach and leave additional constraints open for the reader.

6   Conclusions

We presented a specification of multi-level modeling within Telos that exploits the existence of the Telos axioms to keep it very simple, yet consistent with the Telos specification of instantiation and specialization. We further presented the implementation of DeepTelos in ConceptBase. Since ConceptBase is a highly optimized implementation of Telos, the extended language DeepTelos also has an efficient implementation. This implementation is available under an open license and can be downloaded to be applied and extended for own research and experimentation. Future work includes the following:

- DeepTelos should be tested with more example models from other multi-level modeling approaches to see its precise limitations.
- The restriction on the *Isa* predicate implementation in ConceptBase should be lifted to avoid the detour via the self-defined ISA relation.
- Additional axioms, e.g. forbidding the cyclicity of *IN* should be investigated.
- The introduction of additional axioms and relations can be guided by Carvalho's work [3] on ontological foundations of multi-level modeling.
- The linguistic and ontological use of the new construct of most general instances deserves more research with respect to utility and consistency.

References

1. Atkinson, C., Kühne, T.: The essence of multilevel metamodeling. In: Gogolla, M., Kobryn, C. (eds.) UML 2001. LNCS, vol. 2185, pp. 19–33. Springer, Heidelberg (2001). doi:10.1007/3-540-45441-1_3
2. Atkinson, C., Kühne, T.: Reducing accidental complexity in domain models. Softw. Syst. Model. **7**(3), 345–359 (2008)
3. Carvalho, V.A., Almeida, J.P.A., Fonseca, C.M., Guizzardi, G.: Extending the foundations of ontology-based conceptual modeling with a multi-level theory. In: Johannesson, P., Lee, M.L., Liddle, S.W., Opdahl, A.L., López, Ó.P. (eds.) ER 2015. LNCS, vol. 9381, pp. 119–133. Springer, Heidelberg (2015). doi:10.1007/978-3-319-25264-3_9
4. Gonzalez-Perez, C., Henderson-Sellers, B.: A powertype-based metamodelling framework. Softw. Syst. Model. **5**(1), 72–90 (2006)
5. Greenspan, S.J., Mylopoulos, J., Borgida, A.: On formal requirements modeling languages: RML revisited. In: ICSE 1994, pp. 135–147. IEEE Computer Society/ACM Press (1994)
6. Gutheil, M., Kennel, B., Atkinson, C.: A systematic approach to connectors in a multi-level modeling environment. In: Czarnecki, K., Ober, I., Bruel, J.-M., Uhl, A., Völter, M. (eds.) MODELS 2008. LNCS, vol. 5301, pp. 843–857. Springer, Heidelberg (2008). doi:10.1007/978-3-540-87875-9_58
7. Henderson-Sellers, B., Gonzalez-Perez, C.: The rationale of powertype-based metamodelling to underpin software development methodologies. In: APCCM 2005, pp. 7–16. Australian Computer Society (2005)
8. Jarke, M., Gallersdörfer, R., Jeusfeld, M.A., Staudt, M., Eherer, S.: ConceptBase - a deductive object base for meta data management. J. Intell. Inf. Syst. **4**(2), 167–192 (1995)

9. Jeusfeld, M.A.: Complete list of O-Telos axioms (2005). http://merkur.informatik.rwth-aachen.de/pub/bscw.cgi/d1228997/O-Telos-Axioms.pdf
10. Jeusfeld, M.A., Jarke, M., Mylopoulos, J. (eds.): Metamodeling for Method Engineering. Cooperative Information Systems. MIT Press, Cambridge (2009)
11. Klas, W., Schrefl, M.: Metaclasses and Their Application: Data Model Tailoring and Database Integration. LNCS, vol. 943. Springer, Heidelberg (1995). doi:10.1007/BFb0027185
12. Lara, J., Guerra, E.: Deep meta-modelling with METADEPTH. In: Vitek, J. (ed.) TOOLS 2010. LNCS, vol. 6141, pp. 1–20. Springer, Heidelberg (2010). doi:10.1007/978-3-642-13953-6_1
13. de Lara, J., Guerra, E., Cuadrado, J.S.: When and how to use multilevel modelling. ACM Trans. Softw. Eng. Methodol. 24(2), 12:1–12:46 (2014)
14. Mylopoulos, J., Borgida, A., Jarke, M., Koubarakis, M.: Telos: representing knowledge about information systems. ACM Trans. Inf. Syst. 8(4), 325–362 (1990)
15. Neumayr, B., Jeusfeld, M.A., Schrefl, M., Schütz, C.: Dual deep instantiation and its ConceptBase implementation. In: Jarke, M., Mylopoulos, J., Quix, C., Rolland, C., Manolopoulos, Y., Mouratidis, H., Horkoff, J. (eds.) CAiSE 2014. LNCS, vol. 8484, pp. 503–517. Springer, Heidelberg (2014). doi:10.1007/978-3-319-07881-6_34
16. Neumayr, B., Schuetz, C.G., Jeusfeld, M.A., Schrefl, M.: Dual deep modeling: multi-level modeling with dual potencies and its formalization in F-Logic. Softw. Syst. Model. 1–36 (2016). doi:10.1007/s10270-016-0519-z
17. Nissen, H.W., Jeusfeld, M.A., Jarke, M., Zemanek, G.V., Huber, H.: Managing multiple requirements perspectives with metamodels. IEEE Softw. 13(2), 37–48 (1996). http://dx.doi.org/10.1109/52.506461
18. Odell, J.J.: Power types. In: Odell, J.J. (ed.) Advanced Object-Oriented Analysis and Design Using UML, pp. 23–32. Cambridge University Press, Cambridge (1998)
19. Pirotte, A., Zimányi, E., Massart, D., Yakusheva, T.: Materialization: a powerful and ubiquitous abstraction pattern. In: VLDB, pp. 630–641 (1994)
20. Rossini, A., de Lara, J., Guerra, E., Rutle, A., Wolter, U.: A formalisation of deep metamodelling. Formal Aspects Comput. 26(6), 1115–1152 (2014)

Pragmatic Quality Assessment for Automatically Extracted Data

Scott N. Woodfield[1], Deryle W. Lonsdale[1], Stephen W. Liddle[1],
Tae Woo Kim[1], David W. Embley[1,2(✉)], and Christopher Almquist[1]

[1] Brigham Young University, Provo, UT 84602, USA
embley@cs.byu.edu
[2] FamilySearch International, Orem, UT 84097, USA

Abstract. Automatically extracted data is rarely "clean" with respect
to pragmatic (real-world) constraints—which thus hinders applications
that depend on quality data. We proffer a solution to detecting pragmatic constraint violations that works via a declarative and semantically
enabled constraint-violation checker. In conjunction with an ensemble of
automated information extractors, the implemented prototype checks
both hard and soft constraints—respectively those that are satisfied or
not and those that are satisfied probabilistically with respect to a threshold. An experimental evaluation shows that the constraint checker identifies semantic errors with high precision and recall and that pragmatic
error identification can improve results.

Keywords: Quality data · Data cleaning · Automated information
extraction · Declarative constraint specification · Automated integrity
checking · Conceptual-model-based extraction ensemble.

1 Introduction

Automated information-extraction systems (and sometimes even humans) can
extract erroneous (even ridiculous) information. Unless extracted information
about entities, values, and relationship assertions among entities and values
is correct, applications that depend on the information being correct—such as
search, marketing, advertising, and hinting applications—quickly degrade.

Perhaps the most important aspect of data quality is whether the data
satisfies real-world constraints—formally, *pragmatic constraints*. In our proposed solution to assessing the quality of automatically extracted data, we
begin by aligning internal conceptual-model constraints—formally, *semantic
constraints*—with pragmatic constraints. Realizing that pragmatic constraints
may be probabilistic and both hard and soft and that verification of accuracy
may require supporting documentation, we semantically enrich conceptual models with constraint specification based on probability distributions, and we add
the possibility of attaching supporting documentation to every object and relationship assertion [1]. Then, contrary to standard practice in business database

© Springer International Publishing AG 2016
I. Comyn-Wattiau et al. (Eds.): ER 2016, LNCS 9974, pp. 212–220, 2016.
DOI: 10.1007/978-3-319-46397-1_16

systems, we allow an ensemble of automated extractors to populate the conceptual schema with data that may violate declared integrity constraints. Checking incoming data against declared constraints is straightforward—indeed, is fully automatic based on the declarations alone. Deciding how to handle constraint violations, however, is application-dependent.

Although these augmented conceptual models are generally applicable for use with machine-learned or rule-encoded expert information-extraction systems, our implemented prototype, Fe6,[1] focuses on family-history applications. In Fe6 we handle constraint violations by flagging them red, yellow, or green depending on the severity of the violation and allow adjudication users to correct errors. Interestingly, because constraint specification is declarative in Fe6 conceptual models, handlers that send warning messages to adjudication users for constraint violations can all be generated automatically.

Figures 1 and 2 show an example. In the text snippet in Fig. 1, observe that Reverend Ely's children belong to two different mothers: Elizabeth who died in 1871 and Abbie, whom Reverend Ely married subsequently. The automated extraction in Fig. 2 has the children all belonging to Elizabeth, but Francis, the last child in the list, was born after Elizabeth died. The automatic extraction engines, which are blind to pragmatics, regularly make these kinds of mistakes. Semantic constraint checkers, however, can assess the extracted information and catch constraint violations. Handlers generate messages and flag potentially erroneous filled-in form-fields with a "circle-?" warning icon. When an adjudication user clicks on the icon, a message like the one in Fig. 2 pops up to warn the user of potential constraint violation(s). (Note that the message refers to birth dates, which are not present in the family-composition form in Fig. 2. They are, however, extracted onto another form.)

The Fe6 constraint checker primarily contributes to increasing data quality, a major concern in information systems and conceptual modeling. Conceptual modeling researchers have proposed various frameworks for assessing model quality (e.g. [2]) from which some level of data quality will presumably follow. Fe6 constraint checkers directly address data quality in ontological conceptualizations by aligning conceptually declared semantic constraints with pragmatic real-world constraints and then checking asserted fact-instances proposed for inclusion in a populated model instance. Moreover, the Fe6 approach to constraint checking harmonizes well with work on information-extraction systems in which inconsistencies and errors are detected and repaired (e.g. [3]). It also harmonizes well with work on data cleaning for database systems [4], but extends this work by allowing contradictory facts to be captured and then reasoning probabilistically over facts to increase data quality.

---

[1] Fe6: **F**orm-based **e**nsemble with **6** pipeline phases that accepts an OCRed document as input and generates a conceptualization of document-asserted facts as output.

243327. Rev. Ben Ezra Stiles Ely, Ottumwa, Ia., b. 1828, son of Rev. Ezra Stiles Ely and Mary Ann Carswell; m. 1848, Elizabeth Eudora McElroy, West Ely, Mo., who was b. 1829, d. 1871, dau. of Abraham McElroy and Mary Ford Radford; m. 2nd, 1873, Abbie Amelia Moore, Harrison, Ill., who was b. 1852, dau. of Porter Moore and Harriet Leonard.   Their children:

1. Elizabeth B., b. 1849.
2. Ben-Ezra Stiles, b. 1856.
3. George Everly Montgomery, b. 1858, d. 1877.
4. Laura Elizabeth, b. 1859.
5. LaRose DeForest, b. 1861.
6. Charles Wadsworth, b. 1863.
7. Mary Anita, b. 1865.
8. Francis Argyle, b. 1876.

Fig. 1. Text snippet from *The Ely Ancestry* [5], p. 421.

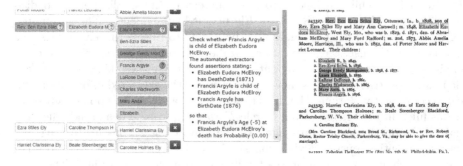

Fig. 2. Screenshot of constraint violation: child born after mother's death.

2   Application System

To serve their customers, family-history web sites such as FamilySearch.org and Ancestry.com provide search and hinting facilities over a large collection of data about individuals and families. They populate their searchable data stores mostly by crowd-sourcing. Hundreds of thousands of volunteers painstakingly fill in forms with data copied from images displayed on a computer screen. Most of the images are of handwritten data, often in pre-created forms (e.g. census records, birth certificates, death certificates, and military records). Some of the images, however, are typeset or typewritten such as are newspaper obituaries and family-history books. To extract genealogical data from these printed sources, providers are turning to OCR and automated information-extraction techniques to make this data available for search and hinting.

Fe6 consists of an ensemble of extractors designed to span the space from fully unstructured text to highly semi-structured text. Extracted data from a page of a document (e.g. Page 421 of *The Ely Ancestry* in Fig. 2) is distributed to a form (e.g. the "Family" form in Fig. 2). An adjudicator checks the filled-in form for correctness and makes corrections as necessary. As an aid to checking, hovering over a record in the form highlights fields as Fig. 2 shows and also displays warning icons on fields for which the system has detected a semantic constraint violation. Clicking on an icon pops open a display window explaining the violation.

2.1 Conceptualization

An evidence-based conceptual model [1] serves as the formal foundation for Fe6 applications. Figure 3 shows an example—a conceptualization with its predicates, constraints, and documenting evidence.

The diagram in Fig. 3 graphically represents a logic database schema. Object sets, depicted as named rectangular boxes, are one-place predicates (e.g. *Person(x)*). Relationship sets, depicted by lines connecting object sets, are *n*-place predicates (e.g. *Person(x) has BirthDate(y)*). Observe that predicates are in infix form and that predicate names come directly from the text and reading direction arrows in the diagram.

Constraints can be hard (returning only either *satisfied* or *not satisfied* when checked) or soft (returning a *probability of being satisfied* when checked). The conceptual-model diagram in Fig. 3 has 28 hard participation constraints specifying a minimum and maximum number of times an object may participate in a relationship set. Each object-set/relationship-set connection has one participation constraint as denoted by the decorations on the ends of the connecting lines. The 2's in Fig. 3 explicitly specify participation constraints that override decoration-specified participation constraints—each specifies that children have two parents. The diagram also shows 4 hard subset constraints (denoted by triangles on connecting lines) specifying that the objects in an object set must be a subset of the objects in another object set—children and spouses are also persons. In addition, Fig. 3 shows one of many possible soft constraints as a probability distribution (*Child being born Years after marriage date of parent Person has Probability*). Figure 3 indicates, as well, that evidence can be associated with

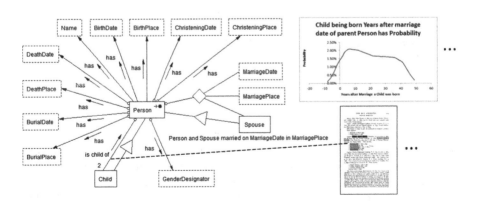

Fig. 3. Depiction of conceptual model features.

(and in Fe6 is associated with) every predicate assertion instance (e.g. *Child is child of Person* statements found in a document).

2.2 Hard Constraints

The conceptual-model diagram itself declaratively specifies hard cardinality constraints [6]. For example, it specifies that a person has at most one death date. The *Person* side of the *Person has DeathDate* relationship set has an "o" ("o" for "optional") on its connection and thus allows for no death date. The *DeathDate* side of the relationship set has an arrowhead, which specifies that the relationship from *Person* to *DeathDate* is functional (at most one death date).

The declaration of a participation constraint is sufficient to generate code that both checks for participation constraint violations and handles them. In a populated model instance, counting the number of times an object participates in a relationship set is straightforward, as is checking whether the count is within a *min–max* range. Similarly, generating a handler that names the object sets involved and lists the violating objects in a statement template is also straightforward.

2.3 Soft Constraints

Soft constraints are based on probability distributions. Since the conceptual model is foundationally predicate calculus, constraint rules can all be Datalog-like implications. The antecedents of an implication are predicates in the model or derived from these predicates or from given probability distributions, and the single consequent gives the probability of a condition being satisfied. For example, we can write a rule about the length of time after a parent's marriage date a child is born:

> $Child(x_1)$ *is child of* $Person(x_2)$,
> $Person(x_1)$ *has* $BirthDate(x_3)$,
> $Person(x_2)$ *and* $Spouse(x_4)$ *married on* $MarriageDate(x_5)$ *in Marriage-Place*(x_6),
> $Years(x_7) = Years(\,YearOf(x_3) - YearOf(x_5))$,
> *child being born* $Years(x_7)$ *after marriage date of parent has Probability*(x_8)
> $\Rightarrow$
> $Child(x_1)$ *being born* $Years(x_7)$ *after marriage date of parent* $Person(x_2)$ *has Probability*(x_8).

Any probability that fails to meet a user-specified threshold is a constraint violation. Violations tell us that one or more of the antecedents must be incorrect.

Each possible constraint violation has an application-dependent handler. Interestingly, given only the Datalog rule, both the code to check for a violation and the code to handle a violation can be generated automatically. The checker code need only run its usual interpreter on the given Datalog statement, which in essence creates a relational table in which each tuple is the join of all predicate instances that satisfy the Datalog statement. These tuples are then fed one at a time to the handler. Given a user-chosen threshold for constraint violation, the handler fills in a message template with extracted instance data found to be in violation. The handler generator substitutes textual instance values for variables in unary predicate-statement phrases (such as $BirthDate(x)$) and formats them for ease of reading. Since non-textual objects (such as *Person* instances and *Child* instances) come into existence by the principle of ontological commitment, the handler generator replaces unary person predicates with the person's name—the trigger for committing the extraction ontology to recognize the existence of a person.

3   Experimental Evaluation

We designed an experiment to test the constraint checker: (1) How well does it identify errors with semantic inconsistencies? (2) Can extraction accuracy be improved by intelligently removing assertions flagged by the constraint checker as possible extraction errors?

For the experiment we selected three books: *The Ely Ancestry* [5] (sample page snippet in Fig. 2), *The Register of Marriages and Baptisms in the Parish of Kilbarchan* [7], and *A Genealogical History of the Harwood Families* [8]. As a development test set, we chose three pages from each book. On these nine pages, we identified extraction errors with semantic inconsistencies made by the ensemble of extractors. For soft errors, we wrote Datalog rules over probability distributions, that would find each of these errors. These soft constraints plus the hard max-participation constraints in the conceptual model in Fig. 3 became the fixed set of constraints for the blind test set. The blind test set consisted of the four pages in each book located 1/5, 2/5, 3/5, and 4/5 of the way through the book (although we took a subsequent page if the page turned out to be a picture page as happened in three cases and also if the page contained essentially no genealogical information as happened in one case).

To determine how well the constraint checker identifies errors, we ran the extraction ensemble on the development test pages, identified the semantic errors encountered, and wrote rules to catch these errors—14 rules in addition to the model-specified participation-constraint rules in Fig. 3. Table 1 shows the results of applying the constraint checker to the twelve blind test pages. Overall, the ensemble extracted 479 records consisting of 1201 filled-in fields. The constraint checker marked 239 of these fields as possibly being in error as a result of finding violations of the 14 probabilistic semantic inference rules and the max-participation-constraint rules in the conceptual model. Looking for additional rules that would have caught errors in the blind test set that did not occur in the development test set, we found three—person names consisting of all digits and two kinds of improbable in-law relationships.

After ground-truthing the extraction for the blind test pages, we again applied the constraint checker to determine whether it would incorrectly identify and erroneously mark fields as possible semantic errors. Table 1 shows the precision, recall, and F-score. True positives are fields marked as possible errors

Table 1. Fields marked as potential errors by the constraint checker.

Book	Records	Filled Fields	Marked Fields	Erroneously Marked Fields	unMarked Fields	% Prec.	Rec.	F-score
Ely	159	410	127	3	25	97.7	83.6	90.1
Kilbarchan	276	694	108	12	0	90.0	100	94.7
Harwood	44	97	4	0	0	100	100	100
Overall	479	1201	239	12	25	94.1	90.5	92.3

Total number of development test-set rules: 14
Total number of new rules needed for blind test set: 3

Table 2. Accuracy (%): Precision, Recall, and F-score.

Book	Ensemble Extraction Results			All Suspect Assertions Retracted			Identifiable Erroneous Assertions Retracted		
	Prec.	Rec.	F-s.	Prec.	Rec.	F-s.	Prec.	Rec.	F-s.
Ely	81.2	65.1	72.2	83.6	44.0	57.6	77.0	59.1	66.8
Person	83.8	93.3	88.3	82.7	75.3	78.8	83.8	93.3	88.3
Couple	78.6	35.5	48.9	84.6	35.5	50.0	84.0	33.9	48.3
Family	78.0	56.8	65.7	86.7	16.0	27.1	61.1	40.7	48.9
Kilbarchan	91.9	90.5	91.2	97.3	85.2	90.8	95.3	91.1	93.2
Person	100	96.4	98.2	100	89.2	94.3	100	94.2	97.0
Couple	87.7	87.7	87.7	94.4	93.2	93.8	88.7	86.3	87.5
Family	85.6	85.6	85.6	96.0	76.0	84.8	94.2	90.4	92.2
Harwood	79.1	79.1	79.1	80.5	76.7	78.6	81.0	79.1	80.0
Person	96.3	86.7	91.2	96.2	83.3	89.3	96.3	86.7	91.2
Couple	75.0	60.0	66.7	85.7	60.0	70.6	85.7	60.0	70.6
Family	25.0	66.7	36.4	25.0	66.7	36.4	25.0	66.7	36.4
Overall	87.3	80.1	83.5	92.1	69.0	78.9	88.2	78.1	82.8

in pre-ground-truthing forms that were not marked in the post-ground-truthing forms. False positives are those marked fields that appeared in both pre- and post-ground-truthing forms. The total number of positives is the number of true-positive marked fields plus the number of unmarked fields that would have been marked had the constraint checker encoded the additional three rules for semantic errors in the blind test set that did not apply to the development test set. In our experiment the constraint checker was 100 % accurate except in a few instances in the Kilbarchan and Ely books where it encountered parents of the same child supposedly having the same gender. Gender is inferred from gender designators such as "son of", "Mrs.", etc. or in the absence of a gender designator by a large list of name/gender-frequency pairs.

Table 2 shows the results of our efforts to determine how well-the constraint checker could repair erroneously extracted data. Overall, the ensemble extracted information with an F-score of 83.5 %. Retracting all suspect assertions improved precision by 4.8 % points at the expense of a large drop in recall (11.1 % points) and a drop in F-score of 4.6 % points. Intelligently retracting just those assertions that are certainly or heuristically identifiable as being erroneous, improved precision slightly to 88.2 % without dropping recall by much, but enough to cause a slight drop in the F-score of 0.7 % points.

Assertions identifiable as certainly erroneous are those from rules with exactly one antecedent assertion such as "parent of self" and "spouse of self". Based on text layout, we heuristically chose to reject assertions violating participation constraints in which the lexical reading distance between the objects being related is more distant than the closest. Thus, for example, when the extractors declared two death dates for an individual, we kept only the date closest to the person's name.

4 Concluding Remarks

Being based on a formal conceptual model whose underlying semantics is predicate calculus makes the specification of constraints and constraint processing declarative. To the extent user-specified inference rules reflect real-world pragmatics, constraint checkers can identify semantically inconsistent extraction errors. Except in a few cases, however, the checker does not know which of the extracted assertions in antecedent predicates is in error. In general, determining which one(s) of several possible antecedent assertions is in error is non-trivial.

References

1. Embley, D.W., Liddle, S.W., Woodfield, S.N.: A superstructure for models of quality. In: Indulska, M., Purao, S. (eds.) ER 2014. LNCS, vol. 8823, pp. 147–156. Springer, Heidelberg (2014). doi:10.1007/978-3-319-12256-4_16
2. Akoka, J., Berti-Equille, L., Boucelma, O., Bouzeghoub, M., Comyn-Wattiau, I., Cosquer, M., Goasdoué-Thion, V., Kedad, Z., Nugier, S., Peralta, V., Cherfi, S.S.: A framework for quality evaluation in data integration systems. In: ICEIS 2007 - Proceedings of the Ninth International Conference on Enterprise Information Systems, pp. 170–175, Funchal, Madeira, Portugal, June 2007
3. Gutierrez, F., Dou, D., Fickas, S., Wimalasuriya, D., Zong, H.: A hybrid ontology-based information extraction system. J. Inf. Sci. (2015). On-line publication number 0165551515610989
4. Rahm, E., Do, H.H.: Data cleaning: problems and current approaches. IEEE Data Eng. Bull. 23(4), 3–13 (2000)
5. Vanderpoel, G.B. (ed.): The Ely Ancestry: Lineage of RICHARD ELY of Plymouth, England, Who Came to Boston, Mass., about 1655 & settled at Lyme, Conn., in 1660. The Calumet Press, New York (1902)
6. Liddle, S.W., Embley, D.W., Woodfield, S.N.: Cardinality constraints in semantic data models. Data & Knowl. Eng. 11(3), 235–270 (1993)

7. Grant, F.J. (ed.): Index to The Register of Marriages and Baptisms in the PARISH OF KILBARCHAN, pp. 1649–1772. J. Skinner & Company, LTD, Edinburgh, Scotland (1912)
8. Harwood, W.H.: A Genealogical History of the Harwood Families, Descended from Andrew Harwood, Whose English Home Was in Dartmouth, Devonshire, England, and Who Emigrated to America, and Was Living in Boston, Mass., in 1643. Watson H. Harwood, M.D., Chasm Falls, New York, 3rd edn. (1911)

UnifiedOCL: Achieving System-Wide Constraint Representations

David Weber[✉], Jakub Szymanek, and Moira C. Norrie

Department of Computer Science, ETH Zurich, Zürich, Switzerland
{weber,norrie}@inf.ethz.ch, jakub.szymanek@alumni.ethz.ch
http://www.globis.ethz.ch

Abstract. Constraint definitions tend to be distributed across the components of an information system using a variety of technology-specific representations. We propose an approach where constraints are managed in a single place using *OCL* with extensions for technology-specific concepts. These constraints are then mapped to technology-specific representations which are validated at runtime. Bi-directional translations of constraint definitions allows existing components to be easily integrated into the system. We present an implementation of the approach and report on a user study with developers from industry and research.

Keywords: Constraints · OCL · Transformations

1 Introduction

Constraints for basic data validation typically are defined in different components of an information system, including client-side form validation, business logic and databases. Further, the set of applicable constraints may depend on a particular configuration or context. For example, different constraints might apply in the mobile and desktop versions of an application due to differences in the functionality offered. Since constraints are derived from software requirements which may evolve over time, especially with agile methods, it can be challenging for developers to keep track of all constraints and maintain consistency throughout an entire system. It would therefore be highly beneficial if constraint definitions could be managed in a single place and automatically mapped to component-specific implementations for runtime validation.

To achieve this, we propose an approach in line with *Model-Driven Architecture (MDA)* [7,9] where a technology-independent model serves as a base for technology-specific code generation. In our model, constraints are expressed in UnifiedOCL, a domain specific language which extends OCL with capabilities to represent technology-specific constraints. To cater for the integration of different technologies, the grammar of UnifiedOCL is extensible by means of so-called *labels* which are grouped into dictionaries.

Furthermore, we studied various approaches and technologies of bi-directional translations between various models and representations. This resulted in an

© Springer International Publishing AG 2016
I. Comyn-Wattiau et al. (Eds.): ER 2016, LNCS 9974, pp. 221–229, 2016.
DOI: 10.1007/978-3-319-46397-1_17

extensible toolkit capable of efficiently translating constraints to and from *UnifiedOCL*. As a consequence, the system allows for translation from any source representation to any target representation, which we call multi-translations. Our proof-of-concept implementation supports three technology-specific representations: object-oriented language (*Java*), relational database (*SQL*) and business rules (*Drools*), which let us explore and cover a broad range of constraints.

After discussing the background and related work in Sect. 2, we introduce our approach in Sect. 3. The details of the unified constraint representation are presented along with our *DSL UnifiedOCL* and pluggable label dictionaries in Sect. 4. In Sect. 5, we describe our multi-translations and we report on the user study that we carried out in Sect. 6. Concluding remarks are given in Sect. 7.

2   Background

The *OCL* [16] plays an important role alongside *UML* in model-centric methodologies and enables concepts such as design by contract to be supported. However, the fact that it is platform independent results in the limitation that not all types of constraints that can be defined in technology-specific representations can be expressed directly. For example, the primary key constraint in relational databases has to be represented by a combination of *not null* and *unique* constraints. Further, it cannot express common restrictions on values such as email addresses or number precision which can be handled in Java using @Email and @Digits annotations, respectively. Additionally, *OCL* is not powerful enough to allow for the validation of numbers that require complex algorithms computing checksums such as the *Luhn algorithm* for a credit card number.

Several approaches have been proposed for translating *OCL* constraints to technology-specific languages. Many of these provide translations to *SQL*, e.g. [11,12]. Others have proposed translations to Java, e.g. [17] and specifically also to the Java Modeling Language (*JML*) [8], e.g. [5]. Aspect-oriented approaches, e.g. [6], translate design constraints defined in *OCL* into aspects that, when applied to a particular implementation, check the constraints at runtime. A comparison of different approaches to constraint validation based on *OCL* is provided in [1]. Their comparison includes direct translation to implementation languages, use of executable assertion languages, and use of aspect-oriented programming languages.

Some projects support translations from *OCL* to any form of assertion, e.g. [2, 10]. Moiseev et al. [10] use the same *MDA* approach as we do, but with the goal of showing how structural similarities can be used to generate additional translations with minimum effort.

Cosentino and Martínez [3] address reverse engineering by translating relational schemas into *OCL* expressions. Since *OCL* constraints are not *context-free*, they also generate the associated *UML* class diagram.

Shimba et al. [13] is one of the few projects that handle bi-directional translations, in their case between *OCL* and *JML*. Like us, their implementation is based on *Eclipse*[1] and *Xtext*[2]. However, although they mention Query/View/-Transformation Operational (QVT)[3] and the ATL Transformation Language (ATL)[4], they do not explicitly state if they use it for writing translation rules. We used QVT for only one case, using *Xtend*[5] for all others.

To the best of our knowledge, ours is the first approach that supports bidirectional translations between an *OCL-like* platform-independent constraint model and multiple technology-specific representations. This is beneficial if legacy systems want to move from one constraint representation to another or if a software developer prefers not to use a specific representation.

3 Approach

Figure 1 presents an overview of our approach. The various technology-specific constraint representations are depicted at the bottom (*JavaBeans Validation, SQL, Drools*). Each representation could be used in one or more components of the information system.

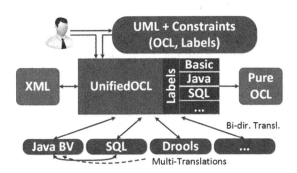

Fig. 1. Approach overview

UnifiedOCL is implemented as a new Domain Specific Language (*DSL*) that allows developers to define a wide variety of constraints using a textual representation that can be extended with labels to provide a compact way of specifying common constraints. This makes it easy for non-programmers to understand.

It combines structural domain information (*UML*), constraint definitions from *OCL* and a set of labels which either represent constraints not available in *OCL* (such as primary key in *SQL*) or simply provide a more convenient representation (such as email and credit card constraints). The syntax and constraint representation capabilities of *UnifiedOCL* will be presented in Sect. 4, while details of the constraint translations will be given in Sect. 5.

---

[1] https://eclipse.org/.
[2] http://www.eclipse.org/Xtext/.
[3] https://projects.eclipse.org/projects/modeling.mmt.qvt-oml.
[4] https://wiki.eclipse.org/ATL.
[5] https://eclipse.org/xtend/.

In our approach, it is possible to model an information system using a *UML* editor, enhancing the model with constraints defined in the standard *OCL* notation or with our label notation as depicted at the top of Fig. 1. This *UML* model can then be converted to a *UnifiedOCL* representation. Nonetheless, it is also possible to create and modify the *UnifiedOCL* representation in a text editor independent of a *UML* model.

By additionally introducing individual translations from all technology-specific representations to *UnifiedOCL* as indicated by the bi-directional arrows in Fig. 1, it is possible to translate between any two constraint representations in an information system. To add an extension for a technology-specific representation, only one single bi-directional translation to and from *UnifiedOCL* has to be provided to achieve multi-translations as depicted at the bottom of Fig. 1. This is possible since *UnifiedOCL* is powerful enough to express most of the constraints from various representations. Furthermore, it is possible to translate *UnifiedOCL* to pure *OCL* and exchange *UnifiedOCL* in an *XML* format.

4   Unified Constraint Representations

UnifiedOCL specifies both the constraints and the contextual data structure in which constraints exist, such as an *SQL* table schema or a Java class. An example is presented in Listing 1 where *OCL* together with our concept of labels are used to define constraints.

Listing 1. Example of UnifiedOCL

```
package org.example {
 public abstract class Employee {
  public attribute id: Integer {primarykey};
  public attribute name: String {notnull};
  public attribute birthDate: Date {past};
  public attribute email: String {email};
  public attribute salary: Real {range(min=2500, max=5300)};

  public reference subordinates: Employee[0..*]{unique};

  invariant IsJunior: self.age<25;
  invariant PersonId: not self.id.oclIsUndefined()
     and Person.allInstances()
     ->forAll(a : Person|a<>self implies a.id<>self.id);

  public operation checkIn (time: in Date,
     checkedIn: inout Boolean): String {
   precondition NotAlreadyCheckedIn: checkedIn=false;
   body CheckInBody: checkedIn=true;
   postcondition SuccessfullyCheckedIn: result=true;
   };
 . . .
```

In the given example in Listing 1 the data structure is class Employee in package (org.example) with the attributes (id, name, etc.) of data types (Integer, String, etc.). UnifiedOCL labels are used to define constraints associated with these. For example, the attribute id is labelled as a primarykey based on the SQL concept. The labels past and email define pattern matches not supported in OCL, while the notnull, range and unique labels provide a convenient way of defining the appropriate constraints.

Additionally, the reference (subordinates) has a label unique to disallow duplicates along with cardinality constraints specifying that any number of subordinates can exist, where the syntax [0..*] is part of the UnifiedOCL grammar. UnifiedOCL also allows directionalities to be specified for the parameters of operations as shown in the definition of the checkIn operation. Pre-, body- and post-conditions are also defined for this operation.

In contrast, the invariant constraints IsJunior and PersonId are defined in OCL. We have included a duplicate definition of the PersonId invariant using the primarykey label just to emphasise the convenience of using UnifiedOCL labels over OCL notation. With labels, the developer only has to name commonly used constraints and not care about the implementation. The technology-specific representation and validation of these constraints is the concern of the constraint translation which is discussed in the next section.

Labels also provide a way of extending the language with technology-specific concepts since the set of labels may be expanded. A list of all labels defined within our current implementation together with their parameters can be found in [15, pp. 163–165].

UnifiedOCL is based on the OCLinEcore syntax which allows an EMF Ecore model [14] to be combined with OCL statements. The OCLinEcore grammar extends the EssentialOCL [4] grammar, which allows OCL expressions to be specified but has no relation to the Ecore (or any other) data model. We derived UnifiedOCL by extending the EssentialOCL language and reusing the OCLinEcore language components and Ecore metamodel. We changed the metamodel by extending OCLinEcore concepts with attributes or relationships required to reflect the structure of a UML class diagram. For example, this involved introducing (1) a grammar element to reflect the concept of encapsulation levels, (2) simple exceptions, (3) a directionality meaning for method parameters, (4) user defined primitive types, (5) a Date built-in primitive type, and (6) a grammar element to allow operations to be specified as multithreaded. Additionally, and most important, we introduced support for the special constraint representation labels described above.

5   Constraint Translations

We distinguish between a formal constraint definition specified in UnifiedOCL and a technology-specific representation which is dependent on the particular programming language used for validation code. Bi-directional translations are concerned with generating the validation code from the formal constraint definition and vice versa.

For example, assume that a `Food` entity has a **name** attribute of type string which must be at least of length 3. The *formal constraint definition* in *UnifiedOCL* is shown in Listing 2.

Listing 2. *UnifiedOCL* translation example

```
package org.example {
  public abstract class Food {
    public attribute name: String {length(min=3)};
  }
}
```

The *technology-specific representations* for *SQL*, *Bean Validation* (*BV*) and *Drools* are given in Listings 3, 4 and 5 respectively:

Listing 3. *SQL* translation example

```
CREATE TABLE Food (
  name VARCHAR NOT NULL,
  CONSTRAINT ck_food_name CHECK (length(name::text) >= 3)
);
```

Listing 4. Java *BV* translation example

```
package org.example;
public class Food {
  @Length(min = 3)
  public String name;
}
```

Listing 5. *Drools* translation example

```
rule "Food_name_minlength"
when Food (name.length < 3)
then
  ...
end;
```

All translations, except for pure *OCL* extractions, use the model-to-text *M2T* [18] approach and consist of three main steps: (1) obtaining a traversable in-memory model instance from the source file(s), (2) model discovery and analysis and (3) performing a model to text serialisation.

Three different approaches have been used for generating an in-memory model such as an abstract syntax tree (*AST*). In some cases, such as *Drools*, an existing parser that accompanies the technology was used. For *SQL*, a parser was generated with the help of the modeling framework *Xtext* which is based on the *ANTLR*[6] parser. Bean Validation is an example where a model discovery tool such as *MoDisco*[7] was used.

Usually, the entire model needs to be analysed before serialisation can begin. For example, constraints in *SQL* can be defined in various places including as part of a column definition, at the table level or as an `ALTER TABLE` statement defined outside of the table, possibly in a different script. Therefore, an intermediary model is generated before being converted to the target textual representation.

When analysing a model, we identify constraint occurrences with regular expressions and create abstract constraint representations (*ACRs*) containing

---

[6] http://www.antlr.org/.
[7] https://eclipse.org/MoDisco/.

all information about the constraint in a technology independent way. Dictionaries define the mapping of positions within regular expressions to constraint parameters. An *ACR* defines the location, type, names, parameters and values of a constraint. To generate a target representation, we use specific target representation producers (*TRPs*) which are also defined in dictionaries and able to serialise the *ACRs* to the target textual representation.

In the *JavaBeans Validation* example of Listing 4 the technology-specific constraint @Length(min = 3) would be matched with an abstract *size* constraint from our *Java2UnifiedOCL* dictionary. The resulting *ACR* would then have the location org.example.Food.name, the type *size*, a unique name and the *lowerBound* parameter with a value of 3. Our *General2UnifiedOCL* dictionary can be used to translate any *ACR* to a specific *UnifiedOCL* representation and would be used to generate the representation in Listing 2. Similarly, the dictionary could also be used for the opposite translation from *UnifiedOCL* to *JavaBeans Validation*.

The extraction of *OCL* statements from *UnifiedOCL* increases the usefulness of our system since tools such as *DresdenOCL*[8] allow objects such as JavaBeans to be validated based on the pure *OCL* specification.

6   Evaluation

We conducted a user study with 20 software engineers from both research and industry (15 male, 5 female). 50 % had studied or worked in a university at some time and 75 % had worked in industry.

The participants had to solve three tasks with the help of our tool. Before each task, additional features of the tool relevant to the task were explained. A feedback questionnaire based on a 5-point Likert-type scale ('totally disagree' to 'totally agree') was used. In this summary of results, we combine the first two values into 'disagree' and the last two into 'agree'.

In the first task, participants had to convert a *UML* diagram with two simple, connected entities without any constraints and a total of eight attributes into their choice of *Java*, *SQL* or *Drools* code. They were then presented with the same *UML* diagram with seven constraint definitions in *UnifiedOCL* label notation, without an explanation of the notation, and were required to extend the code accordingly. Finally, they had to generate the same code using our tool and edit it if it did not meet their expectations.

For the second task, they were given a short introduction to *UnifiedOCL* and asked to add a field to one of the classes along with a specific constraint. The third task, required them to combine a definition in Java with one in *SQL* to give a single definition in Java, *SQL* or *UnifiedOCL* using our tool.

85 % of the participants chose Java in task 1 and 15 % *SQL*. Only 30 % were able to manually solve the task completely, even though 80 % of all users had a good or very good understanding of *UML* and almost half (43 %) of those with

---

[8] http://www.dresden-ocl.org/index.php/DresdenOCL.

partial solutions declared their knowledge in the selected technology as very good.

The average time users spent writing initial code was 185 s (std. dev. 70 s), while the average for extending it was 224 s (std. dev. 73 s). The average time required using our tool was significantly less at 46 s (std. dev. 21 s). Moreover, all agreed that the generated code met their expectations, with only five of them editing it slightly to adjust formatting, organise imports, or alter names. All agreed that the tool was easy to learn and use.

Task two was successfully solved by almost all participants (90 % knew how to define the field and 85 % the constraint) with failures due to a misunderstanding about what to do rather than not knowing how to do it. 90 % of users agreed that the *UnifiedOCL* syntax is intuitive. Similarly, almost all (75 %) agreed that they would remember the *UnifiedOCL* syntax required to solve this task.

In task three, there were no errors in the use of the system. Most users (60 %) chose *UnifiedOCL* as the common format used for the comparison with stated reasons including '*UnifiedOCL* can represent all constraints whereas Java and *SQL* will have some problems with certain constraints' and 'this translation is easier and more obvious'. Of those selecting conversion to Java or *SQL*, most justified it in terms of familiarity, with one stating that *UnifiedOCL* would be the preferred choice if they had more experience with it.

All participants agreed that the tool was efficient and convenient to use, and 85 % were satisfied with the results. Those who were not satisfied were missing some sort of order of the attributes in the target representation. We decided to maintain the same order of attributes as in the source representation, but nevertheless it is one of the extensions that should be considered since it was mentioned by seven participants (35 %).

Full details of the results are provided in [15, pp. 136–143].

7   Conclusions

We have presented an approach that allows constraints validated in different components of an information system to be managed in a central repository, with technology-specific validation code generated automatically. Constraints are specified in *UnifiedOCL* using a mix of *OCL* and *UnifiedOCL* labels which provide a shorthand for common technology-specific constraints. *UnifiedOCL* is extensible as new labels can be introduced at any time.

References

1. Avila, C., Sarcar, A., Cheon, Y., Yeep, C.: Runtime constraint checking approaches for OCL. a critical comparison. In: SEKE (2010)
2. Baresi, L., Young, M.: Toward translating design constraints to run-time assertions. Electr. Notes Theor. Comput. Sci. **116**, 73–84 (2005)
3. Cosentino, V., Martínez, S.: Extracting UML/OCL integrity constraints and derived types from relational databases. In: MoDELS International Workshops (2013)

4. EssentialOCL. http://help.eclipse.org/juno/index.jsp?topic=%2Forg.eclipse.ocl.
   doc%2Fhelp%2FEssentialOCL.html. Accessed 04 Apr 2016
5. Hamie, A.: Using patterns to map OCL constraints to JML specifications. In: Ham-
   moudi, S., Pires, L.F., Filipe, J., Neves, R.C.D. (eds.) Model-Driven Engineering
   and Software Development. Communications in Computer and Information Science, vol. 506, pp. 35–48. Springer, Switzerland (2015)
6. Khan, M.U., Arshad, N., Iqbal, M.Z., Umar, H.: AspectOCL: extending OCL
   for crosscutting constraints. In: Taentzer, G., Bordeleau, F. (eds.) ECMFA
   2015. LNCS, vol. 9153, pp. 92–107. Springer, Heidelberg (2015). doi:10.1007/
   978-3-319-21151-0_7
7. Kleppe, A., Warmer, J., Bast, W.: MDA explained - the model driven architecture:
   practice and promise. Addison-Wesley, Reading (2003)
8. Leavens, G.T., Baker, A.L., Ruby, C.: JML: a notation for detailed design. In:
   Kilov, E., Rumpe, B., Simmonds, I. (eds.) Behavioral Specifications of Businesses
   and Systems. The Springer International Series in Engineering and Computer Science, vol. 523, pp. 175–188. Springer, New York (1999)
9. Mellor, S.J., Scott, K., Uhl, A., Weise, D.: Model-driven architecture. In: Bruel,
   J.-M., Bellahsene, Z. (eds.) OOIS 2002. LNCS, vol. 2426, pp. 290–297. Springer,
   Heidelberg (2002). doi:10.1007/3-540-46105-1_33
10. Moiseev, R., Hayashi, S., Saeki, M.: Using hierarchical transformation to generate
    assertion code from OCL constraints. IEICE Trans. 94(3), 612–621 (2011)
11. Obrenovic, N., Popovic, A., Aleksic, S., Lukovic, I.: Transformations of check con-
    straint PIM specifications. Comput. Inf. 31(5), 1045–1079 (2012)
12. Oriol, X., Teniente, E.: Incremental checking of OCL constraints with aggregates
    through SQL. In: Johannesson, P., Lee, M.L., Liddle, S.W., Opdahl, A.L., López,
    Ó.P. (eds.) ER 2015. LNCS, vol. 9381, pp. 199–213. Springer, Heidelberg (2015).
    doi:10.1007/978-3-319-25264-3_15
13. Shimba, H., Hanada, K., Okano, K., Kusumoto, S.: Bidirectional translation
    between OCL and JML for round-trip engineering. In: APSEC (2013)
14. Steinberg, D., Budinsky, F., Paternostro, M., Merks, E.: EMF: Eclipse Modeling
    Framework 2.0. Addison-Wesley Professional, Reading (2009)
15. Szymanek, J.: Achieving unified data quality representation by constraints trans-
    formation. http://dx.doi.org/10.3929/ethz-a-010510131 (2015)
16. Warmer, J., Kleppe, A.: The Object Constraint Language: Getting Your Models
    Ready for MDA, 2nd edn. Addison-Wesley Longman Publishing Co. Inc., Boston
    (2003)
17. Wilke, C.: Java code generation for Dresden OCL2 for eclipse. Technische Univer-
    sität Dresden, Germany (2009)
18. Wimmer, M., Burgueño, L.: Testing M2T/T2M transformations. In: Moreira, A.,
    Schätz, B., Gray, J., Vallecillo, A., Clarke, P. (eds.) MODELS 2013. LNCS, vol.
    8107, pp. 203–219. Springer, Heidelberg (2013). doi:10.1007/978-3-642-41533-3_13

Semantic Annotations

Building Large Models of Law with NómosT

N. Zeni[1(✉)], E.A. Seid[1], P. Engiel[2], S. Ingolfo[1], and J. Mylopoulos[1]

[1] Department of Information Engineering and Computer Science,
University of Trento, Trento, Italy
{nicola.zeni,elias.seid,silvia.ingolfo,john.mylopolous}@unitn.it
[2] Programa de Pós-Graduação em Informática, PUC-Rio, Rio de Janeiro, Brazil
pengiel@inf.puc-rio.br

Abstract. Laws and regulations impact the design of software systems, as they introduce new requirements and constrain existing ones. The analysis of a software system and the degree to which it complies with applicable laws can be greatly facilitated by models of applicable laws. However, laws are inherently voluminous, often consisting of hundreds of pages of text, and so are their models, consisting of thousands of concepts and relationships. This paper studies the possibility of building models of law semi-automatically by using the NómosT tool. Specifically, we present the NómosT architecture and the process by which a user constructs a model of law semi-automatically, by first annotating the text of a law and then generating from it a model. We then evaluate the performance of the tool relative to building a model of a piece of law manually. In addition, we offer statistics on the quality of the final output that suggest that tool supported generation of models of law reduces substantially human effort without affecting the quality of the output.

1 Introduction

Laws and regulations impact the design of software systems, as they constrain their features and their operations. The analysis of a software system, intended to ensure that it complies with applicable laws can be greatly facilitated by conceptual models of applicable laws. However, laws are inherently voluminous, often consisting of hundreds of pages of text. This suggests that their models will also be voluminous, consisting of thousands of concepts and relationships. For example, for the two laws studied in this work, generated models had approximately 6,000 and 11,000 elements (concepts, relationships) respectively. This paper studies the possibility of building conceptual models of law semi-automatically by using a tool-supported process.

In particular, we present the NómosT tool, its architecture and the process by which a user constructs a model of law semi-automatically. The process consists of first annotating the text of a law with semantic tags, and then generating from it a conceptual model, with supplementary input from the user. To evaluate NómosT, we have compared models constructed semi-automatically using NómosT with manually constructed models. In addition, we offer statistics on

© Springer International Publishing AG 2016
I. Comyn-Wattiau et al. (Eds.): ER 2016, LNCS 9974, pp. 233–247, 2016.
DOI: 10.1007/978-3-319-46397-1_18

the quality of the final output that suggest that tool-supported generation of models of law reduces human effort by more than 400 % without affecting the quality of the output. For the two laws we have included in our study, this means that instead of requiring about 50 h of manual labour to construct a full model of the law manually, one can use the NómosT tool and reduce manual effort to approximately 10 h. Precise statistics on our experiments are presented in the sequel.

The rest of the paper is structured as follows. Section 2 presents the research baseline for our work, while Sect. 3 presents the NómosT tool. In Sects. 4 and 5 we present the two experiments and report and discuss derived results. Section 6 compares our results to related research in the literature, and Sect. 7 concludes and discusses future work.

2   Research Baseline

This section presents the GaiusT framework for semantic annotation of legal documents, as well as the Nómos modeling language, intended for modeling law.

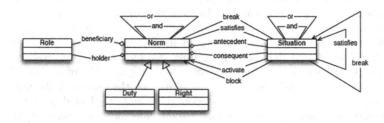

Fig. 1. A meta-model for the Nómos modeling language

GaiusT. The GaiusT tool automates the semantic annotation of legal documents. The tool has been successfully applied for the annotation of different legal documents in both English and Italian and has proven useful in supporting legal text analysis [16]. GaiusT uses structural and semantic patterns to extract and annotate text fragments that describe legal concepts from documents. Structural analysis identifies legal document structure, including cross references. Using a metamodel of legal concepts, GaiusT identifies instances of complex deontic concepts, such as actors, rights and obligations. The metamodel constitutes a core element for semantic analysis. From it, one can derive an annotation schema that specifies the rules for identifying instances of legal concepts by listing concept identifiers with their syntactic indicators and patterns to represent complex concepts. Syntactic indicators can be single words, phrases, or references previously parsed basic entities, while patterns are collection of concepts related by regular expressions. Patterns are also useful in identifying relationships among concepts. The output of GaiusT is an XML file that lists all annotations generated by the tool.

Nómos. Nómos is a modeling language for law, intended to support compliance analysis for software requirements [8,15]. The modeling framework is founded on the concept of a *norm*, an atomic fragment of law with deontic status. A norm is characterized by: (1) a type which can be right or duty, (2) a holder – a role responsible for complying with the norm, (3) a beneficiary who profits from the norm, (4) an antecedent situation that makes the norm applicable, and (5) a consequent situation that has to be achieved for the satisfaction of the norm A *situation* is a state-of-affairs, such as being in a public building or sending personal information. In addition to the primitive concepts of norm and situation, Nómos includes relationships between norms and/or situations. In particular, the following relationships are included: Activate, Block, Break and Satisfy. Activate and Block relate situations to norms and determine the applicability of a norm, while Break and Satisfy determine the satisfiability of a norm or situation. Nómos has been developed over several years, and includes several dialects (Nómos, Nómos 2 and Nómos 3). For our purposes, we are using the Nómos 2 dialect. Figure 1 presents the metamodel of Nómos2.

3 NómosT

NómosT was developed upon the GaiusT framework to semi-automate the generation of Nómos models. NómosT supplements GaiusT with four new modules that support the entire model generation process:

1. A library module including helper functions and data for managing different legal document type templates (e.g. American regulations, European law, Italian law etc.); for each template, the module includes annotation patterns for document structure, concepts, and syntactic indicators;
2. An extended semantic annotation module over what is available in GaiusT; this supports nested patterns defined in the NómosT metamodel;
3. A new visualization module that applies XSLT transformations on XML annotated documents and generates an HTML report; and
4. A new module that computes statistics on legal concepts and annotated elements.

The architecture of NómosT is presented in Fig. 2, the components presented in dark gray constitute GaiusT while, the components in light gray represent the additional functionalities of NómosT. The core component of the tool uses and manipulates on the metamodel of GaiusT and Nómos. The meta-model of Nómos contains five concepts namely: *Role, Norm, Duty, Right* and *Situation* (see Fig. 1). In the tool we add a set of auxiliary patterns – Actor, Resource, Exception, Antecedent, Consequent, PositiveVerb, NegativeVerb, Holder and Beneficiary – used to extract instances of the five concepts. A pattern can be nested within other patterns. For example, the Role concept has syntactic indicators that identify instances of actor, beneficiary and holder in the document while the concept of *Situation* has been defined as a combination of an *Actor* or *Role*, an *Action* and a *Resource*. PositiveVerb identifies instances of a modal

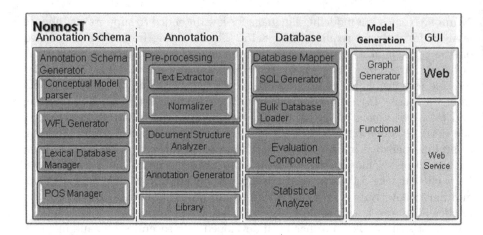

Fig. 2. NómosT system architecture

verb that express permission, while NegativeVerb identifies instances of obligation and prohibition. Figure 3 reports the main patterns used in the mapping of
concepts and relationships. Concepts, patterns and relationships are described in
the annotation schema and are the basis for semantic annotation, and the generation of Nómos models. The annotation schema includes not only concepts,
patterns and relationships but also structural elements that capture the structure of laws such as Part, Title, Chapter, Section and their sub items. Every
concept of the conceptual model has a correspondence concept or pattern in the
annotation schema.

Each pattern is represented in an extended BNF notation (aka eBNF) and
describes allowable combinations of concepts, sub-patterns and structural elements. Turning to the identification of relationships, instances of Activate and
Block are identified through new patterns derived through a manual analysis of
four Sections of annotated legal documents of Italian and German laws. These
patterns are highly heuristic and need to be augmented by manual inspection of
the legal text. Table 1 reports the list of new syntactic indicators and patterns
identified[1].

3.1   Generation Process

The process of generating a Nómos model requires three steps.

Set Up of the Annotation Schema. Tune the syntactic indicators for actor,
role and resource, since these can vary for different laws.

This step requires the analysis of the target legal document, concerning the
Definition Part, where main actors, roles, and terms are defined precisely and

---

[1] The tool is available at http://www.fastsas.com/.

$$
\begin{aligned}
\langle Right\rangle &::= (\ \langle Actor\rangle\ |\ \langle Role\rangle\ )^+ \\
&|\ \langle PositiveVerb\rangle\ \langle Action\rangle^+\ \langle Resource\rangle^+ \\
\langle Obligation\rangle &::= (\ \langle Actor\rangle\ |\ \langle Role\rangle\ )^+ \\
&|\ \langle NegativeVerb\rangle\ \langle Action\rangle^+\ \langle Resource\rangle^+ \\
\langle Norm\rangle &::= \langle Right\rangle\ |\ \langle Obligation\rangle \\
\langle ExceptionNorm\rangle &::= \langle Exception\rangle\ \langle Norm\rangle \\
\langle ConditionNorm\rangle &::= \langle Condition\rangle\ \langle Norm\rangle \\
\langle Situation\rangle &::= (\ \langle Actor\rangle\ |\ \langle Role\rangle\ )^+\ \langle Action\rangle\ \langle Resource\rangle \\
\langle Antecedent\rangle &::= \langle ConditionNorm\rangle\ \langle Situation\rangle \\
\langle Consequent\rangle &::= \langle Situation\rangle\ \langle ConditionNorm\rangle \\
\langle RelActivate\rangle &::= \langle Antecedent\rangle\ \langle Norm\rangle_x^+\ |\ \langle Antecedent\rangle\ \langle Norm\rangle_y^+ \\
\langle RelSatisfy\rangle &::= \langle Consequent\rangle\ \langle Norm\rangle_x^+\ |\ \langle Consequent\rangle\ \langle Norm\rangle_y^+ \\
\langle RelBreak\rangle &::= \langle Consequent\rangle\ \langle Norm\rangle_x^+\ |\ \langle Consequent\rangle\ \langle Norm\rangle_y^+ \\
\langle RelBlock\rangle &::= \langle Norm\rangle_x^+\ \langle Norm\rangle_y^+ \\
\langle RelDerogation\rangle &::= \langle Norm\rangle_x^+\ \langle Norm\rangle_y^+ \\
\langle RelEndorsment\rangle &::= \langle Norm\rangle_x^+\ \langle Norm\rangle_y^+
\end{aligned}
$$

Fig. 3. EBNF patterns used to generate Nómos model

Table 1. Syntactic indicators, and patterns extrapolated with heuristic approach

Syntactic indicators	Antecedent/consequent
Where, as long as, if then, as far as, given than, only when, subject to	Activate/block
In cases referred to, in which	Activate
As referred to, in this case, when	Activate/satisfy
In accordance	Activate/consequent
Only to fulfil, to ensure, in order to	Consequent/satisfy
Nómos relation type	Patterns
Activate	<Antecedent> + <Obligation>
Satisfy	<Consequent> + <Right>
Block	<Antecedent + NegativeModalVerb>
Break	<Consequent> + <NegativeModalVerb>

a reference synonym is assigned. The step is supported by statistical analysis using word and n-grams frequency.

Semantic Annotation of the Document. The second step performs the semantic annotation of the document. The step consists of several sub-steps of normalizing and parsing. In particular we have: (1) Normalize and flatten the input document by removing leading and unprintable characters, trailing spaces, to produce a text document where each line represents a phrase; (2) the annotation of text units of a given document with XML tags delimiting its text unit

```
- <Antecedent Id="64" Type="B" Value="Antecedent" IdE="98">
  - <GerSubSubSection Value="1." Id="11" Type="S" IdE="74">
    - <Right Id="759" Type="B" Value="Right" IdE="94">
        <Resource Value="the data" IdE="12416" Id="56" Type="C"/>
        <Action Value="allow" IdE="1229" Id="304" Type="C"/>
        the identification of
        <Actor Value="persons" IdE="12417" Id="285" Type="C"/>
        who are or were professionally involved as
        <Role Value="journalists" IdE="12417" Id="585" Type="C"/>
        in preparing,
        <Action Value="producing" IdE="12687" Id="113" Type="C"/>
        or disseminating broadcasts,
    </Right>
  </GerSubSubSection>
</Antecedent>
```

Fig. 4. Excerpt of output of Nómos model

boundaries – structure identification – and annotating cross references; (3) the identification of concepts, by using syntactic indicators and grammar rules. Every concept is annotated with a XML tag; (4) the identification of relationships, by using the heuristic patterns. (5) the annotation of nested patterns; (6) lastly, a statistical analysis resulting in a conceptual model. The final output consists of both an XML and and HTML report with all elements annotated, the graphical model, the statistical analysis and the input document browsable within annotated elements. The output of step two is an annotated text document (see an example in Fig. 4), along with a conceptual model.

Improve and Validate the Models. In the final step, human modellers improve and validate the final models by going through the XML and HTML documents checking all identified elements.

4   Evaluation of NómosT

Two experiments have been conducted to evaluate the tool by comparing the Nómos model generated by the tool-supported process, against the golden standard Nómos models created by Nómos experts. We adopt the same evaluation strategy as we used for GaiusT tool by comparing the output of the tool with gold standard [16]. With these experiments we evaluated how tool-constructed models compare with the gold standard with respect to quality and how the tool improves productivity. For both studies, the comparison is twofold: on one hand we evaluate the effectiveness of NómosT in reducing human effort, and on the other hand we evaluate the quality of the output, measured in terms of precision and recall. The evaluation does not consider overhead to set up NómosT resources, such as the construction of the conceptual model, time used for tuning the syntactic elements of the annotation schema and relationship patterns. After all, this is an one-time only overhead for a given language or normative system of a country and can be at least partially offset by overhead to train people, so that they are comfortable with legal concepts and the annotation process for legal documents. The experiments conducted are intended to answer the following research questions:

– RQ1: Does the semi-automatic extraction of Nómos model reduce manual effort?
– RQ2: What is the quality of the model produced by NómosT process compared to the models produced through a manual process?

To answer these questions, we use two measures. The first measures the manual effort it takes to build a model of law with/without the NómosT tool, measured in min/h. The second measure evaluates the correctness of the models generated relative to a golden standard. We assume that quality of manual generated models constitutes an upper bound, however, in order to take into account human disagreement and obtain a more realistic estimate of system performance, we calibrate automatic results relative to human performance. Thus recall and precision have been calibrated taking into account human disagreement. Correctness was measured in terms of precision and recall in the identification of elements (concepts, relationships) that constitute the output conceptual model.

4.1 Italian Law Experiment

In this study we used four Sections of the official English translation of the Italian privacy law "Italian Personal Data Protection Code": Sections 37, 43, 54 and 78 (see http://www.garanteprivacy.it/home_en/italian-legislation). The Sections have been chosen for pragmatic reasons[2]. In this experiment we used four participants (three are authors of this paper). Two participants were Nómos experts involved in building the golden standard for evaluating the accuracy of the NómosT tool in generating Nómos models. Two of the participants were given the original legal text of the selected four sections of the Italian privacy law. The other two participants had background in processing legal text with NLP techniques. These generated models of law semi-automatically using the NómosT tool.

To answer **RQ1** we evaluate how much the tool improves manual performance by comparing the time taken to build manually the golden standard with the time taken to build models with the help of the tool. Table 2 reports the time taken by human experts to manually annotate the four Sections and produce a Nómos model. The table also reports on the time taken to generate models semi-automatically. In the table we can observe that Section 78 takes much longer than others Sections. This happens because Section 78 is much more dense in

---

[2] Section 37 has 507 words, 14 sentences, Section 43 has 438 words, 12 sentences, Section 54 has 343 words, 10 sentences and Section 78 has 373 words, 13 sentences.

Table 2. Time efforts for the creation of the models

Sections of law	Manual annotation (min)	Manual generation of graphical model (min)	Manual generation annotation and model (min)	Tool supported generation of the model (min)
37	8	38	46	12
43	9	32	41	8
54	7	26	33	14
78	35	53	88	23
Average	15	37	52	14

the concepts and relationships it describes. The golden standard models have been built by experts in an average of 15 min for each Section. The process of producing annotated documents by the tool requires in total 32 ms while the average time for checking a model is 14 min. As expected, checking models for consistency and completeness (column 5 on Table 2) takes much less than generating models (column 3). Also note that the Italian law included many instances of Satisfy which had to be added manually because they are not handled by NómosT.

The time reported for the Tool assisted includes the effort to improve and validate the model generated by the tool. Our preliminary results indicate that the NómosT tool largely reduces human effort in building Nómos model.

To answer **RQ2** we have analyzed the models produced with the help of the tool, against a golden standard. The model produced by the expert has been evaluated pairwise with the model produced by tool and refined manually adopting the following criteria: (1) first, annotated concepts were considered correct when they overlapped on most meaningful words, so that minor divergences in text fragment boundaries were ignored; (2) concepts identified by NómosT and missed by expert were manually revisited and validated; (3) concepts that the tool annotates using more than one annotation are count as valid (for example human annotator mark a sentence as situation while NómosT mark the same sentence with two situations). Nómos relationships were the most troublesome to identify in the text. Indeed in the results from the tool-supported process relationships such as activate and block were often mis-identified or missing altogether[3]. Table 3 reports qualitative results of the Italian law. Results have been calibrated considering human disagreement which was 13.3 %, reporting an overall performance of 81 %. As aspected, Section 78 reports a drop in performance due to the complexity of the content. Section 54 reports similar results as Section 78 since the the tool did not captured relationships.

4.2   German Law Experiment

To gather further evidence about the performance of NómosT, we run a second experiment using The German Data Protection Act. The goal was to test the effectiveness of the tool with a law from a different jurisdiction. The hierarchi-

---

[3] Generated models are available at http://www.fastsas.com/Experiments/Ita.

Table 3. Evaluation rates for the Nómos concepts retrieved semi-automatically with the use of the NómosT tool.

Measure	Section				Avg
	37	43	54	78	
Recall	0.84	0.90	0.54	0.55	0.71
Precision	0.96	0.97	1.00	1.00	0.98
Fallout	1.00	1.00	0.00	0.00	0.50
Accuracy	0.82	0.88	0.54	0.55	0.69
Error	0.18	0.13	0.46	0.45	0.31
F-measure	0.90	0.93	0.70	0.71	0.81

cal structure of the document contains Part, Title, Chapter and Sections, Subsection, Sub-sub-section and List. The German Data Protection Act contains 48 Sections which are categorised into four parts. The tool annotates and generates Nómos models for all 48 Sections. For the evaluation, we used Sections 13 and 14 of part II and Sections 41 and 42 of part IV of the official English translation of the German Data Protection Act (see http://www.gesetze-im-internet.de)[4] to annotate and generate models, for purposes of comparison. The four Sections have been chosen randomly, without using specific criteria. In this experiment we used two participants (both authors of this paper). These participants were given a printed document with the original legal text of the selected four Sections. The two participants did the annotation and in second stage they checked the correctness of the models generated by the tool. These participants have experience in modeling and Nómos language.

To evaluate the human effort, **RQ1**, we compared the time taken to build manually the model with the time taken with the help of the tool. Table 4 summarizes the time that annotators spent to do the task. In particular, to manually annotate and build a model for a Section of German law, annotators take an average of 52 min. On the other hand, annotators spent an average of 11.5 min to check and verify the model generated by the tool. The time used by the tool to generate the final graphical model is an average of ten for an increase in productivity of more than 400 %. We have a four-fold improvement in productivity. By extrapolating from the results concerning the four sections, we estimate that to build Nómos models manually for the entire German law would require 42 h, but with the use of NómosT, manual effort can be reduced to 9.5 h.

To answer **RQ2**, we have compared the models produced with the help of the tool with ones manually generated by analysts. To calculate human disagreement we compared the models generated manually to each other noting the differences (number of concepts and relationships) and calculating the percentage of agreement.

---

[4] Section 13 has 303 words with 12 sentences, Section 14 has 572 words, 21 sentences, Section 41 has 264 words, 12 sentences and Section 42 has 249 words, 13 sentences.

Table 4. Time required to build the Model

Sections of law	Manual annotation (min)	Manual generation of graphical model (min)	Manual generation annotation and model (min)	Tool supported generation of the model (min)
13	15	40	55	8
14	10	36	46	15
41	15	40	55	10
42	15	30	45	13
Average	14	37	51	12

Table 5. Evaluation rates for the Nómos model with the use of the NómosT tool.

Measure	Section				Avg
	13	14	41	42	
Recall	1.00	0.78	0.73	0.83	0.84
Precision	0.85	0.89	0.94	0.95	0.91
Fallout	1.0	1.00	1.13	1.00	1.00
Accuracy	0.83	0.69	0.65	0.80	0.74
Error	0.22	0.36	0.48	0.20	0.31
F-measure	0.92	0.83	0.82	0.89	0.86

Table 5 reports the results of the second experiment. Results of the tool have been calibrated with both human annotated models, considering the rate of agreement in average around 83.0 %. F-measure in average is 86.6 % with an accuracy of 74.2 %, showing that the generated models have a good quality and with a small human effort can be improved. The overall quality compared with the Italian experiment shows a better result for this experiment, because of the way German laws are structured and phrased.

5 Discussion

The comparison of the two laws in terms of size shows that they have a different density with respect to concepts and style. This is because of the different structure of Italian vs German laws. The statistics reported in Table 6 indicate that, for example in the Italian privacy law, the number of extracted actions is much higher than the number of rights and duties. Italian laws do not use modal verbs to express right and duty explicitly, but our syntactic indicators refer to modal verbs. On the other hand, the number of obligations in the German law is four times the number of rights. This is because the law is written using the perspective of the actor who must comply with the law[5].

---

[5] Generated models are available at http://www.fastsas.com/Experiments/Ger.

Table 6. Comparison of elements of the two laws.

Elements	German (44 pages)	Italian (101 pages)
Antecedent	70	313
Beneficiary	28	0
Obligation	61	276
Right	50	145
Situation	257	748
Actor	847	940
Auxuliary patterns	5,229	8,263
Relationships	775	Not applicable
Overall elements	7,317	10,685

During the study we observed a number of limitations of the NómosT that we will addressed in future development of the tool. In particular: (1) The pattern for the *Situation* concept must be refined with other grammar rules; (2) The identification of other Nómos relationships must be addressed by expanding the current set of implemented patterns for identifying relationships. (3) The use of data-mining techniques to discover regularities – patterns – in concepts and structure of input document.

Threats to Validity. The objective of this evaluation was to assess the benefits of using the NómosT tool for the semi-automatic generation of large models of law. The use of Nómos experts to generate the golden standard for our study, lends confidence to the correctness of the models used in our experiments, and limit risks for construct validity. External validity for our study is concerned with the generalizability of the results to other cases. The results of our investigation are encouraging but we consider them preliminary, so they need to be confirmed by other experiments including a larger set of participants, both expert and non-expert, and laws from other jurisdictions. More importantly, our results depend critically on the modelling language used for laws. Nómos is a light-weight propositional language lacking quantifiers, modal operators and other features present in languages used to formalize law. It would be very difficult to extend our results to other law-modelling languages that are more expressive than Nómos.

Internal validity—factors affecting subject performance during the study—is also very important. The skills of the subjects involved in the experiments were appropriate to the objective of our preliminary investigation. Moreover, there was no bias of the subjects towards the topics covered by the Sections used for the experiments.

6   Related Work

The problem of tool-supported generation of models of law is particularly challenging because it combines the difficulties of analyzing legal documents to extract deontic concepts with those of relating these concepts with semantic relationships to generate a complete conceptual model. Generally speaking, the NómosT tool supports the semi-automatic generation of Nómos models and as such is not comparable with any of the existing tools, even though the techniques used for semantic annotation, syntactic patterns and model element identification are shared by many of the approaches reviewed below.

The extraction of normative concepts from legal documents is an old, and still open, research problem. Several approaches have been proposed in the past decade [1,2], though none deals explicitly with the problem of tool-supported generation of full-fledged models of law. A related, and equally old, problem addressed in the literature is the automation of software requirements extraction from text. On this front, [12] proposes a tool named LOLITA to preprocess user requirements using full natural language analysis, while [9] proposes another tool NL-OOPS, based on LOLITA, to automatically derive class diagrams. More recently, [10] presents a system to fully analyze legal documents using a deep syntactic analysis to produce automatic annotations of normative documents. [14] proposes a methodology that applies NLP techniques using grammatical patterns to analyse textual requirement documents and extract conceptual models.

[5] proposes a name entity recognition approach based on NLP techniques to extract automatically actors from legal document. NómosT tool uses word and n-grams frequency of the Definition Part of law to identify instances of actors and roles. [3,4] propose a framework for acquiring legal requirements using a systematic frame-based requirements analysis methodology. The framework uses an upper ontology to classify regulatory statements, context-free mark-ups to annotate natural language fragments with XML, and document models to handle the structural organization of regulatory documents. Their approach for extracting legal requirements is similar to ours, however our work goes farther in generating full models of law.

[13] presents a system called SALOMON to summarize Belgian criminal cases, while [2] proposes EuNómos, a management service that uses semantic text classication and ontologies to enable users to view legal documents from different sources and find legal concepts. Along similar lines, [7] proposes a methodology to extract legal norms from laws using a set of pattern that helps in the extraction of the conditions and logical structure of legal rules for modelling and reasoning with obligations for compliance checking. Similarly to our approach, they use patterns to identify relevant case summaries from legal documents, though we focus on the generation of full models of law, taking also into account the strucuture of the document.

[11] proposes a tool and a methodology for assessing the compliance of software requirements with relevant laws and regulations, while [1] proposes a framework for extracting normative elements? such as provisions, obligations, and sanctions? from a legal document. NómosT goes a step farther by extracting

conditions (antecedents and consequents) for norms using a heuristic approach. Our approach go a step further, extracting conditions (antecedent and consequent) using again an heuristic approach. In this regard our tool processes the normative elements and conditions which motivates the norm to be applicable or satifiable.

[6] proposes to build goal models from legal documents with the objective to compare the compliance of goals of organizations with respect to legal requirements. Towards this end, a goal oriented language is applied to extract goal models from the legal documents. The modeling framework does not include the norm and situation relationships included in NómosT.

NómosT tool supports the semi-automatic generation of Nómos models and as such is not comparable with any of the existing tools, even if, the techniques used for semantic annotation, syntactic patterns and model element identification are shared by many of the approaches reviewed here.

7   Conclusions and Future Work

Building conceptual models of laws is a hard and time consuming process that requires legal knowledge as well as modeling skills. Moreover, laws are intricate and voluminous thus resulting in models with thousands of elements. The NómosT tool supports the semi-automatic construction of models of law by first annotating legal text and then generating a conceptual model. It is then up to the user of the tool to check the model against the legal text for soundness and completeness. The effectiveness of NómosT has been evaluated with two experiments that measured the reduction of human effort in time saved, and the quality of the resulting models. Experiments have been conducted on two different laws, the Italian Personal Data Protection Code, and the German Data Protection Act, both available in English. The results from the two experiments are encouraging: human effort was reduced by more than 400 % without affecting the quality of the output. Testing the tool on two different laws demonstrates that the tool is easily adaptable with few adjustments, even when the laws come from different jurisdictions.

However, the tool needs to be extended and improved since it lacks patterns to cover the break and satisfy relationships of Nómos. The tool also needs to be further extended with a graphical representation of the model, and better traceability of annotated concepts, in order to better support the analyst as she is comparing a generated model with corresponding text. In addition, the tool is missing the functionality of generating a model using the XMI interchangeable format for better tool interoperation.

Acknowledgment. This research has been partially supported by the ERC advanced grant 267856 'Lucretius: Foundations for Software Evolution'.

References

1. Biagioli, C., Francesconi, E., Passerini, A., Montemagni, S., Soria, C.: Automatic semantics extraction in law documents. In: 10th International Conference on Artificial Intelligence and Law, ICAIL 2005, pp. 133–140. ACM, New York (2005). http://doi.acm.org/10.1145/1165485.1165506

2. Boella, G., di Caro, L., Humphreys, L., Robaldo, L., van der Torre, L.: NLP challenges for eunomos a tool to build and manage legal knowledge. In: Proceedings of the Eight International Conference on Language Resources and Evaluation (LREC 2012). ELRA, Istanbul, May 2012

3. Breaux, T.D., Anton, A.I.: A systematic method for acquiring regulatory requirements: a frame-based approach. In: RHAS-6: Proceedings of the 6th International Workshop on Requirements for High Assurance Systems (RHAS-6). Software Engineering Institute (SEI), Pittsburgh, September 2007

4. Breaux, T.D.: Legal requirements acquisition for the specification of legally compliant information systems. Ph.D. thesis, North Carolina State University (2009)

5. Dozier, C., Kondadadi, R., Light, M., Vachher, A., Veeramachaneni, S., Wudali, R.: Named entity recognition and resolution in legal text. In: Francesconi, E., Montemagni, S., Peters, W., Tiscornia, D. (eds.) Semantic Processing of Legal Texts. LNCS (LNAI), vol. 6036, pp. 27–43. Springer, Heidelberg (2010). doi:10.1007/978-3-642-12837-0_2

6. Ghanavati, S., Amyot, D., Peyton, L.: Compliance analysis based on a goal-oriented requirement language evaluation methodology. In: 17th IEEE International Requirements Engineering Conference, RE 2009, Atlanta, Georgia, USA, 31 August–4 September 2009, pp. 133–142 (2009). http://dx.doi.org/10.1109/RE.2009.42

7. Hashmi, M.: A methodology for extracting legal norms from regulatory documents. In: 2015 IEEE 19th International Enterprise Distributed Object Computing Workshop (EDOCW), pp. 41–50, September 2015

8. Ingolfo, S., Siena, A., Mylopoulos, J., Susi, A., Perini, A.: Arguing regulatory compliance of software requirements. Data Knowl. Eng. **87**, 279–296 (2013). http://www.sciencedirect.com/science/article/pii/S0169023X1200105X

9. Kiyavitskaya, N., Zeni, N., Mich, L., Mylopoulos, J.: Experimenting with linguistic tools for conceptual modelling: quality of the models and critical features. In: Meziane, F., Métais, E. (eds.) NLDB 2004. LNCS, vol. 3136, pp. 135–146. Springer, Heidelberg (2004). doi:10.1007/978-3-540-27779-8_12

10. Lesmo, L., Mazzei, A., Palmirani, M., Radicioni, D.: Tulsi: an NLP system for extracting legal modificatory provisions. Artif. Intell. Law **21**(2), 139–172 (2013). http://dx.doi.org/10.1007/s10506-012-9127-6

11. Massey, A.K.: Legal requirements metrics for compliance analysis. Ph.D. thesis, North Carolina State University (2012)

12. Mich, L.: NL-OOPS: from natural language to object oriented requirements using the natural language processing system LOLITA. Nat. Lang. Eng. **2**(2), 161–187 (1996). http://dx.doi.org/10.1017/S1351324996001337

13. Moens, M., Uyttendaele, C., Dumortier, J.: Information extraction from legal texts: the potential of discourse analysis. Int. J. Hum. Comput. Stud. **51**(6), 1155–1171 (1999). http://dx.doi.org/10.1006/ijhc.1999.0296

14. Rolland, C., Proix, C.: A natural language approach for requirements engineering. In: Loucopoulos, P. (ed.) CAiSE 1992. LNCS, vol. 593, pp. 257–277. Springer, Heidelberg (1992). doi:10.1007/BFb0035136

15. Siena, A., Jureta, I., Ingolfo, S., Susi, A., Perini, A., Mylopoulos, J.: Capturing variability of law with *Nómos* 2. In: Atzeni, P., Cheung, D., Ram, S. (eds.) ER 2012. LNCS, vol. 7532, pp. 383–396. Springer, Heidelberg (2012). doi:10.1007/978-3-642-34002-4_30
16. Zeni, N., Kiyavitskaya, N., Mich, L., Cordy, J., Mylopoulos, J.: GaiusT: supporting the extraction of rights and obligations for regulatory compliance. Requir. Eng. **20**, 1–22 (2013). http://dx.doi.org/10.1007/s00766-013-0181-8

An Efficient and Simple Graph Model for Scientific Article Cold Start Recommendation

Tengyuan Cai, Hongrong Cheng$^{(\boxtimes)}$, Jiaqing Luo, and Shijie Zhou

School of Computer Science and Engineering,
University of Electronic Science and Technology of China,
No. 2006, Xiyuan Ave, West Hi-Tech Zone, Chengdu, China
tycai1@sina.com, hrcheng@uestc.edu.cn

Abstract. Since there is little history information for the newly published scientific articles, it is difficult to recommend related new articles for users. Although tags of articles can provide important information for new articles, they are ignored by existing solutions. Moreover, the efficiency of these solutions is unsatisfactory, especially on the big data situation. In this paper, we propose an efficient and simple bi-relational graph for new scientific article recommendation called user-article based graph model with tags (UAGMT), which can integrate various valuable information (e.g., readership, tag, content and citation) into the graph for new article recommendation. Since the structure of the bi-relational graph model is simple and the model incorporates only a few similarity relationships, it can ensure high efficiency. Besides, the tags' information of articles which summarizes the main content is integrated to enhance the reliability of the similarity of articles. It is especially helpful for improving the cold start recommendation performance. A series of experiments on CiteULike dataset show that the recommendation efficiency is greatly improved by using our UAGMT with the guaranteed performance on the cold-start situation.

Keywords: New article recommendation · Cold start problem · Bi-relational graph · Tags' information

1 Introduction

Recently, websites like CiteULike[1] and Mendeley[2] allow users to organize the scientific articles which they are interested in and share them with other users. These websites have paved the way for using recommendation methods to help researchers find their interested articles.

There have existed various recommendation methods, such as collaborative filtering (CF), content-based and hybrid recommendation methods. The collaborative filtering techniques [1,2] base on the rating matrixes created from the

---

[1] http://www.citeulike.org.
[2] http://www.mendeley.com.

© Springer International Publishing AG 2016
I. Comyn-Wattiau et al. (Eds.): ER 2016, LNCS 9974, pp. 248–259, 2016.
DOI: 10.1007/978-3-319-46397-1_19

user readership or the paper citation network [3], while the textual content of articles is hardly accessed. Especially, when the articles are newly published, the rating matrixes and usage histories are extremely sparse which makes the traditional collaborative filtering methods become inapplicable. This is the so-called cold start problem in recommendation systems. In contrast, the content-based methods [4,5] mainly use the content of items (e.g., title and abstract of articles, description of images and synopsis of movies etc.) for recommendation. However, the content-based methods can not solve the cold start problem satisfactorily either, because they only exploit the content information of items but miss other behaviour information (e.g., citation information of articles). The hybrid recommendation methods [6–9] try to combine the advantages of both collaborative and content-based recommendation methods. These models can solve the cold start problem in a certain degree, but ignore the important tags' information of the articles which is helpful for covering the shortage of new articles for lack of the historical information. Thus, it is likely lead to hinder the further improvement of the recommendation performance. Moreover, the efficiency of the hybrid models is not satisfactory, especially on the big data situation.

In this paper, we propose an efficient and simple bi-relational graph model for new scientific article recommendation. The main contributions of this paper can be summarized as follows:

- A user-article based graph model with tags is proposed, which appends only a few similarity relationships. Thus, it can greatly reduce the data dimensions. In this way, UAGMT can ensure high efficiency of recommendation.
- UAGMT integrates tags' information into it. Due to the tags' information can make up the deficiency of lacking of historical information for new articles, via integrating tags' information, UAGMT can enhance the reliability of intrinsic links between the content of articles, which is conducive to guarantee the recommendation performance.
- UAGMT combines multiple relationships for new article recommendation, which can easily allow us to explore how these types of existed information can be better combined.
- An extensive evaluation is conducted using the real-world dataset gathered from CiteULike to show that the importance of tag information and the highly efficiency of our proposed model on the cold-start situation.

The rest of the paper is organized as follows. In Sect. 2, we review related work about new article recommendation and the random walk with restart (RWR) method used in this paper. In Sect. 3, we describe our graph model. In Sect. 4, we present the evaluation results in detail. Finally, we conclude the paper with a summary and future work in Sect. 5.

2   Related Work

New Article Recommendation. Cold-start problem recommendation refers to either new items or new users, and we focus on the former case in this paper.

For new articles, the content information (e.g., title, abstract, text and author etc.) of articles is important for making recommendation. Blei et al. [10] propose Latent Dirichlet Allocation (LDA) and use it to find the hidden thematic structures based on the content information of the articles. They use the hidden theme to compute the similarity of articles, and then recommend most appropriate new articles for users. Sugiyama et al. [11] extend scholar paper recommendation with citation and reference information. By combining potential reference information with article content, they show that how they can improve the results. Jiwoon et al. [12] presented a Belief Propagation based method to predict the likelihood of new published articles' relevance to a target user, and use citation relationship to infer probabilistically of the user interest. Then, they can recommend most interesting new articles for a target user. Wang et al. [8] present a probabilistic graphical models called collaborative topic regression (CTR) to recommend articles. When the article is new, they use the resulting topics and proportions of LDA to initialize the CTR model. Then they can help users to find new articles which they are interested in. However, these hybrid models have not considered the tags' information in the field of cold-start recommendation. The tags' information of articles can be integrated in a graph-based approach, that is one of the research focus in UAGMT.

Random Walk with Restart. Several studies exist in the field of applying Random Walk with Restart (RWR) [13,14] on graphs. RWR is a good choice to measure vertex-to-vertex relevance. Although other random walk based theories are also applicable, RWR has been proven to be a powerful tool, and has recently been applied in recommendation systems [9,15–18]. Konstas et al. [16] propose a recommendation technique that is based on RWR over a graph which connects both users to tags and tags to items. They merge additional information such as friendship and social tagging embedded in social knowledge to perform item recommendation. Meng et al. [17] propose a unified graph-based model with RWR that integrates the content information, authorship and citation into a graph, which can provide personal item recommendation. For a similar application, Tian et al. [9] propose an approach to recommend old and new articles which based on RWR in a user-item graph that combines the similarity of users and items as well as user preferences together. Bagci et al. [18] propose a random walk based context-aware friend recommendation algorithm (RWCFR), which considers the current context (e.g., current social relations, personal preferences and current location) of the user to provide personalized recommendations. In this paper, we also build a graph model with users and articles. However, we make up the deficiency of lacking of historical information for new articles with integrating tags' information into the bi-relational graph. Thus, our work is different from previous works.

3 Proposed Method

To investigate the effects of tags' information, we analyze the combination of primary content (title and abstract) and all existed information (title, abstract and tag). In this section, we describe our proposed UAGMT for handling the cold-start problem on scientific article recommendation with different combination.

3.1 Similarity Computation

In the article recommendation system, we represent the user information with the symbol $U = \{U_1, U_2, \cdots, U_m\}$, where m is the number of users on the dataset. Similarly, the articles can be represented by a n-dimensional vector like $A = \{A_1, A_2, \cdots, A_n\}$. Each article can be represented by its feature vector with n vocabulary words. As we all known, for new articles, there is few ratings and little usage history information, thus their contents are especially significant for appropriate recommendation. Since the role of tags' information is similar to the keywords of the articles, we regard that the tags' information as one part of its content information can be combined with other content information for new article recommendation. In order to explore the effects of tags' information, we compare the performance of recommended results using different combination of resources, whether or not the tags' information is merged in the resource.

Firstly, we only use the articles' title and abstract to constitute its primary content. Let A_{i_w} be the vector of v primary words given by Eq. 1. Then we use the cosine similarity to compute the relevance of articles, and use symbol S_{pri} to indicate the relevance.

$$A_{i_w} = \{w_1, w_2, \cdots, w_v\}, \tag{1}$$

As we mentioned above, the content information of articles is important for marking recommendation. Since the tags' information with short words summarizes the main idea of the articles, it may be better and more quickly help users discover the articles in their own research areas or they are interested. Here, we can enhance the reliability of the similarity of articles and improve the performance of recommendation via integrating tags' information to the content of articles. We use a l-dimensional vector A_{i_t} to represent the tags' information, where the l is the number of tags in this article.

$$A_{i_t} = \{t_1, t_2, \cdots, t_l\}, \tag{2}$$

Then each article can be represented by a feature vector with $v + l$ words. Because a tag uses the words that are effective in capturing the idea of the articles, whose role is similar to the keywords, we assume that the tags' information is more important than the primary content. Here, we set the w_T weight of tags in the feature vector. Thus, the finally feature vector of articles is defined by Eq. 3.

$$A_i = \{A_{i_w}, w_T A_{i_t}\}, \tag{3}$$

After that, we use the cosine similarity to compute the pairwise similarities among articles. These similarities can be represented by a symbol S_{mix} which has integrated the tags' information into the bi-relational graph model.

3.2   Graph Construction

The UAGMT as illustrated in Fig. 1 has two parts corresponding to the two different types of objects. We use an undirected graph $G = <V, E>$, where $V = V_U \cup V_A$. V_U and V_A indicate the user and article vertices, respectively. As we can see, two types of links are needed in this graph, which are intra-layer links and inter-layer links. Obviously, the edges connecting user with article describe the inter-layer links, contrarily other edges describe the intra-layer links.

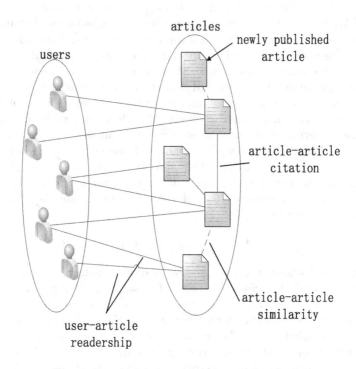

Fig. 1. User-article based graph model with tags

For the inter-layer links, we construct them based on the user-article relationships. Each article is associated with $u_i(u_i \leq m)$ users libraries. So we define Eq. 4 to judge whether there is an edge between them.

$$W_{UA}(U_i, A_j) = \begin{cases} 1, \text{ if } A_j \text{ appears in the library of } U_i \\ 0, \text{ otherwise} \end{cases} . \tag{4}$$

Our model is an undirected graph, so its adjacency matrix is symmetric. Thus, we can get that $W_{AU} = W_{UA}^T$.

The intra-layer links denote the relations between the same types of objects. To make the model easier, now we only consider article relations. In Sect. 4.5, we will further explore the impact of user networks and article relations.

For article relations, we define two types of links in this model. One type of links denote the citation information among the articles, we abbreviate it as *CI-links*, another type of links denote the similarity among articles which can be represented by *SI-links*. In UAGMT, we construct the *CI-links* based on the citation data.

$$W_{AA_{CI}}(A_i, A_j) = \begin{cases} 1, \text{ if } A_j \text{ is one of citations of } A_i \\ 0, \text{ otherwise} \end{cases} . \tag{5}$$

Analogously, *SI-links* are determined by the pairwise similarities S_{pri} (or S_{mix}) and a pre-defined parameter k.

$$W_{AA_{SI}}(A_i, A_j) = \begin{cases} 1, \text{ if } A_j \text{ is one of the } k \text{ most similar to } A_i \\ 0, \text{ otherwise} \end{cases} . \tag{6}$$

3.3   Random Walk with Restart Based Recommendation

Based on the multiple information embedded in UAGMT, we apply a random walk with restart based algorithm to recommend new articles. In order to adopt random walk with restart learning method on UAGMT, we use a matrix to represent G, which can be taken as the transition probability matrix M for a random walk.

As we discussed in Sect. 3.2, now we only consider article relationships which can be represented by the symbol M_{AA} when we construct the intra-layer links. Therefore the user relations $M_{UU} = 0$ in the transition probability matrix M. Let M_{UA} and M_{AU} represent the inter-layer links between the subgraph G_U and G_A, respectively. The edge chosen by a random walker is proportional to its weight in the adjacency matrix. So we get the normalized transition probability matrix $\widetilde{M}$ through its row regularization [19]. Then we use the method proposed by [14] to iteratively calculate Eq. 7 until the ranking vector r converges.

$$r = (1 - c)\widetilde{M}r + cq, \tag{7}$$

Where the vector q is the starting vector, and the index of the seed node in it sets to 1 and others to 0. During initialization, we set the nodes in the graph which corresponds to new articles to 1, others to 0. As a result, the ranking scores of all of the vertices, represented by r, are determined. Finally, the top-N highly ranked vertice that includes one article vertex and other user vertexes.

4   Experiments

We evaluate UAGMT on a real dataset for new article recommendation and conduct several experiments to compare the performance of our proposed model with the state-of-art models.

4.1 Dataset

The real dataset used in our experiments is from CiteULike and extends by Wang and Blei [8] by adding the tag information into original dataset [20]. The content information of the article in the dataset is extracted from its title and abstract. After removing the stop words, for all articles, we choose the top 8000 distinct words with high tf-idf value as the vocabulary. Since the content of articles can be easily summarized by the brief tags, which is similar to the role of keywords, we regard tags' information as a part of its content information, and then each article can be represented as a vector of vocabulary. In order to reduce noise and dimension of the vector, we remove the little-used tags which are used less than 5 times. After that each element (word or tag) can be denoted by a binary value val, such that $val = 1$ if the word or tag occurs in the current article, otherwise, $val = 0$. A brief description of final dataset is presented in Table 1.

Table 1. Statistics of the dataset

Users	Items	Tags	User-item	Citations
5551	16980	7386	20498	44709

Here, we only consider the problem of new article recommendation. In this case, we use 5-fold cross validation. First, we evenly group all articles into 5 folds, and then we iteratively treat one fold as the testing set and other as the training set. We form predictive ratings for the test set, and then record the average performance. Notice that in this case, for the articles appearing in the training set, all article-tag pairs and user-article relationships are kept, while the articles in the testing set do not have any user information.

4.2 Evaluation Scheme

In our experiment, the aim of recommender system is to find good new articles for users, so a set of articles and user libraries are analyzed. We will present each article with N users which are sorted by the predicted rating for the entries in the testing set and evaluate those users who are actually interested in this article.

Two possible metrics are precision and recall. However, zero ratings are uncertain. Since zero entries can be caused either by irrelevance between the user and the article or by users who may do not know the articles in the prediction progress, the *precision* is not a proper metric here. Therefore, as in [8], we use *recall* as one evaluation metric. Like most recommender systems, the recall metric only considers the positively rated users within the top N. Note that a higher recall with lower N implies a better model. The *recall@N* for each articles is defined as:

$$recall@N = \frac{number\ of\ relevant\ users\ in\ topN}{total\ number\ of\ relevant\ users}.$$

Besides, we also use $success@N$ as in [20] as our another evaluation metric. The $success@N$ metric is the probability of finding a true user among the top N recommended users for each articles. It is defined as:

$$success@N = \begin{cases} 1, \text{if a true user in the recommended users} \\ 0, \text{otherwise} \end{cases}.$$

Since recommendations should not only be *recall* and *success* but also be provided the computational costs, we evaluate the computational costs of the methods in terms of Runtime and Memory. Both runtime and memory are measured for the complete workflow of the parameter optimization using a PC with a 2-core Intel i5-2410 2.3 GHz CPU and 16 GB memory.

4.3 Baselines and Experimental Settings

Depending on whether to add tags' information to calculate the similarity of articles, two approaches are supported by UAGMT. These approaches are formulated as follows:

- **UAGMT-P:** Based on the primary content of articles, we use the S_{pri} to compute the $W_{AA_{SI}}$ and build graph model for recommendation.
- **UAGMT-M:** Based on the additional tags' information, we use the S_{mix} to compute the $W_{AA_{SI}}$ and build graph model for recommendation.

Since both articles' content and user-article relationships are used in the UAGMT-P, we use CTR [8] and BG-IteRWR [9] as the baselines for comparison to show the performance of UAGMT.

We use 5-fold cross-validation to search for the optimal parameters in validation sets. More specifically, we find that CTR achieves good prediction performance when $v = 100$, $u = 0.01$, $a = 1$, $b = 0.01$, and $K = 200$. For UAGMT, we set the both weight of tag w_T and k to 5, the restart probability c to 0.25.

4.4 Computational Cost

In the first set of experiments, we ignore the tags' information, and put our focus on the role of the articles' primary content. So, we compare the computational costs for parameter optimization of UAGMT-P with CTR and BG-IteRWR.

However, since BG-IteRWR uses all the similarity of users and articles, the graph model is extremely dense. Thus, BG-IteRWR requires large amount of computing resources for matrix inversion. Due to the space limitation, UAGMT-P and CTR successfully process in the dataset, while BG-IteRWR fails due to its high memory requirement. So, there are only two models in Table 2, which shows that the time and space are required by these models for parameter optimization.

By looking at the results presented in Table 2, we can find that the UAGMT-P requires less time and is almost up to 2 faster than that of CTR. In addition, we measure the memory required for parameter optimization of each method.

Table 2. Computational costs for parameter optimization.

Methods	Memory (MB)	Runtime (s)
UAGMT-P	**2118.33**	**4545.96**
CTR	5164.21	8139.25

Obviously, UAGMT-P nearly saves 50 % memory space, which results in the superior efficiency of UAGMT-P compared with CTR.

In order to compare our model with BG-IteRWR, we compare the edges of graph, the space and time are required when the graph data is read into memory. The final result can be seen in Table 3.

Table 3. Computational costs of UAGMT-P vs. BG-IteRWR

Methods	N	m	Memory (MB)	Runtime (s)
UAGMT-P	22531	**259444**	7	**0.65**
BG-IteRWR	22531	249646622	5713.8	1063.5

From Table 3, we can see that UAGMT-P not only achieves 1636× speedup for on-line response $(0.65/1063.5\,\text{s})$, but also saves 816× on storage $(7/5713.8\,\text{M})$ compared with BG-IteRWR.

4.5   Effects of Tags' Information

As what we have declared, the tags' information can enhance the reliability of the similarity of articles and is more important than the primary content, we would expect that UAGMT-M recommends more interesting articles to users than UAGMT-P. Now, it is great interest to us to look at whether this is true. Here, we compare the *recall* and *success* of UAGMT-M with UAGMT-P. At the same time, we also compare UAGMT-P with CTR.

Figure 2(a) and (b) show the overall *recall@N* and *success@N* of all models on the dataset when we set $N = 5, 10, 20, 40, 60$, respectively.

As we can see, using the same resource, the UAGMT-P achieves better performance than CTR. Besides, UAGMT-M is clearly superior to UAGMT-P, which indicates that UAGMT-M is expert in finding the potential users who are really interested in the corresponding articles. UAGMT-M improves the performance by 21 % and 6 % on average in terms of *recall* and *success* compared to that of UAGMT-P which ignores the tags' information of articles. To understand what makes such changes, we compare the recommended results of UAGMT-M and UAGMT-P. The former enhances the reliability of intrinsic links between the content of articles, and find out more interesting new articles for users.

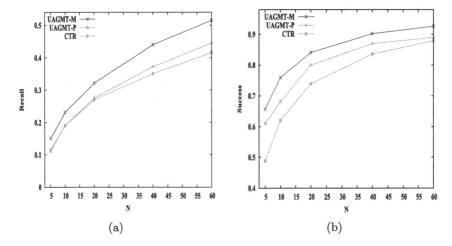

(a)   (b)

Fig. 2. Experimental results on dataset for new article recommendation. (a) shows the *recall@N* of all methods when N ranges from 5 to 60. (b) shows the *success@N* of all methods when N ranges from 5 to 60.

4.6   Further Analysis of User Networks and Article Relations

To understand the impact of user networks and article relations, we conduct additional experiments by adding the user networks or removing the similarities of articles from UAGMT-M. Here, the + (or −) indicate adding (or removing) related information to graph model. Additionally, we use symbol **UU** and **AAS** to denote the user networks and article similarities information, respectively.

Table 4. The impact of user networks and article relations

	Recall					Success				
	@5	@10	@20	@40	@60	@5	@10	@20	@40	@60
UAGMT-M	**0.15**	**0.231**	**0.326**	**0.44**	**0.515**	**0.657**	**0.759**	**0.841**	**0.902**	**0.926**
UAGMT-M(+UU)	0.12	0.19	0.27	0.38	0.45	0.56	0.67	0.77	0.84	0.88
UAGMT-M(-AAS)	0.09	0.14	0.20	0.28	0.33	0.45	0.53	0.60	0.66	0.70

By comparing UAGMT-M with UAGMT-M(-AAS), we can find the graph model benefits a lot from the similarities of articles, which means that the content information of articles is absolutely important on the cold-start situation. By looking at the results presented in Table 4, the approach (UAGMT-M) with the similarities of articles improves 60 % on average in terms of *recall* compared to the approach (UAGMT-M(-AAS)) without the similarities. In contrast, UAGMT-M(+UU) appears that the relations among users do not work very well on our dataset. The relations among users may introduce more noise and seems to have negative impact on this dataset.

5   Conclusions

In this paper, we propose an efficient and simple bi-relational graph model, which integrates various valuable information into the bi-relational graph as a solution to handle cold-start problem in the article recommendation. We conduct a series of experiments on the real world dataset. The experimental results demonstrate that our model takes less time and requires less memory space than other baseline models. Meanwhile, our model also achieves better performance than the CTR. Once the tags' information is integrating, the graph model achieves the best performance for new article recommendation. Besides, comparing with BG-IteRWR, our model can balance the processing cost and recommendation quality. It can preserve 90 % quality, while dramatically saving the stored cost and the computation time.

For future work, the information of authors is worth integrating into graph to make better predictions for personalized recommendation. Our future work direction also aims at producing such a novel tag's weighting scheme suitable for old article recommendation.

Acknowledgments. This research is supported by National Nature Foundation under Grant 61300094 and the Fundamental Research Funds for the Central Universities under Grant ZYGX2013J083.

References

1. Sarwar, B., Karypis, G., Konstan, J., et al.: Item-based collaborative filtering recommendation algorithms. In: Proceedings of the 10th International Conference on World Wide Web, pp. 285–295. ACM (2001)
2. Mnih, A., Salakhutdinov, R.: Probabilistic matrix factorization. In: Advances in Neural Information Processing Systems, pp. 1257–1264 (2007)
3. McNee, S.M., Albert, I., Cosley, D., et al.: On the recommending of citations for research papers. In: Proceedings of the 2002 ACM Conference on Computer Supported Cooperative Work, pp. 116–125. ACM (2002)
4. El-Arini, K., Veda, G., Shahaf, D., et al.: Turning down the noise in the blogosphere. In: Proceedings of the 15th ACM SIGKDD International Conference on Knowledge Discovery and Data Mining, pp. 289–298. ACM (2009)
5. He, Q., Pei, J., Kifer, D., et al.: Context-aware citation recommendation. In: Proceedings of the 19th International Conference on World Wide Web, pp. 421–430. ACM (2010)
6. Basilico, J., Hofmann, T.: Unifying collaborative and content-based filtering. In: Proceedings of the Twenty-First International Conference on Machine Learning, p. 9. ACM (2004)
7. Xia, F., Asabere, N.Y., Liu, H., et al.: Folksonomy based socially-aware recommendation of scholarly papers for conference participants. In: International World Wide Web Conferences Steering Committee, pp. 781–786 (2014)
8. Wang, C., Blei, D.M.: Collaborative topic modeling for recommending scientific articles. In: Proceedings of the 17th ACM SIGKDD International Conference on Knowledge Discovery and Data Mining, pp. 448–456. ACM (2011)

9. Tian, G., Jing, L.: Recommending scientific articles using bi-relational graph-based iterative RWR. In: Proceedings of the 7th ACM Conference on Recommender Systems, pp. 399–402. ACM (2013)

10. Blei, D.M., Ng, A.Y., Jordan, M.I.: Latent Dirichlet allocation. J. Mach. Learn. Res. **3**, 993–1022 (2003)

11. Sugiyama, K., Kan, M.Y.: Exploiting potential citation papers in scholarly paper recommendation. In: Proceedings of the 13th ACM/IEEE-CS Joint Conference on Digital Libraries, pp. 153–162. ACM (2013)

12. Ha, J., Kwon, S.H., Kim, S.W., et al.: Recommendation of newly published research papers using belief propagation. In: Proceedings of the 2014 Conference on Research in Adaptive and Convergent Systems, pp. 77–81. ACM (2014)

13. Tong, H., Faloutsos, C., Pan, J.Y.: Fast random walk with restart and its applications. In: Proceedings of ICDM, pp. 613–622 (2006)

14. Shin, K., Jung, J., Lee, S., et al.: BEAR: block elimination approach for random walk with restart on large graphs. In: Proceedings of the 2015 ACM SIGMOD International Conference on Management of Data, pp. 1571–1585. ACM (2015)

15. Eto, M.: Random Walk with Wait and Restart on Document Co-citation Network for Similar Document Search. RecSys Posters (2014)

16. Konstas, I., Stathopoulos, V., Jose, J.M.: On social networks and collaborative recommendation. In: Proceedings of the 32nd International ACM SIGIR Conference on Research and Development in Information Retrieval, pp. 195–202. ACM (2009)

17. Meng, F., Gao, D., Li, W., et al.: A unified graph model for personalized query-oriented reference paper recommendation. In: Proceedings of the 22nd ACM International Conference on Information and Knowledge Management, pp. 1509–1512. ACM (2013)

18. Bagci, H., Karagoz, P.: Context-aware friend recommendation for location based social networks using random walk. In: Proceedings of the 25th International Conference Companion on World Wide Web, pp. 531–536. ACM (2016)

19. Pan, J.-Y., Yang, H.-J., Faloutsos, C., Duygulu, P.: Automatic multimedia cross-modal correlation discovery. In: KDD, pp. 653–658. ACM (2004)

20. Wang, H., Chen, B., Li, W.J.: Collaborative topic regression with social regularization for tag recommendation. In: Proceedings of the Twenty-Third International Joint Conference on Artificial Intelligence, pp. 2719–2725. AAAI Press (2013)

Keyword Queries over the Deep Web

Andrea Calì[1], Davide Martinenghi[2(✉)], and Riccardo Torlone[3]

[1] Birkbeck, University of London, London, UK
andrea@dcs.bbk.ac.uk
[2] Politecnico di Milano, Milano, Italy
davide.martinenghi@polimi.it
[3] Università Roma Tre, Roma, Italy
torlone@dia.uniroma3.it

Abstract. The Deep Web is constituted by data that are accessible through Web pages, but not indexable by search engines as they are returned in dynamic pages. In this paper we propose a conceptual framework for answering keyword queries on Deep Web sources represented as relational tables with so-called access limitations. We formalize the notion of optimal answer and characterize queries for which an answer can be found.

Keywords: Keyword query · Access pattern · Deep web

1 Introduction

It is well known that the portion of the Web indexed by search engines constitutes only a very small fraction of the data available online. The vast majority of the data, commonly referred to as *Deep Web*, is "hidden" in local databases whose content can only be accessed by manually filling up Web forms. This happens for instance when we need to find a flight from Italy to Japan on the Web site of an airline company. This immediately poses an interesting challenge, i.e., how to automatically retrieve relevant information from the Deep Web – a problem that has been deeply investigated in recent years (see, e.g., [2,3,6,17] for discussion). Usually, a data source in the Deep Web is conceptually modeled by a relational table in which some columns, called *input* attributes, represent fields of a form that need to be filled in so as to retrieve data from the source, while all the others, called *output* attributes, represent values that are returned to the user. Consider for instance the following relations in which the i superscript denotes the input attributes.

$$r_1 = \begin{array}{|c c|} \hline Dept^i & Emp \\ \hline IT & John \\ AI & Mike \\ \hline \end{array} \begin{array}{l} t_{11} \\ t_{12} \end{array} \quad r_2 = \begin{array}{|c c|} \hline Emp^i & Proj \\ \hline John & P1 \\ Ann & P2 \\ Mike & P2 \\ \hline \end{array} \begin{array}{l} t_{21} \\ t_{22} \\ t_{23} \end{array} \quad r_3 = \begin{array}{|c c c|} \hline Proj^i & Emp & Role \\ \hline P1 & John & DBA \\ P1 & Ann & Analyst \\ \hline \end{array} \begin{array}{l} t_{31} \\ t_{32} \end{array}$$

© Springer International Publishing AG 2016
I. Comyn-Wattiau et al. (Eds.): ER 2016, LNCS 9974, pp. 260–268, 2016.
DOI: 10.1007/978-3-319-46397-1_20

Relation r_1 represents a form that, given a department, returns all the employees working in it; relation r_2 a form that, given an employee, returns all the projects he/she works on; and relation r_3 a form that, given a project, returns the employees working in it along with their role. These access modalities are commonly referred to as *access limitations*, in that data can only be queried according to given patterns. Different approaches have been proposed in the literature for querying databases with access limitations: conjunctive queries [4,5], natural language [15], and SQL-like statements [13]. In this paper, we address the novel problem of accessing the Deep Web by just providing a set of keywords, in the same way in which we usually search for information on the Web with a search engine. Consider for instance the case in which the user only provides the keywords "DBA" and "IT" for querying the portion of the Deep Web represented by the relations above. Intuitively, he/she is searching for employees with the DBA role in the IT department. Given the access limitations, this query can be concretely answered by first accessing relation r_1 using the keyword *IT*, which allows us to extract the tuple t_{11}. Then, using the value *John* in t_{11}, we can extract the tuple t_{21} from relation r_2. Finally, using the value *P1* in t_{21}, we can extract the tuples t_{31} and t_{32} from relation r_3. Now, since t_{31} contains *DBA*, it turns out that the set of tuples $\{t_{11}, t_{21}, t_{31}\}$ is a possible answer to the input query in that the set is connected (every two tuples in it share a constant) and contains the given keywords. However, the tuple t_{21} is somehow redundant and can be safely eliminated from the solution, since the set $\{t_{11}, t_{31}\}$ is also connected and contains the keywords. This example shows that, in this context, the keyword query answering problem can be involved and tricky, even in simple situations. In the rest of this paper, we formally investigate this problem in depth. We first propose, in Sect. 2, a precise semantics of (optimal) answer to a keyword query in the Deep Web. We then tackle, in Sect. 3, the problem of finding an answer to a keyword query by assuming that the domains of the keywords are known in advance. This allows us to perform static analysis to immediately discard irrelevant cases from our consideration. Section 4 ends the paper with some conclusions and future works.

Related work. To our knowledge, this is the first paper that proposes a comprehensive approach to the problem of querying the Deep Web using keywords. In an earlier work [7], we have just defined the problem and provided some preliminary insights on query processing. The problem of query processing in the Deep Web has been widely investigated in the last years, with different approaches and under different perspectives including: data crawling [18], integration of data sources [11], query plan optimization [5], and generic structured query models [13]. However, none of them has tackled the problem that we have addressed in this paper. The idea of querying structured data using keywords emerged more than a decade ago [1] as a way to provide high-level access to data and free the user from the knowledge of query languages and data organization. Since then, a lot of work has been done in this field (see, e.g., [20] for a survey) but never in the context of the Deep Web. This problem has been investigated in the context of various data models: relational [14], semi-structured [16],

XML [10], and RDF [19]. Within the relational model, the common assumption is that an answer to a keyword query is a graph of minimal size in which the nodes represent tuples, the edges represent foreign key references between them, and the keywords occur in some node of the graph [12]. Our definition of query answer follows this line but it is more general, since it is only based on the presence of common values between tuples, while not forcing the presence of foreign keys. The various approaches to keyword query answering over relational databases are commonly classified into two categories: *schema-based* and *schema-free*. Schema-based approaches [1,12] make use, in a preliminary phase, of the database schema to build SQL queries that are able to return the answer. Conversely, schema-free approaches [9,14] rely on exploration techniques over a graph-based representation of the whole database. Since the search for an optimal answer consists in finding a minimal *Steiner tree* on the graph, which is known to be an NP-Complete problem [8], the various proposals rely on heuristics aimed at generating approximations of Steiner trees. Our approach makes use of the schema of the data sources but cannot be classified in any of the approaches above since, given the access limitations, it rather relies on building a minimal query plan of accesses to the data sources.

2   Preliminaries and Problem Definition

We model data sources as relations of a relational database and we assume that, albeit autonomous, they have "compatible" attributes. For this, we fix a set of *abstract domains* $\mathbf{D} = \{D_1, \ldots, D_m\}$, which, rather than denoting concrete value types (such as string or integer), represent data types at a higher level of abstraction (for instance, *car* or *country*). Therefore, in an abstract domain an object is uniquely represented by a value. The set of all values is denoted by $\mathscr{D} = \bigcup_{i=1}^{n} D_i$. For simplicity, we assume that all abstract domains are disjoint. We then say that a *(relation) schema* r, customarily indicated as $r(A_1, \ldots, A_k)$, is a set of attributes $\{A_1, \ldots, A_k\}$, each associated with an abstract domain $dom(A_i) \in \mathbf{D}$, $1 \leq i \leq k$. A *database schema* $\mathscr{S}$ is a set of *schemas* $\{r_1, \ldots, r_n\}$. As usual, given a schema r, a *tuple* t over r is a function that associates a value $c \in dom(A)$ with each attribute $A \in r$, and a *relation instance* $r^{\mathscr{J}}$ of r is a set of tuples over r. For simplicity, we also write $dom(c)$ to indicate the domain of c. A (database) instance $\mathscr{J}$ of a database schema $\mathscr{S} = \{r_1, \ldots, r_n\}$ is a set of relation instances $\{r_1^{\mathscr{J}}, \ldots, r_n^{\mathscr{J}}\}$, where $r_i^{\mathscr{J}}$ denotes the relation instance of r_i in $\mathscr{J}$. For the sake of simplicity, in the following we assign the same name to attributes of different schemas that are defined over the same abstract domain.

Definition 1 (Access pattern). *An access pattern Π for a schema $r(A_1, \ldots, A_k)$ is a mapping $\Pi : \{A_1, \ldots, A_k\} \to M$, where $M = \{i, o\}$ is called access mode, and i and o denote* input *and* output*, respectively; A_i is correspondingly called an* input *(resp.,* output*) attribute for r wrt Π.*

Henceforth, we denote input attributes with an 'i' superscript, e.g., A^i. Moreover, we assume that each relation has exactly one access pattern.

Definition 2 (Binding). *Let $A'_1, \ldots, A'_\ell$ be all the input attributes for r wrt Π; any tuple $\mathscr{b} = \langle c_1, \ldots, c_\ell \rangle$ such that $c_i \in dom(A'_i)$ for $1 \leq i \leq \ell$ is called a binding for r wrt Π.*

Definition 3 (Access). *An* access *is a pair $\langle \Pi, \mathscr{b} \rangle$, where Π is an access pattern for a schema r and $\mathscr{b}$ is a binding for r wrt Π. The output of such an access on an instance $\mathscr{I}$ is the set $\mathscr{T}$ of all tuples in the relation $r^{\mathscr{I}} \in \mathscr{I}$ over r that match the binding, i.e., such that $\mathscr{T} = \sigma_{A_1 = c_1, \ldots, A_\ell = c_\ell}(r)$.*

Intuitively, we can only access a relation if we can provide a binding for it, i.e., a value for every input attribute.

Definition 4 (Access path). *Given an instance $\mathscr{I}$ for a database schema $\mathscr{S}$, a set of access patterns Π for the relations in $\mathscr{S}$, and a set of values $\mathscr{C} \subseteq \mathscr{D}$, an* access path *on $\mathscr{I}$ (for $\mathscr{S}$, Π and $\mathscr{C}$) is a sequence $\xrightarrow{\mathscr{b}_1}_{r_1^{\mathscr{I}}} \mathscr{T}_1 \xrightarrow{\mathscr{b}_2}_{r_2^{\mathscr{I}}} \cdots \xrightarrow{\mathscr{b}_n}_{r_n^{\mathscr{I}}} \mathscr{T}_n$, where, for $1 \leq i \leq n$ (i) $\mathscr{b}_i$ is a binding for a relation $r_i \in \mathscr{S}$ wrt a pattern $\Pi_i \in \Pi$ for r_i (ii) $\mathscr{T}_i$ is the output of access $\langle \Pi_i, \mathscr{b}_i \rangle$ on $\mathscr{I}$, and (iii) each value in $\mathscr{b}_i$ either occurs in $\mathscr{T}_j$ with $j < i$ or is a value in $\mathscr{C}$.*

Definition 5 (Reachable portion). *A tuple t in $\mathscr{I}$ is said to be* reachable given $\mathscr{C}$ *if there exists an access path P (for $\mathscr{S}$, Π and $\mathscr{C}$) such that t is in the output of some access in P; the* reachable portion $reach(\mathscr{I}, \Pi, \mathscr{C})$ of $\mathscr{I}$ is the set of all reachable tuples in $\mathscr{I}$ given $\mathscr{C}$.*

In the following, we will write $\mathscr{S}^{\Pi}$ to refer to schema $\mathscr{S}$ under access patterns Π.

Example 1. Consider the following instance $\mathscr{I}$ of a schema $\mathscr{S}^{\Pi} = \{r_1(A_1^i, A_2), r_2(A_2^i, A_1), r_3(A_1^i, A_2, A_3)\}$.

$$r_1 = \begin{array}{|c|c|}\hline A_1^? & A_2 \\\hline c_0 & c_1 \\\hline c_2 & c_3 \\\hline\end{array}\begin{array}{l} t_{11} \\ t_{12}\end{array} \quad r_2 = \begin{array}{|c|c|}\hline A_2^i & A_1 \\\hline c_1 & c_2 \\\hline c_4 & c_2 \\\hline c_1 & c_6 \\\hline\end{array}\begin{array}{l} t_{21} \\ t_{22} \\ t_{23}\end{array} \quad r_3 = \begin{array}{|c|c|c|}\hline A_1^i & A_2 & A_3 \\\hline c_2 & c_1 & c_8 \\\hline c_5 & c_4 & c_8 \\\hline c_6 & c_7 & c_9 \\\hline\end{array}\begin{array}{l} t_{31} \\ t_{32} \\ t_{33}\end{array}$$

Then, for instance, $\{t_{11}\}$ is the output of the access with binding $\langle c_0 \rangle$ wrt $r_1(A_1^i, A_2)$, and $\xrightarrow{\langle c_0 \rangle}_{r_1^{\mathscr{I}}} \{t_{11}\} \xrightarrow{\langle c_1 \rangle}_{r_2^{\mathscr{I}}} \{t_{21}, t_{23}\}$, is an access path for $\mathscr{S}$, Π and $\mathscr{C} = \{c_0\}$, since, given $\mathscr{C}$, we can extract t_{11} from r_1 and, given $\{c_1\}$ from t_{11}, we can extract t_{21} and t_{23} from r_2. The reachable portion of $\mathscr{I}$, given $\mathscr{C}$, is $reach(\mathscr{I}, \Pi, \mathscr{C}) = \{t_{11}, t_{12}, t_{21}, t_{23}, t_{31}, t_{33}\}$, while $\{t_{22}, t_{32}\} \cap reach(\mathscr{I}, \Pi, \mathscr{C}) = \emptyset$. Figure 1a shows the reachable portion $\mathscr{I}'$ of $\mathscr{I}$ given $\mathscr{C}$ along with the access paths used to extract it, with dotted lines enclosing outputs of accesses. ∎

The definition of answer to a keyword query in our setting requires the preliminary notion of join graph.

Definition 6. (Join graph). *Given a set $\mathscr{T}$ of tuples, the* join graph *of $\mathscr{T}$ is a node-labeled undirected graph $\langle N, E \rangle$ constructed as follows: (i) the nodes N are labeled with tuples of $\mathscr{T}$, with a one-to-one correspondence between tuples of $\mathscr{T}$ and nodes of N; and (ii) there is an arc between two nodes n_1 and n_2 whenever the tuples labeling n_1 and n_2 have at least one value in common.*

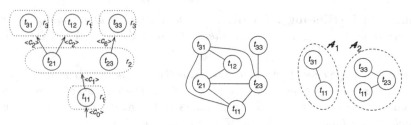

(a) Reachable portion $\mathcal{I}'$, given $\{c_0\}$. (b) Join graph of $\mathcal{I}'$. (c) Two answers to KQ q.

Fig. 1. Illustration of Examples 1, 2, and 3.

Example 2. Consider instance $\mathcal{I}$ of Example 1 and the reachable portion $\mathcal{I}'$ of $\mathcal{I}$ given $\{c_0\}$, shown in Fig. 1a. The join graph of $\mathcal{I}'$ is shown in Fig. 1b.   ∎

A *keyword query* (KQ) is a non-empty set of values in $\mathcal{D}$ called *keywords*.

Definition 7 (Answer to a KQ). *An answer to a KQ q against a database instance $\mathcal{I}$ over a schema $\mathcal{S}^{\Pi}$ is a set of tuples $\mathcal{A}$ in reach$(\mathcal{I}, \Pi, q)$ such that: (i) each keyword $k \in q$ occurs in at least one tuple t in $\mathcal{A}$; (ii) the join graph of $\mathcal{A}$ is connected; (iii) no proper subset $\mathcal{A}' \subset \mathcal{A}$ satisfies both Conditions (i) and (ii) above.*

It is straightforward to see that there could be several answers to a KQ; below we give a widely accepted criterion for ranking such answers [20].

Definition 8. *Let $\mathcal{A}_1, \mathcal{A}_2$ be two answers to a KQ q on an instance $\mathcal{I}$. We say that $\mathcal{A}_1$ is better than $\mathcal{A}_2$ if $|\mathcal{A}_1| \leq |\mathcal{A}_2|$. The optimal answers are those of minimum size.*

Example 3. Consider a KQ $q = \{c_1, c_8\}$ over the instance $\mathcal{I}$ of Example 1. Figure 1a shows two possible answers: $\mathcal{A}_1 = \{t_{11}, t_{31}\}$ and $\mathcal{A}_2 = \{t_{11}, t_{23}, t_{33}\}$. $\mathcal{A}_1$ is better than $\mathcal{A}_2$ and is the optimal answer to q.   ∎

3   Detecting Non-answerable Queries

For convenience of notation, we sometimes write $c: D$ to denote value c and indicate that $dom(c) = D$. In addition, in our examples, the name of an attribute will also indicate its abstract domain.

3.1   Compatible Queries

In order to focus on meaningful queries, we semantically characterize queries for which an answer might be found.

Definition 9 (Compatibility). *A KQ q is said to be compatible with a schema $\mathcal{S}$ if there exist a set of access patterns Π and an instance $\mathcal{I}$ over $\mathcal{S}^{\Pi}$ such that there is an answer to q against $\mathcal{I}$.*

Example 4. The KQ $q_1 = \{a\colon A, c\colon C\}$ is not compatible with schema $\mathcal{S}_1 = \{r_1(A, B), r_2(C, D)\}$, since no set of tuples from $\mathcal{S}$ containing all the keywords in q_1 can ever be connected, independently of the access patterns for $\mathcal{S}_1$. Conversely, q_1 is compatible with $\mathcal{S}_2 = \{r_1(A, B), r_3(B, C)\}$, as witnessed by a possible answer $\{r_1(a, b), r_3(b, c)\}$ and patterns Π such that $\mathcal{S}_2^{\Pi} = \{r_1(A^i, B), r_3(B, C)\}$. Similarly, KQ $q_2 = \{a\colon A, a'\colon A\}$ is compatible with a schema $\mathcal{S}_3 = \{r_1(A, B)\}$, as witnessed by a possible answer $\{r_1(a, b), r_1(a', b)\}$ and patterns Π such that $\mathcal{S}_3^{\Pi} = \{r_1(A^i, B)\}$. However, q_2 is not compatible with a schema $\mathcal{S}_4 = \{r_4(A)\}$, since a unary relation, alone, can never connect two keywords. ∎

Checking compatibility of a KQ with a schema essentially amounts to checking reachability on a graph. The main idea is that in order for an answer to ever be possible, we must find an instance that exhibits a witness (i.e., a set of tuples) satisfying all the conditions of Definition 7.

3.2 Answerable Queries

A stricter requirement than compatibility is given by the notion of answerability.

Definition 10 (Answerability). *A KQ q is* answerable *against a schema $\mathcal{S}^{\Pi}$ if there is an instance $\mathcal{I}$ over $\mathcal{S}^{\Pi}$ such that there is an answer to q against $\mathcal{I}$.*

Example 5. Consider KQ $q = \{a\colon A, c\colon C\}$ and schema $\mathcal{S}_1^{\Pi} = \{r(A^i, B), s(B, C, D^i)\}$. Although q is compatible with $\mathcal{S}_1$, it is not answerable against $\mathcal{S}_1^{\Pi}$, since no tuple from $\mathcal{S}_1$ can be extracted under Π (no values for domain D are available). Conversely, q is answerable against $\mathcal{S}_2^{\Pi} = \{r(A^i, B), s(B^i, C, D)\}$, since an answer like $\{r(a, b), s(b, c, d)\}$ could be extracted by first accessing r with binding $\langle a \rangle$, thus extracting value b, and then s with binding $\langle b \rangle$. ∎

In order to check answerability, we need to check that all the required relations can be accessed according to the access patterns. To this end, we first refer to a schema enriched with unary relations representing the keywords in the KQ[1].

Definition 11 (Expanded schema). *Let q be a KQ over a schema $\mathcal{S}^{\Pi}$. The expanded schema $\mathcal{S}_q^{\Pi}$ of $\mathcal{S}^{\Pi}$ wrt. q is defined as $\mathcal{S}_q^{\Pi} = \mathcal{S}^{\Pi} \cup \{r_c(C) | c \in q\}$, where r_c is a new unary relation, not occurring in $\mathcal{S}^{\Pi}$, whose only attribute C is an output attribute with abstract domain $dom(C) = dom(c)$.*

Then, we use the notion of dependency graph (d-graph) to denote output-input dependencies between relation arguments, indicating that a relation under access patterns needs values from other relations.

Definition 12 (d-graph). *Let q be a KQ over a schema $\mathcal{S}^{\Pi}$. The d-graph $G_q^{\mathcal{S}^{\Pi}}$ is a directed graph $\langle \mathcal{N}, \mathcal{E} \rangle$ defined as follows. For each attribute A of each*

---

[1] If other values are known besides the keywords, this knowledge may be represented by means of appropriate unary relations with output mode in the schema.

relation in the expanded schema $\mathcal{S}_q^{\Pi}$, there is a node in $\mathcal{N}$ labeled with A's access mode and abstract domain. There is an arc $u \frown v$ in $\mathcal{E}$ whenever: (i) u and v have the same abstract domain; (ii) u is an output node; and (iii) v is an input node.

Some relations are made invisible by the access patterns and can be discarded.

Definition 13 (Visibility). An input node $v_n \in \mathcal{N}$ in a d-graph $\langle \mathcal{N}, \mathcal{E} \rangle$ is visible if there is a sequence of arcs $u_1 \frown v_1, \ldots, u_n \frown v_n$ in $\mathcal{E}$ such that (i) u_1's relation has no input attributes, and (ii) v_i's and u_{i+1}'s relation are the same, for $1 \leq i \leq n-1$. A relation is visible if all of its input nodes are.

Example 5 (cont.). Consider the KQ and the schemas from Example 5. The d-graphs $G_q^{\mathcal{S}_1^{\Pi}}$ and $G_q^{\mathcal{S}_2^{\Pi}}$ are shown in Figs. 2a and b, respectively. ■

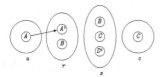

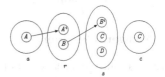

(a) D-graph $G_q^{\mathcal{S}_1^{\Pi}}$ from Example 5; s is not visible.

(b) D-graph $G_q^{\mathcal{S}_2^{\Pi}}$ from Example 5; all relations are visible.

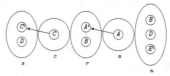

(c) D-graph $G_q^{\mathcal{S}^{\Pi}}$ from Example 6; u is not visible.

Fig. 2. D-graphs from the examples.

Answerability of a KQ q is checked by means of compatibility with a schema in which all non-visible relations have been eliminated.

Example 6. Consider a KQ $q = \{a : A, c : C\}$ and a schema $\mathcal{S}^{\Pi} = \{r(A^i, B), s(C^i, D), u(B, D, E^i)\}$. Relation u is not visible in $G_q^{\mathcal{S}^{\Pi}}$ (Fig. 2c). Then, q is not answerable in $\mathcal{S}^{\Pi}$, since q is not compatible with schema $\{r(A, B), s(C, D)\}$ (i.e., $\mathcal{S}$ without relation u). ■

4   Conclusions and Future Work

In this paper, we have defined the problem of keyword search in the Deep Web. We are currently working on an algorithmic solution for query answering in this context that aims at minimizing the number of accesses to the data sources. We believe that several interesting issues can be studied in the framework defined in this paper. We plan, e.g., to leverage known values (besides the keywords) and ontologies to speed up the search for an optimal answer as well as to consider the case in which nodes and arcs of the join graph are weighted to model source availability and proximity, respectively.

Acknowledgments. A. Calì acknowledges support from the EPSRC grant EP/E010865/1 ("LIQUID") and from the EU COST Action IC1302 ("KEYSTONE"). D. Martinenghi acknowledges support from the EC's FP7 "CUbRIK" and "SmartH2O" projects, and the FESR project "Proactive".

References

1. Agrawal, S., Chaudhuri, S., Das, G., DBXplorer: a system for keyword-based search over relational databases. In: ICDE, pp. 5–16 (2002)
2. Bienvenu, M. et al.: Dealing with the deep web and all its quirks. In: Proceedings of VLDS, pp. 21–24 (2012)
3. Calì, A., Calvanese, D., Martinenghi, D.: Dynamic query optimization under access limitations and dependencies. J. UCS **15**(1), 33–62 (2009)
4. Calì, A., Martinenghi, D.: Conjunctive query containment under access limitations. In: Li, Q., Spaccapietra, S., Yu, E., Olivé, A. (eds.) ER 2008. LNCS, vol. 5231, pp. 326–340. Springer, Heidelberg (2008). doi:10.1007/978-3-540-87877-3_24
5. Calì, A., Martinenghi, D.: Querying data under access limitations. In: ICDE, pp. 50–59 (2008)
6. Calì, A., Martinenghi, D.: Querying the deep web. In: EDBT, pp. 724–727 (2010)
7. Calì, A., Martinenghi, D., Torlone, R.: Keyword search in the deep web. In: Proceedings of the 9th AMW (2015)
8. Garey, M.R., Graham, R.L., Johnson, D.S.: The complexity of computing steiner minimal trees. SIAM J. Appl. Math. **32**(4), 835–859 (1977)
9. Golenberg, K., Kimelfeld, B., Sagiv, Y.: Keyword proximity search in complex data graphs. In: SIGMOD, pp. 927–940 (2008)
10. Guo, L., Shao, F., Botev, C., Shanmugasundaram, J.: XRANK: ranked keyword search over xml documents. In: SIGMOD, pp. 16–27 (2003)
11. He, B., Zhang, Z., Chang, K.C.-C., Metaquerier: querying structured web sources on-the-fly. In: Proceedings of SIGMOD, pp. 927–929 (2005)
12. Hristidis, V., Papakonstantinou, Y.: Discover: keyword search in relational databases. In: VLDB, pp. 670–681 (2002)
13. Jamil, HM, Jagadish, HV.: A structured query model for the deep relational web. In: CIKM, pp. 1679–1682 (2015)
14. Kimelfeld B., Sagiv Y.: Finding and approximating top-k answers in keyword proximity search. In: PODS, pp. 173–182 (2006)
15. Lehmann, J., Furche, T., Grasso, G., Ngomo, A.-C.N., Schallhart, C., Sellers, A., Unger, C., Bühmann, L., Gerber, D., Höffner, K., Liu, D., Auer, S.: DEQA: deep web extraction for question answering. In: Cudré-Mauroux, P., et al. (eds.) ISWC 2012. LNCS, vol. 7650, pp. 131–147. Springer, Heidelberg (2012). doi:10.1007/978-3-642-35173-0_9
16. Guoliang Li, E., et al.: EASE: an effective 3-in-1 keyword search method for unstructured, semi-structured and structured data. In: SIGMOD, pp. 903–914 (2008)

17. Madhavan, J., Afanasiev, L., Antova, L., Halevy, A.Y.: Harnessing the deep web: present and future. In: CIDR (2009)
18. Raghavan, S., Garcia-Molina, H.: Crawling the hidden web. In: VLDB, pp. 129–138 (2001)
19. Tran, T., Wang, H., Rudolph, S., Cimiano, P.: Top-k exploration of query candidates for efficient keyword search on graph-shaped (rdf) data. In: ICDE, pp. 405–416 (2009)
20. Yu, J.X., Qin, L., Chang, L.: Keyword search in relational databases: a survey. IEEE Data Eng. Bull. **33**(1), 67–78 (2010)

Sensor Observation Service Semantic Mediation: Generic Wrappers for In-Situ and Remote Devices

Manuel A. Regueiro[1], José R.R. Viqueira[1(✉)], Christoph Stasch[2],
and José A. Taboada[1]

[1] Computer Graphics and Data Engineering Group (COGRADE),
Centro de Investigación en Tecnoloxías da Información (CITIUS),
Universidade de Santiago de Compostela (USC), Santiago de Compostela, Spain
{manuelantonio.regueiro,jrr.viqueira,manel.cotos}@usc.es
[2] 52° North Initiative for Geospatial Open Source Software GmbH,
Martin-Luther-King-Weg 24, 48155 Muenster, Germany
c.stasch@52north.org

Abstract. In-situ and remote sensors produce data that fit different data modeling paradigms, namely, Entity/Relationship paradigm for the former and Multidimensional Array paradigm for the latter. Besides, different standardized data access services are used in practice. Therefore their integrated access is still a major challenge. This paper describes a solution for the development of generic semantic data access wrappers for observation datasets generated by in-situ and remote sensing devices. Those wrappers are key components of data mediation architectures designed for the semantic integrated publishing of observation data.

Keywords: Semantic mediation · Interoperability · Data integration · Observation data · Environmental data

1 Introduction

The amount of environmental observation datasets generated nowadays is increasing due to the advances in sensing technologies. In-situ devices, like meteorological stations, generate data that fit well the Entity/Relationship paradigm and relevant relational technologies. Remote devices, like radars, generate array data, which are generally managed with ad-hoc implementations on top of standardized array file formats.

This article is based upon work from COST Action KEYSTONE IC1302, supported by COST (European Cooperation in Science and Technology). It has been partially funded by the Galician Government (Xunta de Galicia) and FEDER funds of the EU under the Consolidation Program of Competitive Research Units (Network ref. R2014/007).

I. Comyn-Wattiau et al. (Eds.): ER 2016, LNCS 9974, pp. 269–276, 2016.
DOI: 10.1007/978-3-319-46397-1_21

The implementation of Spatial Data Infrastructures (SDIs) demands from data providers standardized data access services. The Open Geospatial Consortium (OGC) proposes the Sensor Observation Service (SOS) specification to provide access to collections of observations. Informally, *Observations* provide values of *Properties* of specific entities (*Feature of Interest - FOI*), which are generated by some observation *Process*. Beyond the above metadata and the observed value, an observation must also record temporal data and some other optional metadata, including the unit of measure (uom), quality information and some other parameters. Mandatory operations of the SOS interface include *DescribeSensor* and *GetObservation*. The former provides a Sensor Modeling Language - SensorML description of a specific *Process*. The later retrieves observation data that matches specific criteria, including filters on space, time and metadata. To minimize the probability of getting an empty result in a GetObservation request, the observations of each *Process* of a SOS are grouped into collections called *Offerings*. Mandatory operation *GetCapabilities* provides appropriate metadata of each available *Offering*.

Integrated access to in-situ and remote observation data sources through SOS has already been reported in [10]. A semantic mediation solution of SOS data sources has also been developed as previous work of these authors [9], where a well-known mediator/wrapper architecture [12] is combined with the use of ontologies. Basic SOS related concepts are defined in a *Core Ontology* as specializations of relevant W3C Semantic Sensor Network (SSN) [5] concepts. *Data Source Ontologies* represent SOS metadata of each dataset by specializing relevant concepts of the *Core Ontology*. Data source classes may be annotated with relationships to classes of some well-known top-level application domain ontology like SWEET [8]. The definition of a *Mediator Ontology* enables the expert to specify required semantic integration knowledge, in the form of relationships between global and local concepts. Those relationships are used to determine which data sources must be queried and which criteria has to be used during global *GetObservation* evaluations. The implementation of the wrappers of the different data sources is always ad-hoc. However, many similarities exist between the different relational sensor observation datasets, and the same applies to those recording array observation data.

Based on the above, this paper describes the implementation of two generic data access wrappers: (i) A wrapper for in-situ geospatial observation data sources, recorded in spatial relational DBMSs and (ii) A wrapper for remote geospatial observation data sources, accessible through NetCDFSubset[1] standardized array data services.

The remainder of this paper is organized as follows. Section 2 discusses on some related pieces of work. The design and implementation of the in-situ sensor observation data wrapper is described in Sect. 3. Section 4 is devoted to the remote sensor observation data wrapper. Finally, Sect. 5 concludes the paper.

---

[1] http://www.unidata.ucar.edu/software/thredds/current/tds/reference/NetcdfSubsetServiceReference.html.

2   Related Work

Most of the current SOS implementations are specialized on observations generated by in-situ devices, recorded in relational databases under specific data models (see the 52° North SOS for a representative example[2]). Only [2] supports array data sources generated by remote sensing devices.

Semantic sensor data discovery and integration are identified as major challenges in [3], in the scope of the Semantic Sensor Web [11] and the Linked Sensor Data. In the *Model Based Mediation* approach for scientific data sources [7], each data source exports its semantics within relevant ontologies and the mediator combines data source ontologies with data integration knowledge provided by the domain expert. An extension of a conventional conceptual model with constructs that incorporate observation semantics is defined in [1]. The result data modeling framework may be used to annotate data sources with observation semantics.

In [4] the semantic annotation of SensorML documents is the base for the semantic registration of sensing devices in SOS services, which enables subsequent semantically integrated access. A semantic SOS (SemSOS) implementation is reported in [6], where sensor data is semantically annotated and transformed to RDF to be recorded with semantic data storage technologies. Next, SPARQL is used to implement SOS requests. It noticed that none of the above approaches intend to provide semantic data mediation between various existing data sources.

3   In-Situ Sensor Observation Data Wrapper

A generic wrapper was developed that enables SOS access to any database of in-situ observations recorded in a spatially enabled DBMS. To illustrate this, let us first describe two real data sources, which were used during the evaluation of the proposed solution.

Meteorological Stations[3] (Fig. 1(a)): Observation data is generated every 10 min (*10MinutesData*), daily (*DalyData*) and monthly (*MonthlyData*). Each *Measurement* represents the fact that a sensing device (*Sensor*) that measures a given property (*Parameter*) is installed in a *Station* at a given *Elevation* above the soil and an aggregation process (*Function*) is next applied with a given time frequency (*Interval*). *Sensors* are classified by *SensorTypes* whereas *Stations* are integrated in *Networks*.

CTD Profiles[4] (Fig. 1(b)): Each data element (*Data*) records a value, a sea depth level and a reference to a *Measurement*. A *Measurement* references a measured property (*Parameter*) and a *Profile*, which represents the use of a specific *CTD-Device* at a given time instant and at a given location in the sea (*Station*).

A uniform view of any database is provided through a generic data model (See Fig. 2).

---

[2] http://52north.org/communities/sensorweb/sos/index.html.
[3] http://www2.meteogalicia.es/galego/observacion/estacions/estacions.asp.
[4] http://www.intecmar.org/Ctd/Default.aspx.

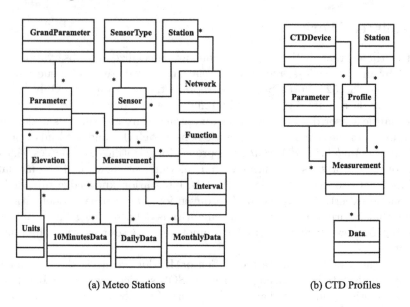

(a) Meteo Stations

(b) CTD Profiles

Fig. 1. Conceptual models of meteorological station and CTD data sources.

The model enables both the generation of the required *Data Source Ontology* and the implementation of the SOS *GetObservation* operation. At the top of the diagram, three UML classes enable the representation of the *Process*, *Property* and *FOI* OWL classes that might be available in the data source (*SensorType*, *GrandParameter* and *Network* elements in the case of meteorological stations). The URI of each class is constructed concatenating its identifier (id) with the data source identifier. Relationships with the selected well-known top-level application domain ontology (SWEET in our case) are also provided. Finally, each OWL class has also a reference to its superclass in the model. This enables the creation of OWL class hierarchies from the data source data.

Individuals of the above classes are represented by relevant UML classes. *ProcessDescriptionTime* represents the temporal evolution o the SensorML description of each *Process*. Finally, the observations of each *Process* and *Property* at each *FOI* are represented by UML class *ObservationInstance*. *ObservationInstanceLatest* is used to enable more efficient access to the last observations, which is a typical data need in many real applications.

The SQL code of the *ProcessInstance* view for the data source of meteorological stations is given below.

```
SELECT CAST(p.id AS VARCHAR)||"_"||replace(p.name, "", "-")||_||
        CAST(e.id AS VARCHAR)||"_"||replace(e.elevation, "", "-") AS id,
      CAST(gp.id AS VARCHAR)||"_"||gp.name AS propertyClass
FROM Paramter AS p, GrandParameter AS gp, Measurement AS m, Elevation AS e
WHERE p.grandParameter=gp.id AND m.parameter=p.id AND m.elevation=e.id
```

Identifiers are generated concatenating appropriate keys of the database elements with other attributes that can be better interpreted by humans. Thus,

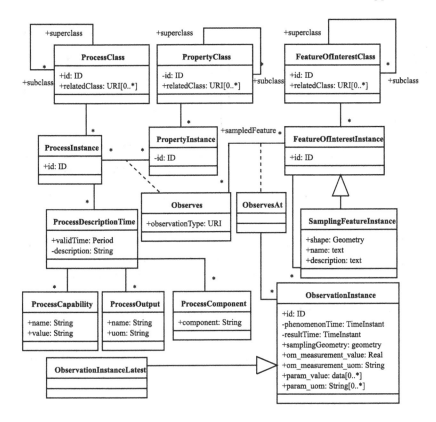

Fig. 2. Generic conceptual model for in-situ observation databases.

Parameter "Temperature" (id = 25), measured at "10 m" (Elevation identifier 15) has identifier "25_Temperature_15_10-m".

A *GetObservation* request that retrieves all the observations of a *Property* with identifier *prop* generated by a *Process* with identifier *proc*, during the period defined by instants *s* and *e* at FOIs located inside a given rectangle *b* is implemented with the following SQL statement[5].

```
SELECT oi.*
FROM ObservationInstance oi JOIN
    SamplingFeatureInstance sfi ON (oi.foi = sfi.id)
WHERE  oi.process = proc AND oi.property = prop
  AND oi.phenomenonTime BETWEEN s AND e
  AND st_intersects(b, sfi.shape)
```

The above initial implementation offered very slow response times. This is due to the fact that potential indexes of the underlying database are not used, because of the way identifiers are constructed. To overcome this problem, the application domain expert must provide the positions inside each identifier

---

[5] Spatial SQL standard ISO/IEC 13249-3:2011 must be supported by the underlying DBMS.

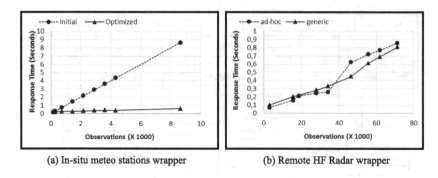

(a) In-situ meteo stations wrapper   (b) Remote HF Radar wrapper

Fig. 3. Performance evaluation.

occupied by key attributes (indexed ones). Thus, the restriction "oi.property = '25_Temperature_15_10-m'" may be replaced by a more efficient "oi.paramId = 25 and oi.elevId = 15". The gain in performance is shown in Fig. 3(a).

4   Remote Sensor Observation Data Wrapper

A generic wrapper was developed that enables the semantically integrated access to array datasets produced by remote sensors and published through NetCDF-Subset services. A specialization of the *Raster Core Ontology*, whose main elements are depicted in Fig. 4, is used by the expert to provide required metadata of each such dataset.

Processes that generate the array data are represented by individuals of core#Process. Each *Offering* of the data source will be defined normally as

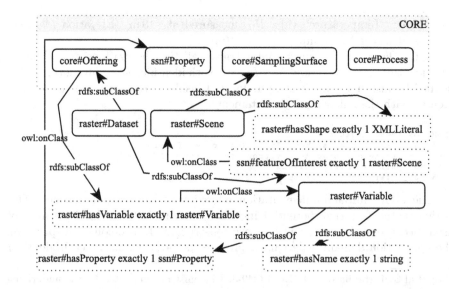

Fig. 4. Raster core ontology.

a subclass of core#Offering, specifying with a relevant restriction the reference to its *Process* and with relevant annotation the reference to the specific catalog of the specific THREDDS data server. Variables of the server are defined as individuals of raster#Variable, referencing their related SOS *Property*. An algorithm is periodically executed to update such ontology with metadata obtained from the THREDDS data server, which is required to solve future *GetCapabilities* and *GetObservation* requests.

SOS *GetCapabilities* requests are implemented using SPARQL over the above ontology. *GetObservation* requests are solved in two steps. First, a SPARQL query is executed to obtain the relevant raster#Dataset classes of the ontology and next a NetCDFSubset request is performed for each such dataset to obtain the required array data. Regarding performance evaluation, it is noticed that the a main difference between the current generic implementation of the wrapper and an ad-hoc one would be given by the time to access the ontology. However, such time is two low in comparison to the time to access the datasets. This comparison between the generic and ad-hoc implementations is given in Fig. 3(b).

5   Conclusion

The design and implementation of generic data access wrappers for in-situ and remote sensor observation data sources was discussed. Those wrappers are key components of a mediator/wrapper architecture for sensor observation semantic data mediation. Generic models and ontologies are designed and based on them SOS operations are implemented. The expert can concentrate now on semantic issues related to the datasets, decreasing this way the development cost of data wrappers, without a sensitive impact in the system performance.

References

1. Bowers, S., Madin, J., Schildhauer, M.: A conceptual modeling framework for expressing observational data semantics. In: Li, Q., Spaccapietra, S., Yu, E., Olivé, A. (eds.) Conceptual Modeling - ER 2008. LNCS, vol. 5231, pp. 41–54. Springer, Heidelberg (2008)
2. Bridger, E., Bermudez, L.E., Maskey, M., Rueda, C., Babin, B.L., Blair, R.: Oostethys - open source software for the global earth observing systems of systems. In: American Geophysical Union Fall 2009 Meeting (2009)
3. Bröring, A., Echterhoff, J., Jirka, S., Simonis, I., Everding, T., Stasch, C., Liang, S., Lemmens, R.: New generation sensor web enablement. Sensors 11(3), 2652 (2011)
4. Bröring, A., Maué, P., Janowicz, K., Nüst, D., Malewski, C.: Semantically-enabled sensor plug & play for the sensor web. Sensors 11(8), 7568 (2011)

5. Compton, M., Barnaghi, P., Bermudez, L., García-Castro, R., Corcho, O., Cox, S., Graybeal, J., Hauswirth, M., Henson, C., Herzog, A., Huang, V., Janowicz, K., Kelsey, W.D., Phuoc, D.L., Lefort, L., Leggieri, M., Neuhaus, H., Nikolov, A., Page, K., Passant, A., Sheth, A., Taylor, K.: The SSN ontology of the W3C semantic sensor network incubator group. Web Semant. Sci. Serv. Agents World Wide Web **17**, 25–32 (2012)

6. Henson, C.A., Pschorr, J.K., Sheth, A.P., Thirunarayan, K.: Semsos: semantic sensor observation service. In: Proceedings of the 2009 International Symposium on Collaborative Technologies and Systems, CTS 2009, pp. 44–53. IEEE Computer Society (2009)

7. Ludascher, B., Gupta, A., Martone, M.: Model-based mediation with domain maps. In: 17th International Conference on Data Engineering, Proceedings, pp. 81–90 (2001)

8. Raskin, R.G., Pan, M.J.: Knowledge representation in the semantic web for earth and environmental terminology (SWEET). Comput. Geosci. **31**(9), 1119–1125 (2005)

9. Regueiro, M.A., Viqueira, J.R., Stasch, C., Taboada, J.A.: Semantic mediation of observation datasets through sensor observation services. Technical report, CITIUS, Universidade de Santiago de Compostela, January 2016

10. Regueiro, M.A., Viqueira, J.R., Taboada, J.A., Cotos, J.M.: Virtual integration of sensor observation data. Comput. Geosci. **81**, 12–19 (2015)

11. Sheth, A., Henson, C., Sahoo, S.: Semantic sensor web. IEEE Internet Comput. **12**(4), 78–83 (2008)

12. Wiederhold, G.: Mediators in the architecture of future information systems. Computer **25**(3), 38–49 (1992)

Modeling and Executing Business Processes

Probabilistic Evaluation of Process Model Matching Techniques

Elena Kuss[1]([✉]), Henrik Leopold[2], Han van der Aa[2], Heiner Stuckenschmidt[1], and Hajo A. Reijers[2]

[1] Research Group Data and Web Science, University of Mannheim,
68163 Mannheim, Germany
{elena,heiner}@informatik.uni-mannheim.de

[2] Department of Computer Science, Vrije Universiteit Amsterdam,
De Boelelaan 1081, 1081 HV Amsterdam, The Netherlands
{h.leopold,j.h.vander.aa,h.a.reijers}@vu.nl

Abstract. Process model matching refers to the automatic identification of corresponding activities between two process models. It represents the basis for many advanced process model analysis techniques such as the identification of similar process parts or process model search. A central problem is how to evaluate the performance of process model matching techniques. Often, not even humans can agree on a set of correct correspondences. Current evaluation methods, however, require a binary gold standard, which clearly defines which correspondences are correct. The disadvantage of this evaluation method is that it does not take the true complexity of the matching problem into account and does not fairly assess the capabilities of a matching technique. In this paper, we propose a novel evaluation method for process model matching techniques. In particular, we build on the assessment of multiple annotators to define probabilistic notions of precision and recall. We use the dataset and the results of the Process Model Matching Contest 2015 to assess and compare our evaluation method. We find that our probabilistic evaluation method assigns different ranks to the matching techniques from the contest and allows to gain more detailed insights into their performance.

Keywords: Process model matching · Non-binary evaluation · Matching performance assessment

1 Introduction

Process models are conceptual models used for purposes ranging from the documentation of organizational operations [6] to the definition of requirements for information systems [19]. Process model *matching* refers to the automatic identification of corresponding activities between such models. The application scenarios of matching techniques are manifold. They include the analysis of model differences [12], harmonization of process model variants [13], process model

© Springer International Publishing AG 2016
I. Comyn-Wattiau et al. (Eds.): ER 2016, LNCS 9974, pp. 279–292, 2016.
DOI: 10.1007/978-3-319-46397-1_22

search [9], and the detection of process model clones [22]. The challenges associated with the matching task are considerable. Among others, process model matching techniques must be able to deal with heterogeneous vocabulary, different levels of granularity, and the fact that typically only a few activities from one model have a corresponding counterpart in the other. In recent years, a significant number of process model matching techniques have been defined to address these problems (cf. [4,10,11,14,23,24]). One central question that concerns all these techniques is how to demonstrate that they actually perform well.

To demonstrate the performance of a matching technique, authors typically conduct evaluation experiments that consist of solving a concrete matching problem. So far, the basis of such evaluation experiments is a binary *gold standard* created by humans, which clearly defines which correspondences are correct. By comparing the correspondences generated by the matching technique against those from the gold standard, it is possible to compute the well-established metrics precision, recall, and F-measure [15]. In this way, the performance of an approach can be quantified and compared against others.

The disadvantage of this evaluation method is that it does not take the true complexity of the matching problem into account. This is, for instance, illustrated by the gold standards of the Process Model Matching Contests (PMMCs) 2013 and 2015. The organizers of the contests found that there was not a single model for which two independent annotators fully agreed on all correspondences [1,3]. A binary gold standard, however, implies that any correspondence that is not part of the gold standard is incorrect and, thus, negatively affects the above mentioned metrics. This raises the question of why the performance of process model matching techniques is determined by referring to a single correct solution when human annotators may not even agree on what this correct solution is.

Recognizing the need for a more suitable evaluation strategy for process model matching techniques, we use this paper to propose a novel *process model matching evaluation method*. Instead of building on a binary gold standard, we define a non-binary gold standard that combines a number of binary assessments created by individual annotators. This allows us to express the *support* that exists for correspondences in the non-binary gold standard as the fraction of annotators that agree that a given correspondence is correct. The *probabilistic* precision and recall metrics we define take these support values into consideration when assessing the performance of matching techniques. As such, correspondences with high support values have a greater impact on precision and recall scores than correspondences with low support.

The rest of the paper is organized as follows. Section 2 illustrates the problems associated with the usage of binary gold standards for process model matching evaluation. In Sect. 3, we define the non-binary gold standard and probabilistic precision and recall metrics. In Sect. 4, we assess and compare the proposed probabilistic evaluation metrics by applying our method on the dataset of the PMMC 2015. Section 5 discusses related work on the evaluation of matching techniques in different application domains. Finally, we conclude the paper and discuss future research directions in Sect. 6.

2   Problem Illustration

Given two process models with their respective sets of activities A_1 and A_2, the goal of process model matching is to automatically identify the activities (or sets of activities) from A_1 and A_2 that represent similar behavior. The result of conducting process model matching, therefore, is a set of activity correspondences. One of the central questions in the context of process model matching is how to assess whether the correspondences identified by a matching technique are correct. To illustrate the problems associated with the *evaluation* of process model matching, consider the example depicted in Fig. 1. It shows two simplified process models from the PMMC 2015 [1], as well as possible correspondences between them.

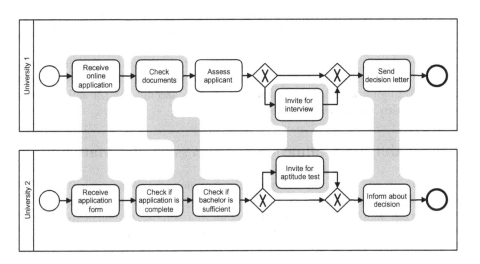

Fig. 1. Two process models and possible correspondences

Upon closer inspection of the correspondences shown in Fig. 1 it becomes clear that many of the correspondences are actually disputable. Consider, for instance, the correspondence between *"Receive online application"* from University 1 and *"Receive application form"* in the process of University 2. On the one hand, we can argue in favor of this correspondence because they both describe the receipt of an application document. On the other hand, we can argue that these activities do not correspond to each other because the former relates to an online procedure, whereas the second refers to a paper-based step. We can bring forward similar arguments for the correspondence between *"Invite for interview"* and *"Invite for aptitude test"*. Both activities aim to assess whether an applicant is suitable for a university. However, an interview is clearly a different assessment instrument than an aptitude test, which makes the correspondence disputable. Lastly, also the correspondence between *"Check documents"* from University 1 and the two activities *"Check if application is complete"* and *"Check if bachelor is sufficient"* from University 2 is controversial. If we consider the activity *"Check documents"* to solely relate to the completeness of the documents, then the activity *"Check if bachelor is sufficient"* should not be part of the correspondence. These examples illustrate that it may be hard and, in some cases, even impossible to agree on a single *correct* set of correspondences. Despite this, the evaluation of process model matching techniques currently depends on the definition of such a single set of correct correspondences, i.e. a binary gold standard. This binary gold standard is needed to compute precision, recall, and F-measure, which are traditionally used to evaluate process model matching techniques (cf. [1,3,14,23,24]).

In this paper, we argue that a binary evaluation of process model matching techniques does not account for the full complexity of the process model matching task. Binary evaluation does not consider disagreements that may exist regarding the correctness of correspondences. Therefore, binary evaluation does not provide a fair assessment of the output generated by a matching technique. We address this problem by defining the first non-binary process model matching evaluation method. We build on a gold standard that has been defined by several annotators and, in this way, allows to account for the subjectivity associated with identifying correspondences.

3 Probabilistic Evaluation of Process Model Matching

In this section, we define our method for non-binary matching evaluation. The starting point of our method is formed by binary assessments created by individual human annotators. Each of these *binary human assessments* captures the correspondences that a single annotator identifies between two given process models.

Definition 1 (Binary Human Assessment). *Let A_1 and A_2 be the sets of activities of two process models. Then, a binary human assessment can be captured by the relation $H : A_1 \times A_2$. Each element $(a_1, a_2) \in H$ specifies that the human assessor considers the activity a_1 to correspond to the activity a_2.*

Note that Definition 1 also allows for one-to-many and many-to-many relationships. If, for instance, the elements (a_1, a_2) and (a_1, a_3) are both part of H, then there exists a one-to-many relationship between the activity a_1 and the two activities a_2 and a_3. Further note that a binary human assessment according to Definition 1 should be created independently and solely reflect the opinion of a single assessor. Based on a number of such independently created binary human assessments, we can then define a non-binary gold standard.

Definition 2 (Non-binary Gold Standard). *A non-binary gold standard is a tuple $\mathcal{GS} = (A_1, A_2, \mathcal{H}, \sigma)$ where*

– *A_1 and A_2 are the sets of activities of two process models,*

- $\mathcal{H} = \{H_1, \ldots, H_n\}$ is a set of independently created binary human assessments, and
- $\sigma : \mathcal{A}_1 \times \mathcal{A}_2 \to \mathbb{R}$ is a function assigning to each $(a_1, a_2) \in \mathcal{A}_1 \times \mathcal{A}_2$ a support value, which is the number of binary human assessments in $\mathcal{H}$ that contain the correspondence (a_1, a_2) divided by the total number of binary human assessments $|\mathcal{H}|$.

The overall rationale of the non-binary gold standard from Definition 2 is to count the individual opinions from the binary human assessments as votes. In this way, we obtain a *support value* σ for each correspondence according to the number of votes in favor of this correspondence. In this way, any correspondence with a support value $0.0 < \sigma < 1.0$ can be regarded as an uncertain correspondence. For these correspondences, there is no unanimous vote about whether or not it is a correct correspondence. Based on these support values, we define non-binary notions of the well-established metrics precision, recall, and F-measure that take the uncertainty of correspondences into account. For convenience, we introduce $\mathcal{C}$ as the set of all unique correspondences based on the union of all binary human assessments from $\mathcal{H}$.

Definition 3 (Probabilistic Precision, Recall, and F-Measure). *Let A_1 and A_2 be the sets of activities of two process models, $M : A_1 \times A_2$ the correspondences identified by a matching technique, and $\mathcal{GS} = (A_1, A_2, \mathcal{H}, \sigma)$ a non-binary gold standard. Then, we define probabilistic precision, recall, and F-measure as follows:*

$$\textit{Probabilistic Precision (ProP)} = \frac{\sum\limits_{m \in M} \sigma(m)}{\sum\limits_{m \in M} \sigma(m) + |M \backslash \mathcal{C}|} \tag{1}$$

$$\textit{Probabilistic Recall (ProR)} = \frac{\sum\limits_{m \in M} \sigma(m)}{\sum\limits_{c \in \mathcal{C}} \sigma(c)} \tag{2}$$

$$\textit{Probabilistic F-Measure (ProFM)} = 2 \times \frac{ProP \times ProR}{ProP + ProR} \tag{3}$$

Probabilistic precision and recall are adaptations of the traditional notions of precision and recall that incorporate the support values from a non-binary gold standard $\mathcal{GS}$. We define *probabilistic precision* ProP as the sum of the support values of the correspondences identified by the matching technique (M) divided by the same value plus the number of correspondences that are not part of the gold standard ($|M \backslash \mathcal{C}|$). This definition gives those correspondences that have been identified by many annotators a higher weight than those that have only been identified by a few. Therefore, it accounts for the uncertainty associated with correspondences in the non-binary gold standard. As a result, the impact of false positives, i.e. correspondences that have been identified by the matching technique but are not part of the gold standard, result in a strong penalty of 1.0. We justify this high penalty by the high coverage of uncertain correspondences included in non-binary gold standards. These gold standards can be expected to contain a broad range of potential correspondences, including those identified by only a single annotator. Any correspondence not included in this broad range can be considered as incorrect with certainty, which is reflected in the penalty of 1.0 for false positives.

Probabilistic recall. ProR follows the same principle as the probabilistic precision. It resembles the traditional definition of recall, but incorporates the support values from the non-binary gold standard respectively. As a result, identifying correspondences with a higher support has a higher influence on the recall than identifying correspondences with a low support. The probabilistic F-measure ProFM presents the harmonic mean of probabilistic precision and recall. It is computed in the same way as the traditional F-measure, though it is here based on ProP and ProR.

To illustrate these metrics, consider the correspondences, their support values, and the output of three matchers depicted in Table 1. The support values reveal that five out of six correspondences are considered to be correct correspondences in one or more binary human assessments. Matcher $\mathcal{M}_1$ identifies exactly these five correspondences. Therefore, $\mathcal{M}_1$ achieves ProP and ProR scores of 1.0. By contrast, matcher $\mathcal{M}_2$ identifies only three of the five correct correspondences. The matcher also includes the incorrect correspondence c_6 in its output. This results in a ProP value of 0.71 and a ProR value of 0.77. Although matcher $\mathcal{M}_3$ correctly identifies four correspondences, instead of the three identified by $\mathcal{M}_2$, it achieves the exact same ProP and ProR values. This occurs because $\mathcal{M}_3$ identifies c_4 and c_5, which have a combined support value of 0.75, i.e. the same support value as correspondence c_3 that is identified by $\mathcal{M}_2$. This demonstrates that correspondences with a high support value have a greater contribution to the metrics than those with low support.

Table 1. Exemplary matcher output and metrics

Corr. ($\mathcal{C}$)	Supp. (σ)	$\mathcal{M}_1$	$\mathcal{M}_2$	$\mathcal{M}_3$
c_1	1.00	1	1	1
c_2	0.75	1	1	1
c_3	0.75	1	1	0
c_4	0.50	1	0	1
c_5	0.25	1	0	1
c_6	0.00	0	1	1

Furthermore, non-binary gold standards allow us to obtain more fine-granular insights into the performance of matchers. We can achieve this by computing probabilistic precision and recall scores for correspondences with a minimal support level. By adapting the equations from Definition 3 in this way, we can differentiate between matchers that identify correspondences with a broad range of support values and those that focus on the identification of correspondences with high support values. We capture this notion of *bounded* probabilistic precision, recall, and F-measure in Definition 4.

Definition 4 (Bounded   Probabilistic   Precision,   Recall,   and   F-measure). *Let A_1 and A_2 be the sets of activities of two process models, $M : A_1 \times A_2$ the correspondences identified by a matching technique, $\mathcal{GS} = (A_1, A_2, \mathcal{H}, \sigma)$ a non-binary gold standard, and $\mathcal{C}_\tau$ refer to the set of correspondences with a support level $\sigma \geq \tau$. Then, we define bounded probabilistic precision, recall, and F-measure as follows:*

$$ProP(\tau) = \frac{\sum\limits_{m \in M} \sigma(m)}{\sum\limits_{m \in M} \sigma(m) + |M \backslash \mathcal{C}_\tau|} \tag{4}$$

$$ProR(\tau) = \frac{\sum\limits_{m \in M} \sigma(m)}{\sum\limits_{c \in \mathcal{C}_\tau} \sigma(c)} \tag{5}$$

$$ProFM(\tau) = 2 \times \frac{ProP(\tau) \times ProR(\tau)}{ProP(\tau) + ProR(\tau)} \tag{6}$$

By computing bounded precision and recall values, we can directly gain insights into the differences between the results obtained by matchers $\mathcal{M}_2$ and $\mathcal{M}_3$. For instance, $\mathcal{M}_2$ and $\mathcal{M}_3$ respectively achieve ProP(0.75) scores which only consider correspondences with $\sigma \geq 0.75$, i.e. 0.71 and 0.50. Similarly, they achieve ProR(0.75) scores of 0.77 and 0.54. These metrics indicate that matcher $\mathcal{M}_2$ is more successful in identifying correspondences with high support values. By contrast, the bounded scores reveal that $\mathcal{M}_3$ identifies more correspondences, although it also includes those with lower support values.

4   Evaluation Experiments

In this section, we apply our probabilistic evaluation method to a dataset from the Process Model Matching Contest 2015. To this end, we create a non-binary gold standard and compute the probabilistic metrics for the matchers that participated in the contest. The overall goal of our experiments is to demonstrate the usefulness of the non-binary perspective and the value of the insights that our evaluation method delivers. Section 4.1 first describes the setup of our experiments. Then, Sect. 4.2 elaborates on the results.

4.1   Setup

To demonstrate the usefulness of our evaluation method, we apply it to the University Admission dataset from the PMMC 2015 [1]. This dataset consists of nine BPMN process models describing the admission processes for graduate study programs of different German universities. The size of the models varies between 10 and 44 activities. The task in the context of the Process Model Matching Contest 2015 was to match these models pairwise, resulting in a total number of 36 matching pairs. Our experiments with this dataset consist of two steps:

1. *Non-binary gold standard creation:* To define a non-binary gold standard, we asked eight different individuals to identify the correspondences for the 36 model pairs from the dataset. The group of annotators involved was heterogeneous and included four researchers being familiar with process model matching and four student assistants from the University of Mannheim in Germany. The student assistants were introduced to the problem of process model matching but not influenced in the way they identified correspondences. The result of this step, was a non-binary gold standard based on eight binary assessments. Note that we did not apply any changes to the individual assessments. We included them in their original form into the non-binary gold standard.

2. *Probabilistic evaluation:* Based on the non-binary gold standard, we calculated probabilistic precision, probabilistic recall, and F-measure for each of the 12 matchers that participated in the PMMC 2015. In line with the report from the PMMC 2015 we distinguish between micro and macro average. Macro average is defined as the average precision, recall, and F-measure of all 36 matching pairs. Micro average, by contrast, is computed by considering all 36 pairs as one matching problem. The micro average scores take different sizes of matching pairs (in terms of the correspondences they consist of) into account. As a result, a poor recall on a small matching pair has only limited impact on the overall micro average recall score.

4.2   Results

This section discusses the results of our experiments. We first elaborate on the characteristics of the non-binary gold standard we created. Then, we present the results from the probabilistic evaluation and compare them to the results of the non-binary evaluation from the PMMC 2015. Finally, we present the insights from the bounded probabilistic evaluation.

Non-binary Gold Standard Creation. The non-binary gold standard resulting from the eight binary assessments consists of a total of 879 correspondences. The binary gold standard from the PMMC 2015 only consisted of 234 correspondences, which is less than a third. The average support value per model pair ranges from 0.33 to 0.91. This illustrates that the models considerably differ with respect to how obvious the contained correspondences are.

Figure 2 illustrates the distribution of the support values. It shows that there are two extremes. On the one hand, there is a high number of correspondences with six or more votes (support value ≥ 0.75). On the other hand, there is also a high number of correspondences with three votes or less (support value ≤ 0.375). Overall, the number of correspondences that would be included based

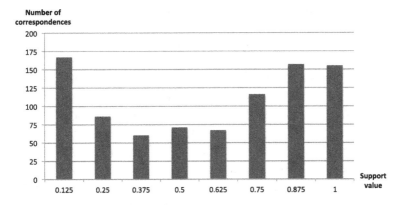

Fig. 2. Distribution of support values in the non-binary gold standard

on a majority vote (support value ≥ 0.5) amounts to 495, which is only a little more than half of the correspondences from the non-binary gold standard. These numbers illustrate the complexity associated with defining a binary gold standard and highlight the risks of a purely binary method. Instead of excluding a high number of possible correspondences, we include them with a respective support value.

Probabilistic Evaluation. Table 2 presents the probabilistic evaluation results based on the non-binary gold standard. It shows the micro and macro values of probabilistic F-measure (ProFM), precision (ProP), and recall (ProR) for each matcher that participated in the PMMC 2015. The column *Rank - New* indicates the rank the matcher has achieved according to the probabilistic F-measure micro value. The column *Rank - Old* shows the rank the systems has achieved according to the binary evaluation from the PMMC 2015 [1].

The results from the table illustrate that the probabilistic evaluation has notable effects on the ranking. Although four matchers remain on the same rank, the ranking changes dramatically for other matchers. For instance, the matcher *AML-PM* moves from rank 10 to 2 and the matcher *RMM-NLM* moves from rank 2 to rank 9. A brief analysis of how the matchers work provides an explanation for this development. The matcher *AML-PM* does not impose strict thresholds on the similarity values it uses for identifying correspondences. As a result, it also identifies correspondences with low support values. In the binary gold standard, however, these correspondences were simply not included and resulted in a decrease of precision. Table 3 illustrates this effect by showing an excerpt from the correspondences generated by the matcher *AML-PM* and the respective entries from the binary and the non-binary gold standard. We can see that from the five correspondences from Table 3 only two were included in the binary gold standard. In the context of an evaluation based on this gold standard these three correspondence would therefore reduce the precision of this matcher. An evaluation based on the non-binary gold standard, however, would come to a different assessment. The non-binary gold standard does not only include the

Table 2. Results of probabilistic evaluation with new gold standard

Rank			Approach	ProFM		ProP		ProR	
New	Old	Δ		Mic	Mac	Mic	Mac	Mic	Mac
1	1	±0	RMM-NHCM	**.431**	.387	**.783**	.751	.297	.302
2	10	+8	AML-PM	.387	.365	.377	.390	**.398**	.399
3	9	+6	KnoMa-Proc	.378	.312	.506	.493	.302	.286
4	4	±0	OPBOT	.369	.322	.648	.666	.258	.256
5	5	±0	KMSSS	.368	.313	.563	.623	.274	.276
6	8	+2	BPLangMatch	.360	.325	.532	.475	.272	.272
7	11	+4	RMM-VM2	.329	.293	.516	.643	.242	.240
8	3	−5	MSSS	.307	.238	.761	.772	.192	.201
9	2	−7	RMM-NLM	.306	.244	.681	.565	.197	.203
10	6	−4	RMM-SMSL	.301	.289	.309	.306	.294	.297
11	7	−4	TripleS	.293	.200	.486	.473	.210	.214
12	12	±0	pPalm-DS	.258	.235	.210	.249	.335	.332

Table 3. Effect of gold standard on assessment of output of matcher *AML-PM*

Correspondence ($\mathcal{C}$)		Gold standard	
Activity 1	Activity 2	Binary	Non-binary
Send documents by post	Send appl. form and documents	0	0.750
Evaluate	Check and evaluate application	0	0.500
Apply online	Complete online interview	0	0.375
Wait for results	Waiting for response	1	0.875
Rejected	Receive rejection	1	0.625

two correspondence from the binary gold standard, but also includes the three other correspondences. It is obvious that this positively affects the ProP of the matcher and improves its overall ProFM respectively.

For the matcher *RMM-NLM* we observe the opposite effect. In the context of the evaluation with the non-binary gold standard it misses a huge range of correspondences. Consequently, the ProR of this matcher decreases considerably.

Bounded Probabilistic Evaluation. The bounded variants of probabilistic precision, recall, and F-measure provide the possibility to obtain more detailed insights into the performance of the matchers. Figure 3 illustrates this by showing the values of ProP, ProR, and ProFM for $\tau = 0.0$, $\tau = 0.375$, $\tau = 0.5$, and $\tau = 0.75$ for five selected matchers from the PMMC 2015.

The results from Fig. 3 show that the effect of a change in the minimum support level τ varies for the different matchers. In general, we observe a decreasing ProP and an increasing ProR for higher values of τ. This is intuitive because

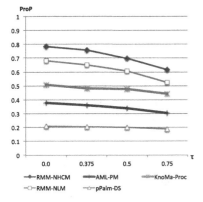

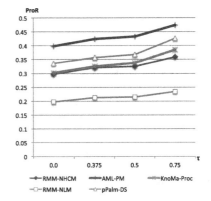

(a) Bounded Probabilistic Precision

(b) Bounded Probabilistic Recall

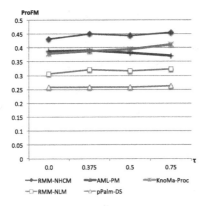

(c) Bounded Probabilistic F-Measure

Fig. 3. ProP, ProR, and ProFM for different values of τ

a higher value of τ results in the consideration of fewer correspondences. However, for some matchers this effect is stronger than for others. For instance, we observe hardly any change in ProP and a strong increase in ProR for the matcher *pPalm-DS*. This means that this matcher mainly identifies correspondences with high support. It therefore benefits from a stricter gold standard. The matcher *RMM-NLM* represents a contrasting case. The ProP of this matcher decreases dramatically with an increase of τ, while its ProR slightly increases. This reveals that this matcher also identifies a considerable number of correspondences with low support. Since these correspondences turn into false positives when we increase τ, the ProP drops respectively.

The consideration of the bounded variants of ProP, ProR, and ProFM illustrate that an evaluation based on a non-binary gold standard facilitates a more detailed assessment of specific matchers. It is possible to identify whether a matcher focuses on rather obvious correspondences (with high support) or whether a matcher also identifies less apparent correspondences (with low support).

5   Related Work

Existing work on process model matching evaluate their approaches using precision, recall, and F-measures, see for example the reports of the Process Model Matching Contests [1,3]. Thus, the used evaluation metrics compare an absolute correspondence list with a binary gold standard. Schema matching and ontology matching techniques are similar to process model matching techniques in the sense that these techniques all set out to identify relations between concepts in different conceptual models [8]. Research in the fields of schema and ontology matching (cf. [18,21]) shows a similar tendency to evaluate the performance of matching techniques based on binary values. However, these fields use a broader range of evaluation metrics to suit needs related to specific applications. For example, aside from the F-measure [2], *error* [17], *information loss* [16], and *overall* [5] are all used to aggregate precision and recall values.

More recently, some metrics have been proposed that relax the binary evaluations of precision and recall metrics. Ehrig and Euzenat [7] propose alternative precision and recall metrics that take into account the closeness of results in ontology matching. Closeness can, for example, exploit the tree structure of ontologies, where the distance between elements in the tree can be computed to determine if a result is close or remote from the expected result. Sagi and Gal [20] adapt precision and recall metrics in order to support non-binary matching results. These metrics can, for instance, be directly applied on first-line-matching results that contain non-binary confidence values. Although this work also specifies that precision and recall could be adapted to support non-binary gold standards, to the best of our knowledge, no works have done this so far.

6   Conclusion

In this paper, we proposed a probabilistic method for assessing the performance of process model matching techniques. Our method is motivated by the insight that it is often hard and in many cases even impossible to define a sensible binary gold standard that clearly specifies which correspondences are correct. Therefore, our evaluation method builds on a number of independent assessments of the correspondences, which are combined into a single probabilistic gold standard. By interpreting the number of votes for each correspondence as support, we defined probabilistic notions of the well-established metrics precision, recall, and F-measure.

To gain insights into the usefulness of our probabilistic evaluation method, we applied it to the University admission data set and the participating twelve matching techniques from the PMMC 2015. To this end, we recruited eight annotators for the creation of a non-binary gold standard and then computed the probabilistic metrics for each of the matching techniques. We found that the non-binary gold standard contained almost three times as many correspondences as the existing binary gold standard and that only for a fraction of these correspondences there was a unanimous agreement. This emphasizes the risk of using a purely binary evaluation method, which is also reflected in the considerable effect of our probabilistic evaluation method on the ranking of the matching techniques. Furthermore, we found that the probabilistic evaluation allows to obtain more detailed insights into the specific strengths and weaknesses of individual matchers.

In future work, we plan to apply our method on additional data sets and to investigate how human experts perceive the probabilistic results. Our overall goal is to establish the proposed method as a new standard for the evaluation of process model matching techniques and to apply it in the context of the next PMMC.

References

1. Antunes, G., Bakhshandeh, M., Borbinha, J., Cardoso, J., Dadashnia, S., Francescomarino, C.D., Dragoni, M., Fettke, P., Gal, A., Ghidini, C., Hake, P., Khiat, A., Klinkmüller, C., Kuss, E., Leopold, H., Loos, P., Meilicke, C., Niesen, T., Pesquita, C., Péus, T., Schoknecht, A., Sheetrit, E., Sonntag, A., Stuckenschmidt, H., Thaler, T., Weber, I., Weidlich, M.: The process model matching contest 2015. In: 6th International Workshop on Enterprise Modelling and Information Systems Architectures (2015)
2. Berlin, J., Motro, A.: Autoplex: automated discovery of content for virtual databases. In: Batini, C., Giunchiglia, F., Giorgini, P., Mecella, M. (eds.) CoopIS 2001. LNCS, vol. 2172, pp. 108–122. Springer, Heidelberg (2001). doi:10.1007/3-540-44751-2_10
3. Cayoglu, U., Dijkman, R., Dumas, M., Fettke, P., Garcıa-Banuelos, L., Hake, P., Klinkmüller, C., Leopold, H., Ludwig, A., Loos, P., et al.: The process model matching contest 2013. In: 4th International Workshop on Process Model Collections: Management and Reuse (PMC-MR 2013) (2013)
4. Cayoglu, U., Oberweis, A., Schoknecht, A., Ullrich, M.: Triple-S: a matching approach for Petri nets on syntactic, semantic and structural level. Technical report, Karlsruhe Institute of Technology (KIT) (2013)
5. Do, H.-H., Melnik, S., Rahm, E.: Comparison of schema matching evaluations. In: Chaudhri, A.B., Jeckle, M., Rahm, E., Unland, R. (eds.) NODe 2002. LNCS, vol. 2593, pp. 221–237. Springer, Heidelberg (2003). doi:10.1007/3-540-36560-5_17
6. Dumas, M., Rosa, M., Mendling, J., Reijers, H.: Fundamentals of Business Process Management. Springer, Heidelberg (2013)
7. Ehrig, M., Euzenat, J.: Relaxed precision and recall for ontology matching. In: Proceedings of K-Cap 2005 Workshop on Integrating Ontology, pp. 25–32. No commercial editor (2005)
8. Giunchiglia, F., Shvaiko, P., Yatskevich, M.: Semantic matching. In: Liu, L., Özsu, M.T. (eds.) Encyclopedia of Database Systems, pp. 2561–2566. Springer, New York (2009)
9. Jin, T., Wang, J., La Rosa, M., Ter Hofstede, A., Wen, L.: Efficient querying of large process model repositories. Comput. Ind. 64(1), 41–49 (2013)

10. Klinkmüller, C., Weber, I., Mendling, J., Leopold, H., Ludwig, A.: Increasing recall of process model matching by improved activity label matching. In: Daniel, F., Wang, J., Weber, B. (eds.) BPM 2013. LNCS, vol. 8094, pp. 211–218. Springer, Heidelberg (2013). doi:10.1007/978-3-642-40176-3_17

11. Kunze, M., Weidlich, M., Weske, M.: Behavioral similarity – a proper metric. In: Rinderle-Ma, S., Toumani, F., Wolf, K. (eds.) BPM 2011. LNCS, vol. 6896, pp. 166–181. Springer, Heidelberg (2011). doi:10.1007/978-3-642-23059-2_15

12. Küster, J.M., Koehler, J., Ryndina, K.: Improving business process models with reference models in business-driven development. In: Eder, J., Dustdar, S. (eds.) BPM 2006. LNCS, vol. 4103, pp. 35–44. Springer, Heidelberg (2006). doi:10.1007/11837862_5

13. La Rosa, M., Dumas, M., Uba, R., Dijkman, R.: Business process model merging: an approach to business process consolidation. ACM Trans. Softw. Eng. Methodol. (TOSEM) 22(2), 11 (2013)

14. Leopold, H., Niepert, M., Weidlich, M., Mendling, J., Dijkman, R., Stuckenschmidt, H.: Probabilistic optimization of semantic process model matching. In: Barros, A., Gal, A., Kindler, E. (eds.) BPM 2012. LNCS, vol. 7481, pp. 319–334. Springer, Heidelberg (2012). doi:10.1007/978-3-642-32885-5_25

15. Manning, C.D., Raghavan, P., Schütze, H.: Introduction to Information Retrieval, vol. 1. Cambridge University Press, Cambridge (2008)

16. Mena, E., Kashyap, V., Illarramendi, A., Sheth, A.: Imprecise answers in distributed environments: Estimation of information loss for multi-ontology based query processing. Int. J. Coop. Inf. Syst. 9(04), 403–425 (2000)

17. Modica, G., Gal, A., Jamil, H.M.: The use of machine-generated ontologies in dynamic information seeking. In: Batini, C., Giunchiglia, F., Giorgini, P., Mecella, M. (eds.) CoopIS 2001. LNCS, vol. 2172, pp. 433–447. Springer, Heidelberg (2001). doi:10.1007/3-540-44751-2_32

18. Rahm, E., Bernstein, P.A.: A survey of approaches to automatic schema matching. VLDB J. 10(4), 334–350 (2001)

19. Rolland, C., Prakash, N., Benjamen, A.: A multi-model view of process modelling. Requir. Eng. 4(4), 169–187 (1999)

20. Sagi, T., Gal, A.: Non-binary evaluation for schema matching. In: Atzeni, P., Cheung, D., Ram, S. (eds.) ER 2012. LNCS, vol. 7532, pp. 477–486. Springer, Heidelberg (2012). doi:10.1007/978-3-642-34002-4_37

21. Shvaiko, P., Euzenat, J.: Ontology matching: state of the art and future challenges. IEEE Trans. Knowl. Data Eng. 25(1), 158–176 (2013)

22. Uba, R., Dumas, M., García-Bañuelos, L., Rosa, M.: Clone detection in repositories of business process models. In: Rinderle-Ma, S., Toumani, F., Wolf, K. (eds.) BPM 2011. LNCS, vol. 6896, pp. 248–264. Springer, Heidelberg (2011). doi:10.1007/978-3-642-23059-2_20

23. Weidlich, M., Dijkman, R., Mendling, J.: The ICoP framework: identification of correspondences between process models. In: Pernici, B. (ed.) CAiSE 2010. LNCS, vol. 6051, pp. 483–498. Springer, Heidelberg (2010). doi:10.1007/978-3-642-13094-6_37

24. Weidlich, M., Sheetrit, E., Branco, M.C., Gal, A.: Matching business process models using positional passage-based language models. In: Ng, W., Storey, V.C., Trujillo, J.C. (eds.) ER 2013. LNCS, vol. 8217, pp. 130–137. Springer, Heidelberg (2013). doi:10.1007/978-3-642-41924-9_12

Context-Aware Workflow Execution Engine for E-Contract Enactment

Himanshu Jain[1(✉)], P. Radha Krishna[2], and Kamalakar Karlapalem[1]

[1] Center for Data Engineering, IIIT-Hyderabad, Hyderabad, India
`himanshu.jain@student.iiit.ac.in`, `kamal@iiit.ac.in`
[2] Infosys Limited, Hyderabad, India
`radhakrishna_p@infosys.com`

Abstract. An e-contract is a contract that is specified, modeled and executed by a software system. E-contract business processes are modeled using workflows and their enactment is mostly dependent on the execution context. Existing e-contract systems lack context-awareness, and thus often face difficulties in enacting when context and requirements of e-contracts change at run-time. In this paper, we (a) present an approach for context pattern discovery and build a context-aware workflow execution engine, (b) develop an approach for context-aware execution-workflow to instantiate and execute context-based workflow instances and (c) provide a framework for context-aware e-contract enactment system. We also demonstrate the viability of our approach using a government contract.

Keywords: E-Contracts · WFMS · Execution-Workflow · Context-aware systems

1 Introduction

An e-contract is an electronic version of the conventional contract which stipulates that the involved parties agree to fulfill specified activities and deliverables. E-contracts are associated with several entities, processes and procedures, and are used to regulate cross-organizational business processes. Usually, e-contract business processes are modeled using workflows and their enactment is mostly dependent on the *execution context*. Workflow systems require capturing such context information for dynamic update of workflows during execution. This necessitates incorporating context information at run-time, which is not feasible for generic workflow management system (WFMS), as it needs to capture, comprehend and act on just-in-time context information. Contracts evolve over a period and the contextual changes influence the e-contract enactment. To provide adequate service for the users, applications and services should be aware of their contexts and should automatically adapt to their changing contexts [1]. Existing e-contract systems (e.g., [2, 3]) do not emphasize the role of contextual information during the specification and execution of e-contracts, but addressed the problem of e-contract enactment as just workflow orchestration. In today's organizations (ex., Government and Health), it is unlikely that application processes are modeled once and executed repeatedly without any changes. Huge cost is

© Springer International Publishing AG 2016
I. Comyn-Wattiau et al. (Eds.): ER 2016, LNCS 9974, pp. 293–301, 2016.
DOI: 10.1007/978-3-319-46397-1_23

incurred to re-model a business process or to change its specification during execution (or, to handle new context information), as these processes and their structures are pre-defined. Several methods have been proposed in the past to overcome these challenges (e.g., [4]. However, those solutions work at the *"workflow instance"* level; where they change/modify the workflow instance itself and follow a *fixed specification and execution procedure* of workflow engine (detailed example with such WFMS is presented in Sect. 4). Hence, there is not much flexibility at the specification and execution level. On the other hand, meta-level execution models dynamically modify and enhance the workflow execution engine procedures [5]. However, such systems require some prior information (such as external information and present resource availability) to adapt them according to the requirement of the workflow instance.

In this work, we introduce a Context-Aware Meta Execution-Workflow (C-MEW) approach, which allows modification of *workflow execution engine procedure* when required, according to the business and technological needs, without changing the workflow engine execution code. Here, the **workflow engine execution procedure is defined as a workflow** so that it can be adapted to the changes [5]. C-MEW generates context-based execution-workflow (CEW) as a workflow engine with *process context information* to dynamically execute the workflow instances and adapt to changes of the environment. The proposed *context-aware e-contract enactment system* draws the contextual information and incorporates it at the CEW which performs the actual workflow instance execution. In this work, we show an e-government contract activity between Internet Service Provider (ISP) and Government of India to illustrate our approach. The rest of the paper is organized as follows. Section 2 presents an overview of our context-aware e-contract enactment system. Context-aware workflow execution engine component is described in Sect. 3. Section 4 illustrates our approach using an example e-contract activity and Sect. 5 concludes the paper.

2 Context-Aware E-Contract Enactment Framework

In this section, we develop a framework for an *information system life cycle starting from collecting and analyzing context information till executing modified workflows to completion in order to support the changes in run-time or requirements during e-contract enactment*. Our system provides the capabilities of defining and selecting different contract flows for contract specification, and is capable of efficiently managing the execution states. The ability to store, update, retrieve, and share the pertinent information by users is an important feature of our system.

Figure 1 shows the framework of our context-aware e-contract enactment system. *Contract Enactor* continuously monitors the contract execution for clause violations or path deviations. Multiple workflows, defined for various individual tasks, are difficult to coordinate among various parties, as there are dependencies between tasks. For instance, in an e-governance project, several activities have dependencies across multiple departments, which require huge coordination, but at the same time need to be satisfied for their successful commitment.

Contract Workflow helps in managing workflows globally for all the parties. It ensures that context change for an inter-dependent activity shall propagate among its

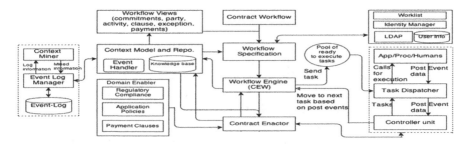

Fig. 1. Framework for context-aware e-contract enactment system

dependents, for example, change of payment details of a user during an activity is used among all its dependent activities. Contract workflow combines activity (or set of tasks) of parties in the required order as per the inputs provided by the contract enactor and with human support, if required. It also allows flexibility of augmenting additional tasks and events. *Workflow Views* are derived from contract workflow, which enable cross-organizational workflow interaction. Workflow views explicitly represent the interdependency in both *data* and *control* between different aspects of e-contract, and focus more on input and output data, conditions and events. A *userId* is associated with every task, which enable only specific user to perform the corresponding task. Hence, a user can only see his tasks on his *worklist*. Workflow views are created by analyzing the task allocated to a user in the XML specification document.

Figure 2 shows workflow views for *"Payment of Subscriber's tariff"* activity. Here, the two workflow views are pertaining to Service provider and Subscriber parties in our example contract (see Sect. 4). First workflow view corresponds to the service provider, who will be initiating the payment collection independent of second party. But, as soon as service provider sends the notification, it triggers the second workflow view, which is associated with the subscriber, using *message* method. These two workflow views will coordinate each other for completion of desired activity (see Sect. 4).

Workflow Specification component performs two steps: (i) create workflows from the activities using XML specification document uploaded by the contract manager, and (ii) provides explicit provisions for representing exceptions, task attributes such as organizational hierarchy and roles. During specification, the workflow tasks are associated with policies and applications mentioned in *domain enabler* component. The workflow specification module retrieves the associated attributes and related

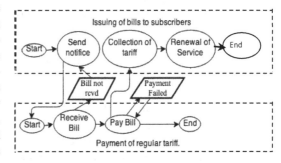

Fig. 2. Workflow views for payment of subscriber's tariff activity

information from the *knowledge base*. Workflow is validated based on tasks' specifications and the data specified to make a workflow executable. Validation criteria include 'after specification of an activity, every node, except start node, shall have at least one incoming node', 'every node except exit node shall have at least one outgoing node' and 'start node has only one path'. During execution, when a task requires human intervention, it appears as a to-do task on **Work-List** of associated user such that user can see what tasks are pending and thereby select them for processing. Other sub-components such as *identity manager* and *user info* manage hierarchical information, task escalation structure, and calendar of users in an organization. **Domain Enabler** has information such as regulatory compliance, policies, payment and procurement clauses related to the domain. Once, the contract enactment starts, it should comply with such domain specific constraints. Contract enactor automatically maps these constraints to clauses and activities depending upon the type of event.

Event Handler consists of Event-Condition-Action (ECA) rules manager. When an event occurs, it checks the conditions, identifies the corresponding rule and executes the action part. Exception handling is done using ECA rule manager in coordination with contract enactor component. When an exception occurs at runtime, a CEW execution definition is dynamically selected from the *knowledge base* depending on the context of the exception and particular workflow instance (Sect. 5). This new definition performs appropriate actions in order to continue execution of e-contract. However, if unknown exception occurs, manual intervention is required to define ECA rule corresponding to this exception. Therefore, both expected and unexpected exceptions are catered in real time by ECA rule manager, so that 'manual handling' is minimized. ECA definition tables are defined as follows:

- Event *(eventID, eventType, description, objectAffected, ruleFires, eventEvaluationLocation)*
- Condition *(conditionID, conditionType, description, conditionEvaluationLocation)*
- Action *(actionID, actionType, description, objectAffected, eventRaise, actionPerf, location)*
- Activity-log *(time, event, object, prevAction, postAction)*

Knowledge Base (KB) is our underlying data and meta data Database component. During execution of an activity workflow, workflow engine generates context variables such as location and time along with events related to that activity. This context information is stored in the KB, which will be further used during execution. All definitions of CEWs are stored in the KB for their re-use. KB also consists of database triggers that are associated with tasks.

Context model determines the schema of the context that is captured. It provides context information to the workflow specification component and helps workflow execution component during run-time. It processes the context data and stores it in a XML format. Our context model is based on *Key-Value* model, where *key* refers to the category of context information such as exceptions and events, and *value* refers to the data collected from internal and external sources. For modeling of context information, we categorize context information into two types: *Type-A (internal)* and *Type-B (external)*. Type-A represents the context generated from internal to the system such as values associated with task parameters, task assignment to resources/users and events/exceptions generated. Type-B represents the context generated by the external to the system during execution of workflow instances such as capabilities of users performing a task and location where the task is executed. Type-B's context information sources are system interfaces which allow capturing external information/events. Similarly, log files and XML specification files are source of context information for Type-A class. After classification of context information, it is stored in a repository from which appropriate as well as task-relevant context information is derived. Both Type-A and Type-B together provides necessary information to update the current workflow instance or selection of an appropriate workflow by the C-MEW. Every task has a unique *task-ID* and parameters associated with it for extracting context information.

Relationships between different kinds of context information have to be identified and established in order to enable further reasoning about context. For example, we can improve task allocation by allocating more tasks to those users who have good success/completion rate. Context miner, which is subcomponent of context model, extracts context information semantics. Derivation and identification of semantics between context information permits correlation and aggregation of context information at the application level. The aggregator maintains an up-to-date list of currently available context-information related to the executing instances based on instance specification and the extrinsic information. *Controller Unit* (see Fig. 1) is responsible for managing and matching the relevant context information.

3   Context-Aware Workflow Execution Engine

C-MEW provide re-usable workflow execution by generating context-aware execution-workflow (CEW) instances. *C-MEW* has the ability to re-configure and manipulates its objects based on the context information. It allows flexible execution control flow and procedure to specify and execute workflows. This procedure is implemented as the workflow engine, and can be modified or enhanced based on the current context.

Figure 3 shows C-MEW generating different CEWs based on the task requirements. CEW executes an activity by executing its individual tasks one-by-one. During execution of a workflow, C-MEW requests for associated context-information, which is retrieved from Context Model, C-MEW's controller validates context information against workflow's requirement. In case the information provided fails to fulfill the desired requirement, C-MEW performs workflow instances using other sources of information such as databases and human resources. Otherwise, if context model provides the desired information, then the information is extracted using "get-context-information" method, which is defined with C-MEW and used against the task requirements. Also, C-MEW has information about the task specification and node arrangements, which helps in monitoring and checking conformance during execution. Execution of an activity is done by using specified transition path, transition condition between the tasks and other parameters related to a task. By designing *context-aware execution-workflow*, we resolve the various dependencies between tasks such as data-dependency from users, temporal event dependency, and dependency of a task on

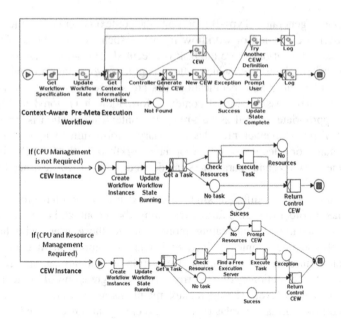

Fig. 3. Context-aware Meta Execution Workflow generating CEWs

external events. Since *instances of an activity usually consists of same definition and prone to similar exceptions*, context-based specification of an instance can result in less redundancy and consumption of time. Similarly, pre-conditions can be evaluated beforehand and execution engine can proceed without allowing it to wait for the evaluation of that condition.

Exceptions are logged in the event-logs. Storing exceptions in the event log helps in determining which task has raised which exception, and these exceptions are well monitored in future instances of such tasks. In case, already handled exceptions occur, another definition of CEW is selected from *knowledge base* based on the past-experience, and accordingly, modify the current CEW to execute the task. But if selected CEW is also not able to handle the exception, *user intervention is required* for defining a *new* ECA rule which acts as a handler for this new exception. Along with exception handling, better user allocation can be carried out using the C-MEW. For instance, based on the users' profile and their related history, it can be easily inferred for "who is the best person to whom this task can be assigned". Each activity has an associated set of variables (stored in database) specified by workflow specification component. These are process variables whose values are set based on context for an instance selected for execution. This feature allows CEW to support *reactive adaptation to context parameters* when their values can change abruptly during the execution. The workflow is executed as if it is a standard one, however, when the engine encounters an activity, it executes using two sub-components: *Meta Execution Controller* and *Task Dispatcher*. These two components interact with each other to execute the user workflows. Meta execution controller, using the workflow definition, move from one task instance to another and complete its execution. It consists of set of programs and routines that execute the tasks. Task dispatcher receives request from the controller to execute task instances. It returns post event data to the controller. After completion of sub-process, the control returns to the CEW in order to perform the next activity.

4 E-Government Contract – Tariff Payment

In this work, we used the e-government contract, which involves four parties namely *Licensor*, *Licensee*, *Subscriber* and *Bank*. Licensor refers to any authorized person, who grants license. Licensee is a registered company that has been awarded license for providing the service. Subscriber is a person or legal entity who avails service from the licensee. The Licensor grant contract to the Licensee on the terms and conditions to establish, maintain and operate internet service in the country. This contract will enable the licensee to provide internet based services to its subscribers and collect tariff from them accordingly. Initially, instance related context information (Type A) is retrieved from its source. Context manager creates/decides appropriate CEW on the basis of combination of base CEW and available context information.

Consider *Payment of tariff by subscriber to the licensee activity*. Table 1 displays the specification of payment activity and also show that several manual (M) tasks in the case of traditional WFMS can be automated (A) using CEW. According to the contract, the periodic payment of the tariff is made by the subscriber. In case the subscriber becomes defaulter for more than a specified period, then system will issue notice. Further, if the number of months of non-payment of tariff crosses a specified limit, then it may terminate the services. Certain task entities (such as exceptions, data variables, resultant event, actions and triggering events) are linked to every activity. When the due date for payment of tariff falls below a deadline, the payment has to be done by the client to the service provider to renew the service. In that process, the context information such as *client Information (last renewal date, due date, type); bill details; provider's bank information for crediting payment, etc.* is needed. Task 'Pay tariff' parameters are:

- **Triggering event:** Due date for payment.
- **Condition:** Payment of tariff should be done strictly by end of every month.
- **Action:** Receive the bill and credit to the Licensee's account.
- **Resultant/Post events:** payment receipt, renew service, bill sent, bill received, payment verified, acknowledgement sent etc.
- **Exception:** Incorrect account info, unable to credit, etc. (see Table 1).
- **Related Variables:** Bank account information of subscriber, number of subscribers paying simultaneously, amount to be paid, bank account information of licensee, last date for payment, mode of payment, past status of subscriber (pending bill, number of defaults, penalty etc.)
- **Applicability condition:** *validSubscriber* = *true*, *currentTime* - *lastPaymentTime* > *1 month*. Here, *currentTime* and *validSubscriber* are context variables included in subscriber's context.

Table 1. Specification of example payment activity (A- Automated, M-Manual)

Id	Task		Input	Output	Exceptions
	CEW	WFMS			
1	Notification		Subscribers address	Notification signal	Communication error
			Bill detail	Sent	Wrong details of subs.
	A	M			Not sent by sender
2	Receive notification		Bill details	None	Notification not received
					Communication error
					Timeout
					Subscriber not checked
	A	M			Wrong bill received
3	Pay bill		Bill detail	Invoke payment sub-workflow	Payment unsuccessful
			Bank information	Payment done	Wrong bank info.
			Due date	Payment failed	Less available amount
	A	M	Method of payment		Due date expired
4	Collection of tariff		Payment information	Payment verified	Payment not received
	A	A		Payment not verified	
5	Renew service		Service renew request	Subscriber id	Renewal request not sent
	A	M		payment verification	

Using the above information, C-MEW generates CEW instance that executes the payment workflow instance. Consider a simple payment workflow as given below for a particular service (say cable subscription):

Start → Enter payee bank details → Enter payee bank account number → Enter amount → Submit → Payee bank sends for reconciliation → Credit the amount to payee account number → End

During the execution of this workflow, suppose (i) the task 'Submit' is done before the due date of payment, (ii) there is a problem at reconciliation center (e.g., system overload due to bulk processing of transactions), and (iii) the amount is not credited to the payee account by the due date. This (i), (ii) and (iii) causes payment not received by the due date causing penalty on payment amount. In the case of traditional workflow execution scenario, the payment task is not in the successful state and expects a human intervention as there is a delay in the credit task operation. This may lead to a cumbersome process (in some cases) as the person in-charge may not have sufficient knowledge and needs to escalate the case. However, in our context oriented approach, the CEW involves (a) capturing execution context (e.g., value of currentTime variable) during the execution of 'Submit' task, (b) capturing context pertaining to the delay at reconciliation center, (c) generating a new workflow instance based on the context information for sending a notification message (that overcomes the additional penalty due to non-payment within the due date) and (d) continuing the execution of previous workflow instance for crediting the amount. This is possible due to availability of context information pertaining to differences in the task execution timings (i.e., Type A - (a) and (d)) as well as the past experience by the concerned staff (i.e., Type B – (b) and (c)), and thus the C-MEW seamlessly handles the late credit of payment and in turn avoiding discontinuity of subscription service. Note that there can be other solutions for this specific issue, but our aim is to show how context oriented solution handles this specific issue. Our solution is capable of handling more complex situations (e.g., new Licensee taken over the existing subscribers of internet service with new terms and conditions).

5   Conclusions

In this paper, a framework is presented to support context-aware electronic contract enactment life-cycle. We showed the viability of context-aware WFMS to coordinate and automate contract enactment. Our CEW approach facilitates building a knowledge base by capturing both internal and external context and model the workflows to support a variety of e-contracts. Further, C-MEWs drives the complete workflow engine so that it can cope with context changes and enact the contracts.

References

1. Dey, A.K.: Understanding and using context. Pers. Ubiquit. Comput. **5**(1), 4–7 (2001)
2. Grefen, P., Aberer, K., Hoffner, Y., Ludwig, H.: Crossflow: cross-organizational workflow management in dynamic virtual enterprises. Int. J. Comput. Syst. Sci. Eng. **15**(5), 277–290 (2000)
3. Krishna, P.R., Karlapalem, K., Chiu, D.K.W.: An ER^{EC} framework for E-contract modeling, enactment and monitoring. Data Knowl. Eng. **51**(1), 31–58 (2004)
4. Murguzur, A., De Carlos, X., Trujillo, S., Sagardui, G.: Context-aware staged configuration of process Variants@Runtime. In: Jarke, M., Mylopoulos, J., Quix, C., Rolland, C., Manolopoulos, Y., Mouratidis, H., Horkoff, J. (eds.) CAiSE 2014. LNCS, vol. 8484, pp. 241–255. Springer, Heidelberg (2014)
5. Sharma, S., Karlapalem, K., Krishna, P.R.: A case for a workflow driven workflow execution engine. In: 22nd Workshop on Information Technology and Systems (WITS) (2012)

Annotating and Mining for Effects of Processes

Suman Roy$^{1(\boxtimes)}$, Metta Santiputri^2, and Aditya Ghose^2

^{1} Infosys Ltd., # 44 Electronics City, Hosur Road, Bangalore 560 100, India
Sunam_Roy@infosys.com
^{2} School of Computer Science and Software Engineering, University of Wollongong,
Wollongong, NSW 2500, Australia
ms804@uowmail.edu.au, aditya@uow.edu.au

Abstract. We provide a novel explicit annotation of a process model
by way of accumulating effects of individual tasks specified by analysts
using belief bases and computing the accumulated effect up to the point
of execution of the process model in an automated manner. This technique permits the analyst to specify immediate effect annotations in a
practitioner-accessible simple propositional logic formulas and generates
a sequence of tasks along with cumulative effects, called effect logs. Further we propose and solve an effect mining problem, that is, given an
effect log discover the process model with effect annotations of individual tasks which is close to the original annotated process model.

Keywords: Business process modeling · Semantic annotation · Effects ·
Belief bases · Annotated processes · Effect logs · Effect mining

1 Introduction

In this work we describe a technique for an explicit semantic annotation of
process models. We require practitioners to provide a description of the immediate effects of each task. An effect of a task becomes true when the latter gets
executed. These effects are propagated across different nodes (tasks and gateways) in the process model and then accumulated in a context-sensitive manner automatically, such that the cumulative effect annotation associated with
any task in a BPMN process model[1] would describe the effects achieved by the
process as if the process were executed up to that point [3]. The cumulative effect
description of a task might be non-deterministic, this non-determinism may be
caused by the execution of parallel gateways resulting in interleaving of paths
in the process model, and belief update leading to multiple alternative means of
resolving inconsistencies generated by the "undoing" of effects. Our effect annotation borrows ideas from Semantic Business Process Validation (SBPV) which

---

S. Roy—This work was done when the author visited University of Wollongong
during July–Dec'14 to work on Infosys-CRC funded project on data-driven process
discovery.
^{1} Process models captured using industry standard notation BPMN.

I. Comyn-Wattiau et al. (Eds.): ER 2016, LNCS 9974, pp. 302–310, 2016.
DOI: 10.1007/978-3-319-46397-1_24

combines concepts from the workflow [6,8,13] and AI action and changes [4,15]. While we adopt the token semantics from workflow literature [14,15] for determining execution traces of processes we use belief operator from AI [5,7] for updating the effect and their accumulation on enabling of nodes. By this way we are able to compute an effect trace of the process which is a sequence of pairs consisting of task and the cumulative effect at this node.

Next we consider an inverse problem: given an effect log, *i.e.*, a set of effect traces, how one can determine the original effects at the tasks? We call this effect mining problem, *aka* process mining problem [11,12]. Although process designers take utmost care in designing process models there is no guarantee that they indeed reflect the correct models under consideration. The goal of process discovery is to derive some sort of model that describes the process as accurately as possible. Similarly, the goal of effect discovery is to generate a semantically annotated process which is close to the original semantic description of the process model. As one solution approach for this effect mining problem we propose a modification of process discovery algorithm, *viz.*, α-mining problem to find out a process model along with the effects associated with each task.

Related Work. There is a rich body of work on semantic annotation for web services. In one of them Weber *et al.* proposed an approach, Semantic Business Process Validation (SBPV) [15], in which axiomatic task descriptions are annotated and propagated across process models. The SBPV approach requires the user to completely specify pre-conditions and post-conditions that are context sensitive. In another approach Hinge *et al.* [3] proposed a technique for obtaining semantic effect descriptions of BPMN process models, without requiring the analyst to express excessive formal specification. Using an approach similar to SBPV in [4] Hoffman *et al.* proposed a framework of annotating processes for capturing the semantics of task execution in which compliance is checked against a set of constraints imposed on process states. Motivated by SBPV [4,15] and the annotation method suggested in [3] we lift ideas from AI and use belief bases to annotate the tasks with effects, propagate these effects across the nodes automatically in a context sensitive manner, and compute the accumulated effects of each task up to the execution point.

There is not much work on effect mining we could find. In [10] Santiputri *et al.* present a data-driven approach for mining semantically annotated business processes. The authors assume event logs in execution histories of business processes describing both task execution events (found in process logs) and state update events (recorded in effect logs) at disposal and mine for immediate effect annotations for each task in the process model to be edited and refined by analysts. In our work we only consider effect logs which is a collection of pairs consisting of tasks and accumulated effects, and discover the process model with effect annotations for each task. While in the previous work the authors use a variant of sequence mining algorithms for effect mining we use a modified process mining algorithm for effect discovery.

The paper is organized as follows. We introduce a semantic annotation of process models in Sect. 2 along with an example of effect annotation. The problem of effect mining is defined in Sect. 3. Finally we conclude in Sect. 4.

2 A Semantic Annotation of Processes

We introduce an annotation framework for business processes where tasks are annotated with effects. An effect of a task is some fact which materializes when the task is executed. It is captured by analysts providing a description of the immediate effects of each process task, i.e., a context independent specification of the functionality of each task. For the sake of easier readability we first introduce a simple process graph without annotation. We use a formalism of a business process which bears close resemblance with those described in [1,4,15] and that of work-flows [8].

A *BPM process* is a graph (also called a process model graph) $\mathbf{P} = (\mathcal{N}, \mathcal{F})$ where $\mathcal{N}$ is a finite set of nodes which is partitioned into the set of tasks $\mathcal{T}$, the set of gateways $\mathcal{G}$, and the set of events $\mathcal{E}$, i.e., $\mathcal{N} \cong \mathcal{T} \uplus \mathcal{G} \uplus \mathcal{E}$; $\mathcal{G}$ can be further partitioned into disjoint sets of decision merges, $\mathcal{G}_M$ ($\mathcal{G}_M^{and}$ (synchronizer) and $\mathcal{G}_M^{xor}$ (merge)) and decision splits, $\mathcal{G}_S$ ($\mathcal{G}_S^{and}$ (fork) and $\mathcal{G}_S^{xor}$ (choice)); a set $\mathcal{E}$ of events which is a disjoint union of two sets of events $\mathcal{E}_s$ and $\mathcal{E}_f$, where $\mathcal{E}_s$ is the set of start events with no incoming edges, $\mathcal{E}_f$ is the set of end events with no outgoing edges; and $\mathcal{F} \subseteq (\mathcal{N} \backslash \mathcal{E} \times \mathcal{N} \backslash \mathcal{E}) \bigcup (\mathcal{E}_s \times \mathcal{N} \backslash \mathcal{E}) \bigcup (\mathcal{N} \backslash \mathcal{E} \times \mathcal{E}_f)$ corresponds to sequence flows connecting tasks with tasks, tasks with gateways, gateways with tasks, start nodes with tasks and tasks with end nodes.

Let $in(n)$ $(out(n))$ be the set of incoming (outgoing) edges to (out of) node $n \in \mathcal{N}$. We impose the following conditions: $\forall n_s \in \mathcal{E}_s, |in(n_s)| = 0$, and $|out(n_s)| = 1$; $\forall n_f \in \mathcal{E}_f, |in(n_f)| = 1$, and $|out(n_f)| = 0$; for every $n \in \mathcal{T}, |in(n)| = |out(n)| = 1$; for every $n \in \mathcal{G}_S, |in(n)| = 1$ and $|out(n)| > 1$; for every $n \in \mathcal{G}_M, |in(n)| > 1$ and $|out(n)| = 1$; any outgoing edge $out(n)$ from a fork node $n \in \mathcal{G}_S^{and}$ will have a task node t appearing immediately after n: $(n, t) \in \mathcal{F}$, and every node is on a path from some start node to some end node. If these conditions hold then we say the business process to be *well-formed*. We shall consider only well-formed business processes henceforth.

Let us now specify the semantics of control elements of a business process. Given a process $\mathbf{P} = (\mathcal{N}, \mathcal{F})$, a *state* of $\mathbf{P}$ is a marking $\mu : \mathcal{F} \to \mathbb{N}$, also called a token mapping. The number of tokes may change during the execution of the process, when the transitions are enabled. A state μ' is reached from state μ via node n, written as $\mu \xrightarrow{n} \mu'$, when n can be a task, AND-split, AND-join or XOR-split or XOR-join, for details see [9,15].

The initial state is given by a marking μ_0 where $\mu_0(e_s) = 1$, for all $e_s \in \mathcal{E}_s$, and $\mu_0(e) = 0$ for all other edges e. A node n is said to be *activated* in a state μ if there exists state μ' such that $\mu \xrightarrow{n} \mu'$. A state μ' is reachable from a state μ, denoted as $\mu \xrightarrow{*} \mu'$ if there exists a (possibly finite) path, $\rho : n_s, n_1, \ldots, n_f \in (\mathcal{N})$ and a finite sequence of markings $\mu_1, \ldots \mu_k$ such that μ is activated in n_s and $\mu \xrightarrow{n_s} \mu_1 \xrightarrow{n_1} \cdots \xrightarrow{n_l} \mu_k$ and $\mu' = \mu_k$.

For a path ρ we denote the projection of ρ on set of tasks $\mathcal{T}$ as $\rho_{|\mathcal{T}}$. A *complete trace* (also called *trace*) of a business process $\mathbf{P}$ is a sequence of tasks $\tau = t_1, \ldots t_l$, $(t_i \in \mathcal{T},\ 1 \leq i \leq l)$ such there is a path $\rho = n_s, n_1, \ldots, n_f \in \mathcal{N}$ in $\mathbf{P}$ and $\tau = \rho_{|\mathcal{T}}$. The set of all traces of a process $\mathbf{P}$ is denoted as $\mathbb{T}_{\mathbf{P}}$. For the remainder of the paper we assume our process to be sound [2,15].

For annotating processes with effects we shall use logical propositions and assume the existence of a countable set $\mathcal{P}$ of propositions. The set of all literals over $\mathcal{P}$ is denoted as $\mathcal{L}_{\mathcal{P}}$. A belief base $\mathcal{B}$ is a conjunction of literals in $\mathcal{P}$ which is logically consistent. It can be written using set-theoretic notation. For example, if a belief base $\mathcal{B} = a \wedge \neg b \wedge c$, where $a, b, c \in \mathcal{P}$ then $\mathcal{B} = \{a, \neg b, c\}$. A theory $\mathbf{T}$ over $\mathcal{P}$ can be taken to be any propositional theory. A knowledge base $\mathcal{K}$ is a pair $(\mathcal{P}, \mathbf{T})$, where $\mathbf{T}$ can be assumed to consist of rules and facts. Wlog we can assume $\mathbf{T}$ to be the conjunction of those rules and facts.

We define an annotated process model/graph as $\mathbb{G}_{\mathbf{P}} = (\mathcal{N}, \mathcal{F}, \mathcal{K}, \mathcal{A})^2$, where $\mathbf{P} = (\mathcal{N}, \mathcal{F})$ is the underlying process model as before, $\mathcal{K} = (\mathcal{P}, \mathbf{T})$ is the underlying knowledge base annotation, $\mathcal{A}$ is a partial function mapping $n \in \mathcal{T}$ to $\mathrm{eff}(n) \subseteq \mathcal{B}(\mathcal{P})$, and mapping $e \in \mathrm{out}(n)$ for $n \in \mathcal{G}_S^{xor}$ to $(\mathrm{con}(e), \mathrm{pos}(e))$ where $\mathrm{con}(e) \in \mathcal{L}_{\mathcal{P}}$ and $\mathrm{pos}(e) \in \{1, \ldots, |\mathrm{out}(n)|\}^3$. The following technical conditions need to be imposed: there does not exist an e such that $\mathbf{T} \wedge \mathrm{con}(e)$ is unsatisfiable; there do not exist n, e, and e' so that $e, e' \in \mathrm{out}(n)$ (e and e' being distinct), $\mathcal{A}(e)$ and $\mathcal{A}(e')$ are defined, and $\mathrm{pos}(e) = \mathrm{pos}(e')$. Moreover, the cardinality of the set of reachable states immediately preceding a choice gateway must be bounded from below by the number of outgoing edges from the gateway.

In an execution of process we shall assume the effects of the activities of the process will be dynamically changed with the corresponding knowledge environment. Let us assume the current available information be represented by an a-priori available knowledge base $\mathcal{K}$; and an accumulated effect B_0 that we assume to be true (*i.e.*, to persist) until the next task has been executed. Suppose that a task t in a process is executed in an instance of a process whose effect can be captured by the belief base $B = \mathrm{eff}(t)$. What would be our knowledge after t is executed? Borrowing concepts from artificial intelligence [5,7], we revise our knowledge using belief update to capture the changing scenario (we treat belief revision and belief update as same). This can be achived using an update operators Δ details of which can be found in [9].

Let us now formally define semantics of an annotated process graph, a similar semantic annotation for business processes is provided in [4,15]. A *state s* of $\mathbb{G}$ is a pair $\iota = (\mu, \mathcal{E}_a)$ where μ is a token mapping as defined before, and $\mathcal{E}_a : 2^{\mathcal{T}} \mapsto 2^{(\mathcal{P})}$ is a cumulative effect accumulation function. Assume that the current set of tasks for which the effects are accumulated till date is $\mathcal{T}_c$ and its accumulated effect is $\mathcal{E}_a(\mathcal{T}_c)$. The updated set of tasks will be $\mathcal{T}_c'$ when a new task is executed. The initial state is $\iota_0 = (\mu_0, \mathcal{E}_{a0})$ where $\mathcal{T}_c = \emptyset$. By default, we assume $\mathcal{E}_{a0}(\emptyset) = \emptyset$. The effects across the tasks/gateways are going to be

---

[2] we shall drop the subscript $\mathbf{P}$ when it is clear from the context.

[3] For the sake of rigor $\mathcal{P}$ can be partitioned into two sets $\mathcal{P} = \mathcal{P}_t \uplus \mathcal{P}_x$, where tasks are annotated with symbols from $\mathcal{P}_t$, and conditions on choices come from $\mathcal{P}_x$.

accumulated in a recursive manner; the accumulated effect will be denoted as $\mathcal{E}'_a(\mathcal{T}'_c)$. Let ι and ι' be two states. A state ι' is reached from state ι via node n, written as $\iota \xrightarrow{n} \iota'$, if and only if $n \in (T \cup g)$ and $(n_i, n) \in \mathcal{F}$. We consider different cases of n being an task, a split gateway, a join gateway etc. in [9]. As before for a given a business process $\mathbf{P}$ we consider a trace $\mathbf{P}$ to be a sequence of tasks $\tau = t_1, \ldots t_l$, where $t_i \in \mathcal{T}$, $1 \le i \le l$. Similarly an *effect trace* is defined to be a sequence $\varepsilon : (t_1, \mathcal{E}_{a1}), (t_2, \mathcal{E}_{a2}), \ldots, (t_m, \mathcal{E}_{am})$, where $\tau = t_1, \ldots t_m$ is called the underlying *trace* of ε. Given an annotated process model we denote $\mathcal{E}_{\mathbb{G}}$ to be the set of its effect traces.

Figure 1 depicts an example of a business process for illustrating effect annotation. This process diagram is drawn using BPM notation. We use this process graph as the running exam-

Table 1. Effect annotations for process model in Fig. 1

Task	Effects
Order (A)	*ordered ∧ received*
Reject order (C)	*rejected*
Fulfill order (B)	*fulfilled*
Send invoice (D)	*invoiceSent ∧ paymentExpected*
Ship order (E)	*shipped*
Receive payment (F)	*paymentReceived*
Accept payment (G)	*paymentAccepted ∧ ¬paymentExpected ∧ paid*
Close order	*closed*

ple throughout this paper. This process contains a start and an end node, and various tasks, such as "order", "reject order", "fulfill order" etc. It also has a number of routing constructs such as an XOR-split after the task order and an AND-split after fulfill order. Only one of the branches after the XOR-split is executed depending on the condition (approved or fulfilled) which is true.

In Fig. 1 the semantic annotation of each task is given in Table 1. The knowledge base is given by $\mathcal{K} = \{\mathcal{P}, \mathbf{T}\}$, where

$\mathbf{P} = \{ordered, received, rejected, fulfilled, invoiceSent, paymentExpected, shipped,$

$\quad paymentReceived, paymentAccepted, closed, approved, cancelled;$ and

$\quad \mathbf{T} = \{closed \rightarrow \neg(ordered \land received \land fulfilled);$

$\quad (cancelled \land rejected) \rightarrow \neg(ordered \land received)\}.$

Assuming an initial state to be $\iota_0 = (\mu_0, \mathcal{E}_{a0})$ where $\mathcal{T}_c = \emptyset$ and $\mathcal{E}_{a0}(\emptyset) = \emptyset$ we can compute the cumulative effect on the execution of each task/gateway. The

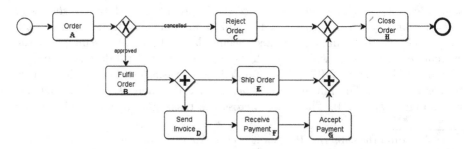

Fig. 1. An example of a process using BPM notation

Table 2. Accumulated effect annotations for process model in Fig. 1

Task	Accumulated effects
Order	$\{ordered, received\}$
Reject order	$\{ordered, received, cancelled, rejected\}$
Fulfill order	$\{ordered, received, approved, fulfilled\}$
Send invoice	$\{ordered, received, approved, fulfilled, shipped, invoiceSent,$ $paymentExpected\}$
	$\{ordered, received, approved, fulfilled, invoiceSent,$ $paymentExpected\}$
Ship order	$\{ordered, received, approved, fulfilled, shipped\}$
	$\{ordered, received, approved, fulfilled, invoiceSent,$ $paymentReceived, paymentAccepted, paid, shipped\}$
Receive payment	$\{ordered, received, approved, fulfilled, shipped, invoiceSent,$ $paymentExpected, paymentReceived\}$
	$\{ordered, received, approved, fulfilled, invoiceSent,$ $paymentExpected, paymentReceived\}$
Accept payment	$\{ordered, received, approved, fulfilled, shipped, invoiceSent,$ $paymentReceived, paymentAccepted, paid\}$
	$\{ordered, received, approved, fulfilled, invoiceSent,$ $paymentReceived, paymentAccepted, paid\}$
Close order	$\{cancelled, rejected, closed, \neg fulfilled\}$
	$\{ordered, received, approved, fulfilled, invoiceSent,$ $paymentReceived, paymentAccepted, paid, shipped, closed\}$

effect accumulation corresponding to the execution of each node is given in the Table 2. The accumulated effect is computed by finding the maximal consistent set computed out of the union of individual effect of the node and the current accumulated effect [9].

3   Effect Log Mining

The log entries that we consider contain event of one type (*viz.*, completion of the event), hence we drop event from the log entries in subsequent discussions and consider only tasks (similar convention is followed in ProM-framework). Let $\mathcal{T}$ to be the set of tasks/activities. We denote a trace as $\sigma \in T^*$, where $\sigma = t_0, t_1, \ldots t_{n-1}$, such that $t_i \in \mathcal{T}, 0 \le i \le n - 1$. A process log is a defined as a set of traces, denoted as $W \in \mathcal{P}(\mathcal{T}^*)$. An effect log $\Theta \subseteq \mathcal{P}(\mathcal{T} \times \mathcal{B}(P))$ is defined as a set of effect traces.

The problem of process mining takes process log as input and produces process models as output. That is given a process log $W \in \mathcal{P}(\mathcal{T}^*)$ over a set $\mathcal{T}$ of activities, find process model $\mathbf{P} = (\mathcal{N}, \mathcal{F})$ such that $\mathbb{T}_{\mathbf{P}} = W$. In this work we propose a variant of process mining problem which we call effect log mining (also called effect discovery). It says, given an effect log $\Theta \subseteq \mathcal{P}(\mathcal{T} \times \mathcal{B}(P))$ find annotated process model $\mathbb{G} = (\mathcal{N}, \mathcal{F}, \mathcal{K}, \mathcal{A})$ such that $\mathcal{E}_{\mathbb{G}} = \Theta$.

We made some simplifications of our effect mining problem. We assume our knowledge base $\mathcal{K}$ is a pair $(\mathcal{P}, \mathbf{T})$, and $\mathbf{T}$ is empty, that is, it contains no facts or no rules. Further we make the unique name assumption for tasks, *i.e.*, a task appears only once in the process model, which is just a matter of renaming. Next we propose an algorithm for effect discovery using log abstractions [12] based on log-based ordering relations. Our log-based ordering relation is defined on annotated task nodes (pairs of tasks with accumulated effects). We also define an edge relation between annotated nodes based on the above ordering relation as part of our discovery algorithm. Using this algorithm it will be possible to discover the process and find effect for each individual task in the discovered process. In this work we choose to use a modified α-algorithm to discover our process model [11] (in spite of its inability to address loops, non-free-choice structures, and limited ability to address variability and closed path). For the details of the algorithm the reader is referred to [9].

We employ our process discovery technique on our example where we assume the knowledge base to be $\mathcal{K} = \{\mathcal{P}, \emptyset\}$, where $\mathcal{P}$ is defined before. We consider the effect log ε of the process model in Table 3. The workflow $\mathcal{W}_{\mathbf{P}}$ discovered thus is shown in Fig. 2. Using our technique we can only recover gross annotation of

Table 3. Effect traces and its underlying trace of the process model

Effect trace ε	The underlying trace
((start, $\emptyset$), (A,{*ordered, received*}), (A,{*ordered, received, cancelled*}), (C,{*ordered, received, cancelled, rejected*}), (H,{*ordered, received, cancelled, rejected, closed*}), (end,{*ordered, received, cancelled, rejected, closed*}))	(start,A,C,H,end)
((start, $\emptyset$), (A, {*ordered, received*}), (A, {*ordered, received, approved*}), (B, {*ordered, received, approved, fulfilled*}), (E, {*ordered, received, approved, fulfilled, shipped*}), (D, {*ordered, received, approved, fulfilled, shipped, invoiceSent, paymentExpected*}), (F, {*ordered, received, approved, fulfilled, shipped, invoiceSent, paymentExpected, paymentReceived*}), (G, {*ordered, received, approved, fulfilled, shipped, invoiceSent, paymentReceived, paymentAccepted, paid*}), (H, {*ordered, received, approved, fulfilled, shipped, invoiceSent, paymentReceived, paymentAccepted, paid, closed*}), (end, {*ordered, received, approved, fulfilled, shipped, invoiceSent, paymentReceived, paymentAccepted, paid, closed*}))	(start,A,B,E,D,F,G,H,end)
((start, $\emptyset$), (A, {*ordered, received*}), (A, {*ordered, received, approved*}), (B, {*ordered, received, approved, fulfilled*}), (D, {*ordered, received, approved, fulfilled, invoiceSent, paymentExpected*}), (F, {*ordered, received, approved, fulfilled, invoiceSent, paymentExpected, paymentReceived*}), (G, {*ordered, received, approved, fulfilled, invoiceSent, paymentReceived, paymentAccepted, paid*}), (E, {*ordered, received, approved, fulfilled, invoiceSent, paymentReceived, paymentAccepted, paid, shipped*}), (H, {*ordered, received, approved, fulfilled, invoiceSent, paymentReceived, paymentAccepted, paid, shipped, closed*}), (end, {*ordered, received, approved, fulfilled, invoiceSent, paymentReceived, paymentAccepted, paid, shipped, closed*}))	(start,A,B,D,F,G,E,H,end)

individual task instead of exact effect, however the satisfiability of the former implies that of the latter.

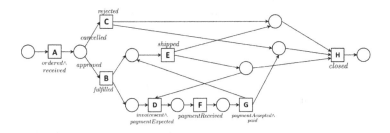

Fig. 2. Discovered workflow $\mathcal{W}_{\mathbf{P}}$

4 Conclusion

Our semantic annotation of process models can help bridge between the high-level process and the actual IT infrastructure as support functions like discovery, composition, mediation can be implemented with concrete services using Semantic Web formalisms. Given an implementation of services and observed snapshots, we should be able to discover the process with its effect annotations using our algorithm. In future we plan to integrate our effect mining technique with data-driven approach to mining effect annotations (and specifically post conditions) from event logs arising in process execution histories [10].

References

1. Dijkman, R.M., Dumas, M., Ouyang, C.: Semantics and analysis of business process models in BPMN. Inf. Softw. Technol. **50**(12), 1281–1294 (2008)
2. Fahland, D., Favre, C., Jobstmann, B., Koehler, J., Lohmann, N., Völzer, H., Wolf, K.: Analysis on demand: instantaneous soundness checking of industrial business process models. Data Knowl. Eng. **70**(5), 448–466 (2011)
3. Hinge, K., Ghose, A.K., Koliadis, G., Process, S.: A tool for semantic effect annotation of business process models. In: Proceedings of the 13th IEEE International Enterprise Distributed Object Computing Conference, EDOC 2009, pp. 54–63 (2009)
4. Hoffmann, J., Weber, I., Governatori, G.: On compliance checking for clausal constraints in annotated process models. Inf. Syst. Front. **14**(2), 155–177 (2012)
5. Katsuno, H., Mendelzon, A.O.: Propositional knowledge base revision and minimal change. Artif. Intell. **52**(3), 263–294 (1991)
6. Kiepuszewski, B., ter Hofstede, A., van der Aalst, W.: Fundamentals of control flow in workflows. Acta Informatica **39**, 143–209 (2003)
7. Liberatore, P.: The complexity of belief update. Artif. Intell. **119**(1–2), 141–190 (2000)

8. Liu, R., Kumar, A.: An analysis and taxonomy of unstructured workflows. In: Aalst, W.M.P., Benatallah, B., Casati, F., Curbera, F. (eds.) BPM 2005. LNCS, vol. 3649, pp. 268–284. Springer, Heidelberg (2005). doi:10.1007/11538394_18
9. Roy, S., Santriputri, M., Ghose, A.: Annotating and mining for effects of processes. Technical report, University of Wollongong, Australia (2015, Available on request)
10. Santiputri, M., Ghose, A.K., Dam, H.K., Wen, X.: Mining process task post-conditions. In: Johannesson, P., Lee, M.L., Liddle, S.W., Opdahl, A.L., López, Ó.P. (eds.) ER 2015. LNCS, vol. 9381, pp. 514–527. Springer, Heidelberg (2015). doi:10.1007/978-3-319-25264-3_38
11. van der Aalst, W.M.P., Weijters, T., Maruster, L.: Workflow mining: discovering process models from event logs. IEEE Trans. Knowl. Data Eng. 16(9), 1128–1142 (2004)
12. Dongen, B.F., Aalst, W.M.P.: Multi-phase process mining: building instance graphs. In: Atzeni, P., Chu, W., Lu, H., Zhou, S., Ling, T.-W. (eds.) ER 2004. LNCS, vol. 3288, pp. 362–376. Springer, Heidelberg (2004). doi:10.1007/978-3-540-30464-7_29
13. Vanhatalo, J., Völzer, H., Koehler, J.: The refined process structure tree. In: Dumas, M., Reichert, M., Shan, M.-C. (eds.) BPM 2008. LNCS, vol. 5240, pp. 100–115. Springer, Heidelberg (2008). doi:10.1007/978-3-540-85758-7_10
14. Vanhatalo, J., Völzer, H., Leymann, F.: Faster and more focused control-flow analysis for business process models through SESE decomposition. In: Krämer, B.J., Lin, K.-J., Narasimhan, P. (eds.) ICSOC 2007. LNCS, vol. 4749, pp. 43–55. Springer, Heidelberg (2007). doi:10.1007/978-3-540-74974-5_4
15. Weber, I., Hoffmann, J., Mendling, J.: Beyond soundness: on the verification of semantic business process models. Distrib. Parallel Databases 27(3), 271–343 (2010)

Business Process Management and Modeling

Automated Discovery of Structured Process Models: Discover Structured vs. Discover and Structure

Adriano Augusto[1,2(✉)], Raffaele Conforti[1], Marlon Dumas[3],
Marcello La Rosa[1], and Giorgio Bruno[2]

[1] Queensland University of Technology, Brisbane, Australia
{a.augusto,raffaele.conforti,m.larosa}@qut.edu.au
[2] Politecnico di Torino, Turin, Italy
giorgio.bruno@polito.it
[3] University of Tartu, Tartu, Estonia
marlon.dumas@ut.ee

Abstract. This paper addresses the problem of discovering business process models from event logs. Existing approaches to this problem strike various tradeoffs between accuracy and understandability of the discovered models. With respect to the second criterion, empirical studies have shown that block-structured process models are generally more understandable and less error-prone than unstructured ones. Accordingly, several automated process discovery methods generate block-structured models by construction. These approaches however intertwine the concern of producing accurate models with that of ensuring their structuredness, sometimes sacrificing the former to ensure the latter. In this paper we propose an alternative approach that separates these two concerns. Instead of directly discovering a structured process model, we first apply a well-known heuristic that discovers more accurate but sometimes unstructured (and even unsound) process models, and then transform the resulting model into a structured one. An experimental evaluation shows that our "discover and structure" approach outperforms traditional "discover structured" approaches with respect to a range of accuracy and complexity measures.

Keywords: Automated process discovery · Process structuring · BPMN

1 Introduction

Automated process discovery refers to a family of methods that generate a business process model from an event log [18]. An event log in this context is a set of traces, each consisting of a sequence of events observed within one execution of a process.

Existing automated process discovery methods strike various tradeoffs between accuracy and understandability [20]. In this setting, accuracy is commonly declined into three dimensions: (i) *fitness*: to what extent the discovered

© Springer International Publishing AG 2016
I. Comyn-Wattiau et al. (Eds.): ER 2016, LNCS 9974, pp. 313–329, 2016.
DOI: 10.1007/978-3-319-46397-1_25

model is able to "parse" the traces in the log; (ii) *precision*: how much behavior is allowed by the model but not observed in the log; and (iii) *generalization*: to what extent is the model able to parse traces that, despite not being present in the input log, can actually be produced by the process under observation. Understandability on the other hand is commonly measured via size metrics (e.g. number of nodes) and structural complexity metrics. The latter quantify either the *amount of branching* in a process model or its degree of *structuredness* (the extent to which a model is composed of well-structured single-entry, single-exit components), which have been empirically shown to be proxies for understandability [11].

Inspired by the observation that structured process models may be more understandable than unstructured ones [6], several automated process discovery methods generate structured models by construction [3,10,12]. These approaches however intertwine the concern of accuracy with that of structuredness, sometimes sacrificing the former to achieve the latter. This paper obviates this tradeoff by presenting an automated process discovery method that generates structured models, yet achieves essentially the same fitness, precision and generalization as methods that generate unstructured models. The method follows a two-phased approach. In the first phase, a model is discovered from the log using a heuristic process discovery method that has been shown to consistently produce accurate, but potentially unstructured or even unsound models. In the second phase, the discovered model is transformed into a sound and structured model by applying two techniques: a technique to maximally block-structure an acyclic process model and an extended version of a technique for block-structuring flowcharts.

The paper reports on an empirical evaluation based on real-life and synthetic event logs that puts into evidence the performance of the proposed method relative to two representative methods that discover structured models by construction.

The rest of the paper is organized as follows. Section 2 introduces existing automated process discovery methods and methods for structuring process models. Section 3 presents the proposed method while Sect. 4 reports on the empirical evaluation. Finally, Sect. 5 summarizes the contributions and outlines future work directions.

2   Background and Related Work

In this section we review existing automated process discovery methods and associated quality dimensions. We also introduce methods for transforming unstructured process models into structured ones, which we later use as building blocks for our proposal.

2.1   Automated Process Discovery Algorithms

The bulk of automated process discovery algorithms are not designed to produce structured process models. This includes for example of the α-algorithm [19], which may produce unstructured models and sometimes even models with disconnected fragments. The *Heuristics Miner* [21] partially addresses the limitations of the α-algorithm and consistently performs well in terms of accuracy and simplicity metrics [20]. However, its output may be unstructured and even unsound, i.e. the produced models may contain deadlocks or gateways that do not synchronize all their incoming tokens. *Fodina*[1] is a variant of the Heuristics Miner that partially addresses the latter issue but does not generally produce structured models.

It has been observed that structured process models are generally more understandable than unstructured ones [6]. Moreover, structured process models are sound, provided that the gateways at the entry and exit of each block match. Given these advantages, several algorithms are designed to produce structured process models, represented for example as *process trees* [3, 10]. A process tree is a tree where the each leaf is labelled with an activity and each internal node is labeled with a control-flow operator: sequence, exclusive choice, non-exclusive choice, parallelism, or iteration.

The *Inductive miner* [10] uses a divide-and-conquer approach to discover process trees. Using the *direct follows dependency* between event types in the log, it first creates a directly-follows graph which is used to identify cuts. A cut represent a specific control-flow dependency along which the log can be bisected. The identification of cuts is repeated recursively, starting from the most representative one until no more cuts can be identified. Once all cuts are identified and the log split into portions, a process tree is generated on top of each portion of the log. The algorithm then applies filters to remove "dangling" directly-follows edges so that the result is purely a process tree.

The *Evolutionary Tree Miner (ETM)* [3] is a genetic algorithm that starts by generating a population of random process trees. At each iteration, it computes an *overall fitness* value for each tree in the population and applies mutations to a subset thereof. A mutation is a tree change operation that adds or modifies nodes. The algorithm iterates until a stop criterion is fulfilled, and returns the tree with highest overall fitness.

Molka et al. [12] proposed another genetic automated process discovery algorithm that produces structured process models. This latter algorithm is similar in its principles to ETM, differing mainly in the set of change operations used to produce mutations.

2.2 Quality Dimensions in Automated Process Discovery

The quality of an automatically discovered process model is generally assessed along four dimensions: *recall* (a.k.a. *fitness*), *precision*, *generalization* and *complexity*.

Fitness is the ability of a model to reproduce the behavior contained in a log. Under trace semantics, a fitness of 1 means that the model can produce every trace in the log. In this paper, we use the fitness measure proposed in [2], which measures the degree to which every trace in the log can be aligned with a trace

---

[1] http://www.processmining.be/fodina.

produced by the model. *Precision* measures the ability of a model to generate only the behavior found in the log. A score of 1 indicates that any trace produced by the model is somehow present in the log. In this paper we use the precision measure defined in [1], which is based on similar principles as the above fitness measure. Recall and precision can be combined into a single F-score, which is the harmonic mean of the two measurements $\left(2 \cdot \frac{Fitness \cdot Precision}{Fitness + Precision}\right)$.

Generalization measures the ability of a discovered model to produce behavior that is not present in the log but that can be produced by the process under observation. To measure generalization we use 10-fold cross validation [9]: We divide the log into 10 parts, discover a model from 9 parts (i.e. we hold-out 1 part), and we measure fitness of the discovered model against the hold-out part. This is repeated for every possible hold-out part. Generalization is the mean of the fitness values obtained for each hold-out part. A generalization of 1 means that the discovered models produce traces in the observed process, even if those traces are not in the log from which the model was discovered.

Finally, *complexity* quantifies how difficult it is to understand a model. Several complexity metrics have been shown to be (inversely) related to understandability [11], including *size* (number of nodes); *Control-Flow Complexity (CFC)* (the amount of branching caused by gateways in the model) and *structuredness* (the percentage of nodes located directly inside a well-structured single-entry single-exit fragment).

2.3 Structuring Techniques

Polyvyanyy et al. [15,16] propose a technique to transform unstructured process models into behaviourally equivalent structured ones. The approach starts by constructing the Refined Process Structure Tree (RPST) [17] of the input process model. The RPST of a process model is a tree where the nodes are the single-entry single-exit (SESE) fragments of the model and an edge denotes a containment relation between SESE fragments. Specifically, the children of a SESE fragment in the tree are the SESE fragments that it directly contains. Fragments at the same level of the tree are disjoint.

Each SESE fragment is represented by a set of edges. Depending on how these edges are related, a SESE fragment can be of one of four types. A *trivial* fragment consists of a single edge. A *polygon* is a sequence of fragments. A *bond* is a fragment where all child fragments share two common gateways, one being the entry node and the other being the exit node of the bond. In other words, a bond consists of a split gateway with two or more sub-SESE fragments all converging into a join gateway. Any other fragment is a *rigid*. A model that consists only of trivials, polygons and bonds (i.e. no rigids) is fully structured. Thus the goal of a block-structuring technique is to replace rigid fragments in the RPST with combinations of trivials, polygons and bonds.

In the structuring technique by Polyvyanyy et al., each rigid fragment is unfolded and an ordering relation graph is generated. This graph is then parsed to construct a modular decomposition tree leading to a hierarchy of components from which a maximally structured version of the original fragment is derived. The technique in [16] produces a maximally-structured version of any acyclic fragment (and thus of any model), but it does not structure rigid fragments that contain cycles.

The problem of structuring behavioral models has also been studied in the field of programming, specifically for flowcharts: graphs consisting of tasks (instructions), exclusive split and exclusive join gateways. Oulsnam [13] identified six primitive forms of unstructuredness in flowcharts. He observed that unstructuredness is caused by the presence either of an injection (entry point) or an ejection (exit point) in one of the branches connecting a split gateway to a matching join gateway. Later, Oulsnam [14] proposed an approach to structure these six forms. The approach is based on two rules. The first rule deals with an injection, and pushes the injection after the join gateway, duplicating everything that was originally between the injection and the join. On the other hand, when the unstructuredness is caused by an ejection, the ejection is pushed after the join gateway and an additional conditional block is added to prevent the execution of unnecessary instructions. These two rules are recursively applied to the flowchart, starting from the innermost unstructured form, until no more structuring is possible.

Polyvyanyy's and Oulsnam's technique are complementary: while Polyvyanyy's technique deals mainly with unstructured acyclic rigids with parallelism, Oulsnam's one deals with rigid fragments without parallelism (exclusive gateways only). This observation is a centrepiece of the approach presented in the following section.

3 Approach

The proposed approach to discovering structured process models takes as input an event log and operates in two phases: (i) discovery & cleaning, and (ii) structuring.

3.1 Discovery and Cleaning

In this phase a process model is discovered from an input log using an existing process discovery algorithm. Any process discovery algorithm can be used in this phase. In this paper we use the Heuristics Miner because of its accuracy [20]. In addition to discovering an initial (unstructured) model, this phase fixes model correctness issues such as disconnected nodes (structural issues) and deadlocks (behavioral issues). This is achieved via 3 heuristics. Before presenting them, we formally define a process model.

Definition 1 (Process model). *A process model is a connected graph $G = (i, o, A, G^+, G^x, F)$, where A is a non-empty set of activities, i is the start event, o is the end event, G^+ is the set of AND-gateways, G^x is the set of XOR-gateways, and $F \subseteq (\{i\} \cup A \cup G^+ \cup G^x) \times (\{o\} \cup A \cup G^+ \cup G^x)$ is the set of arcs. A split gateway is a gateway with one incoming arc and multiple outgoing arcs, while a join gateway is a gateway with multiple incoming arcs and one outgoing arc.*

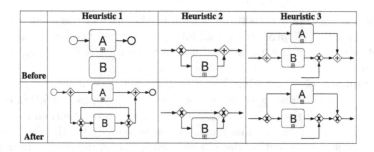

Fig. 1. Examples of application of the three cleaning heuristics.

A process model starts with a unique start event, representing the process trigger (e.g. "order received") and concludes with a unique end event, representing the process outcome (e.g. "order fulfilled"). The model may contain activities, which capture actions that are performed during the process (e.g. "check order") and gateways, which are used for branching (split) and merging (join) purposes. Gateways can be of type XOR, to model exclusive decisions (XOR-split) and simple merges (XOR-join), and AND, to model parallelism (AND-split) and synchronization (AND-join).

The first heuristic (cf. Fig. 1) ensures that a model contains a single start and a single end event, and that every activity in the model is on a path from the start to the end. In case of multiple start or end events, these events are connected via an XOR gateway. In case of activities not on a path from start to end, the heuristic places the activity in parallel with the rest of the process, in such a way that the activity can be skipped and repeated any number of times. The second heuristic ensures that for every bond, the split and the join gateways are of the same type – both AND or both XOR but not mixed (cf. Fig. 1). In the case of an acyclic bond (a bond where all paths go from the entry to the exit gateway), the heuristic matches the exit gateway type with that of entry gateway type. If the bond is cyclic (there is a path from the exit to the entry gateway), the heuristic converts all gateways into XORs. The third heuristic addresses cases of unsoundness related to *quasi-bonds*. A quasi-bond is a bond with an injection via a join gateway or an ejection via a split gateway, along a path connecting the entry and exit gateways of the bond. The heuristic replaces the entry and exit gateways of the quasi-bond as well as the join (split) causing the injection (ejection), with XOR gateways.

3.2 Structuring

The second phase of our approach deals with the structuring of the discovered process model by removing injections and ejections. Before discussing this phase, we need to formally define the notions of activity path, injection and ejection. An activity path is a path containing activity nodes only (no gateways), between two gateways.

Definition 2 (Activity Path). *Given two gateways g_{entry} and g_{exit} and a sequence of activities $S = \langle a_1, \ldots, a_n \rangle$, there is a path from g_{entry} to g_{exit}, i.e. $g_{entry} \leadsto^S g_{exit}$ iff $g_{entry} \to a_1 \to a_2 \to \cdots \to a_n \to g_{exit}$, where $a \to b$ holds if there is an arc connecting a to b. Using the operator $\leadsto$ we define the set of all paths of a process model as $P \triangleq \{(g_1, g_2, S) \in G \times G \times A^* \mid g_1 \leadsto^S g_2\}$. The set of incoming paths of a gateway g_x is defined as $\circ g_x = \{(g_1, g_2, S) \in P \mid g_x = g_2\}$. Similarly the set of outgoing paths is defined as $g_x \circ = \{(g_1, g_2, S) \in P \mid g_x = g_1\}$.*

Definition 3 (Injection). *Given four different gateways g_1, g_2, g_3, g_4, they constitute an injection $i = (g_1, g_2, g_3, g_4)$ iff $\exists (S_1, S_2, S_3) \in A^* \times A^* \times A^* \mid g_1 \leadsto^{S_1} g_2 \wedge g_2 \leadsto^{S_2} g_3 \wedge g_4 \leadsto^{S_3} g_2$ (see "before" column in Fig. 2).*

Definition 4 (Ejection). *Given four different gateways g_1, g_2, g_3, g_4, they constitue an ejection $e = (g_1, g_2, g_3, g_4)$ iff $\exists (S_1, S_2, S_3) \in A^* \times A^* \times A^* \mid g_1 \leadsto^{S_1} g_2 \wedge g_2 \leadsto^{S_2} g_3 \wedge g_2 \leadsto^{S_3} g_4$ (see "before" column in Fig. 2)*

According to [17], a rigid is *homogeneous*, if for all injections and ejections in the rigid, the gateways are of the same type, otherwise it is *heterogeneous*.

Moreover, if an injection or ejection is part of a cycle the rigid is *cyclic*, otherwise it is *acyclic*. Now we have all ingredients to describe the structuring phase. In this phase, the RPST of the discovered process model is generated and all its rigids identified. Once all rigids have been identified, the

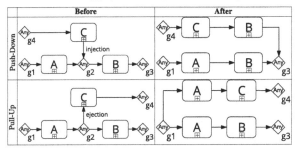

Fig. 2. Structuring of injection and ejection.

RPST is traversed bottom-up, and each rigid is structured along the way.

Algorithm 1 shows how the RPST is traversed and each node is structured. The algorithm uses a bottom-up traversal strategy implemented via a queue. First, all leaves of the RPST are inserted in the queue. At each step a node from the queue is removed, and structured if it is a rigid. The structuring is performed using BPStruct [15] if the rigid is *sound* and consists only of AND gateways (*sound AND-homogeneous*) or a mixture of AND and XOR gateways (*sound heretogeneous*) – cf. line 8. Otherwise the structuring is performed using an extended version of Oulsnam's algorithm [14] (line 9) as discussed later. Then the node is marked as visited and if the parent node has not been visited yet, it is added to the queue (cf. line 11). This is repeated until the queue is empty.

We decided to use two different structuring techniques since BPStruct guarantees optimal results when applied on *sound AND-homogeneous* or *heterogeneous* rigids only, whilst it produces suboptimal results for *acyclic XOR-homogeneous* rigids and it fails in case of *cyclic XOR-homogeneous* or *unsound* rigids. The structuring of these types of rigids is achieved instead using an

---

Algorithm 1. Structuring flow

---

input: RPST *rpst*

1 Queue *Queue* := getLeaves(*rpst*);
2 Set *Visited* := ∅;
3 **while** *Queue* ≠ ∅ **do**
4   *node* := remove(*Queue*);
5   *parent* := getParent(*node*);
6   **if** *isRigid(node)* **then**
7   **if** *isSoundANDHomogeneous(node) OR isSoundHeterogeneous(node)* **then**
8   BPStruct(*node*);
9   **else** EOStruct(*node*);
10   *Visited* := *Visited* ∪ {*node*};
11   **if** *parent* ∉ *Visited* **then** insert(*Queue, parent*);

Algorithm 2. Push-Down

---

input: Injection $i = (g_1, g_2, g_3, g_4)$
input: Set of all Paths P
input: Set of all Gateways G

1 **if** $g_2 \circ \ \subseteq \ \circ \ g_3$ **then**
2     $g_2' := \text{copy}(g_2)$;
3     $G := G \cup \{g_2'\}$;
4     $P := P \cup \{(g_4, g_2', S) \in G \times G \times A^* \mid \exists (g_4, g_2, S_x) \in (g_4 \circ \ \cap \ \circ g_2)[S_x = S]\}$;
5     $P := P \setminus (g_4 \circ \ \cap \ \circ g_2)$;
6     $P := P \cup \{(g_2', g_3, S') \in G \times G \times A^* \mid \exists (g_2, g_3, S) \in (g_2 \circ \ \cap \ \circ g_3)[S' = \text{copy}(S)]\}$;
7   **if** $(|g_2 \circ| = 1)$ AND $(|\circ g_2| = 1)$ **then** $G := G \setminus \{g_2\}$;
8   **if** $(|g_2' \circ| = 1)$ AND $(|\circ g_2'| = 1)$ **then** $G := G \setminus \{g_2'\}$;

Algorithm 3. Pull-Up

---

input: Ejection $e = (g_1, g_2, g_3, g_4)$
input: Set of all Paths P
input: Set of all Gateways G

1 **if** $\circ \ g_2 \subseteq g_1 \circ$ **then**
2     $g_2' := \text{copy}(g_2)$;
3     $G := G \cup \{g_2'\}$;
4     $P := P \cup \{(g_2', g_4, S) \in G \times G \times A^* \mid \exists (g_2, g_4, S_x) \in (g_2 \circ \ \cap \ \circ g_4)[S_x = S]\}$;
5     $P := P \setminus (g_2 \circ \ \cap \ \circ g_4)$;
6     $P := P \cup \{(g_1, g_2', S') \in G \times G \times A^* \mid \exists (g_1, g_2, S) \in (g_1 \circ \ \cap \ \circ g_2)[S' = \text{copy}(S)]\}$;
7   **if** $(|g_2 \circ| = 1)$ AND $(|\circ g_2| = 1)$ **then** $G := G \setminus \{g_2\}$;
8   **if** $(|g_2' \circ| = 1)$ AND $(|\circ g_2'| = 1)$ **then** $G := G \setminus \{g_2'\}$;

---

extended version of Oulsnam's algorithm. Before presenting this latter algorithm, we need to introduce two operators.

The first operator is the *push-down* operator (see Algorithm 2). Given an Injection $i = (g_1, g_2, g_3, g_4)$, Push-Down(i) can be applied if

$g_2 \circ \subseteq \circ g_3$ (see line 1). The operator removes the input injection in four steps: (i) it creates a copy of g_2, namely g_2'; (ii) for each path from g_4 to g_2, it changes the end node of the path from g_2 to the new gateway g_2' (lines 4 and 5); (iii) for each path from g_2 to g_3, it duplicates the path, setting g_2' as the starting node of the path, instead of g_2 (line 6); and (iv) it removes any of g_2 and g_2' if it is a trivial gateway (see Fig. 2).

The second operator is the *pull-up* operator (see Algorithm 3). Given an Ejection $e = (g_1, g_2, g_3, g_4)$, Pull-Up(e) can be applied if $\circ g_2 \subseteq g_1 \circ$ (see line 1). The operator removes the input ejection in four steps: (i) it creates a copy of g_2, namely g_2'; (ii) for each path from g_2 to g_4, it changes the starting node of the path from g_2 to the new gateway g_2' (lines 4 and 5); (iii) for each path from g_1 to g_2, it duplicates the path, setting g_2' as the end node of the path, instead of g_2 (line 6); and (iv) it removes any of g_2 and g_2' if it is a trivial gateway (see Fig. 2).

While the push-down operator is an adaptation of Oulsnam's technique [14], the pull-up operator is a new operator. Despite the pull-up operator preserves trace equivalence it does not preserve weak bisimulation equivalence, because it does not preserve the moment of choice (it may pull a choice to an earlier point). Indeed, referring to Fig. 2, given a generic ejection $e = (g_1, g_2, g_3, g_4)$, the pull-up operator by definition can be applied iff $\circ g_2 \subseteq g_1 \circ$, this means g_2 can be reached only from g_1, and consequentially the only way to reach g_4 from g_2 is passing through g_1. Considering this latter and that by definition the pull-up operator generates a path $S_{24}' \in g_2' \circ \cap \circ g_4$ for each previously existing path $S_{24} \in g_2 \circ \cap \circ g_4$ (step ii), and creates a duplicate path $S_{12}' \in g_1 \circ \cap \circ g_2'$ for each previously existing path $S_{12} \in g_1 \circ \cap \circ g_2$ (step iii), it follows that for each concatenation of S_{12} and S_{24} existing before the pull-up operator, after the pull-up operator there will exist a concatenation of S_{12}' and S_{24}' that is its duplicate. Therefore, the nature of the pull-up operator does not introduce nor remove executable traces. The only drawback of the pull-up operator is that the decision to take the path that will lead to g_4 is anticipated at g_1, whilst before was at g_2 (i.e. earlier point of choice). Due to this tradeoff, we make the use of the pull-up operator optional as discussed below.

Algorithm 4 (Extended Oulsnam) shows how the two operators are used to structure a rigid fragment. The inputs of the algorithm are an unstructured rigid and a boolean value to indicate whether the pull-up operator is to be used. First, the algorithm detects every injection on top of which the push-down operator can be applied (see line 2), and if the pull-up is enabled, every ejection on top of which the pull-up can be applied (line 4). Second, it selects the cheapest injection and the cheapest ejection (lines 5 and 6). The cheapest injection (ejection) is the injection (ejection) generating the minimum number of duplicates after a push-down (pull-up). Third, the cheapest among these two is then chosen (line 8) and the corresponding operator is applied. The algorithm iterates over these three steps until no more ejections or injections can be removed, which results in a fully structured or maximally structured rigid. Selecting the cheapest injection or ejection at each step does not ensure that the final model will have the minimum

---

Algorithm 4. EOStruct (Extended Oulsnam)

---

input: Rigid r
input: Boolean *pullup*

1 **do**
2   Set $I :=$ detectInjections(r);
3   Set $E := \varnothing$;
4   **if** *pullup* **then** Set $E :=$ detectEjections(r);
5   **if** $I \neq \varnothing$ **then** Injection $i :=$ cheapestInjection(I);
6   **if** $E \neq \varnothing$ **then** Ejection $e :=$ cheapestEjection(E);
7   **if** *(i not $\perp$) OR (e not $\perp$)* **then**
8   **if** *((e = $\perp$) OR ((i not $\perp$) AND (cost(i) $\leq$ cost(e))))* **then**
            Push-Down(i);
9   **else** Pull-Up(e);
10 **while** $I \neq \varnothing$ OR $E \neq \varnothing$;

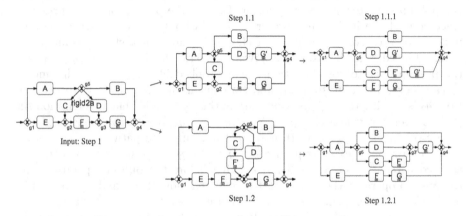

Fig. 3. An example application of the A^* search tree with our structuring method.

number of duplicates. In order to achieve the latter property, we embed the Extended Oulsnam algorithm inside an A^* search [8], where each state in the search tree is a transformed version of the initial rigid fragment, and the cost function associated with each state is defined as $f_{(s)} = g_{(s)} + h_{(s)}$ with $g_{(s)} = \#duplicates$ and $h_{(s)} = 0$. We set function $h_{(s)}$ to zero since it is not possible to predict how many duplicates are needed in order to structure a rigid.

Figure 3 illustrates an example where a rigid is structured using Algorithm 4 within an A^* search. In this example, the rigid has two injections, i.e. $i_1 = (g_1, g_2, g_3, g_5)$ and $i_2 = (g_2, g_3, g_4, g_5)$. Assuming i_2 is the cheapest of the two injections (i.e. the size of subprocess G is smaller than the size of subprocess F), if we first remove i_2 and then i_1 (see Step 1.1 and Step 1.1.1) we will have to duplicate sub-process G twice. This would not happen if we first removed i_1 and then i_2 (see Step 1.2 and Step 1.2.1). The use of an A^* search helps us avoid these situations since it takes care of exploring the search tree and selecting the sequence of removals of injections and ejections, that leads to the minimum number of duplicated elements.

For unsound rigids, we only apply the push-down operator in order to preserve the moment of choice of the split gateways of the quasi-bonds that will be turned into bonds when structuring the rigid (not shown in Algorithm 4 for brevity). After the structuring procedure has been completed, we match the type of the join gateways of the acyclic bonds with the type of their corresponding split gateways (e.g. if the split is an AND gateway the join will be turned into an AND gateway). In case of cyclic bonds, we turn both split and join gateways into XOR to avoid soundness issues. If multiple bonds share the same join gateway, this is replaced with a chain of gateways, one for each bond, maintaining the original bonds hierarchy. Finally, since we disable the use of the pull-up operator on unsound rigids, we cannot guarantee that these will be fully structured, hence we cannot guarantee that they will be turned into sound fragments.

Complexity. The complexity of the push-down and pull-up operators is linear on the number of activity paths to be duplicated when structuring an injection or ejection, i.e. $O(|g_2 \circ \cap \circ g_3|)$. This is bounded by $O(n^2)$, where n is the number of nodes in the model. The complexity of the Extended Oulsnam algorithm is linear on the number of injections and ejections, which is $O\left(\binom{g}{4}\right)$ where g is the number of gateways, which is bounded by the number of nodes n. Hence, $O\left(\binom{n}{4}\right) + O(n^2) \approx O(n^4)$. Finally, the complexity of A^* is $O(b^q)$ where b is the branching factor and q is the depth of the solution. In our case the branching factor is the number of injections and ejections, and so is the depth of the solution. Hence the complexity of our method is $O(n^{4^{n^4}}) \cdot O(n^4) \approx O(n^n)$. This does not include the complexity of the baseline discovery method.

4   Evaluation

We implemented our method as a standalone tool as well as a ProM plugin, namely the *Structured Miner* (hereafter SM).[2] The tool takes a log in MXML or XES format (currently it supports Heuristics Miner (HM) and Fodina (FM) as baseline discovery algorithms), and returns a maximally structured process model in BPMN format.

Using this tool, we conducted a series of experiments to evaluate the accuracy of our discovery approach compared to that of methods that structure the model during discovery. We selected two representative methods: Inductive Miner (IM) and Evolutionary Tree Miner (ETM), and compared the results with our approach on top of HM and FM. As the results obtained with FM were consistently similar to those obtained with HM and due to space reasons, this section only reports the results using HM.

We measured accuracy using the fitness, precision, F-score and generalization metrics and model complexity via size, CFC and structuredness as defined

---

[2] Available from http://apromore.org/platform/tools.

in Sect. 2.2. The experiments were done on an Intel dual-core i5-3337U 1.80 Ghz with 12 GB of RAM running JVM 7 with 8 GB of heap, except for the experiments using ETM, which were done on a 6-core Xeon E5-1650 3.50 Ghz with 128 GB of RAM running JVM 7 with 40 GB of heap, time-bounded to 30 min as the ETM algorithm is computationally very expensive and can otherwise take several hours per log.

4.1   Datasets

We generated three sets of logs using the ProM plugin "Generate Event Log from Petri Net". This plugin takes as input a process model in PNML format and generates a distinct log trace for each possible execution sequence in the model. The first set (591 Petri nets) was obtained from the SAP R/3 collection, SAP's reference model to customize their R/3 ERP product [4]. The log-generator plugin was only able to parse 545 out of 591 models, running into out-of-memory exceptions for the others. The second set (54 Workflow nets[3]) was obtained from a collection of sound and unstructured models extracted from the IBM BIT collection [6]. The BIT collection is a publicly-available set of process models in financial services, telecommunication and other domains, gathered from IBMs consultancy practice [7]. The third set contains 20 artificial models, which we created to test our method with more complex forms of unstructuredness, not observed in the two real-life collections. These are: (i) rigids containing AND-gateway bonds, (ii) rigids containing a large number of XOR gateways (>5); (iii) rigids containing rigids and (iv) rigids being the root node of the model. Out of these 619 logs we only selected those for which

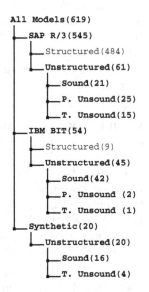

Fig. 4. Taxonomy of models discovered by HM from the logs (P. = partially, T. = totally).

HM produced an unstructured model, as our approach does not add value if the resulting model is already structured. This resulted in 126 logs, of which 61 came from SAP, 45 from IBM and 20 were synthetic. These logs range from 4,111 to 201,758 total events (avg. 49,580) with 3 to 4,235 distinct traces (avg. 137). From the models discovered with HM, we identified 79 sound models, 31 partially unsound models, i.e. models for which there is at least one complete trace, and 16 totally unsound models, i.e. models whose traces always deadlock. A taxonomy of the datasets used is shown in Fig. 4.

4.2   Results

Tables 1 and 2 report the average value and standard deviation for each quality measure across all discovery algorithms, for the models mined from the real-life

---

[3] This collection originally counted 59 models, but we discarded five duplicates.

Table 1. Quality of models discovered from real-life data.

Log class (Class size)	Discovery method	Accuracy				Complexity		
		Fitness	Precision	F-score	Gen. (10-fold)	Size	CFC	Struct.
Sound (63)	IM	1.00 ± 0.01	0.69 ± 0.31	0.77 ± 0.26	1.00 ± 0.01	23.8 ± 7.9	11.2 ± 5.0	1.00 ± 0.00
	ETM	0.91 ± 0.08	0.93 ± 0.06	0.92 ± 0.06	0.90 ± 0.06	26.4 ± 8.6	8.6 ± 4.3	1.00 ± 0.00
	HM	1.00 ± 0.00	0.99 ± 0.05	0.99 ± 0.03	1.00 ± 0.01	25.0 ± 7.7	8.7 ± 4.2	0.50 ± 0.16
	SM$_{HM}$	1.00 ± 0.00	0.99 ± 0.02	1.00 ± 0.01	1.00 ± 0.00	29.7 ± 13.3	10.2 ± 6.5	0.90 ± 0.21
P. unsound (27)	IM	0.98 ± 0.03	0.73 ± 0.27	0.80 ± 0.22	0.98 ± 0.03	22.1 ± 5.9	11.6 ± 5.0	1.00 ± 0.00
	ETM	0.90 ± 0.09	0.86 ± 0.11	0.87 ± 0.07	0.89 ± 0.06	21.7 ± 7.8	7.5 ± 5.2	1.00 ± 0.00
	HM	0.69 ± 0.21	0.85 ± 0.10	0.75 ± 0.16	0.66 ± 0.21	21.9 ± 7.3	9.0 ± 5.1	0.53 ± 0.21
	SM$_{HM}$	0.97 ± 0.04	0.93 ± 0.11	0.95 ± 0.08	0.97 ± 0.04	24.6 ± 10.5	10.0 ± 6.7	0.97 ± 0.15
T. unsound (16)	IM	0.99 ± 0.03	0.82 ± 0.21	0.88 ± 0.14	0.99 ± 0.03	24.1 ± 12.0	9.6 ± 6.7	1.00 ± 0.00
	ETM	0.90 ± 0.10	0.87 ± 0.09	0.88 ± 0.07	0.89 ± 0.09	25.0 ± 4.2	9.2 ± 0.7	1.00 ± 0.00
	HM	-	-	-	-	22.3 ± 9.4	7.8 ± 3.6	0.72 ± 0.19
	SM$_{HM}$	0.96 ± 0.06	0.92 ± 0.14	0.93 ± 0.11	0.96 ± 0.06	23.2 ± 10.4	7.7 ± 3.3	1.00 ± 0.00

Table 2. Quality of models discovered from artificial data.

Log class (Class size)	Discovery method	Accuracy				Complexity		
		Fitness	Precision	F-score	Gen. (10-fold)	Size	CFC	Struct.
Sound (16)	IM	1.00 ± 0.01	0.53 ± 0.31	0.64 ± 0.26	1.00 ± 0.01	18.7 ± 4.5	10.7 ± 3.7	1.00 ± 0.00
	ETM	0.89 ± 0.07	0.96 ± 0.05	0.92 ± 0.04	0.89 ± 0.05	22.1 ± 7.7	7.3 ± 3.2	1.00 ± 0.00
	HM	1.00 ± 0.00	1.00 ± 0.00	1.00 ± 0.00	1.00 ± 0.00	21.6 ± 5.2	8.2 ± 3.1	0.32 ± 0.17
	SM$_{HM}$	1.00 ± 0.00	1.00 ± 0.00	1.00 ± 0.00	1.00 ± 0.00	25.1 ± 7.7	9.1 ± 3.5	1.00 ± 0.00
P. unsound (4)	IM	1.00 ± 0.00	0.44 ± 0.27	0.56 ± 0.22	1.00 ± 0.00	23.5 ± 10.4	11.5 ± 1.1	1.00 ± 0.00
	ETM	0.83 ± 0.12	0.88 ± 0.09	0.84 ± 0.07	0.78 ± 0.15	25.5 ± 1.5	10.0 ± 1.0	1.00 ± 0.00
	HM	0.61 ± 0.16	0.84 ± 0.06	0.69 ± 0.14	0.61 ± 0.16	27.8 ± 9.1	8.8 ± 1.5	0.30 ± 0.15
	SM$_{HM}$	0.89 ± 0.13	0.98 ± 0.02	0.93 ± 0.07	0.89 ± 0.13	30.0 ± 12.3	11.0 ± 3.3	1.00 ± 0.00

data, respectively, artificial data. When HM generates sound models its output is already of high quality along fitness, precision and generalization, with a marginal standard deviation. In this case, our approach only improves the structuredness of the models, at the cost of a minor increase in size and CFC, due to the duplication introduced by the structuring. IM instead, despite having similarly high values of fitness and generalization, loses in precision with an average of 0.69 with high standard deviation, meaning that the actual precision may be much better or worse depending on the specific log used. As expected, these models are structured by construction, but CFC still remains higher than that of HM (and its structured variant SM) due to IM's tendency to generate flower models (which is also the cause for low precision). Finally, the quality of the models discovered by ETM ranks in-between that of IM and HM both in terms of accuracy and complexity, at the price of sensibly longer execution times.

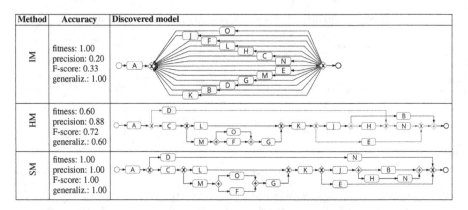

Fig. 5. A model from the SAP R/3 logs, discovered by IM, HM and SM (injections and gateways causing unsoundness in the HM model are highlighted).

The improvement of our method on top of HM is more evident when the latter discovers unsound models. Here HM's accuracy dramatically worsen compared to IM and ETM. For example, in the case of partially unsound models, on average fitness is 0.69 for HM vs. 0.98 for IM on real-life data, and 0.61 vs. 1 on artificial data, while for totally unsound models, fitness and precision for HM cannot even be measured. Our approach does not only notably increases structuredness (e.g. 0.53 vs. 0.97), but it also repairs the soundness issues and recovers the accuracy lost by HM, significantly outperforming both IM and ETM in terms of precision and F-score without compromising fitness and generalization, which get very close to those obtained by IM, e.g. fitness increases from 0.69 to 0.97, as opposed to 0.98 for IM, with an F-score of 0.95 instead of 0.80 in the case of partially unsound models discovered from real-life data. In the case of "sound models", ETM strikes a better tradeoff between accuracy and complexity compared to IM, but again, at the price of long execution times.

To illustrate when our approach outperforms IM, Fig. 5 shows the BPMN model generated by IM, HM and SM from one of the SAP R/3 logs and the corresponding quality measures.[4] In this example, the precision of the model produced by IM is low due to the presence of a large "flower-like" structure, which causes overgeneralization. Precision is higher with HM, though fitness and generalization suffer from the model being unsound. By structuring and fixing the behavioral issues of this model, SM improves on all metrics, scoring a perfect 1 for both F-score and generalization.

The negative effects of overgeneralization brought by IM are higher when the models used for generating the logs exhibit complex unstructured patterns, such as those introduced in the artificial data (cf. Table 2). For example, the precision of IM is 0.53 for sound models (with a high standard deviation), as opposed to

---

[4] The original labels are replaced with letters for the sake of compactness.

1 with HM. In these cases, SM consistently outperforms IM and ETM, while significantly improving over HM in terms of structuredness (0.3 vs. 1).

In these experiments we disabled the pull-up operator of our method in order to ensure weak bisimulation equivalence between the model discovered by HM and the structured one. As a result, we could not fully structure 15 models from real-life data, which explains a value of structuredness less than 1 for SM in Table 1. When we enable the pull-up operator, all the discovered models are fully structured, at the price of losing weak bisimilarity.

Time performance. Despite having exponential complexity in the worst case scenario, the time SM took to structure the models used in this evaluation was well within acceptable bounds, taking on average less than one second per model (avg = 894 ms, min = 2 ms, max = 109 s, 95 % percentile = 47.65 ms).

4.3 Threats to Validity

A potential threat to internal validity is the use of process model complexity metrics as proxies for assessing the understandability of the discovered process models, as opposed to direct human judgement. However, the three chosen complexity metrics (size, CFC and structuredness) have been empirically shown to be highly correlated with perceived understandability and error-proneness [6,11]. Further, while the process models obtained with our method are affected by the individual accuracy (fitness, precision and generalization) of the baseline algorithm used (HM or FM), Structured Miner is independent of these algorithms, and our experiments show that the method significantly improves on structuredness while keeping the same levels of accuracy. In addition, the method can often fix issues related to model correctness.

The evaluation reported above is based on two real-life datasets. This poses a threat to external validity. It should be noted though that these two datasets collect models from a variety of domains, including finance, sales, accounting, logistics, communication and human resources, and that the resulting logs are representative of different characteristics (number of events and number of distinct traces). Moreover, the use of an additional dataset artificially generated allowed us to evaluate our method against a large variety of unstructured model topologies, including some complex ones not observed in the two real-life datasets.

5 Conclusion

We presented a two-phased method to extract a structured process model from an event log wherein a process model is first extracted without any structural restriction, and then transformed into a structured one if needed. The experimental results show that this two-phased method leads to higher F-score than existing methods that discover a structured process model by design. In addition, the proposed method is more modular, insofar as different discovery and block-structuring methods can be plugged into it.

In this paper, we used the Heuristics Miner and Fodina for the first phase. In future work, we will experiment with alternative methods for discovering (unstructured) process models to explore alternative tradeoffs between model quality metrics. In the second phase, we employed a structuring method that preserves weak bisimilarity (if the pull-up operator is disabled). A direction for future work is to explore the option of partially sacrificing weak bisimilarity (while still keeping trace equivalence) to obtain models with higher structuredness. Another direction for future work is to use process model clone detection techniques [5] to refactor duplicates introduced by the structuring phase. This may allow us to strike better tradeoffs between size and structuredness.

Acknowledgments. This research is partly funded by the Australian Research Council (grant DP150103356) and the Estonian Research Council (grant IUT20-55).

References

1. Adriansyah, A., Munoz-Gama, J., Carmona, J., Dongen, B.F., Aalst, W.M.P.: Alignment based precision checking. In: Rosa, M., Soffer, P. (eds.) BPM 2012. LNBIP, vol. 132, pp. 137–149. Springer, Heidelberg (2013). doi:10.1007/978-3-642-36285-9_15
2. Adriansyah, A., van Dongen, B.F., van der Aalst, W.M.P.: Conformance checking using cost-based fitness analysis. In: Proceedings of EDOC. IEEE (2011)
3. Buijs, J.C.A.M., Dongen, B.F., Aalst, W.M.P.: On the role of fitness, precision, generalization and simplicity in process discovery. In: Meersman, R., Panetto, H., Dillon, T., Rinderle-Ma, S., Dadam, P., Zhou, X., Pearson, S., Ferscha, A., Bergamaschi, S., Cruz, I.F. (eds.) OTM 2012. LNCS, vol. 7565, pp. 305–322. Springer, Heidelberg (2012). doi:10.1007/978-3-642-33606-5_19
4. Curran, T., Keller, G.: SAP R/3 Business Blueprint: Understanding the Business Process Reference Model. Prentice-Hall, Inc., Upper Saddle River (1997)
5. Dumas, M., García-Bañuelos, L., La Rosa, M., Uba, R.: Fast detection of exact clones in business process model repositories. Inf. Syst. **38**(4), 619–633 (2013)
6. Dumas, M., Rosa, M., Mendling, J., Mäesalu, R., Reijers, H.A., Semenenko, N.: Understanding business process models: the costs and benefits of structuredness. In: Ralyté, J., Franch, X., Brinkkemper, S., Wrycza, S. (eds.) CAiSE 2012. LNCS, vol. 7328, pp. 31–46. Springer, Heidelberg (2012). doi:10.1007/978-3-642-31095-9_3
7. Fahland, D., Favre, C., Koehler, J., Lohmann, N., Völzer, H., Wolf, K.: Analysis on demand: instantaneous soundness checking of industrial business process models. Data Knowl. Eng. **70**(5), 448–466 (2011)
8. Hart, P.E., Nilsson, N.J., Raphael, B.: A formal basis for the heuristic determination of minimum cost paths. IEEE Trans. Syst. Sci. Cybern. **4**(2), 100–107 (1968)
9. Kohavi, R.: A study of cross-validation and bootstrap for accuracy estimation and model selection. In: Proceedings of IJCAI, pp. 1137–1145. Morgan Kaufmann (1995)
10. Leemans, S.J.J., Fahland, D., Aalst, W.M.P.: Discovering block-structured process models from event logs - a constructive approach. In: Colom, J.-M., Desel, J. (eds.) PETRI NETS 2013. LNCS, vol. 7927, pp. 311–329. Springer, Heidelberg (2013). doi:10.1007/978-3-642-38697-8_17
11. Mendling, J.: Metrics for Process Models: Empirical Foundations of Verification, Error Prediction, and Guidelines for Correctness. Springer, Heidelberg (2008)

12. Molka, T., Redlich, D., Gilani, W., Zeng, X.-J., Drobek, M.: Evolutionary computation based discovery of hierarchical business process models. In: Abramowicz, W. (ed.) BIS 2015. LNBIP, vol. 208, pp. 191–204. Springer, Heidelberg (2015). doi:10. 1007/978-3-319-19027-3_16

13. Oulsnam, G.: Unravelling unstructured programs. Comput. J. **25**(3), 379–387 (1982)

14. Oulsnam, G.: The algorithmic transformation of schemas to structured form. Comput. J. **30**(1), 43–51 (1987)

15. Polyvyanyy, A., García-Bañuelos, L., Dumas, M.: Structuring acyclic process models. Inf. Syst. **37**(6), 518–538 (2012)

16. Polyvyanyy, A., García-Bañuelos, L., Fahland, D., Weske, M.: Maximal structuring of acyclic process models. Comput. J. **57**(1), 12–35 (2014)

17. Polyvyanyy, A., Vanhatalo, J., Völzer, H.: Simplified computation and generalization of the refined process structure tree. In: Bravetti, M., Bultan, T. (eds.) WS-FM 2010. LNCS, vol. 6551, pp. 25–41. Springer, Heidelberg (2011). doi:10. 1007/978-3-642-19589-1_2

18. van der Aalst, W.M.P.: Process Mining - Discovery, Conformance and Enhancement of Business Processes. Springer, Heidelberg (2011)

19. van der Aalst, W.M.P., Weijters, T., Maruster, L.: Workflow mining: discovering process models from event logs. IEEE Trans. Knowl. Data Eng. **16**(9), 1128–1142 (2004)

20. De Weerdt, J., De Backer, M., Vanthienen, J., Baesens, B.: A multi-dimensional quality assessment of state-of-the-art process discovery algorithms using real-life event logs. Inf. Syst. **37**(7), 654–676 (2012)

21. Weijters, A.J.M.M., Ribeiro, J.T.S.: Flexible heuristics miner (FHM). In: Proceedings of CIDM. IEEE (2011)

Detecting Drift from Event Streams of Unpredictable Business Processes

Alireza Ostovar[1($\boxtimes$)], Abderrahmane Maaradji[1], Marcello La Rosa[1],
Arthur H.M. ter Hofstede[1,2], and Boudewijn F.V. van Dongen[2]

[1] Queensland University of Technology, Brisbane, Australia
{alireza.ostovar,abderrahmane.maaradji,m.larosa,
a.terhofstede}@qut.edu.au
[2] Eindhoven University of Technology, Eindhoven, The Netherlands
b.f.v.dongen@tue.nl

Abstract. Existing business process drift detection methods do not
work with event streams. As such, they are designed to detect inter-
trace drifts only, i.e. drifts that occur between complete process executions (traces), as recorded in event logs. However, process drift may also
occur *during* the execution of a process, and may impact ongoing executions. Existing methods either do not detect such *intra-trace* drifts, or
detect them with a long delay. Moreover, they do not perform well with
unpredictable processes, i.e. processes whose logs exhibit a high number of distinct executions to the total number of executions. We address
these two issues by proposing a fully automated and scalable method for
online detection of process drift from event streams. We perform statistical tests over distributions of behavioral relations between events, as
observed in two adjacent windows of adaptive size, sliding along with
the stream. An extensive evaluation on synthetic and real-life logs shows
that our method is fast and accurate in the detection of typical change
patterns, and performs significantly better than the state of the art.

1 Introduction

Business processes tend to evolve due to various types of changes in the business
environment in which they operate. For example, these can be changes in regulations, competition, supply, demand and technological capabilities, as well as
internal changes in resource capacity or workload, or simply changes in seasonal
factors. Some of these changes may not be documented at all, e.g. those initi-
ated by individual process participants due to replacement of staff, or exceptions
that in some cases give rise to new workarounds that over time become common
practices. In the long run, undocumented process changes may affect process
performance and more in general, hamper process improvement initiatives.

This motivated academics to devise methods and tools that allow business
analysts to pinpoint process changes as early as possible. *Business process drift
detection* [1–5] is a family of process mining techniques which aim at detecting changes based on observations of business process executions recorded in
event logs. Event logs consist of *traces*, each representing one execution of the

© Springer International Publishing AG 2016
I. Comyn-Wattiau et al. (Eds.): ER 2016, LNCS 9974, pp. 330–346, 2016.
DOI: 10.1007/978-3-319-46397-1_26

business process. Accordingly, a business process drift is defined as a statistically significant change in the process behavior [5].

Still, state-of-the-art methods in this area suffer from two major limitations. First, they do not work in online settings with streams of events that incrementally record the executions of a business process. As such, they are designed to detect inter-trace drifts only, i.e. drifts that occur between complete process executions (traces), as recorded in event logs. Even if some approaches work in online settings (e.g. [5]), they still deal with streams of complete traces or abstractions thereof. However, process drift may also occur *during* the execution of a process, and may impact ongoing executions. Existing methods either do not detect such *intra-trace* drifts, or detect them with a long delay, as they need to wait for the trace to complete. A related problem is that they do not perform well with *unpredictable* processes, i.e. processes whose logs exhibit a high number of distinct traces over the total number of traces – a typical characteristic of healthcare logs. This is because they rely on statistical tests over trace distributions, which may not have sufficient data samples when the proportion of distinct traces over the total number of traces is very high, in other words, where there is high variability in the log.

To address these two limitations, we propose a fully automated, online method for detecting process drifts from event streams. We perform statistical tests over distributions of behavioral relations between events such as conflict, causality and concurrency, as observed from two adjacent windows of adjustable size, which we slide over the stream. Given that behavioral relations between events are a type of sub-trace features, the method does not suffer from low accuracy when the log is highly variable (i.e. for unpredictable processes). We extensively evaluate the accuracy and scalability of our method by simulating event streams from artificial and real-life logs. The results show that the approach is fast and highly accurate in detecting common change patterns, and significantly better than the state of the art in process drift detection.

The paper is structured as follows. Section 2 discusses related work. Section 3 introduces the proposed method while Sects. 4 and 5 present its evaluations on synthetic and real-life logs respectively. Section 6 concludes the paper.

2   Related Work

Various methods have been proposed to detect process drifts from event logs [1–5]. These methods are based on the idea of extracting *features* (e.g. patterns) from the traces of an event log. For example, Carmona et al. [1] propose to represent a log as a polyhedron. This representation is computed for prefixes in a random sample of the initial traces in the log. The method checks the fitness of subsequent trace prefixes against the constructed polyhedron. If a significant number of these prefixes does not lie in the polyhedron, a drift is declared. The method guarantees that drifts of certain types will always be detected. However, to find a second drift after the first one, the entire detection process must be restarted, thus adversely affecting on the scalability of the method.

In previous experiments we conducted [5], the execution of this implemented method took hours to complete. Another drawback is its inability to pinpoint the exact moment of the drift.

Accorsi et al. [2] propose to cluster the traces in a moving window of the log, based on the average distance between each pair of events in the traces. This method heavily depends on the choice of the window size: a low window size may lead to false positives while a high size may lead to false negatives (undetected drifts), as drifts happening inside the window go undetected. In addition the method is not designed to deal with loops, and may fail to detect types of changes that do not cause significant variations to the distances between activity pairs, e.g. changes involving an activity being skipped.

Bose et al. [3] propose a method to detect process drifts based on statistical testing over feature vectors. The method is not fully automated, as the user is asked to identify the features to be used for drift detection, implying that they have some a-priori knowledge of the possible nature of the drift. Further, this method is unable to identify certain types of drifts such as inserting a conditional branch or a conditional move, even if the relevant process activities are selected as features. Finally, similar to Accorsi et al. [2], the user is required to set a window size for drift detection. Depending on how this parameter is set, some drifts may be missed. This latter limitation is partially lifted in a subsequent extension [4], which introduces a notion of *adaptive window*. The idea is to increase the window size until it reaches a maximum size or until a drift is detected. However, this technique requires the user to set a minimum and a maximum window size. If the minimum window size is too small, minor variations (e.g. noise) may be misinterpreted as drifts (false positives). Conversely, if the maximum window size is too large, the execution time is affected and some drifts may go undetected.

All these methods may miss certain types of changes that are not covered by the types of features used. Moreover, their scalability is constrained by the need to extract and analyze a feature space that is potentially very large. Hence, they are not suitable for online settings. This motivated us to propose a new method [5] for detecting process drifts determined by a wide range of typical process change patterns [6]. The method is based on statistical tests over the distribution of *runs* (an abstraction of complete traces), as observed in two consecutive time windows. The size of these windows is adjusted based on changes in log variability. This method outperforms all the above methods in terms of detection accuracy and scalability. As such, we selected it as a baseline for the experiments in this paper. As shown in the experiments, this method also does not cater for highly variable event logs. In such logs each distinct run occurs only a few times, leading to a less reliable statistical test, to hence to many false negatives. Further, the method cannot detect intra-trace drifts from event streams.

To the best of our knowledge, the only method that deals with event streams has been proposed by Burattin et al. [7]. However, this work mainly focuses on the online discovery of process models captured as a set of business constraints (formulated in Linear Temporal Logic) between events. Any change in the extracted constraints over time may be considered as a drift. Nonetheless, there is no statistical support for detecting whether changes are in fact significant, and the exact positions of the identified drifts are not reported. As such, drift detection accuracy is not evaluated. In another study, Burattin et al. [8] adapt an automated process discovery method, namely the Heuristics Miner, to handle incremental updates as new events are produced. Our proposal is complementary to this as it allows drifts to be detected accurately and efficiently, and can be used as an oracle to identify points in time when the process model should be updated.

Drift detection has been studied in the field of data mining [9], where a widely studied challenge is that of designing efficient learning algorithms that can adapt to data that evolves over time (a.k.a. *concept drift*). This includes for example changes in the distributions of numerical or categorical variables. However, the methods developed in this context deal with simple structures (e.g. numerical or categorical variables and vectors thereof), while in business process drift detection we seek to detect changes in more complex structures, specifically behavioral relations between process events (e.g. concurrency, conflicts, loops). Thus, methods from the field of concept drift detection in data mining cannot be readily transposed to business process drift detection.

3 Drift Detection Method

From a statistical viewpoint, the problem of business process drift detection can be formulated as follows: *identify a time point before and after which there is a statistically significant difference between the observed process behaviors.* Therefore, to detect a drift we need features that properly capture the behavior of a process. By monitoring and analyzing the feature vectors over time, we can identify the time points where the feature vectors exhibit statistically significant changes. We explored a few different features including *Direct Follow relations* (direct succession), *Follow relations* (succession), *Block Structures* (extracted from *process trees* produced by the Inductive Miner [10]) and α^+ *Relations* [11]. We found that while the direct follow and follow relations are over-fitting features, block structures were under-fitting features. However, α^+ relations proved to be the suitable level of abstraction for capturing the behavior of unpredictable processes represented in an event stream.

To detect a process drift we perform a statistical test, namely the G-test of independence,[1] over distributions of α^+ relations observed in two adjacent time windows of adaptive size, sliding along with a stream of events. Basically, the most recent events are equally divided into reference window (less recent events), and detection window (more recent events). Each time a new event enters the event stream, the two windows shift forward so that the new event is in the detection window. The set of events within each window is used to build a corresponding sub-log. This sub-log represents the process behavior observed

---

[1] The G-test is a non-parametric hypothesis statistical test which assumes no a-priori knowledge of the statistical distributions. The G-test is a better approximation to the theoretical chi-squared distribution than the chi-squared test [12].

within the respective window. The sliding window is a well-established technique in the concept drift community [9].

Then the α^+ relations and their frequencies are extracted from each sub-log, and used to populate a $2 \times n$ matrix, the so-called *contingency matrix*, where n is the number of distinct relations. Each column in the contingency matrix corresponds to a category of a statistical variable, here an α^+ relation. The first row in the contingency matrix contains the frequencies of the relations in the detection window, i.e. the *observed* frequencies, while the second row contains the frequencies of the relations in the reference window, i.e. the *expected* frequencies.

The result of applying the G-test of independence on the contingency matrix is the significance probability (*P-value*) that the populations of α^+ relations over the two windows come from the same distribution. A *P-value* above a predefined threshold[2] accepts the null hypothesis, i.e. the frequency distributions of the α^+ relations in the two windows are similar. However, a *P-value* below the threshold rejects the null hypothesis, meaning that the α^+ relations in the two windows come from different distributions. In other words, they reflect different process behaviors (process drift).

3.1   Intra-trace vs. Inter-trace

A drift may occur between complete executions of a process. We call this an *inter-trace* drift. For example, a new legislation requires an insurance company to perform a more stringent verification on new claims, while old claims are exempted. These however are not the only type of drift. In reality, a drift may also occur *during* the execution of a process and may impact ongoing process instances [6]. We call these *intra-trace* drifts. For example, an insurance check may need to be removed altogether due to a contingency plan triggered by severe weather conditions (e.g. a flood). Such a change may impact new process instances as well as the instances that have already started, but that have not yet gone through the check to be removed.

In addition, in order to detect a drift using a stream of traces, we have to wait until each trace completes before we can use it. This delays the detection of the drift. On the other hand, working on a stream of events allows us to instantly use each observed event, thereby detecting a drift as soon as possible during the execution of the process.

3.2   Event Stream and α^+ Relations

An event log is a set of traces, each capturing the sequence of events originated from a given process instance. Each event represents an occurrence of an activity. The configuration where these events are read individually from an online source is known as event streaming. An event stream is a potentially infinite sequence of events, where events are ordered by time and indexed. Events of the same trace do not need to be consecutive in the event stream, i.e. traces can be "overlapping". Formally:

---

[2] The typical value of the threshold, i.e. significance level, for the G-test is 0.05 [13].

Definition 1 (Event log, Trace, Event stream). Let L be an *event log* over the set of labels $\mathcal{L}$, i.e. $L \in \mathbb{P}(\mathcal{L}^*)$. Let $\mathcal{E}$ be the set of event occurrences and $\lambda : \mathcal{E} \to \mathcal{L}$ a labelling function. An *event trace* $\sigma \in L$ is defined in terms of an order $i \in [0, n-1]$ and a set of events $\mathcal{E}_\sigma \subseteq \mathcal{E}$ with $|\mathcal{E}_\sigma| = n$ such that $\sigma = \langle \lambda(e_0), \lambda(e_1), \ldots, \lambda(e_{n-1}) \rangle$. An *event stream* is a function $S : \mathbb{N}^+ \to \mathcal{E}$ that maps every element from the index $\mathbb{N}^+$ to $\mathcal{E}$.

In this paper, we use the α^+ relations, as an extension of the α relations, to capture the behavior of a process. The α-algorithm defines three exclusive relations: *conflict*, *concurrency* and *causality*. The α^+-algorithm adds two more relations: *length-two loop* and *length-one loop*. The α^+ relations are formally defined as follows:

Definition 2 (α^+ relations from [11]). Let L be an event log over $\mathcal{L}$. Let $a,b \in \mathcal{L}$:

- $a\triangle_L b$ if and only if there is a trace $\sigma = l_1 l_2 l_3 \ldots l_n$ and $i \in 1, \ldots, n-2$ such that $\sigma \in L$ and $l_i = l_{i+2} = a$ and $l_{i+1} = b$,
- $a \diamond_L b$ if and only if $a\triangle_L b$ and $b\triangle_L a$,
- $a >_L b$ if and only if there is a trace $\sigma = l_1 l_2 l_3 \ldots l_n$ and $i \in 1, \ldots, n-2$ such that $\sigma \in L$ and $l_i = a$ and $l_{i+1} = b$,
- $a \to_L b$ if and only if $a >_L b$ and $(b \not>_L a$ or $a \diamond_L b)$,
- $a\#_L b$ if and only if $a \not>_L b$ and $b \not>_L a$, and
- $a \parallel_L b$ if and only if $a >_L b$ and $b >_L a$, and $a \not\diamond_L b$.

A length-two loop relation, including a and b, is denoted with $a\triangle_L b$. The frequency of this relation in a log is the number of occurrences of the substring aba. A causality relation from a to b is denoted with $a \to_L b$. The frequency of this relation in a log is the number of occurrences of the substring ab. A parallel relation between a and b is denoted with $a \parallel_L b$. The frequency of this relation in a log is the minimum of the frequencies of the two substrings, ab and ba. A conflict relation between a and b is denoted with $a\#_L b$, and indicates that there is no trace with the substring ab or ba. The frequency of this relation in a log is the number of occurrences of a and b. The α^+-algorithm also discovers length-one loop relations as a pre-processing operation. For example, there is a length-one loop including the activity a in a log if there is a trace with the substring aa. The frequency of this relation in a log is the number of occurrences of the substring aa.

3.3   Statistical Testing over Event Streams

This section describes our online drift detection algorithm as presented in Algorithm 1. The drift detection algorithm has three parameters: 1. *eventStream*: a stream of events. 2. *initWinSize*: initial size of the detection and reference windows. 3. *maxBufSize*: maximum available memory for the event buffer storing the incoming events, namely *eventBuf*. Since the algorithm works online the size of this buffer must not exceed *maxBufSize*. Therefore, each time a new event e arrives we first check if the buffer has reached its maximum size, and if so we shift the events in the buffer and discard the least recent event (lines 10–11). We then insert the new event into the buffer (line 12).

The first statistical test should be performed when the number of events in the buffer is $2 \times initWinSize$ (line 14). Before each statistical test we adapt the size of the two windows to improve the accuracy of the approach (line 15). The notion of adaptive window is explained in Sect. 3.4. The method *updateSublogs* updates the sub-logs related to the detection and reference windows, namely *detSubLog* and *refSubLog*, respectively, using the events within their corresponding windows (line 16). The first time this method is called the sub-logs are built from scratch. The α^+ relations and their frequencies are extracted from the two sub-logs and populated in a contingency matrix (line 18). We then perform the G-test of independence on this contingency matrix and obtain the P-value (line 19). The value of the G-test threshold, *GtestThreshold*, is set to the typical value of the G-test, which is 0.05.

Each time the P-value drops below the threshold *GtestThreshold*, we store the current event and the current window size in *pbtEvent* and *pbtWinSize*, respectively (lines 23–24). Since any statistical test is subject to sporadic stochastic oscillations, we introduced an additional filter, namely *oscillation filter*. The P-value drops have to be consistent over many consecutive statistical tests in order to avoid reporting incidental drops in the P-value (oscillations). The size of the oscillation filter is calculated by function Φ which uses the window size w as input. The number of consecutive tests in which the P-value is below the threshold *GtestThreshold* is stored in *pbtLen*. We detect a drift only if *pbtLen* is at least equal to $\Phi(w)$ (line 25). Our experiments showed that a value of $\Phi(w) = w/2$ provides the best results in terms of accuracy (cf. Sect. 4.3). The drift is localized at the event where the P-value dropped consistently below the threshold, stored at *pbtEvent* (line 26). Whenever the P-value exceeds the threshold we reset *pbtLen*, *pbtEvent* and *pbtWinSize* (lines 28–30).

3.4 Adaptive Window

Best practices of using the G-test recommend that no more than 20 % of the expected frequencies in the contingency matrix have less than 5 occurrences, to have a reliable statistical test [12]. Thus, each time before performing the statistical test we ensure the size of the two windows is large enough to fulfil this requirement. Even though the larger the window size is the higher the chances that the requirement of the statistical test is met, a very large window size may increase the number of new events needed to detect a drift, so-called *mean delay*. Furthermore, it may also cause the detection and reference windows to span over multiple drifts, thereby letting some of the drifts go undetected. Therefore, we need to balance between improving the reliability of the statistical test, by increasing the window size, and reducing the detection delay of the method, by decreasing the window size.

The idea behind our adaptive window originates from the requirement of the statistical test mentioned above, meaning that on average we aim to have a frequency of no less than 5 for each of the α^+ relations in the contingency matrix. Given that the maximum number of possible relations over the set of labels

Algorithm 1. Drift Detection Algorithm

Input: *eventStream*; *initWinSize*; *maxBufSize*.

1 *eventBuf*   // Event buffer
2 $w \longleftarrow$ *initWinSize*   // Current window size
3 *detSubLog, refSubLog*   // List of sub-traces within detection and
  reference windows, respectively
4 *GtestThreshold* $\longleftarrow$ 0.05   // Typical threshold value of G-test
5 *pbtEvent* $\longleftarrow$ *NIL*   // Current event when P-*value* drops below
  GtestThreshold
6 *pbtWinSize* $\longleftarrow$ -1 // Value of w when P-*value* drops below
  GtestThreshold
7 *pbtLen* $\longleftarrow$ 0   // # of consecutive tests that P-*value* remains below
  GtestThreshold

8 **while** *true* **do**
9     $e \longleftarrow$ *fetch*(*eventStream*)   // Fetch a new event e
10   **if** *size*(*eventBuf*) = *maxBufSize* **then**
11   *shift*(*eventBuf*)
12   *insert*(*eventBuf*, *e*)
13   *ebLength* $\longleftarrow$ length of *eventBuf*
14   **if** *ebLength* $\geq 2 \cdot$ *initWinSize* **then**
15   *newWinSize* $\longleftarrow$ *adWin*(*eventBuf*, *w*)
16   *updateSublogs*(*eventBuf*, *detSubLog*, *refSubLog*, *w*, *newWinSize*)
17       $w \longleftarrow$ *newWinSize*
18   *conMat* $\longleftarrow$ *buildContingencyMatrix*(*detSubLog*, *refSubLog*)
19   *pValue* $\longleftarrow$ *Gtest*(*conMat*)
20   **if** *pValue* < *GtestThreshold* **then**
21   *pbtLen* $\longleftarrow$ *pbtLen* + 1
22   **if** *pbtEvent* = *NIL* **then**
23   *pbtEvent* $\longleftarrow$ *e*
24   *pbtWinSize* $\longleftarrow$ *w*
25   **if** *pbtLen* = Φ(*pbtWinSize*) **then**
26   *reportDrift*(*pbtEvent*)   // Drift detected and reported
27   **else**
28   *pbtLen* $\longleftarrow$ 0
29   *pbtEvent* $\longleftarrow$ *NIL*
30   *pbtWinSize* $\longleftarrow$ -1

(activity names) $\mathcal{L}$ is $|\mathcal{L}|^2$, we calculate $|\mathcal{L}|$ over both detection and reference windows, denoted by $|\mathcal{L}_{det}|$, $|\mathcal{L}_{ref}|$, respectively. By multiplying $max(|\mathcal{L}_{det}|, |\mathcal{L}_{ref}|)^2$ by 5 it is likely to have enough events in both windows to fulfil the requirement of the statistical test. Hence window size w is defined as $w = max(|\mathcal{L}_{det}|, |\mathcal{L}_{ref}|)^2 \cdot 5$.

The expansion and the shrinkage of the windows is performed recursively. This is because each time the windows are, for example, expanded there may be a need to expand the windows again due to changes in $|\mathcal{L}_{det}|$ and/or $|\mathcal{L}_{ref}|$. It is worth mentioning that our adaptive window is not dependent on the initial window size, since starting from any initial value the window sizes converge to the length needed to fulfil the requirement of the statistical test. The maximum size each window could grow to is the length of the event buffer divided by two.

It is worth mentioning that in the unlikely extreme scenario where the overlapping between traces is to the extent that each event within a window comes from a distinct trace, data streaming techniques with a gradual forgetting strategy [9] should be used.

Time complexity. Each time a new event is received from the stream, we first extract the α^+ relations in each sliding window and count their frequencies, and then perform the G-test of independence. The worst-case complexity of computing the α^+ relations is quadratic in the cardinality of the label set, i.e. $O(|\mathcal{L}|^2)$. Given a contingency matrix of maximum size $2 \times |\mathcal{L}|^2$, the complexity of the G-test is $O(|\mathcal{L}|^2)$. Since the two mentioned operations have the same complexity and are executed in a sequence, the complexity of our method is $O(|\mathcal{L}|^2)$ for every new event read from the stream.

4   Evaluation on Synthetic Logs

We implemented the proposed method as a plug-in, namely *ProDrift 2.0*,[3] and used this tool to assess the goodness of our method in terms of accuracy and scalability in a variety of settings. The tool can read a continuous stream of events or an event log replayed as an event stream. In the rest of this section we discuss the design of the experiments, the datasets used, the impact that oscillation filter and inter-drift distance have on our method, and conclude by comparing our method with the method in [5].

4.1   Evaluation Design

To evaluate the effectiveness of our method, we created a variety of synthetic logs with different configurations, and then replayed these logs as event streams. We first modeled a base business process using CPN tools and then used this model to generate the logs.[4] The model features 28 different activities, combined with different intertwined structural patterns: three XOR structures, four AND structures, two loops of length two, and one loop of length four. We built this model in a way that the resulting log is highly variable. To produce logs that include drifts, we then injected different types of control-flow changes into the base CPN model.

We applied in turn one out of twelve *simple change patterns* [6] to the base model. These patterns, summarized in Table 1, describe different change operations commonly occurring in business process models, such as adding/removing a model fragment, putting a model fragment in a loop, swapping two fragments,

---

[3] Available at http://apromore.org/platform/tools.

[4] http://cpntools.org.

or parallelizing two sequential fragments. Similarly to our previous work [5], we organized the simple changes into three categories: Insertion ("I"), Resequentialization ("R") and Optionalization ("O") (cf. Table 1). These categories make six possible *composite change patterns* ("IOR", "IRO", "OIR", "ORI", "RIO", and "ROI") by nesting the simple patterns within each other. For example, the composite pattern "ROI" can be obtained by first adding a new activity ("I"), then making this activity parallel to an existing activity ("O") and finally by putting the whole parallel block into a loop structure ("R").

Each of these change patterns were applied locally on the base model in such a way that it is possible during log replay to choose between the base model execution path and the altered one. For instance, if the applied change pattern was to replace a process fragment (*rp*), the CPN model would have a branching point, called *drift toggle*, right before this fragment, that allows the execution to follow either the initial model fragment or the new process fragment. A drift is injected by switching the toggle on or off. In this way, we can generate intra-trace drifts. For instance, if the toggle is switched on when trace #500 starts, the traces that started before that trace and have not yet reached the branching point, will follow the new process behavior, thus exhibiting the change. These traces will therefore have an intra-trace drift. In the remainder, whenever we say that a drift has been injected at a given trace number (after a given number of traces) it means that the drift toggle has been switched on at the first event of that given trace number (resp. after that given number of traces have started).

Finally, in order to vary the distance between drifts, for each change pattern we generated three logs of 2,500, 5,000 and 10,000 traces, and injected drifts by switching the drift toggle on and off every 10% of the log. This led to an inter-drift distance of 250, 500 and 1,000 traces per change pattern, with 9 drifts per log. The position of an injected drift is given by the index of the first event

Table 1. Simple control-flow change patterns

Code	Simple change pattern	Category
re	Add/remove fragment	I
cf	Make two fragments conditional/sequential	R
lp	Make fragment loopable/non-loopable	O
pl	Make two fragments parallel/sequential	R
cb	Make fragment skippable/non-skippable	O
cm	Move fragment into/out of conditional branch	I
cd	Synchronize two fragments	R
cp	Duplicate fragment	I
pm	Move fragment into/out of parallel branch	I
rp	Substitute fragment	I
sw	Swap two fragments	I
fr	Change branching frequency	O

in the event stream, after the drift toggle has been switched on. These indexes are used as the true positives of our evaluation (the *gold standard*). Further, for each of the 6 composite change patterns, we created 3 possible combinations, by changing the type of pattern used. This led to 12 (simple patterns) + 18 (complex patterns) = 30 different variants of the CPN model times three inter-drift distances, resulting in a total of 90 logs.[5] All these logs exhibit a very high *trace*

---

[5] All the CPN models used for this simulation, the resulting synthetic logs, and the detailed evaluation results are available with the software distribution.

variability (80 % ± 2), measured as the ratio between the number of distinct traces and the number of total traces in the log. According to our analysis of real-life logs, this value is very indicative of logs of unpredictable processes, such as the one used in the second part of this evaluation.

To assess the scalability of our method for online drift detection, we measured the execution time per each new event read from the stream. To evaluate accuracy, we used F-score and mean delay. The *F-score* is computed as the harmonic mean of recall and precision, where recall measures the proportion of actual drifts that have been detected and precision measures the proportion of detected drifts that are correct. The *mean delay* [14] assesses the ability of the method to find drifts as early as possible in an event stream, and is measured as the number of events between the actual position of the drift and the end of the detection window.

4.2 Execution Times

We conducted all tests on an Intel i7 2.20 GHz with 16 GB RAM (64 bit), running Windows 7 and JVM 7 with standard heap space of 2 GB, and a stream buffer (*maxBufSize*) of 1 GB. The time required to update the α^+ relations and perform the G-test, ranges from a minimum of 10 ms to a maximum of 50 ms with an average of 14 ms. These results show that the method is suited for online drift detection, including scenarios where the inter-arrival time between events is in the order of milliseconds.

4.3 Impact of Oscillation Filter

In the first experiment, we measured the impact of the oscillation filter $\Phi(w)$ on F-score and mean delay, by varying its value from $w/4$ to w, where w is the window size. Figure 1 shows the obtained F-score and mean delay averaged over all change patterns. As expected, we observe that the F-score increases as the filter value grows and eventually plateaus when it reaches the sliding window size, by filtering out false positives. However, a larger filter value causes a much higher delay. On the other hand, while a smaller filter value leads to a smaller delay, it may induce our method to consider incidental changes as actual drifts, causing the F-score to drop, though this still remains above 0.9. As a tradeoff, for the remainder of this evaluation, we used $\Phi(w) = w/2$. With this parameter being set empirically, our method is completely automated, and no parameter setting is required from the user.

4.4 Inter-drift Distance

In the second experiment, we compared the F-score and mean delay obtained on logs of different inter-drift distances (250, 500 and 1,000), in order to assess the minimum distance that our method can handle. The results, averaged over all change patterns, indicate that the method performs similarly for the logs

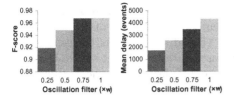
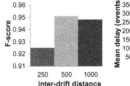

Fig. 1. F-score and mean delay using different oscillation filter values.

Fig. 2. F-score and mean delay using different inter-drift distances.

with 500 and 1,000 traces of inter-drift distance, achieving an F-score of about 0.95 and mean delay of about 2,500 (cf. Fig. 2). There is a slight decrease in the F-score and a notable increase in the mean delay when using a distance of 250 traces. In this case, the two sliding windows may contain two drifts as these are very close. In such cases, the method may miss one of the two drifts, leading to a lower recall. These cases however are not very common, as evidenced by the value of the F-score, which does not go below 0.92.

4.5 Comparison with Baseline per Process Change Pattern

In the third experiment, we evaluated the accuracy of our method in detecting each of the 18 change patterns. Figure 3 shows the F-score and mean delay for each change pattern in Table 1, averaged over the three log sizes, in comparison with those obtained with our previous run-based method [5] (the baseline).

Our method could find all the change patterns with a high F-score (above 0.9 in all but four cases), and a delay in the range of 2,500 events (approximately 100 traces), peaking at 4,000 events. When compared to the baseline method, our method outperforms the baseline in terms of F-score in the majority of change patterns (cf. Fig. 3(left)), while the baseline fails to detect half of the simple change patterns (*lp*, *pl*, *cb*, *cd*, *pm* and *sw*). Since in highly variable logs each distinct run is observed only a few times, the result of the statistical test is less reliable. Thus, in such logs, the run-based method can only find drift types whose occurrences replace the current set of runs with a considerably new set of runs, e.g. when removing a process fragment (pattern *re*). On the other hand, our current method considers events (as opposed to traces) and extracts fine-

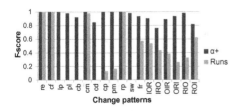
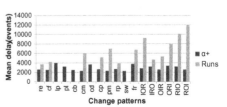

Fig. 3. F-score and mean delay per change pattern, obtained with our method vs. [5].

grained, yet abstract features that capture the process behavior into a few basic relations. Each drift type would be represented in a handful of α^+ relations, and any change in its frequency would be "echoed" through its correspondent basic relations, making it easier for the statistical test to detect such a change. Moreover, our method could always detect the drift faster than the baseline (cf. Fig. 3(right)) as it does not need to wait until a trace is completed to consider it as an input for the statistical test.

4.6   Comparison with Baseline over Different Log Variability Rates

In this last experiment with artificial logs, we evaluated our method in comparison with the baseline, when changing the variability rate of the log. As said before, the trace variability of a log is the ratio between distinct traces and the total number of traces. It varies from close to 0 %, where all traces are the same, to 100 %, where every trace is distinct. Similarly, we define the *run variability* as the ratio between distinct runs and the total number of runs. Depending on the concurrency oracle used, a high trace variability does not necessarily imply a high run variability. On the other hand, a high run variability always implies an equal or higher trace variability. For instance, a log with 50 % trace variability results in a run variability of 10 % (i.e. on average each run is repeated 10 times). This is due to the aggregation of traces into runs based on the concurrency oracle. The baseline method performs relatively well with a log with 10 % run variability. Thus, we studied how F-score and mean delay vary as we increase the run variability of a log.

For this purpose, we generated a new set of synthetic logs as described in Sect. 4.1 with different run variability rates, achieved by varying the loopback branching probability in the CPN model. For each run variability rate and change pattern, we generated logs of 10,000 traces. The results of this evaluation are reported in Fig. 4.

As the variability of the log increases, the baseline method's accuracy drops significantly. This is because the statistical test adopted by this method is inadequate when the number of distinct runs is large, as their frequency will be low. In contrast, capturing the process behavior at a lower level of abstraction, as done by the $\alpha+$ relations, as opposed to runs, leads to much higher frequencies in the contingency table of the statistical test, ensuring its reliability.

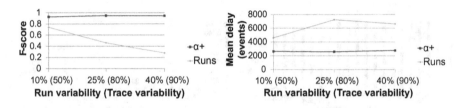

Fig. 4. F-score and mean delay per log variability, obtained with our method vs. [5].

This property is valid regardless of the variability of the log which explains the steady performance of our method.

5 Evaluation on Real-Life Log

In addition to the experiments with artificial logs, we evaluated out method on the BPI Challenge (BPIC) 2011 log, and compared the results with those obtained by the baseline.[6] This log records patient treatments in the Gynaecology department of a Dutch academic hospital. It contains 150,291 events in over 1,143 traces, of which 981 are distinct, and 623 labels. We first filtered the noise from this event log, using an offline noise filter [15], which basically removes infrequent activities.[7] This operation reduced the number of traces to 1,121, of which 798 are distinct, and the number of labels to 42, resulting in the same trace and run variability of 71 %.

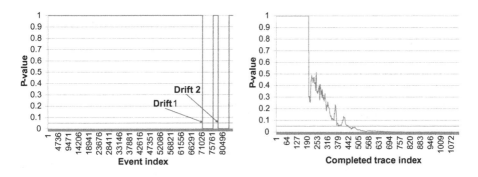

Fig. 5. P-value in our method (left) and in the baseline (right) for the BPIC 2011 log.

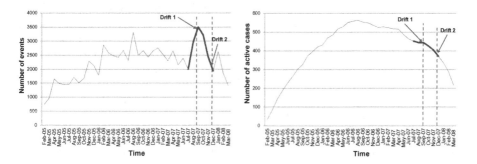

Fig. 6. Number of events (left) and active cases per month (right) in the BPIC 2011 log.

We applied our method on the stream of events obtained by replaying the filtered log. The average execution time for each new event in the stream was 44 ms. As shown in Fig. 5(left), two drifts were detected at the event indexes of 71,321 and 78,541, corresponding to the dates 6/9/2007 and 29/11/2007 respectively. The baseline could not detect any drift as the p-value quickly dropped and remained under the threshold, as shown in Fig. 5(right).

In order to validate the results, we profiled the number of events per month, shown in Fig. 6(left). The plot exhibits a sharp and consistent increase in the number of events between July and Sept. 2007 followed by a sharp and consistent decrease between Sept. and Dec. 2007. We investigated the log and found that the frequencies of five activities do increase and then decrease notably over the period in question. Moreover, the number of active cases per month (cf. Fig. 6(right)) decreases gradually after August 2006. Thus, this variation in the number of events cannot be explained because of new cases. Rather, this phenomenon could be the result of some rework in the business process. A rework may manifest itself with looping behavior and/or duplicate activities, which are change patterns our method is able to detect.

In conclusion, while these observations support the hypothesis of the presence of two drifts in the log, the results should be validated with domain experts.

6   Conclusion

We presented a fully automated method for online detection of business process drifts from event streams. The method relies on a statistical test over distributions of behavioral relations observed in two adjacent windows sliding along the event stream. We proposed an adaptive window technique in order to automatically adjust the sliding windows size, striking a good tradeoff between accuracy and detection delay.

We evaluated our method against different degrees of log variability and varying inter-drift distance, by injecting various change patterns into synthetic logs. The results showed that the method is able to scale up to online settings and detect drifts very accurately, while outperforming a state-of-the-art baseline for all the change patterns. A second evaluation on a healthcare log with very high variability showed that our method could detect two drifts that were supported by observations from the log.

In future we plan to empirically evaluate our technique with domain experts. Moreover, we plan to work on drift characterization in order to provide process stakeholders with relevant explanations on the detected drifts. A possible direction to tackle this problem is to apply the log delta analysis technique in [17] in order to retrieve diagnostics of the behavioral differences between the pre-drift and the post-drift sub-streams. Another avenue for future work is to study the interplay between changes in the process control flow and changes in other process perspectives, such as in the resources behavior or data involved in the execution of the process. In this respect, a starting point is to look at the work in [18], which analyses the dynamics of human resource behavior as observed from event logs.

Acknowledgments. This research is partly funded by the Australian Research Council (grant DP150103356).

References

1. Carmona, J., Gavaldà, R.: Online techniques for dealing with concept drift in process mining. In: Hollmén, J., Klawonn, F., Tucker, A. (eds.) IDA 2012. LNCS, vol. 7619, pp. 90–102. Springer, Heidelberg (2012). doi:10.1007/978-3-642-34156-4_10
2. Accorsi, R., Stocker, T.: Discovering workflow changes with time-based trace clustering. In: Aberer, K., Damiani, E., Dillon, T. (eds.) SIMPDA 2011. LNBIP, vol. 116, pp. 154–168. Springer, Heidelberg (2012)
3. Bose, R.P.J.C., van der Aalst, W.M.P., Zliobaite, I., Pechenizkiy, M.: Dealing with concept drifts in process mining. IEEE Trans. NNLS **25**(1), 154–171 (2014)
4. Martjushev, J., Bose, R.P.J.C., Aalst, W.M.P.: Change point detection and dealing with gradual and multi-order dynamics in process mining. In: Matulevičius, R., Dumas, M. (eds.) BIR 2015. LNBIP, vol. 229, pp. 161–178. Springer, Heidelberg (2015). doi:10.1007/978-3-319-21915-8_11
5. Maaradji, A., Dumas, M., Rosa, M., Ostovar, A.: Fast and accurate business process drift detection. In: Motahari-Nezhad, H.R., Recker, J., Weidlich, M. (eds.) BPM 2015. LNCS, vol. 9253, pp. 406–422. Springer, Heidelberg (2015). doi:10.1007/978-3-319-23063-4_27
6. Weber, B., Reichert, M., Rinderle-Ma, S.: Change patterns and change support features-enhancing flexibility in process-aware information systems. DKE **66**(3), 438–466 (2008)
7. Burattin, A., Cimitile, M., Maggi, F.M., Sperduti, A.: Online discovery of declarative process models from event streams. IEEE Trans. Serv. Comput. **8**, 833–846 (2015)
8. Burattin, A., Sperduti, A., van der Aalst, W.M.P.: Control-flow discovery from event streams. In: IEEE Congress on Evolutionary Computation (CEC), pp. 2420–2427. IEEE (2014)
9. Gama, J., Žliobaitė, I., Bifet, A., Pechenizkiy, M., Bouchachia, A.: A survey on concept drift adaptation. ACM Comput. Surv. (CSUR) **46**(4), 1–37 (2014)
10. Leemans, S.J.J., Fahland, D., Aalst, W.M.P.: Discovering block-structured process models from event logs - a constructive approach. In: Colom, J.-M., Desel, J. (eds.) PETRI NETS 2013. LNCS, vol. 7927, pp. 311–329. Springer, Heidelberg (2013). doi:10.1007/978-3-642-38697-8_17
11. de Medeiros, A.A., van Dongen, B.F., Van der Aalst, W.M.P., Weijters, A.: Process mining: extending the α-algorithm to mine short loops. Technical report, BETA Working Paper Series, WP 113, Eindhoven University of Technology, Eindhoven (2004)
12. Harremoës, P., Tusnády, G.: Information divergence is more χ^2-distributed than the χ^2-statistics. In: IEEE ISIT, pp. 533–537 (2012)
13. Nuzzo, R.: Statistical errors. Nature **506**(13), 150–152 (2014)
14. Ho, S.S.: A martingale framework for concept change detection in time-varying data streams. In: Proceedings of ICML, pp. 321–327. ACM (2005)
15. Conforti, R., La Rosa, M., ter Hofstede, A.H.: Noise filtering of process execution logs based on outliers detection (2015)

16. Bifet, A., Gavaldà, R.: Kalman filters and adaptive windows for learning in data streams. In: Todorovski, L., Lavrač, N., Jantke, K.P. (eds.) DS 2006. LNCS (LNAI), vol. 4265, pp. 29–40. Springer, Heidelberg (2006). doi:10.1007/11893318_7

17. Beest, N.R.T.P., Dumas, M., García-Bañuelos, L., Rosa, M.: Log delta analysis: interpretable differencing of business process event logs. In: Motahari-Nezhad, H.R., Recker, J., Weidlich, M. (eds.) BPM 2015. LNCS, vol. 9253, pp. 386–405. Springer, Heidelberg (2015). doi:10.1007/978-3-319-23063-4_26

18. Pika, A., Wynn, M.T., Fidge, C.J., Hofstede, A.H.M., Leyer, M., Aalst, W.M.P.: An extensible framework for analysing resource behaviour using event logs. In: Jarke, M., Mylopoulos, J., Quix, C., Rolland, C., Manolopoulos, Y., Mouratidis, H., Horkoff, J. (eds.) CAiSE 2014. LNCS, vol. 8484, pp. 564–579. Springer, Heidelberg (2014). doi:10.1007/978-3-319-07881-6_38

Modeling Structured and Unstructured Processes: An Empirical Evaluation

Evellin Cardoso[1](✉), Katsiaryna Labunets[1], Fabiano Dalpiaz[2],
John Mylopoulos[1], and Paolo Giorgini[1]

[1] University of Trento, Trento, Italy
{evellin.souzacardoso,katsiaryna.labunets,john.mylopoulos,
paolo.giorgini}@unitn.it
[2] Utrecht University, Utrecht, The Netherlands
f.dalpiaz@uu.nl

Abstract. Imperative process languages, such as BPMN, describe business processes in terms of collections of activities and control flows among them. Despite their popularity, such languages remain useful mostly for structured processes whose flow of activities is well-known and does not vary greatly. For unstructured processes, on the other hand, the verdict is still out as to the best way to represent them. In our previous work, we have proposed Azzurra, a specification language for business processes founded on social concepts, such as roles, agents and commitments. In this paper, we present the results of an experiment that comparatively evaluates Azzurra and BPMN in terms of their ability to represent structured and unstructured processes. Our results suggest that Azzurra is better suited than BPMN for unstructured business processes.

Keywords: Azzurra · BPMN · Specification languages · Empirical evaluation

1 Introduction

Business Process Management (BPM) is founded on the premise that process behavior has to be explicitly modeled, analyzed and managed along with software as a means for improving enterprise operations. In order to support such models, many process modeling languages have been proposed, including BPMN, EPCs, BPEL and more. Such languages are predominantly activity-centered [5,12], in the sense that their modeling primitives [5] are founded on the notion of activity. Within this paradigm, imperative models express business processes as a set of activities inter-connected by control flow primitives inspired by Petri nets, finite state machines, and other system modeling frameworks dating back to the 50 s and 60 s. The distinguishing feature of imperative models is that they explicitly capture all possible execution paths for a business process.

Despite the popularity of activity-centered, imperative models—as evidenced by large industrial and academic adoption of the BPMN modeling language as

© Springer International Publishing AG 2016
I. Comyn-Wattiau et al. (Eds.): ER 2016, LNCS 9974, pp. 347–361, 2016.
DOI: 10.1007/978-3-319-46397-1_27

de facto standard for process representation [10,16]—activity-centered languages remain especially useful for routine, structured processes defined in terms of a specific set of behaviors. For unstructured processes, however, execution order is context-dependent and even the activities needed are unclear and/or undefined at design time. For such processes, as also pointed out by van der Aalst [1], activity-centered languages are an inflexible solution as they demand the identification of activities and control flows for the construction of a process model.

In our previous research, we have introduced Azzurra [6], a specification language for business processes that shifts the focus of representation from activities to *social commitments*. Formally, a commitment $C(x,y,p,q)$ is a promise with contractual validity made by an agent x (debtor) to another agent y (creditor) that, if proposition p is brought about (antecedent), then proposition q will be brought about (consequent). By introducing correctness criteria for the enactment of a process, Azzurra abstracts away from specific activities (operationalizations) for achieving a goal; rather, Azzurra focuses on the outcomes of a process through the notion of a commitment's consequent. The elements of Azzurra suggest the hypothesis that it is more appropriate than its imperative cousins for unstructured processes, as they require more flexible specifications. To confirm/deny this hypothesis, we have conducted a preliminary study using scenarios that have been elaborated in [6], hoping to gain insights on the suitability of Azzurra for modeling unstructured processes.

The contribution of this paper is to report the results of a preliminary experiment performed with master's students at the University of Trento, to examine the suitability of Azzurra for unstructured processes. To this purpose, we designed and enacted an experiment to test two propositions about quality of structured and unstructured processes models represented in both Azzurra and BPMN. Here, model quality is defined in terms of the metrics of *precision* and *coverage* used in Ontology Engineering for evaluating the quality of ontologies [19]. Our results suggest that Azzura is less usable than BPMN in the sense that the social concepts it is founded on are less familiar to master's-level students in Computer Science. On the other hand, Azzura leads to better models, where "better" is defined in terms of the metrics of precision and coverage.

The rest of the paper is structured as follows: Sect. 2 provides the research baseline for our work, including classifications of processes from the BPM literature, together with a sketchy overview of current process modeling languages. Section 3 describes the experimental process, covering scope, plan, execution, analysis and interpretation of the results, including a general discussion of the findings. Finally, Sect. 4 summarizes the results and outlines future work.

2   Baseline

We discuss classifications for business processes in Sect. 2.1, and we briefly review the most prominent business process modeling languages in Sect. 2.2.

2.1 The Spectrum of Work in BPM

There exist several classifications for business processes according to their characteristics [2,8]. A common classification scheme considers the level of structuring or predictability, thus dividing business processes into a spectrum of work of four types (see Fig. 1) [2,4,8]. The level of structuring and predictability basically considers the extent to which the behavior of a given business process is predictable at modeling time:

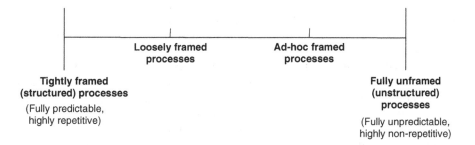

Fig. 1. The spectrum of work in BPM adapted from [17]

In the leftmost extreme of the spectrum, a *tightly framed (or structured) process* comprehends those processes whose execution of activities consistently follows a predefined process model [2,8]. Since a formal representation of these processes can be easily described prior to their execution, tightly framed processes are characterized as fully predictable and repetitive and after their design-time description they can be repeatedly instantiated at runtime. Examples of this category are production and administrative processes [7] and as well as bank transactions that are executed in an exact sequence to comply with legal norms.

Even though tightly framed processes usually have a predictable behavior, a certain degree of unpredictability is expected due to the occurrence of exceptions and evolutions within the domain. Therefore, a *loosely framed process* corresponds to a process in which it is possible to represent the process behavior and a set of constraints a priori [2], such that the process model describes the "standard way of doing things" while requiring additions, removals or generation of alternative sequence of activities during runtime [7].

Differently from a tightly and loosely framed processes that can be described a priori by an explicit process model, the behavior of *ad-hoc framed process* cannot be determined in terms of a explicit process logic during design time due to a lack of domain knowledge or the complexity of task combinations. Instead, only structured fragments can be identified a priori and properly composed on a per-case basis, while process parts that are undefined or uncertain can only be specified and incorporated as the process evolves [7].

Finally, within the rightmost category of the spectrum, *fully unframed (or unstructured) processes* have sufficient variability in such way that no process description can be pre-defined at all [2,7]. As a result, process participants need to make decisions using their knowledge to create activities on demand. The creation of such activities is based on situation-specific parameters whose values are determined as the process execution proceeds. Besides choosing activities on demand, they also dynamically decide the execution order of such activities.

2.2   Process Modeling Languages

Although the disparities regarding the nature of process behavior in reality trigger process modeling languages to accommodate such diversity, contemporary techniques for process modeling are predominantly *activity-centered* [5,12], although over the past years an *artifact-centered* approach has also emerged [12].

The activity-centered paradigm elects the concept of *activity* as its first class modeling construct [5] in order to express business processes as a set of activities. Within activity-centered models, a plethora of conceptual languages like BPMN, BPEL, UML, EPCs represent business processes within an imperative (or procedural) paradigm that is basically founded on the notions of activities and a number of causal dependencies among such activities. The paradigm requires modelers to explicitly represent the causal activations of activities and therefore, all possible paths executed by the business process have to be also exhaustively enumerated during modeling time.

The rigidity imposed by the imperative paradigm triggered the development of (activity-centered) declarative languages. In this context, declarative workflows [1] have arisen as a more flexible alternative for the specification of business processes by enabling the representation of behavior in terms of minimal precedence constraints among activities. By default, all execution paths are allowed and prohibited execution paths are specified by constraints on the execution order between activities.

Unlike the activity-centered paradigm, the artifact-centered paradigm represents the states of artifacts (also denominated as data objects) that are used throughout the process and how these states are changed/updated by activities [17]. Further, the paradigm also complements the representation of processes in relation to declaratives languages as it focuses on a hybrid approach of the representation of data and activities that update such data objects.

Deviating from the current trends of process representation, we introduced the Azzurra [6] specification language for business processes that shifts the focus from activities and data objects to agents, roles, *social commitments* and protocols. In Azzurra, business processes are represented as protocols that are carried out by intentional agents and roles. Such agents and roles have expectations in relation to each other that are modeled in terms of *social commitments*. Formally speaking, a social commitment $C(x,y,p,q)$ is a promise with contractual validity made by an agent x (debtor) to another agent y (creditor) that, if proposition p is brought about (antecedent), then proposition q will be brought about (consequent). Commitments' consequents specify correctness criteria that have to be respected, rather than capturing how to achieve a determined business goal through a prescription of a number of steps (activities). This shift in the modeling paradigm opens up the possibility of providing more flexible specifications for business processes as it allows the participating agents to decide the best operationalizations to achieve the outcomes during runtime.

In light of the assumption that Azzurra provides a more flexible solution for the specification of business processes, we have performed a preliminary evaluation of the language by means of two scenarios in [6]. Both scenarios have been extracted from the BPM literature as representatives of business processes that require flexible specifications. More specifically, Scenario 1 (Fracture treatment) intended to compare Azzurra's representational features with the representational features of current modeling languages, namely procedural, declarative and data-centered approaches. The conclusion of such comparison led us to the realization that Azzurra focuses on different aspects of current modeling languages in order to represent business processes. As a consequence of that, our intuition rests on the realization that this shift of focus can better capture the features of unstructured business processes. Therefore, Scenario 2 (Transient Ischemic Attack (TIA) Clinical Guideline) has been chosen due to its unstructured nature to check this intuition that Azzurra better supports the representation of such kind of processes. In this context, we enumerated the domain representational needs of unstructured processes such as the absence of genuine activities to be executed as well as the lack of ordering constraints between such activities and compared both representations in Azzurra and BPMN of the TIA clinical guideline. A direct conclusion of such comparison indeed established that Azzurra is better than BPMN for unstructured processes.

With these insights at hand, in this paper we perform an experiment with students to check the validity of our insights regarding the suitability of Azzurra and BPMN for structured and unstructured processes. BPMN has been chosen for the comparison under consideration due to its wide acceptance and popularity as a standard for business processes representation [10,16]. More specifically, with this experiment, we want to acquire objective and statistically significant evidence regarding the suitability of Azzurra for unstructured processes. In order to perform the experiment, we elaborated the following propositions:

P1. Azzurra produces models of better quality than BPMN in the representation of unframed (unstructured) business processes;

P2. BPMN produces models of better quality than Azzurra in the representation of tightly framed (structured) business processes.

3 The Experiment Process

The design of our experiment has been conducted on the basis of guidelines for experimentation in software engineering [13,20]. According to such guidelines, the experiment process can be divided into five main activities depicted in Fig. 2.

Within the **Scoping** activity, the experiment is defined in terms of problem statement and goals, defining *why* the experiment is needed. According to the

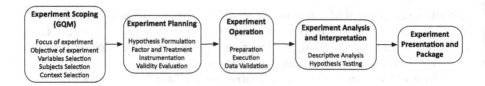

Fig. 2. The experimentation process according to [20]

Wöhlin's guidelines [20], the Goal, Question, Metric (GQM) template [3] comprehends a suitable instrument for defining the scope of a given experiment. Our GQM template is described in Sect. 3.1.

The **Planning** activity is the phase in which the foundation of the experiment is laid, defining *how* it is conducted. The steps conducted in the scope of our planning activity are described in Sect. 3.1.

The **Operation** activity encompasses the preparation of subjects and required material on which the experiment in executed (i.e., *objects*), the actual execution of the experiment as well as the collection of measurements (see Sect. 3.2). The **Analysis and Interpretation** activity focuses on qualitatively and quantitatively processing the outcomes of the experiment (Sect. 3.3 and Sect. 3.4). Finally, the results are presented in the course of the **Presentation and Package** (leading to the present paper).

3.1 Experiment Scoping and Planning

Our experiment starts by scoping its objectives using the GQM template depicted in Table 1:

Table 1. GQM for our experiment

Focus of the experiment: Analyze Azzurra specification language and compare it with the BPMN modeling language.
Objective of the experiment: Checking the adequacy of the Azzurra and BPMN languages for the representation of structured and unstructured business processes.
Variables selection: We compare Azzurra and BPMN modeling languages in terms of model quality.
Subject: From the point of view of M.Sc. students enrolled in classes of Organizational Information Systems.
Context of the experiment: M.Sc. students creating Azzurra and BPMN models.

In the following, the planning phase of our experiment required us to elaborate the *hypotheses* (together with the *independent* and *dependent variables*), *factors* and *treatments* applied to our experiment.

Hypothesis Formulation. As we intend to compare Azzurra and BPMN for structured and unstructured processes, we construct three null hypotheses, one for each factor and a third one for the interaction between the factors [20].

- **Null Hypothesis H_{0-1}:** There is no significant difference in model quality of Azzurra and BPMN modeling languages.
- **H_{a-1}:** There is significant difference in the model quality of Azzurra and BPMN modeling languages.
- **Null Hypothesis H_{0-2}:** There is no significant difference in model quality of structured and unstructured scenarios.
- **H_{a-2}:** There is significant difference in model quality of structured and unstructured scenarios.
- **Null Hypothesis H_3:** There are no significant interactions between the type of modeling language and types of business processes in terms of model quality.
- **H_{a-3}:** There are significant interactions between the type of modeling language and types of business processes in terms of model quality.

Note that our hypotheses are elaborated in terms of model quality (*dependent variable*). In order to select the metrics for measuring model quality in our evaluation, we get inspiration from the field of Ontology Engineering; more precisely, we use a formal evaluation framework [19] that defines the dimensions of *precision* and *coverage* to define the quality of a given ontology (model).

In [19], a conceptualization comprehends a set of conceptual relations about a certain portion of reality perceived by an agent, defining a set of intended models I_K. In this context, the role of an ontology is to provide a specification of such conceptualization, precisely capturing the intended models according to such conceptualization and excluding the non-intended ones. Considering that it is not always easy to find the right set of entities so that an ontology admits only the intended models [9], ontologies are considered only approximations of conceptualizations. Consequently, the formal framework of Staab et al. [19] proposes a schema for evaluating ontologies with respect to the degree of approximation they can provide to their respective conceptualizations. To evaluate such degree of approximation, the *precision* and *coverage* metrics are introduced and can be mathematically defined as:

$$P = \frac{|I_K \cap O_K|}{|O_K|} (precision) \quad C = \frac{|I_K \cap O_K|}{|I_K|} (coverage)$$

In Ontology Engineering, *precision* measures how much the represented models O_K are relevant according to the set of intended models I_K, while *coverage* measures how much of the intended models I_K are represented by the ontology O_K. We use analog reasoning for our evaluation of Azzurra and BPMN modeling languages. In our case, business processes are considered the target conceptualization that can be represented by two distinct ontologies, i.e., the Azzurra and BPMN modeling languages. Every business process has a natural language description that admits a number of execution paths (in our case, the set of intended models I_K corresponds to the set of intended execution paths $I_{execPath}$)

and specifications in BPMN and Azzurra provide representation of such execution paths ($R_{execPath}$). Therefore, *precision* measures how many paths which are represented in the model are correct in relation to the intended paths prescribed by the natural language description, while *coverage* measures how many paths provided in the natural language description are indeed captured in the model representation. In our case, *precision* and *coverage* are mathematically defined as follows:

$$P = \frac{|I_{execPath} \cap R_{execPath}|}{|R_{execPath}|} (precision) \quad C = \frac{|I_{execPath} \cap R_{execPath}|}{|I_{execPath}|} (coverage)$$

Factor and Treatment. As the aim of our experiment is to investigate whether the Azzurra modeling language has a more faithful representation of unstructured business process than the BPMN modeling language, we have two factors: factor A is the type business process modeling language (whose treatments are Azzurra and BPMN modeling languages) and factor B is the type of business process under consideration (whose treatments are unstructured and structured business processes). Factors and treatments are depicted in Table 2:

Table 2. Factors and treatments applied in our experiment

BP Type (Factor B) \ Language Type (Factor A)	Azzurra	BPMN
Structured		
Unstructured		

Instrumentation. Participants used a free online modeling tool[1] for the elaboration of BPMN 2.0 models and a plug-in[2] developed at University of Trento for the elaboration of Azzurra models. In the end of the experiment, they provided the source of Azzurra and BPMN models for later evaluation of the results.

Validity evaluation. We enumerate the main threats to the validity of our experiment using the Wohlin's categorization [20]:

Threats to construct validity. The threats in this category are: (i) a major threat to construct validity is that the chosen business processes may not be representative samples for the structured and unstructured types of business processes. To mitigate this issue, we have chosen already consolidated scenarios within the BPM literature as representatives from structured and unstructured processes; (ii) furthermore, the domain knowledge involved in the description of the scenarios may entail some difficulty during the modeling process; (iii) the fact that

---

[1] www.lucidchart.com.

[2] https://trinity.disi.unitn.it/azura/azura/.

BPMN is an imperative language, while Azzurra is declarative may also entail additional difficulties as there is some evidence that imperative languages are more understandable than declarative ones [15]; (iv) hypothesis guessing may also represent a threat as subjects can be conditioned by the results they are providing. We mitigated this threat by carefully formulating questions on the basis of correct usage and preference of modeling languages.

Threats to external validity. Here, our largest threat is the usage of students as subjects in our experiment. Further, they had prior training in BPMN and UML activity diagrams during the course lectures. To mitigate these issues and make their background more uniform, we have provided preliminary training in both Azzurra and BPMN languages by means of one example. In order to encourage subjects to participate, they could earn at most one point in the overall course grade on the basis of the correct usage of languages constructs.

Threats to conclusion validity. The two threats to conclusion validity are the low number and homogeneity of the samples (students) that may impact our ability to reveal patterns in the data. Besides that, the first author of this paper evaluated the number of admissible execution paths for each scenario, together with their respective representations in Azzurra and BPMN.

Threats to internal validity. This type of validity is threatened by the effect of order in which the subjects apply the treatments (structured and unstructured) as students may learn the content of natural languages descriptions, and the second models are easier to produce. To mitigate the effect of order, the order is assigned randomly to each subject. By having the same number of subjects starting with the first treatment as with the second, the design is balanced [20].

3.2   Experiment Operation

Preparation. We continue following the same rationale of evaluation through modeling scenarios. In particular, we have used same business process from Scenario 2 used in [6] (i.e., the TIA clinical guideline) as a representative of unstructured business process and the X-Ray Medical Order (extracted from [17]) as the representative of structured business process. The selection of both scenarios as representatives of unstructured and structured business process has been supported by BPM literature that positions clinical guidelines as unstructured processes [7] and the X-Ray Medical Order as a structured process [17].

Next, a natural language description[3] has been extracted from literature in order to be applied on the subjects. Further, the corresponding Azzurra and BPMN models have been built in advance for each scenario by the first author with the purpose of ensuring that process models to be built in each scenario indeed covered the core concepts of both modeling languages.

---

[3] Scenario descriptions, experimental results and data analysis are available at https://www.dropbox.com/s/8qlwd5svqbt3hmw/Empirical%20evaluation.zip?dl=0.

Experiment execution. The experiment has been conducted in July 2015 with master's students in Computer Science in the scope of the Organizational Information Systems Course at University of Trento. In total, 17 subjects participated in this empirical test. The experiment has been structured in different parts:

- **Introduction Phase (15 min)**: General instructions about the experiment and introduction to Azzurra modeling language and modeling tool together with a presentation about BPMN. It is also important to note that students had prior contact with BPMN along the course lectures;
- **Experiment phase (40 min, i.e., 20 min for each language)**: Group 1 models the structured scenario using Azzurra and BPMN, whereas group 2 models the unstructured scenario using Azzurra and BPMN;
- **Questionnaire phase (15 min)**: General questions concerning the background of the subject and questions regarding the elaboration of models relative to scenario 1 and 2.

Data validation. The obtained data were checked for consistency and plausibility. We discarded the inputs from two students due to incompleteness; thus, we could employ data from 15 students in the data analysis.

3.3   Experiment Analysis and Interpretation

To report experimental results, Table 3 shows mean, median and standard deviation values for precision and coverage by language and process type:

Table 3. Precision and coverage by language and process type

		Azzurra			BPMN		
		Mean	Median	Std. dev.	Mean	Median	Std. dev.
Unstructured	Precision	1.00	1.00	0.00	1.00	1.00	0.00
	Coverage	0.89	1	0.18	0.34	0.36	0.07
Structured	Precision	1.00	1.00	0.00	0.95	1.00	0.13
	Coverage	0.82	0.75	0.19	0.82	0.75	0.19
Overall	Precision	1.00	1.00	0.00	0.97	1.00	0.09
	Coverage	0.85	1.00	0.18	0.60	0.50	0.28

We conducted statistical analysis to test whether the null hypothesis H_0 can be rejected, thereby allowing us to draw conclusions about our studied phenomenon: the modeling of structured and unstructured business processes.

For the selection of the statistical tests, we followed the guidelines prescribed by Harvey [11, Chap. 37]. As the participants of our experiment applied both methods, to test H_{0-1}, we can use paired t-test or its non-parametric analog,

Wilcoxon test. However, the participants did not switch scenario type and, therefore, to test H_{0-2} we use unpaired t-test or its non-parametric analog, Mann-Whitney (MW) test. Finally, to test H_{0-3} we need to investigate the difference between the combination of two factors (type of language and type of process), which requires ANOVA test or its non-parametric analog, Kruskal-Wallis (KW) test [20]. We checked the normality of data by Shapiro-Wilk test which returned p-$value = 0.0013$ for coverage and p-$value = 6.8 \cdot 10^{-11}$ for precision. Thus, we used non-parametric tests for all three hypothesis. Further, for all statistical tests we use a threshold of 5 % for α, the probability of committing Type-I error [20].

Null Hypothesis H_{0-1} (Azzurra vs. BPMN): The results of the Wilcoxon test revealed a statistically significant difference between two modeling languages with respect to coverage (test results: $W = 7$, $Z = 2.09$, p-$value = 0.04$, Cohen's $d = 1.06$) and no significant difference in precision (p-$value = 0.32$). The power of the Wilcoxon test for coverage is 0.72. Therefore, we cannot reject the null hypothesis both for coverage and precision. However, to achieve 80 % power for coverage we would need a sample size of 16 participants, while we had 13 participants. For Azzurra, the overall mean coverage is 0.85, whereas for BPMN the overall mean coverage is 0.6. As coverage describes the percentage of the intended interpretations (according to the natural language description) that are indeed captured by the model, a mean coverage of 0.85 means that 85 % of all intended paths are captured in the model, whereas 15 % of them are not. In fact, this is a reasonable advantage from Azzurra, once the language specifies process paths in terms of correctness criteria, whereas BPMN requires a more verbose style of specification, demanding exhaustive specification of all potential process paths. It is natural that some intended process paths are not captured in the BPMN representation. Observe also the significant difference in terms of coverage between Azzurra (0.893) and BPMN (0.345) for unstructured processes. As unstructured processes potentially have a large number of process paths, this difference in terms of coverage between both languages becomes even more evident for such kind of processes.

Null Hypothesis H_{0-2} (Structured vs. Unstructured): To test this hypothesis, we should use MW test which assumes the equality of variance. However, the Levene's test for homogeneity of variance returned p-$value = 0.37$ for precision and p-$value = 0.04$ for coverage. Therefore, we cannot rely on the results of the MW test for coverage. To mitigate this issue, we cross-validate the results of MW test with KW test which does not require equal variance. The MW test results did not reveal significant difference between two process types both for precision (p-$value = 0.35$) and coverage (p-$value = 0.11$). The KW test returned p-$value = 0.11$ for coverage, which supported the results of MW test. In order to achieve statistically significant results for coverage with 80 % power we would need a sample size of 54 participants. The results show that the process type did not affect the performance of the participants. The null hypothesis H_{0-2} cannot be rejected for any of the variables.

Null Hypothesis H_{0-3} (Language and Process type): The results of KW test revealed a statiscally significant effect of the combination of language and process type on coverage ($\chi^2(3) = 15$, *p-value* $= 0.002$) and no effect on precision (*p-value* $= 0.44$). Therefore, the null hypothesis H_{0-3} can be rejected only for coverage. A post-hoc test using MW test with Holm correction showed the significant differences between coverage of the results produced by participants who used BPMN on unstructured process and other participants who used BPMN on structured process (MW test results: *p-value* $= 0.002$, Cohen's d $= 3.23$) or Azzurra on unstructured (*p-value* $= 0.003$, Cohen's d $= 4.02$) and structured process (*p-value* $= 0.002$, Cohen's d $= 3.23$). It means that there is a significant difference in terms of coverage between Azzurra and BPMN for unstructured processes, as described above, whereas for structured processes both Azzurra and BPMN have equal performance in terms of coverage.

3.4 Discussion

Our aim is to investigate the suitability of the Azzurra language for representing unstructured processes and its superiority in terms of model quality in relation to BPMN. In our approach, model quality is measured in terms of *precision* and *coverage*, two metrics extracted from the field of Ontology Engineering for the evaluation of ontology quality. Regarding our propositions introduced in Sect. 2.2, our findings suggest that:

P1. The Azzurra modeling language is significantly better than BPMN in terms of coverage for the representation of unstructured processes, but the power of the test is not enough to completely reject null hypothesis H_{0-1} (see the discussion of null hypothesis H_{0-1}).

P2. No definite conclusion can be drawn, due to the absence of statistically significant difference between the two modeling languages with respect to precision (see the discussion of null hypothesis H_{0-1}).

The superiority of Azzurra over BPMN in terms of coverage for unstructured processes can be explained by the representational style of Azzurra and BPMN: Azzurra requires correctness criteria to be specified as commitment's consequents, whereas BPMN imposes the need of exhaustive specification of all activities and paths. First, if we consider the advantage of Azzurra over BPMN in terms of coverage—therefore measuring how many intended paths are indeed captured by its corresponding representation—, an Azzurra representation "covers" more paths than its counterpart in BPMN, as Azzurra's correctness criteria captures all possible paths in an implicit way as opposed to explicitly capturing all paths. Therefore, there is a higher chance that some paths are indeed forgotten during the modeling process in a BPMN representation.

Second, considering Azzurra's suitability for unstructured processes, these processes are characterized by an "on-the-fly" creation of activities, lacking also a pre-defined execution order among activities. Therefore, their textual description allows several interpretations regarding the potential paths to be captured (e.g., for three activities A, B and C, it is possible to capture 3! paths). Azzurra's features can cope better than BPMN with both aspects of unstructured processes:

via commitments, modelers can specify obligations to be fulfilled and participants can dynamically select which activities to perform to fulfill such obligations at runtime. Further, a commitment-based representation also allows one to specify lack of structure necessary for unstructured processes, refraining from capturing a specific order to fulfill them. Differently, as we have noticed during the evaluation of experiment's results, students commonly captured only the most trivial sequence of activities in BPMN, missing all the other possible interpretations according to the natural language description.

Our experimental evaluation considered the metrics of *precision* and *coverage* to determine the quality of models representations in terms of domain faithfulness and language expressiveness, rather than the focusing on the modelers' perception. To overcome this issue, we distributed a questionnaire among participants. In this survey, there is significant preference of BPMN in relation to Azzurra. This answer should be interpreted with care for two reasons. First, the questionnaire revealed prior process modeling experience of subjects in BPMN both in academia and industry. Second, imperative process modeling has its roots in imperative and declarative computer programming languages which have been used in computer science since the 50s and 60s. Third, there is evidence that imperative languages are more understandable than declaratives ones [15]. As familiarity is a very important aspect for the usability of modeling languages, preference of BPMN seems to natural in this case.

Although we effectively conducted the experiment with a homogeneous group of master's students, some limitations must be considered. In particular, the relatively low number of experimental subjects constitutes a limitation in terms of statistically significance of our conclusions. Moreover, while BPMN models have been produced on the basis of a professional tool, the usage of a prototypical implementation of the Azzurra modeling tool may be also considered a disadvantage in relation to its respective counterpart in BPMN models.

4   Conclusion

In this paper, we empirically evaluated the Azzurra and BPMN modeling languages for the representation of structured and unstructured processes in terms *precision* and *coverage*, two metrics used in the evaluation of ontology quality in the field of Ontology Engineering. Our empirical results indicate that Azzurra can be considered superior to BPMN for the representation of unstructured processes. However, no further claims can be stated concerning the superiority of BPMN over Azzurra for the representation of structured processes.

A very natural direction for our future work is the replication of our experiment. In that respect, we first envision an experimental design that encompasses a higher number os students in order to be able to validate some of our hypothesis (e.g., the difference of structured and unstructured processes). Alternatively, we would be also interested in repeating the similar experiment with BPM experts within an industrial setting. The adoption of industrial experts would allow us to not only gain more statistical power in our analysis, but could be also instrumental for acquiring insights regarding the acceptance of Azzurra within the industry. A second future work direction for our work concerns the elaboration of modeling patterns and guidelines for process representation using Azzurra, similarly as the existent ones for BPMN [14]. Finally, the usage of the same dataset with different metrics for the evaluation of process models (as the one proposed in [18]) could yield us different conclusions regarding the suitability of both process languages.

Acknowledgement. The research leading this paper has been funded by ERC advanced grant 267856 "Lucretius: Foundations for Software Evolution", unfolding during the period of April 2011 – March 2016. It has also received fundings from the SESAR Joint Undertaking under grant agreement No 699306 under the European Union's Horizon 2020 research and innovation program.

References

1. van der Aalst, W.M.P., Pesic, M., Schonenberg, H.: Declarative workflows: balancing between flexibility and support. Comput. Sci. Res. Dev. **23**(2), 99–113 (2009)
2. van der Aalst, W.M.P.: Business process management: a comprehensive survey. In: ISRN Software Engineering (2013)
3. Basili, V.R., Caldiera, G., Rombach, H.D.: The goal question metric approach. In: Encyclopedia of Software Engineering. Wiley, New York (1994)
4. vom Brocke, J., Rosemann, M.: Handbook on Business Process Management 1: Introduction, Methods, and Information Systems (2010)
5. Cohn, D., Hull, R.: Business artifacts: a data-centric approach to modeling business operations and processes. IEEE Data Eng. Bull. **32**(3), 3–9 (2009)
6. Dalpiaz, F., Cardoso, E., Canobbio, G., Giorgini, P., Mylopoulos, J.: Social specifications of business processes with Azzurra. In: Proceedings of the International Conference on Research Challenges in Information Science, pp. 7–18 (2015)
7. Di Ciccio, C., Marrella, A., Russo, A.: Knowledge-intensive processes: characteristics, requirements and analysis of contemporary approaches. J. Data Semant. **4**(1), 29–57 (2015)
8. Dumas, M., van der Aalst, W.M., ter Hofstede, A.H.: Process-Aware Information Systems: Bridging People and Software Through Process Technology. Wiley, New York (2005)
9. Guarino, N.: Formal ontology and information systems. In: Proceedings of Formal Ontology in Information Systems (1998)
10. Harmon, P.: The State of Business Process Management 2016. Technical report, BPTrends (2016)
11. Harvey, M.: Intuitive Biostatistics. Oxford University Press, New York (1995)
12. Hull, R.: Artifact-centric business process models: brief survey of research results and challenges. In: Meersman, R., Tari, Z. (eds.) OTM 2008. LNCS, vol. 5332, pp. 1152–1163. Springer, Heidelberg (2008). doi:10.1007/978-3-540-88873-4_17
13. Juristo, N., Moreno, A.M.: Basics of Software Engineering Experimentation. Springer, New York (2010)
14. Mendling, J., Reijers, H.A., van der Aalst, W.M.P.: Seven process modeling guidelines (7PMG). Inf. Softw. Technol. **52**(2), 127–136 (2010)

15. Pichler, P., Weber, B., Zugal, S., Pinggera, J., Mendling, J., Reijers, H.A.: Imperative versus declarative process modeling languages: an empirical investigation. In: Daniel, F., Barkaoui, K., Dustdar, S. (eds.) BPM 2011. LNBIP, vol. 99, pp. 383–394. Springer, Heidelberg (2012). doi:10.1007/978-3-642-28108-2_37

16. Recker, J.: BPMN research: what we know and what we don't know. In: Proceedings of the International Workshop on Business Process Model and Notation, pp. 1–7 (2012)

17. Reichert, M., Weber, B.: Enabling Flexibility in Process-Aware Information Systems - Challenges, Methods, Technologies. Springer, Heidelberg (2012)

18. Rozinat, A., De Medeiros, A.A., Günther, C.W., Weijters, A., van der Aalst, W.M.: Towards an Evaluation Framework for Process Mining Algorithms. BPM Center Report BPM-07-06, BPMcenter.org, p. 10 (2007)

19. Staab, S., Gomez-Perez, A., Daelemana, W., Reinberger, M.L., Noy, N.F.: Why evaluate ontology technologies? Because it works! IEEE Intell. Syst. 19(4), 74–81 (2004)

20. Wohlin, C., Runeson, P., Höst, M., Ohlsson, M.C., Regnell, B., Wesslén, A.: Experimentation in Software Engineering: An Introduction. Kluwer Academic Publishers, Norwell (2000)

Applications and Experiments of
Conceptual Modeling

MetaScience: An Holistic Approach for Research Modeling

Valerio Cosentino[1], Javier Luis Cánovas Izquierdo[2(✉)], and Jordi Cabot[2,3]

[1] AtlanMod Team, Inria, Mines Nantes, LINA, Nantes, France
valerio.cosentino@mines-nantes.fr
[2] UOC, Barcelona, Spain
jcanovasi@uoc.edu
[3] ICREA, Barcelona, Spain
jordi.cabot@icrea.cat

Abstract. Conferences have become primary sources of dissemination in computer science research, in particular, in the software engineering and database fields. Assessing the quality, scope and community of conferences is therefore crucial for any researcher. However, digital libraries and online bibliographic services offer little help on this, thus providing only basic metrics. Researchers are instead forced to resort to the tedious task of manually browsing different sources (e.g., DBLP, Google Scholar or conference sites) to gather relevant information about a given venue. In this paper we propose a conceptual schema providing a holistic view of conference-related information (e.g., authors, papers, committees and topics). This schema is automatically and incrementally populated with data available online. We show how this schema can be used as a single information source for a variety of complex queries and metrics to characterize the ER conference. Our approach has been implemented and made available online.

Keywords: Conference analysis · Data mining · MetaScience · Scientometrics

1 Introduction

Conferences play a key role in the research community specially in many areas of Computer Science (CS) where they are the primary source for researchers to present and discuss new results and ideas [1,2]. Availability of conference analytics is therefore a fundamental information for both researchers, looking for a venue to submit their work, and organizers (e.g., steering and program committee chairs), in need of monitoring its health (e.g., evolution of papers accepted and community).

Current analytics so far are mostly limited to assessment of basic common indicators such as ranking, citation indexes and acceptance rates, usually available in digital libraries and bibliographic services. However, relevant information on the author community (e.g., openness towards new researchers), author profiling (e.g., most prolific authors, author clustering) or composition of the Program

© Springer International Publishing AG 2016
I. Comyn-Wattiau et al. (Eds.): ER 2016, LNCS 9974, pp. 365–380, 2016.
DOI: 10.1007/978-3-319-46397-1_28

Committee (PC) are often not available or scattered thus forcing researchers to perform tedious and manual browsing to get the information they need in a process that does not scale.

In this paper we propose a conceptual schema that provides an holistic, homogeneous and detailed representation of all kinds of conference-related information. A relational database is derived from our conceptual schema and populated through an extraction mechanism that collects and integrates data from different heterogeneous sources such as bibliographic metadata, conference websites, quality indicator services and a number of digital libraries by applying a plethora of extraction techniques (i.e., database import, web scraping and file processing) tailored to the nature of each data source. Our approach incorporates an incremental update mechanism that can be triggered at any moment to refresh and keep the database updated with the latest information available online.

The obtained data can therefore be used to better understand how conferences behave by automatizing the calculation of conference analytics. Thanks to our homogeneous and integrated representation, we can perform this calculation at a massive scale (e.g., to compare conference results across subfields) and going beyond pure publication analysis (e.g., studying publication patterns of PC members when compared with non-PC members), something that was not feasible until now. We illustrate some of the metrics on the ER conference itself. Tool support for the whole process is provided and a web service focusing on individual summary metrics is also available.

The remainder of the paper is organized as follows. Section 2 introduces our approach together with the conceptual and database schemas. Section 3 describes the data collection while Sect. 4 focuses on conference metrics. Section 5 discusses implementation details. We conclude by presenting the related work in Sect. 6 and future research directions in Sect. 7.

2 Approach

We propose a conceptual schema to model all relevant aspects of research conferences. This schema is materialized as a relational database and populated from a variety of partial sources through an incremental update mechanism. The resulting database can then be queried to calculate a number of quality metrics for the conferences (individually or to compare them). Figure 1 shows an overview of our approach. Both layers can be easily extended to add new data sources and metrics.

In the remainder of this section, we describe the conceptual schema and the corresponding database schema, key components of our approach. Next sections describe the other elements of the data collection and data analytics layers.

2.1 Conceptual Schema

Figure 2 shows the conceptual schema depicted as a UML class diagram. The main concepts include: *Researcher*, *Paper*, *Conference* and *ConferenceEdition*.

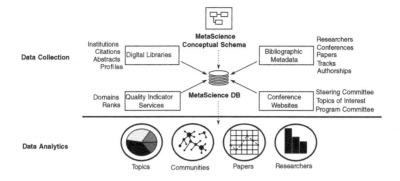

Fig. 1. Overview of METASCIENCE.

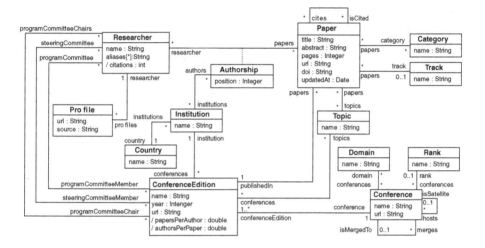

Fig. 2. METASCIENCE conceptual schema.

They represent respectively, individuals involved in a conference (publishing or being part of committees), publications, conferences and the corresponding editions. The associations among these concepts allow representing the authors of the publications (see *papers* association), where papers were published (see *publishedIn* association), their citations (*cites*), the conference committees (*programCommitteeChairs*, *programCommittee* and *steeringCommittee*) and the conference editions (*conferenceEdition*).

The schema also models the order of the authors and their affiliation in each paper (see *Authorship* association class). Researchers can also be identified with different aliases (see *aliases*) and have several profiles (see *Profile*) like Google Scholar or ResearchGate. Conference editions are organized by an institution (see association between *ConferenceEdition* and *Institution*) and define a set of topics of interest (see association between *ConferenceEdition* and *Topic*). Conferences can be a satellite event of others (see association *isSatellite*) or the result of merging two or more conferences (see association *merges*).

Additionally, the schema embeds a set of concepts to facilitate the classification of papers and conferences. The concepts *Category, Topic, Track* define respectively the category of a paper (e.g., short paper, long paper), the topics assigned to it, and the conference track where it was assigned. The concepts *Domain* and *Rank* describe the domains and rank assigned to a conference. Finally, concepts in the schema can be enriched with some calculated metrics, expressed as derived attributes like the number of citations for researchers (see the attribute *citations*) or the ratio of papers per author and authors per paper for each conference edition (attributes *papersPerAuthor* and *authorsPerPaper*).

2.2   Database Schema

The database schema shown in Fig. 3 is derived from the conceptual schema previously presented. In a nutshell, concepts/attributes in the conceptual schema are mapped into tables/columns in the database schema and associations are mapped into foreign keys (e.g., *track* in *Paper* concept is mapped to *track_id* foreign key in *paper* table) or new tables (e.g., *topic_paper* table) depending on the cardinality of the association, following the typical translation strategies. Note that the association class has been mapped into a new table (see *authorship* table).

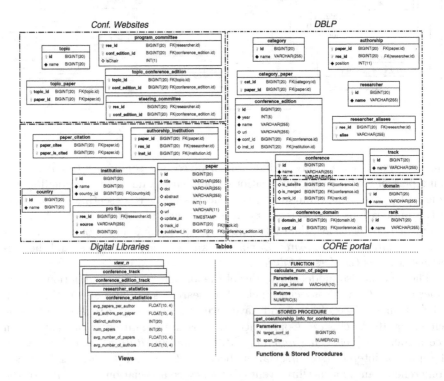

Fig. 3. METASCIENCE database schema.

Additionally, several views have been created in the database to store the derived attributes (e.g., *conference_statistics* view). Auxiliary methods have been implemented as either functions or stored procedures (e.g. *calculate_num_of_pages*). These elements calculate basic aggregated data that will be frequently accessed when defining more complex metrics. Full description of these views and methods can be found in the repository hosting the tool.

3   Data Collection

The data collection layer includes several components to collect specific information from different data sources. In particular, we consider (1) bibliographic metadata, (2) conference websites, (3) digital libraries and (4) quality indicator services. Bibliographic metadata includes information about papers, researchers, authorship, conferences, their editions and tracks, obtained from DBLP[1]. Conference websites are used to retrieve committee members (e.g., steering and program committees) and topics of interest. Digital libraries are accessed to collect data about paper abstracts and citations as well as researchers' profiles and affiliation institutions. Finally, conference ranking information and conference domains can be derived, for instance, from the CORE Rankings portal[2]. In the following we give details about the import process for each source.

3.1   DBLP

Figure 4 shows an overview of the extraction process for DBLP data. It concerns both the DBLP database[3] and website[4] since the database dump does not contain all information available in the website, e.g., conference tracks.

In a nutshell, the DBLP database includes a set of relational tables to store information about publications and authors. Publication details are stored in the table *dblp_pub_new* and include, among others, its type, title, page intervals, year and the link to the DBLP web page where the publication is located. Author tables keep track of their position in papers (table *dblp_author_ref_new*), their names (table *dblp_authorid_ref_new*) and possible name aliases (table *dblp_aliases_new*). In the following, we describe how information contained in the DBLP database and website are processed and imported in our database.

Researchers, Papers and Authorship Data. Authors and their aliases stored in the DBLP database are mapped into the tables *researcher* and *research_alias* of our database. A similar approach is followed to populate papers

---

[1] DBLP is a popular online reference for open bibliographic information in computer science with over 3M publication records.
[2] CORE (http://www.core.edu.au/index.php/conference-portal) provides assessment of conferences in computing disciplines according to a mix of indicators such as citation and acceptance rates.
[3] Dumps of the DBLP database are released periodically at http://dblp.l3s.de.
[4] http://dblp.uni-trier.de.

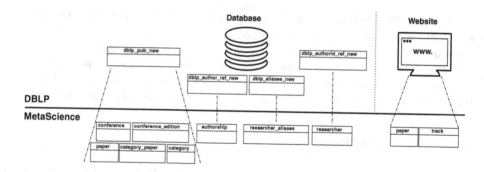

Fig. 4. Overview of the extraction process for DBLP.

and authorship details, thus filling the *paper* and *authorship* tables. Additionally, at this stage, also the tables *category* and *category_paper* are populated. Currently, the papers are categorized according to their number of pages (e.g., less than 11 pages as short papers) since there is no explicit information about a paper category in DBLP. This value can be configured to adapt to specific page lengths for a given conference.

Conference Data. We rely on the analysis of the proceedings of each conference in the DBLP database to fill the tables regarding the information for conferences (*conference*, their editions *conference_edition*) and conference relationships (attributes *is_satellite* and *is_merged* in table *conference*). The actual name of the conference is retrieved by web scraping the conference page on the DBLP website, since, surprisingly, this information is not present in the database.

Tracks Data. Tracks assigned to papers are obtained by a web crawler visiting the DBLP web page of the conference edition where the paper metadata is located. For each paper, its position on the web page is retrieved according to its title and then the name of the assigned track is collected by selecting the first HTML header that precedes it. The obtained information is finally stored in the table *track* and linked to the corresponding paper (attribute *track_id* in table *paper*), and then aggregated in the views *conference_edition_track* and *conference_track*.

3.2 Conference Websites

Topics of interest and committees (e.g., program and steering committees) are listed on the conference website, but each website follows a different structure (e.g., number of pages, content of each page, completeness of the data). Given this heterogeneity we have devised a semi-automatic extraction process that leverages on web scraping techniques and a Domain Specific Language (DSL) to configure the scraping process.

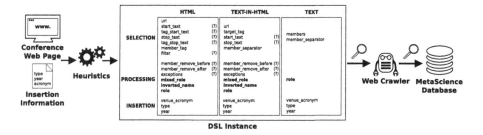

Fig. 5. DSL attributes for *HTML, TEXT-IN-HTML* and *TEXT* modes.

Figure 5 shows an overview of the extraction process. It takes as input the URL of the conference web page where the target information is located, and additional information about the conference (i.e., its acronym and the edition under analysis) and type of data to be extracted (e.g., topics, steering committee). Then, a set of heuristics based on text mining techniques generate an instance of our DSL, i.e., an initial configuration. This configuration is then used to (1) instruct a crawler to locate and return the topics/committee members in the web page and (2) drive the insertion of the data obtained to our database. Both the DSL instance and the data collected by the crawler can be manually checked and tuned if needed by the user.

The current defined heuristics are able to locate the list of elements required in the extraction process (i.e., topics or committee members) and isolate the single elements by using a pattern-based search. The location of the target data is achieved by searching for specific words that may precede (e.g., *topic, committee, PC*) and follow it (e.g., *important dates, submission*). Then, the target data is analyzed to determine the single elements and the contained relevant text by leveraging on the most frequent HTML tags and non-alphanumeric symbols used.

The DSL, shown in Fig. 5, can be executed in three different modes, namely, *HTML* (when information is encoded in HTML format), *TEXT* (pure text) and *TEXT-IN-HTML* (a mixture of both), depending on the availability of the target information and how it is coded in the web page. Each mode is composed by a set of parameters that can be mandatory, optional (see question marked attributes) or specific to extract committee members (see bold attributes). These attributes are grouped in 3 blocks: (1) *selection block*, which drives the location of the target elements; (2) *processing block*, which defines text processing rules to remove extra data that may appear together with the target elements; and (3) *insertion block*, which specifies where to insert the elements to our database.

The selection block contains the link of the web page to analyze, the HTML tag (*member_tag*) enclosing the target elements and, optionally, other tags and text used as delimiters (e.g., *ol* tags in enumerations) and/or a filter (e.g., to select HTML tags with a given id). The processing part defines regular expressions applied to each single element to isolate the target information (*member_remove_before* and *member_remove_after*). However, exceptions can be defined for elements for which the regular expression fails. When dealing with committee members, the parameter *role* defines the type of role to retrieve (i.e., normal member or chair), the parameter *inverted_name* is used when the first and last names are inverted and the parameter *mixed_roles* is used when normal members and chairs are listed together. On the other hand, the insertion parameters are used to insert the selected elements in our database for a specific venue, year and type (i.e., type of committee or topic).

This process is repeated at least twice for each conference website of a given edition, one targeting the topics and the other targeting the PC. If available, we can also used it to extract the Steering Committee (SC). When dealing with the PC, an important step is the matching between the names in the web page and researcher names in our database (stored in our database (*researcher* and *researcher_alias* tables). We use well-known identity matching/entity resolution algorithms (e.g., [3,4]) for this.

3.3 Digital Libraries

Information about paper abstracts, institutions, citations and profiles can be obtained by mining popular digital libraries. Our extraction process relies on Google Scholar, a free public search engine for academic papers and literature. For each paper, the platform provides links to the digital library hosting it, to the papers citing it and to the author profiles on the platform. However, as the platform does not provide any API to execute queries programmatically, we have devised an extraction process based on web-scraping techniques as well though using a different approach than for conference websites.

The extraction process takes as input a list of paper titles and their identifiers from our database. A crawler then visits Google Scholar, sends each title as query string and locates the corresponding hit by measuring the Levenshtein distance[5] between the title hit and the input title. Once the title is matched, first the attribute *updated_at* of the paper being analyzed is set to the current timestamp (this information will be used for the update process). Then, the links to (1) the web page of the digital library hosting the paper, (2) the citations page and (3) the profiles of the authors, are passed to three different processes together with the paper identifier. Such processes, described below, collect the desired information.

Paper Abstract and Institution. Abstracts and institutions are obtained by launching a crawler able to deal with a battery of popular digital libraries (i.e., *IEEE Xplore, Springer Link, ScienceDirect, IEEE Computer Society, ACM*), depending on the publishing source for the conference. The collected abstracts are used to update the corresponding paper stored in the table *paper*. Affiliation information is first assigned to the authors according to their position in the

---

[5] The Levenshtein distance represents the minimum number of single-character changes (i.e. insertions, deletions or substitutions) required to change one word into the other.

paper, and then processed and inserted in the tables *country*, *institution* and *authorship_institution*.

Citations. The citation information is collected by a crawler that navigates through the papers listed in the citations pages. The titles are matched with those ones stored in our database by measuring their resulting Levenshtein distance. For each match, the identifiers of the citing and cited papers are stored in the table *paper_citation*.

Profiles. The process to extract the Scholar profile relies on a crawler that accesses the link passed as input and collects the name of the researcher visible on his profiles. Next, the obtained name is used to retrieve the corresponding identifier stored in our database, by relying on his position in the paper being analyzed. The identifier and the link are then stored in the table *profile*. Additionally, the name collected from the web crawler is used to enrich the aliases in our database (*researcher_alias* table) if it has not been tracked before.

3.4 CORE Rankings Portal

CORE classifies over 1,700 conferences and workshops in computer science. No conference rankings are perfect nor we claim CORE is the best one. But as the most popular one we chose it as the input source to populate this section of the database. Each venue is represented by a name and acronym and is associated to a rank and one or more domains, also called fields of research. This information can be exported as a CSV file. Thus, we have defined an extraction process that processes this CSV to first match the conferences with those ones included in the database based on equal acronyms and, if needed, on the Levenshtein distance calculated between their names. The matched conferences with their rank and domain information are serialized to a textual format to allow a manual verification if so desired. Once the match has established, the rest of the CSV data is used to populate the tables *domain*, *rank*, *conference_domain* and the attribute *rank* in the table *conference*.

3.5 Incremental Update Process

The goal of the update operation is two-fold: it refreshes the data concerning paper citations and researcher profiles already stored in our database, and it completes the database by adding information about new conference editions, conferences and researchers. Due to lack of space we cannot describe herein the details of the process but in a nutshell, for the synchronization of papers we use the attribute *update_at* of the table *paper* to know when that paper was updated for the last time while for full conferences/editions we compare their identifiers with those in DBLP to detect new elements to import, and then trigger the process to recover all the related data for them.

4   Data Analytics

In this section we illustrate how METASCIENCE can be used to (1) automate the calculation of quality metrics that so far had to be manually processed, and (2) enable more ambitious analysis that were not feasible before. Due to space limitations, we show a variety of analysis that can be achieved with META-SCIENCE, however by leveraging on the data stored in our database, the user is free to compute any metric he/she wants.

In particular, we discuss four possible dimension analysis: (1) general, (2) co-authorship, (3) program committee and (4) topics. Next we present how each one may be addressed[6] and illustrate them by applying the metrics to this same *Int. Conf. on Conceptual Modeling*. It is worth noting that the same metrics can be replicated for any conference, and be used to compare conferences each other.

4.1   General

We define four basic metrics to characterize essential information for each conference edition, namely: *Num_papers* (number of accepted papers); *Num_authors* (number of unique authors); *Papers_per_Author* (ratio of papers per author); and *Authors_per_Paper* (ratio of authors per paper). The result of applying those metrics on the 34 editions of ER is shown in Table 1. The table also includes the trend of the metric value along the editions. To measure metric trends we compute the Spearman correlation (ρ) between the value of the metric in each edition and the time axis. Spearman correlation allows us to quantify monotone trends: as the time axis is monotonically increasing, strong correlation indicates presence of a trend in the metric. It is interesting to note the remarkable positive trend for the metrics *Num_authors* and *Authors_per_Paper*.

Among all possible general metrics, we believe the ones related to conference openness, measuring how easy is for new researchers to become part of the community, are of special interest. For this, we use the metrics *Newcomers* (percentage of authors who are new to the conference in each edition, an author

Table 1. Summary of the metric values.

Metric	Min	1st Qu.	Median	Mean	3rd Qu.	Max.	SD (σ)	Trend ρ
Num_papers	25.00	34.00	40.00	40.79	47.00	75.00	10.14	0.37
Num_authors	49.00	79.00	87.00	97.94	122.00	216.00	36.50	0.82
Papers_per_Author	1.00	1.03	1.06	1.07	1.01	1.16	0.04	0.30
Authors_per_Paper	1.70	2.18	2.43	2.54	3.00	3.50	0.54	0.88
Newcomers	55.95 %	66.67 %	70.73 %	70.51 %	75.00 %	84.16 %	7.19	−0.52
Newcomers_papers	22.22 %	38.46 %	47.37 %	46.81 %	56.25 %	66.67 %	12.40	−0.74
Community_papers	7.41 %	12.00 %	14.76 %	14.76 %	18.52 %	29.73 %	5.16	−0.19
Mixed_papers	20.83 %	25.00 %	37.50 %	38.43 %	48.72 %	62.96 %	13.13	0.73

---

[6] The queries to calculate the metrics for each dimension are available at the tool website.

is new when she has not published a full paper in the previous 5 editions), *Newcomer_papers* (papers authored by only newcomers), *Community_papers* (papers where no newcomer author participated) and *Mixed_papers* (the rest). Last four rows in Table 1 shows the summary statistics of the results of these metrics. The moderate negative trend on the metric *Newcomers* and the positive trend for the metric *Mixed_papers* may reveal that new authors are joining the conference with the help of community members.

4.2   Authorship Analysis

We propose to study the authorship relations among the authors by means of building a global co-authorship graph with information from all the editions of a conference. In this kind of graphs, authors who have published a paper in the conference are represented as nodes while co-authorship is represented as an edge between the involved author nodes. Weight of nodes and edges represent the number of papers and number of coauthorship of the authors represented by those nodes, respectively. Figure 6 shows the co-authorship graph for the ER conference. The graph includes 2,158 nodes (i.e., unique authors) and 3,766 edges (i.e., co-authorship relations).

Once we have this graph, a number of graph-based metrics can be calculated to get a feeling of the collaboration patterns of the ER community. For instance, the average degree is 3.49, the average path length is 8.042 and there are 460 connected components (each connected component identifies a sub-community of authors that work together). Most of the components (394 in total) are composed by 1 to 4 author nodes but there is one component (sub-graph with black-filled

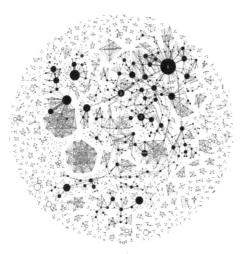

Fig. 6. Co-authorship graph for all the editions of the ER conference. Numbered nodes represent the three nodes with the highest betweenness centrality value: (1) John Mylopoulos, (2) Juan Carlos Trujillo and (3) Veda C. Storey.

nodes) that includes 828 author nodes (almost 40 % of the total number of authors), thus revealing the main core of authors in the conference and showing they tend to work together at least from time to time instead of ER being the composition of a set of isolated groups.

To expand on this, we also calculated the betweenness centrality value for each node, which measures the number of shortest paths between any two nodes that pass through a particular node and allows to identify prominent authors in the community that act as bridges between group of authors. The author node with the highest betweenness centrality value is John Mylopoulos (largest black node in the graph, tagged with the value (1), followed by Juan Carlos Trujillo (node tagged with number (2) and Veda C. Storey (node tagged with number (3). John Mylopoulos also has 5 as average distance to other authors within its connected component. Finally, we also measured the graph density, which is the relative fraction of edges in the graph, that is, the ratio between the actual number of edges (actual collaboration values) and the maximum number of possible edges in the graph (potential collaboration relationships). In our graph, the graph density is 0.002, which is a very low value.

4.3   Program Committee Analysis

This is one of the least explored areas due to the challenges other authors found to automatically collect PC information in the past (i.e., [5–7]). With our approach, data regarding the PC can be leveraged to calculate PC evolution metrics like (1) PC_Size (size of the PC per conference edition) or (2) PC_Age (number of consecutive editions for which a researcher has been member of the PC). Table 2 shows the results for these metrics for the last 10 editions of the ER conference. It is worth noting that the minimum and maximum sizes of the PC are 73 (in 2010) and 105 (in 2013), respectively. On the other hand, only 2 members (i.e., Barbara Pernici and Il-Yeol Song) stayed as part of the PC for the last 10 editions.

METASCIENCE can also help in deciding who should become part of the PC and choose the PC Chairs. For instance, we define the metrics (1) Inactive_Members (number of PC members that have not published a paper in the previous 3 editions); and (2) Active_Authors (counting the number of authors who have published in each of the previous 3 conference editions and are not yet PC members). When applying these metrics on the 2015 conference edition. we have that Inactive_Members reports that 60 out of the 99 members in the PC from 2015 did not publish in the previous 3 editions (a high value, though

Table 2. Summary for the metrics PC_Size and PC_Age.

Metric	Min	1st Qu.	Median	Mean	3rd Qu.	Max.	SD (σ)	Trend ρ
PC_Size	73.00	82.75	90.00	90.80	99.75	105.00	10.921	0.32
PC_Age	1.00	1.00	1.33	1.94	2.46	10.00	1.38	N.A

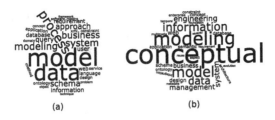

Fig. 7. Comparison between the top 30 keywords extracted from (a) paper abstracts and (b) topics of interest, for the last 10 editions of the ER conference.

some of them did publish in workshops or had other responsibilities). The metric *Active_Authors* tells us that only 7 researchers published constantly from 2012 to 2014 and from them only 3 were PC members in 2015, while the remaining 4 were not (but some of their co-authors were, which at least indicates that their expertise was somehow represented).

4.4   Topics Analysis

Information regarding the topics of interest can be used to study the main working areas of a conference. We believe it is specially interesting to compare the theoretical list of topics (those published in the call for papers) with the actual list of topics (those addressed by accepted papers, inferred from the analysis of their titles and abstracts). This information is useful to gauge the actual interest of topics by the community and use that when deciding on the conference evolution path (e.g., what topics to cover in the future).

Figure 7 shows a visual comparison between the tag clouds of keywords extracted from (a) the paper abstracts published in the last 10 editions of ER and (b) the topics of interests of the corresponding conference editions. For the sake of clarity, the generated clouds include the top 30 keywords. As can be seen, keywords such as *model*, *modeling* and *data*, which can be considered part of the core concepts of the conference, are representative for both clouds. Instead, keywords *process* and *business* appear to be more relevant in actual papers than they are in the call for papers, while keywords *enterprise* and *reverse* only appear in the conference topics but no paper tackled them directly. This analysis reveals a possible discrepancy between the conference topics and the actual trend in the paper topics. Surprisingly enough, the relevance of the keywords *ontology* and *web* seem to point out that the corresponding topics receive little attention from both conference and papers.

5   Tool Support

All artifacts developed in this paper for the extraction process and the metrics calculation are available in the METASCIENCE repository[7]. The steps to initialize, enrich and update the database have been implemented in Python 2.7.6.

---

[7] https://github.com/SOM-Research/metaScience.

The crawlers rely on *Selenium*, a portable software testing framework tuned to collect information from conference web pages and digital libraries, while the database integrated in METASCIENCE uses MySQL. We also developed a free online service[8] that leverages part of the presented infrastructure to offer individual research reports.

6   Related Work

There are several online services offering basic bibliographic data on CS conferences and journals like DBLP, ACM Portal, CiteSeerX and IEEE Xplore. Platforms such as ResearchGate and Academia.edu provide social networks that allow researchers to disseminate their work and measure their impact according to basic publication statistics (e.g., co-author index, citation count, publication count). Other services provide more complex bibliometrics information. Arnetminer extracts and mines academic social networks, Google Scholar provides bibliometric analysis of the research performance of individuals and papers, as well as rating and ranking for journals and conferences, while Microsoft Academic Search offers information about institutions and fields of study for researchers, conferences and journals. However, each of them focuses on part of the information that is required to perform a complete conference analysis (e.g., none of them integrates information about program committees, topics of interest or its core ranking) with different degrees of completeness.

Once the conference information is gathered, several authors have proposed metrics to analyze the data. The most common form to assess a conference quality is through citation analysis [8–11]. Since exclusive focus on citation analysis is controversial [12,13], other authors have proposed additional metrics taking into account other aspects such as program committee members [6] and co-authorship networks [14]. For instance, [5] determines the health of a small set of software engineering conferences by combining several metrics such as openness to new authors, introversion/inbreeding and program committee turnover. Nevertheless, these analysis are limited in terms of the scope and the number of metrics since they are forced to manually extract part of the data. In contrast, our infrastructure would make this analysis scalable and offer the chance to quickly come up with new metrics combining richer data sources as shown in the previous sections. A similar approach to ours with regard to the analysis of conferences was presented in [15] but focused on the co-authorship graphs and citations of the CAiSE conference, some of their metrics could be integrated in our approach to make them available to any other conference.

7   Conclusion

In this paper we have presented a conceptual schema for the integrated analysis of conference research activities. Based on this schema, we have devised a

---

[8] http://som-research.uoc.edu/tools/metaScience.

database-driven infrastructure incrementally populated with data coming from different heterogeneous sources (DBLP, CORE rankings, web scraping on conference websites, etc.). This information enables the definition of a variety of complex metrics mixing the different sources information and their automatic calculation on a large set of CS conferences. In particular, we have illustrated these metrics via the analysis of this own ER conference to shed some light on its co-authorship graph, PC membership and topics of interest.

As future work, we would like to extend this work to journal analysis and integrate additional information sources (e.g., PubMed) to tackle areas outside CS. This would enable comparing typical values of CS conferences (which themselves should also be compared based on their subfields) with, for instance, biology ones. We will also work on the extension of our heuristics for web scraping to increase their success rate (currently around 70 % on average of conference websites we have tested can be automatically parsed, while the rest require small tunings on the initial generated configuration), a better suppport for semantic analysis when studying the topics and the use of other quality indicator services (e.g., GII-GRIN[9]). Finally, we plan to use our data to conduct an exhaustive study of research conferences and work with SC members to interpret the results in order to (1) help them take corrective actions if needed and (2) consolidate a set of metrics that we see useful across fields in order to use them as quick and public summary of key performance indicators of conferences.

References

1. Patterson, D.A.: The health of research conferences and the dearth of big idea papers. Commun. ACM **47**(12), 23–24 (2004)
2. Chen, J., Konstan, J.A.: Conference paper selectivity and impact. Commun. ACM **53**(6), 79–83 (2010)
3. Goeminne, M., Mens, T.: A comparison of identity merge algorithms for software repositories. Sci. Comput. Program. **78**(8), 971–986 (2013)
4. Christen, P.: A comparison of personal name matching: techniques and practical issues. In: ICDM Conference, pp. 290–294 (2006)
5. Vasilescu, B., Serebrenik, A., Mens, T., van den Brand, M.G., Pek, E.: How healthy are software engineering conferences? Sci. Comput. Program. **89**, 251–272 (2014)
6. Zhuang, Z., Elmacioglu, E., Lee, D., Giles, C.L.: Measuring conference quality by mining program committee characteristics. In: Digital Libraries Conference, pp. 225–234 (2007)
7. Vasilescu, B., Serebrenik, A., Mens, T.: A historical dataset of software engineering conferences. In: MSR Conference, pp. 373–376 (2013)
8. Hirsch, J.E.: An index to quantify an individual's scientific research output. Natl. Acad. Sci. USA **102**(46), 16569–16572 (2005)
9. Amin, M., Mabe, M.: Impact factors: use and abuse. Int. J. Environ. Sci. Tech. **1**(1), 1 (2004)
10. Martins, W.S., Gonçalves, M.A., Laender, A.H., Ziviani, N.: Assessing the quality of scientific conferences based on bibliographic citations. Scientometrics **83**(1), 133–155 (2010)

---

[9] http://valutazione.unibas.it/cs-conference-rating.

11. Van Eck, N.J., Waltman, L.: CitNetExplorer: a new software tool for analyzing and visualizing citation networks. J. Informetrics **8**(4), 802–823 (2014)
12. Saha, S., Saint, S., Christakis, D.A.: Impact factor: a valid measure of journal quality? J. Med. Libr. Assoc. **91**(1), 42 (2003)
13. Bornmann, L., Daniel, H.D.: Does the H-index for ranking of scientists really work? Scientometrics **65**(3), 391–392 (2005)
14. Montolio, S.L., Dominguez-Sal, D., Larriba-Pey, J.L.: Research endogamy as an indicator of conference quality. ACM SIGMOD Rec. **42**(2), 11–16 (2013)
15. Jarke, M., Pham, M.C., Klamma, R.: Evolution of the CAiSE author community: a social network analysis. In: Seminal Contributions to Information Systems Engineering, 25 Years of CAiSE, pp. 15–33 (2013)

Comparison and Synergy Between Fact-Orientation and Relation Extraction for Domain Model Generation in Regulatory Compliance

Sagar Sunkle[✉], Deepali Kholkar, and Vinay Kulkarni

Tata Consultancy Services Research, 54B Hadapsar Industrial Estate,
Pune 411013, India
{sagar.sunkle,deepali.kholkar,vinay.vkulkarni}@tcs.com
http://www.tcs.com/

Abstract. Modern enterprises need to treat regulatory compliance in a holistic and maximally automated manner, given the stakes and complexity involved. The ability to derive the models of regulations in a given domain from natural language texts is vital in such a treatment. Existing approaches automate regulatory rule extraction with a restricted use of domain models counting on the knowledge and efforts of domain experts. We present a semi-automated treatment of regulatory texts by automating in unison, the key steps in fact-orientation and relation extraction. In addition, we utilize the domain models in learning to identify rules from the text. The key benefit of our approach is that it can be applied to any legal text with a considerably reduced burden on domain experts. Early results are encouraging and pave the way for further explorations.

Keywords: Regulatory compliance · Rule extraction · Fact-orientation · Relation extraction · Natural language processing · Machine learning

1 Introduction

Modern enterprises face an unprecedented regulatory regime. Non-compliance often results in personal liability and risk for top management and to shareholders. Compliance management needs to be holistic in nature, because the same regulations may vary based on geography and over time and different units of an enterprise may have to be compliant with different regulations [12]. Equally importantly, it needs to be automated to the extent possible, so that compliance can be proved quickly, reliably, and maintained through time- and geography-specific variations.

With a formal representation of regulatory rules, it becomes possible for enterprises to check compliance with more reliable and thorough proofs/evidence [22]. Significant literature exists focusing on formal compliance checking [13,20]. But these solutions presuppose existence of rules.

© Springer International Publishing AG 2016
I. Comyn-Wattiau et al. (Eds.): ER 2016, LNCS 9974, pp. 381–395, 2016.
DOI: 10.1007/978-3-319-46397-1_29

Several approaches use natural language processing (NLP) and machine learning (ML) techniques to extract the rules from legal NL texts in a semi-automated manner. Even so, complexity of legal texts leads most of these approaches to formulate targeted solutions. For instance, these approaches require the domain experts to identify structural arrangements like chapters, sections, paragraphs, etc., specific to legal texts [7], to simplify complex legal sentences and making them amenable to analyses [3, 14, 25], and to annotate legal texts to identify rules and various other aspects specific to given approaches [24].

Interestingly, many of these approaches either do not use a conceptual modeling method or it is done in a way that restricts its applicability to rule extraction. We believe that the lack of a conceptual modeling method targeted at obtaining domain-specific regulation model in a generic manner results in most of these approaches being (a) specific to a regulation and specific to a given natural language [2, 16], and (b) not being able to scale due to continued reliance on the domain experts in various activities.

We argue in this paper that a more generic approach that uses a conceptual modeling method should drive the legal rule extraction. We present an automation of fact-orientation enhanced with relation extraction aimed at domain model generation. We consider the automated rule extraction to be a 3-step process consisting of (1) domain model generation, (2) rule identification using the domain model, and (3) rule authoring based on identified rules. Our specific contributions with respect to the first 2 steps are as follows:

1. We compare fact-orientation and relation extraction for their suitability toward regulatory domain model generation. Focusing on the commonality between them that both utilize *examples/instances* of core concepts, we provide an interactive synergistic treatment for the same.
2. We use the domain model and the dictionary obtained thus to identify rules in an automated manner.

We begin in Sect. 2 by reviewing related work and presenting the technical overview of our approach. The focus of this paper is on the first 2 steps, which are detailed in Sects. 3 and 4 respectively. The third step is similar to existing approaches but less reliant on domain experts. Results of an ongoing case study are discussed along with key issues in Sect. 5. We present future work and conclude the paper in Sect. 6.

Departing from most of the work in ontology learning as well as legal rule extraction, we aim to obtain a simple list of domain concepts and as many mentions of these concepts as possible. Once this list is available, we also use open information extraction techniques to obtain relations. We do not focus on any legal text-specific aspects such as segmentation, cross-referencing, identification of modalities, types of provisions and so on. Our idea is to only obtain a domain model and a dictionary with which to identify rules and defer the consideration of legal text-specific aspects till we obtain the logical specifications which provide appropriate level of abstraction at which to treat the aspects. Both the generation of logical specification and treatment of legal text-specific aspects are out of the scope of this paper.

2   Related Work and Technical Overview

Legal texts are unique from other NL texts mainly because legal texts are *prescriptive* in nature [25] and present details of modalities like permissions, obligations, and prohibitions.

2.1   Complexity of Legal Texts

Legal texts are different from other NL texts in the following ways [24]:

- Legal NL texts contain long sentences with complex clauses with a number of lists representing characteristics of norms and their applicability in specific conditions.
- They use cross references such that various details of a norm may be found in different chapters/sections/subsections.
- The changes to the definitions of norms over time in terms of exceptions, and variety of repeals and amendments are often placed in supplementary annexes.

At the same time, some studies have found that specific kinds of provisions follow typical sentential forms, at the least in a given regulation [15]. This peculiarity can be exploited as in some ML-driven approaches which use patterns of sentence structures in their learning techniques [16].

2.2   Current Approaches to Rule Extraction/Authoring

The complexity of legal NL texts has compelled the existing approaches in rule extraction research to come up with targeted solutions. In particular the NL-driven approaches use steps that include (a) identifying language patterns like *juridical natural language constructs* as in [7] and coming up with specialized parsing mechanisms for the same, (b) manually transforming statements in legal NL texts to simplified form such as *restricted natural language statements* as in [3] for easier processing, and (c) utilizing structural characteristics of legal NL texts by identifying sections of text at varying granularity from phrases to chapters and annotating cross references as in [25].

The approaches that do refer to a conceptual model use it in a restricted sense. For instance, the approach in [25] uses a *conceptual (meta) model of deontic concepts*. This model represents legally oriented concepts such as an actor, a right, an obligation, an exception, and so on. It is used as a basis of the semantic annotations, but is not a core artifact that drives the rule extraction process. The approach in [11] is similar to the approach in [25] in that it uses what it refers to as a *governance extraction model*, which again focuses on legal concepts alone rather than business domain concepts.

Similar to NL-driven approaches, ML-driven approaches too focus on classifying the sentences/paragraphs from the legal texts into different kinds of provisions without informing the features of the classifiers with a representation of domain model. For instance, approaches like [2] implemented in the context of

Norme in Rete and [16] from the project E-POWER use classifiers based on word frequency with a training set labeled by the domain expert. When such features are used to train classifiers, the reason of classification remains hard to understand and improve upon as demonstrated in [15,18].

Below, we describe how we enable generating a domain model of regulations and a dictionary and how both are used in learning rules from the legal text. We choose fact-orientation as a domain modeling method. This choice is influenced to some extent by our previous work. We used a realization of fact-orientation known as Semantics of Business Vocabulary and Rules (SBVR) to manually create vocabulary of regulations which we use to generate NL explanations of proofs of (non-) compliance [22]. Our previous work was in the context of Indian Know Your Customer (KYC)[1] regulations. KYC regulations aim to prevent money laundering (ML) and financing of terrorism (FT). They require the financial institutions like banks to take new customers following strict identity and address checks while transactions of existing customers need to be monitored based on their risk profiles. We use running examples from KYC henceforth. Note that we use the principles of fact-orientation without aiming specifically to generate SBVR formulations of the regulations.

2.3   Technical Overview

Our approach is illustrated in Fig. 1. As mentioned in Sect. 1, we consider the semi-automated rule extraction to be a 3-step process.

We make no assumption about the legal text like NL-driven approaches as described above, rather we use one peculiarity of legal texts that they contain definitions of key concepts referred in the text. We use fact-orientation as an overall modeling method. In step ①, we implement relation extraction (RE) as an adapted version of an RE technique called *Dual Iterative Pattern Relation*

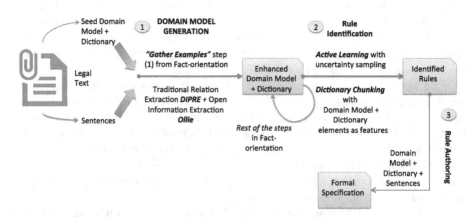

Fig. 1. Technical overview

---

[1] https://rbi.org.in/scripts/BS_ViewMasCirculardetails.aspx?id=9848.

Extraction (DIPRE) [4]. We also use a recent cousin of RE called open information extraction (open IE) implemented using Ollie tool [17]. Step ① uses sentences from legal NL text along with a seed domain model created from the definitions and an initial dictionary.

Once we obtain an enhanced domain model and dictionary, in step ② we use them to inform the features of *active learning*, a semi-supervised ML technique to classify legal NL text sentences into rules and non-rules rather than variety of provisions. Once the classifier is trained with the required precision and recall, in step ③ we can use a rule authoring environment along with all the artifacts so far obtained to author the rules.

In the next section, we first review each of fact-orientation and relation extraction and then describe how they are used in step ① of our approach.

3   Fact-Orientation and Relation Extraction

While our familiarity with fact-orientation (FO) is one reason, the other more substantial reason is the focus in FO on enabling the domain-expert to partake in domain modeling.

3.1   Role of Fact-Orientation in Domain Model Generation

FO bears many advantages over entity relationship and object-orientation when it comes to modeling the domain at conceptual level as enlisted below:

1. All ground assertions of interest are non-decomposable *facts* which are instances of *fact types*. Fact types can be unary to n-ary. This attribute free approach facilitates advantages such as semantic stability, an analysis of which the interested reader is invited to refer in [9].
2. FO models are validated by domain experts in two ways: verbalization [6] and population. It means that verbalization of fact types has to be agreed upon by the domain expert using populations of the same from the NL texts. This makes FO apt in the context of legal NL texts.
3. Being more generic, FO models can be transformed to other modeling formats if required. For instance, the freeware NORMA tool enables exporting the models in object role model specification to many other formats including relational views and even Datalog [5].

The first step of the conceptual schema design procedure (CSDP) prevalent in FO is that of *(Gather and) Transform familiar information examples into elementary facts (and apply quality checks)*. The second step applies population check, meaning that the fact types indeed are valid with respect to examples from NL texts. Step 3 to 7 refine the concept types and add constraints of various kinds.

The first step essentially abstracts from examples to create fact types. In general, the process of collecting population examples and abstracting from them is manual. This is where we make use of relation extraction as described next.

3.2   Role of Relation Extraction in Domain Model Generation

Relation extraction (RE) or traditional information extraction (IE) is the task of discovering assertions of a particular relation between two or more concepts in NL texts [1]. Supervised approaches to RE require completely labeled training sets of sentences and unsupervised methods use trained named entity taggers to identify concepts thereby being able to identify relations between more prevalent pairs of concepts like persons and locations [1].

Since we wish to be able to identify relations specific to a domain, we are interested in semi-supervised approaches which learn from a small set of tagged seed instances or few hand-crafted extraction patterns. Given a known pair of concepts and their handful of mentions, semi-supervised RE techniques like Dual Iterative Pattern Relation Extraction (DIPRE) [4] enable finding the rest of the mentions.

At this point, we bring to notice that FO and RE operate in opposite directions. Figure 2 illustrates this with concept types Bank, Customer, and Document and population examples containing mentions of these types from KYC text. While the first step in FO uses population examples to abstract to concept types, RE enables finding all mentions of given related concept types and their seed instances. For instance, given the known concept types Customer and Document related through *submits* relation and a handful of mentions so related as in Fig. 2, DIPRE can find other mentions with patterns induced from sentences containing the known mentions.

To automate the first step of FO, we still need to take care of two more aspects:

1. We need a way to find unknown concept types.
2. We need a way to find relations between all concept types found so far.

We describe in the following how we automate these two aspects in sync with RE so that by the end of the processing the text for mentions and new concept types, we generate a basic domain model and a dictionary that maps all concepts to their mentions throughout the text thus automating the first step of FO.

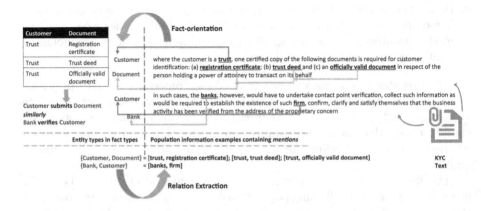

Fig. 2. Comparative view of fact-orientation and relation extraction

3.3   Our Approach for Domain Model Generation

We use the LingPipe[2] toolkit for processing text, which implements several algorithms from computational linguistics.

Finding Unknown Mentions of Known Concept Types. In order to identify known mentions in the text, we use an implementation of approximate dictionary chunker from [23] implemented in LingPipe. This chunker produces chunks based on weighted edit distance of strings from entries of a dictionary in which we store known pairs of concept types and their mentions. In order to seed this dictionary, we refer to the *definitions* section of the legal text, in our case KYC. This chunker forms an important module of our system, since it is used in both finding unknown concept types and finding relations between all concept types. It is also used in creating a specialized feature representation in learning to identify rules in legal text as explained later in Sect. 4.

Finding Unknown Mentions of Unknown Concept Types. In order to find concept types that could be part of the domain model but not yet known, we again use mentions of concepts that we have so far found. We use a hypothesis known as *distributional semantics* [10], which suggests that counting the contexts that two words share improves the chance of correctly guessing whether they express the same meaning, in other words, semantically similar expressions occur in similar contexts (Fig. 3).

We cluster the contexts, i.e., n characters to the left and right of mentions of each concept type so far known and then cluster these to suggest to the domain expert, what looks like other possible mentions. This is illustrated in Fig. 4.

The domain expert either adds to the dictionary, a new mention of a known concept type as in the case of (A) in Fig. 4 or as in the case of (B) has the option to add a new concept type along with the mention(s), if she recognizes that the mention(s) refers to different concept type not in the current set of

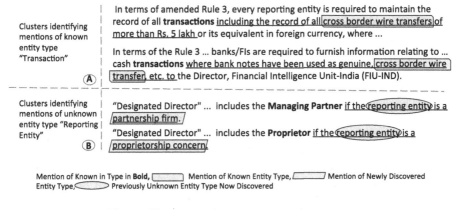

Fig. 3. Clustering of contexts around mentions

[2] http://alias-i.com/lingpipe/index.html.

known concept types. In (A), clustering the contexts of mentions of the concept type Transaction reveals a mention *cross border wire transfer* which the domain expert deems to be of the same concept type Transaction. In (B), clustering the contexts of mentions of the concept type Designated Officer reveals the mentions *partnership firm* and *proprietorship concern*, which the domain expert adds along with previously unknown type Reporting Entity of which they are mentions.

Finding Relations Between Known Concept Types. In order to find relations between concept types identified in the domain model, we use Ollie[3], an open IE implementation. Open IE differs from traditional RE in that open IE systems extract a diverse set of relational tuples without requiring any relation-specific human input. Whereas traditional RE like DIPRE requires concept type pairs representing a relation as shown in Fig. 2, open IE works where target relations are not known in advance. Open IE systems identify relation phrases, i.e., phrases that denote relations in English sentences.

The implementation we use, Ollie, is able to avoid uninformative and incoherent extractions. As an example of the former, whereas other open IE systems incorrectly extract *made(Faust,deal)* from the sentence "Faust made a deal with the devil.", Ollie (as successor of Reverb [8]) correctly extracts *made a deal with(Faust, the devil)*. Ollie is better than other open IE systems also because it extracts relations mediated by nouns, adjectives, and other verbal structures and a context-analysis step increases precision of relations extracted by including contextual information from the sentence in the extractions [17].

We input the concept types and mentions found so far to Ollie along with all the sentences in the legal text. Whenever existing mentions match with phrases that Ollie has found to be in relation, that relation is considered to exist between the concept types of the mentions.

Overall Approach to Domain Model Generation. We present the use of RE, context clustering, and open IE in Algorithm 1. The seed domain model and dictionary are obtained from *definitions* section of the regulation. In most of financial services regulations that we have encountered apart from KYC, we have found that definitions of key concept types are provided along with their subtypes and terms with which they are referred to in the text.

The procedure searchMentions implements semi-supervised RE. We implemented an adaptation of DIPRE wherein instead of looking for mentions on the web, we search the sentences for mentions to induce patterns using inducePatterns. Since compared to web, legal text is very small, the number of patterns that can be induced is also small. Whenever searchMentions finds possible mentions in the same relation via apply-re-patterns, we ask the domain expert to verify if the mentions are indeed in relation.

The procedure contextClustering implements clustering of contexts via apply-Clustering around mentions of all known concepts. In our experiments, we use length of 80 characters when capturing contexts via computeContexts to make single link clusters. Examples shown in Fig. 4 show results where the underlined

---

[3] https://github.com/knowitall/ollie.

text is a context under consideration. We involve the domain expert to verify and add to domain model and dictionary only the concepts and mentions she knows to be relevant.

Finally, the procedure searchRelations implements open IE over sentences of the text via runOpenIE. In our case, this is a call to Java wrapper around Ollie. If mentions of two different concepts are found in the subject and object of IE relation, then that relation is taken to exist between the two concepts.

Algorithm 1. DOMAIN MODEL GENERATION

Input: Text, Seed Domain Model (DM), Dictionary of Mentions (DoM)
Output: DM, DoM

1 $sentences \leftarrow sentenceDetection(text)$
2 **procedure** searchMentions($Sentences\ sents,\ DM\ dm,\ DOM\ dom$)
3   **for** *each conceptPair cp in dm* **do**
4        $mentionPair \leftarrow mentionsOfConcept(cp, dom)$
5   **while** $apply\text{-}re\text{-}pattern(sents, re\text{-}Patterns) > 0$ **do**
6           $re\text{-}Patterns \leftarrow inducePatterns(sents, mentionPair)$
7           $de\text{-}Input \leftarrow apply\text{-}re\text{-}pattern(sents, re\text{-}Patterns)$
8           $dom \leftarrow dom + de\text{-}Input$

10   **return** dom ;
11 **procedure** contextClustering($Sentences\ sents,\ DM\ dm,\ DOM\ dom$)
12   **for** *each concept cn in dm* **do**
13   **for** *each conceptMention cm of cn in dom* **do**
14          $mentionContextList \leftarrow computeContexts(sents, cm)$
15          $de\text{-}Input \leftarrow applyClustering(mentionContextList)$
16          $dm \leftarrow dm + de\text{-}Input$
17          $dom \leftarrow dom + de\text{-}Input$

19   **return** dm, dom ;
20 **procedure** searchRelations($Sentences\ sents,\ DM\ dm,\ DOM\ dom$)
21   **for** *each sent in sents* **do**
22       $open\text{-}IE\text{-}Relation \leftarrow runOpenIE(sent)$
23   **for** *each conceptPair cp(cn1, cn2) in dm* **do**
24   **for** *each mentionPair mp of cp in dom* **do**
25   **if** *open-IE-Relation.subject contains mp.mention1 and open-IE-Relation.object contains mp.mention2* **then**
26                $dm \leftarrow open\text{-}IE\text{-}Relation.relation(cn1, cn2)$

28   **return** dm ;
29 **while** $dm.hasChanged()$ *or* $dom.hasChanged()$ **do**
30    $dom \leftarrow$ searchMentions($sents,\ dm,\ dom$)
31    $dm, dom \leftarrow$ contextClustering($sents,\ dm,\ dom$)

32 $dm \leftarrow$ searchRelations($sents,\ dm,\ dom$)
33 **return** dm, dom

At this juncture, the domain model does not contain constraints or sub-types. We revert back to fact-orientation and follow step 2 to 7. Step 2 of FO applies population check. Since we take domain experts' input on each of RE, clustering, and IE stages in terms of mentions and concepts, step 2 of FO is implicitly supported in our approach. We provide a view to the domain expert into the sentences of the legal text, where a pair of concept is under consideration for combining or sub-typing. Similarly, the domain expert refers to the occurrences of concepts and their mentions in the text via specialized view to add and refine constraints.

4   Regulatory Rule Identification

Active Learning. To automate manual rule identification, we use semi-supervised active learning. Active learning techniques can learn from very less number of labeled sentences, by querying the domain expert on possible classes of a sentence. In our case, the classes are rule sentences and non-rule sentences.

The process of active learning involves taking a small set of labeled examples (sentences) as input, as well as a larger set of unlabeled examples, and generating a classifier and a relatively small set of newly labeled data. The learning process aims at keeping the domain expert annotation effort to a minimum, only asking for advice where the training utility of the result of such a query is high [21].

Representing Features based on Domain Model and Dictionary. We intend to make the use of the domain model and the dictionary mimic the way a domain expert actually identifies regulations in the text. We use a specialized FeatureExtractor[4] from LingPipe called ChunkerFeatureExtractor. A feature extractor provides a method of converting generic input objects into feature vectors. A ChunkerFeatureExtractor implements a feature extractor for character sequences based on a specified chunker. Here, we utilize the same approximate dictionary chunker we referred to in Sect. 3.3. This arrangement helps us in uniquely representing features in terms of concepts and their mentions from the domain model and the dictionary respectively.

To implement an active learner for rule identification, we use LogisticRegressionClassifier from LingPipe. It is a scored classifier that provides conditional probability classifications of input objects. It uses an underlying logistic regression model and feature extractor which in our case is the ChunkerFeatureExtractor. We implement the prototypical active learning algorithm from [19].

5   Results and Discussion

We present the results of applying our approach from Algorithm 1 to KYC text as well as applying active learning to the task of identifying rules in KYC below along with the discussion of key pointers.

---

[4] http://alias-i.com/lingpipe/docs/api/com/aliasi/util/FeatureExtractor.html.

Applying RE, Clustering, and IE to KYC Text. We copy pasted the text of KYC from the link shared earlier. We use LingPipe's IndoEuropeanSentenceModel to split the text into sentences. We obtained 525 sentences. From the *definition* section, we obtained 4 concepts.

We get 4 more concepts and their mentions through contextual clustering. Table 1 shows the mentions from definitions (#2) and from the application of RE and clustering (#3). We only specify 5 mentions of concepts in the table for the want of space. The column #4 indicates no. of sentences out of 525 where mentions of concepts were found.

Figure 4 shows some of the relations discovered between concepts based on the mentions that actually occurred in the corresponding sentences using Ollie.

Applying FO to Domain Model and Dictionary. Fig. 5 shows a fact-oriented model of KYC regulations. We used NORMA[5] tool to draw the object role model displayed on the right in Fig. 5.

Figure 6 shows the verbalization of concept Bank as well as fact types verifies and submitsForVerification generated automatically from the model. The relations or the fact types were adapted in consultation with the domain expert from initial set of relations from definitions sections and relations obtained from IE, a few of which were shown in Fig. 4.

Using the Dictionary with the Active Learner. Out of 525 sentences, we use 300 sentences to teach the active learner in a 10-fold cross validation setup with 225 sentences to test the learner. We annotated 10 sentences as denoting rules and 5 sentences as denoting non-rules before starting the learning sessions.

To identify how the use of domain model and dictionary affect recall and precision, we show the feature representations (a) when dictionary is used, i.e., when the learner is informed, (b) when instead of the dictionary, only a feature extractor based on n-gram tokenizer is used, i.e., the learner is uninformed, and (c) when dictionary is used along with a feature extractor based on n-gram tokenizer, i.e., the learner is semi-informed.

[individuals] CUSTOMER < may be categorised as > RISK CATEGORY [low]
[individuals/entities] CUSTOMER < be regulated by > REPORTING ENTITY [insurance companies]
[officially valid document in respect of] DOCUMENT < may be required by > CUSTOMER [fi]
[document] DOCUMENT < would be submitted to > BANK [bank]
[banks] BANK < should closely monitor especially accounts of multi-level marketing (mlm) companies in > CUSTOMER[firms]
[banks] BANK < should obtain ovd for > DOCUMENT [proof of address and identity of the relative]
[banks] BANK < to submit feedback on > TRANSACTION [deposits]
[banks] BANK < should categorise their customers into > RISK CATEGORY [low]
[exchanges] TRANSACTION < be reported by > BANK [banks]

Fig. 4. Relations found with IE; mentions in [ ] brackets, concepts in **bold**, relations in <>

We used InteractionFeatureExtractor from LingPipe which produces interaction features between two feature extractors to create the combined extractor

---

[5] https://www.ormfoundation.org/files/folders/norma_the_software/default.aspx.

Table 1. KYC concepts and mentions; #1: concept present in seed domain model, #2: no. of seed mentions, #3: no. of total mentions found with RE and IE, #4: no. of sentences where concept mention occurs

Sr.	Concepts	#1	#2	#3	Mentions	#4
1	Reporting entity	N	0	9	All India financial institutions, local area banks, primary (urban) co-operative banks, scheduled commercial banks, state and central co-operative banks	14
2	Bank	N	0	1	Bank	257
3	Account	N	0	2	Client accounts, small accounts	5
4	Customer	Y	12	30	Foreign portfolio investors, politically exposed persons, artificial juridical person, association of persons, body of individuals	123
5	Document	Y	33	51	Certificate of incorporation, certificate/licence issued by the municipal authorities under shop and establishment act, complete income tax return, licence/certificate of practice issued in the name of the proprietary concern by any professional body incorporated under a statute	128
6	Transaction	Y	15	17	Creating a legal person, cross-border wire transfer, deposits, withdrawal, fiduciary relationship	111
7	Risk category	N	0	3	High, low, medium	23
8	Designated director	Y	4	4	Managing partner, managing director, managing trustee, whole-time director	2

for case c. The value of an interaction feature is the product of the values of the individual features.

We found that when we used domain model and dictionary exclusively to represent features, we obtained consistently higher recall than the other two extractors. On the other hand, using n-grams of lengths 3 to 5 exclusively, we obtained higher precision than the other two extractors. Recall represents retrieval coverage. Because the dictionary captures mentions of concepts, the recall or coverage of dictionary extractor is comprehensive.

In our case, the extractor based on n-grams consistently has higher precision, which measures retrieval specificity but has correspondingly lower recall than the dictionary extractor. These results may be attributed to capturing concepts via dictionary of mentions against n-grams which do not make sense (*ther, nci,*

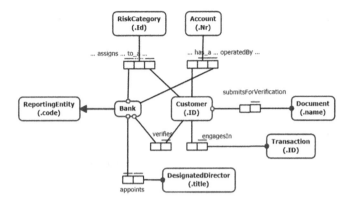

Fig. 5. KYC domain model using fact-orientation

Bank **is an entity type.**
Reference Scheme: ReportingEntity has ReportingEntity_code.
Reference Mode: .code.
Data Type: Text: Fixed Length (0).

Fact Types:
Bank appoints DesignatedDirector.
Each Bank **is an instance of** ReportingEntity.
Customer has_a Account operatedBy Bank.
Bank assigns RiskCategory to_a Customer.
Bank **verifies** Customer.

Bank verifies Customer.
For each Customer, **at most one** Bank verifies **that** Customer.
It is obligatory that each Bank verifies **some** Customer.
It is possible that some Bank verifies **more than one** Customer.

Fig. 6. KYC verbalization using fact-orientation

nanci, cash, and so on). The combined extractor achieves recall of dictionary extractor and reaches the precision of n-gram extractor. Our results indicate that for rule identification, a semi-informed approach performs better.

Summary. Our initial foray using FO, RE, context clustering, and IE indicates that we can do away with simplified paraphrasing of legal NL texts and other annotations used in existing approaches while reliably generating a domain model and a dictionary. The domain model and the dictionary can be used in unison with extractors focused on precision to achieve a better combination of precision and recall.

6   Future Work and Conclusion

We presented an approach and an algorithm to domain model generation using fact-orientation (FO) and flavors of relation extraction (RE) based on how each treats mentions of concepts in NL texts. In our ongoing experiments, we are trying to create an integrated development environment that shows views of FO, RE, context clustering, and open information extraction (IE) to the domain expert. Further work also includes giving more immersive treatment to rule authoring whereby knowledge latched so far can be utilized by the domain expert.

We are also experimenting with MiFID II[6] regulations, which presents more than 5000 sentences.

Our approach has shown to be generic in the sense that no regulation-specific structuring, simplification, or annotation is needed to capture the domain model and the rules. Also compared to existing approaches, it has the potential to scale well.

References

1. Bach, N., Badaskar, S.: A review of relation extraction. Lit. Rev. Lang. Stat. II (2007)
2. Biagioli, C., Francesconi, E., Passerini, A., Montemagni, S., Soria, C.: Automatic semantics extraction in law documents. In: Sartor, G. (ed.) ICAIL, Italy, 6–11 June 2005, pp. 133–140. ACM (2015). http://doi.acm.org/10.1145/1165485
3. Breaux, T.D., Antón, A.I.: Deriving semantic models from privacy policies. In: 6th Policy Workshop, Sweden, pp. 67–76. IEEE Computer Society (2005)
4. Brin, S.: Extracting patterns and relations from the world wide web. In: Atzeni, P., Mendelzon, A., Mecca, G. (eds.) WebDB 1998. LNCS, vol. 1590, pp. 172–183. Springer, Heidelberg (1999). doi:10.1007/10704656_11
5. Curland, M., Halpin, T.: The NORMA software tool for ORM 2. In: Soffer, P., Proper, E. (eds.) CAiSE Forum 2010. LNBIP, vol. 72, pp. 190–204. Springer, Heidelberg (2011). doi:10.1007/978-3-642-17722-4_14
6. Curland, M., Halpin, T.: Enhanced verbalization of ORM models. In: Herrero, P., Panetto, H., Meersman, R., Dillon, T. (eds.) OTM 2012. LNCS, vol. 7567, pp. 399–408. Springer, Heidelberg (2012). doi:10.1007/978-3-642-33618-8_54
7. van Engers, T.M., van Gog, R., Sayah, K.: A case study on automated norm extraction. In: Gordon, T. (ed.) The Seventeenth Annual Conference on Legal Knowledge and Information Systems, JURIX 2004, pp. 49–58. Frontiers in Artificial Intelligence and Applications. IOS Press, Amsterdam (2004)
8. Fader, A., Soderland, S., Etzioni, O.: Identifying relations for open information extraction. In: Proceedings of the Conference on Empirical Methods in Natural Language Processing, EMNLP 2011, pp. 1535–1545. ACL, Stroudsburg (2011)
9. Halpin, T.A.: Fact-orientation and conceptual logic. In: Proceedings EDOC 2011, Finland, pp. 14–19. IEEE Computer Society (2011)
10. Harris, Z.S.: Mathematical Structures of Language. Wiley, New York (1968)
11. Hassan, W., Logrippo, L.: Governance requirements extraction model for legal compliance validation. In: RELAW 2009, USA, pp. 7–12 (2009)
12. Kaminski, P., Robu, K.: Compliance and control 2.0: emerging best practice model. McKinsey Working Papers on Risk 33, October 2015
13. Kharbili, M.E., de Medeiros, A.K.A., Stein, S., van der Aalst, W.M.P.: Business process compliance checking: current state and future challenges. In: MobIS. LNI, vol. 141, pp. 107–113. GI (2008)
14. Kiyavitskaya, N., Zeni, N., Breaux, T.D., Antón, A.I., Cordy, J.R., Mich, L., Mylopoulos, J.: Automating the extraction of rights and obligations for regulatory compliance. In: Li, Q., Spaccapietra, S., Yu, E., Olivé, A. (eds.) ER 2008. LNCS, vol. 5231, pp. 154–168. Springer, Heidelberg (2008). doi:10.1007/978-3-540-87877-3_13

---

[6] http://eur-lex.europa.eu/legal-content/EN/TXT/HTML/?uri=CELEX:32014L0065&from=EN.

15. de Maat, E., Krabben, K., Winkels, R.: Machine learning versus knowledge based classification of legal texts. In: Proceedings of JURIX 2010, pp. 87–96. IOS Press, Amsterdam (2010)
16. de Maat, E., Winkels, R.: Automatic classification of sentences in Dutch laws. In: Proceedings JURIX 2008, pp. 207–216. IOS Press, Amsterdam (2008)
17. Mausam, S., M., Bart, R., Soderland, S., Etzioni, O.: Open language learning for information extraction. In: Proceedings of EMNLP-CONLL (2012)
18. Moens, M.F., Boiy, E., Palau, R.M., Reed, C.: Automatic detection of arguments in legal texts. In: ICAIL 2007, pp. 225–230. ACM, New York (2007)
19. Olsson, F.: A literature survey of active machine learning in the context of natural language processing. Technical report, Kista, Sweden, April 2009
20. Racz, N., Weippl, E.R., Bonazzi, R.: IT governance, risk & compliance (GRC) status quo and integration: an explorative industry case study. In: SERVICES 2011, USA, 4–9 July 2011, pp. 429–436. IEEE Computer Society (2011)
21. Settles, B.: Active learning literature survey. Computer Sciences Technical report 1648, University of Wisconsin-Madison (2009)
22. Sunkle, S., Kholkar, D., Kulkarni, V.: Explanation of proofs of regulatory (non-)compliance using semantic vocabularies. In: Bassiliades, N., Gottlob, G., Sadri, F., Paschke, A., Roman, D. (eds.) RuleML 2015. LNCS, vol. 9202, pp. 388–403. Springer, Heidelberg (2015). doi:10.1007/978-3-319-21542-6_25
23. Tsuruoka, Y., Tsujii, J.: Boosting precision and recall of dictionary-based protein name recognition. In: Proceedings of the ACL 2003 Workshop on Natural Language Processing in Biomedicine, BioMed 2003, vol. 13, pp. 41–48. ACL, Stroudsburg (2003)
24. Wyner, A., Peters, W.: On rule extraction from regulations. In: Atkinson, K. (ed.) Legal Knowledge and Information Systems - JURIX, Vienna, Austria. Frontiers in Artificial Intelligence and Applications, vol. 235, pp. 113–122. IOS Press (2011). http://www.booksonline.iospress.nl/Content/View.aspx?piid=26386
25. Zeni, N., Kiyavitskaya, N., Mich, L., Cordy, J.R., Mylopoulos, J.: GaiusT supporting the extraction of rights and obligations for regulatory compliance. Requir. Eng. 20(1), 1–22 (2015)

Development of a Modeling Language for Capability Driven Development: Experiences from Meta-modeling

Janis Stirna[✉] and Jelena Zdravkovic

Department of Computer and Systems Sciences,
Stockholm University, Postbox 7003, 164 07 Kista, Sweden
{js,jelenaz}@dsv.su.se

Abstract. Changing business environments related to constant variations in customers' demand, situational conditions, regulations, emerging security threats, etc. may be addressed by approaches that integrate organizational development with information system development taking into account changes in the application context. This paper presents experiences from Method Engineering of the Capability Driven Development (CDD) methodology with a focus on the CDD meta-model and the modeling activities that led to it. CDD consists of several method components. Hence, a conceptual meta-model of CDD and a meta-model of the modeling language based on the 4EM approach are presented together with a number of lessons learned.

Keywords: Method engineering · Meta-modeling · Enterprise Modeling · Capability driven development

1 Introduction

Modern Information System (IS) designs have to support dynamic adaptations because new and unexpected business opportunities and threats arise, demands change drastically, as well as environmental and security risks increase. To respond to this challenge of continuous adaptation, the EU FP7 project "Capability as a Service in digital enterprises" (CaaS) [1] developed a methodology for capturing and analyzing the influence of the business application context on the IS using the notion of capability. Capability is generally seen as a fundamental abstraction to describe what a core business does [2]. The methodology developed by CaaS is called *Capability Driven Development* (CDD). It consists of a modeling language and a way of working. The areas of modeling as part of CDD are Enterprise Modeling (EM), context modeling, variability modeling, adjustment algorithms and patterns for capturing best practices. The development of the CDD methodology followed the following principles, which were defined during analysis of use case requirements and are documented in [3]:

- The CaaS project should not develop a single methodology mandatory for all business cases, but a reference methodology for using in majority of cases and pathways of extending the reference methodology to proprietary methodologies.

© Springer International Publishing AG 2016
I. Comyn-Wattiau et al. (Eds.): ER 2016, LNCS 9974, pp. 396–403, 2016.
DOI: 10.1007/978-3-319-46397-1_30

- All types of concepts, i.e. patterns, context, process, and enterprise models should be based on a same meta-model.
- The CDD methodology should not be a monolithic block but component-oriented to allow flexible selection and use of method components depending on the organization's intentions and a particular development situation.
- Integration of existing methods or method components should be given preference before substituting them with new.
- The CDD methodology is to be supported by the CDD Environment, a part of which is the *Capability Design Tool* (CDT) implemented in Eclipse.

Following these preconditions, one of the first steps of the CDD methodology development was to seek approaches that would be useful for the modeling activities that CDD needed to cover. One such activity was EM and specially Goal Modeling. For this we selected the 4EM [4, 5] approach to be included in CDD. In this respect, the objectives of this paper are (1) to present the CDD methodology development with a particular focus on the meta-modeling activity that took place, and (2) to retrospectively reflect on the experiences and lessons learned.

The research approach followed the principles of design science [6] consisting of several design and evaluation cycles. The CDD methodology is the main design artifact. It is composite because the methodology components, such as the meta-model, are design artifacts in their own right. This paper presents experiences from the development of the meta-model for the CDD methodology. It has been used and validated in four use case companies of the CaaS project.

The rest of the paper is organized as follows. Section 2 gives background to method development. Section 3 summarizes the CDD approach and outlines how it was developed. Section 4 presents the meta-models created, while Sect. 5 summarizes the lessons learned. Concluding remarks are given in Sect. 6.

2   Background to Method Development

Method engineering (ME) is *the engineering discipline to design, construct and adapt methods, techniques and tools for the development of information systems* [7]. One of the first efforts in modeling of modeling methods (meta-modeling) was proposed by [8] and development of customizable tools for supporting various methods (meta-tools) by [9]. A key activity of ME is designing method parts, denoted method chunks [10] or method components [11], for supporting specific IS development activities. Development of the CDD methodology concerned with correct identification of the main method parts and their relevant concepts, which motivated the choice of [11] as the approach for describing the CDD components in terms of the following aspects: purpose, overview and relationships, method component in terms of semantics, notation and language, as well as forms of cooperation.

The process of conceptualization of CDD was based on meta-modeling to specify the modeling language in a declarative manner and to develop a tool for its support. A key challenge was to base ME and tool development on common modeling constructs and structure. In this regard MOF meta-modeling architecture [12] defining four modeling layers, from M3 meta-meta model layer to M0 instance layer, proved useful. Modeling languages are typically specified at M2 (meta-model layer). Once they are used to describe models reflecting reality, M1 model layer is populated. When the models at M1 level are instantiated M0 level is reached. The CDD methodology was defined by an M2 model.

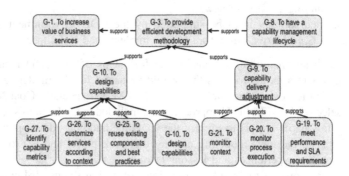

Fig. 1. A goal model fragment for the CDD methodology, adapted from [3]

3 Background to Capability Driven Development

The motivation for the CDD methodology development was analyzed in the initial requirements elicitation phase of the project. This was done by interviews with the use case companies, survey with a large number of external companies, as well as by several iterations of methodology development and capability designs for the four use case companies in order to validate the initial versions of the modeling language. This allowed us elaborating the overall goals (see Fig. 1) and requirements for the CDD methodology, defining an initial conceptual meta-model for representing capability designs, and outlining method components. Results of this work are reported in [3].

The CDD methodology defines both aspects that comprise a modeling methodology, namely, (1) the modeling language in terms of concepts, relationships, and notations used to represent the modeling product, i.e. the models of capability designs created, and (2) the way of working, the procedures and tools used, in order to arrive at a capability design of good quality i.e. the modeling process. The CDD methodology consists of a number of interlinked method components [4] each of which is described according to a framework presented in [11].

The CDD method components are divided into *upper-level method components* and *method extensions*. Upper-level components describe modeling a certain part of the capability design – Capability Design Process, EM, Context Modeling, Reuse of Capability Designs, and Run-time Delivery Adjustments. Method extensions address specific business challenges to which the CDD methodology can be applied. The overall CDD process includes three cycles – capability design; capability delivery; and capability refinement/updating [10].

The theoretical and methodological foundation for CDD is provided by the conceptual *core capability meta-model* (CMM). Simplified version is shown on Fig. 2; c.f. [4]

for full version with definitions. CMM was developed on the basis of requirements from the industrial project partners, and related research on capabilities. CMM has three main sections: (a) *Enterprise model* representing organizational designs with Goals, KPIs, Processes (with concretizations as Process Variants) and Resources; (b) *Context model* represented with Context Set for which a Capability is designed and Context Situation at runtime that is monitored and according to which the deployed solutions should be adjusted. Context Indicators are used for measuring the context properties (Measuring Property); and (c) *Patterns and variability model* for delivering Capability by reusable solutions for reaching Goals under different Context Situations. Each pattern describes how a certain Capability is to be delivered in a certain Context Situation and what Processes Variants and Resources are needed.

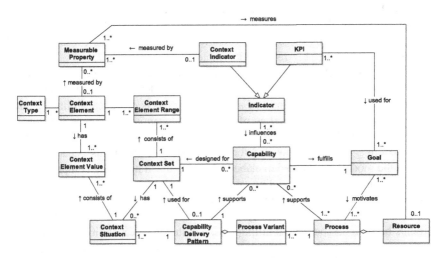

Fig. 2. The core capability meta-model (CMM) for supporting CDD [4].

4 CDD Meta-model Development

The work started by iterative development of the CMM. It was validated by applying it in four companies: SIV AG (Germany) for business processes outsourcing; FreshT Ltd. (UK) for maritime compliance capability; CLMS Ltd (UK) for collaborative software development using MDD; Everis (Spain) for service promotion capability and government SOA platform management capability.

During this process it became clear that capability design is based on EM and that the CMM contains elements commonly used in EM. Hence, following the overall stance of the project of preferring the use of existing methodology components, we decided incorporating an existing EM approach for the CDD tasks with similar purpose. The 4EM approach was chosen because of three main reasons: (1) it has six interlinked sub-models addressing the key perspectives of an organizational design (goals, business rules, processes, concepts, actors, and IS requirements), (2) the 4EM meta-model is formally defined, and (3) two of its developers participated the project.

After the assessment of the suitability of 4EM for integration with CDD, we investigated how the elements in the capability meta-model correspond to the elements of the 4EM sub-models. On a conceptual level three strong similarity links were identified suggesting which sub-models of CDD can be supported by 4EM.

Link-1 between 4EM Goals Model and the EM part of the CDD model: goals and KPIs represent the intentional dimension of capability design and they correspond to the Goals Model in 4EM. There are explicit components devoted to goal modeling in 4EM such as goal, problem, opportunity, cause, as well as supports, hinders, and AND and OR refinement relationships, which are also needed for capability design.

Link-2 between 4EM Business Process Model and CDD Processes and Resources: CDD business process, process variants and resources correspond to the operational dimension of capability design. In 4EM there are two specific sub-models devoted to this, namely Business Process Model and Actors and Resources Model, which might be useful for capability design. Later it was decided to use BPMN instead of 4EM Business Process Modeling because an existing Eclipse plugin was chosen for modeling tool, which considerably reduced its implementation costs.

Link-3 between 4EM Concepts Model and CDD Context model: CDD modeling constructs used for representing context, such as context element, context indicator, and measurable property can be considered as the static aspects of the capability design in the sense that they reflect properties of things and phenomena. Hence they can, in principle, be modeled with the Concepts Model of 4EM. But since we observed that specific modeling guidance is needed for each of these components because of their purpose in the model, we decided to elaborate a specialized modeling component and a distinct notation for context modeling, available in [4].

The main purpose of CMM is to present the various modeling components of CDD and how they are related conceptually. It also implicitly includes the main integrity constraints based on association multiplicities, e.g. that each capability is motivated by exactly one goal. The CMM was extensively used in discussions with the use case partners and within the methodology development team. It was the main reference model for the development of the methodology steps.

This version of the meta-model, i.e. the CMM, is however insufficiently detailed for developing a modeling language to the full extent as well as to develop a modeling tool. Hence, the meta-model containing detailed components the modeling language was created. Figure 3 shows a meta-model of the modeling language. Due to the lack of space we have only presented 4EM Goal Model extended with the core components of CDD (in grey). The main difference between the language meta-model in Fig. 3 and the CMM in Fig. 2 is that associations and association roles are modeled as classes. This is needed to specify which association types are permitted between which modeling component types. It also allows specifying graphical symbols for the symbolic association types, such as AND, OR, and AND/OR goal refinement associations. This version of the meta-model was developed analytically – by considering the purpose of each component in the CMM and how it could be represented by the modeling language taking the constructs and notation of 4EM as a starting point. The resulting meta-model proved to be useful in discussions between method and tool developers. It was later implemented in the CDT and extended to represent information needed for other parts of the CDD methodology, such as variables and calculations used for capability adjustment algorithms, which were not part of the modeling language but were needed for capability monitoring.

5 Summary of Lessons Learned

The CMM was used throughout the project from setting the vision to iterative validation at the use case companies. The following experiences can be summarized.

Meta-modeling was an important ME activity designing method components with a clear purpose and semantics. A notable property of CDD in comparison with other methodologies is that the same CMM constructs were used by a fairly large number of methodology components and extensions. E.g. context modeling constructs are used by almost all CDD components. Other methodologies more often have dedicated method components based on specific fragments of the meta-model, e.g. 4EM goals modeling uses the meta-model of the Goals sub-model.

The CMM development went through many iterations. The initial version was fine-tuned during the early requirements elicitation and validation phases, c.f. [3]. Further refinements were introduced during applications at the use case companies and in interactions with the tool development team. The most frequent changes were concerning multiplicities representing integrity constraints of the CDD methodology.

Some modeling constructs were difficult to understand by some method and tool developers in the project and discussing them from the point of view of the CMM and creating examples of capability models based on the meta-model proved useful.

The CMM represented integrity and quality constraints assumed to be useful in the CDD methodology, e.g. each capability requires exactly one context set. This however does not take into account temporal states of the model, i.e. the fact that once a capability component is placed in a model it will exist without a link to a context set until such a modeling component is created and association to it defined.

The meta-model on Fig. 3 represents the CDD (in grey) and 4EM language components. It essentially served as the reference point for tool development. But it was not useful for conceptual discussions, e.g., when developing the different method components. For this purpose the CMM was used. Referring to the MOF levels, the language meta-model (Fig. 3) followed the principles of M2 level, while Ecore (meta-model of Eclipse Modeling Framework) provided M3 level components.

The meta-models were drawn using Vision and System Architect for the purpose of documentation only. It was then manually transferred to Eclipse for implementation into the tool. This process proved somewhat inefficient, and using a meta-tool such as Troux Architect or MetaEdit + would have been more efficient.

The CDD methodology was developed iteratively – the initial version was validated and then refined and extended by additional method components in three development-validation cycles. Development of all new method components started with the inclusion of the new modeling components in the CMM, which included certain restructuring and defining links to the existing components.

The parts of the meta-model related to runtime monitoring and adjustments were supported by other components of the CDD environment. E.g., Capability Context Platform was used for monitoring measurable properties and context elements, as well

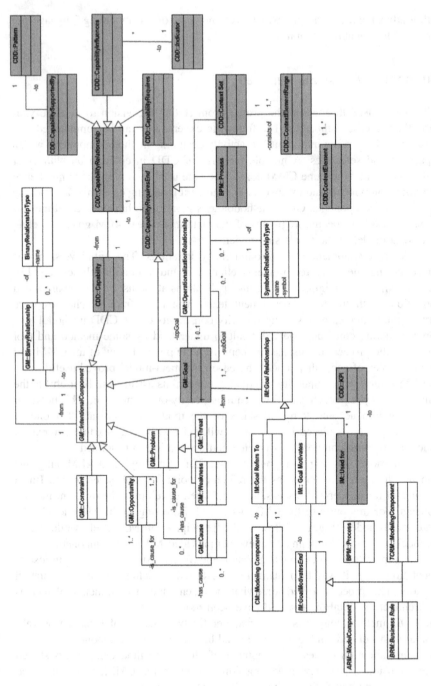

Fig. 3. CDD and 4EM goal model language meta-model

as Capability Navigation Application was used for performing calculations based on context elements and KPI in order to execute capability adjustment algorithms.

6 Concluding Remarks

ME of the CDD methodology included meta-modeling of the modeling language with a particular effort on integration with concepts of the 4EM approach and on supporting the development of a modeling tool. The CDD methodology and environment have been applied to real capability design projects at four use case companies as part of design-evaluation cycles of the project. The validation results show that the methodology and the environment are useful for the companies for adjusting business designs to context changes to address their business challenges.

References

1. EU FP7 CaaS Project: Capability as a service for digital enterprises, proj. no. 611351. http://caas-project.eu/
2. Ulrich, W., Rosen, M.: The business capability map: building a foundation for business/it alignment. Cutter Consortium for Business and Enterprise Architecture (2012)
3. Bērziša, S., Bravos, G., Gonzalez, T., Czubayko, U., España, S., Grabis, J., Henkel, M., Jokste, L., Kampars, J., Koc, H., Kuhr, J., Llorca, C., Loucopoulos, P., Juanes, R., Sandkuhl, K., Simic, H., Stirna, J., Zdravkovic, J.: Deliverable D1.4: requirements specification for CDD. CaaS – Capability as a Service for Digital Enterprises, FP7 proj. 611351, Riga Technical University (2014). http://caas-project.eu/deliverables/
4. Bērziša, S., España, S., Grabis, J., Henkel, M., Jokste, L., Kampars, J., Koç, H., Sandkuhl, K., Stirna, J., Valverde, F., Zdravkovic J.: Deliverable 5.2: the initial version of capability driven development methodology, FP7 proj. 611351. CaaS – Capability as a Service in digital enterprises, Stockholm University (2015). doi:10.13140/RG.2.1.2399.4965
5. Sandkuhl, K., Stirna, J., Persson, A., Wißotzki, M.: Enterprise Modeling – Tackling Business Challenges with the 4EM Method. Springer, Heidelberg (2014). ISBN 978-3-662-43724-7S
6. Hevner, A.R., March, S.T., Park, J., Ram, S.: Design science in information systems research. MIS Q. 28(1), 75–105 (2004)
7. Brinkkemper, S.: Method engineering: engineering of information systems development methods and tools. Inform. Softw. Tech. 38(4), 275–280 (1996)
8. Smolander, K.: OPRR: a model for modelling systems development methods. In: Lyytinen, K., Tahvanainen, V.-P. (eds.) Next Generation CASE tools. IOS Press, Amsterdam (1991)
9. Bergsten, P., Bubenko, J., Dahl, R., Gustafsson, M.R., Johansson, L.A.: RAMATIC - A CASE Shell for Implementation of Specific CASE Tools. SISU, Stockholm (1989)
10. Ralyté, J., Backlund, P., Kühn, H., Jeusfeld, M.A.: Method chunks for interoperability. In: Embley, D.W., Olivé, A., Ram, S. (eds.) ER 2006. LNCS, vol. 4215, pp. 339–353. Springer, Heidelberg (2006)
11. Goldkuhl, G., Lind, M., Seigerroth, U.: Method integration: the need for a learning perspective. IEEE Proc. Softw. 145(4), 113–118 (1998)
12. OMG: OMG Meta Object Facility (MOF) Core Specification, Version 2.5 (2015). http://www.omg.org/mof/

Applying Conceptual Modeling to Better Understand the Human Genome

José F. Reyes Román[1,2(✉)], Óscar Pastor[1], Juan Carlos Casamayor[1],
and Francisco Valverde[3]

[1] Research Center on Software Production Methods (PROS),
Universitat Politècnica de València, Valencia, Spain
{jreyes,opastor}@pros.upv.es, jcarlos@dsic.upv.es
[2] Department of Engineering Sciences, Universidad Central del Este (UCE),
San Pedro de Macorís, Dominican Republic
[3] Computer Science Department, Universitat de València, Valencia, Spain
girome@uv.es

Abstract. The objective of the work is to present the benefits of the application of *Conceptual Modeling (CM)* in complex domains, such as genomics. This paper explains the evolution of a *Conceptual Schema of the Human Genome (CSHG)*, which seeks to provide a clear and precise understanding of the human genome. We want to highlighting all the advantages of the application of CM in a complex domain such as *Genomic Information Systems (GeIS)*. We show how over time this model has evolved, thus we have discovered better forms of representation. As we advanced in exploring the domain, we understood that we should be extending and incorporating the new concepts detected into our model. Here we present and discuss the evolution to reach the current version (CSHG v2). A solution based on conceptual models gives a clear definition of the domain with direct implications for the medical context.

Keywords: Conceptual modeling · CSHG · Evolution · GeIS · Human genome

1 Introduction

Why is Conceptual Modeling (CM) [1] *essential to design and develop correct information systems?* This is a fundamental question for the CM community, which is interested in demonstrating that only through the use of CM techniques can the design and development of quality of information systems be achieved. The need for such a CM-based design and development strategy should be more evident, the greater the complexity of the system under study.

Understanding the human genome is a good example of such an extremely complex problem. Using CMs to provide a solution to deal with the human genome, it has been initially explored in previous works (see for instance [2, 3]), but a holistic perspective of the whole picture has still not been provided. The use of advanced information system engineering approaches is required in this domain due to the huge amount of biological information. An important part of modern Bioinformatics science is devoted

© Springer International Publishing AG 2016
I. Comyn-Wattiau et al. (Eds.): ER 2016, LNCS 9974, pp. 404–412, 2016.
DOI: 10.1007/978-3-319-46397-1_31

to the management of genomic data, but because its continuous evolution it is difficult to find convincing solutions.

However, we were surprised to discover that when we questioned our bio-colleagues about their conceptual data models, the answer was—*in the best case*— simply a relational logical design: a description located in the solution space with no abstract or conceptual design perspective at all. Therefore, we suggested to our bioinformatics colleagues to build a CSHG with the main goal of understanding how life—*as we understand it in our planet*—works.

Our aim in this papers is thus to demonstrate the need for a CM:

- to share the understanding of the essential domain concepts—*in our case the* human *genome*, and
- to guide the design and development of the corresponding databases, which normally support only a part of the CM. This means that using the CM only as a holistic, conceptual DB, it will be possible to integrate different data sources that represent different perspectives of genomic knowledge.

To report all the work done following this research line, we firstly introduce a first conceptual representation of the relevant genomic knowledge, which we call Conceptual Schema of the Human Genome version 1 (CSHG v1). In this paper we do not focus on the details of the *conceptual schema* (CS), but on the conceptual architectural decisions taken for building it. After this conceptual exercise, we show more in-depth discussions about how to better represent basic concepts whose associated knowledge is in constant evolution. The result of this work is the proposal of an alternative version of the conceptual schema, which we call CSHG v2. We also discuss in this paper the conceptual analysis that guided the design of a new version of the CS. The outcome is a sound understanding of the relevant information to achieve more efficient data management policies.

The paper is divided into the following sections: Sect. 2 presents the initial structure for the conceptual schema of the human genome. Section 3 shows the evolution of our CSHG from v1 to v2. Finally, Sect. 4 contains the conclusions and outlines future work.

2 An Initial Conceptual Schema for the Human Genome: CSHG v1

One of the essential benefits of using CM is that it accurately represents the relevant concepts of the analyzed domain. After performing an initial analysis of the problem domain, the next step is to design a domain representation in the form of a CSHG. In this first representation, important decisions are taken to adequately represent the concepts that are basic to understanding the domain.

The first important decision is how to structure the representation of the analyzed domain. Considering the complexity of the information contained in the human genome, we decided to divide the CS representation into three main parts, each one related to a specific domain view:

1. The *Gene-Mutation view* is focused on the gene [5] structure, together with its possible, relevant variations and the determination of the data sources.
2. The *Genome view* is focused on how we go from the whole genome to its relevant component (*chromosomes*) and the type of DNA segments they are made up.
3. The *Transcription view* is centered around the actors that participate in the essential processes of transcription and translation, in order to identify the components that guide the process of going from the DNA-based genotype, to the protein synthesis that is related to the phenotype (*external gene manifestation*).

Next, we introduce the selected CSHG following in order these three views (*you can see the full view of this release in* [11]).

2.1 The Gene-Mutation View

To represent the essential *"Gene"* concept, we assume that the different possible variants—called *"alleles"*—for a gene, are associated to a primary Gene class through using an *"Allele"* class that has two specializations: (1) One representing the sequence considered of reference for the gene and (2) Another representing a possible variated version of the previous one.

The sequence of reference contains an attribute *"sequence"* that gets the specific DNA sequence for a Gene. The variated versions of the Gene that are included in the *"Allelic Variant"* class use a derived attribute which represents a change in the sequence of reference. *What structure has an allele? Is it a sufficiently well-defined structure for it to be included in our Conceptual Schema?* The answer that we give to this question uses the concept of *"Transcription Unit"*. This is represented through an association between the selected allelic version of a Gene, and the set of DNA pieces that compose it—called *"Segments"* in our model. Going further, the structure of a Segment contains the following components: (a) A *promoter*: describes the sequence of DNA that marks the beginning of the transcription. (b) *Transcribable sequences*: is responsible for describing the DNA sequence transcribed by RNA polymerase. (c) A *terminator*: describes the end of the transcription process in the DNA sequence. (d) *Regulatory sequence*: describes an allelic segment containing the nucleotide sequences of the regulatory functions of one or more processes of transcription.

To characterize in detail, the possible variants, the conceptual schema introduces a *"Variation"* class, where the changes to be applied to the reference sequence are specified. The next important aspect is to identify the type of variations that are considered relevant. Summarizing what is currently known, we distinguish three main types of variations:

- The first, focused on the effect that the variation has (it is either a mutation—associated to a disease—or it is simply a neutral variation in the sense that it has no bad effect in clinical terms—we refer to it as *"Neutral Polymorphism"* in biological language.
- The second considers the location of the variation—i.e. if it is variation whose scope is either the chromosome or the gene.

- The third considers whether the variation has a description associated with it. The description could take two forms: (a) A *"precise variation"* when the structure and the nucleotides that are involved are clearly known, or (b) if the variation structure is not known, we talk about an *"imprecise variation"* whose effects are probably still to be discovered.

It is important to fix how many precise variations do exist: *insertions, deletions, Indel* and *inversion* [7].

In this version of our schema the concept of SNPs[1] it was not explicitly represented because it was considered as a normal variation. In the development of our CSHG v1 we detected an important point to consider: the use of reference sequences from external sources. Unfortunately, gene identifiers sometimes depend on the external data source. It is therefore important to represent in our CS the external data sources used for the identification of a gene and an allele (represented in the CS using the *"Gene Data Bank Identification"* and *"Allele Data Bank Identification"* classes respectively). It is also important for this view to know the origin of the data considered as *"relevant"*, because its health implications. The aim is to support this relevance with bibliographic data and present a clear view about the knowledge source.

2.2   The Genome View

The next view is introduced with the goal of including individual genomes that could be compared structurally with the previous gene-mutation view. This view provide a general perspective related to the whole Genome notion, and characterizing its concrete composition. In fact, the genome is composed of chromosomes—*in the human's case 23 pairs of chromosomes as is well-known*. They are represented by the *"Chromosome"* class in our CS. The sequences of chromosomes are long, and to manage them with functional unity criteria, they are divide into, smaller *"pieces"* (components with a functional identity). We will use the notion of *"Segment"* to account for this fact. Introducing this element as a basic component of a global genomic sequence identifies which specific parts of chromosomal DNA have an important meaning. The composition of all these chromosome segments represents the sequence of the entire *chromosome*.

The segments of chromosomes can be of two types: *"coding"* and *"non-coding"*, depending on whether or not they are associated with protein synthesis. In our CS we label them as *"GenicSegment"* and *"NonGenicSegment"* respectively. Genic Segments represent the coding parts that are traditionally considered most significant for the chromosome and that are related to genes. But it is increasingly clear that the *"non-genic"* DNA components also have vital functions in explaining the genomic operation. This is why there is a need to distinguish between gene segments (related to a gene and

---

[1] A *single nucleotide polymorphism* (SNP), is a variation at a single position in a DNA sequence among individuals. Recall that the DNA sequence is formed from a chain of four nucleotide bases: A, C, G, and T [*Scitable by Nature Education*].

connected through the gene concept with the previous Gene-Mutation view) and non-genic segments.

Similarly, it is necessary to distinguish between different types of non-genic segments. According to current knowledge, two types were identified: (a) *intergenic regions* that represent the space between genes, and, (b) those that are part of the *chromosome elements structure*. Among these chromosomal elements, we found three elements considered of interest: *centromere, telomere* and *ORI* [4, 8]. This view thus makes it feasible to represent complete genomes of individuals, and allows introducing the information associated with two aspects: Research Centers responsible for sequencing genomes and the final result of the sequencing process of a given sample (represented in the CS by the "*ResearchCenter*" and "*Genome*" classes respectively).

2.3   The Transcription View

The main purpose of this view is to represent the process of "*protein synthesis*" [9], by integrating a definition of the internal structure of the alleles in order to describe how the aforementioned elements are involved in the process of DNA transcription.

The first aspect we studied was the representation of the transcribed RNA copy of DNA from the transcriptable sequence (related to a "*transcribable sequence*" and thus linked to the Gene-Mutation view). This RNA product that is obtained immediately after transcription is known as "*primary transcript*" in the biological vocabulary. The primary transcript is constituted by one or more partitions (represented as main components of a class called "*Primary Transcript Path*"), and each partition has two types of transcription elements: *Exons* and *Introns* [4].

The exons present different combinations for a certain partition of the primary transcript. In the CS we represent the different combinations of exons by means of the class "*Spliced Transcript*" (related to a "*alelle*" and hereby again connected with the Gene-Mutation view). The process of "*Splicing*" is based on the elimination of introns and union of exons on the mRNA before leaving the core. The results of this process represented by the *Splicing Transcript* class can produce two different splicing results: *the mRNA* and the *alternative splicing* (represented in the CS as "*Others RNA*") [6].

The mRNA is then the result of the transcription of a gene and it carries the information needed to synthesize a protein. To complete this transcription view, we need to model the path from the mRNA to the resulting protein translation process. Within the mRNA we found the open reading frames (*ORF*) ([4]). After finishing the translation of an ORF, an amino acid chain is generated by the primary structure of the protein ("*Primary Polipeptide*" class). The chemical transformations of the chain of amino acids produce as final result a functional protein (represented in the CS as "*Protein*"). The combination of these three views makes our first version of the CSHG.

3   From v1 to v2: CSHG v2

While applying in the real practice the initial version of the CSHG, we identified a set of questions to address:

1. We were not sure about the suitability of mixing a Genome view related to the storage of individual genomes—the so-called Genome view in v1, with a more theoretical, structural Genomic view related to the Genome configuration and characterization as a whole—the so-called Gene-Mutation and Transcription view.
2. Concerning the core concept of gene, it is not always feasible to describe DNA structure in terms of genes as basic constructs. We concluded that the most suitable structure is suing chromosome elements as the basic building blocks.
3. More relevant concepts were needed, for instance, the concept of SNPs.

The development of these three ideas led us to the evolution of the conceptual schema CSHG v2 that we explain in detail below. (*the full view of this schema is available in* [11]).

3.1   Removing Individual Genomes Data Bank

Reviewing the knowledge represented in our CSHG v1, the generic genome template— *which is the precise human genome structure and how to characterize it*—and the genome data bank perspective—how to store individual genomes that are to be analyzed—was mixed: the gene-mutation and transcription views appear together in the conceptual schema.

For representing accurately, the domain knowledge, the generic properties of the genome and the individual samples should be clearly distinguished. By separating the individual sample of a patient from the genome template taken as reference, it would be easier to find—for instance—significant variations related with diseases. The CSHG v2 thus omits the so-called Genome view, focusing on a more precise description of a generic genome template to collect all the relevant genome information. We decided to organize it in five mains "*views*" (see for instance [11]):

- *Structural:* describes the genome structure.
- *Transcription:* shows the components and concepts related to protein synthesis.
- *Variation:* describes the changes in the sequence of reference.
- *Pathways* (not analyzed in this work for reasons of space): describes information about metabolic pathways.
- *Bibliography and data bank view:* describes where any given data comes from.

3.2   The Chromosome Elements as Basic Modeling Units

The use of chromosome elements as basic building DNA elements has a direct influence on the way in which variations and their DNA origin were represented in the CS.

In v1 the notion of allele was represented as an explicit derived notion—through the class *Allelic Variant*. Additionally, all the variations were related to genic segments, as it was not possible to register variations whose source were in other—*non genic*—genome parts. To overcome this problem, our conceptual proposal is to directly relate a variation with a specific DNA chromosome position, as this solution better represents the real genome structure. The benefit of not having the variation directly related to an *Allelic Variant* is twofold:

- Firstly, it allows the variation to be defined with more precision, as it is associated with a unique genome sequence where the variation occurs. The variation is not dependent on the Allelic Variant and the corresponding many-to-many association as was done in the previous v1.
- Secondly, the Allelic Variant concept is no longer needed explicitly. As we have no individual genomes in the model, the absence of individual genomes eliminates the need for managing Allelic Variants. As our knowledge of the genomic domain increased, we wondered if reference Allelic Variants do really exist. This would mean that there is a catalogue of well-determined variants whose structure and behavior should be perfectly known. The introduction of this knowledge into the model could be accomplished at any time. But while a precise answer for this question does not exist, we conclude that omitting the Allelic Variant class provides a clearer description, conceptually speaking.

In any case, it is possible to generate allele instances using the adequate combinations of variations, because it can be seen as derived information obtained by applying a set of selected variations on the source sequence of reference. To have instances of an Allelic Variant class involves characterizing the specific set of variations that *"create"* the considered allele. We argue that this v2 representation is more precise because the separation of these conceptual concerns is made explicit, the conceptual schema is in a—semantically-speaking—clearer state, and it enables incorporating new knowledge, as satisfactory answers to the open questions are provided by the progress in the genome understanding process. The representation of this allelic knowledge is left out until the next version of the conceptual schema.

3.3 Modeling SNPs

In the initial version, a highly relevant genome concept as the SNP was not explicitly represented in our conceptual definition. The specialization of different variations accomplished in version 2 is more precise, as it distinguishes between two categories: the *frequency* of the variation, and its known, *precise* or *imprecise* description.

Beyond this conceptual simplification, it is important to take into account how SNPs are stored in current, widely-used data sources (as *dbSNP* [10]). Looking at their current representations, we performed a reverse conceptual engineering exercise to include in the CSHG a set of classes that represent this knowledge. We discovered that an SNP is specified in this domain as a potential set of variations in which one nucleotide changes into another one. This change is open, meaning that the notion of variation in this case is that one position in the sequence of reference may have different values depending on the studied population, and with a given frequency. This fact has been addressed using a specialization hierarchy for SNPs.

This change leaded to a new discussion. Any precise variation is modeled as an individual variation where the sequence of reference *"suffers"* a change. But the way in which SNPs are treated is somewhat different: an SNP defines which nucleotide is altered. It appears in the source reference sequence (through the attribute *"allele"* for the homozygous case, *"allele1"* and *"allele2"* for the heterozygous case). This representation preserves the way in which SNP data appears in real genomic settings. But the view of SNPs as a set of individual variations suggests that a better representation could be to model SNP as an aggregation of precise (*indel*) variations. This change will better represent conceptually what an SNP is, but the change has to be carefully analyzed because data management of current SNPs data repositories should be properly adapted to the new data representation.

4 Conclusions and Future Work

Using conceptual modeling—CM—techniques is a basic strategy to design and develop sound and efficient *Genomic Information Systems* (GeIS). This is the central issue of our work. The CM applied to this type of environment facilitates the generation of systems that support the decision making processes in the Bioinformatics domain. The domain knowledge always required to be extended in order to meet with the new needs that.

The initial version (v1) focused on modeling *"Genotyping"* then sought to create a semantic and content description (on existing sources to *"capture"* and *"represent"* good information data). The reality is that we faced and discussed multiple decisions before moving on to our next CSHG v2. The version 2 of the CS is characterized by the change in its central axis based on *"genes"* and takes as its axis the concept of *"Chromosome (and chromosome elements)"*. This change was made to simplify the schema and provide a more flexible approach to extend it according to the domain evolution. This new version gives us greater precision, and allows us to manipulate data in a more direct way.

Future research work is oriented to the integration of haplotypes and statistical factors in our conceptual schema. We also contemplate the implementation of an ETL process using our CS.

Acknowledgements. This work has been supported by the Ministry of Higher Education, Science and Technology (*MESCyT*). Santo Domingo, Dominican Rep. and by Spanish Ministry of Economy and Competitiveness under the project PI13/02247 cofinanced with ERDF.

References

1. Olivé, A.: Conceptual Modeling of Information Systems. Springer, Heidelberg (2007)
2. Bornberg-Bauer, E., Paton, N.W.: Conceptual data modelling for bioinformatics. Briefings Bioinform. **3**(2), 166–180 (2002)
3. Ram, S., Wei, W.: Modeling the semantics of 3D protein structures. In: Atzeni, P., Chu, W., Hongjun, L., Zhou, S., Ling, T.-W. (eds.) ER 2004. LNCS, vol. 3288, pp. 696–708. Springer, Heidelberg (2004)
4. Glossary of Genetic Terms: NHGRI (2016). http://www.genome.gov/glossary/
5. Rodden, R.T.: Genetics for Dummies, 2nd edn. Wiley Publishing, Inc., Indianapolis (2010)

6. Tazi, J., Bakkour, N., Stamm, S.: Alternative splicing and disease. Biochim. Biophys. Acta (BBA) Mol Basis Dis. **1792**(1), 14–26 (2009)
7. den Dunnen, J.T., Antonarakis, S.E.: Recommendations for the description of DNA seq. variants - v2.0. Hum. Mutat. **15**, 7–12 (2000)
8. Craig, N., Green, R., Greider, C., Cohen-Fix, O., Storz, G., Wolberger, C.: Molecular Biology: Principles of Genome Function. Oxford University Press, Oxford (2014)
9. Spirin, A., Swartz, J.: Cell-Free Protein Synthesis: Methods and Protocols. Wiley, Weinheim (2014). ISBN 9783527691502/9783527691500
10. Sherry, S.T., Ward, M.H., Kholodov, M., Baker, J., Phan, L., Smigielski, E.M., Sirotkin, K.: dbSNP: the NCBI database of genetic variation. Nucleic Acids Res. **29**(1), 308–311 (2001)
11. Pastor, O., Reyes Román, J.F., Valverde, F.: Conceptual schema of the human genome (CSHG). Technical report (2016). http://hdl.handle.net/10251/67297

Schema Mapping

Data Analytics: From Conceptual Modelling to Logical Representation

Qing Wang[(✉)] and Minjian Liu

Research School of Computer Science,
Australian National University, Canberra, Australia
{qing.wang,minjian.liu}@anu.edu.au

Abstract. In recent years, data analytics has been studied in a broad range of areas, such as health-care, social sciences, and commerce. In order to accurately capture user requirements for enhancing communication between analysts, domain experts and users, conceptualising data analytics tasks to provide a high level of modelling abstraction becomes increasingly important. In this paper, we discuss the modelling of data analytics and how a conceptual framework for data analytics applications can be transformed into a logical framework that supports a simple yet expressive query language for specifying data analytics tasks. We have also implemented our modelling method into a unified data analytics platform, which allows to incorporate analytics algorithms as plug-ins in a flexible and open manner, We present case studies on three real-world data analytics applications and our experimental results on an unified data analytics platform.

Keywords: Data analytics · Conceptual modelling · Logical model · Query language

1 Introduction

Data analytics is rapidly growing in popularity, with a variety of applications in many areas, e.g., health-care, social sciences, commerce, etc. This has led to the recent development of a large number of data analytics tools and systems, most of which are built upon graph models, such as GraphLab [11] and Pregel [12]. Nonetheless, in practice, many data analytics applications are still conducted in an ad-hoc way, due to the lack of general principles to design, develop and implement data analytics applications. For example, the decision on choosing data models for data analytics applications often relies on individuals' own expertise, rather than a systematic consideration of requirements. This calls for a formal design paradigm that can provide a high level of modelling abstraction to support users in understanding their data analytics requirements. In particular, with the increasing complexity of data analytics applications, the

---

Q. Wang and M. Liu—Contributed equally to this work.

© Springer International Publishing AG 2016
I. Comyn-Wattiau et al. (Eds.): ER 2016, LNCS 9974, pp. 415–429, 2016.
DOI: 10.1007/978-3-319-46397-1_32

need to explicitly represent data analytics requirements into a conceptual model is pressingly required [6].

Recently, several methods for conceptually modelling data analytics applications have been reported [2,15,16]. A conceptual modelling paradigm for network analytics applications, called the Network Analytics ER model (NAER), was proposed in [15]. In a nutshell, the NAER model extends the concepts of the traditional ER models [4] in three aspects: (a) the *structural* aspect - analytical entity and relationship types are added to represent first-class entities and relationships from the data analytics perspective; (b) the *manipulation* aspect - topological constructs are added to explicitly represent different topological structures of interest; and (c) the *integrity* aspect - constraints are added for governing integrity among different data analytics tasks. Based on this conceptual modelling paradigm, a set of design guidelines has further been provided in [15], through which users can benefit from establishing a conceptual framework that provides a coherent and comprehensive view on data analytics applications. As depicted in Fig. 1, such a conceptual framework may consist of a *core schema*, which has basic entity and relationship types to capture data requirements as in the traditional ER modelling, *topology schemas*, which have analytical entity and relationship types to capture query requirements of data analytics applications, and *query topics*, which describe the structure of queries in query requirements and are associated with both the core schema and the topology schemas.

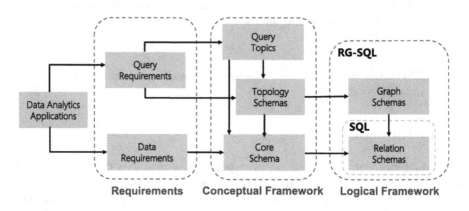

Fig. 1. A general process of modelling data analytics applications

Nonetheless, how can we transform such a conceptual framework into a logical framework which is well suited to model the logical structure of data analytics applications without ambiguities? Although basic entity and relationship types in the core schema can be easily transformed into relation schemas following the existing rules [14], it is not yet clear: (1) How can analytical entity and relationship types be accurately defined at the logical level? (2) What logical structure can topology schemas be translated into? (3) How can topological constructs be specified using a query language, ideally in a declarative way? These questions are left unanswered in the previous works [15,16]. This paper aims to answer these questions by exploring the connections between such a conceptual framework for data analytics and its corresponding logical representation.

Contributions. We have the following contributions in this paper:

- We discuss how a conceptual framework for data analytics as introduced in [15] can be effectively transformed into a logical framework.
- We introduce a novel query language for data analytics, which extends SQL with the ability to query topological properties of interest.
- We have implemented our modelling method into a unified data analytics platform, which allows to incorporate analytics algorithms as plug-ins in a flexible and open manner.
- We present three real-world data analytics applications to illustrate the expressive power and simplicity of our modelling method, and the experimental results of evaluating the performance of our data analytics platform.

Outline. In the following, Sect. 2 discusses the modelling of data analytics and Sect. 3 introduces our query language for data analytics. We discuss three data analytics applications in Sect. 4, and present our experimental results in Sect. 5. The paper is concluded in Sect. 6.

2 Modelling Data Analytics

In this section, we discuss data analytics from a modelling perspective. This is because, in practice, many organisations are facing the challenges of managing data analytics tasks in a complex environment, and using modelling techniques can bring in several advantages to addressing these challenges, including: enhancing communications among multiple stakeholders, understanding connections among complex analysis requirements, and detecting design flaws earlier and right from the start before implementing any code.

We first recall the Network Analytics ER (NAER) modelling method [15], then elaborate on the transformation from a conceptual model into the logical representation for data analytics applications.

Generally, the NAER modelling method supports two kinds of entities and relationships [15]: (1) *base entities and relationships* which specify first-class entities and relationships that should be stored in a database system from a data management perspective, as in the traditional ER modelling; (2) *analytical entities and relationships* which specify first-class entities and relationships used for the data analytics purpose. In the NAER model, base types are the ground from which analytical types can be derived, and the base types that define an analytical type are called the *support* of the analytical type.

To conceptualise data analytics tasks, not only data requirements (i.e., what kind of data is needed) but also query requirements (i.e., what kinds of queries are used) are considered in the conceptual modelling process. Base entity and relationship types are used to capture data requirements, leading to a core schema, while analytical entity and relationship types are used to capture query requirements, which yields a number of topology schemas. That is, a *core schema* contains a set of base types, and each *topology schema* contains a set of analytical types, and the support of each analytical type in a topology schema is a subset of base types in the core schema. In general, each conceptual framework for data analytics applications contains a core schema which is relatively large, and a number of topology schemas which are often small. Although being small, topology schemas can be flexibly composed into larger schemas if needed [16].

After a conceptual framework has been established as previously discussed, the question arising is: how can such a conceptual framework be transformed into a logical framework? Although, in principle, it is possible to choose any logical data model, e.g., the relational data model, a graph model or a combination of several data models, data in many real-world applications is stored in relational databases. Moreover, data analytics tasks often require sophisticated analysis on both relational and topological properties of data. For these reasons, we develop the following data model at the logical level:

- Transform basic entities and relationships in the core schema into a set of relations for storage, as in the traditional ER modelling approach [14];
- Transform analytical entities and relationships in the topology schemas into a set of *entity-relationship (ER) graphs* for analytics [9]. That is, one topology schema corresponds to one type of ER graphs in which each vertex represents an analytical entity and each edge between two vertices represents an analytical relationship between two analytical entities.

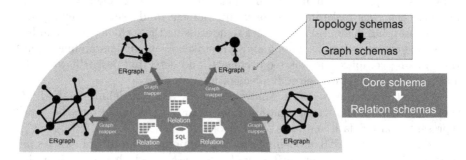

Fig. 2. A hybrid data model at the logical level

Figure 2 illustrates a hybrid data model, in which a collection of ER graphs are constructed on top of relations through graph mappers either on the fly or in a materialized manner, as will be formally defined in Sect. 3. Accordingly, the core schema and topology schemas in a conceptual model are transformed into a set of relation schemas and graph schemas in a logical model. In practice, such a hybrid data model can be easily built by applying the above transformation rules to a conceptual model that describes data analytics tasks. Since data analytics tasks often require additional querying capability over graphs, for example, finding paths, detecting communities, clustering, ranking, etc., in order to implement such a hybrid data model at the logical level, we would need a query language that can support joint analytics of relations and graphs.

3   A Query Language for Data Analytics

We present a SQL-like query language for data analytics, called RG-SQL, which extends the standard SQL with new features to facilitate joint analytics of relations and graphs. More specifically, RG-SQL provides data definition statements that can create graphs from relations in a flexible way, and data manipulation statements to conduct various data analytics operations over relations and graphs. In the following, we explain these new features of RG-SQL in detail.

Creating graphs. RG-SQL can create two types of graphs: undirected graphs and directed graphs, through the specification on graph types using UNGRAPH and DIGRAPH, respectively. Graphs can be created either on the fly or in a materialized manner with the following syntax:

– *Graphs on the fly*
     SELECT <attribute list>
     FROM <relations | graphs>
     WHERE <graph name> IS <graph type> AS (graph mapper);
– *Materialized graphs*
     CREATE <graph type> <graph name> AS (graph mapper);

where <graph type> := UNGRAPH | DIGRAPH, and a graph mapper is a SQL query that extracts an *edge list* (i.e., a list of edges of a graph, which is a common data structure for representing a graph) from relations in the underlying databases for graph construction.

Ranking. To assess the importance of vertices within a graph, RQ-SQL provides a RANK operator with the following syntax:

     RANK(<graph name>, <measure>)
     <measure> := degree | indegree | outdegree | betweenness |
              closeness | pagerank

A number of measures are available for determining the importance of vertices [3]. One may choose the most suitable measure for a specific query based on the type of the graph and desired properties. Each RANK(<graph name> , <measure>) yields a relation with two attributes: vertexid, and value.

Clustering. To explore the clustering structure of vertices over a graph, RG-SQL provides a CLUSTER operator with the following syntax:

     CLUSTER(<graph name>, <algorithm>)
     <algorithm> := CC | SCC | GN | CNM | MC

where CC refers to an algorithm of finding connected components, SCC an algorithm of finding strongly connected components, and GN, CNM and MC three algorithms for community detection, which respectively correspond to Girvan-Newman algorithm [7], Clauset-Newman-Moore Algorithm [5] and Peixoto's modified Monte Carlo Algorithm [13]. Each CLUSTER(<graph name>, <algorithm>) yields a relation with three attributes: clusterid, size and members.

Path finding. To find paths among two or more vertices, RG-SQL provides a PATH operator with the following syntax:

PATH(<graph name>, <path expression>)
<path expression> := . | V | <path expression>/ <path expression>|
                         <path expression>// <path expression>

where V is a vertex expression that imposes certain condition on the vertices of a path, . is a *do-not-care* symbol indicating that any vertex is allowed in its position, / represents one edge, and // represents any number of edges. A path expression is *valid* if it contains a vertex expression in the first and last positions. For example, an expression V1//V2 specifies a path between two vertices V1 and V2, regardless of the length of the path. Each PATH(<graph name> , <path expression>) yields a relation with three attributes: pathid, length and path.

3.1 Discussion

We now briefly discuss the expressive power of RG-SQL in comparison with the relational query language SQL and the graph query language Cypher used in Neo4j (http://neo4j.com). Since RG-SQL extends the standard SQL with the additional operations, such as ranking, clustering and path finding, RQ-SQL is strictly more expressive than SQL and has the expressive power beyond the first order logic [1], for example, recursion in a path finding expression V1//V2 cannot be expressed by SQL but can be expressed by RG-SQL. For Cypher, it is a query language designed to express graph patterns, which can nonetheless be expressed by RG-SQL or its variations through a combination of path finding operations. However, not all operations of RG-SQL can be expressed by Cypher, e.g., ranking operations using betweenness and clustering operations using GN.

4   Data Analytics Applications

In this section we study data analytics tasks in three real-world applications and explain how data analytics requirements can be conceptualized in our work.

4.1 ACM Digital Library

ACM Digital Library (http://dl.acm.org/) is a bibliographical network containing a collection of articles, authors, and publishers. Each article is written by one or more authors, one article may cite a number of other articles, and articles are included in conference proceedings or journals published by publishers. Figure 3 depicts a conceptual schema for this data analytics application, which includes the topology schemas S_{a1} and S_{a2} required by the following queries:

Q1: [Collaborative communities] *Find the communities that consist of authors who collaborate with each other to publish articles together.*

Q2: [Influential articles] *Find the top 3 most influential articles.*

For Q1, we may use RQ-SQL to create a materialized coauthorship graph for coauthorship over S_{a1}, then find the collaborative communities in the coauthorship graph by applying the MC algorithm in CLUSTER.

```
CREATE UNGRAPH coauthorship AS
    (SELECT w1.aid, w2.aid AS coaid
     FROM WRITE AS w1, WRITE AS w2
     WHERE w1.aid!=w2.aid AND w1.pid=w2.pid);

SELECT clusterid, size, members
FROM CLUSTER(coauthorship, MC);
```

For Q2, we may create a citation graph over S_{a2} on the fly and then to find influential articles in the citation graph using the measure betweenness.

```
SELECT vertexid, value
FROM RANK(citation, betweenness)
WHERE citation IS DIGRAPH AS (SELECT aid, citedaid FROM CITE)
LIMIT 3;
```

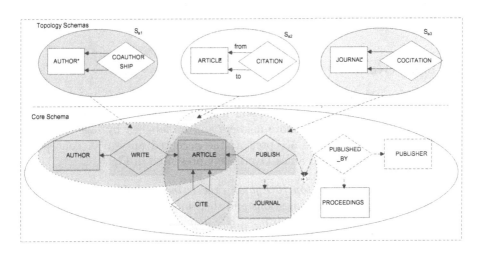

Fig. 3. A conceptual schema for ACM Digital Library

4.2   Twitter

Twitter (https://twitter.com/) is a social network which enables users to post tweets. Users may follow one another. A tweet can mention one or more users and be labelled by one or more tags. Figure 4 depicts a conceptual schema for data analytics in Twitter. Typical data analytics tasks in Twitter include to analyse how users follow each other and to find the most followed people as described by the following queries:

Q3: [Shortest path] *Find the shortest path between Jack and Max.*

Q4: [Most followed people] *Find the most followed people who have posted at least one tweet about ANU.*

Firstly, the `following` graph over the topology schema S_{t1} is created based on entities of USER* and their relationships in FOLLOWING. Then for Q3 we may find the shortest path between Jack and Max using the following RG-SQL query:

```
SELECT *
FROM PATH(following, v1//v2)
WHERE v1 AS (SELECT uid FROM USER WHERE name = 'Jack')
      AND v2 AS (SELECT uid FROM USER WHERE name = 'Max')
ORDER BY length ASC LIMIT 1;
```

For Q4, we need to not only find the most followed people in the `following` graph but also people who have posted a tweet tagged by @ANU from the relations over the core schema, as illustrated by the following RG-SQL query.

```
SELECT uid, value
FROM RANK(following, pagerank) AS p1, POST AS p2, LABELLED_BY AS l
WHERE p1.vertexid=p2.uid AND p2.twid=l.tid AND l.label='ANU'
ORDER BY value DESC;
```

4.3   Stack Overflow

Stack Overflow (http://stackoverflow.com/) is a collaboratively edited question and answer site for programmers. Users may ask questions or post answers. A question may have zero or more answers and be labelled by tags. For each question, one answer can be accepted as the accepted answer. A conceptual schema for data analytics in Stack Overflow is presented in Fig. 5.

Q5: [Python experts] *Find top 10 Python experts in Stack Overflow* (i.e. users who often reply Python questions and their answers are often accepted).

Q6: [Most influential expert] *Find the influential expert in Stack Overflow who is involved in one of the top 3 largest question-answer communities.*

Similarly, we first create the `getting_answers` graph over the topology schema S_{s1}. Then the RQ-SQL query for Q5 is follows:

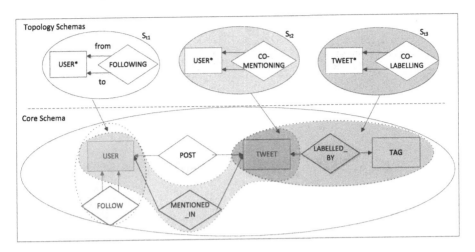

Fig. 4. A conceptual schema for Twitter

```
SELECT * FROM RANK(getting_answers, pagerank) WHERE vertexid IN
    (SELECT owner_id FROM ANSWER AS a, LABELLED_BY AS l, TAG AS t
        WHERE a.parent_qid=l.qid AND l.tid=t.tid AND tag_label = 'python')
LIMIT 10;
```

For Q6, we have the following RQ-SQL query, in which both RANK and CLUSTER operators are applied over two different graphs and their results can be flexibly combined to support further analytics.

```
SELECT r.vertexid
FROM RANK(getting_answers, pagerank) AS r,
     (SELECT members FROM CLUSTER(co-answering, MC)
      ORDER BY size DESC LIMIT 3) AS c
WHERE r.vertexid=ANY(c.members);
```

5   Experiments

We have implemented our modelling method into a unified data analytics platform, called *Rogas*, which allows to incorporate analytics algorithms as plug-ins in a flexible and open manner [10]. To understand how well Rogas can perform in comparison with other database systems, we have conducted experiments to compare the expressive power of query languages and the time efficiency of query execution in three different systems: PostgreSQL (http://www.postgresql.org/), Neo4j (http://neo4j.com) and Rogas. These experiments were performed on a Dell Optiplex 9020 desktop computer with the Intel(R) Core(TM) i7-4790 CPU 3.6 GHz 8 cores processor, 16 GB of memory and 256 GB disk. Rogas extends the query engine of PostgreSQL 9.4.4, with additional functionalities implemented using Python 2.7.6. The version of Neo4j we used is community 2.2.5.

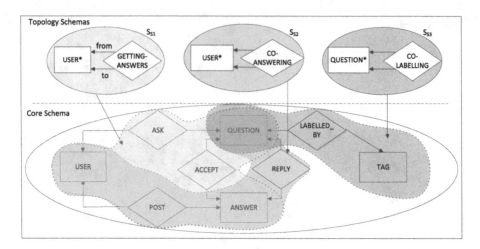

Fig. 5. A conceptual schema for Stack Overflow

In our experiments, we used the data sets from the data analytics applications discussed in Sect. 4: (1) ACM Digital Library (ACM DL) data set provided by the ACM Digital Library (http://dl.acm.org/), (2) Stack Overflow data set from the Stanford Network Analytics Platform (http://snap.stanford.edu/proj/snap-icwsm/), and (3) Twitter data set provided by Haewoon Kwak (http://an.kaist.ac.kr/traces/WWW2010.html). Table 1 presents more details about these three data sets.

Table 2 depicts the queries used in our experiments, which can be generally divided into three categories: (1) Q1–Q3 are relational queries including join, sorting, and aggregate operations; (2) Q4–Q10 are queries about graph properties, including: triangle counting, pagerank centrality, path finding and community detection; (3) Q11–Q12 are sophisticated queries that may combine several graph properties, e.g., Q11 combines pagerank centrality with finding connected components and Q12 combines pagerank centrality with path finding.

Our first experiment is to illustrate the expressive power of the three query languages: PostgreSQL, RG-SQL and Cypher in terms of the queries Q1–Q12. As shown in Table 3, PostgreSQL, RG-SQL and Cypher do have different expressive powers. SQL cannot be used to specify Q6–Q12 and Cypher cannot be used to specify Q10–Q12. Nonetheless, RG-SQL is expressive enough to specify all these queries.

Our second experiment is to evaluate the time efficiency of query execution in Rogas, PostgreSQL and Neo4j. As not all queries can be expressed by PostgreSQL and Neo4j, we have thus compared Q1-Q5 over the three systems, and Q6-Q9 only over Rogas and Neo4j. Note that, for Q6 and Q7, Neo4j needs to use an extension, called *Neo4j Mazerunner*, to run graph analytics algorithms at scale with Hadoop HDFS and Apache Spark (http://neo4j.com/developer/apache-spark/#mazerunner), and is thus required to send an HTTP

Table 1. Three data sets used in our experiments

Data set	Raw data size	No of vertices in graphs (Neo4j)	No of edges in graphs (Neo4j)	No of records in relations (PostgreSQL)	
ACM DL	14.9 GB (XML)	1,128,243	2,488,849	PUBLISHER	50
				JOURNAL	128
				PROCEEDINGS	6,421
				ARTICLE	337,006
				AUTHOR	784,638
				WRITE	932,400
				CITE	1,212,894
Stack Overflow	30.6 GB (XML)	21,713,109	31,747,662	QUESTION	7,990,787
				ANSWER	13,684,117
				TAG	38,205
				LABELLED_BY	13,466,686
Twitter	29.7 GB (TXT)	13,250,196	264,368,797	TWEET	10,762,104
				TAG	210,121
				USER	2,277,971
				FOLLOW	259,602,970
				MENTIONED_IN	3,108,776
				LABELLED_BY	1,657,051

GET request to Neo4j Mazerunner. In such cases, the time of executing queries in Neo4j includes the time for sending and receiving the requests. For each query, we ran it 5 times in each system and took the average time for plotting. Figure 6 presents our experimental result. The key observations are as follows:

- For Q1–Q5, Rogas performed equally well with PostgreSQL, and better than Neo4j in most queries except for Q4. This is because Q4 is about pattern matching which requires to navigate hyper-connectivity on graphs, and Neo4j has been particularly optimised for such queries whereas we have not yet implemented any query optimisation techniques. For Q5, it is not surprising that Rogas performed better than Neo4j since it handles the problem of triangle counting, for which the study in [8] has also experimentally verified that relational databases can perform the triangle counting task very efficiently through expressing a three-way self-join.
- For Q6–Q7, as Neo4j needs to use Neo4j Mazerunner, it requires time on sending and receiving the requests. Thus, Rogas performed better than Neo4j. However, for Q8–Q9, similar to Q4, these queries need to navigate hyper-connectivity on graphs and Neo4j performed better than Rogas.

In addition to Q1–Q12, we have also run several queries about closeness centrality over Twitter using Rogas and Neo4j. Rogas can successfully complete the queries and return the query results, while Neo4j failed and the system reported the "OutOfMemory" error. The reason for this is that the graphs created in Twitter are large so that processing these queries exceeded the memory limitation of Neo4j.

Table 2. Queries used in our experiments

Query	Data set	Query description
		Join Operation + Sorting Operation
Q1	Stack Overflow	Show the question id, the owner id and the tag label of top 10 questions that have the most view count.
		Join Operation + Sorting Operation + Aggregate Operation
Q2	Stack Overflow	Show the top 5 answerers and their latest reputation score in an descending order based on the number of their answers that accepted by questions.
		Join Operation + Sorting Operation + Aggregate Operation
Q3	ACM DL	Show the number of articles of each journal and proceeding along with the journal name and the proceeding title in a descending order.
		Pattern Matching
Q4	Twitter	Recommend 10 twitter users for Jack who currently does not follow these users but Jack follows somebody who are following them.
		Triangle Counting
Q5	ACM DL	Count the number of triangles of the co-authorship network.
		PageRank Centrality
Q6	ACM DL	Find the top 10 influential authors according to the pagerank centrality in the co-authorship network.
		Connected Component
Q7	ACM DL	Count the number of connected components of the co-authorship network.
		Path Finding
Q8	ACM DL	Find paths with length less than 2, which connect two author V1 and V2 in the co-authorship network where author V1 is affiliated at ANU and author V2 is affiliated at UNSW.
		Shortest Path
Q9	ACM DL	Find a shortest paths between two authors Michael Norrish and Kevin Elphinstone in the co-author network.
		Community Detection
Q10	Stack Overflow	Find a group of tags that they are often used together to label a question.
		PageRank Centrality + Connected Component
Q11	ACM DL	According to the pagerank centrality, find the top 3 authors of the biggest collaborative community in the co-authorship network.
		PageRank Centrality + Path Finding
Q12	ACM DL	According to the pagerank centrality, show how the top 2 authors connect with each other in the co-authorship network.

Table 3. Comparison on the expressive power of the query languages PostgreSQL, RQ-SQL and Cypher over the queries Q1–Q12, where √ and × indicate "expressible" and "not expressible", respectively

	Q1	Q2	Q3	Q4	Q5	Q6	Q7	Q8	Q9	Q10	Q11	Q12
PostgreSQL	√	√	√	√	√	×	×	×	×	×	×	×
RG-SQL	√	√	√	√	√	√	√	√	√	√	√	√
Cypher	√	√	√	√	√	√	√	√	√	×	×	×

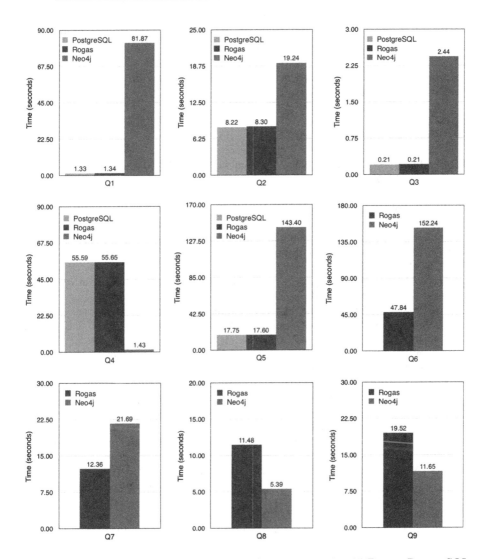

Fig. 6. Comparison on the time efficiency of query execution in Rogas, PostgreSQL and Neo4j over the queries Q1–Q9

6   Conclusions

In this paper, we have discussed how data analytics tasks can be conceptualised by a conceptual model and then transformed into a logical model. We have also proposed a query language for data analytics, and implemented the proposed methods into a data analytics platform that can unify various data analytics tasks and algorithms. This work was based on our case studies on several real-world data analytics applications.

In the future, we plan to add query topics into our data analytics platform and investigate the development of a query language at a higher level through query topics. We will also study network dynamics and develop techniques to analyse and visualise networks that dynamically change over time.

Acknowledgement. We thank the ACM Digital Library for providing the data set of the ACM bibliographical network.

References

1. Abiteboul, S., Hull, R., Vianu, V.: Foundations of Databases. Addison-Wesley, Reading (1995)
2. Bao, Z., Tay, Y., Zhou, J.: sonSchema: a conceptual schema for social networks. In: Conceptual Modeling, pp. 197–211 (2013)
3. Brandes, U., Erlebach, T.: Network Analysis: Methodological Foundations. Springer Science & Business Media, New York (2005)
4. Chen, P.: The entity-relationship model - toward a unified view of data. ACM TODS **1**(1), 9–36 (1976)
5. Clauset, A., Newman, M.E., Moore, C.: Finding community structure in very large networks. Phys. Rev. E **70**(6), 066111 (2004)
6. Embley, D.W., Liddle, S.W.: Big data—conceptual modeling to the rescue. In: Ng, W., Storey, V.C., Trujillo, J.C. (eds.) ER 2013. LNCS, vol. 8217, pp. 1–8. Springer, Heidelberg (2013). doi:10.1007/978-3-642-41924-9_1
7. Girvan, M., Newman, M.E.: Community structure in social and biological networks. PNAS **99**(12), 7821–7826 (2002)
8. Jindal, A., Madden, S.: GRAPHiQL: a graph intuitive query language for relationaldatabases. In: IEEE International Conference on Big Data, pp. 441–450 (2014)
9. Kasneci, G., Ramanath, M., Sozio, M., Suchanek, F.M., Weikum, G.: Star: steiner-tree approximation in relationship graphs. In: ICDE, pp. 868–879 (2009)
10. Liu, M., Wang, Q.: Rogas: a declaratice framework for network analysis. In: VLDB (2016)
11. Low, Y., Gonzalez, J.E., Kyrola, A., Bickson, D., Guestrin, C.E., Hellerstein, J.: Graphlab: a new framework for parallel machine learning. arXiv preprint arXiv:1408.2041 (2014)
12. Malewicz, G., Austern, M.H., Bik, A.J., Dehnert, J.C., Horn, I., Leiser, N., Czajkowski, G.: Pregel: a system for large-scale graph processing. In: ACM SIGMOD, pp. 135–146 (2010)
13. Peixoto, T.P.: Efficient Monte Carlo and greedy heuristic for the inference of stochastic block models. Phys. Rev. E **89**(1), 012804 (2014)

14. Thalheim, B.: Entity-relationship Modeling: Foundations of Database Technology. Springer Science & Business Media, New York (2013)
15. Wang, Q.: Network analytics ER model-towards a conceptual view of network analytics. In: ER, pp. 158–171 (2014)
16. Wang, Q.: A conceptual modeling framework for network analytics. Data Knowl. Eng. **99**, 59–71 (2015)

UMLtoGraphDB: Mapping Conceptual Schemas to Graph Databases

Gwendal Daniel[1]([✉]), Gerson Sunyé[1], and Jordi Cabot[2,3]

[1] Atlanmod Team, Inria, Mines Nantes, Lina, Nantes, France
{gwendal.daniel,gerson.sunye}@inria.fr
[2] ICREA, Barcelona, Spain
[3] Internet Interdisciplinary Institute, UOC, Barcelona, Spain
jordi.cabot@icrea.cat

Abstract. The need to store and manipulate large volume of (unstructured) data has led to the development of several NoSQL databases for better scalability. Graph databases are a particular kind of NoSQL databases that have proven their efficiency to store and query highly interconnected data, and have become a promising solution for multiple applications. While the mapping of conceptual schemas to relational databases is a well-studied field of research, there are only few solutions that target conceptual modeling for NoSQL databases and even less focusing on graph databases. This is specially true when dealing with the mapping of business rules and constraints in the conceptual schema. In this article we describe a mapping from UML/OCL conceptual schemas to Blueprints, an abstraction layer on top of a variety of graph databases, and Gremlin, a graph traversal language, via an intermediate Graph metamodel. Tool support is fully available.

Keywords: Database design · UML · OCL · NoSQL · Graph database · Gremlin

1 Introduction

NoSQL databases have become a promising solution to enhance scalability, availability, and query performance of data intensive applications. They often rely on a *schemaless* infrastructure, meaning that their schemas are implicitly defined by the stored data and not formally described. This approach offers great flexibility since it is possible to use different representations of a same concept (non-uniform data), but client applications still need to know (at least partially) how conceptual elements are stored in the database in order to access and manipulate them. Acquiring this implicit knowledge of the underlying schema can be an important issue, for example in data integration processes, where each data source has to be inspected to find its underlying structure [13].

Graph databases are a particular type of NoSQL databases that represent data as a set of vertices linked together by edges where both vertices and edges

© Springer International Publishing AG 2016
I. Comyn-Wattiau et al. (Eds.): ER 2016, LNCS 9974, pp. 430–444, 2016.
DOI: 10.1007/978-3-319-46397-1_33

can be labeled with a number of property values. Graph databases often provide advanced and expressive query languages that are particularly optimized to compute traversals of highly interconnected data. Recently, the graph database ecosystem is gaining popularity in several engineering fields such as social network [11] or data provenance [1] analysis, and the leading graph database vendor Neo4j[1] is used in production by several companies [16].

In order to take full benefit of NoSQL solutions, designers must be able to integrate them in current code-generation architectures to use them as target persistence backend for their conceptual schemas. Unfortunately, while several solutions provide transformations from ER and UML models to relational database schemas, the same is not true for NoSQL databases as discussed in detail in the related work. Moreover, NoSQL databases present an additional challenge: data consistency is a big problem since the vast majority of NoSQL approaches lack any advanced mechanism for integrity constraint checking [21].

To overcome this situation, we propose the UMLtoGraphDB framework, that translates conceptual schemas expressed using the Unified Modeling Language (UML) [24] into a graph representation, and generates database-level queries from business rules and invariants defined using the Object Constraint Language (OCL) [23]. The framework relies on a new GraphDB metamodel, as an intermediate representation to facilitate the integration of several kinds of graph databases. Enforcement of (both OCL and structural) constraints is delegated to an intermediate software component (middleware) in charge of maintaining the underlying database consistent with the conceptual schema. External applications can then use this middleware to safely access the database. This is illustrated in Fig. 1.

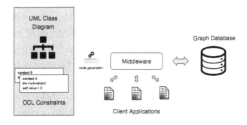

Fig. 1. Conceptual model to graph database

The rest of the paper is structured as follows: Sect. 2 presents the UMLtoGraphDB framework and its core components, Sect. 3 introduces the GraphDB metamodel and details the model-to-model transformation which creates an instance of it from a UML model. Section 4 presents the transformation that creates graph database queries from OCL expressions, and Sect. 5 introduces the code generator. Finally, Sect. 6 describes our tool support, Sect. 7 presents the related works and Sect. 8 ends up with the conclusions and future work.

---

[1] http://neo4j.com/.

2   UMLtoGraphDB Approach

UMLtoGraphDB is aligned with the OMG's MDA standard [22], proposing a structured methodology to systems development that promotes the separation between a specification defined in a platform independent way (Platform Independent Model, PIM), and the refinement of that specification adapted to the technical constraints of the implementation platform (Platform Specific Model, PSM). A model-to-model transformation (M2M) generates PSM models from PIMs while a model-to-text transformation typically takes care of producing the final code out of the PSM models. This PIM-to-PSM phased architecture brings two important benefits: (i) the PIM level focuses on the specification of the structure and functions, raising the level of abstraction and postponing technical details to the PSM level. (ii) Multiple PSMs can be generated from one PIM, improving portability and reusability. Moreover, using an intermediate PSM model instead of a direct PIM-to-code approach allows designers to tune the generation when needed and simplify the transformations by reducing the semantic gap between their input and output artefacts.

In our scenario, the initial UML and OCL models would conform to the PIM level. UMLtoGraphDB takes care of generating the PSM and code from them. Figure 2 presents the different component of the UMLtoGraphDB framework (light-grey box).

In particular, **Class2GraphDB** (1) is the first M2M of the UMLtoGraphDB framework. It is in charge of the creation of a low-level graph representation (PSM) from the input UML class diagram (PIM). The output of the Class2GraphDB transformation is a **GraphDB Model** (2), conforming to the GraphDB metamodel (Sect. 3). This metamodel is defined at the PSM level, and describes data structures in terms of graph primitives, such as *vertices* or *edges*. The **OCL2Gremlin** transformation (3) is the second M2M in the UMLtoGraphDB framework. It is in charge of the translation of the OCL constraints, queries, and business rules defined at the PIM level into graph-level queries. It produces a **Gremlin Model**, conforming to the Gremlin language metamodel that complements the previous GraphDB one.

The last step in MDA processes is a PSM-to-code transformation, which generates the software artifacts (database schema, code, configuration files . . .) in the target platform. In our approach, this final step is handled by the **Graph2Code** (5) transformation (Sect. 5) that processes the generated GraphDB and Gremlin models to create a set of Java Classes wrapping the structure of the database, the associated constraints, and the business rules. These Java classes compose the **Middleware** layer (6) presented in Fig. 1, and contain the generated code to access the physical **Graph Database** (7).

To illustrate the different transformation steps of our framework we introduce as a running example the conceptual schema presented in Fig. 3 representing a simple excerpt of an e-commerce application. This schema is specified using the UML notation, and describes *Client*, *Orders*, and *Products* concepts. A *Client* is an abstract class defined by a name and an address. *PrivateCustomers* and *CorporateCustomers* are subclasses of *Client*. They contain respectively a

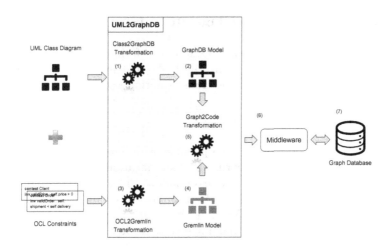

Fig. 2. Overview of the UMLtoGraphDB infrastructure

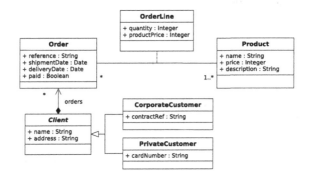

Fig. 3. Class diagram of a simple e-commerce application

cardNumber and a *contractRef* attribute. *Clients* own *Orders*, that are defined by a *reference*, a *shipmentDate*, and a *deliveryDate*. In addition, an *Order* maintains a *paid* attribute, that is set to true if the *Order* has been paid. *Products* are defined by their *name*, *price*, and a textual *description* and are linked to *Orders* through the *OrderLine* association class, which records the *quantity* and the *price* of each *Product* in a given *Order*.

In addition, the conceptual data model defines three textual OCL constraints (presented in Listing 1), which represent basic business rules. The first one checks that the *price* of a *Product* is always positive, the second one verifies that the *shipmentDate* of an *Order* precedes its *deliveryDate*, and the last one ensures a *Client* has less than three unpaid *Orders*.

```
context Product inv validPrice: self.price > 0
context Order inv validOrder: self.shipmentDate < self.deliveryDate
context Client inv maxUnpaidOrders:
    self.orders → select(o | not o.paid) → size() < 3
```

Listing 1. Textual Constraints

3   Mapping UML Class Diagram to GraphDB

In this section we present the Class2Graph transformation, which is the initial step in the approach presented in Fig. 2. We first introduce the GraphDB metamodel and then, we focus on the transformation itself.

3.1   GraphDB Metamodel

The GraphDB metamodel defines the possible structure of all GraphDB models. It is compliant with the Blueprints [26] specification, which is an interface designed to unify NoSQL database access under a common API. Initially developed for graph stores, Blueprints has been implemented by a large number of databases such as Neo4j, OrientDB, and MongoDB. The Blueprints API is, to our knowledge, the only interface unifying several NoSQL databases[2]. Blueprints is the base of the Tinkerpop stack: a set of tools to store, serialize, manipulate, and query graph databases. Among other features, it provides Gremlin [27], a traversal query language designed to query Blueprints databases.

Figure 4 presents the GraphDB metamodel. A *GraphSpecification* element represents the top-level container that owns all the objects. It has a *baseDB* attribute, that defines the concrete database to instantiate under the Blueprints API. In our prototype, the baseDB can be either Neo4j or OrientDB, two well known graph databases. *GraphSpecification* contains all the *VertexDefinitions* and *EdgeDefinitions* through the associations *vertices* and *edges*.

A *VertexDefinition* can be *unique*, meaning that there is only one vertex in the database that conforms to it. *VertexDefinitions* and *EdgeDefinitions* can be linked together using *outEdges* and *inEdges* associations, meaning respectively that a *VertexDefinition* has outgoing edges and incoming edges. In addition, *VertexDefinition* and *EdgeDefinition* are both subtypes of *GraphElement*, which can define a set of *labels* that describe the type of the element, and a set of *PropertiesDefinition* through its *properties* reference. In graph databases, properties are represented by a *key* (the name of the property) and a *Type*. In the first version of this metamodel we define four primitive types: *Object, Integer, String*, and *Boolean*.

3.2   Class2GraphDB Transformation

Intuitively, the transformation consists of mapping UML *Classes* to *VertexDefinitions*, *Associations* to *EdgeDefinitions*, and *AssociationClasses* to new *VertexDefinitions* connected to the ones representing the involved classes. The mapping also creates *PropertyDefinitions* for each *Attribute* in the input model, and add them to the corresponding mapped element.

Note that GraphDB has no construct to represent explicitly inheritance, and thus, the mapping has to deal with inherited attributes and associations. To handle them, the translation finds all the attributes and associations in the parent

---

[2] Implementation list is available at https://github.com/tinkerpop/blueprints.

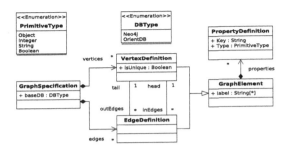

Fig. 4. GraphDB metamodel

hierarchy of each class, and adds them to the mapped *VertexDefinition*. While this creates duplicated elements in the GraphDB model, it is the more direct representation to facilitate queries on the GraphDB model. In the following, we describe this transformation in more detail.

A class diagram CD is defined as a tuple $CD = (Cl, As, Ac, I)$, where Cl is the set of classes, As is the set of associations, Ac is the set of association classes, and I the set of pairs of classes such as $(c1, c2)$ represents the fact that $c1$ is a direct or indirect subclass of $c2$. Note that the first version of UMLtoGraphDB transforms only a subset of the class diagram, for example enumerations and interfaces supports are planned as future work.

A GraphDB diagram GD is defined as a tuple $GD = (V, E, P)$, where V is set of vertex definitions, and E the set of edge definitions, and P the set of property definitions that compose the graph.

– **R1:** each class $c \in Cl, not\ c.isAbstract$ is mapped to a vertex definition $v \in V$, where $v.label = c.name \cup c_{parents}.name$, with $c_{parents} \subset Cl$ and $\forall p \in c_{parents}, (c, p) \in I$.

– **R2:** each attribute $a \in (c \cup c_{parents}).attributes$ is mapped to a property definition p, where $p.key = a.name$, $p.type = a.type$, and added to the property list of its mapped container v such as $p \in v.properties$.

– **R3:** each association $as \in As$ between two classes $c_1, c_2 \in Cl$ is mapped to an edge definition $e \in E$, where $e.label = as.name$, $e.tail = v_1$, and $e.head = v_2$, where v_1 and v_2 are the *VertexDefinitions* representing c_1 and c_2. Note that $e.tail$ and $e.head$ values are set according to the direction of the association. If the association is not directed, a second edge definitions $e_{opposite}$ is created, where $e_{opposite}.label = as.name$, $e_{opposite}.tail = v_2$, and $e_{opposite}.head = v_1$, representing the second possible direction of the association. Aggregation associations are mapped the same way, but their semantic is handled differently in the generated code. In order to support inherited associations, *EdgeDefinitions* are also created to represent associations involving the parents of c.

– **R4:** each association $as \in As$ between multiple classes $c_1...c_n \in Cl$ is mapped to a vertex definition v_{asso} such as $v_{asso}.label = as.name$ and a set of *EdgeDefinitions* $e_i.tail = v_i$ and $e_i.head = v_{asso}$, associating the created vertex definition to the ones representing $c_1...c_n$.

- **R5:** each association class $ac \in Ac$ between classes $c_1...c_n$ is mapped like an association between multiple classes using a vertex definition v_{ac} such as $v_{ac}.label = ac.name$. As for a regular class, v_{ac} contains the properties corresponding to the attributes $ac.attributes$, and a set of $EdgeDefinitions$ $e_i \in E$ where $e_i.tail = v_i$ and $e_i.head = v_{ac}$.

To better illustrate this mapping, we now describe how the GraphDB model shown in Fig. 5 is created from the example presented in Fig. 3. Note that for the sake of readability we only show an excerpt of the created GraphDB model. To begin with, all the classes are translated into *VertexDefinition* instances following *R1*. This process generates the elements v1, v2, v3, and v4, with the labels *(Client, PrivateCustomer)*, *(Client, CorporateCustomer)*, *Order*, and *Product*. Then, *R2* is applied to transform attributes into *PropertyDefinitions*. For example, the attribute *name* of the class *Client* is mapped to the *PropertyDefinition* p1, which defines a key *name* and a type *String*. These *PropertyDefinition* elements are linked to their containing *VertexDefinition* using the *properties* association. Once this first step has been done, *R3* is applied on the association *orders*, mapping it to the *EdgeDefinitions* e1 and e2, containing the name of the association. *VertexDefinitions* representing *PrivateCustomer* and *CorporateCustomer* classes are then linked to the one representing *Order*, respectively with e1 and e2. Since the association *orders* is directed, the transformation puts v1 and v2 as the tail of the edge, and v3 as its head. Then, the association class *OrderLine* is transformed by *R5* to the *VertexDefinition* v5, and its attributes *productPrice* and *quantity* are transformed into the *PropertyDefinitions* p6 and p7. Finally, two *EdgeDefinitions* (e3 and e4) are also created to link the *VertexDefinition* v3 and v4 to it.

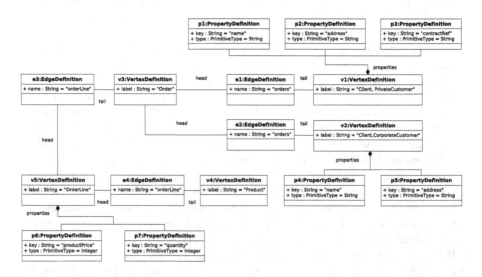

Fig. 5. Excerpt of the mapped GraphDB model

These mapping rules have also been specified in ATL [14], which is a domain-specific language for defining model-to-model transformations aligned with the QVT standard [15]. ATL provides both declarative (rule-based) and imperative constructs for transforming and manipulating models. As an example, Listing 2 shows the ATL transformation rule that maps a UML *Class* to a *VertexDefinition*. It is applied for each non-abstract *Class* element, excepted *AssociationClasses*, which have a particular mapping, as explained in Sect. 3. The rule creates a *VertexDefinition* element, and sets its label attribute with the *name* of each *Class* in its parent hierarchy. The set of parent *Classes* is computed by the helper **getParentClassHierarchy**, which returns a sequence containing all the parents of the current *Class*. Finally, *VertexDefinition properties* are set, by getting all the attributes from the parent hierarchy, and are transformed by the abstract *lazy rule* **GenericAttribute2Property**. The full ATL transformation is available in the project repository[3].

```
rule Class2VertexDefinition {
    from
        class : UML! Class (not(class.oclIsTypeOf(UML! AssociationClass)) and
            not(class.abstract))
    to
        vertex : Graph! VertexDefinition (
        labels  ← class.getParentClassHierarchy()→collect(cc | cc.name)
        -- Generate a property for each Attribute in the class hierarchy
        properties  ← class.getParentClassHierarchy()
            →collect(cc | cc.attribute)
            →collect(att | thisModule.GenericAttribute2Property(att))
        )
}
```

Listing 2. Class2VertexDefinition ATL Transformation Rule

4   Translating OCL Expressions to Gremlin

Once the GraphDB model has been created, another transformation is performed to translate the OCL expressions defined in the conceptual schema into a Gremlin query model. The mapping presented in this Section is adapted from the one presented in [8] dedicated to OCL query evaluation on NeoEMF, a scalable model persistence framework designed to store models into graph databases [2]. In this Section, we present the Gremlin language and describe how OCL expressions are transformed into Gremlin queries according to the UML to GraphDB mapping.

4.1   The Gremlin Query Language

Gremlin is a Groovy domain-specific language built over *Pipes*, a data-flow framework on top of *Blueprints*. We have chosen Gremlin as the target query language for UMLtoGraphDB due to its adoption in several graph databases.

Gremlin is based on the concept of process graphs. A process graph is composed of vertices representing computational units and communication edges

---

[3] https://github.com/atlanmod/UML2NoSQL.

which can be combined to create a complex processing flow. In the Gremlin terminology, these complex processing flows are called *traversals*, and are composed of a chain of simple computational units named *steps*. Gremlin defines four types of steps: **Transform steps** that map inputs of a given type to outputs of another type, **Filter steps**, selecting or rejecting input elements according to a given condition, **Branch steps**, which split the computation into several parallel sub-traversals, and **side-effect steps** that perform operations like edge or vertex creation, property update, or variable definition or assignment.

In addition, the *step* interface provides a set of built-in methods to access meta information: number of objects in a step, output existence, or first element in a step. These methods can be called inside a traversal to control its execution or check conditions on particular elements in a step.

4.2   OCL2Gremlin Transformation

Table 1 presents the mapping between OCL expressions and Gremlin concepts. Supported OCL expressions are divided into four categories based on Gremlin step types: transformations, collection operations, iterators, and general expressions. Note that due to lack of space we only present a subset of the OCL expressions which are supported by our approach. A complete version of this mapping is available in previous work [8].

These mappings are systematically applied on the input OCL expression, following a postorder traversal of the OCL Abstract Syntax Tree. As an example, Listing 3 shows the Gremlin queries generated from the OCL constraints of the running example (Sect. 2). The v variable represents the vertex that is being currently checked, and the following steps are created using the mapping. Note that generated expressions are queries that return a boolean value. These queries are embedded in checking methods during the generation phase (Sect. 5).

```
v.property("price") > 0;  // validPrice
v.property("shipmentDate") < self.property("deliveryDate");  //
    validOrder
v.outE("orders").inV.filter{it.property("paid")==false}
    .count() < 3;  // maxUnpaidOrders
```

Listing 3. Generated Gremlin Queries

5   Code Generation

Our code-generator relies on the Blueprints API for interacting with the graph database in a vendor neutral way. We first briefly review this API and then we show how we leverage it to enforce that any application aiming to query/store data through the created middleware does it so according to the its initial UML/OCL conceptual schema.

Table 1. OCL to Gremlin mapping

OCL expression	Gremlin step
Type	"Type.name"
C.allInstances()	g.V().hasLabel("C.name")
collect(attribute)	property(attribute)
collect(reference)	outE('reference').inV
oclIsTypeOf(C)	o.hasLabel("C.name")
$col_1 \rightarrow union(col_2)$	col_1.fill(var_1); col_2.fill(var_2); union(var_1, var_2);
including(object)	gather{it << object;}.scatter;
excluding(object)	except([object]);
size()	count()
isEmpty()	toList().isEmpty()
select(condition)	c.filter{condition}
reject(condition)	c.filter{!(condition)}
exists(expression)	filter{condition}.hasNext()
$=, >, >=, <, <=, <>$	$==, >, >=, <, <=, ! =$
$+, -, /, \%, *$	$+, -, /, \%, *$
and, or, not	&&, ‖, !
variable	variable
literals	*literals*

5.1   Blueprints API

The Blueprints API is composed of a set of Java classes to manipulate graph databases in a generic way. These classes are wrappers for database-level elements, such as *vertices* and *edges*, providing methods to access, update, and delete them. A Blueprints database is instantiated using a `GraphFactory`, that takes a configuration file containing the properties of the databases (type of the underlying graph engine, allocated memory ...) and creates the corresponding graph store.

The Blueprints `Vertex` class provides the methods `addEdge(String label, Vertex otherEnd)` and `removeEdge(otherEnd)` that allow to connect/disconnect two vertices by creating/deleting an edge between the current vertex and *otherEnd* with the given *label*. Blueprints also defines the vertex method `property(String key)`, that retrieve the value of the vertex property defined by the given key. In addition, the Blueprints API provides the `traversal()` method, that allows to send Gremlin traversals to the database and return the subgraph resulting from that query.

A complete reference of the Blueprints API is available in [26].

5.2   Graph2Code Transformation

The final step in our UMLtoGraphDB process is the database and code artifacts generation. Figure 6 presents the infrastructure generated by the Graph2Code transformation. In short, the generator processes the GraphDB model to retrieve all the *VertexDefinition* elements and, for each one, it creates a corresponding Java class with the relevant *getters* and *setters* for its attributes (derived from the properties definitions linked to the vertex) and associations (derived from the input/output edges of the vertex).

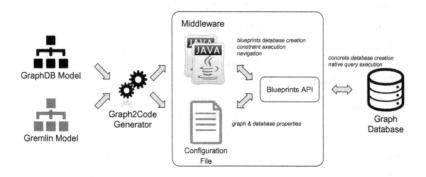

Fig. 6. Generated infrastructure

Listing 4 presents an excerpt of the Java class generated from the *Client* element. Note that this class extends *BlueprintsBean*, which is a generic class that we provide as part of the UMLtoGraphDB infrastructure. *BlueprintsBean* provides auxiliary methods to connect the class with the Graph database via the Blueprints API and facilitates the creation and management of graph elements.

Once this basic Java class structure is completed, the generator starts processing the *Gremlin Model* to create additional methods. Each method is in charge of checking one of the OCL constraints (or queries) in the conceptual schema. As usual, checking methods return a boolean value (*false* if the constraint is violated). As an example, Listing 4 includes the method `checkMaxUnpaidOrder` executing the Gremlin traversal mapped from the OCL expression self.orders→select(o | not o.paid)→size() < 3 (this mapping is detailed in Sect. 4). The generated expression follows the syntax variant of the Gremlin internal DSL and not the Groovy-based syntax, both versions can be generated by our infrastructure. Note that the task of calling the generated constraint-checking method is responsibility of the client application. Automatic and incremental checking of these constraints is left for future work.

Finally, the Graph2Code generator creates a *Configuration File* that contains the graph and database properties, and is used by the Blueprints API to instantiate the concrete graph engine.

```
public class Client extends BlueprintsBean {
  public String getName() {
    return (String)this.vertex.property("name").value();
  }
  public String getAddress() {
    return (String)this.vertex.property("address").value();
  }
  public void setName(String newName) {
    this.vertex.property("name",newName);
  }
  public void setAddress(String newAddress) {
    this.vertex.property("address",newAddress);
  }
  public void addOrder(Order order) {
    this.vertex.addEdge("orders", order.getVertex());
  }
  public void removeOrder(Order order) {
    this.vertex.removeEdge(order.getVertex());
  }
  public boolean checkMaxUnpaidOrders() {
    return this.graph.traversal().V(this.vertex).outE("orders")
      .inV().filter(v → v.get().<Boolean>property("paid").value())
      .count().is(P.lt(3)).hasNext();
  }
}
```

Listing 4. Generated Client Java Class

6   Tool Support

UMLtoGraphDB has been implemented as a collection of open-source Eclipse plugins, available on Github[4]. UMLtoGraphDB takes as input the UML and OCL files (defined, for instance, using Eclipse-based UML editors such as Papyrus[5]), that are then translated, respectively, by the Class2GraphDB and OCL2Gremlin ATL transformations seen before. These transformations add up to a total of 110 rules and helper functions.

The code-generator is implemented using the XTend programming language [3]. Even if this language was initially designed as a template-based language for generation tasks it has now evolved to a more general programming language that provides syntactic sugar, lambda expressions and other useful extensions on top of Java. The generator takes the GraphDB and Gremlin models and processes them as described in Sect. 5.

The time needed by the entire transformation chain to produce the Java code from the input UML and OCL specifications is in the order of a few seconds for the several examples we have tested. A precise analysis of the scalability of the transformation performance according to the size of the input for very large conceptual model is left for future work.

---

[4] https://github.com/atlanmod/UML2NoSQL.
[5] https://eclipse.org/papyrus/.

7   Related Work

Mapping conceptual schemas to relational databases is a well-studied field of research [19]. A few works also cover schemas that include (OCL) constraints. For example, Demuth and Hussman [9] propose a mapping from UML (augmented with OCL constraints) to SQL that covers most of OCL and implement it via a code generator [10] that automates the process. Brambilla et al. [4] propose a methodology to implement integrity constraints into relational databases recommending alternative implementations based on performance parameters. While these approaches are well-suited for relational databases, they all rely on the generation of database constraints. In a NoSQL environment, and especially for graph databases, there is a lack of support for built-in constraint constructs, and data validation must be delegated to the application layer as UMLtoGraphDB does.

Li et al. proposed an approach to transform UML class diagrams into a HBase data model [18], by mapping classes to tables, attributes to columns, and providing transformation rules for associations, compositions, and generalization. Still, it is only applicable to column-based datastores, and does not support the definition of custom OCL constraints and business rules.

More specific to NoSQL databases, the NoSQL Schema Evaluator [20] generates query implementation plans from a conceptual schema and workload definition. For now, the approach is limited to Cassandra, but authors intend to adapt it to different data models, such as key-values and document stores. However, this solution does not take into account constraints specified in the conceptual model. Sevilla et al. [25] presented a tool to infer versioned schemas from NoSQL databases. The resulting model is then used to automatically generate a viewer and validator for the schema but they do not aim to provide support for a full-fledged application nor consider the addition of constraints on the reversed schema. Bugiotti et al. [5] propose a database design methodology for NoSQL databases. It relies on NoAM, an abstract data model that aims to represent NoSQL systems in a system-independent way. NoAM models can be implemented in several NoSQL databases, including key-value stores, document databases, and extensible record stores. Instead, we focus on generating NoSQL databases from higher-level UML models, and thus, designers do not need to learn a new language/platform. Nevertheless, NoAM could be integrated in our approach if we manage to extend it with constraint support. In that case, NoAM could be seen as a PSM derived from UML models and OCL constraints, and can be used to implement non-graph databases, which are not supported by our approach for now.

8   Conclusion and Future Work

In this article we have presented the UMLtoGraphDB framework, a MDA-based approach to implement (UML) conceptual schemas in graph databases, including the generation of the code required to check the OCL constraints defined in the schema. Our approach is specified as a chain of model transformations that use a new intermediate GraphDB metamodel. This metamodel can also be regarded as a kind of UML profile (and could be easily reexpressed as such) for graph databases.

As future work, we plan to provide refactoring operations on top of the GraphDB model to allow designers to tune the data representation according to specific needs, such as query execution performance or memory consumption. We also plan to extend our approach to cover reverse engineering scenarios, by adapting existing work on schema extraction from relational databases [7] to graph databases. Another ongoing work pursues adapting our framework to cover multiple database types. More precisely, we aim to support conceptual schema fragmentation between several databases (even mixing NoSQL and SQL ones). This requires a mechanism to evaluate constraints over several persistence solutions and query languages. Apache Drill [12] or Hibernate OGM [17] could be reused for this.

Finally, we plan to reuse existing work on the integration of incremental constraint checking [6] as part of the code-generation phase so that the scalable performance of the graph database is not hampered by the constraint evaluation phase.

References

1. Anand, M.K., Bowers, S., Ludäscher, B.: Techniques for efficiently querying scientific workflow provenance graphs. In: EDBT, vol. 10, pp. 287–298 (2010)
2. Benelallam, A., Gómez, A., Sunyé, G., Tisi, M., Launay, D.: Neo4EMF, a scalable persistence layer for EMF models. In: Cabot, J., Rubin, J. (eds.) ECMFA 2014. LNCS, vol. 8569, pp. 230–241. Springer, Heidelberg (2014). doi:10.1007/978-3-319-09195-2_15
3. Bettini, L.: Implementing Domain-Specific Languages with Xtext and Xtend. Packt Publishing Ltd., Birmingham (2013)
4. Brambilla, M., Cabot, J.: Constraint tuning and management for web applications. In: Proceedings of the 6th ICWE Conference, pp. 345–352. ACM (2006)
5. Bugiotti, F., Cabibbo, L., Atzeni, P., Torlone, R.: Database design for NoSQL systems. In: Yu, E., Dobbie, G., Jarke, M., Purao, S. (eds.) ER 2014. LNCS, vol. 8824, pp. 223–231. Springer, Heidelberg (2014). doi:10.1007/978-3-319-12206-9_18
6. Cabot, J., Teniente, E.: Incremental integrity checking of UML/OCL conceptual schemas. JSS **82**(9), 1459–1478 (2009)
7. Chiang, R.H.L., Barron, T.M., Storey, V.C.: Reverse engineering of relational databases: extraction of an EER model from a relational database. Data Knowl. Eng. **12**(2), 107–142 (1994)
8. Daniel, G., Sunyé, G., Cabot, J.: Mogwaï: a framework to handle complex queries on large models. In: Proceedings of the 10th RCIS Conference. IEEE (2016, to appear). http://tinyurl.com/zx6cfam
9. Demuth, B., Hussmann, H.: Using UML/OCL constraints for relational database design. In: France, R., Rumpe, B. (eds.) UML 1999. LNCS, vol. 1723, pp. 598–613. Springer, Heidelberg (1999). doi:10.1007/3-540-46852-8_42

10. Demuth, B., Hussmann, H., Loecher, S.: OCL as a specification language for business rules in database applications. In: Gogolla, M., Kobryn, C. (eds.) UML 2001. LNCS, vol. 2185, pp. 104–117. Springer, Heidelberg (2001). doi:10.1007/3-540-45441-1_9

11. Fan, W.: Graph pattern matching revised for social network analysis. In: Proceedings of the 15th ICDT, pp. 8–21. ACM (2012)

12. Hausenblas, M., Nadeau, J.: Apache drill: interactive ad-hoc analysis at scale. Big Data 1(2), 100–104 (2013)

13. Cánovas Izquierdo, J.L., Cabot, J.: Discovering implicit schemas in JSON Data. In: Daniel, F., Dolog, P., Li, Q. (eds.) ICWE 2013. LNCS, vol. 7977, pp. 68–83. Springer, Heidelberg (2013). doi:10.1007/978-3-642-39200-9_8

14. Jouault, F., Allilaire, F., Bézivin, J., Kurtev, I.: ATL: a model transformation tool. SCP 72(1–2), 31–39 (2008)

15. Jouault, F., Kurtev, I.: On the architectural alignment of ATL and QVT. In: Proceedings of the 21st SAC Conference, pp. 1188–1195. ACM (2006)

16. Lal, M.: Neo4j Graph Data Modeling. Packt Publishing Ltd., Birmingham (2015)

17. Leonard, A.: Pro Hibernate and MongoDB. Apress, Berkeley (2013)

18. Li, Y., Gu, P., Zhang, C.: Transforming UML class diagrams into HBase based on meta-model. In: Proceedings of the 4th ISEEE Conference, vol. 2, pp. 720–724. IEEE (2014)

19. Marcos, E., Vela, B., Cavero, J.M.: A methodological approach for object-relational database design using UML. SoSyM 2(1), 59–72 (2003)

20. Mior, M.J., Salem, K., Aboulnaga, A., Liu, R., NoSE: schema design for NoSQL applications. In: 32nd ICDE Conference. IEEE (2016, accepted). http://tinyurl.com/hqoxddx

21. Okman, L., Gal-Oz, N., Gonen, Y., Gudes, E., Abramov, J.: Security issues in NoSQL databases. In: Proceedings of the 10th TrustCom Conference, pp. 541–547. IEEE (2011)

22. OMG: MDA Specifications (2016). http://www.omg.org/mda/specs.htm

23. OMG: OCL Specification (2016). www.omg.org/spec/OCL

24. OMG: UML Specification (2016). www.omg.org/spec/UML

25. Sevilla Ruiz, D., Morales, S.F., García Molina, J.: Inferring versioned schemas from NoSQL databases and its applications. In: Johannesson, P., Lee, M.L., Liddle, S.W., Opdahl, A.L., López, Ó.P. (eds.) ER 2015. LNCS, vol. 9381, pp. 467–480. Springer, Heidelberg (2015). doi:10.1007/978-3-319-25264-3_35

26. TinkerPop: Blueprints API (2016). blueprints.tinkerpop.com

27. TinkerPop: The Gremlin Language (2016). gremlin.tinkerpop.com

Facilitating Data-Metadata Transformation by Domain Specialists in a Web-Based Information System Using Simple Correspondences

Scott Britell[1]($\boxtimes$), Lois M.L. Delcambre[1], and Paolo Atzeni[2]

[1] Department of Computer Science, Portland State University,
PO Box 751, Portland, OR 97207, USA
britell@cs.pdx.edu, lmd@pdx.edu
[2] Dipartimento di Ingegneria, Università Roma Tre,
Via della Vasca Navale 79, 00146 Roma, Italy
atzeni@dia.uniroma3.it

Abstract. We seek to empower domain specialists and non-technical web designers to be able to design and configure their system directly, without necessarily requiring interaction with a software developer or DB specialist. We observe that structured information shown on a web page presents a conceptual model of the information shown; and, that such web pages make a variety of choices regarding whether or not application information is presented in the data (with or without schema labels) or in the metadata (schema). Also, the same application may present the same data in different schemas on different pages. In this paper, we extend our earlier work—on providing generic widgets for structured information that can be easily used and configured by domain specialists—to also include data/metadata transformation. Thus, we put data/metadata transformation (from one conceptual model to another) in the hands of domain specialists without database expertise. The contributions of this paper are: showing how our approach can be used to support data/metadata transformation in both directions and demonstrating this capability in a non-trivial case study. The paper also provides evidence that non-expert users can successfully provide simple correspondences through the results of a small-scale user study.

1 Introduction

The overall goal of this research is to empower non-technical users to easily configure their web-based information system without requiring a programmer or DB/SQL expert. We believe that domain specialists understand the semantics of their data and are in the best position to decide how to display and manipulate their data. Modern content management systems (CMSs) share the same goal; they typically allow the domain specialist to consider their data in an entity-centric conceptual model where each entity has (single- or multi-valued) attributes and outbound references/links. While a CMS may also offer view or

© Springer International Publishing AG 2016
I. Comyn-Wattiau et al. (Eds.): ER 2016, LNCS 9974, pp. 445–459, 2016.
DOI: 10.1007/978-3-319-46397-1_34

template mechanisms that allow complex data structures to be displayed, they offer somewhat limited flexibility and need to be modified by software developers. We provide more sophisticated widgets, written in a generic fashion (by software developers), that can be easily configured by domain specialists, on their own. Our approach distinguishes the *local* schema (e.g., an entity-centric, conceptual view of domain data typically offered by a CMS), a *canonical structure* (i.e., a generic schema for widget developers), and a *domain structure* that sits between the two.

Take, for example, the university personnel widgets shown in Fig. 1. The *local* schemas are shown in the entity-centric tables on the left. For presentation on the web page, the widget transforms data from the local schema into the form of the *domain structures* (here represented as the schema of the table on the right). In the example of a university we consider university staff and administrators as specialists in this domain. The domain specialist provides correspondences (the lines in Fig. 1) between the *local* schema and the *domain structure*. The widget (shown below each set of tables) is built using a generic schema (the *canonical structure*). Domain specialists should be able to easily provide correspondences since they are working with their own local schema (which they are very familiar with) and a domain structure (which they should be able to understand). (The correspondences shown in the top of Fig. 1 are (almost trivially) straightforward. Actual correspondences may be more complex/interesting.) We offer feedback dynamically by displaying a preview of the widget as each correspondence is defined. This may remove the delay or miscommunication that might occur when a domain specialist must interact with a DB or software developer to make changes to their site.

Our work to date has focused on generic widgets that display complex structures [4] and on generic widgets that allow create/edit capability of the underlying local data through the widgets [5]. The focus of this paper is on allowing domain specialists to fluidly move data of interest in and out of the schema, using what is typically called data/metadata transformation, including the ability to pivot and unpivot data. The contributions of this paper are: (1) showing how correspondences with domain and canonical structures can support data/metadata transformations, (2) presenting a case study that shows a complex, faceted browse widget that uses data/metadata transformation, and (3) extending our simple correspondences to include a condition in order to support the classical DB pivot operation. This paper also provides evidence that non-technical domain users can supply correspondences while using our mapping tool (with dynamic widget previews) based on our user study.

The paper is organized as follows. Section 2 provides the motivation for our focus on data/metadata transformation as well as a brief description of our earlier work that provides the foundation for the work in this paper. Section 3 shows how we are able to support the classical unpivot operation (metadata to data transformation) and presents our case study that shows how structured information can be easily mapped to a domain structure that enables the use of our faceted browse widget. Section 4 generalizes our correspondences to support

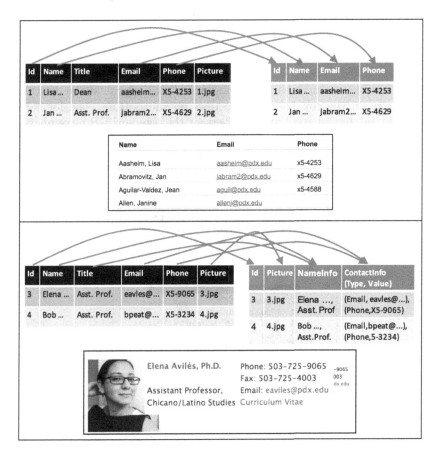

Fig. 1. Local schemas (left tables above and below) are transformed into the domain structures (schema of the right tables) via the shown correspondences (arrowed lines). The transformed data is then used to populate widgets (shown below tables).

the classical pivot operation as well as other data to metadata transformations. Section 5 evaluates this work by comparing it to the range of work from the DB community to support data/metadata transformations including unpivot and pivot. Section 5 also presents results from our user study that shows that non-technical domain specialists can easily supply the correspondences that our work depends on. Related work and conclusions with future work are presented in Sects. 6 and 7, respectively.

2   Background

Motivation. The standard DB unpivot operation has been studied extensively in relation to databases [6, 18] and information/schema integration/exchange [11, 12, 19]. The operation moves information from schema (metadata) to data as shown in Fig. 2, moving from top to bottom. The classical schema for an employee table (simplified here) is on the top of the figure with attributes for id, name, email, ext (extension), home (phone), and cell (phone). The unpivoted version of this table is shown on the bottom of the figure; *email, ext, home,* and *cell* (formerly attribute names) have been unpivoted and appear in the data. Each employee row on the top has multiple rows on the bottom—one for each of the non-null, unpivoted attributes. Conversely, the standard DB pivot operation transforms data with a schema similar to the one on the bottom (consisting of id, attribute name, attribute value triples) into data with a schema like the one on the top, moving information from data to schema (metadata).

employee					
id	name	email	ext	home	cell
1	Alice	a@pdx.edu	5-3456	555-9823	555-2342
2	Bob	b@pdx.edu	5-2414	555-0394	

gen_emp			
id	name	contact	contact_type
1	Alice	a@pdx.edu	email
1	Alice	5-3456	ext
1	Alice	555-9823	home
1	Alice	555-2342	cell
2	Bob	b@pdx.edu	email
2	Bob	5-2414	ext
2	Bob	555-0394	home

Fig. 2. Above, a standard schema; below, a schema where the email and phone number attributes have been unpivoted into a single *contact* attribute and the metadata (i.e., attribute names) from the employee table is transformed into data in the *contact_type* attribute in the gen_emp table.

We believe that structured information shown on a web page presents a conceptual model of the data being displayed. Even for simple, structured data, e.g., contact information on a public web site for employees at a university, the conceptual model can vary based on the choices made with regard to data vs. metadata. Consider the widgets from public web pages showing directory information for university personnel in Fig. 1. The upper widget shows a classical conceptual model for an employee where the schema is shown as column headers. The bottom widget in Fig. 1 shows a mix of classical, combined, and unpivoted data. Notice that the attribute names Phone, Fax, and E-mail are shown immediately preceding the data value rather than in a column header, analogous to the DB unpivot operation followed by a nest operation. We also see that the faculty name, and title have been combined into a single unnamed attribute—with only the data values shown (without schema information).

These web pages suggest that these models, with varying amounts of combined and unpivoted data, can be easily understood by end-users. One important contribution of this paper is allowing domain specialists to easily transform data to metadata and metadata to data, to decide whether or not to include schema, and to easily combine nesting, pivot, and unpivot operations.

Foundation. This paper builds on our prior work [3–5] called information integration with local radiance[1] comprised of four main parts: (1) canonical structures (generic schema fragments), (2) domain structures (schema fragments with appropriate names), (3) mappings comprised of simple correspondences from local schemas to domain structures, and (4) a query algebra based on the extended relational algebra [8] and the nested relational algebra [17].

Domain structures are (small) schema fragments consisting of entities, attributes, and relationships with domain-appropriate names (like those shown in the upper part of Figs. 4, 6, 9, and 10, later in the paper); we also use a straightforward translation to the relational model to represent them (like those shown in tabular form in Fig. 1).

Our query language extends the nested relational algebra (σ, π, $\bowtie$, ν, ..., plus γ for grouping [8]) with two new operators: apply (α) and type (τ) [3]. Our *apply* operator ($\alpha(DT)$) is the basis of every query in our system. The *apply* operator uses correspondences between local schemas and a domain structure to perform information integration/transformation. Given a domain entity type or domain relationship type, from a domain structure, DT, *apply* will generate table scan queries for all local structures that the domain type has been mapped to and then take the union of the results. The *apply* operator is designed to work with the underlying (local) schema of multiple databases and then integrate the results in the form of a global schema (the domain structure). The result of the *apply* operator is a set of relational tuples which can be passed to other relational algebra operators to create more complex queries. Consider the bottom half of Fig. 1, an *apply* operation on a domain structure (of the form of the schema of the right table) will use the correspondences drawn to populate the Picture, NameInfo, and the Value portion of the ContactInfo Columns. (The *apply* operator does not perform the nest operation; the nest operator of the nested relational algebra can be used subsequent to the apply). The local *type* operator ($\tau_n(\chi)$) takes a domain structure component (n) and a query (χ) and introduces an attribute into the query result containing the local structure names to which the domain structure component (entity, attribute, or relationship) was mapped. For example, in the bottom half of Fig. 1, the type information in ContactInfo would be added using a query like $\tau_{ContactInfo}(\alpha(DT))$, where we first use our *apply* operator to populate the data then use τ to get the correct local type.

A canonical structure is a generically named schema fragment used by a widget developer. As an example, Fig. 3 shows the canonical structure that can be used to build the widget shown in the top half of Fig. 1—a generically named entity, an id attribute, and a number of generic attributes. The widget can then be built by writing a query in our algebra against the canonical structure and then writing code to display the results. A site developer can then instantiate

---

[1] In our earlier papers, we called it local dominance.

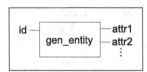

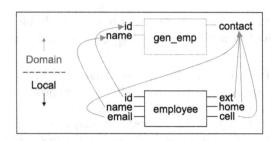

Fig. 3. A canonical structure used to build a wid-
get like that shown in the
top of Fig. 1.

Fig. 4. A local employee schema (below) is
mapped to perform an unpivot operation to
a generic employee domain structure (top).

the widget by specifying a domain structure to work with the widget, in this
example the structure for the table on the right side of Fig. 1. A widget may be
instantiated multiple times in a site using different domain structures. Once a
widget has been instantiated with a domain structure, a domain specialist can
map their local schema to the domain structure for use by the widget; where a
mapping consists of a set of simple correspondences from a local schema to the
domain structure (like the lines shown in Fig. 1).

3   Unpivot

To see how simple correspondences and domain structures used in our system can
support an unpivot operation, consider Fig. 4. The local schema, shown at the
bottom of the figure, has a classical structure with five descriptive attributes plus
the *id* attribute for the *employee* entity. The domain structure at the top shows a
generic employee entity (named *gen_emp*) with an *id* and *name* attribute and an
attribute called *contact*. In this example, the local *id* and *name* attributes have
been mapped to the *id* and *name* attributes in the domain structure, respectively.
(Corresponding attributes in the local schema and domain structure need not
have the same name.) The *email*, *ext*, *home*, and *cell* attributes are all mapped
to the *contact* attribute in the domain structure. These four correspondences to
the *contact* attribute do part of the unpivot operation; they combine data from
the four local attributes into a single attribute in the domain structure.

The queries needed to transform the employee table based on these correspondences are shown in Fig. 5. The *apply* (α) operator operates on the generic
employee entity in the domain structure (*gen_emp*) to produce the intermediate
result shown in the middle of the figure. Here we see that the correspondences
have been used, as expected. The type operator (τ) is then applied to this intermediate result with a parameter of *contact* to extract the local type (schema)
name from the local schema for the data values that appears in the *contact*
attribute. The final result is shown at the bottom of the figure.

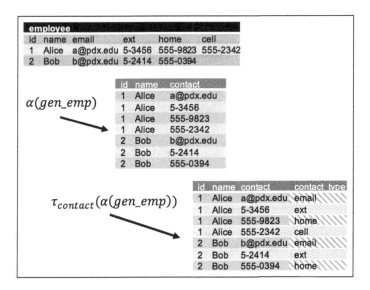

Fig. 5. An unpivot using our query operators and the correspondences and domain structure shown in Fig. 4

3.1 Case Study: Ensemble and Faceted Browse

As part of the Ensemble[2] project we helped develop a number of digital library collections in the Ensemble portal. The portal was limited to standard browsing and searching features. The bottom half of Fig. 6 shows the basic ER model of collections in Ensemble (with a subset of the full attribute set). The portal has two entities (*collection* and *dublin core record*) with the single *contains* relationship.

A collection of digital library records is shown in the standard Ensemble hierarchical navigation widget in Fig. 7 with the collection entity instance entitled "The Beauty and Joy of Computing"[3], a curriculum for introductory computer science, with all of its educational resources. Given the simple ER structure in the local schema, browsing resources was limited to a basic list of resources in a collection (the circled 1).

To facilitate browsing of collections we leverage the combination and unpivot features of IILR to implement a faceted browse widget—where the collection in the hierarchical navigation widget can be partitioned at any level by any of the attributes of the resources in the collection. Figure 8 shows the same collection after it has been faceted by class week. The new symbol to the left of the ±symbol is our facet symbol. After being faceted by week, we see that we can now also facet each week by any of the remaining attributes that have been mapped to the *facet* domain attribute (as shown in Fig. 6). For example, we see

---

[2] http://computingportal.org.
[3] http://computingportal.org/node/11172.

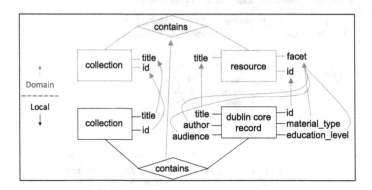

Fig. 6. The local schema (bottom) for collections in the Ensemble portal and the domain structure (top) used for the faceted browse widget.

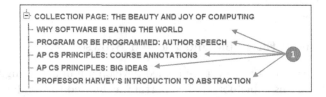

Fig. 7. An hierarchical navigation widget in the Ensemble portal without faceting.

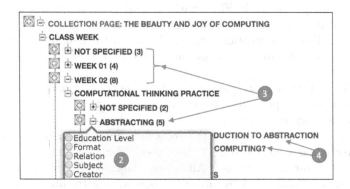

Fig. 8. A faceted browse widget in the Ensemble portal where the collection has been faceted by "Class Week" and then "Computational Thinking Practice".

that "WEEK 02" has been faceted by computational thinking practice. Each level of the hierarchy is able to be faceted differently enabling users to quickly see resources partitioned by any combination of facets. The "Abstracting" computational thinking practice could be further faceted by the facets listed in the drop down menu (the circled 2) shown in the figure, e.g., "Education Level", "Format", etc.

We show how we can use the domain structure and correspondences from Fig. 6 and our query language to build our faceted browsing interface. Note that the query numbers shown on the right margin correspond to the circled numbers shown in Figs. 7 and 8.

First, to build the original hierarchal browsing structure (Fig. 7) we return all resources in the collection with id of id:

$$Resources = \pi_{resource\_id}(\sigma_{collection\_id=id}(\alpha(Contains))) \tag{1}$$

The $apply$ operator on the $Contains$ domain structure returns all resource_ids (the projection) in the correct collection (the selection).

Next, we find all facet types and values used in the collection with id id by joining the $Contains$ domain relationship[4] with the $Resource$ domain entity on $resource\_id$ for a collection with id id. This query gives us all the facet types and values in the given collection using the τ operator.

$$Facets(id) = \tau_{Facet}(\alpha(Resource) \bowtie_{resource\_id=resource\_id} Resources \tag{2}$$

Once we have all of the facet types and values (i.e., an unpivot) we create the faceted browse interface in Fig. 8 using the extended relational algebra [8] to populate the facet values and counts (the circled 3) and the resources corresponding to each facet (the circled 4):

$$Facet\_Counts(id) = \gamma_{Facet\_type,Count(Facet)}$$
$$(\sigma_{Facet\_type=ftype}(Facets(id)))) \tag{3}$$

$$FResources(id, ftype, fvalue) = \pi_{resource\_id}(\sigma_{Facet\_type=ftype}(Facets(id)))$$
$$\wedge Facet=fvalue$$
$$\tag{4}$$

4   Pivot

In this section we show how our system can be used for the standard pivot operation and more generally for data to metadata transformation. Figure 9 shows a transformation in the reverse direction from Sect. 3. We have a local schema where all contact information is stored in the $contact$ attribute and the corresponding type is in the $contact\_type$ attribute. We would like this data to appear in a pivoted form where contact information is broken out into the $email$, ext, $home$, and $cell$ domain attributes.

---

[4] We use a straightforward translation of the ER model of the domain structures into the relational model.

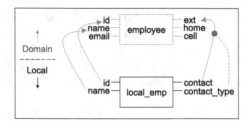

Fig. 9. An example of the pivot correspondence.

In order for this to work we must tell the system which data from the local schema should end up in the *ext* domain attribute, for example. A traditional correspondence in our system is of the form

$$C = (id, A, DA)$$

where each correspondence has an id, a local attribute A, and a corresponding domain attribute DA.

A conditional correspondence adds a conditional predicate P to the correspondence and has the form

$$C = (id, A, DA, P)$$

such that when the correspondence is used in an apply operation, data from local attribute A will only be in the query result for domain attribute DA when the predicate P evaluates to true.

We developed the visual syntax for (a limited form of) the predicate, shown in Fig. 9; a regular correspondence (the solid line) is augmented by the dot with a dotted line. This visual syntax is translated into a predicate for the correspondence where data from the local attribute with the solid line will appear in the domain attribute only when data in the local attribute with the dotted line is equal to the name of the domain attribute. The correspondence shown in Fig. 9 results in the predicate

$$P = (contact\_type = \text{``}ext\text{''})$$

In Fig. 10 we show the complete set of correspondences to pivot from the local schema to the domain structure. The end-user can easily combine regular correspondences and conditional (dotted) correspondences in a single mapping. In this case the *id* and *name* attributes are mapped directly while the *email*, *ext*, *home*, and *cell* attributes are pivoted from the local *contact* attribute.

Once mappings are created, an *apply* operation on the domain structure (as shown in Fig. 11) will use the correspondences and can combine multiple tuples in the source database into a single tuple in the query answer based on the correspondences. For example, in the figure we see that four tuples for "Alice" in the *local_emp* table are combined to make one tuple in the output query; these tuples are joined based on the *id* attribute.

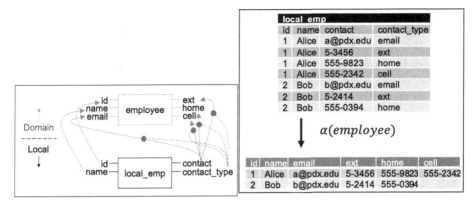

Fig. 10. The complete set of correspondences to pivot the local schema into the domain structure. A user can create a regular correspondence and then chose to add a condition (in this case the specific pivot conditions) for the contact attribute correspondences.

Fig. 11. The pivot operation, using the local and domain structures from Fig. 10 with example employee data.

5   Evaluation

Comparison to Other Systems. Table 1 shows a comparison of our our system (IILR) to SchemaSQL [12], FIRA/FISQL [18,19], Clio [11], and the unpivot/pivot operations supported in SQL (in systems like Oracle and SQL Server).

Table 1. Comparison of data-metadata transformation systems

	SQL	SchemaSQL	FIRA/FISQL	CLIO	IILR
Can perform Pivot/Unpivot	✓	✓	✓	✓	✓
Can perform arbitrary metadata-data transformations	✗	✓	✓	✓	✓
Can perform arbitrary data-metadata transformations	✗	✓	✓	✓	✓
Has a simple visual syntax	✗	✗	✗	✓	✓
Has a non-ambiguous result	✓	✓	✗	✗	✓
Has preview capability	✗	✗	✗	✗	✓

While all these systems can do pivot/unpivot operations, we see that SQL is quite limited; the syntax is complex. The other three systems allow more generalized transformations and Clio provides a simple visual syntax. SQL, SchemaSQL, and our system produce a single non-ambiguous result, whereas FIRA and Clio can potentially have ambiguous or non-intended results; FIRA relies on the optimal tuple merge (which may not be unique) and Clio generates many different mappings that may or may not be correct. Our system avoids the ambiguity problem by limiting users to simple correspondences and maintaining ids. We have also explicitly built in the preview mechanism for our system; while this could be implemented on top of the other systems it is not by default.

User Study. We evaluated whether or not non-technical users can supply correspondences (for our structured navigation widget) based on a small-scale user study. The study consisted of three tasks. The first task was a training task, where participants were shown how to use the mapping system and how to map a simple hierarchical local schema to the hierarchical navigation widget. The second task mirrored the first task but the local schema names were changed and the participants were left to create mappings on their own. For the final task, once again on their own, participants were given a complex university schema with entities for colleges, departments, research labs, professors, and students and then asked to create mappings as they saw fit. We did not require users to create any specific mappings but, rather, were interested in seeing which mappings users would create.

Participants were also asked to complete: a pre-test survey about background knowledge and technical experience; a task-specific survey after each of the non-training tasks; and, a post-test survey at the end of the study. Table 2 shows results of the survey. The first two rows show responses to the technical experience survey. Participants' database experience ranged from less than 1 year to over ten years while all had at least three years of web development experience. In asking about database experience we include using spreadsheets or databases as experience. While all respondents had at least some experience with databases we did have a broad range of experience from non-expert to expert. The task-specific survey asked participants to respond to statements using a five point Likert scale with one being "Strongly Disagree" and five being "Strongly Agree". Tasks are indicated by T1 and T2 in Table 2.

Table 2 shows that all users found it easy to create mappings and all were positive or neutral about the ability to preview mappings using widgets before saving a mapping. Two of the users disliked using the tool and one user (who reported liking the tool verbally) failed to complete the post-test survey (the null cells in the last two rows of the table). There appears to be no correlation between previous experience or technical knowledge and the ability to create mappings; both experienced and non-experienced users reported liking and not liking the tool.

6   Related Work

Like Clio [9], we want users to be able to create mappings by simply drawing lines from local schemas to domain structures. Some users may map only small

Table 2. User study results (T1/T2 indicate tasks; U1 etc. indicate users)

Question	U1	U2	U3	U4	U5	U6	U7	Average
Years of DB experience	10+	<1	5	8	<1	4	10+	
Years of Web development experience	10+	3	5	10+	3	5	10	
"I consider myself an advanced Drupal user"	3	1	3	1	2	3	5	2.57
T1 "When I created a mapping with the tool, it was easy"	4	5	3	5	5	5	5	4.57
T1 "Seeing a preview of mapping results helped me determine if the mappings were what I wanted"	2	5	5	5	5	3	2	3.86
T2 "When I created a mapping with the tool, it was easy"	4	5	5	5	3	5	5	4.57
T2 "Seeing a preview of mapping results helped me determine if the mappings were what I wanted"	3	5	5	3	5	2	5	4
"I enjoyed creating mappings"	2		2	4	4	5	5	3.67
"It would be useful to have mappings and widgets in websites that I work with regularly."	2		2	5	4	5	4	3.67

parts of their local schema (enough for use within a widget) to (typically small) domain structures. This is in contrast to the typical use case of schema/data exchange [7,15] and model management systems [2], where an entire source schema/model is mapped to a target/global schema/model. The flexibility of our mappings is also inspired by pay-as-you-go data integration such as that proposed by Madhavan [13].

While our conditional mappings add complexity to our system, we believe that keeping them simple enough for non-technical users is important. While we cannot meet the complexity provided by Fagin [7] we believe that the subset of mappings we can provide is sufficient for what our users want to do.

Exploratory and faceted search [14] has been shown to be a popular method for navigating digital libraries. A large number of hierarchical search interfaces have been created [1,10,20] that allow facets to be chosen dynamically. Dynamic taxonomies [16] can be used to update facets based on the corpora. But these systems often focus on processing unstructured text. In contrast we focus on structure; our facets may come from any attribute, from heterogeneously structured resources. These other systems require technical expertise to configure and expand, while our widget can be updated by domain specialists by adding or removing simple correspondences.

7   Conclusion

We have shown how IILR can be extended to encompass standard pivot/unpivot operations and how our system can used to perform a combination of these operations. We believe that the combination of feedback and easy-to-use systems will allow non-technical users to take more responsibility for their data management. We plan to extend this work by incorporating all of the new mapping syntax into our mapping interface. In addition, we plan to provide a formal characterization of pivot/unpivot using our system.

Acknowledgments. This work was supported in part by National Science Foundation grants 0840668 and 1250340. Any opinions, findings, and conclusions or recommendations expressed in this material are those of the author(s) and do not necessarily reflect the views of the National Science Foundation.

References

1. Allen, R.B.: Two digital library interfaces that exploit hierarchical structure. In: Proceedings of DAGS 1995. Electronic Publishing and the Information Superhighway (1995)
2. Bernstein, P.A., Melnik, S.: Model management 2.0: manipulating richer mappings. In: Proceedings of the 2007 ACM SIGMOD International Conference on Management of Data, SIGMOD 2007, pp. 1–12. ACM, New York (2007)
3. Britell, S., Delcambre, L.M.L., Atzeni, P.: Flexible information integration with local dominance. In: International Conference on Information Modelling and Knowledge Bases, Kiel, Germany (2014)
4. Britell, S., Delcambre, L.M.L.: Mapping semantic widgets to web-based, domain-specific collections. In: Atzeni, P., Cheung, D., Ram, S. (eds.) ER 2012. LNCS, vol. 7532, pp. 204–213. Springer, Heidelberg (2012). doi:10.1007/978-3-642-34002-4_16
5. Britell, S., Delcambre, L.M.L., Atzeni, P.: Generic data manipulation in a mixed global/local conceptual model. In: Yu, E., Dobbie, G., Jarke, M., Purao, S. (eds.) ER 2014. LNCS, vol. 8824, pp. 246–259. Springer, Heidelberg (2014). doi:10.1007/978-3-319-12206-9_20
6. Cunningham, C., Galindo-Legaria, C.A., Graefe, G.: Pivot and unpivot: optimization and execution strategies in an RDBMs. In: VLDB 2004, pp. 998–1009. VLDB Endowment (2004)
7. Fagin, R., Kolaitis, P.G., Miller, R.J., Popa, L.: Data exchange: semantics and query answering. Theor. Comput. Sci. **336**(1), 89–124 (2005)
8. Gupta, A., Harinarayan, V., Quass, D.: Generalized projections: a powerful approach to aggregation. In: Proceedings of 21st VLDB Conference, pp. 11–15 (1995)
9. Haas, L.M., Hernández, M.A., Ho, H., Popa, L., Roth, M.: Clio grows up: from research prototype to industrial tool. In: Proceedings of the 2005 ACM SIGMOD International Conference on Management of Data, SIGMOD 2005, pp. 805–810. ACM, New York (2005)
10. Hearst, M.A.: Design recommendations for hierarchical faceted search interfaces. In: Proceedings of SIGIR 2006 Workshop on Faceted Search (2006)
11. Hernández, M.A., Papotti, P., Tan, W.C.: Data exchange with data-metadata translations. Proc. VLDB Endow. **1**(1), 260–273 (2008)

12. Lakshmanan, L.V.S., Sadri, F., Subramanian, I.N.: SchemaSQL - a language for interoperability in relational multi-database systems. In: VLDB 1996, pp. 239–250. Morgan Kaufmann Publishers Inc., San Francisco (1996)
13. Madhavan, J., Jeffery, S.R., Cohen, S., Dong, X.L., Ko, D., Yu, C., Halevy, A.: Web-scale data integration: you can only afford to pay as you go. World Wide Web Internet Web Inf. Syst. **7**, 342–350 (2007)
14. Marchionini, G.: Exploratory search: from finding to understanding. Commun. ACM **49**(4), 41 (2006)
15. Papotti, P., Torlone, R.: Schema exchange: generic mappings for transforming data and metadata. Data Knowl. Eng. **68**(7), 665–682 (2009)
16. Sacco, G.: Dynamic taxonomies: a model for large information bases. IEEE Trans. Knowl. Data Eng. **12**(3), 468–479 (2000)
17. Schek, H.J., Scholl, M.H.: The relational model with relation-valued attributes. Inf. Syst. **11**(2), 137–147 (1986)
18. Wyss, C.M., Robertson, E.L.: A formal characterization of pivot/unpivot. In: Proceedings of the 14th ACM International Conference on Information and Knowledge Management, CIKM 2005, pp. 602–608. ACM, New York (2005)
19. Wyss, C.M., Robertson, E.L.: Relational languages for metadata integration. ACM Trans. Database Syst. **30**(2), 624–660 (2005)
20. Yee, K.P., Swearingen, K., Li, K., Hearst, M.: Faceted metadata for image search and browsing. In: CHI 2003, p. 401, April 2003

Conceptual Modeling Guidance

Visualizing User Story Requirements at Multiple Granularity Levels via Semantic Relatedness

Garm Lucassen[(✉)], Fabiano Dalpiaz, Jan Martijn E.M. van der Werf,
and Sjaak Brinkkemper

Utrecht University, Utrecht, The Netherlands
{g.lucassen,f.dalpiaz,j.m.e.m.vanderwerf,s.brinkkemper}@uu.nl

Abstract. The majority of practitioners express software requirements using natural text notations such as user stories. Despite the readability of text, it is hard for people to build an accurate mental image of the most relevant entities and relationships. Even converting requirements to conceptual models is not sufficient: as the number of requirements and concepts grows, obtaining a holistic view of the requirements becomes increasingly difficult and, eventually, practically impossible. In this paper, we introduce and experiment with a novel, automated method for visualizing requirements—by showing the concepts the text references and their relationships—at different levels of granularity. We build on two pillars: (i) *clustering techniques* for grouping elements into coherent sets so that a simplified overview of the concepts can be created, and (ii) state-of-the-art, corpus-based *semantic relatedness algorithms* between words to measure the extent to which two concepts are related. We build a proof-of-concept tool and evaluate our approach by applying it to requirements from four real-world data sets.

1 Introduction

Natural language (NL) is the most popular notation to represent software requirements: around 60 % of practitioners employ NL as their main artifact [12]. Moreover, the trend in agile development has boosted the adoption of the semi-structured NL notation of *user stories* [11,14,31]: "As a ⟨*role*⟩, I want ⟨*goal*⟩, so that ⟨*benefit*⟩". Recent research [14] shows that 90 % of practitioners in agile development adopt user stories.

NL requirements are easy to read but have a major drawback: as their number increases, the quantity of the involved concepts grows rapidly, making it increasingly harder for humans to construct an accurate mental model of those concepts. A possible solution is the (semi-)automated generation of an explicit conceptual model [6,10,19].

Inspired by these works, we have previously proposed the *Visual Narrator* tool that automatically extracts conceptual models from sets of user stories with satisfactory accuracy (80 %–90 %) [23]. However, our evaluation with practitioners indicated that the extracted models quickly become too large to be effectively explored by analysts.

© Springer International Publishing AG 2016
I. Comyn-Wattiau et al. (Eds.): ER 2016, LNCS 9974, pp. 463–478, 2016.
DOI: 10.1007/978-3-319-46397-1_35

The problem of model comprehensibility can be generalized to the conceptual modeling field [3, 17]: humans' working-memory capacity restricts the ability to read models and leads to *cognitive overload* when the same model includes too many concepts.

To tackle this problem, we build upon Shneiderman's *visual information seeking* mantra: *"overview first, zoom/filter, details on demand"* [26]. We propose and experiment with a mechanism for improving the visualization of conceptual models that are generated by the *Visual Narrator* from user stories. We make use of clustering techniques to group the concepts so to obtain an initial *overview*.

We go beyond existing clustering approaches in literature (see Sect. 5) by leveraging on state-of-the-art, corpus-based *semantic relatedness* algorithms based on neural networks to determine the similarity between concepts [8, 28]. The significant improvements in accuracy of these recent approaches trigger our experimentation of these techniques for guiding the clustering of the concepts in user stories.

Our approach is novel in that it does not require additional documentation about the system under development; indeed, it relies on publicly available corpuses of data from the Web. Moreover, we focus on conceptual models generated from user stories, which have a limited expressiveness compared to full-fledged conceptual models.

Specifically, this paper makes two contributions:

- We devise a method for creating an overview of the concepts in a conceptual model by creating clusters that contain semantically related concepts;
- We propose a proof-of-concept tool for generating clusters and for zooming them; we evaluate its feasibility by applying it to user story sets from 4 real-world cases.

The rest of the paper is structured as follows. Section 2 outlines our background: the *Visual Narrator*, semantic similarity, and clustering techniques. Section 3 presents our method. Section 4 applies our proof-of-concept tool to real-world user story data sets. Section 5 reviews related work, and Sect. 6 presents our conclusions and future directions.

2   Background

To ease constructing a mental image of a software system, we propose to take requirements expressed as user stories and derive a conceptual model that enables inspecting system functionality with different degrees of granularity. We review the background work that will later be combined as part of our method in Sect. 3.

2.1   From User Stories to Conceptual Models

User stories are a textual language for expressing requirements that uses a compact template. A user story captures *who* the requirement is for, *what* it is expected from the system, and (optionally) *why* it is important [33]. Although many different templates exist, 70 % of practitioners use the Connextra template [14]: *"As a ⟨type of user⟩, I want ⟨goal⟩, [so that ⟨some reason⟩]"*. For example: *"As an Event Organizer, I want to receive an email when a contact form is submitted, so that I can respond to it"*.

In previous work, we created a tool that automatically extracts a conceptual model from a set of user stories using NLP heuristics: the *Visual Narrator*. This tool is itself built upon a conceptual model of user stories that distinguishes between *role*, *means* and *ends* parts of a user story [13]. By parsing the user stories with SpaCy's part-of-speech tagging[1] and applying eleven state-of-the-art heuristics, the Visual Narrator creates conceptual models of a user story set with up to 86 % recall and 81 % precision. The output of Visual Narrator is an OWL 2 ontology or a Prolog program including the concepts and relationships extracted from a set of user stories.

2.2   Novel Approaches to Semantic Similarity

As we aim to group concepts in order to facilitate comprehension, we need to identify concepts that are similar or related to one another. We rely on the *semantic similarity* (more precisely, *semantic relatedness*) of word pairs. This is a number—typically in the [0,1] range—that captures the distance between the two words, with 0 being no relatedness and 1 being full relatedness. For any given word, this technique can be used to identify a list of similar words or to calculate its semantic similarity score with a collection of words. If the process is repeated for all words in a collection C, one obtains a matrix that defines the pairwise similarity between all concepts in C.

Among the many approaches to calculating semantic similarity [9], we focus on a family of novel, state-of-the-art algorithms: *skip-gram* by Google [16] and *GloVe* by Stanford [20]. Both algorithms parse huge quantities of unannotated text to generate *word embeddings* without requiring supervision. A word embedding maps some attributes of a word to a *vector* of real numbers that can then be used for a variety of tasks, similarity being one of them. Both skip-gram and GloVe adhere to the distributional hypothesis: *"linguistic items with similar distributions have similar meanings"*.

These techniques constitute the most accurate state-of-the-art and provide significant improvements even on other word embedding approaches [16, 20]. Moreover, the innovative vector-based approach of word2vec enables basic "semantic arithmetics" on words: vector("King") - vector("Man") + vector("Woman") results in a vector which is most similar to vector("Queen"). These new methods have not yet been applied in the conceptual modeling and requirements engineering literature, while they are slowly but steadily being adopted in industry, also thanks to their excellent performance.

---

[1] https://spacy.io/.

2.3   Clustering Algorithms

Clustering refers to the process of taking a set of concepts and grouping them so that concepts in the same group are similar and concepts in different groups are different. We aim to adopt clustering in the context of user stories and on the basis of the semantic similarity/relatedness between concepts. Since word embeddings and semantic similarity scores are expressed as numbers, we can easily use pre-existing tools to apply the existing variety of clustering algorithms.

The go-to algorithm for most clustering needs is k-means , but through experimentation with many of the available algorithms we found it to be less applicable for our use case. This is mostly due to the randomness of the algorithm: the resulting clusters differentiate too much between runs.

Instead, we choose an algorithm that leads to similar accuracy results but uses a consistent approach: Ward's minimum variance method [32]. Ward's algorithm starts by assigning all concepts to their own cluster and then iterating over the cluster collection until it finds the two clusters that, when merged, lead to a minimum increase in within-cluster variance of the collection of clusters. It keeps repeating this step until k clusters have been formed. Although Ward's method is slower than k-means, the impact is negligible for the relatively small data sets that one extracts from a set user stories, and in extreme cases the clustering over the entire data set can be executed once the tool starts.

3   Visualization Method for User Stories

We describe our approach to visualizing concepts and relationships between user stories based on the theory introduced in Sect. 2. Our method features three main functionalities: the generation of an overview (Sect. 3.1), zooming in and out mechanisms (Sect. 3.2), and filtering techniques (Sect. 3.3). To illustrate, we use a publicly available set of 104 user stories from the Neurohub project[2], an information environment for neuro-scientists developed by three British universities.

3.1   Overview Generation

The purpose of an overview is to *"provide a general context for understanding the data set"* [5]. By abstracting from all the details of the data, filtering extraneous information and highlighting specific patterns and themes in the data, the overview supports the end-user in understanding the information. To achieve this goal for a user story set, we propose a 6-step process visualized in Fig. 1 and elaborated below.

1. **Extraction from User Stories.** The Visual Narrator extracts a set of relevant concepts C from the user stories and a set of relationships $R \subseteq C \times C$ between those concepts. In our example, the output consists of 124 concepts

---

[2] http://neurohub.ecs.soton.ac.uk/index.php/All_User_Stories.

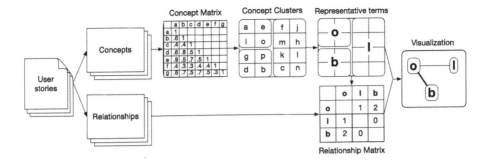

Fig. 1. Our method for generating the overview

in C and 144 relationships between these concepts in R as shown in the following Prolog lines:

concept('Neuroscience').
concept('Researcher').
...
isa(concept('Book Page'),concept('Page')).
rel(concept('Researcher'),'Create',concept('Book Page')).

2. **Concept Similarity Calculation.** We use the skip-gram implementation *word2vec*[3] to calculate the semantic similarity/relatedness scores—in the range $[0, 1]$—for each concept with all other concepts in the list C. As explained in Sect. 2, the use of skip-grams combines efficiency and accuracy. This step results in a similarity matrix SM of size $|C| \times |C|$ such that $\forall i, j \in [0, |C|)$. $SM_{i,j} = skipgram(c_i, c_j)$. In the following example, it is possible to see how some couples of words are much more semantically related than others: compare researcher and neuroscience (0.5134) with neuroscience and booking (0.1667).

SM	neuroscience	researcher	book	booking	...
neuroscience	1.0000	0.5134	0.3446	0.1667	...
researcher	0.5134	1.0000	0.3362	0.2055	...
book	0.3446	0.3362	1.0000	0.2301	...
booking	0.1667	0.2055	0.2301	1.0000	...
...	...	...	...	...	...

3. **Concept Clustering.** We utilize Ward's clustering algorithm to group all the concepts according to their similarity in SM. This results in a high-level disjoint clustering WC that forms the basis for our visualization. In our experimentation, inspired by the cognitive principles by Moody [18], we generate nine clusters.

---

[3] https://code.google.com/p/word2vec/.

0: ['acceptance test', 'acceptance', 'analysis', 'behaviour', 'dependency', 'description', 'drug response', 'experiment description', 'experiment', 'input', 'knowledge', 'neurohub dependency', 'neuroscience', 'paper', 'provenance', 'research paper', 'research', 'response ', 'search result', 'search', 'southampton neuroscience', 'test result', 'test', 'work', 'worm analysis']
1: ['control system', 'equipment booking', 'equipment', 'installation', 'lts machine', 'lts', 'lab administrator', 'lab member', 'lab', 'mri operator', 'mri', 'neurohub installation', ' neurohub workspace', 'spreadsheet', 'system administrator', 'system', 'workspace']
2: ['behaviour video', 'calendar', 'directory', 'google calendar', 'google', 'inventory', 'link', 'log ', 'machine', 'meta', 'reference', 'script', 'table', 'tag', 'type', 'ups', 'version', 'video', ' web', 'worm', 'write ups', 'write']
3: ['browser', 'client', 'interface graphics/colour', 'interface', 'mendeley client', 'neurohub node', 'node', 'operator', 'protocol', 'user', 'web browser']
4: ['booking', 'control', 'cost', 'drug', 'event', 'field', 'forward', 'minimal', 'others', 'period', ' release', 'result', 'run', 'share', 'sharing', 'southampton', 'time', 'track', 'what']
5: ['data file', 'data', 'file type', 'file', 'html tag', 'html', 'information', 'keywords', 'meta data' , 'metadata', 'minimal information', 'share data', 'template']
6: ['administrator', 'engineer', 'investigator', 'member', 'release engineer', 'researcher', ' supervisor']
7: ['graphics/colour', 'mendeley', 'neurohub']
8: ['book entry', 'book page', 'book', 'entry', 'log book', 'neurohub page', 'page']

Note how the clusters are of different sizes: for example, while cluster 0 has size 25, cluster 7 has size 3. Also note how cluster 6 neatly relates roles/professions such as administrator, engineer, etc. This is one of the key differences of employing corpus-based similarity as opposed to looking at the graph structure.

4. **Representative Term Selection.** From each cluster c_i in WC, we identify the concept which is most similar to the collection of concepts in cluster c_i. We do so by using the analogy capabilities of skip-gram as introduced in Sect. 2.2: we compute the sum of the word vectors swv of the concepts in a cluster; then, we set the cluster label by choosing the name of concept in the cluster whose vector model is most similar to the vector swv. For example, consider a cluster with concepts administrator, visitor and individual. We compute the sum vector swv = vector("Administrator") + vector("Visitor") + vector("Individual"). Among these concepts, the word whose vector is closest to the sum of the vectors is individual. To avoid meaningless labels, we remove stop words—such as he, a, from, ... —before we execute this step. For the Neurohub case, we obtain the following results:

0: analysis 1: lab   2: web 3: user 4: time
5: data   6: engineer 7:   8: book

Note that for cluster 7 no label could be assigned because word2vec does not have any of the cluster's terms in its dictionary.

5. **Inter-cluster Relationships Matrix Generation.** Since the concepts in a cluster are represented by one term, intra-cluster relationships do not need to be visualized. Starting from the list of relationships R, we derive a matrix ICR of size $|WC| \times |WC|$ that determines the strength of the relationships between the clusters by counting how many relationships exist between the concepts in those clusters. Formally, $\forall i, j \in [0, |WC|)$:

$$ICR(c_i, c_j) = \begin{cases} 0, \text{if } i = j \\ |r(x,y)| \in R. \ (x \in c_i \wedge y \in c_j) \vee (x \in c_j \wedge y \in c_x), else \end{cases}$$

In our example, we obtain the following matrix:

ICR	c0	c1	c2	c3	c4	c5	c6	c7	c8
c0	0	2	2	4	5	0	3	1	0
c1	2	0	2	3	3	1	5	2	0
c2	2	2	0	8	0	4	4	0	1
c3	4	3	8	0	7	10	1	3	2
c4	5	3	0	7	0	2	5	0	0
c5	0	1	4	10	2	0	14	0	0
c6	3	5	4	1	5	14	0	0	1
c7	1	2	0	3	0	0	0	0	1
c8	0	0	1	2	0	0	1	1	0

The remarkably large number of relationships between 5 and 6 is caused by the concentration of role concepts in cluster 6 who perform an action on the concepts related to data in cluster 5.

6. **Visualization Drawing.** Each cluster $c \in WC$ becomes a vertex (a circle) with the representative term as its label. The diameter of the circle increases with the number of concepts in the cluster. Lines are drawn for each inter-cluster relationship in ICR; the width of a link increases with the number of relationships between the connected clusters. An example of the generated overview is shown in Fig. 2.

3.2 Zooming

The purpose of zooming is to reduce the complexity of the data presentation by having the user adjust the data element size and selection on the screen [5]. We propose two zooming views that enable exploring distinct details of the overview; these views are accessed by clicking on either (1) a concept or (2) a relationship.

When a user clicks on a concept, that concept will be zoomed in and the steps outlined in Sect. 3.1 are re-run on the concepts within the cluster. The

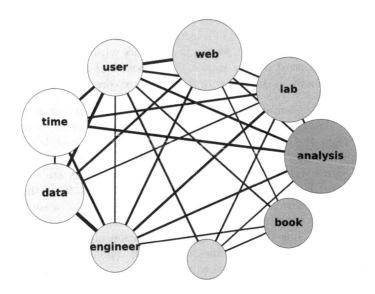

Fig. 2. Example overview of the user stories from the Neurohub project

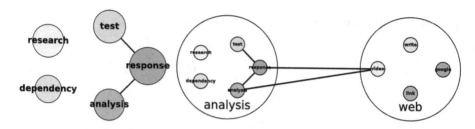

Fig. 3. Zooming examples for Neurohub: concept zoom on the *analysis* cluster (on the left), and relationship zoom between the *analysis* and the *web* clusters (on the right)

only difference is that we set the number of sub-clusters to the square root of the number of elements within the cluster[4]. The outcome is a more granular view of the concepts in the cluster and showing new inter-cluster relationships that were previously hidden as intra-cluster relationships. See the left image of Fig. 3 for an example. In case the number of concepts in that cluster is lower or equal than 9 (see [18]), all concepts will be shown.

Clicking on a relationship will simultaneously zoom in on the two clusters that the relationship connects, showing the same more granular view of the concepts as when clicking on a concept. Furthermore, zooming in on the relationship displays all underlying relationships individually and connects the smaller underlying concept clusters on both sides. See the right image of Fig. 3 for an example.

3.3   Filtering

The purpose of filtering is the same as zooming: reducing the complexity of the presented data. However, instead of selecting a specific region, filtering controls enable the user to change whether the data points with a given attribute are visible [5]. In the context of user stories, we propose four filters that enable the user to further simplify a data view or to further explore some specific details:

1. *Relationships:* by default any view is drawn with its relevant relationships. Optionally, the user can turn this off the relationships clicking, allowing complete focus on the concept clusters. Alternatively, it is possible to filter out specific relationship types, e.g., visualizing only or hiding is-a relationships.
2. *Role:* a central and prominent aspect of user stories, roles are the most frequently occurring concepts in any user story set. Indeed, 96 of the 123 relationships in the Neurohub example (78 %) connect a role to some concept. We propose two ways of filtering roles: (i) removing all roles from the set of concepts C, enabling the user to focus on relationships between other concepts; (2) selecting a specific role to focus on, removing all concepts and relationships that are not related to that role.

---

[4] Determining the number of clusters is still a work-in-progress part of our approach.

3. *Search:* users can query for concept terms to find the cluster related to that concept. For example, searching for *file* will highlight the data cluster and its relationships while slightly blurring all unrelated concepts and relationships.
4. *Agile Artifacts:* In agile software development, user stories are organized into meaningful chunks: epics, themes and sprints. The user can select any combination of these in order to explore specific parts of the system (via epics and themes) or to focus on certain development periods (sprints).

4   Prototype Demonstration

We demonstrate the feasibility of our approach by applying a prototype implementation to three real-world case studies. The prototype is available online including the Neurohub user stories[5]. Unfortunately, we cannot release the confidential case study user stories. For each case, we present four views of their user story concepts and relationships: overview, concept zoom, relationship zoom and a role filter. Finally, we evaluate and discuss the output.

4.1   Case 1: CMSCompany

The company developing this complex CMS product for large enterprises is located in the Netherlands, serving 150 customers with 120 employees. Their supplied data consists of 32 syntactically correct user stories, which represents a snapshot of approximately a year of development in 2011. Visual Narrator extracted 96 concepts and 114 relationships, exemplifying that despite the small size of the user story set, the use of long user stories with non-trivial sentence structuring means many concepts and relationships are present.

Applying the prototype to *CMSCompany*'s user stories results in Fig. 4. Upon examination of the overview on the left, one thing immediately stands out: the clusters are highly interrelated and none of them clearly has the majority of relationships. This is likely a consequence of the long, non-trivial structuring of these user stories. Furthermore, some of the representative terms are highly relevant to the CMS domain: site, marketeer, text, business & analytics are important aspects of CMSCompany's product.

By contrast, the concept zoom of the *result* cluster has no intercluster relationships at all. In fact, none of the subclusters contain such a relationship. Intuitively, the authors believed this to be a bad result but upon closer examination this phenomenon actually turns out to be the ideal situation. Indeed, there actually *are* relationships between concepts in this subcluster but they are all within their own subsubcluster, demonstrating that at this level the semantic clustering approach is very effective at grouping related user story concepts.

---

[5] https://github.com/gglucass/Semantic-Similarity-Prototype.

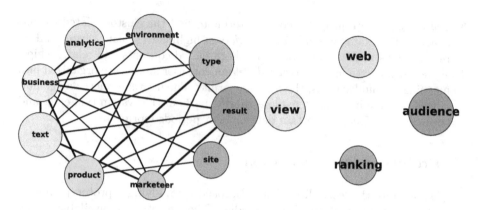

Fig. 4. Overview for CMSCompany user stories and concept zoom on the *result* cluster

4.2   Case 2: WebCompany

This is a young Dutch company that creates tailor-made web applications for businesses. The team consists of nine employees who iteratively develop applications in weekly Scrum sprints. WebCompany supplied 98 user stories covering the development of an entire web application focused on interactive story telling that was created in 2014. Although the data set is 3× as big as CMSCompany's, these user stories are very simple, concise and contain very few complex sentence structures. Because of this, Visual Narrator extracts just 106 concepts and 123 relationships.

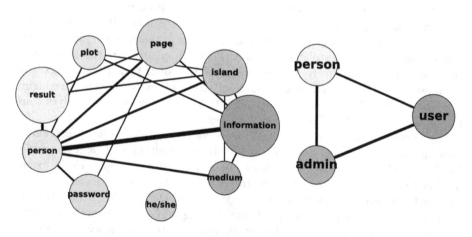

Fig. 5. Overview for WebCompany user stories and concept zoom of *person* cluster

In CMSCompany's overview in Fig. 5 the *person* cluster clearly has the most relationships with other clusters. This is a direct consequence of two factors:

(1) the person clusters contains all roles defined in the user stories and (2) because the user stories are simple, the majority of relationships in this set are role(action, object). However, for this case not all representative terms are meaningful. In particular, *result* is strongly related to merely 3 or 4 out of 22 concepts in that cluster. This exemplifies the approach's weakness of selecting very general terms for large, less coherent clusters because they are at least somewhat related to many of the terms in the cluster.

In some cases, previously intracluster relationships do become intracluster relationships when zooming in on a cluster. The subclusters in *person* are all related to one another in some way. Because this user story concerns an entire web application, this is to be expected. Indeed, if admin was not related to a user a human analyst should be triggered to investigate if the user story set is incomplete. This exemplifies a possible real-world use case of the prototype output.

4.3   Case 3: SCMCompany

This case concerns stories from a company that delivers a leading Supply Chain Management (SCM) suite for large companies in the logistics, healthcare, technology and consumer sectors. To support development in keeping up with double digit revenue growth, the company has started to embrace user stories. This set consists of 54 high quality user stories of moderate size and complexity. In total, Visual Narrator extracted 91 concepts and 114 relationships.

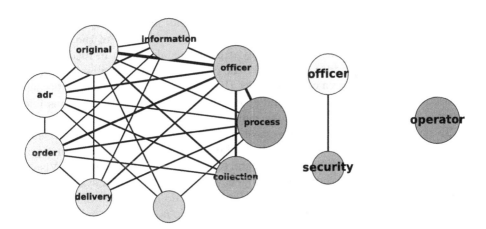

Fig. 6. Overview for SCMCompany user stories and concept zoom of *officer* cluster

Nearly all of the representative terms in the overview in Fig. 6 are strongly related to the SCM domain. Furthermore, the relationship between concepts *security* and *officer* in the concept zoom is actually an accurate representation of the relationship in the source data. Considering that the sub clusters contain multiple concepts, this example demonstrates a positive result of our approach for selecting a representative term.

5 Related Literature

We review the relevant literature about RE visualization, clustering techniques for generic conceptual models, and extraction of conceptual models from requirements.

5.1 RE Visualization

Requirements engineering visualization (REV) is concerned with creating effective visualizations of RE artifacts. Cooper et al. [4] review the papers appeared in the REV workshops between 2006 and 2008. They distinguish between different types of visualizations: tabular, relational, sequential, hierarchical, and metaphorical/quantitative. The most relevant categories for our work are the relational—i.e., (hyper-)graphs—and hierarchical—decomposing a system into its parts. While many relational approaches exist, very few focus on hierarchal aspects, which are the key in our work.

We deliberately exclude from this section the vast body of literature on requirements modeling languages: this important family of requirements visualization approaches goes beyond the scope of our paper, as we aim at visualizing the main concepts that can be extracted from NL requirements.

Reinhard et al. [22] propose an improved Fisheye zoom algorithm for the visualization and editing of hierarchical requirements models. The most interesting feature of their algorithm is that is guarantees stability of the adjusted layouts and runs in linear time. We may exploit this algorithm in future work. Gandhi and Lee [7] use visualizations in the context of requirements-driven risk assessment. They extract a concept lattice that relates risk-related concepts such as assets, threats, vulnerabilities and countermeasures. The lattice is a possible criterion for a zoom-in/zoom-out mechanism.

To date, ReCVisu+ [21] is the most effective tool for requirements visualization. ReCVisu+ supports different visual exploration tasks and, like our approach, is based on clustering techniques and semantic similarity. While RecVisu+ determines similarity based on the frequency of co-occurrence in system documentation, we rely on corpus-based techniques that do not require the existence of additional system documentation. Moreover, we do not consider only concepts but also relationships.

5.2 Conceptual Modeling Clustering

The conceptual modeling and databases community is well aware that (E)ER diagrams are often large and cluttered. Teorey et al. have studied this problem already in the late 80s [27]: they proposed collapse/expand mechanisms that can be used to hide/view entities and relationships that are secondary to some primary entities; for example, 'journal address' and 'journal note' can be collapsed into a cluster labeled 'journal'.

Akoka and Comyn-Wattiau [1] propose automated clustering techniques that can be used to realize Teorey's vision and that derives non-overlapping clusters. They experiment multiple distance indicators with different semantics (visual, hierarchical, cohesive, etc.) and compare their strengths and weaknesses. Moody and Flitman [18] combine and refine principles from previous work and include cognitive aspects, such as the maximum size of a cluster being nine elements, in order to facilitate human comprehension. Tzitzikas and Hainaut [29] use link analysis from web searching to generate a smaller diagram that includes only the major entity and relationships; they also propose an automated 2D visualization that uses force-directed drawing algorithms.

Summarization techniques exist for database schemas. Yu and Jagadish [34] formalize the notion of a schema summary and define its quality in terms of complexity (number of elements), importance (inclusion of the most important elements), and coverage (are all major chunks of the original schema represented?). Based on these notions, they propose algorithms that optimize each of these quality criteria. Yuan et al. [35] go further by proposing elaborate metrics to determine table similarity and importance.

All these techniques inspire our work. The main novelty of our proposal is that we focus on conceptual models that represent requirements, and that we use novel corpus-based techniques to determine similarity. The significant advances that these algorithms provide make it possible for us to experiment clustering based on the co-occurrence of words in corpora of data on the Web with promising results.

5.3 Extracting Conceptual Models from Requirements

There is a long tradition in generating conceptual models from NL requirements. Already in 1989, Saeki et al. [24] proposed a method for the automatic extraction of verbs and nouns from NL. The ideas of this method were operationalized by numerous (semi-)automated tools, including NL-OOPS [15], CM-Builder [10], CIRCE [2], aToucan [36], and the tool by Sagar and Abirami [25].

All these approaches use NL processing algorithms such as tokenization, part-of-speech tagging, morphological analysis and parsing. These tools show promising precision and recall—comparable if not better than human experts—, although they often require restricted NL to do so. In previous work [23], we leveraged these tools and proposed an approach that is specifically suited for requirements expressed as user stories.

6   Discussion, Conclusion and Future Work

This paper explored the potential of applying semantic relatedness algorithms for visualizing user stories. After studying and experimenting with state-of-the-art algorithms such as skip-gram, we presented a novel, automated method for visualizing user stories at different levels of granularity. We applied a prototype implementation of this method to four real-world user story sets, studied the output and observed that:

- The generated visualizations are capable of highlighting relevant information classifications for the system. For example, the central role of the person cluster in the WebCompany overview is easily recognizable.
- For the majority of clusters, the generated representative term is meaningful and relevant within the application domain.
- When an intercluster relationship is present on the zoom level, it is generally relevant within that (sub-)domain. The analysis subcluster of Neurohub for example relates test, response and analysis.
- On the overview level, too many intercluster relationships are visible, effectively rendering them useless for further human analysis.
- The prototype tends to select irrelevant common denominator terms for large clusters with low internal coherence.
- Word2Vec does not include all words in meaningful clusters, resulting in residual clusters that cannot be assigned any label.

Based on these observations, we envision possible applications for our visualization approach to include: (1) discovering missing relationships between clusters that may result in further user stories; (2) teaching system functionality by exploring simplified, manageable chunks; and (3) analyzing expected system changes after introducing new sets of user stories (e.g., new epics). However, further practitioner evaluation is necessary to confirm the validity of our observations and the potential of these applications.

In future work, we intend to experiment with these possible use cases as well as investigate how to substantially improve the generated output. A necessary next step is to combine and compare our work with existing state-of-the-art clustering techniques that do not rely on semantic relatedness. Additionally, future work should incorporate state-of-the-art group structure visualization techniques [30]. We expect this to produce outputs that are even more usable in real-world scenarios. Additionally, we are investigating the potential benefits of applying machine learning to enhance the accuracy of semantic relatedness scores for specific application domains.

References

1. Akoka, J., Comyn-Wattiau, I.: Entity-relationship and object-oriented model automatic clustering. Data Knowl. Eng. **20**(2), 87–117 (1996)
2. Ambriola, V., Gervasi, V.: On the systematic analysis of natural language requirements with CIRCE. Autom. Softw. Eng. **13**(1), 107–167 (2006)
3. Aranda, J., Ernst, N., Horkoff, J., Easterbrook, S.: A framework for empirical evaluation of model comprehensibility. In: Proceedings of MiSE (2007)
4. Cooper Jr., J.R., Lee, S.W., Gandhi, R.A., Gotel, O.: Requirements engineering visualization: a survey on the state-of-the-art. In: Proceedings of REV, pp. 46–55 (2009)

5. Craft, B., Cairns, P.: Beyond guidelines: what can we learn from the visual information seeking mantra? In: Proceedings of IV, pp. 110–118, July 2005
6. Du, S., Metzler, D.P.: An automated multi-component approach to extracting entity relationships from database requirement specification documents. In: Kop, C., Fliedl, G., Mayr, H.C., Métais, E. (eds.) NLDB 2006. LNCS, vol. 3999, pp. 1–11. Springer, Heidelberg (2006). doi:10.1007/11765448_1
7. Gandhi, R.A., Lee, S.W.: Discovering and understanding multi-dimensional correlations among certification requirements with application to risk assessment. In: Proceedings of RE, pp. 231–240 (2007)
8. Goldberg, Y., Levy, O.: Word2vec explained: deriving Mikolov et al.'s negative-sampling word-embedding method. arXiv preprint arXiv:1402.3722 (2014)
9. Harispe, S., Ranwez, S., Janaqi, S., Montmain, J.: Semantic Similarity from Natural Language and Ontology Analysis. Morgan & Claypool Publishers, San Rafael (2015)
10. Harmain, H., Gaizauskas, R.: CM-Builder: a natural language-based CASE tool for object-oriented analysis. Autom. Softw. Eng. 10(2), 157–181 (2003)
11. Kassab, M.: The changing landscape of requirements engineering practices over the past decade. In: Proceedings of EmpiRE (2015)
12. Kassab, M., Neill, C., Laplante, P.: State of practice in requirements engineering: contemporary data. Innov. Syst. Softw. Eng. 10(4), 235–241 (2014)
13. Lucassen, G., Dalpiaz, F., van der Werf, J.M., Brinkkemper, S.: Improving agile requirements: the quality user story framework and tool. Requir. Eng. 21, 383–403 (2016)
14. Lucassen, G., Dalpiaz, F., Werf, J.M.E.M., Brinkkemper, S.: The use and effectiveness of user stories in practice. In: Daneva, M., Pastor, O. (eds.) REFSQ 2016. LNCS, vol. 9619, pp. 205–222. Springer, Heidelberg (2016). doi:10.1007/978-3-319-30282-9_14
15. Mich, L.: NL-OOPS: from natural language to object oriented requirements using the natural language processing system LOLITA. Nat. Lang. Eng. 2, 161–187 (1996)
16. Mikolov, T., Sutskever, I., Chen, K., Corrado, G.S., Dean, J.: Distributed representations of words and phrases and their compositionality. In: Advances in Neural Information Processing Systems, vol. 26, pp. 3111–3119 (2013)
17. Moody, D.: The "Physics" of notations: toward a scientific basis for constructing visual notations in software engineering. IEEE Trans. Softw. Eng. 35(6), 756–779 (2009)
18. Moody, D.L., Flitman, A.: A methodology for clustering entity relationship models — a human information processing approach. In: Akoka, J., Bouzeghoub, M., Comyn-Wattiau, I., Métais, E. (eds.) ER 1999. LNCS, vol. 1728, pp. 114–130. Springer, Heidelberg (1999). doi:10.1007/3-540-47866-3_8
19. Omar, N., Hanna, J., McKevitt, P.: Heuristics-based entity-relationship modelling through natural language processing. In: Proceedings of AICS, pp. 302–313 (2004)
20. Pennington, J., Socher, R., Manning, C.D.: GloVe: global vectors for word representation. In: Proceedings of EMNLP, pp. 1532–1543 (2014)
21. Reddivari, S., Rad, S., Bhowmik, T., Cain, N., Niu, N.: Visual requirements analytics: a framework and case study. Requir. Eng. 19(3), 257–279 (2014)
22. Reinhard, T., Meier, S., Glinz, M.: An improved fisheye zoom algorithm for visualizing and editing hierarchical models. In: Proceedings of REV. IEEE (2007)
23. Robeer, M., Lucassen, G., Van der Werf, J., Dalpiaz, F., Brinkkemper, S.: Automated extraction of conceptual models from user stories via NLP. In: Proceedings of RE (2016)

24. Saeki, M., Horai, H., Enomoto, H.: Software development process from natural language specification. In: Proceedings of ICSE, pp. 64–73. ACM (1989)
25. Sagar, V.B.R.V., Abirami, S.: Conceptual modeling of natural language functional requirements. J. Syst. Softw. **88**, 25–41 (2014)
26. Shneiderman, B.: The eyes have it: a task by data type taxonomy for information visualizations. In: Proceedings of VL, pp. 336–343 (1996)
27. Teorey, T.J., Wei, G., Bolton, D.L., Koenig, J.A.: ER model clustering as an aid for user communication and documentation in database design. Commun. ACM **32**(8), 975–987 (1989)
28. Trask, A., Michalak, P., Liu, J.: sense2vec-a fast and accurate method for word sense disambiguation in neural word embeddings. arXiv preprint arXiv:1511.06388 (2015)
29. Tzitzikas, Y., Hainaut, J.-L.: How to tame a very large ER diagram (using link analysis and force-directed drawing algorithms). In: Delcambre, L., Kop, C., Mayr, H.C., Mylopoulos, J., Pastor, O. (eds.) ER 2005. LNCS, vol. 3716, pp. 144–159. Springer, Heidelberg (2005). doi:10.1007/11568322_10
30. Vehlow, C., Beck, F., Weiskopf, D.: The state of the art in visualizing group structures in graphs. In: Borgo, R., Ganovelli, F., Viola, I. (eds.) Eurographics Conference on Visualization (EuroVis) - STARs. The Eurographics Association (2015)
31. Wang, X., Zhao, L., Wang, Y., Sun, J.: The role of requirements engineering practices in agile development: an empirical study. In: Zowghi, D., Jin, Z. (eds.) Requirements Engineering. CCIS, vol. 432, pp. 195–209. Springer, Heidelberg (2014). doi:10.1007/978-3-662-43610-3_15
32. Ward, J.H.: Hierarchical grouping to optimize an objective function. J. Am. Stat. Assoc. **58**(301), 236–244 (1963)
33. Wautelet, Y., Heng, S., Kolp, M., Mirbel, I.: Unifying and extending user story models. In: Jarke, M., Mylopoulos, J., Quix, C., Rolland, C., Manolopoulos, Y., Mouratidis, H., Horkoff, J. (eds.) CAiSE 2014. LNCS, vol. 8484, pp. 211–225. Springer, Heidelberg (2014). doi:10.1007/978-3-319-07881-6_15
34. Yu, C., Jagadish, H.: Schema summarization. In: Proceedings of VLDB, pp. 319–330 (2006)
35. Yuan, X., Li, X., Yu, M., Cai, X., Zhang, Y., Wen, Y.: Summarizing relational database schema based on label propagation. In: Chen, L., Jia, Y., Sellis, T., Liu, G. (eds.) APWeb 2014. LNCS, vol. 8709, pp. 258–269. Springer, Heidelberg (2014). doi:10.1007/978-3-319-11116-2_23
36. Yue, T., Briand, L.C., Labiche, Y.: aToucan: an automated framework to derive UML analysis models from use case models. ACM Trans. Softw. Eng. Methodol. **24**(3), 13:1–13:52 (2015)

User Progress Modelling in Counselling Systems: An Application to an Adaptive Virtual Coach

Nuria Medina-Medina$^{(\boxtimes)}$, Zoraida Callejas, Kawtar Benghazi,
and Manuel Noguera

Department of Languages and Computer Systems, University of Granada,
Avda. Daniel Saucedo Aranda sn., 18071 Granada, Spain
{nmedina,zoraida,benghazi,mnoguera}@ugr.es

Abstract. Counselling systems such as recommendation systems and virtual coaches assist users to gradually achieve their goals. For that purpose, it is usual to devise a progression plan consisting of intermediate, possibly interrelated, tasks or goals to be accomplished in order to guide counselees from their current state to a (desirable) target state, whilst taking into account their circumstances and needs. Users may also strive to progress in several dimensions or aspects at the same time. However, existing goal modelling proposals are mainly focused on processes and object flows, and do not reflect the variable manner in which user progression may actually take place. In this paper, we propose a user-goal oriented metamodel to represent progressions between user states that serves as a knowledge basis for the construction of adaptive counselling systems. The proposal is exemplified with the design of a virtual coach to promote active ageing in which personalization plays a key role.

Keywords: Progression states · User adaptation · Virtual coach

1 Introduction

Modern Systems and Software Engineering (SSE) has widely recognized the importance of specifying and representing goals and intentions in different types of architectural models (i.e., enterprise, system and software models, etc.), so as to improve the alignment of systems and software to be built with the objectives of the organizations they support [10]. As a matter of fact, in the last years, several approaches have appeared in order to specify the link of the entities of a conceptual model with the purpose they were conceived for [13]. Likewise, it is common to plan the achievement of goals and objectives in terms of a structured sequence of steps and/or the occurrence of events. This point of view has resulted in that most current modelling languages and approaches exhibit a process and activity-centric nature and frequently they do not even provide specific constructs for representing goals [18]. This is also largely due to the increasing popularity of business process management techniques and tools, which provide organizations with tangible benefits in terms of process and activity flow analysis, discovery, improvement, simulation, and prediction [8].

© Springer International Publishing AG 2016
I. Comyn-Wattiau et al. (Eds.): ER 2016, LNCS 9974, pp. 479–487, 2016.
DOI: 10.1007/978-3-319-46397-1_36

Some examples of process modelling notations are UML Activity Diagrams [12], BPMN [11], YAWL [3] and Map [15]. They have proven their appropriateness for fully representing and structuring activities within processes and, thus, conveying behavioural aspects of organizational environments [1,2]. However, there exist situations in which models can become more meaningful when focusing on the structure and inter-dependencies between intermediate objectives or user states to be reached, rather than on the specification of a predefined sequence in which they should be achieved. This is because the particular sequencing (1) may not be so relevant; (2) may take place in so many different ways that, if specified, the model readability and understanding would be reduced [14]; or (3) may even be unknown a priori. Other reasons that may discourage the usage of rich process modelling notations in some contexts derive from the complexity they introduce [17]. For example, most existing notations allow information and object flows, as well as rich control flow gateways, to be represented with specific constructs. However, when paying attention to sequencing the fulfilment of the intermediate goals, these constructs are not required in most cases since such type of information and complex control flows are usually not present [2]. Finally, sometimes it is needed to represent goals about performing the same activity, but an increasing (or decreasing) number of times, rather than a sequenced list of different activities one after another.

This is the case of modelling the progression of a user (or a group of them) to achieve a set of objectives that allows he/she to reach a desired state from his/her current state. In these situations, the main interest is on the specification of the starting point, the intermediate states or goals the progressing individual is expected to go through, and his/her intended end point or general goal. The general objective may encompass different partial objectives or dimensions of the users and their context, but not in a strict, predefined order. Moreover, inter-dependencies between goals in different dimensions and the circumstances that rule the transitions between these partial objectives should be also reflected when modelling user progressions. For example, the fulfilment of a goal in a dimension may trigger or force the advancement of the progressing entity toward the achievement of another goal in a different dimension.

Goal orientation is extensively addressed in the literature [6,9]. Examples of goal oriented modelling and design approaches are the NFR [5], TROPOS [4] and KAOS frameworks [7]. However, these approaches are focused on business and information systems goals rather than on user goals, since goal specification drives several activities related to systems requirements engineering processes [16]. Thus, these approaches can be considered as system-goal oriented. A user-goal modelling focus could be more appropriate for counselling systems, such as coaching systems, where the adaptation to user objectives is usually required. In this paper we present a user-goal oriented proposal for modelling the progressions of users towards a desired objective in counselling systems. Section 2 describes a user progression metamodel and Sect. 3 exemplifies its application to develop a virtual coach for active ageing within the context of a Spanish National Project. Finally, Sect. 4 presents conclusions and outlines ideas for future work.

2   A Metamodel to Represent Progression in Counselling Systems

We introduce a metamodel to represent the progression of users toward a desired objective that can be used as a basis for adaptive counselling systems. Figure 1 illustrates our proposal, which includes two interrelated parts: a user state metamodel and a progression metamodel. Users have a *global objective/goal* that can be decomposed into partial objectives with associated *progression lines*. A *partial objective* is a sub-objective that deals with a particular dimension or aspect included in the global objective. A *progression line* is a series of steps or progression states that must be performed to achieve each partial objective. For example, in an addiction counselling system the global objective may be to stop unhealthy habits, one of the partial objectives may be smoking cessation, and the corresponding progression line could be a sequence of six progression states to gradually reduce the number of cigarettes to zero. Another partial objective could be to control alcohol intake and it would have its own progression line. The number of progression states may differ for different partial objectives.

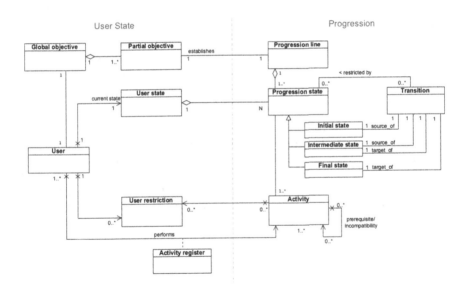

Fig. 1. Metamodel proposed to represent the user progression

Each *progression state* represents a level of achievement of its corresponding partial objective (e.g. the user smokes less than 20 cigarettes per day, the user has stopped smoking, etc.) and there exist *transitions between states* that represent the order in which the states corresponding to a particular progression line precede one another in order to achieve the partial objective (e.g. a reduction in the number of cigarettes smoked per day may determine the transitions).

The transitions may be ruled by *restrictions* that take place between progression states that belong to different progression lines, that is, progression states corresponding to different partial objectives. For instance, it may be required to achieve a good handling of the urge to drink before starting to significantly reduce the number of daily cigarettes. In this case, a state of the drinking progression line restricts a certain transition within the smoking progression line. In some contexts, achieving a certain level in a partial objective may prevent or advice against the transition to another particular progression state in another progression line. Consequently, restrictions can establish a *prerequisite* or an *incompatibility* between a *source state* and a *target state* in a progression line.

The metamodel differentiates between progression states and the specific *activities* that can be performed to achieve them. For example, in the smoking scenario a state may have different activities including *"reducing by half the cigarettes smoked in a week timespan"* or *"throwing away all cigarettes at home today"* depending on its position in the progression line. Each progression state must have at least one associated activity and there is no maximum number of activities. Incompatibility and prerequisite restrictions are also permitted between activities. Consequently, the metamodel defines a set of possible progression states for each partial objective (an *initial state*, a *final state* and one or several *intermediate states*), the activities to perform in order to achieve these states, the transitions between them, and others relations between the progressions of different objectives. To model users, the metamodel defines the *user state* as a set of progression states. It also includes a *registry* of all activities completed by the user (annotated with their performance and satisfaction) as well as the *user restrictions* that may prevent them from performing certain activities.

Sample instance of the metamodel. Figure 2 shows an abstract instance of the metamodel where the first progression line corresponds to an objective "s" and the second to an objective "t". Usually, progressing towards a certain objective requires achieving a certain degree of completion of another objective, e.g. the transition from state *t1* to *t2* requires that the user has achieved *s2*.

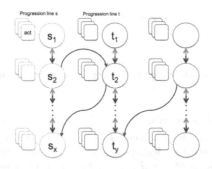

Fig. 2. A sample instance of the metamodel

At an operational level, in a system built on top of an instance of the proposed metamodel, it is necessary to establish the rules that determine user progression. The transition between two successive states of the same progression line must be enriched with: (a) a progression rule that sets the progression conditions; and (b) a regression rule indicating under which circumstances the user returns to a previous progression state, if applicable. Besides, an update rule associated with each activity must be defined to compute the level of progression achieved by the user after successfully completing the activity (progression factor).

At each time, the user state comprises a set of progression states representing the degree to which the user has advanced towards each partial objective. It may happen that the current state for each progression line is different (i.e. the user has advanced faster in some partial objectives with respect to others). To allow personalization, once the current user state has been specified (e.g. in the smoking addiction domain, the initial state of the user may be computed from physical addiction parameters), the following aspects could be subsequently adapted: (a) *target user state*, the set of adapted progression states that a particular user should achieve (e.g. it may not be desirable for very heavy smokers to aim for total cessation); (b) *set of activities to progress to the following state* that may differ between users; and (c) *personalized update, progression, and regression rules*, e.g. the update rule that computes the progression factor may be more relaxed with recent smokers compared to long-trajectory smokers.

3   Case Study: Designing a Virtual Coach for Active Ageing

We have instantiated the proposed metamodel to design a virtual coach that aims at fostering healthy habits for active ageing. The coach will offer advice about nutrition, rest, locomotion, and training routines (although only the last two are discussed in this paper). When targeting ageing populations there are specific conditions and physical problems that must be considered and it is important to account for their particularities when interpreting progresses and preferences. Thus, adaptivity to users is key to success in this application domain. The adaptive architecture of the virtual coach comprises the three modules shown in Fig. 3: (a) *progression model*, stores and manages the progression lines; (b) *user model*, stores and manages the relevant user features; and (c) *adaptation engine*, manages the adaptation rules and strategies used to personalize the advices.

As shown in Fig. 3, the adaptation rules are evaluated within an adaptation engine whose inputs are the user model attributes. These rules generate the adjustments that the progression model demands to personalize the recommendations. Both the progression model and the adaptation rules must be specified initially by human experts. To make it easier, the progression model is expressed in terms of routines (progression states) and exercises (activities), which are frequent concepts in this domain. Similarly, the adaptive rules have the structure: *if <condition> then <action>*, where the *condition* is built upon user attributes and the *action* establishes a shift in the routines and exercises

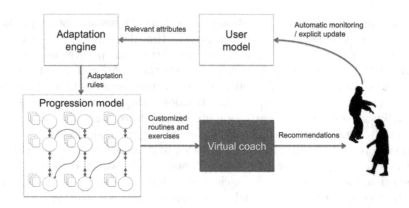

Fig. 3. Architecture for an adaptive virtual coach

of the progression model. Finally, each time the user follows the coach's recommendations, the user model is updated to reflect the progressions (update rules). Progression rules determine whether the user can advance to the next routine or requires further exercises in the current routine.

Following the metamodel, the virtual coach considers eight progression lines: walk, run, go up/downstairs, resistance, strength, balance, speed and coordination. For each of them, there are a series of routines determined by a progression factor in the range [1–100] indicating the degree of attainment of the partial objective. We have established a lower number of progression states (10 routines per line) considering ranges (walking progression 1 to 10, walking progression 11 to 20...) rather than specific values of progression.

Transitions connect consecutive progression states (e.g. "walking progression 1 to 10" with "walking progression 11 to 20") within each progression line ("walk") and a set of progression and regression rules determine the execution of these transitions (forwards or backwards respectively). At the same time, restrictions connect progression states from different progression lines to prevent the execution of a routine until other routines are achieved. For example, the state "running progression 1 to 10" cannot be started until the state "walking progression 31 to 40" has been achieved, that is, users cannot start running until they have shown a certain expertise in walking.

Each routine is performed by means of a series of activities corresponding to physical exercises that unambiguously define the steps to be followed. Each exercise is tagged with a list of user restrictions that make it impracticable or not recommended. For example, running with a prominent slope may be not advisable for a user with an injured ankle.

Counselling systems must adapt their advices to their users and thus must know all user aspects relevant to the counselling. In the case of our virtual coach, the system manages a user model that registers the progression factor of the user in each routine and for each type of exercise stores: satisfaction, duration, repetitions, intensity and frequency as well as a detailed log for each specific exercise performed. Additionally, illnesses and postural deficiencies are annotated. This way, once the progression model and a set of adaptation rules have been defined, they will guide the search for personalized routines according to three steps: (1) filtering the general progression model according to the user's physical condition ignoring the exercises that are not recommendable; (2) identifying the current user state querying the user model; and (3) selecting exercises corresponding to the current user progression state considering the adaptation strategies (e.g. the system may decide not to suggest exercises that have been frequently performed before, or to foster the user's preferred ones).

4   Conclusions and Future Work

Counselling systems are being increasingly used to provide medical, educational, professional or psychological advise, among other purposes. These systems act as an intermediary between professionals and those individuals who need guidance, combining expert knowledge about the domain and the user. Thus, the functional core of any counselling system is given by the objectives that the user intends to achieve and it is expected that the user goes through a series of progression stages before achieving their ultimate objective.

With the aim of facilitating the design of these systems, we present a meta-model to represent and manage the progress of users that encompasses a dual perspective through the combination of a progression and a user model. In our metamodel, progression guidelines are defined through sets of progression states. The connection of these successive states draws a line of progression for each partial objective or dimension. Each progression state has several associated activities that, once completed, enable the user to advance to the next state. The user model records the activities that the user performs over time, extracting performance and satisfaction statistics that can be used for adaptation. It also stores the general state of progression of users and their restrictions and preferences.

On the basis of instantiations of the proposed metamodel, adaptation engines of counselling systems can generate personalized advice either locally (indicating the activities that the user must perform in the next step) or globally (guiding them from their current state to the desired one). With this purpose, two types of adaptations are designed: those that are established by means of semantic annotations on the progression model (restrictions between progression states and restrictions on exercises) and those defined separately in adaptive rules that set conditions on user attributes and derive actions on the progression model. As a proof-of-concept we have presented a virtual coach to promote active ageing that is based on the metamodel contributed and aims to assist users to achieve their objectives of locomotion and training.

For future work, we plan to conduct user studies with the virtual coach. This way, we will be able to evaluate the effectiveness of the adaptation engine and validate the progression and user models. We also intend to implement a module of unsupervised learning that extracts valuable information on possible improvements based on usage patterns. To facilitate the integration of the improvements discovered, we will study the possibility of developing an authoring tool that allows a consistent evolution of both the progression model and the adaptive counselling strategies.

Acknowledgements. This research is supported by the project DEP2015-70980-R of the Spanish Ministry of Economy and Competitiveness and European Regional Development Fund (ERDF), the COST Action $IC1303AAPELE$ and the Andalusian project P11-TIC-7486.

References

1. van der Aalst, W.M.P., ter Hofstede, A.H.M.: Workflow patterns put into context. Softw. Syst. Model. **11**(3), 319–323 (2012)
2. van der Aalst, W.M.P., ter Hofstede, A.H.M., Kiepuszewski, B., Barros, A.: Workflow patterns. Distrib. Parallel Databases **14**(1), 5–51 (2003)
3. van der Aalst, W., ter Hofstede, A.: YAWL: yet another workflow language. Inf. Syst. **30**(4), 245–275 (2005)
4. Bresciani, P., Perini, A., Giorgini, P., Giunchiglia, F., Mylopoulos, J.: TROPOS: an agent-oriented software development methodology. Auton. Agent. Multi-Agent Syst. **8**(3), 203–236 (2004)
5. Chung, L., Nixon, B.A., Yu, E., Mylopoulos, J.: Non-functional Requirements in Software Engineering, vol. 5. Springer Science & Business Media, New York (2012)
6. Chung, L., Supakkul, S., Subramanian, N., Garrido, J.L., Noguera, M., Hurtado, M.V., Rodríguez, M.L., Akhlaki, K.B.: Goal-oriented software architecting. In: Avgeriou, P., Grundy, J., Hall, J.G., Lago, P., Mistrík, I. (eds.) Relating Software Requirements and Architectures, pp. 91–109. Springer, Heidelberg (2011)
7. Dardenne, A., van Lamsweerde, A., Fickas, S.: Goal-directed requirements acquisition. Sci. Comput. Program. **20**(1), 3–50 (1993)
8. Dumas, M., Rosa, M.L., Mendling, J., Reijers, H.A.: Fundamentals of Business Process Management. Springer, Heidelberg (2013)
9. Neiger, D., Churilov, L.: Goal-oriented business process modeling with EPCS and value-focused thinking. In: Proceedings of 2nd International Conference on Business Process Management, BPM 2004, Potsdam, Germany, 17–18 June 2004, pp. 98–115 (2004)
10. Nurcan, S., Salinesi, C., Souveyet, C., Ralyté, J. (eds.): Intentional Perspectives on Information Systems Engineering. Springer, Heidelberg (2010)
11. OMG: Business Process Model and Notation. http://www.bpmn.org/
12. OMG: Unified Modeling Language. http://www.omg.org/spec/UML/2.4.1
13. Poels, G., Decreus, K., Roelens, B., Snoeck, M.: Investigating goal-oriented requirements engineering for business processes. J. Database Manag. **24**(2), 35–71 (2013)
14. Reijers, H.A., Mendling, J.: A study into the factors that influence the understandability of business process models. IEEE Trans. Syst. Man Cybern. Part A Syst. Hum. **41**(3), 449–462 (2011)
15. Rolland, C., Prakash, N., Benjamen, A.: A multi-model view of process modelling. Requirements Eng. **4**(4), 169–187 (1999)
16. Rolland, C., Salinesi, C.: Modeling goals and reasoning with them. In: Aurum, A., Wohlin, C. (eds.) Engineering and Managing Software Requirements, pp. 189–217. Springer, Heidelberg (2005)

17. Salinesi, C., Wäyrynen, J.: A methodological framework for understanding IS adaptation through enterprise change. In: Bellahsène, Z., Patel, D., Rolland, C. (eds.) OOIS 2002. LNCS, vol. 2425, pp. 211–222. Springer, Heidelberg (2002). doi:10. 1007/3-540-46102-7_26
18. Soffer, P., Rolland, C.: Combining intention-oriented and state-based process modeling. In: Delcambre, L., Kop, C., Mayr, H.C., Mylopoulos, J., Pastor, O. (eds.) ER 2005. LNCS, vol. 3716, pp. 47–62. Springer, Heidelberg (2005). doi:10.1007/ 11568322_4

Stepwise Refinement of Software Development Problem Analysis

Tsutomu Kobayashi[1](✉), Fuyuki Ishikawa[2], and Shinichi Honiden[1,2]

[1] The University of Tokyo, Tokyo, Japan
t-kobayashi@nii.ac.jp
[2] National Institute of Informatics, Tokyo, Japan
{f-ishikawa,honiden}@nii.ac.jp

Abstract. The Problem Frames approach has attracted attention because it enables developers to carefully analyze problems in a reasonable manner. Despite that this approach decomposes a problem into subproblems before the analysis is conducted, developers are still faced with a complex analysis when they consider interactions between the various subproblems. Moreover, progressive evolution of requirements is important for flexible development. In this paper, we propose methods to analyze multiple abstraction layers of a problem. Our methods help developers to construct abstract versions of a problem and find relationships between abstract problems and concrete problems. Moreover, our methods support refinement of arguments such that the properties of the abstract problem are preserved in the concrete problem. Therefore, our methods enable developers to divide up arguments into multiple abstraction layers and thus mitigate the complexity of argumentation. We carried out preliminary experiments on abstracting problems and constructing reasonable arguments. Our methods are expected to enable developers to analyze problems in a reasonable manner with less complexity and thus make problem analysis easier.

1 Introduction

Much attention has been focused on the Problem Frames [1] approach to problem analysis. At the beginning of the software development process, this approach supports careful analysis of problems that should be solved with software.

In this paper, we use an example of a controller of traffic lights on the mainland and a small island [2]. The two areas are connected with a one-way bridge, and the traffic lights regulate cars that leave the mainland and the island (Fig. 1). Cars move from the mainland or the island to the bridge (LeaveML, LeaveIL), and vice versa (EnterML, EnterIL). The controller detects the number of cars going left and right on the bridge (#L and #R, respectively) and number of cars on the island (#I), and sends pulses according to the number of cars to the traffic lights (PulseMTL, PulseITL) to change their colors (MLRed, MLGreen, ILRed, ILGreen). The bridge and island together have a capacity (Cap). Thus, the controller should prevent cars on the mainland from entering bridge when

© Springer International Publishing AG 2016
I. Comyn-Wattiau et al. (Eds.): ER 2016, LNCS 9974, pp. 488–495, 2016.
DOI: 10.1007/978-3-319-46397-1_37

the bridge and the island are full of cars ($\#I + \#L + \#R = $ Cap). It also should ensure that all cars on the bridge go in the same direction ($\#L = 0 \vee \#R = 0$).

The approach is based on *problem diagrams*, which shows the relationships of problems and phenomena related to them. The problem diagram of our example is shown on the left side of Fig. 1. The diagram describes the relationship between the *machine domain* (controller) that represents the implementation, *problem domains* (other rectangles) that represent related parts of the world, and *problem requirements* (oval). Labeled lines between domains represent interfaces, which are phenomena shared between domains. A prefix with an exclamation mark indicates the domain that controls the interface. The goal of the analysis is to construct a specification of the machine such that it satisfies the requirements.

In the Problem Frames approach, the constructed problem diagram is decomposed into *subproblem diagrams*, which are then matched to known diagram forms (*problem frames*), and analyzed through arguments on the matched frames. Argumentation involves constructing descriptions of the machine's specifications, domains' properties, and requirements. For example, the right side of Fig. 1 is a snippet of a domain description of cars in the form of a state machine diagram. It describes only the behavior of cars that are going toward the island.

Because software systems have become complex, mitigation of complexity is a crucial consideration in analysis. Although there are a number of methods for decomposing problems [1,3], they all provide decompositions at the same level of abstraction, and they do not consider abstraction of phenomena. Abstraction and refinement play a key role in widely used requirements engineering methods [4,5], but abstraction of phenomena used in discussion of systems' behavior has not been proposed.

In this paper, we propose methods to support developers when they construct and argue abstract versions of a problem that comprises abstract phenomena. Henceforth, we consider several abstraction levels of the same problem, and we call a problem at a higher abstraction level an *abstract problem* and one at a lower abstraction level a *concrete problem*. We use terms such as *abstract phenomena*, *concrete phenomena*, and so forth in the same manner.

By following our methods, developers can first argue an abstract problem, and then gradually elaborate the abstract problem and construct concrete ones. Our methods help developers to refine abstract problems such that the refinement preserves their properties. They enable developers to avoid arguing about abstract properties in concrete problems and divide the complexity of argumentation into several steps.

2   Methods

2.1   Overview

An overview of our methods is depicted in Fig. 2. In the original Problem Frames approach, developers construct a problem diagram before decomposing it into subproblem diagrams and analyzing them. The diagram needs to be concrete enough to include all phenomena that should be considered for construction of

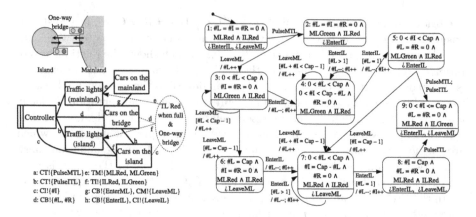

Fig. 1. Problem diagram (left) and part of the domain descriptions (right) of the example

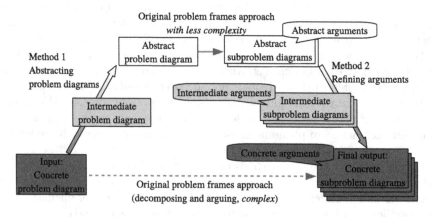

Fig. 2. Overview of our methods

the machine. However, the arguments are often too complex because of concreteness. Our approach to dealing with complexity is analyzing the problem in a stepwise manner. Moreover, it is twofold: method 2 is a process of stepwise argumentation, while method 1 is a preparation for method 2.

By using method 2, developers can analyze an abstract version of the problem first and analyze more concrete versions based on the analyses of the abstract versions later. Method 2 is designed so that consistency between abstract arguments and concrete arguments can be guaranteed.

In the Problem Frames approach, developers have a *concrete*, understanding of the problem and start their analysis by identifying *concrete* phenomena of a problem in a diagram. Therefore, we chose a *concrete* problem diagram as the input of our methods and devised a method to make abstract versions of the input that are suitable for argumentation in abstract layers (method 1). In method 1, developers find semantic relationships between an abstract problem and a concrete problem, which is used for checking consistency in method 2.

A (concrete) problem diagram constructed using the original Problem Frames approach is the input of our methods. First, developers progressively construct abstract versions of the input with method 1. Then, they follow the original Problem Frames approach to analyze the most abstract problem. After that, they progressively make the arguments more concrete with method 2.

2.2   Method 1: Abstraction of Problem Diagrams

This method stepwisely constructs abstract versions of a given diagram by using patterns. New information related to an abstraction is obtained in this process. A possible abstraction of the traffic example is shown in Fig. 3. The intermediate diagram shows that the controller directly informs cars about the number of cars in the every area in intermediate problem. In the abstract diagram, #I, #L, and #R are grouped as "the number of cars outside the mainland" (#O).

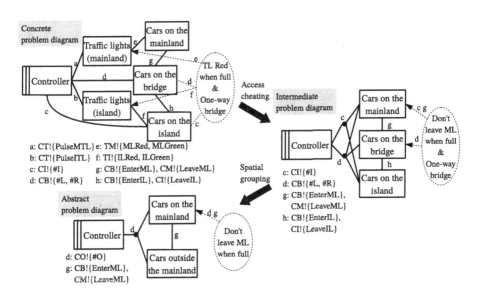

Fig. 3. Stepwise abstraction of a problem diagram

A pattern comprises a target, concrete phenomena, abstract phenomena, gluing concerns, and diagram modifications. The *target* describes parts in a concrete problem diagram that can be changed through an abstraction using the pattern. Modifications made to the problem diagram using the pattern are described in terms of phenomena, namely domains and interfaces. Through the abstraction, developers can omit *concrete phenomena* and adds *abstract phenomena*. Relationships between abstract phenomena and concrete phenomena are described in *gluing concerns*, which are instantiated as gluing descriptions. Modifications made to the problem diagram through the abstraction are described in *diagram modifications*. Developers need to convert requirements that refer to concrete phenomena into abstract requirements by considering gluing descriptions. Abstract requirements can be equivalent to or weaker than their concrete versions, but cannot be stronger than the concrete version.

For example, a pattern named *spatial grouping* is defined as follows:

Target. Several domains of the same class.
Concrete phenomena. Domains in the target and their interfaces.
Abstract phenomena. A domain that is a combination of domains and interfaces that are combinations of concrete interfaces of the same class.
Gluing concerns. For every abstract phenomenon a that represents combinations of concrete phenomenon (c_i), the value of a is equal to the (numerical, set-theoretical, etc.) sum of values of (c_i).
Diagram modifications. Concrete phenomena are replaced with abstract phenomena. Domains that have interfaces with concrete domains become to have interfaces with the abstract domain.

Figure 4 illustrates the application of spatial grouping pattern to the example. First, the target domains ("Cars on the bridge" and "Cars on the island") are replaced with an abstract domain "Cars outside the mainland". Moreover, concrete phenomena (#I, #L, and #R) are grouped as an abstract phenomenon #O. By instantiating the gluing concern, a gluing description "#O = #I + #L + #R" is obtained. Concrete phenomena EnterIL and LeaveIL are omitted, because they are shared within the target domains. A requirement "#I + #L + #R ≤ Cap" is abstracted as "#O ≤ Cap" by considering the gluing description.

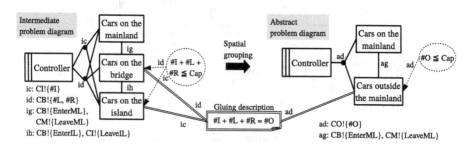

Fig. 4. Application of spatial grouping pattern

We analyzed fourteen problems that comprise safety properties as their key properties, and defined three patterns. Two other patterns are *Temporal grouping*, which is for grouping multiple sequential event phenomena as a single event phenomenon, and *Access cheating*, for constructing an abstract problem without a connection domain.

2.3   Method 2: Refinement of Arguments

Method 2 helps developers to augment abstract subproblem diagrams and construct concrete subproblem diagrams that are consistent with abstract ones.

In this method, developers refine arguments such that they preserve the properties of the abstract problem. Such refinements mitigate the complexity of argumentation, since abstract properties do not need to be confirmed again in the concrete problem. If a refinement adds state transitions that are not described in an abstract problem, the abstract properties may no longer hold in the concrete problem. Method 2 is designed to prevent such a refinement and guarantee that concrete arguments *respect* abstract ones. In other words, refinements using method 2 preserve abstract properties.

Specifically, every state transition that has its abstract version should satisfy two conditions, namely *guard strengthening* and *state change simulation*. Figure 5 describes part of the domain descriptions of cars in the abstract problem and intermediate problem. By considering the gluing concern ($\#O = \#I + \#L + \#R$), state I0 can be viewed as the concrete version of A0. States I10-I12 are concrete versions of A1, and states I20-I22 are concrete versions of A2.

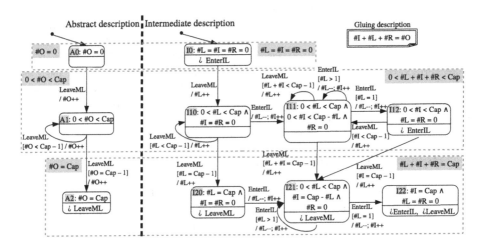

Fig. 5. Example of respectful refinement of the domain description

Guard strengthening. Guards of events in a concrete problem need to be stronger than or equivalent to the corresponding abstract events' guards. For example, by considering the gluing concern ($\#O = \#I + \#L + \#R$) and state ($\#I = \#R = 0$), the guard of the transition from I10 to I20 ($\#L = \text{Cap} - 1$) can be recognized as being equivalent to the guard of the transition from A1 to A2 ($\#O = \text{Cap} - 1$).

State change simulation. State changes through a concrete event should not be contradictory with their abstract event's state changes. For example, event

LeaveML causes a state change #O++ in the abstract problem. In the concrete event, LeaveML causes a state change #L++, which, through the gluing concern (#O = #I + #L + #R), is a limited version of #O++.

All abstract properties hold in the concrete problem when guard strengthening and state change simulation are guaranteed in a refinement. For instance, in our example, developers first confirm the preservation of a property "#O ≤ Cap" in the abstract problem, and then confirm the concrete version "#L + #I ≤ Cap" in an *implicit* way by constructing descriptions in the concrete problem that are consistent with the abstract problem.

3   Preliminary Experiments

We carried out preliminary experiments on three problems including the traffic example described above. First, we described the problems and our methods to four students who study computer science, and requested them to abstract them while finding gluing descriptions. Although participants had never tried the Problem Frames approach, they constructed abstract problems without being puzzled. In addition, one of the authors referred to the documents of the target problems and constructed arguments for problems by following method 2 according to abstract problems and gluing descriptions obtained by the participants. As a result, he succeeded in constructing reasonable arguments for problems at multiple abstraction levels in all cases. Some of the target problems' properties were verified on abstract problems, inherited by concrete problems, and used as lemmas in concrete argumentation. Thus, we consider that our methods make argumentation easier. Our primary future work will be to conduct experiments with larger-scale problems and carefully designed settings.

4   Related Work and Conclusion

Our methods attempt to make problem constituents abstract in a systematic way and refine abstract arguments with abstract properties that are preserved in concrete problems. They mitigate the complexity of argumentation by separating it into multiple steps. As far as we know, this is the first study to tackle the subject. Our methods complement other methods for decomposing problems.

In [6], the notion of *problem transformation* is proposed in a formal way. Problem transformation is an operation to derive a problem P1 from another problem P2 such that P1 describes the solution of P2 in a more detailed way. Our methods can be viewed as a problem transformation over multiple levels of abstraction. Integrating our methods into a problem transformation foundation will be part of our future work.

Goal-oriented requirements engineering approaches such as NFR framework [7], i* [4], and KAOS [5], have been widely studied. Although they effectively use abstraction and refinement of goals to discuss goals, phenomena that are related to systems' behavior are not the subject of abstraction. Moreover, these

approaches do not focus on directly describing or analyzing the behavioral interactions of the various components of a problem. An important aspect of such
methods is their effectiveness in analyzing the variability of systems [8]. Integrating our methods with such methods would be an interesting future topic.

Stepwise refinement is a popular approach in the area of formal methods.
For example, the formal specification method called Event-B [2] supports users
who want to prove the consistency of models at different abstraction levels. Our
methods, which are inspired by the refinement mechanism of Event-B, enable
argumentation over abstract layers of problems in Problem Frames for the purpose of conducting problem analysis.

We devised methods of constructing problems with abstract phenomena from
a concrete problem. By providing a way to construct consistent concrete problems, our methods enable developers to construct concrete problems that inherit
abstract properties. We believe that our methods can help software developers
through incremental and careful argumentation and that they should enable flexible and comprehensible development. Our future work will include integrating
our approach into the formal foundation for Problem Frames [6], finding more
patterns of abstraction, and dealing with changing requirements.

References

1. Jackson, M.: Problem Frames: Analysing and Structuring Software Development
   Problems. Addison-Wesley, Harlow (2001)
2. Abrial, J.R.: Modeling in Event-B: System and Software Engineering. Cambridge
   University Press, New York (2010)
3. Laney, R., Barroca, L., Jackson, M., Nuseibeh, B.: Composing requirements using
   problem frames. In: 12th IEEE International Requirements Engineering Conference, pp. 122–131. IEEE (2004)
4. Yu, E.S.K.: Towards modelling and reasoning support for early-phase requirements
   engineering. In: The Third IEEE International Symposium on Requirements Engineering, pp. 226–235 (1997)
5. Darimont, R., Delor, E., Massonet, P., van Lamsweerde, A.: GRAIL/KAOS: an
   environment for goal-driven requirements engineering. In: 19th International Conference on Software Engineering, pp. 612–613. ACM (1997)
6. Hall, J.G., Rapanotti, L., Jackson, M.: Problem-oriented software engineering.
   Technical report, The Open University (2010)
7. Chung, L., Nixon, B.A., Yu, E., Mylopoulos, J.: Non-functional Requirements in
   Software Engineering, vol. 5. Springer Science & Business Media, New York (2012)
8. Angelopoulos, K., Souza, V.E.S., Mylopoulos, J.: Capturing variability in adaptation spaces: a three-peaks approach. In: Johannesson, P., Lee, M.L., Liddle, S.W.,
   Opdahl, A.L., López, Ó.P. (eds.) ER 2015. LNCS, vol. 9381, pp. 384–398. Springer,
   Heidelberg (2015). doi:10.1007/978-3-319-25264-3_28

Tailoring User Interfaces to Include Gesture-Based Interaction with gestUI

Otto Parra[1,3]([✉]), Sergio España[2], and Oscar Pastor[3]

[1] Computer Science Department, Universidad de Cuenca, Cuenca, Ecuador
otpargon@upv.es
[2] Department of Information and Computing Science, Utrecht University,
Utrecht, The Netherlands
s.espana@uu.nl
[3] PROS Research Centre, Universitat Politècnica de València, Valencia, Spain
opastor@dsic.upv.es

Abstract. The development of custom gesture-based user interfaces requires software engineers to be skillful in the use of the tools and languages needed to implement them. gestUI, a model-driven method, can help them achieve these skills by defining custom gestures and including gesture-based interaction in existing user interfaces. Up to now, gestUI has used the same gesture catalogue for all software users, with gestures that could not be subsequently redefined. In this paper, we extend gestUI by including a user profile in the metamodel that permits individual users to define custom gestures and to include gesture-based interaction in user interfaces. Using tailoring mechanisms, each user can redefine his custom gestures during the software runtime. Although both features are supported by models, the gestUI tool hides its technical complexity from the users. We validated these gestUI features in a technical action research in an industrial context. The results showed that these features were perceived as both useful and easy to use when defining/redefining custom gestures and including them in a user interface.

Keywords: Gesture-based interaction · Model-driven development · Technical action research · Custom gesture · User interface · Human-computer interaction

1 Introduction

User interface development with gesture-based interaction (GBI) is still a complicated process because software engineers need to use tools (e.g. software development kits, CASE tools) and related programming languages, typically third-generation languages, to write code to recognize and respond to application-specific gestures [1]. As a solution to this situation, some of the challenges can be tackled by using a model-driven development (MDD) approach [2], which has been fairly popular in the academic community [3] to develop different software proposals.

In the software development life cycle (SDLC) the requirements specification involves the participation of the stakeholders (e.g. software engineers, end-users). Software engineers usually consider a "representative user" to define the end-user's

© Springer International Publishing AG 2016
I. Comyn-Wattiau et al. (Eds.): ER 2016, LNCS 9974, pp. 496–504, 2016.
DOI: 10.1007/978-3-319-46397-1_38

interaction requirements [4]. However, the concept of the "representative user" does not allow for the individuality and diversity of each user [5]. It is possible to define customized interaction elements for each user on the same user interface (UI) instead of defining the same interaction elements for all users. This decision provides an appropriate level of satisfaction when using the UI, as each user employs his interaction elements to execute an action on the interface.

According to Won et al. [6], *tailoring* is any activity that modifies a software within its context of use and can be a simple or complex activity. At higher levels of complexity, users have more skills to redesign the interaction and functionality of a software. At the most basic level, tailoring involves specifying parameters to an existing software in a way that changes its behaviour at a high level of granularity [7]. Software engineers should thus provide users with tools so that they can change the interaction definition by modifying interaction elements on a UI.

In this paper we describe the extended version of gestUI [8] containing tailoring mechanisms that allow users to define custom gestures and to modify this definition during the execution stage. gestUI is a model-driven, iterative and user-centric method of defining custom gestures and including GBI in UI by code generation. In this context, each user decides the GBI elements at the beginning of the SDLC. The software engineer then includes this specification in the UI, and when the UI is ready, the user performs actions using the GBI. However, if the user wants to change the initial specification of the gestures, then he needs the tools to consider the modification of the gesture catalogue specification to improve the interaction process.

Since our purpose was to gather new knowledge and to design new artefacts (method and tools), we used the design science methodology [9]. This methodology is structured into regulative cycles to perform an initial problem investigation that characterises the problem to be solved, to provide a solution design suitable for solving the problem, and to verify whether the proposed solution satisfies the previously analysed problem.

The contributions of this paper are two-fold. First, we extend gestUI to include tailoring mechanisms in the process to obtain gesture-based interfaces. Secondly, we validate these new features during the execution of a Technical Action Research (TAR) [10] to validate gestUI in an industrial context.

2 The Importance of User-Based Tailoring: Related Work

In the existing literature on tailoring UIs, for instance, Zamborlin et al. [11] describe the Gesture Interaction Designer, which allows users to design their own gestures, making interaction more natural and also allowing the applications to be tailored to the user's requirements. Mayer et al. [12] provide a framework for designing and deploying UIs that are tailored to a particular user group, considering a multi-step adaptation process. Ghiani et al. [13] describe the design and implementation of a tool to allow people with no programming experience to customize the functionality and UI of a multi-device museum guide. González et al. [5] describe a UI management system able to design different versions of a UI according to the cognitive, perceptive and motive skills of each user of the application. They employ a tailoring mechanism to produce a UI according to the user's interaction requirements, avoiding the specification of an "ideal user". Kristiansen [14] suggests a systematic way of defining what needs to be included in the UI for one particular user, based on the user's participation in the overall workflow, using a combination of workflow models and models typically developed in the field of model-based UI design. Won et al. [6] describe FLEXIBEANS, designed specifically to develop highly flexible and tailorable applications. They employ component technology in the design of tailorable systems by providing a complete set of component-based tailoring operations that can be applied to already deployed applications. Maceli et al. [15] suggest some guidelines for designing in use, one of which refers to adapting software to the user's personal needs, employing a tailoring mechanism applied by the users.

This paper describes the extended version of gestUI, which permits users to define custom gestures and include the GBI using a model-driven paradigm. A tailoring mechanism is provided to redefine custom gestures and to include them in the gesture-based software UI.

3   Basic Capabilities of gestUI

This section contains a short description of the improvements made to gestUI. More information on the gestUI method can be found in [8]. gestUI is based on a model-driven paradigm and comprises three layers containing a set of activities and products.

gestUI can be inserted into an existing UI implementation method according to the description included in [8]. By using gestUI, in the first step, a platform-independent gesture catalogue is defined which is conforms to a metamodel defined in our work. Model transformations are then employed to obtain platform-specific gesture specification and the source code of the UI containing the GBI.

In order to verify the applicability of the proposed method, we implemented a tool support using Eclipse and Java programming language. This tool requires an existing UI source code as input and allows users to define custom gestures, to specify action-gesture correspondence and to generate source code including GBI. Considering the actions included in the UI and the previously defined custom gestures, we generate a new version of the source code including GBI. In this version of gestUI, all the users share the same definition of the gestures in a UI and it is not possible to redefine gestures in the execution stage. New features which help to solve these problems are described here.

4   Empowering Users with New gestUI Features

We opted to improve our method by considering two new features:

The first feature is related to the extended version of the gestUI metamodel (Fig. 1) in order to include the user's definition, which permits individual users to define their own gesture catalogue to include GBI in the UI. In this metamodel, the *UserInterface* class denotes the link to an existing UI metamodel containing an element related to the *action* to execute GBI. A UI can then be used by one or more users. Each *user* defines his own *catalogue* containing one or more gestures; each *gesture* permits an action contained in the UI to be executed. Each gesture is formed by one or more *strokes* defined by *postures*, and in turn described by means of coordinates (X, Y). The sequence of these strokes has an order of *precedence*. Each posture is related to a *figure* (e.g. line, circle) with an orientation (up, down, left, right) and is qualified by a state (initial, executing, final).

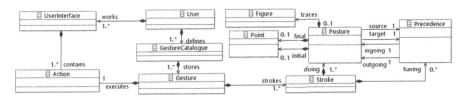

Fig. 1. Extended version of the metamodel

The second feature concerns the redefinition of gestures. We use the map representation proposed by Rolland [16] to describe this process (Fig. 2). This process starts when the user has logged in to the software and obtained a user identification (UID) related to a previously defined gesture catalogue included in a UI to support GBI. To redefine a gesture, the user selects it from the gesture catalogue and proceeds with the redefinition. At the end, the redefined gesture must be included in the UI.

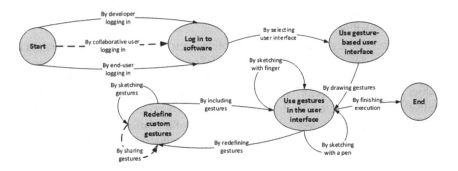

Fig. 2. Map representation of gestUI, including redefinition feature

5 Implementing the New Features

In order to implement the first feature of gestUI, we added a module to define user profiles containing information on each user to specify a UID that is used to relate a gesture catalogue with a user, i.e. a customized gesture catalogue containing gestures identified by the UID plus the name of the gesture.

Fig. 3. Platform-independent gesture catalogue

As a demonstration of the implementation of this feature, Fig. 3 shows a gesture catalogue included in a UI (DrawingDiagrams) with two users (User1 and User2). Each one has a gesture catalogue containing custom gestures. Observe that each gesture is formed by one or more strokes and has an action to execute. The second feature must be included as an option in the software menu. In the case shown, this feature was implemented using Java programming language. Some tool screenshots are included in the next section, as part of the running example.

6 Validating gestUI in a Technical Action Research

gestUI's new features were validated during the execution of a TAR, with the collaboration of Everis, a multinational firm offering business consulting and IT development, maintenance and improvements. The TAR was performed in the context of the CaaS Project (FP7 ICT Programme Collaborative Project no. 611351). The CaaS tools include the Capability Design Tool (CDT) [17], a CASE tool that supports capability modelling according to the CDD meta-model, which includes goal, context, process and concept modelling.

In this paper, we report the results of applying gestUI's tailoring mechanism to the CDT. The first step in the process was to define the gesture catalogue. The users defined the gesture catalogue (Table 1) containing the primitives to be used in the TAR (a subset of the primitives of the CDT), the symbol included in its palette for these primitives, and the gesture selected by the users. Each user defines custom gestures that are stored in a repository. With the aim of defining the platform-independent gesture catalogue, the user selects some of these gestures to be inserted in the model defined in our work [8]. By applying a model transformation, we obtain the platform-independent gesture catalogue for each user.

Table 1. Excerpt of the gesture catalogue for CDT

Primitive	Symbol	Gesture	Primitive	Symbol	Gesture
Context Set	Context Set 1 1		Capability	Capability 2	
Context Element	Context Element 1.1 1.1		Goal	Goal 3 3	

This catalogue is transformed into the platform-specific gesture catalogue by another model transformation. The relation between gesture and action contained in a UI must be defined to specify the GBI required in this process. The users define the gesture-action correspondence by specifying a pair (Gesture, Action). Finally, the source code containing this type of interaction is generated. The target platform decides the programming language to be used in generating the source code.

In order to include GBI in the CDT, we added options to the palette and the main CDT menu and also some source code modules to support this interaction type on the CDT. This process permits users to draw diagrams on the CDT using gestures (Fig. 4). When using the CDT, the user sketches the previously defined gestures in the drawing area to execute actions, in this case sketches gestures corresponding to primitives with the aim of drawing diagrams.

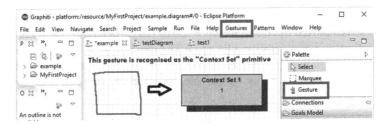

Fig. 4. CaaS project CDT with gesture-based interaction included

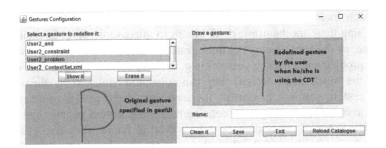

Fig. 5. Redefinition of gestures in CDT

If gestures are hard to remember or to draw, the software provides the option of redefining them (Fig. 5). In this option, the user must select the gesture to be redefined. By clicking the "Show it" button, the current gesture definition appears. On the right-hand panel the user can redraw the previously selected gesture. When the gesture definition agrees with the user's preferences, he includes it in the catalogue by clicking "Save". At the end of this process, the user must reload the gesture catalogue to include the new definition of the gestures in the software.

7 Discussion

In this paper we describe the extended version of gestUI with an extended metamodel and implementing two new features to improve the process of obtaining gesture-based interfaces considering tailoring mechanisms.

In a TAR we analysed the user experience (UE) of redefining custom gestures and the inclusion of GBI in software UIs. Employing a UE Questionnaire (UEQ) [18] we obtained an overall score of 81 % for the impression of the product for the gesture redefinition feature. Regarding efficiency (46 %) and dependability (54 %), we think that these lower values were probably due to the users' lack of experience in using gestures, as reported in the demographic questionnaire. Both scales consider factors such as fast/slow, inefficient/efficient, impractical/practical, and organized/cluttered. We also analysed the perceived ease of use (PEOU) and perceived usefulness (PU) of gestUI using a MEM [19] post-task questionnaire with questions on a 7-point Likert scale. We obtained a PEOU of 5.5 in the custom gesture definition/redefinition and a PU of 5.4. We employed Microsoft Reaction Cards [20] to determine the users' opinion by means of positive and negative adjectives. The most frequent positive adjectives to describe the UE with gestUI were: innovative, useful and simplistic, while some of the more negative adjectives used by the participants were: too technical and slow.

8 Conclusions and Future Work

gestUI permits users to include GBI in existing UIs, using automatic transformations that extend the interface source code. In this paper we describe the improved version of gestUI, which includes tailoring mechanisms to redefine previously defined custom gestures. Using these mechanisms, gestUI helps to improve the level of desirability of the software, as the user employs custom gestures that he has defined himself. If the users have problems when using gestures (e.g. they are difficult to remember or hard to sketch on the touch-based screen) they can solve this situation by themselves by redefining custom gestures. In general, the users considered gestUI's ease of use and usefulness as its main advantages for defining/redefining custom gestures and including GBI in a UI. Some of the challenges to be solved in future work are: (i) to include additional platforms (e.g. mobile platforms) as a target to produce gesture-based UIs (currently we support desktop-computing); (ii) to include additional programming languages as the target language to generate source code (currently we support Java) in order to give support for GBI to other types of software.

Acknowledgments. This work has been supported by Universidad de Cuenca and SENESCYT of Ecuador, and received financial support from Generalitat Valenciana under Project IDEO (PROMETEOII/2014/039).

References

1. Khandkar, S.H., Sohan, S.M., Sillito, J., Maurer, F.: Tool support for testing complex multi-touch gestures. In: ACM International Conference on Interactive Tabletops and Surfaces, ITS 2010, NY, USA (2010)
2. Rodrigues da Silva, A.: Model-driven engineering: a survey supported by the unified conceptual model. Comput. Lang. Syst. Struct. **43**, 139–155 (2015)
3. Papotti, P.E., do Prado, A.F., de Souza, W.L., Cirilo, C.E., Pires, L.F.: A quantitative analysis of model-driven code generation through software experimentation. In: Salinesi, C., Norrie, M.C., Pastor, Ó. (eds.) CAiSE 2013. LNCS, vol. 7908, pp. 321–337. Springer, Heidelberg (2013)
4. Schlobinski, S., Denzer, R., Frysinger, S., Güttler, R., Hell, T.: Vision and requirements of scenario-driven environmental decision support systems supporting automation for end users. In: Hřebíček, J., Schimak, G., Denzer, R. (eds.) Environmental Software Systems. IFIP AICT, vol. 359, pp. 51–63. Springer, Heidelberg (2011)
5. González Rodríguez, M., Pérez Pérez, J.R., Paule Ruíz, M.P.: Designing user interfaces tailored to the current user's requirements in real time. In: Miesenberger, K., Klaus, J., Zagler, W.L., Burger, D. (eds.) ICCHP 2004. LNCS, vol. 3118, pp. 69–75. Springer, Heidelberg (2004)
6. Won, M., Stiemerling, O., Wulf, V.: Component-based approaches to tailorable systems. In: Lieberman, H., Paternò, F., Wulf, V. (eds.) End-User Development, pp. 115–141. Springer, Heidelberg (2006)
7. Burnett, M.M., Scaffidi, C.: End-USer Development. The Encyclopedia of Human-Computer Interaction, 2nd edn. The Interaction Design Foundation, Aarhus (2013)
8. Parra, O., España, S., Pastor, O.: GestUI: a model-driven method and tool for including gesture-based interaction in user interfaces. Complex Syst. Inform. Model. Q. (CSIMQ) **6**, 73–92 (2016)
9. Wieringa, R.: Design science as nested problem solving. In: DESRIST 2009, Malvern, PA, USA (2009)
10. Wieringa, R., Moralı, A.: Technical action research as a validation method in information systems design science. In: Peffers, K., Rothenberger, M., Kuechler, B. (eds.) DESRIST 2012. LNCS, vol. 7286, pp. 220–238. Springer, Heidelberg (2012)
11. Zamborlin, B., Bevilacqua, F., Gillies, M., D'inverno, M.: Fluid gesture interaction design: applications of continuous recognition for the design of modern gestural interfaces. J. ACM Trans. Interact. Intell. Syst. (TiiS) **3**(4), 22:1–22:30 (2014)
12. Mayer, C., Zimmermann, G., Grguric, A., Alexandersson, J., Sili, M., Strobbe, C.: A comparative study of systems for the design of flexible user interfaces. J. Ambient Intell. Smart Environ. **8**(2), 125–148 (2016)
13. Ghiani, G., Paternò, F., Spano, L.D.: Cicero designer: an environment for end-user development of multi-device museum guides. In: Pipek, V., Rosson, M.B., de Ruyter, B., Wulf, V. (eds.) IS-EUD 2009. LNCS, vol. 5435, pp. 265–274. Springer, Heidelberg (2009)
14. Kristiansen, R., Atle Gulla, J., Troetteberg, H.: Use of tailored process models to support ERP end-users. In: Information Systems Technology and Its Applications, 5th International Conference, ISTA 2006, Klagenfurt, Austria (2006)
15. Maceli, M., Atwood, M.E.: "Human Crafters" once again: supporting users as designers in continuous co-design. In: Dittrich, Y., Burnett, M., Mørch, A., Redmiles, D. (eds.) IS-EUD 2013. LNCS, vol. 7897, pp. 9–24. Springer, Heidelberg (2013)

16. Rolland, C.: Capturing system intentionality with maps. In: Krogstie, J., Opdahl, A.L., Brinkkemper, S. (eds.) Conceptual Modelling in Information Systems Engineering, pp. 141–158. Springer, Heidelberg (2007)
17. Sandkuhl, K., Stirna, J.: CaaS Base Methodology, UR (2014)
18. Schrepp, M., Hinderks, A., Thomaschewski, J.: Applying the user experience questionnaire (UEQ) in different evaluation scenarios. In: Marcus, A. (ed.) DUXU 2014, Part I. LNCS, vol. 8517, pp. 383–392. Springer, Heidelberg (2014)
19. Moody, D.L.: The method evaluation model: a theoretical model for validating information systems design methods. In: Proceedings of the 11th European Conference on IS (ECIS), pp. 1327–1336 (2003)
20. Merčun, T., Žumer, M.: Dimensions of user experience and reaction cards. In: The Emergence of Digital Libraries - Research and Practices, 16th International Conference on Asia-Pacific Digital Libraries, Chiang Mai, Thailand (2014)

Unlocking Visual Understanding:
Towards Effective Keys for Diagrams

Nicolas Genon[1(✉)], Gilles Perrouin[1], Xavier Le Pallec[2], and Patrick Heymans[1]

[1] PReCISE, University of Namur, Namur, Belgium
{nicolas.genon,gilles.perrouin,patrick.heymans}@unamur.be
[2] University of Lille, Villeneuve-d'Ascq, France
xavier.le-pallec@univ-lille1.fr

Abstract. Diagrams are (meant to be) effective communication supports to convey information to stakeholders. Being communication supports, they have to be quickly and accurately understood. To enable immediateness, many disciplines such as cartography rely on keys, which categorise diagram symbols and bind them to their meaning. Software engineering extensively relies on visual languages such as UML to communicate amongst the many stakeholders involved in information systems' life-cycle. Yet, keys are barely used in these diagrams, hindering (immediate) understanding and limiting it to language experts. We provide a disciplined approach to design effective keys, by adapting graphic semiology theory and cartographers' know-how to software diagrams. We illustrate our method on a UML class diagram. Designing effective keys raises questions about the concerns and tasks to be addressed by the diagram, and even, reveals issues about the language itself.

Keywords: Key · Caption · Legend · Diagram understandability · Visual immediacy · Visual effectiveness · Visual modelling language

1 Keys in Visual Languages

While understandability is a major preoccupation in Software Engineering (SE) modelling, it still lacks a precise but consensual definition. Based on these references [7,8,14], an understandable diagram is a diagram that provides all (and only) the pieces of information the stakeholders look for, immediately perceptible and in a way suitable to the stakeholders' questions or tasks. We propose a definition of understandability that encompasses those notions but at a more operational level. Understandability is thus a combination of *accuracy* and *speed* at which the stakeholder processes the information conveyed by the diagram. Relying on a visual modelling language does not automatically make diagrams understandable or immediate. Understandability is a quality that requires diagrams to be designed in the appropriate way.

Over time, a series of theories about modelling language visual qualities have emerged but only a handful of them goes beyond the stage of a collection of

© Springer International Publishing AG 2016
I. Comyn-Wattiau et al. (Eds.): ER 2016, LNCS 9974, pp. 505–512, 2016.
DOI: 10.1007/978-3-319-46397-1_39

abstract guidelines. The two most complete theories so far are the Cognitive Dimensions of Notations (CDs) [5] and the Physics of Notations (PoN) [10]. While the CDs provide a large set of high-level properties that help make visual languages cognitively effective (and hence, more easily comprehensible), PoN focusses on evidence-based principles formulated to address SE visual languages in practice. However, both theories still lack a detailed procedure to apply their properties/principles. Our work contributes to make up for this lack of support by proposing a disciplined method to design effective diagramming keys.

Keys – also called legends or captions – are usually thought about to be anecdotal pieces of documentation. On the contrary, we argue that designing effective keys is a real challenge that is worth the effort. Indeed, a key designed according to the method described in this work allows *(i)* to identify the questions to which the diagram can provide answers, *(ii)* to indicate the diagram context, and *(iii)*, to show how the components of the information are visually depicted. Software engineers may consider keys unnecessary given their mastering of modelling languages. However, it would restrict diagrams to information storage artefacts only, whereas they are also communication supports to non-expert stakeholders.

While keys are present on various kinds of documents that we consult in our every-day life, it is surprising that they are most of the time missing from SE diagrams. We searched several sources (Google Scholar, Dblp) and dedicated venues in computer visualisation (VL/HCC, VIS, EuroVIS, SIGGraph, and in Journals like the IEEE Transactions on Visualization and Computer Graphics) as well as cartographic domains. The searched keywords were: *key, legend, caption*, combined to the terms *model understandability, diagram understandability, model comprehensibility, diagram comprehensibility*. We finally unearthed three main articles, focussing on interactive environments. Interactive environments are a sub-category of dynamic environments where visual representations contain animations and the tool hosting the diagram is equipped with functions allowing the user to directly interact on the diagram.

Dykes *et al.* elicit high-level guidelines to design keys for maps in a dynamic environment [3]. These guidelines are driven by distinct strategies governing the display of the key (e.g. embedding the key in the map itself, or revealing the information on demand). Most of their guidelines involve dynamism, which is not easily transferable to the diagrams we target. More importantly, they do not cover fundamental constituents (such as shapes and colors), which are essential for a principled approach to keys design. Tudoreanu and Kraemer's work suffer from the same limitations, with a greater focus on user interaction [17]. Interaction is also the focus of cartographers ([9,12,15]).

Riche *et al.* [6] present and evaluate interactive keys by mentioning fundamental notions. They demonstrate how these notions can be used to empirically assess keys in dynamic environments. In contrast, we use these notions to focus on (static) key design, thus both works are complementary.

2   What Should Be in a Key?

What elements should appear on a diagramming key and how (or where) to place these elements on the diagram are the 'true questions to be asked when designing a key. Our approach is based on the Semiology of Graphics (SoG), a cartography theory published in 1963 by Bertin [1]. In a nutshell, keys designed according to the SoG make the stakeholder (i.e., the reader of the visual representation) able to understand a map without any kind of prior learning (except for the notion of coordinates conveyed by the map). We pursue the same objective but for SE diagrams, independently of the visual modelling language.

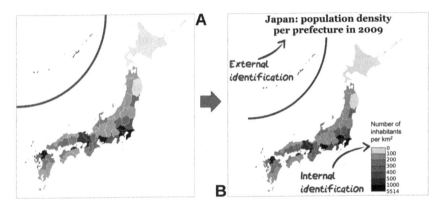

Fig. 1. On the left, a map without any key – on the right, a map with a well designed key

We introduce the elements that compose a key by referring to a (cartography) map example. Considering Fig. 1(a) on its own, the stakeholder can recognize the country under consideration (i.e., Japan). He can also identify distinct levels of colour brightness that seem to express distinct values, but nothing can be certifiably inferred about the semantics of these values. Providing a key to the map actually solves these issues. A key is the visual information added to a visual representation that allows to perform the *external* and *internal* identifications. The internal identification indicates the *components* and their *categories*. *Categories* are the distinct values depicted by visual artefacts on the representation. As depicted by Fig. 1(b), the categories are the numeric ranges associated to each level of colour brightness. In this example, all these ranges are related to a common concern – the number of inhabitants per km^2, which is called a *component*. The external identification provides information about the context (i.e., the *invariant*) of the information conveyed by the visual representation and it consists in wording (i.e., by providing a title to the representation). Referring to the example, the context of Fig. 1(b) is the Japanese population density per prefecture in 2009.

Hereafter, we introduce the hypothesis that structures the relationships among the three core notions. It states that the information conveyed by a visual representation consists of a set of pieces of information. All pieces of information (aka., tuples) are specific combinations of *categories* taken from the same set of *components*. The *components* are defined for the entire visual representation in the context of the given *invariant* and each combination has to be composed of at least one *category* of each *component*. A *component* is defined by several properties: a **name** which is a string denoting the concern that is modelled by the component, a **length**, which is an integer indicating the number of categories defined for this component, and a **organizational level**, which is a value from the set {qualitative, ordered, quantitative} that means that the categories of this component are not naturally ordered (i.e., qualitative), or that there exists a natural order (i.e., ordered), or that it is ordered and the distance between two categories is significant (i.e., quantitative). The *categories* are described by exhaustively eliciting their values.

Referring to the Japan map, we can now define the properties of the component and its categories. The component is labelled *inhabitants/km²*, has a length of *seven*, and its organizational level is *ordered*. The categories for this component are the ranges: [0–99], [100–199], [200–299], [300–399], [400–499], [500–999], [1000–5514]. Every piece of information displayed in the Japan map (see Fig. 1) is a tuple (coordinates, density range). This is a particularity of maps: the (x, y) coordinates are part of the primary notation, even if they do not usually appear in the key.

Components are visually depicted by visual variables. There are eight variables that belong to two distinct categories (Fig. 2): two *planar* variables and six *retinal* variables. The planar variables locate any graphic artefact on the 2D plane as a pair of two *coordinates* (x, y). The six retinal variables are: the *shape*, the *size*, the *colour*, the *orientation*, the *value*, and the *texture*. Every variable is characterised by three properties: *steps*, *length*, and *level*. We do not detail them due to space limitation (see [1]).

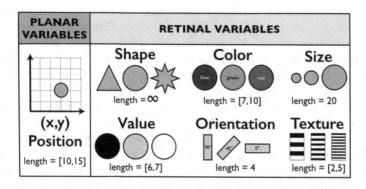

Fig. 2. The 8 visual variables from Bertin [1]

The mapping of a component to a visual variable actually defines the *primary notation* of the modelling language. Every step of the variables from the *primary notation* is semantically meaningful. Hence, it is not allowed to introduce a new step (or change current steps) of those bound variables to carry extra semantics or perceptual attitudes. This is actually the purpose of the *secondary notation*. It is composed of the visual variables that are not bound to any component. These free variables are available to draw attention to certain locations of the diagram, to annotate the diagram, or to add extra (i.e., not part of the modelling language) concerns on the diagram.

3   Method

1. External identification. Wording the diagram (i.e., providing a title).
2. Internal identification. Performed after or in parallel with the external identification. It is composed of three sub-stages:

(a) **category elicitation:** the visual artefacts depicted on the diagram are elicited and those that are visually distinct (i.e., text excluded) are kept.
(b) **component elicitation:** the categories are gathered according to their semantic proximity in order to form components. The components' label, length, and organizational level are also provided (as defined in Sect. 2).
(c) **pre-mapping of visual variables:** potentially appropriate visual variables are elicited. The final choice is postponed to after secondary notation requirements elicitation.

3. Identification of secondary notation requirements. Visual techniques (e.g., perceptual pop-out effect [13,16]) to support foreseen uses of the diagram are elicited. Candidate visual variables are chosen according to their length and level.
4. Mapping components to visual variables. Given the list of variables eligible to the primary notation and the candidate secondary notation variables, the designer selects the variables that constitute the primary notation.
5. Selection of the visual variables to be part of the secondary notation. Using the outcome of Stages 3 and 4, the choice of variables for the secondary notation is ratified.
6. Writing down the key onto the diagram. The component to visual variable mapping is depicted on the diagram itself, because it is required to correctly interpret the meaning of the conveyed information. It is visually structured in this way: *(i)* each component is labelled; *(ii)* the categories and the steps of the visual variable(s) to which each category is mapped are placed below or beside the corresponding component (only those appearing on the diagram); *(iii)* the secondary notation is added (i.e., the addressed concern(s), and below or beside, its/their categories and steps).

4   Running Example: SuperElectronicMarket

In this section, we give an overview of the result of applying our method. We consider a UML class diagram representing an excerpt of the static domain of the SuperElectronicMarket information system. There are four classes, Product, Producer, Customer, Order, one association class, OrderDetail, two binary associations and one composition. A Customer orders Products that are built by a Producer. For each Order, there is a series of OrderDetails, each one corresponding to the purchase of a certain quantity of a given Product. Every Order is at least composed of one OrderDetail. This example does not strive to be realistic w.r.t. to an actual information system: we focus on visual representation of the information, not its relevance.

Let's now assume that we are free to change the UML class diagram concrete syntax (but neither its semantics nor its abstract syntax). We detail each step of our method:

Stage 1. The diagram is given a title: the invariant relate to the (static) concepts of the SuperElectronicMarket domain.

Stage 2. As we do not afford to change the language semantics, this component elicitation may be puzzling and lead to ill-formed components (e.g., a component with a length of one, or a component whose categories are not mapped to the same visual variable(s)). There are four categories and their associated steps:

- classes that are depicted with rectangles (visual variable: shape); Enumerations are distinguished from classes by a textual annotation (i.e., ≪ enumeration ≫), which is not visually discriminant according to the SoG;
- associations that are depicted with plain lines (visual variable: shape);
- association classes that are depicted with a rectangle and a dashed line (visual variable: shape);
- compositions that are depicted with plain lines with a diamond head at the source of the relationship (visual variable: shape).

Grouping these four categories together is not allowed because *(i)* classes and enumerations are implanted as a point on the diagram, while the relationship types adopt a linear implantation (for details about implantation types, see [1]); *(ii)* class diagrams are SoG networks, which implies that the existence of relationships prevails over nodes. Hence, we define two components: *concept types*, which comprises the *class* and *enumeration*, and *relationship types* that gathers the association, composition and association class relationships[1].

Stage 3 (and 5). We choose to not use any secondary notation.

Stage 4. The *concept types* has a length of 2 and is qualitative. The *shape* variable is suitable, but *class* and *enumeration* symbols are visually speaking identical. Hence, we provide a new shape to the *enumeration* that is a rectangle whose vertical sides are curved. We also add a special mark at the top left corner. The rationale sustaining our choice is the following: rectangle with curved sides

---

[1] According to the UML standard [11], association classes are associations with specific properties.

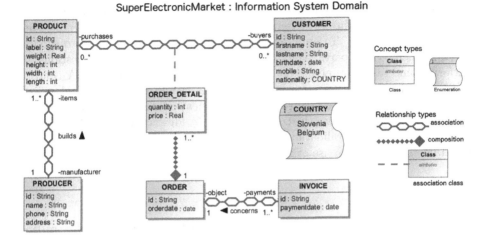

Fig. 3. SuperElectronicMarket UML class diagram with a revised concrete syntax

suggests the meaning of a sheet of paper and the special mark denotes a list of items. The *relationship types* is qualitative, and it counts three categories. Again, any retinal variable could be appropriate. One of the major issues when reading a class diagram is to distinguish between association types. Associations do not carry any head, while compositions and aggregations have a black (respectively, white) diamond. We choose to increase the discrimination of those association types by using colour and by changing the step of the shape variable. Associations are now red, compositions are blue and association classes are green. The shape of the lines is changed this way: chain link shape for associations, diamond link with a large diamond head at the source side for compositions, and a dashed line for the association class. We have chosen to use two variables for the *association types* because it allows to perform redundant coding.

Stage 6. We design the component to visual variable mapping as described in Sect. 3. The resulting diagram is depicted in Fig. 3.

5   Discussion

In this paper, we presented a method to systematically design diagramming keys, which gives concrete validation rules to ensure the diagram is SoG-compliant. SoG is a theory to design visually effective representations in which the information is understood accurately and (almost) immediately. Inspired by cartography, we argue that it is useful for SE diagrams in which neophytes get accustomed with the language concepts progressively and experts are given dedicated reminders on complex notations (such as UML). We improved the concrete syntax of UML class diagrams to make information quickly and accurately perceptible (other examples: https://staff.info.unamur.be/nge/effective-keys). Full power of the SoG can be unleashed when designing a new language: in this context, even abstract syntax (metamodel) will be impacted when performing the internal identification. To empirically validate our method, we plan to set up an experiment where participants would have to answer a series of questions or perform some tasks by relying on a set of diagrams with their keys. A control group would be asked the same actions but they would work with regular diagrams (i.e., without keys). Evaluation and empirical validation of visual concerns have been shown feasible in the context of [2,4]. Additionally, CASE tools could ensure the automatic validation of SoG's constraints. Finally, diagram design could be assisted by the use of interactive keys.

References

1. Bertin, J.: Sémiologie graphique: Les diagrammes - Les réseaux - Les cartes. Gauthier-VillarsMouton & Cie (1973)
2. Caire, P., Genon, N., Heymans, P., Moody, D.: Visual notation design 2.0: towards user comprehensible requirements engineering notations. In: RE 2013 (2013)
3. Dykes, J., Wood, J., Slingsby, A.: Re-thinking map legends with visualization. IEEE Trans. Vis. Comput. Graph. **16**(6), 890–899 (2010)
4. Genon, N., Heymans, P., Amyot, D.: Analysing the cognitive effectiveness of the BPMN 2.0 visual notation. In: Proceedings of SLE 2010, vol. 6563, pp. 377–396 (2010)
5. Green, T., Blandford, A., Church, L., Roast, C., Clarke, S.: Cognitive dimensions: achievements, new directions, and open questions. VLC **17**, 328–365 (2006)
6. Riche, N.H., Lee, B., Plaisant, C.: Understanding interactive legends a comparative evaluation with standard widgets. CGF **29**(3), 1193–1202 (2010)
7. Houy, C., Fettke, P., Loos, P.: Understanding understandability of conceptual models - what are we actually talking about? In: Proceedings of ER, pp. 64–77 (2012)
8. ISO, IEC: ISO 9126. Software Engineering - Product Quality. ISO/IEC 9126 (2001)
9. Kraak, M., Edsall, R., MacEachren, A.: Cartographic animation and legends for temporal maps: exploration and or interaction. In: Proceedings of ICC 1997, pp. 23–27 (1997)
10. Moody, D.L., Heymans, P., Matulevičius, R.: Visual syntax does matter: improving the cognitive effectiveness of the i* visual notation. RE **15**(2), 141–175 (2010)
11. OMG, Inc.: UML 2.4.1 Superstructure Specification, August 2011
12. Peterson, M.P.: Active legends for interactive cartographic animation. Int. J. Geogr. Inf. Sci. **13**(4), 375–383 (1999)
13. Quinlan, P.T.: Visual feature integration theory: past present and future. Psychol. Bull. **129**(5), 643–673 (2003)
14. Selic, B.: The pragmatics of MDD. IEEE Softw. J. **20**(5), 19–25 (2003)
15. Sieber, R., Schmid, C., Wiesmann, S.: Smart legends - smart Atlas. In: Proceedings of the 22nd International Cartographic Conference (ICC 2005), pp. 11–16 (2005)
16. Treisman, A., Gelade, G.: A feature integration theory of attention. Cogn. Psychol. **12**(1), 97–136 (1980)
17. Tudoreanu, M.E., Kraemer, E.: Legends as a device for interacting with visualizations. Technical report WUCS-01-44 (2001)

Goal Modeling

MEMO GoalML: A Context-Enriched Modeling Language to Support Reflective Organizational Goal Planning and Decision Processes

Alexander Bock$^{(\boxtimes)}$ and Ulrich Frank

Research Group Information Systems and Enterprise Modeling,
University of Duisburg-Essen, Essen, Germany
{alexander.bock,ulrich.frank}@uni-due.de

Abstract. Conceptual models of goal systems promise to provide an apt basis for planning, analyzing, monitoring, and (re-)considering goals as part of management processes in the organization. But although a great deal of conceptual goal modeling languages are available, these take only limited account of the organizational dimension of goals, including authorization rights, responsibilities, resources, and, in particular, related decision processes. This paper presents a goal modeling language which is integrated with a method for multi-perspective enterprise modeling, such that context-enriched models of goal systems can be constructed. Aside from organizational aspects, particular emphasis is placed on conceptualizations that clearly distinguish different (meta) levels of abstraction.

Keywords: Goal modeling · Enterprise modeling · Organizational goals · Organizational decision processes · Domain-specific modeling language

1 Introduction

Goals are ordinarily regarded as a prerequisite for the management of the firm. The formulation of organizational goals has been placed at the core of managerial responsibilities for long [28,30], and goal orientation is key to the classical economic theory of decision making [29]. At the same time, explicit goals have often been found to be absent from organizational action [33], and the design of goal systems has for decades been recognized as a challenging task (e.g., [14]).

In order to support organizations in reflectively setting and (re-)assessing goals, conceptual models promise to provide an apt foundation. Explicit models of organizational goal systems may serve as a central reference for different actors and related decision processes, contributing to organizational transparency, consistency, and efficiency. To create goal models, numerous conceptual goal modeling languages (e.g., [4,7,16,26,34,35]) have been brought forward in recent decades. However, existing languages mostly aim to support requirements analysis and largely abstract from organizational aspects of using goals:

© Springer International Publishing AG 2016
I. Comyn-Wattiau et al. (Eds.): ER 2016, LNCS 9974, pp. 515–529, 2016.
DOI: 10.1007/978-3-319-46397-1_40

- The managerial analysis of goals requires accounting for the *context* of goals, including resources, organizational units, business processes, and IT infrastructures. Existing languages consider this context only to a limited extent.
- The *organizational dimension* of goal planning, including authorization rights and fulfillment responsibilities, is widely omitted by existing languages.
- Goals are intimately related to *decision making*. Yet, many languages do not include concepts to interrelate goals with organizational decision processes.
- The concept of a goal holds a variety of *conceptual intricacies*, considered only partly by existing languages (e.g., decompositions of goal contents).

Against this background, the purpose of this paper is to present a domain-specific modeling language (DSML), called MEMO Goal Modeling Language (MEMO GoalML), which, compared to existing languages,

- enables a richer specification and analysis of goals because it integrates goal models with multi-perspective enterprise models that represent the context of goals, especially including organizational-regulatory aspects;
- offers a more elaborate conception of goals because, e.g., it permits to decompose goal contents and distinguishes a larger number of goal relationships;
- provides support for analyzing and aligning goals and decisions because it is integrated with a language to describe organizational decision processes;
- contributes to model consistency, reuse, and flexibility because its language specification explicitly distinguishes between aspects on M_1 and M_0.

The proposed language is designed as part of a comprehensive, multi-perspective method for enterprise modeling (MEMO) [12]. Versions of GoalML have been introduced before [19,24], which we here condense and augment, especially in regard to decision processes, to provide a coherent modeling framework.

The paper proceeds as follows. First, we discuss the theoretical background and synthesize requirements (Sect. 2). Then we present the enterprise modeling method in which the language is embedded (Sect. 3). Meta models and graphical notations of the language are introduced in Sects. 4 and 5. Finally, results and related work are discussed (Sect. 6), and future research routes are outlined (Sect. 7).

2   Theoretical Background, Aims, and Requirements

A research-based construction of a DSML requires a systematic design process, while considering particularities of the artifact 'modeling language'. To this end, we applied a method to design DSMLs [11]. At a macro level, this method consists of seven (iterative) phases [11]: (1) *'Clarification of scope and purpose'*, (2) *'analysis of generic requirements'*, (3) *'analysis of specific requirements'*, (4) *'language specification'*, (5) *'design of graphical notation'*, (6) *'development of modeling tool'*, and (7) *'evaluation and refinement'*. In this paper, we focus on the most salient phases—(1), (3), (4), and (7). We start with an account of scope and purpose (phase 1; Sect. 2.1) and specific requirements (phase 3; Sect. 2.2).

2.1   Aims and Assumptions: Theoretical Considerations

In long debates, the concept of a goal has become recognized as an example of what Simon calls "value elements [...] in decision making" [31, pp. 59–60], describing "states of affairs [that] ought to be" [31, p. 47]. This places goals amidst what March has summarized as "one of the most elaborate terminologies in the professional literature [including] 'values', 'needs', 'wants', 'goods', 'tastes', 'preferences', 'utility', 'objectives'" [20, p. 254]. But in contrast to broader terms such as 'value', goals are ordinarily construed as specific visions of desired future states to guide decision making and problem solving (cf. [21, p. 315] [14, p. 45]).

From this vantage point, goals have been taken as part of the classical economic conception of rationality, where a "rational" decision is one which maximizes goal measures such as expected utility (e.g., [29]). This view is reflected in wide parts of decision theory (e.g., [25, pp. 33–73]) and in goal model analysis techniques that maximize goal attainment (for a review, see [15]). However, when considering goals in organizations, a different picture emerges. First of all, organizations often do not explicate and maintain goal systems at all (e.g., [33]). Second, even in case explicit goals have been defined, it has long been argued that "optimal" alternatives, due to limited cognitive capacities and epistemological issues, cannot be identified [29] [31, pp. 79–109]. Furthermore, many organizational goals, intendedly or unintendedly, are not formulated precisely enough to permit clear evaluation, but rather serve as a broad orientation (e.g., high-level goals related to profits [30, pp. 17, 21–22]) or "sense-making" and inspiration (e.g., goals related to 'social responsibility', [28, p. 73]). Finally, although the customary rhetoric often portrays goals as outcomes of an ubiquitous "organizational mind" [6, p. 26], goals result from social (decision) processes involving individual actors. Thus, it can be assumed that goal planning processes are not only in need of coordinative measures, but that they will also often be affected by hidden agendas and political maneuvering (see, e.g., [6] [30, pp. 11–12]).

Against this background, we do not assume that goal models are, or should be, capable of controlling individual behavior in a mechanistic sense, or that they can ensure "optimal" rational decisions. Instead, we assume that goal models can serve as a possible reference point, among many others, for individual and collaborative decision making in organizations. The main aim of the desired language, then, is to support actors in formulating, discussing, critically (re-)considering, and monitoring goals. As an outcome, the modeling language is sought to contribute to organizational *transparency* (because selected premises and assumptions of decision making can be made explicit), *consistency* (because different actors can refer to, and communicate by means of, a common linguistic structure and related models), and *efficiency* (because distributed goal planning processes can be coordinated and documented by means of a central instrument). In parallel to this main aim, the language specification is intended to support the development of related software systems, including goal modeling tools and enterprise systems, that are aware of, and which can monitor, corporate goals.

2.2   Specific Requirements

Having considered general assumptions and aims, we analyze specific requirements for the desired language in this section. The requirements are based on two grounds. First, they result from the above-indicated extensive literature review that has been conducted as part of a dissertation project [19, pp. 13–100]. Second, in line with the method used to design the language [11], some requirements are derived from considering application scenarios in which the desired method should be applicable [19, pp. 121–130]. The following requirements emerged from considering four application scenarios (cf. [19, pp. 108–114]), namely (1) *goal system analysis* (R_1–R_4, R_8), (2) *organizational goal planning* (R_5, R_6), (3) *goal monitoring* (R_4, R_6), and (4) *coordinating decision processes* (R_7, R_8). Compared to the original requirements [19,24], application scenario 4 is new, and continues work from [2]. For space reasons, we discuss and illustrate the scenarios together with the final specification of the language in Sects. 4 and 5.

R_1—*Goal content.* A goal modeling language should enable to describe the content (or 'substance') of a goal in detail. This can include decomposing the real-world aspects referred to by a goal into different elements, distinguishing between different kinds of aspects (e.g., qualitative and quantitative aspects), and specifying what reaching the different parts of a goal content may imply.

R_2—*Goal functions.* The language should allow to express the function a goal is supposed to serve. At least, it should be possible to explicate whether a goal is sought to specify a concrete, to-be-evaluated performance target for specific actors or whether it aims at inspiration, information, and legitimization.

R_3—*Goal relationships.* A goal modeling language should enable to clearly differentiate between distinct kinds of relationships that can be recognized between goals. For instance, it should be possible to distinguish between logical (de-)composition, assumed causal dependencies between possible actions to attain goals, and means-ends relationships expressing that certain goals have been formulated exclusively to incite actions as a means to attain another goal.

R_4—*Goal abstraction levels.* A language for goal modeling should sharply differentiate different levels of abstraction. In particular, meaningful notions of goal meta types (M_2), types (M_1), and instances (M_0) need to be developed, and the meta model of the language needs to prescribe accurately at which level of abstraction (meta) model elements are to be instantiated. For elements at all levels, the language specification should be oriented towards implementation languages to support the development of modeling tools and software systems.

R_5—*Organizational context.* A language to model organizational goals should permit to interrelate goals with relevant parts of the organizational context. This includes, but is not limited to, general reference points to help interpret a goal (e.g., IT infrastructures or business processes assumed to be affected by goal-related actions), resources allocated to reach a goal, organizational units that formulate, evaluate, or work towards goals, and decision processes (see below).

R_6—*Organizational regulations.* A modeling language to describe organizational goals should provide conceptual means to capture the organizational dimension of goals. In particular, this includes authorization regulations (describing what kind of goals a unit or position may release), goal ownerships (describing which unit or position has formulated, and monitors, a goal), and goal attainment responsibilities (describing who is responsible for reaching a goal).

R_7—*Interrelation with decision processes.* A goal modeling language should be integrated with concepts to describe organizational decision processes to enable analyzing how goals are, or should be, considered in organizational decisions. The language should differentiate between different kinds of relationships, including, e.g., whether goals are subject of, or reference points for, decisions.

R_8—*Reflective use.* A language to model organizational goals should promote a reflective and critical stance towards the formulation, interpretation, and use of goals for purposes of organizational decision making and managerial control. For example, a language should help make explicit underlying (and perhaps simplistic or otherwise problematic) assumptions of the modelers.

3   Context: Multi-perspective Enterprise Modelling

To clarify the foundation on which the GoalML is based, in this section, we first give a brief overview of MEMO. Second, we introduce the MEMO meta modeling language MEMO MML. For an in-depth discussion of MEMO, see [12].

Generic framework. Enterprise modeling is motivated by the insight that analyzing and re-designing enterprises requires accounting for both the organizational action system and the related information system. Accordingly, enterprise models integrate models of the organizational action system (e.g., business process models) and models of information systems (e.g., models of the IT infrastructure). This general idea is reflected in the design of MEMO. MEMO includes a generic, yet adjustable framework to structure any kind of enterprise, as well as a set of DSMLs to describe details of all parts of that framework. The generic framework of MEMO offers three *perspectives* on an enterprise: strategy, organization, and information system. A perspective corresponds to a professional view and is represented by domain-specific concepts. Perspectives can be further differentiated into *aspects* such as resources, structure, process, and goals. This generic framework provides a "ballpark view" of an enterprise, serving as a high-level starting point to identify more specific analysis areas. In order to describe and analyze selected areas in detail, MEMO provides an extensible set of integrated DSMLs. These include languages to model organizational structures and business processes (OrgML, [8,9]), a language to model IT infrastructures (ITML, [18]), a language to model resources (ResML, [17]), and a language to model business indicators (MetricML, [32]). More recent additions include a language to model decision processes [2] and the GoalML presented here. The integration of MEMO DSMLs is accomplished through a language architecture that features a common meta modeling language (MEMO MML; see below) and through common concepts shared by the DSMLs (as illustrated in Sect. 4).

Meta modeling language. We decided to define our own meta modeling language, MEMO MML [10], because existing languages such as the MOF [22] lack concepts we regard as important. Two MEMO MML concepts are especially relevant for the GoalML. First, modeling languages usually consist of meta types at level M_2, which will be instantiated into types at level M_1. However, sometimes it is also known at M_2 what attributes are required for instances at M_0. For example, a language to model processes may include the meta type 'Process' (M_2). For a 'Process', it is obvious that every instance (M_0) has a start and end date. But without dedicated meta concepts, it is not possible to define these attributes at M_2, because they would otherwise be instantiated at M_1 rather than M_0. In MEMO MML, *'intrinsic features'*, similar to 'power types' [23] and 'deep instantiation' [1], enable to define entity types, attributes, and associations at M_2 that are to be instantiated at M_0 only. Second, using MEMO MML, attributes of meta types can be marked as *'derivable'*. This expresses that an attribute's value may be calculated from the states or values of other model elements. In meta models, *intrinsic features* are marked with a white 'i' on a black square, while *derivable* attributes are marked with a black 'd' on a white square. The use of these (meta) concepts is illustrated in the next section.

4   Language Specification

In this section, we discuss the design process of the GoalML (Sect. 4.1) and we present the final specification of the GoalML (Sect. 4.2).

4.1   Design Process, Guidelines, and Design Decisions

In the method applied to design a DSML [11], *'language specification'* comprises several steps. First, the method advises to create a glossary of all concepts identified as relevant elements of the considered domain of discourse. Our resultant glossary included numerous terms, such as 'goal', 'symbolic goal', 'goal content', 'sales target', and 'key goal'. In a second step, it needs to be decided for each concept in the glossary whether it should be part of the language or rather be specified *with* the language [11, p. 146]. This decision cannot be made unambiguously. As an orientation, however, the method we followed provides a set of criteria as guidelines (see [11, pp. 146–147]). For example, criterion Cr_a states that language concepts should be expected to have widely the same meaning within the desired application scope. When applying this criterion to a term like 'key goal', it can be determined that this example would not qualify as a language candidate, as in contrast to the more general term 'goal', it cannot be assumed that there is a largely similar understanding of 'key goal' across different enterprises. As another example, criterion Cr_c states that a meta type which can be instantiated into types of little semantic difference only usually should not become part of a language. When applying this criterion to a term such as 'sales goal', it becomes apparent that possible instantiations into types (e.g., 'sell x units' or 'sell units for a sum total of y M\$') appear too similar, discouraging this term as a language concept. For all language concepts presented in the next section (Sect. 4.2), the assessment of criteria indicated that they should become part of the DSML (see [19, pp. 191–196]). In a following step [11, pp. 147–148], the method advises to design a draft meta model that includes all selected concepts. This step involves the decision whether or not to define a meta model element as 'intrinsic'. While this decision was relevant for all elements, it was particularly significant with respect to *time-related* attributes [19, pp. 197–198]. For example, a goal type could already instantiate most time-related attributes. This would permit to describe goals at a high level of detail at the type level already (e.g., 'Sell 25.000 units until March 31, 2018'). However, in this case, there would be little reuse (as a similar goal like 'Sell 25.000 units until March 31, 2019' would result in another goal type). In consequence, it has been decided to define most time-related attributes as 'intrinsic', to be instantiated at M_0 at model runtime only. Final outcomes of the last step of the method (revise and evaluate the meta model; [11, pp. 148–150]) are presented in Sects. 4.2 and 6.

4.2   Final Language Specification

The language specification of the GoalML will be presented in three steps. First, we present the meta model of the modeling language. Second, we provide a language overview, and clarify the rationales underlying the main concepts. Third, to offer a concise language summary, all language concepts, attributes, and relationships are explained in Tables 1 and 2. While we present a fully coherent, current, and self-contained meta model of the GoalML, the list of language constraints (cf. top left in Fig. 1) as well as a few auxiliary concepts and attributes cannot be presented here for space reasons. These are found in [19].

Meta model. Figure 1 shows the GoalML meta model, defined with MEMO MML. To improve readability, the meta model has been divided into six areas. As explained in Sect. 3, several attributes are marked with either an 'i' or a 'd', expressing that they are 'intrinsic' or 'derivable'. Furthermore, small colored squares are attached to several concepts. These concepts are part of other MEMO languages, representing the aforementioned inter-language integration points.

Language overview. When taken together, the concepts from the six areas shown in the meta model (Fig. 1) are intended to support the four key application scenarios mentioned in Sect. 2, namely (1) goal system analysis, (2) organizational goal planning, (3) goal monitoring, and (4) coordinating decision processes. First of all, the *core concepts* provide the basic way to describe goals in detail (application scenario 1 and 3), offering numerous attributes, while explicitly distinguishing several levels of abstraction (by means of 'intrinsic features'). The two main goal concepts are called *'EngagementGoal'* and *'SymbolicGoal'* (see Table 1). Concepts found in the area *goal content* allow to define goal contents (called *'GoalMatter'*) by decomposing them into any number of *'SituationalAspects'* of varied nature (see the specializations). Furthermore, we propose several *goal relationships*. Beyond common relationships such as AND/OR *'DecompositionRelations'*, we distinguish at a nuanced level between various related, but subtly different inter-goal relationships, explained in Table 2.

Next, of crucial importance, the GoalML enables to interlink goals with the organizational context. This is accomplished by the meta model parts *general*

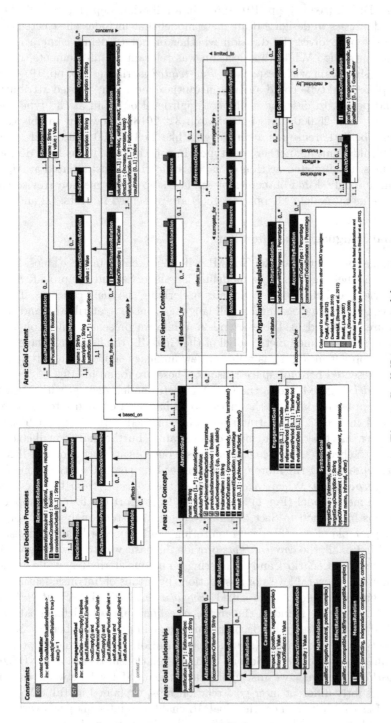

Fig. 1. GoalML meta model

context, *organizational regulations*, and *decision processes*. Here, the GoalML is integrated with concepts of various existing MEMO languages. First, goals can be linked to *'RessourceAllocations'*, taken from MEMO ResML [17], describing resources such as monetary assets or production factors. Second, each goal can be related to any number of *'ReferenceObjects'* that may exist in a MEMO enterprise model, including (but not limited to) *'BusinessProcesses'* [9], *'UnitsOfWork'* [8], and *'InformationSystems'* [18]. Similarly, *'ObjectAspects'* can be associated with *'ReferenceObjects'*, describing a goal content component in more detail. More specifically, in the area *organizational regulations*, the integration with *'UnitOfWork'* [8] (an abstraction of entities like organizational units, positions, and boards) is intended to support organizational goal planning processes (application scenario 2). In particular, the *'InitiationRelation'*, *'Accountability-Relation'*, and *'AuthorizationRelation'* can answer questions regarding different forms of responsibilities and regulations (see Table 2). Finally, the conjoint analysis of *decision processes* and goals (application scenario 4) is achieved through integration with a language to describe decision processes [2]. This integration aids both analyses which take goals as *reference points* for decisions (via *'RelevanceRelation'*) as well as *outcomes* of decisions (via *'ActionVariable'*).

Concept description. Augmenting the general overview, a full description of all GoalML concepts, attributes, and relationships is provided in Tables 1 and 2. Obvious (e.g., 'name') and duplicate attributes (e.g., 'justification') are omitted.

5 Illustration of an Application Case

To illustrate how the GoalML can be applied, and also in order to introduce the concrete syntax of the GoalML, an example application case is discussed in this section. Furthermore, the case exemplifies the integration of the GoalML with other MEMO DSMLs that have been mentioned in the previous sections.

Figure 2 shows an excerpt of an enterprise model of a fictious medium-sized traveling company which offers escorted travel tours for individuals and groups. The included goal model is presented at the center of the figure. In addition, the goal model is integrated with partial models of the organizational structure (using [8]; pt. 1), decision processes (using [2]; pt. 3), and a business process map that includes business process types and their interrelations (using [9]; pt. 4). All contents can be regarded as partial elements of a larger enterprise model, ideally managed and navigable in a modeling tool (for a related tool, see [3]).

To begin, the goal model shows at a glance the use of the central concepts introduced in Sect. 4. As can be found, both broad symbolic goals and more concrete engagement goals have been defined. All goal symbols are further enriched by dynamic notational elements showing current values for selected attributes (e.g., goal priorities). While most elements in the goal model are located at type level, there are also examples related to the instance level (see the textbox at the right-hand goal). Taking a wider perspective, it can also be noted how the inter-model integration enables various domain-spanning analyses. For example,

Table 1. MEMO GoalML: Concept and attribute descriptions

Concepts and attributes	Explanation
AbstractGoal	Abstraction of the two specific goal kinds, summarizing common attributes.
justification	Requires the modeler to justify why a goal is seen as worth striving for.
absolutePriority	An ordinal goal priority.
avgAchievementExpectation	A calculable average of *'achievementExpectation'* of goal instances at M_0.
previousInstancesAchieved	A calculable aggregate of *'result'* of goal instances at level M_0.
valueDevelopment	A calculable trend indicator for *'value'* of target *'SituationalAspects'*.
stateOfInstance	Lifecycle-related attribute to record the state of a goal instance.
achievement-Expectation	An estimation of goal attainment success for a specific goal instance (where the *'values'* of all linked *'TargetSituationRelations'* represent the partial target values of a goal).
result	Records whether or not a goal has been attained successfully; can be determined once a goal instance has been terminated (i.e., once its evaluation date has been reached).
EngagementGoal	Represents a goal which defines a concrete state of affairs to be achieved by particular actors within a given time frame (e.g., 'Negotiate 25 new contracts until May, 2016').
dueDate	When should the goal be fulfilled (i.e., when should all *'values'* be achieved)?
referencePeriod	In what period must phenomena occur to be considered in goal attainment evaluation?
fulfillmentPeriod	In what period may actions to reach the goal be performed?
evaluationDate	When will the goal be evaluated?
SymbolicGoal	Represents a goal which functions as a broad reference point for action, inspiration, information, and legitimization (e.g., 'Increase ecological sustainability').
targetGroup	General classification of the stakeholders to whom the goal will be communicated.
targetGroupDescrip.	Detailed description of the stakeholders to whom the goal will be communicated.
typeOfAnnouncement	The way in which the goal should be communicated to the defined stakeholders.
GoalMatter	Defines the goal content of a goal; composed of several *'SituationalAspects'*.
SituationalAspect	Abstraction of any real-world aspect that may represent (a part of) a goal content.
value	Defines an instance level value for a *'SituationalAspect'* (e.g., '25 M\$' or '25.000 units').
Indicator (from [32])	Describes a quantitative performance indicator representing (a part of a) goal content.
QualitativeAspect	Represents (a part of) a goal content which cannot be measured quantitatively.
ObjectAspect	Defines (a part of) a goal content that depends on the existence or properties of selected real-world phenomena or ideas (as represented in an enterprise model).
GoalConfiguration	Defines what sort of goals are in the scope of a defined *'AuthorizationRelation'*.
goalType	Defines the goal kinds that are encompassed by a goal configuration.
goalMatter	Defines the possible goal contents that are encompassed by a goal configuration.
DecisionProcess (from [2])	Represents an abstraction of similar recurring organizational decision processes.
DecisionPremise (from [2])	Auxiliary abstraction that describes any kind of assertion (or assumption) that may be considered in the context of a decision process. This includes *value*-related and *factual* assertions (for a classical discussion of the distinction, see, e.g., [31, pp. 4–5, 47ff.]).
FactualDecisionPremise ([2])	Describes non-value-related assertions considered in decision processes.
ValueDecisionpremise ([2])	Describes value-related assertions considered in decisions, an example being goals.
ActionVariable (from [2])	Describes factors that can be varied in a decision process (e.g., 'Number of employees to hire'). In goal setting decisions, *goals* will be referenced by an *'ActionVariable'*.

the model enables to analyze organizational regulations, answering questions such as "Who is responsible for achieving a goal?" The answer to this question, e.g., for the goal 'Achieve 25 bonus activity contracts during a travel', could reveal that 'Travel Attendants' are responsible but have communicated only a low level of commitment. Further analyses, then, could trace connections to modeled reference objects, such as business process types (see the bottom-right side), which MEMO would allow to further decompose into control flow diagrams. Beyond that, it can be analyzed and (re-)assessed how goals are related to decision processes (pt. 3). For one thing, this may guide decisions of organizational actors (see, e.g., the *'RelevanceRelation'* at the topmost decision process). For another thing, the decision processes in which certain goals are determined (e.g., the 'performance targets' for travel attendants; bottom-left in Fig. 2) can be analyzed with respect to involved actors, basic assumptions, and available information (as discussed in [2]). In sum, the GoalML provides a model-based ground on which ample analyses of organizational goals and decision processes can be done.

6   Discussion and Related Work

The field of conceptual modeling has brought forward a sizable set of goal modeling languages in recent years, including i^* [34,35], *KAOS* [7], *Tropos* [4],

Table 2. MEMO GoalML: Relationship descriptions

Relationship	Explanation
GoalMatterSituationRelation	Enables the detailed composition of one *'GoalMatter'* from several *'SituationalAspects'*.
isFocalRelation	Defines whether the given *'SituationalAspect'* is the most important one of a *'GoalMatter'*.
AbstractSituationRelation	A common abstraction of *'TargetSituationRelation'* and *'InitialSituationRelation'*.
value	Specifies a target (*'TargetSituationRelation'*) or an initial value (*'InitialSituationRelation'*).
InitialSituationRelation	Optional; may record the initial state of a *'SituationalAspect'* when a goal is released.
dateOfRecording	The date at which the initial state of a *'SituationalAspect'* has been recorded.
TargetSituationRelation	Specifies how a *'SituationalAspect'* has to be qualified in order to consider it met.
valueForm	States if the target value must, e.g., be 'satisfied', reached 'exactly', or 'maintained'.
direction	Indicates the general desired direction of change.
valueJustification	Asks to justify why a target state is seen as adequate (e.g., reachable, yet ambitious).
resultValue	Captures a final result value for a *'SituationalAspect'*, for documentation and analysis.
InitiationRelation	Specifies the unit that has formulated a goal, and monitors and evaluates its progress.
satisfactionWithProgress	Records the satisfaction of the monitoring unit with a *'SituationalAspect's'* current *'value'*.
AccountabilityRelation	Enables to record which organizational unit or position is advised to reach this goal.
commitmentToGoalType	Records a responsible unit's stated commitment to a goal for accountability purposes.
commitmentToGoalInstance	Parallel to the attribute above, but for a goal *instance* (and its specific details).
GoalAuthorizationRelation	Enables to specify in detail the authorization rights of different units for certain goals. First, this includes units and positions that are concerned with an authorization rule (including the roles *'may authorize'*, *'will be affected'*, and *'should be involved'*). Second it is related to a *'GoalConfiguration'* concept to define the scope of authorization.
AbstractGoalRelation	An abstraction of all possible goal relationships.
descriptionIfComplex	If a relationship is assumed to have exceptional qualities, these should be explained.
AbstractDecompositionRelation	Specifies that a goal can be decomposed logically and completely into at least two distinct goals; includes the two specializations *'AND-Relation'* and *'OR-Relation'*.
decompositionCriterion	Defines the criterion by which a goal can be decomposed (e.g., 'regional area').
FinalRelation	Expresses that a goal has been defined only as means to reach a more final other goal.
CausalRelation	Expresses that actions to attain one goal are assumed to affect reaching another.
impact	Defines whether the assumed impact is 'positive", negative', or 'complex'.
intensity	Can be used to document the assumed strength of the causal dependency.
levelOfReliance	Meant to record the reliance of the assumption (e.g., on a scale from 1 to 10).
AbstractInterdependenceRelation	An abstraction of all goal relationships that describe interdependencies between goals.
MathRelation	States that value changes for one goal *by definition* (formally) change those of another.
qualifier	Specifies the direction of the *'MathRelation'* (e.g., 'positive' or 'negative').
EffectRelation	Expresses that actions to reach two goals will likely affect reaching a third goal.
qualifier	Specifies how the attainment of the third goal is affected (e.g., 'compatibly').
MeansRelation	Expresses that actions to reach one goal will likely affect actions to reach another.
qualifier	Specifies the way in which actions to reach one goal interfere with those of another.
RelevanceRelation (from [2])	Specifies that a decision process is, or should be, oriented towards a specific goal.
considerationRequired	Specifies whether the consideration of a goal is 'optional', 'suggested', or 'required'.
hasBeenConsidered	To record *whether* a goal has been considered in a specific decision process (instance).
considerationDetails	To document (in detail) *how* a goal has been considered in a specific decision process.

URN [16], *4EM* [27], and *ARMOR* [26]. Below, we discuss the GoalML and related work in the light of the requirements elucidated in Sect. 2.2. The discussion focuses on support for organizational goal planning. It does not account for other application areas of goal modeling, such as requirements analysis.

Most languages are limited to specifying the goal content with a textual description (e.g., [35, pp. 46–57] [26, p. 9]). In KAOS, a target state can be defined with a formal description *'FormalDef'*, but this is not part of the meta model (cf. [7, pp. 14, 32]). In contrast, the GoalML provides concepts to decompose the goal content into distinct situational aspects of varied nature (R_1). Regarding goal functions (R_2), all languages apart from 4EM provide at least two goal concepts, similar to those proposed here, including, e.g., *'SystemGoal'* and *'PrivateGoal'* in KAOS, or *'Goal'* and *'Soft-Goal'* in i*, Tropos, and URN [34, pp. 229–231] [4, p. 230] [16, pp. 23–24]. When it comes to inter-goal relationships (R_3), every language offers AND/OR decomposition relationships (e.g., [7, p. 32] [26, p. 9]). In addition, i*, Tropos, and URN include *'means-ends'* and *'contribution'* (e.g., [35, pp. 46–57]), KAOS offers *'conflicts'* [7, p. 32], and 4EM includes *'supports'*, *'hinders'*, and *'conflicts'* relationships [27, p. 91]. But no language distinguishes possible goal relationships at a level of detail comparable to that of the GoalML. With respect to abstraction levels (R_4), as incorporated in

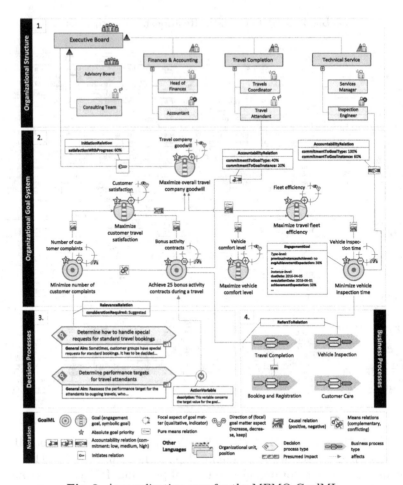

Fig. 2. An application case for the MEMO GoalML

the GoalML, extant work conveys an ambivalent picture. Although some publications discuss abstraction levels (e.g., [7, p. 9] [35, pp. 30–32] [4, pp. 227–228]), no related meta model found in the literature contains details as to inter-level instantiations (e.g., [7, p. 14] [35, pp. 29, 54] [27, pp. 88–91]). With regard to R_5, most languages permit to describe the goal context in a limited way. For example, i* enables to link goals to *'Actors'*, *'Tasks'*, and *'Resources'* [35, pp. 46–57], where Tropos adds concepts like *'Plan'* and *'Capability'* [4, pp. 206–207]. URN allows to integrate goals with 'Use Case Maps', including *'Components'* like *'Objects'*, *'Processes'* or *'Actors'* [16, pp. 102–110]. ARMOR and 4EM allow to link goals to varied concepts like *'BusinessService'* and *'BusinessProcess'* [26, pp. 9–10] [27, pp. 142–145]. But the GoalML is the only language that enables to embed goals in models created from an extensible set of comprehensive DSMLs. With an eye on organizational regulations, most languages, aside from GoalML, offer only indirect concepts. i*, Tropos, and URN permit to model actor dependencies (e.g., [4, p. 229]), but these do not describe organizational responsibilities. ARMOR uses generic links like 'used by' [26, pp. 9–10]. Only 4EM, but without further attributes, offers the relations 'defines' and 'is responsible for' [27, pp. 142–145]. Similarly, other languages only implicitly cover decision processes (R_7), e.g., by concepts like 'Task' in i* [35, pp. 46–57] or 'Problem' in 4EM [27, p. 88]. Finally, several authors seek to convey a reflective account (R_8) of the social context of goals (e.g., [35]). But aside from an 'assumptions' attribute in ARMOR [26, p. 10], the languages do not offer explicit means to stimulate a reflective stance, as the GoalML intends, e.g., by attributes to record 'justifications' or causal assumptions.

7 Conclusions

In this paper, we presented a comprehensive goal modeling language, called GoalML. The language is integrated with other DSMLs as part of a multi-perspective enterprise modeling method, enabling to model organizational goal systems at a level of detail that, to the best of our knowledge, goes beyond any other language. Furthermore, the language places emphasis on a clear distinction of different (meta) levels of abstraction. A modeling tool that implements an educational version of MEMO, including parts of GoalML, is freely available [3]. Future research is aimed at conceptual (enterprise) models, including models of goals and decision situations, which can be used and *modified* at different levels of abstraction at runtime [13]. For example, goal models could be used to enrich enterprise systems, making them "aware" of their goals—and, at best, enabling them to adapt to new goals in a flexible way. For this purpose, we use a (meta) modeling environment, the XModeler [5], which enables an arbitrary number of classification levels and a common representation of models and code.

Acknowledgments. We wish to acknowledge the major contribution of Christian Köhling, who has developed the original version of the GoalML.

References

1. Atkinson, C., Kühne, T.: Model-driven development: a metamodeling foundation. IEEE Softw. **20**(5), 36–41 (2003)
2. Bock, A.: Beyond narrow decision models: toward integrative models of organizational decision processes. In: 17th IEEE Conference on Business Informatics (CBI 2015), pp. 181–190. IEEE Computer Society (2015)
3. Bock, A., Frank, U.: Multi-perspective enterprise modeling - conceptual foundation and implementation with ADOxx. In: Karagiannis, D., Mayr, H.C., Mylopoulos, J. (eds.) Domain-Specific Conceptual Modeling. Springer, Berlin (2016)
4. Bresciani, P., Perini, A., Giorgini, P., Giunchiglia, F., Mylopoulos, J.: Tropos: an agent-oriented software development methodology. Auton. Agent. Multi-Agent Syst. **8**(3), 203–236 (2004)
5. Clark, T., Sammut, P., Willans, J.: Applied Metamodelling: A Foundation for Language Driven Development (3rd edn.). ArXiv e-prints 1505.00149 (2015)

6. Cyert, R.M., March, J.G.: A Behavioral Theory of the Firm. Prentice-Hall, Englewood Cliffs (1963)
7. Dardenne, A., van Lamsweerde, A., Fickas, S.: Goal-directed requirements acquisition. Sci. Comput. Program. **20**(1–2), 3–50 (1993)
8. Frank, U.: MEMO organisation modelling language (1) - focus on organisational structure. ICB Research report 48, University of Duisburg-Essen, Essen
9. Frank, U.: MEMO Organisation Modelling Language (2) - Focus on Business Processes. ICB Research report 49, University of Duisburg-Essen, Essen
10. Frank, U.: The MEMO Meta Modelling Language (MML) and language architecture: 2nd edn. ICB Research report 43, University of Duisburg-Essen, Essen
11. Frank, U.: Domain-Specific modeling languages: requirements analysis and design guidelines. In: Reinhartz-Berger, I., Sturm, A., Clark, T., Cohen, S., Bettin, J. (eds.) Domain Engineering, pp. 133–157. Springer, Heidelberg (2013)
12. Frank, U.: Multi-perspective enterprise modeling: foundational concepts, prospects and future research challenges. Softw. Syst. Model. **13**(3), 941–962 (2014)
13. Frank, U.: Multilevel modeling: toward a new paradigm of conceptual modeling and information systems design. Bus. Inf. Syst. Eng. **6**(6), 319–337 (2014)
14. Heinen, E.: Grundlagen betriebswirtschaftlicher Entscheidungen: Das Zielsystem der Unternehmung. Gabler, Wiesbaden (1966)
15. Horkoff, J., Yu, E.: Comparison and evaluation of goal-oriented satisfaction analysis techniques. Requirements Eng. **18**(3), 199–222 (2013)
16. ITU-T: User Requirements Notation (URN) – Language definition. Series ZZ.151 (2012). www.itu.int/rec/T-REC-Z.151/
17. Jung, J.S.: Entwurf einer Sprache für die Modellierung von Ressourcen im Kontext der Geschäftsprozessmodellierung. Logos, Berlin (2007)
18. Kirchner, L.: Eine Methode zur Unterstützung des IT-Managements im Rahmen der Unternehmensmodellierung. Logos, Berlin (2008)
19. Köhling, C.: Entwurf einer konzeptuellen Modellierungsmethode zur Unterstützung rationaler Zielplanungsprozesse in Unternehmen. Cuvillier, Göttingen (2013)
20. March, J.G.: The technology of foolishness. In: March, J.G. (ed.) Decisions and organizations, pp. 253–265. Blackwell, New York (1988)
21. Medin, D.L., Ross, B.H., Markman, A.B.: Cognitive Psychology, 4th edn. Wiley, Hoboken (2005)
22. Object Management Group: Meta Object Facility (MOF) Core Specification: OMG Available Specification Version 2.0. OMG Document formal/06-01-01
23. Odell, J.J.: Advanced Object-Oriented Analysis and Design Using UML. Cambridge University Press and SIGS Books, Cambridge and New York (1998)
24. Overbeek, S.J., Frank, U., Köhling, C.: A language for multi-perspective goal modelling: challenges, requirements and solutions. Comput. Stan. Interfaces **38**, 1–16 (2015)
25. Parmigiani, G., Inoue, L.Y.T., Lopes, H.F.: Decision Theory: Principles and Approaches. Wiley, Chichester (2009)
26. Quartel, D., Engelsman, W., Jonkers, H., van Sinderen, M.: A goal-oriented requirements modelling language for enterprise architecture. In: Proceedings of 13th IEEE International EDOC Conference (EDOC 2009), pp. 3–13. IEEE, Piscataway (2009)
27. Sandkuhl, K., Stirna, J., Persson, A., Wißotzki, M.: Enterprise Modeling: Tackling Business Challenges with the 4EM Method. Springer, Berlin (2014)
28. Shetty, Y.K.: New Look at Corporate Goals. Calif. Man. Rev. **2**(2), 71–79 (1979)
29. Simon, H.A.: Theories of decision-making in economics and behavioral science. Am. Econ. Rev. **49**(3), 253–283 (1959)

30. Simon, H.A.: On the concept of organizational goal. Adm. Sci. Q. **9**(1), 1–22 (1964)
31. Simon, H.A.: Administrative Behavior: A Study of Decision-Making Processes in Administrative Organization, 3rd edn. Free Press, New York (1976)
32. Strecker, S., Frank, U., Heise, D., Kattenstroth, H.: MetricM: a modeling method in support of the reflective design and use of performance measurement systems. Inf. Syst. E-Bus. Manage. **10**(2), 241–276 (2012)
33. Weick, K.E.: The Social Psychology of Organizing, 2nd edn. McGraw-Hill, Reading (1979)
34. Yu, E.S.: Towards modelling and reasoning support for early-phase requirements engineering. In: 3rd International Symposium on RE, pp. 226–235. IEEE, Los Alamitos (1997)
35. Yu, E.S.: Modeling strategic relationships for process reengineering. In: Yu, E.S., Giorgini, P., Maiden, N., Mylopoulos, J. (eds.) Social Modeling for Requirements Engineering, pp. 11–152. MIT Press, Cambridge (2011)

Can Goal Reasoning Techniques
Be Used for Strategic Decision-Making?

Elda Paja[1]([⊠]), Alejandro Maté[2], Carson Woo[3], and John Mylopoulos[1]

[1] University of Trento, Trento, Italy
elda.paja@unitn.it
[2] University of Alicante, Alicante, Spain
[3] University of British Columbia, Vancouver, Canada
http://disi.unitn.it/~paja/

Abstract. Business strategies aim to operationalize an enterprise's mission and visions by defining initiatives and choosing among alternative courses of action through some form of strategic analysis. However, existing analysis techniques (e.g., SWOT analysis, Five Forces Model) are invariably informal and sketchy, in sharp contrast to the formal and algorithmic counterparts developed in Conceptual Modeling and Software Engineering. Among such techniques, goal models and goal reasoning have become very prominent over the past twenty years, helping to model stakeholder requirements and the alternative ways these can be fulfilled. In this work we explore the applicability of goal models to conceptualize strategic business problems and capture viable alternatives in support of formal strategic decision-making. We show through a comparative study how analysis can be conducted on a realistic case adopted from the literature using existing goal modeling techniques, and identify their weaknesses and limitations that need to be addressed in order to accommodate strategic business analysis.

Keywords: Business intelligence · Strategic decision-making · Requirements engineering · Goal modeling · Strategic analysis · Risk analysis

1 Introduction

Strategic decision-making is crucial in enterprises, as it results in decisions that shape the future, and even the fate, of an enterprise [6]. Many economic and managerial models exist that support strategic decision-making, such as cost-benefit analysis [22], SWOT analysis [2], and Porter's Five Forces Model [21], in combination with data gathered and presented by Business Intelligence (BI) systems [15]. Despite an increasing range of services, techniques and languages available, managers still lack a systematic process for considering all their options in assessing their firm's situation with respect to its strategic objectives and the business environment. Whether due to the difficulties of gathering and organizing all necessary information or due to time constraints, they often end up with hand-waving arguments and heavy use of intuition to make and justify their decisions

© Springer International Publishing AG 2016
I. Comyn-Wattiau et al. (Eds.): ER 2016, LNCS 9974, pp. 530–543, 2016.
DOI: 10.1007/978-3-319-46397-1_41

in picking the best alternative among different courses of action, resulting often in wrong or sub-optimal solutions [3].

We propose to take a different perspective on strategic analysis by grounding it on formal reasoning techniques based on *goal models* and *goal reasoning* [12], both well known in Requirements Engineering (RE). These techniques are suitable for this task due to their conceptual proximity to the problem, they deal with multiple goals and multiple courses of action that are evaluated relative to objectives, such as cost, return-on-investment, etc. The evaluation is often qualitative in the absence of concrete numbers. In this paper we focus on existing goal reasoning techniques, and conduct a study *to evaluate their suitability for strategic analysis* on a realistic case study from the literature, in order to arrive at a list of desiderata for formal strategic analysis over strategic goals.

In order to conduct our study, we have performed a review of existing goal modeling and reasoning techniques [4,8,10] and select the most representative and suitable ones by defining inclusion and exclusion criteria, to apply to the case at-hand for comparison. Our selection criteria focuses on goal modeling techniques which allow us to (i) capture decision points, (ii) provide reasoning, and (iii) allow the introduction of human judgment in the final decision. We exclude techniques that belong to the same family (based on the same core model) to avoid redundancies. As a result, we focus on existing goal models, including i* [25], and a business goal modeling language, BIM (Business Intelligence Model) [10], designed specifically for strategic decision-making within an organizational setting. Our findings suggest that goal models do capture the space of alternatives for fulfilling strategic objectives, while goal reasoning capabilities are not sufficient by themselves to support decision-making in full depth and breadth. Moreover, existing techniques provide only an abstract of the situations, aspects, or threats that might hinder the strategic objectives of the company. Instead, a more concrete view is needed that takes into account specific business qualities, such as ones advocated by the Five Forces Model [21] or the Balanced Scorecard [14].

With this paper we make the following contributions: (i) analyze the suitability of existing goal modeling and reasoning techniques for strategic decision-making by applying our inclusion and exclusion criteria to identify representative techniques; (ii) compare the said goal modeling and reasoning approaches in terms of their modeling and analysis capabilities by means of a case study from literature; (iii) derive a list of desiderata or needs for languages and formal strategic analysis over strategic models.

The rest of the paper is organized as follows. Section 2 presents the motivating case and the actual decision-making problem to be tackled. Section 3 presents existing work in both managerial and goal-modeling areas to support decision-making before introducing our method in Sect. 4. Section 5 introduces the comparative study. We performed step by step modeling and analysis with various goal modeling and reasoning techniques, to lead to the identification of limitations of existing work. Finally, Sect. 6 presents some remarks, and discusses potential improvements and open needs for future work.

2   The Royal Caribbean Cruise Ltd Case

Background. The Royal Caribbean Cruise Ltd (RCCL) [18] is a leisure cruise company aiming at being competitive in the luxury leisure cruise business. Its business strategy aims at (i) enhancing the customer travel and trade experience, (ii) reducing costs, and (iii) increasing revenues. The core idea is that RCCL customers pay a higher price, and in return they are provided with a unique cruising and vacation experience.

However, over the years the company has encountered difficulties in achieving its objectives due to a number of external factors combined with technical ones, such as isolated corporate systems that are unable to provide timely information.

To address these issues, Tom Murphy, the RCCL CIO, proposed the Leapfrog Project, which builts on three main pillars with respect to IT: supply chain, employee system, and customer. Specifically, the first pillar calls for the automation of the shoreside purchasing and procurement process, with the intention to reduce costs, leverage RCCL's bargaining power with vendors to get better prices, and improve inventory planning. The second pillar focuses on tracking employees and having an automated and efficient Human Resources (HR) management tool that is able to handle a growing headcount. Finally, the third pillar, customer, is concerned with building a web-enabled reservation system to give the company a full picture of customer preferences and customer history.

Business problem. Murphy sets a five-year plan of the company through which RCCL can develop fully integrated systems where authorized users can access data anytime anywhere, and cuts costs by consolidating and simplifying existing systems. But, the ambitious Leapfrog Project was negatively affected by the 9/11 tragedy, as the project was halfway through its implementation at the time. When the market begins to turn around, RCCL finds itself with limited budget and manpower, and Murphy faces the challenge of making a decision on where to invest on IT for the short term.

The alternatives that confront him are [18]:

1. Do nothing beyond current expenditure levels;
2. Make an additional $8 million infrastructure investment in the next 12 months to untangle the seven reservation systems as a step to rapidly developing a single reservation system;
3. Introduce change quickly with a much sharper increase in budget than envisioned in option 2.

Among these alternatives, Murphy has to make a decision that will help preserve innovation while keeping in mind company objectives, ensuring that the alternative chosen contributes to the achievement of the main RCCL goals. However, the information about current projects, priorities, etc., is distributed over different exhibits, and there are no guidelines as to how to integrate this information for making a decision. Under these circumstances, a technique is needed to organize and integrate information and facilitate decision-making.

3   Related Work

There is a large and broad set of techniques designed to support decision-making in different contexts. For the scope of this paper, we review *managerial* and *algorithmic* techniques for decision-making, as well as *goal-oriented requirements engineering* approaches.

Management frameworks for strategic decision-making. They are often tailored towards specific types of decision-making and are generally informal and non-algorithmic. Porter proposed several frameworks in this area, including the generic strategies [20] and the Five Forces Model [21]. Generic strategies [20] aim to help a company position itself in the market, while the Five Forces Model [21] considers driving forces in the business environment where the company operates. Similar to the Five Forces, Dynamic SWOT (Strengths, Weaknesses, Opportunities, Threats) Analysis [5] links the firm's capabilities to its relevant competitive environment, allowing the company to potentially turn weaknesses into strengths and threats into opportunities. Next, are the works focused on strategic modeling and monitoring, including Strategy Maps [15] and the Business Motivation Model [19]. Due to their informal nature, these approaches do not support formal analysis, where a well-defined space of alternatives is searched for a solution. In addition, their concepts have been included in the formal Business Intelligence Model framework (BIM) [10], which will be introduced later on in the paper. Finally, there are several works that aim to support decision-making based on performance management, the most prominent being [14]. These approaches are based on measuring the performance of the company, and cannot help in the case that data is not readily available.

Algorithmic techniques. They are designed to automatically select the best alternative between two or more options based on multiple criteria. The largest body of work is centered around MCDM (Multi-Criteria Decision-Making) [7,9, 23], where the Analytical Hierarchy Process is included [9], with multiple surveys comparing the different techniques [7]. MCDM techniques have been applied to quantitative, fuzzy, or qualitative alternative selection in various domains, such as supplier assessment [9]. The basis for MCDM techniques consists in ranking the alternatives according to a set of criteria and selecting the best alternative. Their main drawback is that they can only explain the impact of the choice based on the criteria and do not allow for exploration. For example, if RCCL increases the budget for IT, what would be the impact on other business units?

Additionally, many MCDM techniques stem from the idea that all criteria and relationships with respect to the alternatives at-hand are well known and established, which is rarely true. To address this drawback, approaches like [16] accommodate uncertainty and information value into the analysis. However, even with the inclusion of uncertainty, the limitations on their exploratory capability still remain.

Strategic Goal Modeling and Reasoning. Modeling, and especially goal modeling, has a long tradition in requirements engineering (KAOS, *i**, NFR,

GRL, Tropos, see [24] for an overview). The importance of considering goals in early requirements is acknowledged by numerous works [4], providing several advantages including support in choosing among alternatives [24].

One of the features of goal-oriented models, independently of their approach, is their *goal reasoning* capability, which is usually implemented on top of off-the-shelf solvers, such as SAT solvers, model checkers and AI planners [8].

Horkoff et al. build on [8] to propose an iterative and interactive goal analysis technique [13], which introduces human judgment in the reasoning process to deal with conflicts. These works have shown that especially for real-world scenarios, it is crucial to follow such an iterative and incremental approach. Thus, in Sect. 4 we do the same for modeling and reasoning over RCCL.

The Business Intelligence Model (BIM) [10] is a goal modeling language expressly tailored for strategic modeling. BIM supports special forms of reasoning, extending the work in [13] to take into account situations and indicators and helping analysts in choosing amongst alternative strategies. The resulting hybrid reasoning procedure combines indicator and goal modeling approaches, to allow an organization to answer strategic or monitoring questions, such as "Which strategy is better to achieve these goals?", "Which option is better for maintaining revenue growth and reducing risks?", etc. Answering such questions requires evaluating alternative strategies, assessing an operational strategy, inferring values for composite indicators, and so on, that cannot be captured in other goal modeling languages.

Comparative studies. The reader interested in a broader survey of goal modeling techniques may refer to [11], while an evaluation of goal-model satisfaction analysis techniques is provided by [12].

4   Goal-Modeling and Analysis Techniques Selection

Our comparison follows the approach proposed in [12]. As such, we first define the inclusion and exclusion criteria to select amongst the goal-oriented approaches proposed in the literature. We are interested in techniques and methods that:

- allow us to perform goal modeling that captures decision points;
- provide reasoning support, required for selecting among alternatives;
- make use of human judgment, since decision-making cannot be a fully automated process, but rather should involve business experts to make the final decision based on the information provided, even in the case of missing information (real data).

Accordingly, we will exclude those techniques or methods that:

- do not provide any reasoning capability;
- are based on the same core or are a subset of another technique, in order to avoid repetition as discussed in [12];
- provide extended models and perform extended analysis other than strategic, such as for risks, trust or security, which are out of the scope of this study.

Among the candidate techniques, we have GRL [1], Tropos [8], and i^* [25] in combination with the reasoning techniques proposed by [13]. Since all these techniques share a common core, and they support the same kind of reasoning, we choose i^* as the representative due to (i) our expertise in i^*, and (ii) tool support, which is important for running automated reasoning.

We also include BIM in our comparison, because of its extended modeling capabilities tailored for strategic decision-making. We will compare these techniques using the RCCL case presented in Sect. 2, so that the modeling and reasoning are performed over the same case and using the same information.

In order to apply these techniques we follow a process based on the standard *elicitation, modeling, analysis* loop for *decision-making* in requirements engineering. We adopt it for assessing the goal modeling and analysis techniques in order to try to determine their capabilities in capturing and deciding over the optimal solution for the RCCL case.

We start with an analysis of the document describing the case to gather the information (*elicitation*) for building the models. In analyzing RCCL's case, we were assisted in the process by a business analyst who has extensive knowledge of the case study. The *modeling* phase is conducted on the basis of the information gathered from elicitation. Through modeling we can compare how beneficial each alternative is for RCCL by capturing how it relates to the rest of RCCL's business strategy (its main business objectives). Once the alternatives have been modeled, we proceed to analyzing the ability of each technique to discriminate alternatives and support the decision-making process. Automated *analysis* is run to identify the viable alternatives, to then make a decision through discussion with the business analyst (*decision-making*), who interprets the results, and in our case played the role of the CIO too, to pick an alternative. Model improvements were performed on the basis of this feedback.

5 The Study in Practice

We describe the process of modeling and reasoning over RCCL's strategy along two main threads, namely using (i) the i^* modeling language, together with three variations of goal reasoning techniques, and (ii) BIM modeling and analysis.

The techniques are evaluated on the basis of **RQ.** "*Can goal reasoning techniques be used for strategic decision-making?*", which we evaluate through two criteria C_1. "*Can the analyst make a decision under the condition of lacking real data?*" and C_2. "*Can the analyst be confident about the decision?*".

5.1 Modeling and Reasoning with i^*

We started the modeling and analysis of RCCL's case with i^*, a prominent goal-oriented requirements modeling language developed by *Eric Yu* [25] to model and reason about organizational environments and their information systems. i^* addresses the need to model and analyze the reasons behind stakeholder requirements and interests during early phase requirements engineering. The

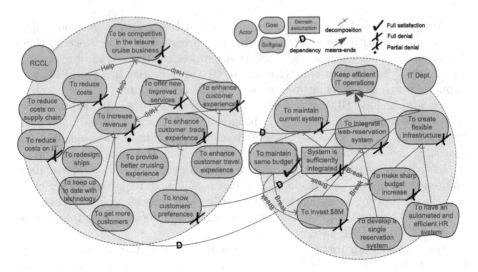

Fig. 1. RCCL business strategy for the alternative maintaining the same budget

basic concept in *i** is that of *intentional actor*, taking into consideration the fact that actors in an organizational environment have to achieve goals, are equipped with certain abilities, have beliefs, etc. The basic constructs offered by this language are: *actor*—together with its associations, *intentional elements*— goals, tasks, and resources, *strategic dependencies*, *decomposition links*, *means-end links*, and *contribution links* among intentional elements.

*i** reasoning techniques support iterative and interactive qualitative procedures [13], qualitative with variables [17], and quantitative reasoning [1].

Modeling RCCL's business strategy in *i.** We model RCCL's business strategy starting from the main business objectives: *reduce costs*, *increase revenue*, and *enhance customer experience*, Fig. 1 provides an excerpt and simplified *i** model of the RCCL case[1]. The model is the result of several iterations and interactions among the business analyst (3rd author) and the modelers (the other authors). Multiple initiatives are implemented to achieve these objectives. First, the reduce costs objective is to be achieved by a combination of cost reductions in the supply chain, IT, and shore-excursion programs. Next, the company aims to increase revenue by redesigning the equipment loaded into ships, keeping up with technology to be more cost-efficient, and offering improved services (for which the customers pay more) in order to attract more customers. Finally, in order to enhance customer experience, RCCL wishes to provide better trading experience, know customer preferences in order to serve them better, and enhance their traveling experience.

Using this model as a baseline for reasoning, there are two ways to model the alternatives available. First, we can represent the three alternatives of

---

[1] Find the complete model at http://disi.unitn.it/~paja/pdf/rccl-diagrams.pdf.

investment as three mutually exclusive alternatives (via *break* relationships) in the goal model, since only one of them will be chosen. Second, we can create a separate model for each alternative ("as-is" and "to-be" models), representing RCCL's objectives in case the represented alternative solution had been chosen. The former approach requires less effort, whereas the latter provides more clarity. Although in practice we went for the second approach, here, due to space constraints, the excerpt model contains all three alternatives, with alternative one being selected as a possible solution for the *what-if* analysis [13].

Picking the best strategy with i^* goal reasoning. Goal reasoning allows analyzing if considering RCCL's strategic goals alone, leads to the selection of one alternative over the others. We explore three subtypes of analysis for comparison:

1. *Qualitative:* the results of the qualitative analysis for the alternative *"To maintain the same budget"* are shown in Fig. 1. Maintaining the same budget does not contribute directly to reducing costs since it does not help to reduce neither IT nor supply chain costs. But, since it involves the continuous use of legacy systems, it entails an increased maintenance cost which threatens to break the system, as denoted in the RCCL case. Furthermore, the lack of new developments in this alternative does not help to offer improved services, nor does it contribute to attract more customers due to the lack of an integrated web reservation or an integrated HR system. As such, if we pick solution one (*"To maintain the same budget"* is fully satisfied, while the other two alternatives are labeled with fully denied), the system is not sufficiently integrated (domain assumption *"System is sufficiently integrated"* is not true, hence fully denied label), and as a result the goal *"To maintain current system"* is fully denied. The results of qualitative analysis are calculated through label propagation following the rules in [13]. According to these results, we can discard this alternative as it fails to meet any of the strategic goals set by RCCL (fully denying *reduce costs* and *enhancing customer experience*, and partially denying *increase revenue*). As far as the other two solutions are concerned, qualitative analysis cannot differentiate between them (not shown in the figure, both yielding to partial satisfaction of RCCL's objectives *increase revenue* and *enhance customer experience*), and thus, this reasoning cannot help us pick the best option among the two.

2. *Qualitative with variables:* A variation of the qualitative analysis inspired by the analytic hierarchy process for decision-making is the analysis with variables [17]. In this kind of analysis, shown in Fig. 2, the process starts by assigning variables that encode the impact of the alternatives to each high-level goal to be pursued. Variables that differ in their qualitative value across alternatives are further refined on each iteration into relationships towards the next set of goals, whereas those variables and goals that do not allow for discriminating between alternatives are discarded. In our case, we initially assign up to three variables (e.g., a,d, and c for *$8M*) per alternative, capturing their contribution to the overall goals. As we can see, *To maintain same budget* (*"As-is"*, Fig. 2(1)) alternative only provides a negative contribution to *reduce costs*, and thus is not an interesting alternative for us. According

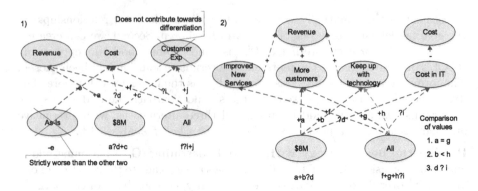

Fig. 2. Qualitative analysis with variables: "$8M" vs "All" (sharp budget increase)

to the description in the RCCL case [18], both remaining alternatives provide the same contribution to *enhance customer experience*. Thus, we need to further refine the contribution to decide between RCCL's objectives *increase revenue* and *reduce costs*.

The refined model (Fig. 2(2)) shows how *"sharp budget increase"* contributes to *improved new services*, whereas the alternative *"invest $8M"* does not. Moreover, it further contributes to RCCL keeping up with technology. The only condition for choosing the alternative *"invest $8M"* as opposed to *"All"* (*sharp budget increase*) would be the difference between the IT cost of both solutions (actual budget cost + unexpected expenses + maintenance cost of the resulting system) outperforms the larger return of investment (ROI) of the sharp budget increase. At this point, a manager with the required information at-hand could make a decision. However, in the case of RCCL this information is not provided, and as a result we cannot make a decision.

3. *Quantitative:* an alternative approach to qualitative analysis is the quantitative analysis (proposed for GRL [1] and adoptable for i^*), which introduces exact values to evaluate the degree of satisfaction of goals. The disadvantage of this approach is that it requires quantitative knowledge about the status of leaf goals and the relationships across goals in the business strategy. For quantitative analysis, we assume that goals are satisfied with a degree between -1 and 1, which can be objectively captured by means of performance indicators attached to the goals. This makes quantitative analysis ideal for companies with scorecards and process indicators readily available. Since the RCCL case only provides partial information about the benefits and costs of each alternative, we cannot run this kind of analysis over the RCCL model.

Results. i^* allows to adequately represent RCCL's objectives (its internal goals) as well as the three alternatives to decide upon its strategy. However, i^* modeling focuses on a company's goals, and not the external factors that might affect a company's strategy. Strategic goal reasoning shows that maintaining the same budget (*"As-is"* goal) is worse than the other two alternatives, but it cannot differentiate between *"invest \$8M"* or *"All"* (*sharp budget increase*). Thus, i^* modeling and reasoning cannot provide an answer to our research question, that is, it does not fulfil criteria C_1 nor C_2.

5.2   BIM Modeling and Analysis

Compared to i^*, BIM was designed for strategic modeling, and offers a richer structure of concepts, including *goals, business processes, situations* (representing SWOT factors), and *indicators* that represent data and criteria used by the company to monitor its goals. Thanks to these constructs, BIM supports various types of reasoning [13], including (i) quantitative and qualitative goal reasoning as in the case of i^*, (ii) indicator-based reasoning with business-rules, both with or without conversion factors by using the values of the indicators, and (iii) hybrid-reasoning, where indicators and goals are intertwined and the propagation alternates between goal satisfaction and indicator performance levels.

Since RCCL does not have any indicators defined, we cannot use indicator-based reasoning techniques. However, goal-based reasoning with BIM does provide an advantage due to the underlying model for its richer and diverse set of concepts, in particular the concepts of internal and external situations. For the sake of simplicity, we will focus on the two alternatives that we could not differentiate before, namely *"invest \$8M"* and *"sharp budget increase"*, and we will omit the analysis of *"to maintain same budget"*.

Modeling RCCL's business strategy in *BIM*. Modeling RCCL's strategy in BIM requires creating a separate model for each alternative. The reason is that there are both alternative-independent and alternative-dependent SWOT factors that help or hurt different goals and amplify or mitigate other factors across the model and, thus, the model for each alternative will contain a different set of situations. As in the case of i^*, we built this model in an iterative way, discovering SWOT factors on each iteration until the model was stable. An excerpt of the model for the alternative *"invest \$8M"* can be seen in Fig. 3.

In this figure, there are both alternative-independent and alternative-dependent factors. On the one hand, we have factors that affect the company as a whole independently of the alternative chosen. For example, the company is affected by *heightened geopolitical uncertainties*, which are increasing *last minute bookings* that are harder to manage and reduce the capability of the company to increase revenue. These factors are useful to determine if the company will achieve its objectives or not, independently of the alternative chosen. On the other hand, we can see the alternative *"invest \$8M"* being affected by the lack of an integrated employee system, which may dampen the increase in revenue and increase the maintenance costs due to the difficulties of managing a large HR base. Second, there could be problems integrating the web reservation system that have been unforeseen, thus affecting all the optimization goals of RCCL. Third, the developed system may not be scalable enough to handle the expected customer volume, thus affecting customer experience. Finally, another factor

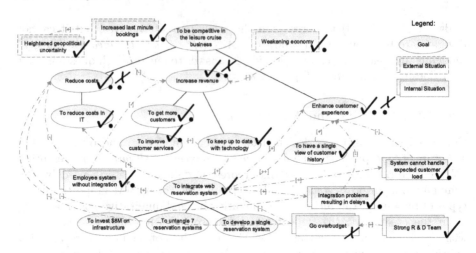

Fig. 3. Excerpt of BIM SWOT-based analysis for the *$8M* alternative

that affects this alternative is *going over-budget*. However, this is mitigated by the factor *strong RCCL's R&D team* (see negative contribution link from the internal situation), making it less likely for RCCL to deviate from the initial planing.

In comparison, the model for *"sharp budget increase"* (omitted due to space constraints[2]) is affected by fewer but more prominent factors than the *"invest $8M"*. First, it is more likely to exceed the estimated budget before achieving its mark than a project with a smaller scope, which is easier to estimate. Furthermore, it is likely to overestimate the ROI generated by the alternative. Finally, there is an increase in the need of trained people to operate the new completely overhauled system.

Picking the best strategy with *BIM*'s goal reasoning. Goal reasoning in BIM operates following the same label-propagation based logic as *i*'s reasoning discussed in Sect. 5.1. However, in this case, we have the added information of situations coming into place. Situations behave in the same way as goals in terms of the reasoning algorithm, but enable BIM SWOT analysis and provide us a better informed result [10].

According to BIM's goal reasoning, neither of the alternatives generates a complete satisfaction of RCCL's goals, which highlights the importance of alternative-independent factors and the need to consider new measures to tackle their effects. Among the alternatives available, the alternative *"invest $8M"* is less likely to fail since the associated factors have a lesser impact than in the case of *"sharp budget increase"*. Using these results the CIO can already make a choice on what alternative to select. However, it is noteworthy that BIM SWOT analysis lacks any guidance to help analyzing the factors that affect the business and the alternatives. In this way, the knowledge included within

---

[2] See http://disi.unitn.it/~paja/pdf/rccl-diagrams.pdf for the complete model.

managerial frameworks could prove to be crucial for ensuring the completeness of the exploratory process, and that critical factors are not overlooked.

Results. BIM allows a broader representation of the RCCL case, for it not only captures the company's strategic objectives in terms of goals, but it also allows representing internal and external factors (via situations) affecting those objectives. BIM does this following a fundamental aspect that influences decision-making, the existence of internal and external factors that affect the outcome of the business objectives and alter the expected contribution of each alternative. This modeling supports strategic goal reasoning that considers SWOT factors too. The advantage of SWOT analysis is that it can aid in evaluating risks while having qualitative information only. Thus, the BIM reasoning indicates the less risky alternative, helping to answer our research question partially, that is, fulfilling the first criteria (C_1), but not the second one (C_2).

6 Discussion

We are exploring the possibility of using goal-based techniques to support strategic decision-making. We performed a study to systematically evaluate existing techniques with the help of a realistic case, namely RCCL. For this task, we have iteratively and incrementally used different modeling and reasoning techniques to pick one of the three alternative strategies. This process has involved the presence and feedback of a business expert playing the role of the CIO.

Our findings show that goal modeling techniques are a good starting point for strategic decision-making, since they provide a global view of the problem at-hand and the alternative courses of action (business strategies). However, the RCCL case shows that, although i*-based analyses allow us to evaluate the alternatives in different ways, they are not able to reach a conclusive decision. It is noteworthy to mention that due to the lack of real data we cannot perform data-driven analysis. This is also true for BIM, which supports indicator-based analysis apart from goal-based reasoning. Nevertheless, the extended modeling language in BIM makes a significant difference when performing goal reasoning. The representation of situations provides further information to the CIO to distinguish among alternatives, favoring the selection of the second, although it still does not provide all the information required for a definitive answer.

The difference in the results provided by $i*$ and BIM denotes the importance of modeling the context of the firm (done via *situations* in BIM). Depending on the context, the optimal decision varies, making goal modeling alone insufficient to reason and explain the best alternative to be followed. These results highlight several desiderata or needs that must be taken into account in the quest for an adequate solution for systematic strategic decision-making.

First, there is a need for a modeling language expressive enough to model not only the firm and its objectives, but also how the context affects strategic goals. As shown by the RCCL case, strategic goals and alternatives can be strongly affected by the context. One can argue that this context may change or be present only in a certain subset of areas where RCCL is operating. Thus, the desired approach should allow decision makers to model under what circumstances each strategic goal will be successful, struggle, or fail, enabling them to make an informed decision. Furthermore, it should also adapt and operationalize each goal in a different way, accounting for the different contexts.

Second, there is a need for a detailed and comprehensive view of both internal and external factors that influence decision-making, which can be difficult to obtain without a systematic exploration process. Therefore, a framework that guides the exploration and evaluates all critical factors is required for achieving a well-informed decision-making process. Such process should be based on well-known management frameworks (Balanced Scorecard [14], Five Forces Model [21], etc.) that encode the knowledge about business drivers (such as competitiveness or differentiation), which go further than cost-benefit analysis, avoiding overlooking factors that will determine the success or failure of strategic goals.

Third, the previous points provide evidence of the need for a flexible reasoning process, one that takes into account the different contexts (via a global or probabilistic view of possible scenaria) and makes the optimal choices not only considering a static model, but the potential evolution of multiple contexts affecting different parts of the company. Such reasoning process would explain to the users why each choice is more adequate for each context, as well as which are the factors that determine the choice (e.g., lowering risks).

Threats to validity. Although our experience has been revealing, there are some threats to validity to the comparative study. The results might be influenced by the selected case (though the RCCL case is quite representative) and the lack of real managers involved in the study. Hence, we plan to consider different cases in the future and test the final hypothesis of performing scenario or context-based analysis and including more criteria to support a systematic and comprehensive approach for strategic decision-making. We also intend to involve actual managers to evaluate the envisioned comprehensive approach.

Specifically, in future work, we intend to augment one of the goal modeling and analysis techniques (e.g., BIM) with a managerial model (e.g., Five Forces, Value Chain, or Balanced Scorecards), in order to support a more systematic and comprehensive strategic decision-making process. In this way we would test our hypothesis that this comprehensive approach fares better, as discussed earlier in terms of open needs. Another possible extension is to enable decision makers to define trade-offs, fine-tuning the degree of satisfaction of strategic objectives. This will allow decision makers to make compromises, where some goals can be sacrificed in quantitative terms in order to excel in other priority goals.

Acknowledgements. This research was partially supported by the ERC advanced grant 267856, 'Lucretius: Foundations for Software Evolution', www.lucretius.eu. A. Maté is funded by Generalitat Valenciana (APOSTD/2014/064).

References

1. Amyot, D., Ghanavati, S., Horkoff, J., Mussbacher, G., Peyton, L., Yu, E.: Evaluating goal models within the goal-oriented requirement language. In: IJIS (2010)
2. Blythe, J.: Principles & Practice of Marketing. Cengage Learning EMEA, Boston (2006)
3. Carroll, P., Mui, C., Lessons, B.D.: What You Can Learn from the Most Inexcusable Business Failures of the Last Twenty-five Years. Penguin, New York (2008)
4. Dardenne, A., van Lamsweerde, A., Fickas, S.: Goal-directed requirements acquisition. Sci. Comput. Program. **20**(1–2), 3–50 (1993)
5. Dealtry, R.: 'Dynamic SWOT Analysis': Developer's Guide. IP (1992)
6. Eisenhardt, K.M., Zbaracki, M.J.: Strategic decision making. SMJ **13**, 17 (1992)
7. Greco, S.: Multiple Criteria Decision Analysis: State of the Art Surveys, vol. 78. Springer Science & Business Media, New York (2005)
8. Giorgini, P., Mylopoulos, J., Sebastiani, R.: Goal-oriented requirements analysis and reasoning in the tropos methodology. EAAI **18**(2), 159–171 (2005)
9. Handfield, R., Walton, S.V., Sroufe, R., Melnyk, S.A.: Applying environmental criteria to supplier assessment: a study in the application of the analytical hierarchy process. Eur. J. Oper. Res. **141**(1), 70–87 (2002)
10. Horkoff, J., Barone, D., Jiang, L., Yu, E., Amyot, D., Borgida, A., Mylopoulos, J.: Strategic business modeling: representation and reasoning. SSM **13**, 1015–1041 (2014)
11. Horkoff, J., Yu, E.: Analyzing goal models: different approaches and how to choose among them. In: ACM SAC, pp. 675–682. ACM (2011)
12. Horkoff, J., Yu, E.: Comparison and evaluation of goal-oriented satisfaction analysis techniques. REJ **18**(3), 199–222 (2013)
13. Horkoff, J., Yu, E.: Interactive goal model analysis for early requirements engineering. In: REJ, pp. 1–33 (2014)
14. Kaplan, R.S., Norton, D.P.: Putting the balanced scorecard to work. Performance measurement, management, and appraisal sourcebook, vol. 66 (1995)
15. Kaplan, R.S., Norton, D.P.: Strategy Maps: Converting Intangible Assets into Tangible Outcomes. Harvard Business Press, Boston (2004)
16. Letier, E., Stefan, D., Barr, E.T.: Uncertainty, risk, and information value in software requirements and architecture. In: ICSE, pp. 883–894. ACM (2014)
17. Liaskos, S., McIlraith, S.A., Sohrabi, S., Mylopoulos, J.: Integrating preferences into goal models for requirements engineering. In: RE, pp. 135–144 (2010)
18. McFarlan, F.W., Massoni, V.: Royal Caribbean Cruises Ltd. HBS (2003)
19. Object Management Group. Business Motivation Model v1.3 specification (2015)
20. Porter, M.E.: Competitive Strategy: Techniques for Analyzing Industries and Competition, vol. 300. Free Press, New York (1980)
21. Porter, M.E.: The five competitive forces that shape strategy (2008)
22. Robinson, R.: Economic evaluation and health care: cost-benefit analysis. Br. Med. J. **307**, 924–924 (1993)
23. Shyur, H.J., Sh Shih, H.: A hybrid MCDM model for strategic vendor selection. Math. Comput. Model. **44**(7), 749–761 (2006)
24. van Lamsweerde, A.: Goal-oriented requirements engineering: a guided tour. In: ISRE, pp. 249–263 (2001)
25. Yu, E.: Towards modelling and reasoning support for early-phase requirements engineering. In: ISRE, pp. 226–235. IEEE (1997)

Requirements Evolution and Evolution Requirements with Constrained Goal Models

Chi Mai Nguyen[(✉)], Roberto Sebastiani, Paolo Giorgini, and John Mylopoulos

DISI, University of Trento, Trento, Italy
chimai.nguyen@unitn.it

Abstract. We are interested in supporting software evolution caused by changing requirements and/or changes in the operational environment of a software system. For example, users of a system may want new functionality or performance enhancements to cope with growing user population (changing requirements). Alternatively, vendors of a system may want to minimize costs in implementing requirements changes (evolution requirements). We propose to use Constrained Goal Models (CGMs) to represent the requirements of a system, and capture requirements changes in terms of incremental operations on a goal model. Evolution requirements are then represented as optimization goals that minimize implementation costs or customer value. We can then exploit reasoning techniques to derive optimal new specifications for an evolving software system. CGMs offer an expressive language for modelling goals that comes with scalable solvers that can solve hybrid constraint and optimization problems using a combination of Satisfiability Modulo Theories (SMT) and Optimization Modulo Theories (OMT) techniques. We evaluate our proposal by modeling and reasoning with a goal model for the meeting scheduling exemplar.

1 Introduction

We have come to live in a world where the only constant is change. Changes need to be accommodated by any system that lives and operates in that world, biological and/or engineered. For software systems, this is a well-known problem referred to as software evolution. There has been much work and interest on this problem since Lehman's seminal proposal for laws of software evolution [3]. However, the problem of effectively supporting software evolution through suitable concepts, tools and techniques is still largely open. And software evolution still accounts for more than 50 % of total costs in a software system's lifecycle.

We are interested in supporting software evolution caused by changing requirements and/or environmental conditions. Specifically, we are interested in models that capture such changes, also in reasoning techniques that derive optimal new specifications for a system whose requirements and/or environment

This research was partially supported by the ERC advanced grant 267856, 'Lucretius: Foundations for Software Evolution' and by SRC GRC Research Project 2012-TJ-2266 WOLF.

© Springer International Publishing AG 2016
I. Comyn-Wattiau et al. (Eds.): ER 2016, LNCS 9974, pp. 544–552, 2016.
DOI: 10.1007/978-3-319-46397-1_42

have changed. Moreover, we are interested in discovering new classes of evolution requirements, in the spirit of [8] who proposed such a class for adaptive software systems. We propose to model requirements changes through changes to a goal model, and evolution requirements as optimization goals, such as "Minimize costs while implementing new functionality". Our research baseline consists of an expressive framework for modelling and reasoning with goals called Constrained Goal Models (hereafter CGMs) [4]. The CGM framework is founded on and draws much of its power from Satisfiability Modulo Theories (SMT) and Optimization Modulo Theories (OMT) solving techniques [1,6].

The contributions of this paper include a proposal for modelling changing requirements in terms of changes to a CGM model, but also the identification of a new class of evolution requirements, expressed as optimization goals in CGM. In addition, we show how to support reasoning with changed goal models and evolution requirements in order to derive optimal solutions.[1]

2 Background: Constrained Goal Models

SMT($\mathcal{LRA}$) and OMT($\mathcal{LRA}$). *Satisfiability Modulo the Theory of Linear Rational Arithmetic (SMT($\mathcal{LRA}$))* [1] is the problem of deciding the satisfiability of arbitrary formulas on atomic propositions and constraints in linear arithmetic over the rationals. *Optimization Modulo the Theory of Linear Rational Arithmetic (OMT($\mathcal{LRA}$))* [6] extends SMT($\mathcal{LRA}$) by searching solutions which optimize some $\mathcal{LRA}$ objective(s). Efficient OMT($\mathcal{LRA}$) solvers like OPTIMATH-SAT [7] allow for handling formulas with thousands of Boolean and rational variables [4,6].

A Working Example. We recall from [4] the main ideas of Constrained Goal Models (CGM's) and the main functionalities of our CGM-Tool through a meeting scheduling example (Fig. 1). We call *elements* both goals and domain assumptions. Labeled bullets at the merging point of the edges connecting a group of source elements to a target element are *refinements* (e.g., (GoodParticipation, MinimalConflict) $\xrightarrow{R_{20}}$ GoodQualitySchedule), while the R_is denote their labels. The label of a refinement can be omitted when there is no need to refer to it explicitly.

Intuitively, requirements represent desired states of affairs we want the system-to-be to achieve (either mandatorily or possibly); they are progressively refined into intermediate goals, until the process produces actionable goals

---

[1] **Note.** This paper was reduced to the current size from its original 14-page length. Accordingly, we have made available an extended version of [5] including *(i)* all figures of the examples which are described only verbally here, *(ii)* the *formalization* of the problem of automatically handling CGM evolutions and evolution requirements for CGMs, *(iii)* an overview of our tool implementing the presented approach, *(iv)* an overview of related work, with a comparison wrt. previous approaches, *(v)* some conclusions and description of future work.

(tasks) that need no further decomposition and can be executed; domain assumptions are propositions about the domain that need to hold for a goal refinement to work. Refinements are used to represent the alternatives of how to achieve an element; a refinement of an element is a conjunction of the sub-elements that are necessary to achieve it.

The main objective of the CGM in Fig. 1 is to achieve the requirement ScheduleMeeting, which is *mandatory*. ScheduleMeeting has only one candidate refinement R_1, consisting in five sub-goals: CharacteriseMeeting, CollectTimetables, FindASuitableRoom, ChooseSchedule, and ManageMeeting. Since R_1 is the only refinement of the requirement, all these sub-goals must be satisfied in order to satisfy it. There may be more than one way to refine an element; e.g., CollectTimetables is further refined either by R_{10} into the single goal ByPerson or by R_2 into the single goal BySystem. The subgoals are further refined until they reach the level of domain assumptions and tasks.

Some requirements can be *"nice-to-have"*, like LowCost, MinimalEffort, FastSchedule, and GoodQualitySchedule (in blue in Fig. 1). They are requirements that we would like to fulfill with our solution, provided they do not conflict with other requirements. To this extent, in order to analyze interactively the possible different realizations, one can interactively mark [or unmark] requirements as satisfied, thus making them mandatory (if unmarked, they are nice-to-have ones). Similarly, one can interactively mark/unmark (effortful) tasks as denied, or mark/unmark some domain assumption as satisfied or denied. More generally, one can mark as satisfied or denied every goal or domain assumption. We call these marks *user assertions*.

In a CGM, elements and refinements are enriched by user-defined *constraints*, which can be expressed either graphically as *relation edges* or textually as *Boolean or SMT ($\mathcal{LRA}$) formulas*. We have three kinds of relation edges. *Contribution edges* $"E_i \xrightarrow{++} E_j"$ between elements (in green in Fig. 1), like "ScheduleAutomatically $\xrightarrow{++}$ MinimalConflicts", mean that if the source element E_i is satisfied, then also the target element E_j must be satisfied (but not vice versa). *Conflict edges* $"E_i \xleftrightarrow{--} E_j"$ between elements (in red), like "ConfirmOccurrence $\xleftrightarrow{--}$ CancelMeeting", mean that E_i and E_j cannot be both satisfied. *Refinement bindings* $"R_i \longleftrightarrow R_j"$ between two refinements (in purple), like $"R_2 \longleftrightarrow R_7"$, are used to state that, if the target elements E_i and E_j of the two refinements R_i and R_j, respectively, are both satisfied, then E_i is refined by R_i if and only if E_j is refined by R_j. Intuitively, this means that the two refinements are bound, as if they were two different instances of the same choice.

It is possible to enrich CGMs with logic formulas, representing arbitrary logic constraints on elements and refinements. In addition to Boolean constraints, it is also possible to use numerical variables to express different numerical attributes of elements (such as cost, worktime, space, fuel, etc.) and constraints over them. For example, in Fig. 1 we associate to UsePartnerInstitutions and UseHotelsAndConventionCenters a cost value of 80 € and 200 € respectively, and we associate "(cost < 100 €)" as a prerequisite constraint for the

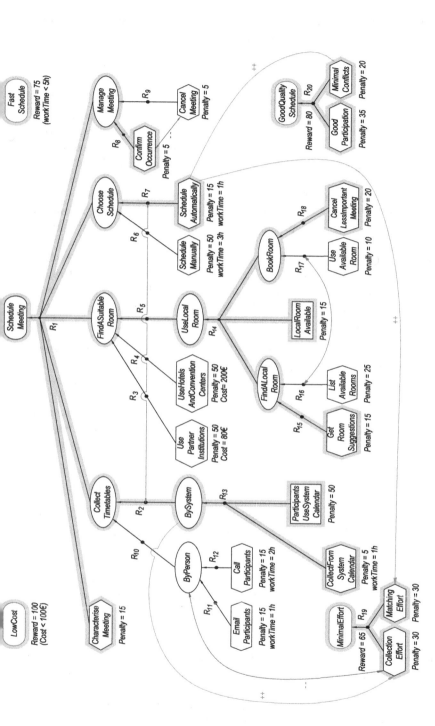

Fig. 1. A CGM $\mathcal{M}_1$, with a realization μ_1 minimizing lexicographically: the difference Penalty-Reward, workTime, and cost. Notationally, round-corner rectangles (e.g., ScheduleMeeting) are root goals, representing stakeholder *requirements*; ovals (e.g. CollectTimetables) are *intermediate goals*; hexagons (e.g. CharacteriseMeeting) are *tasks*, i.e. non-root leaf goals; rectangles (e.g., ParticipantsUseSystemCalendar) are *domain assumptions*. (Color figure online)

nice-to-have requirement LowCost. Implicitly, this means that no realization involving UseHotelsAndConventionCenters can realize this requirement.

We suppose now that ScheduleMeeting is asserted as satisfied (i.e. it is mandatory) and that no other element is asserted. Then the CGM in Fig. 1 has more than 20 possible *realizations*. The sub-graph which is highlighted in yellow describes one of them. Intuitively, a realization of a CGM under given user assertions (if any) represents one of the alternative ways of refining the mandatory requirements (plus possibly some of the nice-to-have ones) in compliance with the user assertions and user-defined constraints. It is a sub-graph of the CGM including a set of satisfied elements and refinements: it includes all mandatory requirements, and [resp. does not include] all elements satisfied [resp. denied] in the user assertions; for each non-leaf element included, at least one of its refinement is included; for each refinement included, all its target elements are included; finally, a realization complies with all relation edges and with all constraints.

In general, a CGM under given user assertions has many possible realizations. To distinguish among them, stakeholders may want to express *preferences* on the requirements to achieve, on the tasks to accomplish, and on elements and refinements to choose. The CGM-Tool provides various methods to express preferences, including:

- attribute *rewards and penalties* to nice-to-have requirements and tasks respectively, so that to maximize the former and minimize the latter; (E.g., satisfying LowCost gives a reward = 100, whilst satisfying CharacteriseMeeting gives a penalty = 15.)
- introduce *numerical attributes, constraints* and *objectives*; (E.g., the numerical attribute Cost not only can be used to set prerequisite constraints for requirements, like "(Cost < 100 €)" for LowCost, but also can be set as objectives to minimize.)

The CGM-Tool provides many automated-reasoning functionalities on CGMs [4].

Search/enumerate minimum-penalty/maximum reward realizations. One can assert rewards to the desired requirements and set penalties of tasks, then the tool finds automatically the optimal realization(s).

Search/enumerate optimal realizations wrt. pre-defined/user-defined objectives. One can define objective functions $obj_1, ..., obj_k$ over goals, refinements and their numerical attributes; then the tool finds automatically realizations optimizing them.

The above functionalities can be combined in various ways. For instance, the realization of Fig. 1 is the one returned by CGM-tool when asked to minimize lexicographically, in order, the difference Penalty-Reward, workTime, and cost.[2]

---

[2] A solution *optimizes lexicographically* an ordered list of objectives $\langle obj_1, obj_2, ... \rangle$ if it makes obj_1 optimum and, if more than one such solution exists, it makes also obj_2 optimum, ..., etc..

They have been implemented by encoding the CGM and the objectives into an SMT($\mathcal{LRA}$) formula and a set of $\mathcal{LRA}$ objectives, which is fed to the OMT tool OPTIMATHSAT [7]. We refer the reader to [4] for a much more detailed description of CGMs and their automated reasoning functionalities.

3   Requirements Evolution and Evolution Requirements

Requirements Evolution. Constrained goal models may evolve in time: goals, requirements and assumptions can be added, removed, or simply modified; Boolean and SMT constraints may be added, removed, or modified as well; assumptions which were assumed true can be assumed false, or vice versa.

Some modifications *strengthen* the CGMs, in the sense that they reduce the set of candidate realizations. For instance, dropping one of the refinements of an element (if at least one is left) reduces the alternatives in realizations; adding source elements to a refinement makes it harder to satisfy; adding Boolean or SMT constraints, or making some such constraint strictly stronger, restricts the set of candidate solutions; changing the value of an assumption from true to false may drop some alternative solutions. Vice versa, some modifications *weaken* the CGMs, augmenting the set of candidate realizations: for instance, adding one of refinement to an element, dropping source elements to a refinement, dropping Boolean or SMT constraints, or making some such constraint strictly weaker, changing the value of an assumption from false to true. In general, however, since in a CGM the goal and/or decomposition graph is a DAG and not a tree, and the and/or decomposition is augmented with relational edges and constraints, modifications may produce combinations of the above effects, possibly propagating unexpected side effects which are sometimes hard to predict.

We consider the CGM in Fig. 1 (namely, $\mathcal{M}_1$) as our starting model, and we assume that for some reasons it has been modified into the CGM $\mathcal{M}_2$ of Fig. 2 in [5] (see Sect. 1). $\mathcal{M}_2$ differs from $\mathcal{M}_1$ for the following modifications:

(a) two new tasks, SetSystemCalendar and ParticipantsFillSystemCalendar, are added to the sub-goal sources of the refinement R_{13};

(b) a new source task RegisterMeetingRoom is added to R_{17}, and the binding between R_{16} and R_{17} is removed; the refinement R_{18} of the goal BookRoom and its source task CancelLessImportantMeeting are removed;

(c) the alternative refinements R_8 and R_9 of ManageMeeting are also modified: two new internal goals ByUser and ByAgent are added and become the single source of the two refinements R_8 and R_9 respectively, and the two tasks ConfirmOccurrence and CancelMeeting become respectively the sources of two new refinements R_{21} and R_{22}, which are the alternative refinements of the goal ByUser; the new goal ByAgent is refined by the new refinement R_{23} with source task SendDecision.

Evolution Requirements. We consider the generic scenario in which a previous version of a CGM $\mathcal{M}_1$ with an available realization μ_1 is modified into a new CGM $\mathcal{M}_2$. As a consequence, μ_1 typically is no more a valid realization of

$\mathcal{M}_2$. E.g., we notice that μ_1 in Fig. 2 in [5] does not represent a valid realization of $\mathcal{M}_2$: not all source tasks of R_{13} are satisfied, BookRoom has no satisfied refinement, and the new goal ByUser and refinement R_{21} are not satisfied. It is thus necessary to produce a new realization μ_2 for $\mathcal{M}_2$.

In general, when one has a sequence $\mathcal{M}_1, \mathcal{M}_2, ..., \mathcal{M}_i, ...$ of CGMs and must produce a corresponding sequence $\mu_1, \mu_2, ..., \mu_i, ...$ of realizations, it is necessary to decide some criteria by which the realizations μ_i evolve in terms of the evolution of the CGMs $\mathcal{M}_i$. We call these criteria, *evolution requirements*. We describe some possible criteria.

Recomputing Realizations. One possible evolution requirement is that of always having the "best" realization μ_i for each $\mathcal{M}_i$, according to some objective (or lexicographic combination of objectives). Let $\mathcal{M}_1$, $\mathcal{M}_2$, and μ_1 be as above. One possible choice for the user is to compute a new optimal realization μ_2 from scratch, using the same criteria used in computing μ_1 from $\mathcal{M}_1$. In general, however, it may be the case that the new realization μ_2 is very different from μ_1, which may displease the stakeholders.

We consider now the realization μ_1 of the CGM $\mathcal{M}_1$ highlighted in Fig. 1 and the modified model $\mathcal{M}_2$ of Fig. 2 in [5]. If we run CGM-Tool over $\mathcal{M}_2$ with the same optimization criteria as for μ_1—i.e., minimize lexicographically, in order, the difference Penalty-Reward, workTime, and cost—we obtain a novel realization μ_2^{lex} (Fig. 3 in [5]). The new realization μ_2^{lex} satisfies all the requirements (both "nice to have" and mandatory) except MinimalEffort. It includes the following tasks: CharateriseMeeting, EmailParticipants, GetRoomSuggestions, UseAvailableRoom, RegisterMeetingRoom, ScheduleManually, ConfirmOccurrence, GoodParticipation, and MinimalConflicts, and it requires one domain assumption: LocalRoomAvailable. This realization was found automatically by our CGM-Tool in 0.059 s on an Apple MacBook Air laptop.

Unfortunately, μ_2^{lex} turns out to be extremely different from μ_1. This is due to the fact that the novel tasks SetSystemCalendar and ParticipantsFillSystemCalendar raise significantly the penalty for R_{13} and thus for R_2; hence, in terms of the Penalty-Reward objective, it is now better to choose R_{10} and R_6 instead of R_2 and R_7, even though this forces ByPerson to be satisfied, which is incompatible with CollectionEffort, so that MinimalEffort is no more achieved. Overall, for μ_2 we have Penalty $-$ Reward $= -65$, workTime $= 4\,h$ and cost $= 0\,\text{€}$.

In many contexts, in particular if μ_1 is well-established or is already implemented, one may want to find a realization μ_2 of the modified CGM $\mathcal{M}_2$ which is as similar as possible to the previous realization $\mathcal{M}_1$. The suitable notion of "similarity", however, may depend on stakeholder's needs. In what follows, we discuss two notions of "similarity" from [2], *familiarity* and *change effort*, adapting and extending them to CGMs.

Maximizing Familiarity. In our approach, in its simplest form, the *familiarity* of μ_2 wrt. μ_1 is given by the number of elements of interest which are common to $\mathcal{M}_1$ and $\mathcal{M}_2$ and which either are in both μ_1 and μ_2 or are out of both of them; this can be augmented also by the number of new elements in $\mathcal{M}_2$ of interest (e.g., tasks) which are denied. In a more sophisticate form, the contribution of each element of interest can be weighted by some numerical value (e.g., Penalty, cost, WorkTime, ...).

For example, if we ask CGM-Tool to find a realization which maximizes our notion of familiarity, we obtain the novel realization μ_2^{fam} (Fig. 4 in [5]). μ_2^{fam} satisfies all the requirements (both "nice to have" and mandatory ones), and includes the following tasks: CharacteriseMeeitng, SetSystemCalendar, ParticipantsFillSystemCalendar, CollectFromSystemCalendar, GetRoomSuggestions, UseAvailableRoom, RegisterMeetingRoom, ScheduleAutomatically, ConfirmOccurrence, GoodParticipation, MinimalConflicts, CollectionEffort, and MatchingEffort; μ_2^{fam} also requires two domain assumptions: ParticipantsUseSystemCalendar and LocalRoomAvailable.

Notice that all the tasks which are satisfied in μ_1 are satisfied also in μ_2^{fam}, and only the intermediate goal ByUser, the refinement R_{21} and the four tasks SetSystemCalendar, ParticipantsFillSystemCalendar, UseAvailableRoom, and RegisterMeetingRoom are added to μ_2^{fam}, three of which are newly-added tasks. Thus, on common elements, μ_2^{fam} and μ_1 differ only on the task UseAvailableRoom, which must be mandatorily be satisfied to complete the realization. Overall, wrt. μ_2^{lex}, we pay familiarity with some loss in the "quality" of the realization, since for μ_2^{fam} we have Penalty $-$ Reward $= -50$, workTime $= 3.5$ h and cost $= 0$ €. This realization was found automatically by our CGM-Tool in 0.067 s on an Apple MacBook Air laptop.

Minimizing Change Effort. In our approach, in its simplest form, the *change effort* of μ_2 wrt. μ_1 is given by the number of newly-satisfied tasks, i.e., the amount of the new tasks which are satisfied in μ_2 plus that of common tasks which were not satisfied in μ_1 but are satisfied in μ_2. In a more sophisticate form, the contribution of each task of interest can be weighted by some numerical value (e.g., Penalty, cost, WorkTime, ...). Intuitively, since satisfying a task requires effort, this value considers the extra effort required to implement μ_2. (Notice that tasks which pass from satisfied to denied do not reduce the effort, because we assume they have been implemented anyway.)

For example, if we ask CGM-Tool to find a realization which minimizes the number of newly-satisfied tasks, we obtain the realization μ_2^{eff} (Fig. 5 in [5]). The realization satisfies all the requirements (both "nice to have" and mandatory), and includes the following tasks: CharacteriseMeeitng, SetSystemCalendar, ParticipantsFillSystemCalendar, CollectFromSystemCalendar, UsePartnerInstitutions, ScheduleAutomatically, ConfirmOccurrence, GoodParticipation, MinimalConflicts, CollectionEffort, and MatchingEffort; μ_2^{eff} also requires one domain assumption ParticipantsUseSystemCalendar.

Notice that, in order to minimize the number of new tasks needed to be achieved, in μ_2^{eff}, FindASuitableRoom is refined by R_3 instead of R_5. In fact, in order to achieve R_5, we would need to satisfy two extra tasks (UseAvailableRoom and RegisterMeetingRoom) wrt. μ_1, whilst for satisfying R_3 we only need to satisfy one task (UsePartnerInstitutions). Besides, two newly added tasks SetSystemCalendar and ParticipantsFillSystemCalendar are also included in μ_2^{eff}.

Thus the total effort of evolving from μ_1 to μ_2^{eff} is to implement three new tasks. Overall, for μ_2^{eff} we have Penalty − Reward $= -50$, workTime $= 3.5$ h and cost $= 80$ €. This realization was found automatically by our CGM-Tool in 0.085 s on an Apple MacBook Air laptop.

Combining Familiarity or Change Effort with Other Objectives. In our approach, familiarity and change effort are numerical objectives like others, and as such they can be combined lexicographically with other objectives, so that stakeholders can decide which objectives to prioritize.

References

1. Barrett, C.W., Sebastiani, R., Seshia, S.A., Tinelli, C.: Satisfiability modulo theories. In: Biere, A., Heule, M.J.H., van Maaren, H., Walsh, T. (eds.) Handbook of Satisfiability, Chap. 26, pp. 825–885. IOS Press, Amsterdam (2009)
2. Ernst, N.A., Borgida, A., Mylopoulos, J., Jureta, I.J.: Agile requirements evolution via paraconsistent reasoning. In: Ralyté, J., Franch, X., Brinkkemper, S., Wrycza, S. (eds.) CAiSE 2012. LNCS, vol. 7328, pp. 382–397. Springer, Heidelberg (2012). doi:10.1007/978-3-642-31095-9_25
3. Lehman, M.M.: Programs, life cycles, and laws of software evolution. In: Proceedings of the IEEE, pp. 1060–1076, September 1980
4. Nguyen, C.M., Sebastiani, R., Giorgini, P., Mylopoulos, J.: Multi object reasoning with constrained goal model. CoRR, abs/1601.07409 (2016, submitted). http://arxiv.org/abs/1601.07409
5. Nguyen, C.M., Sebastiani, R., Giorgini, P., Mylopoulos, J.: Requirements evolution and evolution requirements with constrained goal models. CoRR, abs/1604.04716 (2016). http://arxiv.org/abs/1604.04716
6. Sebastiani, R., Tomasi, S.: Optimization modulo theories with linear rational costs. ACM Trans. Comput. Logics **16**(2) (2015)
7. Sebastiani, R., Trentin, P.: OptiMathSAT: a tool for optimization modulo theories. In: Kroening, D., Păsăreanu, C.S. (eds.) CAV 2015. LNCS, vol. 9206, pp. 447–454. Springer, Heidelberg (2015). doi:10.1007/978-3-319-21690-4_27
8. Souza, V.E.S.: Requirements-based software system adaptation. Ph.D. thesis, University of Trento (2012)

RationalGRL: A Framework for Rationalizing Goal Models Using Argument Diagrams

Marc van Zee[1]([✉]), Diana Marosin[2], Floris Bex[3], and Sepideh Ghanavati[4]

[1] Computer Science and Communication, University of Luxembourg,
Esch-sur-Alzette, Luxembourg
`marc.vanzee@uni.lu`
[2] Luxembourg Institute of Science and Technology, Esch-sur-Alzette, Luxembourg
`diana.marosin@list.lu`
[3] Information and Computing Sciences, Utrecht University, Utrecht, The Netherlands
`f.j.bex@uu.nl`
[4] Texas Tech University, Lubbock, Texas, USA
`sepideh.ghanavati@ttu.edu`

Abstract. Goal modeling languages, such as $i*$ and the Goal-oriented Requirements Language (GRL), capture and analyze high-level goals and their relationships with lower level goals and tasks. However, in such models, the rationalization behind these goals and tasks and the selection of alternatives are usually left implicit. To better integrate goal models and their rationalization, we develop the RationalGRL framework, in which argument diagrams can be mapped to goal models. Moreover, we integrate the result of the evaluation of arguments and their counter-arguments with GRL initial satisfaction values. We develop an interface between the argument web tools OVA and TOAST and the Eclipse-based tool for GRL called jUCMNav. We demonstrate our methodology with a case study from the Schiphol Group.

Keywords: Goal modeling languages · Decision rationalization · Argumentation theory · Argument diagrams

1 Introduction

The Goal-oriented Requirements Language (GRL) is part of the User Requirements Notation (URN), which is an ITU-T standard [8]. GRL [1] consists of several intentional elements (such as softgoals, goals, tasks and resources) and links between them. While GRL models, and goal models in general [19], are useful tools for motivating architectural choices in enterprise and software architecture, they miss important parts of the architecture design rationalization. As a result, GRL models are only the end product of a modeling process, and they do not provide any insight on how the models were created, i.e., what reasons were used to choose certain elements in the model and to reject the others and what evidence was given as the basis of this reasoning.

© Springer International Publishing AG 2016
I. Comyn-Wattiau et al. (Eds.): ER 2016, LNCS 9974, pp. 553–560, 2016.
DOI: 10.1007/978-3-319-46397-1_43

In this paper, we integrate various existing and newly developed interfaces and algorithms into the RationalGRL framework. This framework facilitates argument construction and analysis on the one hand and the rationalization and evaluation of goal models on the other hand. More specifically, RationalGRL framework combines an existing argument diagramming tool[1] [4] based on a formal theory of practical (i.e. goal-driven) argumentation [2,10,16,17] with a standardized goal modeling language and its tool support [1].

The core of RationalGRL is a concrete set of mapping rules from the formal argumentation framework to a GRL model. The mapping rules allow for the automatic translation of arguments and evidence about goals to GRL models. Furthermore, the formal semantics [5] of arguments and counterarguments underlying the argumentation theory helps determining whether the elements of a GRL model are acceptable given the potential contradictory evidence and stakeholders' opinions. In other words, we can compute the initial satisfaction level of IEs in GRL based on the acceptability status of arguments for or against IEs. RationalGRL framework is implemented as an online tool[2].

The rest of this paper is structured as follows. In Sect. 2, we briefly introduce the RationalGRL framework. Due to space constraints we omit technical details. In Sect. 3, we evaluate the framework via a case study of the Schiphol Group. First, we model the discussions about a change in the set of architecture principles of the Schiphol Group. Second, we evaluate the framework and the resulted models with enterprise architects of the Group. In Sect. 4 we present the current literature and the related work.

2   The RationalGRL Framework

The main components of the RationalGRL framework are shown in Fig. 1. The four main parts of the framework, Argumentation, Translation, Goal Modeling, and Update, are numbered and depicted in **bold**. For each component, the technology used to implement it, is marked in a filled rectangle. The last step (*Update*) is out of the scope of this paper. We, now, briefly explain the process of how a goal model is developed in the RationalGRL framework.

In **Step 1 - Argumentation**, stakeholders discuss the requirements of their organization. In this process, stakeholders put forward arguments for or against certain elements of the model (e.g. goals, tasks, ...). Arguments about why certain tasks can contribute to the fulfillment of goals and an evidence to support a claim are also part of this process. Furthermore, stakeholders can challenge claims by forming counterarguments. The complete set of claims, arguments and counterarguments can be represented in an argument diagram.

In **Step 2 - Translation**, the argument diagram is translated to a goal model, in our case GRL. In addition to the structure of arguments and counterarguments, this step also provides means to translate the evaluation of arguments

---

[1] http://ova.arg-tech.org/.

[2] All implementation details/sources as well as the case study descriptions and models can be found on Github: http://github.com/RationalArchitecture/RationalGRL.

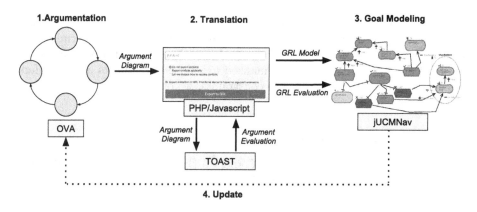

Fig. 1. Overview of the RationalGRL framework

in the argument diagrams to the initial satisfaction values of the GRL intentional elements, which can be positive or negative. A positive evaluation indicates that the element is supported by one or more arguments, while a negative evaluation indicates that the element is not a good alternative in GRL.

In **Step 3 - Goal Modeling**, the goal model that is generated by the Translation process, is evaluated by the stakeholders. These models can be used as a discussion means to investigate whether the goals in the model are in line with the original requirements of the stakeholders. This allows a better rationalization of the goal modeling process, with a clear traceability from the goals of the organization to the arguments and evidence that were used in the discussions.

Step 4 - Update involves translating GRL models with its analysis back into an argument diagram. This falls outside the scope of the current paper.

3 Evaluation

3.1 Case Study Description

Schiphol Group is the owner of an international airport and it operates on both national and international scales. Schiphol Group started using enterprise architecture principles to drive their architecture program in 2003. Principles are generally defined as "a family of guidelines (...) for design" [7] or "general rules and guidelines, intended to be enduring and seldom amended, that inform and support the way an organization fulfils its mission" [14]. In 2003, the principle Adhere to the Corporate Data Model was advocating the use of a company-wide defined data model, such that it provided a high level insight on all the data that were used in the processes and applications. In 2007, the principles were evaluated by a team of five architects and it was concluded that the principle was not very successful, and was conceptually conflicting with another architecture principle Package selection before custom development.

We use these principles as the base of our case study and we provide *a posteriori* analysis of the discussions and evidence that were used in forming the architecture principles and present the goal models generated using the RationalGRL framework. In total, we formalized around 60 arguments and 30 inferences/attack relation. Due to space constraints, we only provide a small subset of the models in this paper.

3.2   Modeling the Case Study in RationalGRL

In 2003, the principle Adhere to the Corporate Data Model was advocating for the use of a company-wide defined data model, such that it provided a high level insight on all the data that is used in the processes and applications. The IT department was assigned the task to define this data model. All applications were supposed to be compatible to this data model. The main motivation for adopting this principle was to obtain a clear and standard approach for information handling. This could improve the way in which customers can be served and to lower the costs.

In 2007, the principles were re-evaluated by a team of five architects. It was concluded that the previous principle was not very successful. Some of the arguments used in this discussion are shown in Fig. 2. An important issue with the corporate data model - principle was the effort needed to be invested by the ICT department to define this data model. Schiphol Group not only focuses on aviation, but also on retail and security. These domains have different needs when it comes to the data they use and their internal processes. In terms of business objects and "on paper" definitions, the data model was agreed upon, but it was never really implemented.

This situation is reflected in a simplified way in the argument diagram by an attack from the argument [EVIDENCE] CorpDM is not defined on [TASK] ICT department defines CorpDM. Two of the other attacks are direct consequences of this issue. Since there was no corporate data model, the principle could not be used ([EVIDENCE] Principle has been used minimally... use it now), and databases between applications were seldom shared ([EVIDENCE] Databases seldom shared).

In addition, the principle was conceptually conflicting with another architecture principle Package selection before custom development. It was virtually impossible to find third-party applications and vendor packages that comply with the corporate data model. This is reflected in the argument diagram as a bi-directional conflict between the principle and [TASK] Use data models of packages applications instead of CorpDM. This task is a direct consequence of the principle Package selection before custom development.

This set of arguments and the evaluation of the real-life situation made architects realize that the focus should be on the exchange of information between applications, not on how the data is stored and managed centrally. This shift of paradigm resulted in creating a new principle Adhere to the canonical data model.

We translate the final argument diagram of the situation in 2007 after introducing the new principle using RationalGRL framework. The result is presented in Fig. 3. Based on the evaluation of GRL IEs, the new principle as well as goals

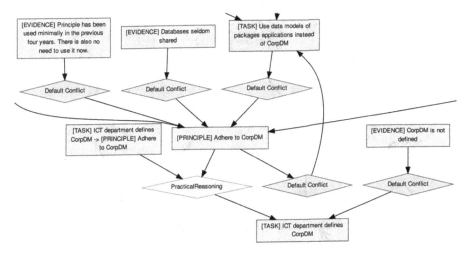

Fig. 2. Part of the argument diagram of the Schiphol Group principles 2007 (visualized in the argument web)

such as Lower diversity and total cost of ownership, Clear and standard way of interfacing, Few dependencies between applications, and Faster time to market receive a positive evaluation. Moreover, the old principle receives a negative evaluation, together with its related goals and tasks. This conclusions can provide insights on how to prioritize from a set of principles, or how to take better informed design decisions when facing alternative solutions.

3.3   Evaluation with Schiphol Group Enterprise Architects

We evaluated our framework and its results with enterprise architects of the Schiphol Group. We first discussed the argument diagrams in order to evaluate whether they represent the situation at 2003 and 2007 correctly. The architects found that argument diagrams are a useful tool to link and reason about arguments. However, they noted that it may be easier to construct the arguments and counterarguments *a postiori* than to do this *a priori*. They felt that it is easier to look back on the process and to extract that relevant arguments, than to do this while the process is still ongoing.

Next, we translated the argument diagrams to GRL models using the translation procedure and evaluated these GRL models with the architects. The architects confirmed that the models are able to represent correctly part of the problem at hand. However, they also noted that some parts were missing from the models, which implies that beside the documents we gathered and used for modeling, there were additional facts we did not consider. However, this partial representation was found useful and the architects consider the usage of formal methods (such as GRL and argumentation) beneficial for "sanity checks", alongside a better formulation of the principles.

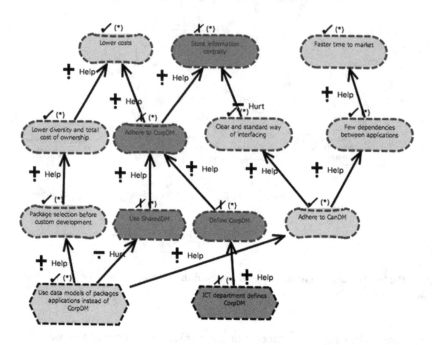

Fig. 3. GRL diagram of the Schiphol Group principles in 2007

4   Related Work

There are several contributions that relate argumentation-based techniques with goal modeling. The contribution most closely related to ours is the work by Jureta *et al.* [9]. This work proposes "Goal Argumentation Method (GAM)" to guide argumentation and justification of modeling choices during the construction of goal models. One of the elements of GAM is the translation of formal argument models to goal models (similar to ours). In this sense, our Rational-GRL framework can be seen as an instantiation and implementation of part of the GAM. One of the main contribution of RationalGRL is that it also takes the acceptability of arguments as determined by the argumentation semantics [5] into account when translating from arguments to goal models. RationalGRL also provides tool support for argumentation, i.e. Argument Web toolset, to which OVA belongs [4], and for goal modeling, i.e. jUCMNav [12]. Finally, Rational-GRL is based on the practical reasoning approach of [3], which itself is also a specialization of Dung's [5] abstract approach to argumentation. Thus, the specific critical questions and counterarguments based on these critical question proposed by [3] can easily be incorporated into RationalGRL.

RationalGRL framework is also closely related to frameworks that aim to provide a design rationale (DR) [13], an explicit documentation of the reasons behind decisions made when designing a system or artefact. DR looks at issues, options and arguments for and against the various options in the design of, for example, a software system, and provides direct tool support for building and analyzing DR graphs. One of the main improvements of RationalGRL over DR approaches is that RationalGRL incorporates the formal semantics for both argument acceptability and goal satisfiability, which allow for a partly automated evaluation of goals and the rationales for these goals.

Arguments and requirements engineering approaches have been combined by, among others, Haley *et al.* [6], who use structured arguments to capture and validate the rationales for security requirements. However, they do not use goal models, and thus, there is no explicit trace from arguments to goals and tasks. Furthermore, like [9], the argumentative part of their work does not include formal semantics for determining the acceptability of arguments, and the proposed frameworks are not actually implemented. Murukannaiah *et al.* [11] propose Arg-ACH, an approach to capture inconsistencies between stakeholders' beliefs and goals, and resolve goal conflicts using argumentation techniques.

Finally, our in previous empirical work we recognized shortcomings in the current state of the art in EA decision rationalization [15]. One of the main shortcomings is that the group decision process is often omitted. This contribution can be seen as way to meet this shortcoming, and in this sense improves on existing EA decision rationalization frameworks. [18]

5   Conclusions and Future Work

There are many directions of future work. There are a large number of different semantics for formal argumentation, that lead to different arguments being acceptable or not. It would be very interesting to explore the effect of these semantics on goal models. Jureta *et al.* develop a methodology for clarification to address issues such as ambiguity, overgenerality, synonymy, and vagueness in arguments. Atkinson *et al.* [2] define a formal set of critical questions that point to typical ways in which a practical argument can be criticized. We believe that critical questions are the right way to implement Jureta's methodology, and our framework would benefit from it. In addition, currently, we have not considered the *Update* step of our framework (Fig. 1). That is, the translation from goal models to argument diagrams is still missing. The *Update* step helps analysts change parts of the goal model and analyze its impact on the underlying argument diagram. Finally, the implementation is currently a browser-based mapping from an existing argument diagramming tool to an existing goal modeling tool. By adding an argumentation component to jUCMNav, the development of goal models can be improved significantly.

References

1. Amyot, D.: Introduction to the user requirements notation: learning by example. Comput. Netw. **42**(3), 285–301 (2003)
2. Atkinson, K., Bench-Capon, T.: Practical reasoning as presumptive argumentation using action based alternating transition systems. Artif. Intell. **171**(10), 855–874 (2007)

3. Atkinson, K., Bench-Capon, T.: Taking the long view: looking ahead in practical reasoning. In: Computational Models of Argument: Proceedings of COMMA, pp. 109–120 (2014)

4. Bex, F., Lawrence, J., Snaith, M., Reed, C.: Implementing the argument web. Commun. ACM **56**(10), 66–73 (2013)

5. Dung, P.M.: On the acceptability of arguments and its fundamental role in non-monotonic reasoning, logic programming and n-person games. Artif. Intell. **77**(2), 321–358 (1995)

6. Haley, C.B., Moffett, J.D., Laney, R., Nuseibeh, B.: Arguing security: validating security requirements using structured argumentation. In: Proceedings of the Third Symposium on RE for Information Security (SREIS 2005) (2005)

7. Hoogervorst, J.A.P.: Enterprise architecture: enabling integration, agility and change. Int. J. Coop. Inf. Syst. **13**(3), 213–233 (2004)

8. ITU-T. Recommendation Z.151 (11, 08): User Requirements Notation (URN) – Language Definition (2008). http://www.itu.int/rec/T-REC-Z.151/en

9. Jureta, I.J., Faulkner, S., Schobbens, P.Y.: Clear justification of modeling decisions for goal-oriented requirements engineering. Requir. Eng. **13**(2), 87–115 (2008)

10. Modgil, S., Prakken, H.: A general account of argumentation with preferences. Artif. Intell. **195**, 361–397 (2013)

11. Murukannaiah, P.K., Kalia, A.K., Telangy, P.R., Singh, M.P.: Resolving goal conflicts via argumentation-based analysis of competing hypotheses. In: 23rd International Requirements Engineering Conference, pp. 156–165. IEEE (2015)

12. Mussbacher, G.,Amyot, D.: Goal and scenario modeling, analysis, and transformation with jUCMNav. In: ICSE Companion, pp. 431–432 (2009)

13. Buckingham Shum, S.J., Selvin, A.M., Sierhuis, M., Conklin, J., Haley, C.B., Nuseibeh, B.: Hypermedia support for argumentation-based rationale. In: Dutoit, A.H., McCall, R., Mistrík, I., Paech, B. (eds.) Rationale Management in Software Engineering, pp. 111–132. Springer, Heidelberg (2006)

14. The Open Group. TOGAF 9 - The Open Group Architecture Framework Version 9 (2009)

15. van der Linden, D., van Zee, M.: Insights from a study on decision making in enterprise architecture. In: PoEM (Short Papers). CEUR Workshop Proceedings, vol. 1497, pp. 21–30 (2015)

16. van Zee, M., Bex, F., Ghanavati, S.: Rationalization of goal models in GRL using formal argumentation. In: Proceedings of RE: Next! Track at the Requirements Engineering Conference 2015 (RE 2015), August 2015

17. van Zee, M., Ghanavati, S.: Capturing evidence and rationales with requirements engineering and argumentation-based techniques. In: Proceedings of the 26th Benelux Conference on Artificial Intelligence (BNAIC2014), November 2014

18. Van Zee, M., Plataniotis, G., van der Linden, D., Marosin, D.: Formalizing enterprise architecture decision models using integrity constraints. In: 2014 IEEE 16th Conference on Business Informatics, vol. 1, pp. 143–150. IEEE (2014)

19. Yu, E.S.K.: Towards modelling and reasoning support for early-phase requirements engineering. In: Proceedings of the 3rd IEEE International Symposium on RE, pp. 226–235 (1997)

Author Index

Printed in the United States
By Bookmasters

and analyzing DR graphs. One of the main improvements of RationalGRL over DR approaches is that RationalGRL incorporates the formal semantics for both argument acceptability and goal satisfiability, which allow for a partly automated evaluation of goals and the rationales for these goals.

Arguments and requirements engineering approaches have been combined by, among others, Haley et al. [6], who use structured arguments to capture and validate the rationales for security requirements. However, they do not use goal models, and thus, there is no explicit trace from arguments to goals and tasks. Furthermore, like [9], the argumentative part of their work does not include formal semantics for determining the acceptability of arguments, and the proposed frameworks are not actually implemented. Murukannaiah et al. [11] propose Arg-ACH, an approach to capture inconsistencies between stakeholders' beliefs and goals, and resolve goal conflicts using argumentation techniques.

Finally, our in previous empirical work we recognized shortcomings in the current state of the art in EA decision rationalization [15]. One of the main shortcomings is that the group decision process is often omitted. This contribution can be seen as way to meet this shortcoming, and in this sense improves on existing EA decision rationalization frameworks. [18]

5 Conclusions and Future Work

There are many directions of future work. There are a large number of different semantics for formal argumentation, that lead to different arguments being acceptable or not. It would be very interesting to explore the effect of these semantics on goal models. Jureta et al. develop a methodology for clarification to address issues such as ambiguity, overgenerality, synonymy, and vagueness in arguments. Atkinson et al. [2] define a formal set of critical questions that point to typical ways in which a practical argument can be criticized. We believe that critical questions are the right way to implement Jureta's methodology, and our framework would benefit from it. In addition, currently, we have not considered the *Update* step of our framework (Fig. 1). That is, the translation from goal models to argument diagrams is still missing. The *Update* step helps analysts change parts of the goal model and analyze its impact on the underlying argument diagram. Finally, the implementation is currently a browser-based mapping from an existing argument diagramming tool to an existing goal modeling tool. By adding an argumentation component to jUCMNav, the development of goal models can be improved significantly.

References

1. Amyot, D.: Introduction to the user requirements notation: learning by example. Comput. Netw. **42**(3), 285–301 (2003)
2. Atkinson, K., Bench-Capon, T.: Practical reasoning as presumptive argumentation using action based alternating transition systems. Artif. Intell. **171**(10), 855–874 (2007)

3. Atkinson, K., Bench-Capon, T.: Taking the long view: looking ahead in practical reasoning. In: Computational Models of Argument: Proceedings of COMMA, pp. 109–120 (2014)
4. Bex, F., Lawrence, J., Snaith, M., Reed, C.: Implementing the argument web. Commun. ACM **56**(10), 66–73 (2013)
5. Dung, P.M.: On the acceptability of arguments and its fundamental role in non-monotonic reasoning, logic programming and n-person games. Artif. Intell. **77**(2), 321–358 (1995)
6. Haley, C.B., Moffett, J.D., Laney, R., Nuseibeh, B.: Arguing security: validating security requirements using structured argumentation. In: Proceedings of the Third Symposium on RE for Information Security (SREIS 2005) (2005)
7. Hoogervorst, J.A.P.: Enterprise architecture: enabling integration, agility and change. Int. J. Coop. Inf. Syst. **13**(3), 213–233 (2004)
8. ITU-T. Recommendation Z.151 (11, 08): User Requirements Notation (URN) – Language Definition (2008). http://www.itu.int/rec/T-REC-Z.151/en
9. Jureta, I.J., Faulkner, S., Schobbens, P.Y.: Clear justification of modeling decisions for goal-oriented requirements engineering. Requir. Eng. **13**(2), 87–115 (2008)
10. Modgil, S., Prakken, H.: A general account of argumentation with preferences. Artif. Intell. **195**, 361–397 (2013)
11. Murukannaiah, P.K., Kalia, A.K., Telangy, P.R., Singh, M.P.: Resolving goal conflicts via argumentation-based analysis of competing hypotheses. In: 23rd International Requirements Engineering Conference, pp. 156–165. IEEE (2015)
12. Mussbacher, G.,Amyot, D.: Goal and scenario modeling, analysis, and transformation with jUCMNav. In: ICSE Companion, pp. 431–432 (2009)
13. Buckingham Shum, S.J., Selvin, A.M., Sierhuis, M., Conklin, J., Haley, C.B., Nuseibeh, B.: Hypermedia support for argumentation-based rationale. In: Dutoit, A.H., McCall, R., Mistrík, I., Paech, B. (eds.) Rationale Management in Software Engineering, pp. 111–132. Springer, Heidelberg (2006)
14. The Open Group. TOGAF 9 - The Open Group Architecture Framework Version 9 (2009)
15. van der Linden, D., van Zee, M.: Insights from a study on decision making in enterprise architecture. In: PoEM (Short Papers). CEUR Workshop Proceedings, vol. 1497, pp. 21–30 (2015)
16. van Zee, M., Bex, F., Ghanavati, S.: Rationalization of goal models in GRL using formal argumentation. In: Proceedings of RE: Next! Track at the Requirements Engineering Conference 2015 (RE 2015), August 2015
17. van Zee, M., Ghanavati, S.: Capturing evidence and rationales with requirements engineering and argumentation-based techniques. In: Proceedings of the 26th Benelux Conference on Artificial Intelligence (BNAIC2014), November 2014
18. Van Zee, M., Plataniotis, G., van der Linden, D., Marosin, D.: Formalizing enterprise architecture decision models using integrity constraints. In: 2014 IEEE 16th Conference on Business Informatics, vol. 1, pp. 143–150. IEEE (2014)
19. Yu, E.S.K.: Towards modelling and reasoning support for early-phase requirements engineering. In: Proceedings of the 3rd IEEE International Symposium on RE, pp. 226–235 (1997)

Author Index

Printed in the United States
By Bookmasters